T0319046

The Handbook of
HIGH FREQUENCY
TRADING

The Handbook of
HIGH FREQUENCY TRADING

GREG N. GREGORIOU
State University of New York (Plattsburgh)

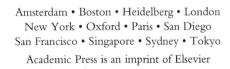

Amsterdam • Boston • Heidelberg • London
New York • Oxford • Paris • San Diego
San Francisco • Singapore • Sydney • Tokyo
Academic Press is an imprint of Elsevier

Academic Press is an imprint of Elsevier
125 London Wall, London EC2Y 5AS, UK
525 B Street, Suite 1800, San Diego, CA 92101-4495, USA
225 Wyman Street, Waltham, MA 02451, USA
The Boulevard, Langford Lane, Kidlington, Oxford OX5 1GB, UK

Notices

Knowledge and best practice in this field are constantly changing. As new research and experience broaden our understanding, changes in research methods, professional practices, or medical treatment may become necessary.

Practitioners and researchers must always rely on their own experience and knowledge in evaluating and using any information, methods, compounds, or experiments described herein. In using such information or methods they should be mindful of their own safety and the safety of others, including parties for whom they have a professional responsibility.

To the fullest extent of the law, neither the Publisher nor the authors, contributors, or editors, assume any liability for any injury and/or damage to persons or property as a matter of products liability, negligence or otherwise, or from any use or operation of any methods, products, instructions, or ideas contained in the material herein.

ISBN: 978-0-12-802205-4

British Library Cataloguing in Publication Data
A catalogue record for this book is available from the British Library

Library of Congress Catalog Number
A catalog record for this book is available from the Library of Congress

For information on all Academic Press publications
visit our website at http://store.elsevier.com/

Typeset by TNQ Books and Journals
www.tnq.co.in

Printed and bound in USA

CONTENTS

LIST OF CONTRIBUTORS

Erdinç Akyıldırım
Akdeniz University, Faculty of Economics and Administrative Sciences, Antalya, Turkey

Paul U. Ali
Melbourne Law School, Parkville, Melbourne, VIC, Australia

David E. Allen
School of Mathematics and Statistics, University of Sydney, and School of Business, University of South Australia, Australia

Albert Altarovici
ETH Zürich, Department of Mathematics, Zürich, Switzerland

Richard G. Anderson
School of Business and Entrepreneurship, Lindenwood University, St Charles, MO, USA

Jane M. Binner
Department of Accounting and Finance, Birmingham Business School, University of Birmingham, Birmingham, UK

Kris Boudt
Solvay Business School, Vrije Universiteit Brussel, Brussels, Belgium

Godfrey Charles-Cadogan
School of Economics, UCT, Rondebosch, Cape Town, South Africa

Giuseppe Ciallella
Law and Economics, LUISS Guido Carli, Rome, Italy

Brittany Cole
University of Mississippi, School of Business, University, MS, USA

Imma Valentina Curato
Ulm University, Ulm, Germany

Jonathan Daigle
University of Mississippi, School of Business, University, MS, USA

Nazmi Demir
Department of Banking & Finance, Bilkent University, Bilkent, Ankara, Turkey

Cumhur Ekinci
ITU Isletme Fakultesi – Macka, Istanbul, Turkey

Dov Fischer
Brooklyn College, School of Business, Brooklyn, NY, USA

Nikola Gradojevic
Lille Catholic University, IÉSEG School of Management, Lille, France

Greg N. Gregoriou
State University of New York (Plattsburgh), NY, USA

George Guernsey
Managing Partner, Insight Mapping, St. Louis, MO, USA

Björn Hagströmer
School of Business, Stockholm University, Stockholm, Sweden

Tobias Hahn
Bond University, Gold Coast, QLD, Australia

Kin-Yip Ho
Research School of Finance, Actuarial Studies and Applied Statistics, ANU College of Business and Economics, The Australian National University, Canberra, ACT, Australia

Hooi Hooi Lean
Economics Program, School of Social Sciences, Universiti Sains Malaysia, Penang, Malaysia

Camillo Lento
Faculty of Business Administration, Lakehead University, Thunder Bay, ON, Canada

François-Serge Lhabitant
CEO and CIO, Kedge Capital, Jersey; EDHEC Business School, Nice, France

Jeffrey G. MacIntosh
University of Toronto, Faculty of Law, Toronto, ON, Canada

Michael J. McAleer
Department of Quantitative Finance, College of Technology Management, National Tsing Hua University, Hsinchu, Taiwan, and Econometric Institute, Erasmus School of Economics, Erasmus University, Rotterdam, The Netherlands

David R. Meyer
Olin Business School, Washington University in St. Louis, St. Louis, MO, USA

Vinod Mishra
Department of Economics, Monash University — Berwick Campus, Berwick, VIC, Australia

Imad Moosa
School of Economics, Finance and Marketing, RMIT, Melbourne, VIC, Australia

Giang Nguyen
Solvay Business School, Vrije Universiteit Brussel, Brussels, Belgium

Birger Nilsson
Department of Economics, Lund University, Sweden

Benedict Peeters
Finvex Group, Brussels, Belgium

Vikash Ramiah
School of Economics, Finance and Marketing, RMIT, Melbourne, VIC, Australia

Erick Rengifo
Fordham University, Bronx, NY, USA

Simona Sanfelici
Department of Economics, University of Parma, Parma, Italy

Martin Scholtus
Econometric Institute and Tinbergen Institute, Erasmus University Rotterdam, Rotterdam, The Netherlands

Tayyeb Shabbir
Department of Finance, CBAPP, California State University Dominguez Hills, Carson, CA, USA and Department of Finance, Wharton School, University of Pennsylvania, Philadelphia, PA, USA

Yanlin Shi
Research School of Finance, Actuarial Studies and Applied Statistics, ANU College of Business and Economics, The Australian National University, Canberra, ACT, Australia

Abhay K. Singh
School of Business, Edith Cowan University, Joondalup, WA, Australia

Russell Smyth
Department of Economics, Monash University, Clayton, VIC, Australia

M. Nihat Solakoglu
Department of Banking & Finance, Bilkent University, Bilkent, Ankara, Turkey

Masayuki Susai
Nagasaki University, Nagasaki, Japan

Rossen Trendafilov
Department of Economics, Truman State University, Kirksville, MO, USA

Dick van Dijk
Econometric Institute and Tinbergen Institute, Erasmus University Rotterdam, Rotterdam, The Netherlands

Bonnie F. Van Ness
University of Mississippi, School of Business, University, MS, USA

Robert A. Van Ness
University of Mississippi, School of Business, University, MS, USA

Bruce Vanstone
Bond University, Gold Coast, QLD, Australia

Camillo von Müller
CLVS-HSG University of St. Gallen, St. Gallen, Switzerland

Yushi Yoshida
Shiga University, Hikone, Japan

Zhaoyong Zhang
School of Business, Faculty of Business and Law, Edith Cowan University, Joondalup, WA, Australia

CONTRIBUTORS BIOGRAPHIES

Erdinç Akyıldırım is a researcher and product developer at Borsa Istanbul. Prior to Borsa Istanbul, he worked as a quantitative analyst and derivatives portfolio manager at Industrial Development Bank of Turkey and as a research and teaching assistant at Bogazici University, Sabanci University, and Swiss Federal Institute of Technology in Zurich. He received a BSc degree in mathematics and MSc degree in financial engineering from Bogazici University. He completed his PhD in banking and finance at University of Zurich and Swiss Finance Institute in 2013. During his PhD, he worked on topics related to financial engineering, financial mathematics, and financial econometrics and has published several papers in international journals and conferences.

Paul U. Ali is Associate Professor at Melbourne University Law School and a member of the Law School's Centre for Corporate Law and Securities Regulation. Paul has published widely on banking and finance law. Paul has worked in the banking and finance and corporate groups of two leading Australian law firms. He has also worked in the securitization team of a bank, and has been a principal of a private capital firm and a consultant with a corporate governance advisory firm.

David E. Allen has a PhD in finance from the University of Western Australia, plus an MPhil in economics from the University of Leicester. In the course of the last 39 years, he has been employed by De Montfort University and the University of Edinburgh in the UK, and the University of Western Australia, Curtin University, and Edith Cowan University in Western Australia where he was Foundation Professor of Finance. He is currently Visiting Professor in the School of Mathematics and Statistics at the University of Sydney and Adjunct Professor at the University of South Australia. He has published 3 books and over 100 other contributions to books and refereed journal publications.

Albert Altarovici is a PhD student in mathematics at ETH Zurich. He specializes in stochastic optimal control and its applications to finance. In a recent paper with J. Muhle-Karbe and H.M. Soner, he studies the asymptotic expansion for the problem of optimal consumption and investment in a market with multiple risky assets, which are correlated Brownian motions and a money market paying constant interest rate where every transaction incurs a fixed transaction cost. He has taught mathematics and finance at the University of Virginia and ETH Zurich.

Richard Anderson is senior research fellow, Center for Economics and the Environment, and Adjunct Professor, School of Business and Entrepreneurship, Lindenwood University, St Charles, Missouri. Previously, he was vice president and economist, Federal Reserve Bank of St Louis, and economist, Board of Governors of the Federal Reserve System, Washington, D.C. Prior to joining the Federal Reserve, he taught at Michigan State University, Ohio State University, and the University of Michigan. He holds a PhD from MIT and a BA in economics from the University of Minnesota. His research focuses on empirical macroeconomics and monetary policy.

Jane M. Binner is Chair of finance, accounting and finance department, Birmingham Business School, Birmingham University, UK. Previously, she was Head of the Accounting and Finance Division at Sheffield Management School, Sheffield, UK and Reader in economics, Aston Business School, Birmingham, UK. She holds PhD, MSc, PGCE, and BA Hons in economics from the University of Leeds. Her research focuses on econometric modeling of financial markets, including asset prices and monetary aggregates.

Kris Boudt is Associate Professor in finance at Vrije Universiteit Brussel and part-time at the econometrics and finance department of the VU University of Amsterdam. He is a research partner of Finvex Group and affiliated researcher at KU Leuven. By training he has an MSc degree in economics from the University of Namur and a PhD from the KU Leuven (2008). Previously, he was Assistant Professor at the KU Leuven (2009–2012) and Guest Lecturer at the University of Illinois at Chicago. The research of Kris Boudt aims at developing econometric methodology for analyzing financial markets and optimizing portfolio risk. He has published in leading international finance and statistics journals including the *International Journal of Forecasting, Journal of Empirical Finance, Journal of Financial Econometrics, Journal of Financial Markets, Journal of Risk, and Statistics and Computing*, among others. Kris Boudt is in the editorial board of quantitative finance letters and is a coauthor of the high-frequency and PortfolioAnalytics packages.

Godfrey Charles-Cadogan is a Research Scientist in risk and uncertainty at the Institute for Innovation and Technology Management (IITM), Ted Rogers School of Management, Ryerson University. His work has been featured in *Financial Research Letters, System Research and Behavioural Science, Proceedings of the American Statistical Association Business & Economics Section, Proceedings of Foundations and Applications of Utility, Risk and Decision Theory, Money Science, All About Alpha, and High Frequency Trading Review*. He is the creator of the Cadogan stock price formula for high-frequency trading, and criterion function for predicting market crash from the probability weighting function implied by index option prices. His research interests are behavioral stochastic processes, financial economics, experimental economics, and decision theory. He holds Bachelor of Science degrees in statistics and actuarial mathematics as well as a Master of Science degree in mathematical statistics from the University of Michigan, and is a PhD candidate in economics at the University of Cape Town in Mathematical Behavioral Economics.

Giuseppe Ciallella graduated with honors at LUISS Guido Carli (Rome) Law School in 2009 and then spent one year as research assistant in Company Law and Securities Regulation at the same university. In 2012, he got an LL.M. from the London School of Economics and Political Science on a "Donato Menichella" Scholarship by the Bank of Italy. His PhD at LUISS Guido Carli is in Law and Economics and his field of research is Banking and Financial Regulation. During his PhD he also worked at Goldman Sachs International, Milan, and at Cleary Gottlieb Steen and Hamilton LLP, Rome.

Brittany Cole is a fifth year finance PhD student at the University of Mississippi. She received a bachelors degree in agriculture economics from the University of Tennessee at Martin and an MBA from the University of Mississippi. Brittany's research interests include corporate and municipal bond trading, information transmission, and market microstructure.

Imma Valentina Curato holds a PhD in mathematics for economic decisions from the University of Pisa, Italy. Currently, she is a Postdoc student at the Institute of Mathematical Finance, Ulm

University, Germany, and an external consultant at the European Central Bank, Frankfurt, Germany. Her main research interests are in the field of nonparametric econometrics: estimation of volatility; of leverage processes in univariate and multivariate frameworks, high-frequency data analysis, calibration/forecast performance of multifactor stochastic volatility models; and of liquidity risk factors models.

Jonathan Daigle is a fourth year finance PhD student at the University of Mississippi. He received his undergraduate degree and MBA from the University of South Alabama. His research interests include private equity, IPOs, and acquisitions.

Nazmi Demir received his MSc and PhD from the University of California, Davis in agricultural economics in 1970 and his associate professorship in economic policy in Turkey, in 2000. Nazmi specialized in Leontief input—output, inefficiency models, and environments in agricultural economics. He was a board member of various international research centers for 18 years. After a long-term government employment at high positions in various departments such as development planning, agrarian reform, and administrative duties in Turkey he joined Bilkent University in the Department of Economics as an instructor first and then as a chairman of the banking and finance department teaching micro- and macroeconomics, statistics, banking, and finance. He has published numerous books and papers in *Developing Economies, Economic Letters, Canadian Journal of Agricultural Economics, and Economic Systems Research.*

Cumhur Ekinci is Assistant Professor of finance at Istanbul Technical University (ITU). He studied economics and finance at Bogazici, Paris I Pantheon-Sorbonne and Aix-Marseille III. Dr Ekinci established and worked in a trading room at CNAM in Paris. He has been teaching financial markets, investment, corporate finance and accounting at ITU, CNAM, Aix-Marseille, and ENPC. His research includes topics in market microstructure, behavioral finance, and risk measurement.

Dov Fischer is Assistant Professor of accounting at Brooklyn College. He holds a doctorate in accounting from University of Colorado at Boulder, and is a CPA in New York State. He researches financial reporting in the banking and pharmaceutical industries, financial derivatives, accounting ethics, International Financial Reporting Standards (IFRS), and accounting education. His research has been recognized and awarded by the American Accounting Association, and he regularly publishes in academic and practitioner journals, including *CPA Journal; Journal of Business & Economic Studies; Journal of Accounting, Ethics, and Public Policy; and Journal of Religion & Business Ethics.*

Nikola Gradojevic received the PhD degree in financial economics from the University of British Columbia, Vancouver, BC, Canada, in 2003. He also holds an MA in economics from University of Essex and Central European University and an MSc in electrical engineering (System Control Major). Currently, he is Associate Professor of finance at the IÉSEG School of Management, Lille Catholic University, in Lille and Paris, France. During his career, he took positions at the University of British Columbia, Bank of Canada, Federal Reserve Bank of St Louis, Lakehead University, and in the private sector as a consultant in the financial and mining industries. He has held visiting appointments at Rouen Business School in France, University of Bologna in Italy, Faculty of Economics in Montenegro and University of Novi Sad, Faculty of Technical Sciences. He is currently a research fellow at the Rimini Center for Economic Analysis in Italy and

Visiting Professor at the University of Essex (The Centre for Computational Finance and Economic Agents) in the United Kingdom. Dr Gradojevic's research interests include empirical asset pricing, market microstructure, high-frequency finance, international finance, nonadditive entropy, artificial intelligence (e.g., neural networks and fuzzy logic), technical trading, asset price volatility and bubbles. He has published his research in journals, such as *Journal of Banking and Finance, Journal of Empirical Finance, Quantitative Finance, Journal of Economic Dynamics and Control, Finance Research Letters, IEEE Signal Processing Magazine, IEEE Transactions on Neural Networks, Physica D, and Journal of Forecasting.*

George Guernsey is Managing Partner of Insight Mapping. He served as group head of strategy, risk and financial reporting at two international banks and two global consulting firms, providing growth strategies to banks and exchanges. Based in London for 17 years, he then developed risk products and strategies for banks and technology companies in Europe and Asia. He cofounded Strategic Insights, a competitive intelligence resource, then launching and directing its Insight Mapping market radar service. Insight Mapping employs customized versions of systems developed for government intelligence services to target emerging threats and opportunities for companies and financial institutions. Early identification provides a competitive advantage for executives seeking to spot needs, design new products and services, mitigate risks, and go to market effectively. He has a BA in political science and economics from Yale University and an MBA with distinction from the Wharton School of the University of Pennsylvania.

Björn Hagströmer is Associate Professor, Stockholm Business School, Stockholm University, Sweden. He holds a PhD from Aston Business School, Birmingham, UK. His research focuses on empirical asset pricing and empirical market microstructure, including high-frequency trading.

Tobias Hahn holds a PhD in computational finance from Bond University. His PhD thesis investigated the application of machine learning to options pricing. He is an active academic researcher, and has practical experience in financial analysis and trading systems development. Tobias's current research interests focus on the modeling of high-frequency financial time series, asset pricing, and model evaluation.

Kin-Yip Ho is currently Assistant Professor at the Research School of Finance, Actuarial Studies and Applied Statistics in The Australian National University. He has held visiting positions, including a fellowship from the Korea Institute of International Economic Policy (KIEP) to work on a research project involving the Chinese financial markets. He has published articles in various international journals, such as *Annals of Actuarial Science, Annals of Financial Economics, China Economic Review, Economie Internationale, Japan and the World Economy, Journal of Applied Econometrics, Journal of Economic Development, Journal of Wealth Management, Mathematics and Computers in Simulation, North American Journal of Economics and Finance, Review of Financial Economics, and World Economy.* He has also published several book chapters on Asian financial markets in the Handbook of Asian Finance. His current research interests lie in the actuarial applications of financial and statistical models, financial econometrics, international finance, and time series analysis. He graduated with a PhD in economics from Cornell University and has an Associate Diploma in Piano Performance from London College of Music.

Hooi Hooi Lean is Associate Professor at the School of Social Sciences (economics program), Universiti Sains Malaysia. She has published more than 80 book chapters and journal articles in many reputed international journals. Dr Lean is listed in the *Who's Who in the World 2009* and Researcher of the Week in GDNet East Asia. She was awarded the ASEAN-ROK Academic Exchange Fellowship Program in 2007, the Democratic Pacific Union Visiting Fellowship in 2008, and the International HERMES Fellowship Program in 2009. Dr Lean also won the "Sanggar Sanjung" Excellence Award for Publication, since 2009 and the "Hadiah Sanjungan" Award for Best Publication, since 2006. There are 1132 citations to her research on Google Scholar.

Camillo Lento is Associate Professor of accounting in the Faculty of Business Administration at Lakehead University. He received his PhD from the University of Southern Queensland, and both his masters (MSc) degree and undergraduate degree (HBComm) from Lakehead University. He is a Chartered Accountant (Ontario), Certified Fraud Examiner, and Chartered Business Valuator. Dr Lento has published numerous articles and book chapters on technical trading models and capital markets. In addition, he is the lead author of the financial accounting casebook entitled *Cases in Financial Accounting*. Dr Lento is also Contributing Editor for Canadian MoneySaver magazine and has authored numerous articles on personal tax planning matters. His tax planning articles have also been featured in many national media outlets. Dr Lento teaches various financial accounting and auditing courses, including contemporary issues in accounting theory, advanced topics in accounting, intermediate accounting, and introductory accounting. Dr Lento continues to practice in the area of accounting, business valuation, and economic loss quantification.

François-Serge Lhabitant is currently the CEO and CIO of Kedge Capital, where he oversees more than $6 billion of capital invested in hedge funds and risk-controlled strategies. He was formerly a member of senior management at Union Bancaire Privie, where he was in charge of quantitative risk management and subsequently, of the quantitative analysis for alternative portfolios. Prior to this, François-Serge was Director at UBS/Global Asset Management, in charge of building quantitative models for portfolio management and hedge funds. On the academic side, François-Serge is currently Professor of finance at the EDHEC Business School (France) and Visiting Professor at the Hong Kong University of Science and Technology. François holds an engineering degree from the Swiss Federal Institute of Technology, a BSc in economics, an MSc in banking and finance, and a PhD in finance from the University of Lausanne.

Jeffrey MacIntosh is the Toronto Stock Exchange Chair of Capital Markets at the Faculty of Law, University of Toronto, and is a past Associate Director and Director of the Capital Markets Institute at the University of Toronto. He specializes in corporation law and finance, securities regulation, venture capital financing, and innovation. He holds law degrees from Harvard and Toronto, and a Bachelor of Science degree from MIT. Professor MacIntosh was appointed a John M. Olin Fellow in law and economics at Yale Law School in 1988–1989. He also served as a member of the Ontario Securities Commission Task Force on small business financing. Professor MacIntosh is the coauthor (with Chris Nicholls) of *Essentials of Securities Regulation* (Toronto: Irwin Law Inc., 2002) and has published numerous articles, book chapters, and commentaries on various topics in his areas of expertise.

Michael J. McAleer holds a PhD in economics from Queen's University, Canada. He is Chair Professor of quantitative finance, National Tsing Hua University, Taiwan; Professor of quantitative finance, Econometric Institute, Erasmus School of Economics, Erasmus University

Rotterdam, The Netherlands; Distinguished Professor, College of Management, National Chung Hsing University, Taiwan; Adjunct Professor, Department of Economics and Finance and Department of Mathematics and Statistics at the University of Canterbury, New Zealand; and Adjunct Professor, Faculty of Economics and Business, Complutense University of Madrid (founded 1293), Spain. He has published more than 600 journal articles and books in econometrics, economics, statistics, finance, risk management, applied mathematics, intellectual property, environmental modeling, and related disciplines. He is presently a member of the editorial boards of 26 international journals, and serves on several as Editor in Chief or Associate Editor in Chief.

David R. Meyer is Senior Lecturer in management at Olin Business School, Washington University in St Louis, teaching international business. Previously, he was Professor of sociology and urban studies at Brown University. His PhD is from the University of Chicago. Meyer's current research examines financial networks, Asian economic development, global business centers, and Asian business networks. Publications include 5 books and monographs and over 50 articles and book chapters. His book, *Hong Kong as a Global Metropolis* (Cambridge University Press, 2000), interpreted that city as the pivot of Asian business networks. The research on network behavior of leading international financiers was funded by the National Science Foundation.

Vinod Mishra is Senior Lecturer in the Department of Economics at Monash University, Australia. He has published more than 40 papers in leading international journals in economics, finance, and related areas. His research interests include applied industrial organization, financial economics, high-frequency financial data analysis, labour economics, development economics, and energy economics. He is particularly interested in studying various aspects of the emerging economies of India and China. There are more than 500 citations to his research on Google Scholar.

Imad Moosa is Professor of finance at RMIT, Melbourne. He has also held positions at Monash University (Melbourne), La Trobe University (Melbourne), and the University of Sheffield (UK). He holds a BA in economics and business studies, MA in the economics of financial intermediaries, and a PhD in financial economics from the University of Sheffield (UK). He has received formal training in model building, exchange rate forecasting, and risk management at the Claremont Economics Institute (United States), Wharton Econometrics (United States), and the Center for Monetary and Banking Studies (Switzerland). Before turning to academia in 1991, he worked as a financial analyst, a financial journalist, and an investment banker for over 10 years. He has also worked at the International Monetary Fund in Washington D.C. and acted as an advisor to the U.S. Treasury. Imad's work encompasses the areas of International Finance, Banking, Risk Management, Macroeconomics, and Applied Econometrics. His papers have appeared in the Journal of Applied Econometrics, Canadian Journal of Economics, IMF Staff Papers, Journal of Futures Markets, Quantitative Finance, Southern Economic Journal, American Journal of Agricultural Economics, Journal of Development Economics, Journal of Comparative Economics, Journal of Economic Organization and Behavior, and Journal of Banking and Finance. He has also written for the prestigious Euromoney Magazine. His recent books include *Quantification of Operational Risk under Basel II: The Good, Bad and Ugly*, *The Myth of Too Big to Fail* (both published by Palgrave in 2008 and 2009, respectively) and *The US-China Trade Dispute: Facts, Figure and Myths*, published by Edward Elgar, in 2012. His recent book, *Quantitative Easing as a Highway to Hyperinflation* has been published by World Scientific.

Giang Nguyen is Doctiris fellow at Finvex Group and Vrije Universiteit Brussel. He was previously responsible for risk management at several major Vietnamese financial institutions (Cement Finance Company and Vietnam bank for Industry and Trade) and worked on the R package highfrequency as a student in the Google Summer of Code project in 2013. He has a bachelor in economics from the National Economics University in Hanoi (Vietnam) and an MBA from the HU Brussels (Belgium). Giang Nguyen is currently a doctoral student at Vrije Unviersiteit Brussel and Finvex Group working on the development of Risk Optimized Portfolio Strategies, with a focus on intraday data, risk factors, and higher order comoments.

Birger Nilsson is Associate Professor, Department of Economics and Knut Wicksell Centre for Financial Research, School of Economics and Management, Lund University, Sweden. He holds a PhD from Lund University. His research focuses on empirical financial economics, including mathematical and statistical methods.

Benedict Peeters is founding partner and CEO of Finvex Group. Finvex Group combines academic research with advanced proprietary technology to analyze all types of financial risks with the aim of adding stability to overall investment portfolios. Its solutions include structured products, funds, and indices. Benedict has gained vast experience in asset management and investment banking in senior positions at BNP Paribas (Global Head of Structured Business, Sales & Investment Division), Morgan Stanley (Managing Director, Head of Structured Products Europe and MENA), and Deutsche Bank (Managing Director, Global Head Fund and Securitization Solutions, Equity Structuring, Global Markets Equities). Benedict publishes frequently in the specialized practitioner-oriented press.

Vikash Ramiah is Associate Professor of finance at RMIT University. He has a Diploma of Management, BSc (Hons) economics, Master of Finance program, and Doctor of Philosophy from RMIT University. He has received numerous awards for outstanding performance in teaching, research, and supervision. Vikash has been teaching economics and finance courses at RMIT, University of Melbourne, La Trobe University, and Australian Catholic University, since 1999. He has published in academic journals (e.g., Journal of Banking and Finance, Journal of Behavioral Finance, European Journal of Finance, Applied Economics, Pacific Basin Finance Journal, and Journal of International Financial Market, Institution and Money), industry reports, one book, book chapters, and over 35 conference papers. Vikash supervises numerous PhD students and regularly attracts research funding. He is an expert reviewer for 13 finance journals and for the Mauritius Research Council. He serves on the editorial board of two finance journals. He was an elected board member of the RMIT University Business Board, Program Director of Open Universities Australia and Acting Board member at the Australian Centre for Financial Studies. He was as a junior auditor at H&A Consultant, manager at Intergate PTY Limited, quantitative analyst at ANZ, Investment Banking Division, provided consultancy services to the Australian Stock Exchange and worked in collaboration with the Finance and Treasury Association of Australia and the Australian Centre for Financial Studies. He is the founder of Researchers Sans Frontiere Network and his research areas are financial markets, behavioral finance, and environmental finance.

Erick Rengifo is Associate Professor in the economics department at Fordham University. Professor Rengifo is an active scholar with interests in market microstructure, behavioral finance, risk management, insurance, microfinance, microinsurance, and econometrics. He is a private consultant in the fields of algorithmic trading, investments, risk management, microfinance, and microinsurance. He is a founder of Spes Nova Inc., a nonprofit corporation whose main goals are to provide funding to microenterprises, assist in market creation, and provide insurance products for the working poor around the world. He is also the founder and director of the Center for International Policy Studies. Professor Rengifo holds a PhD in economics with a concentration in finance and econometrics from Catholic University of Louvain-Belgium.

Simona Sanfelici is Associate Professor of mathematical methods for economics, actuarial sciences, and finance at the Department of Economics, University of Parma, Italy (since December 2005). Her background is in numerical analysis and her main research interests are volatility estimation for high-frequency financial data under market microstructure effects, option pricing, asset allocation, stochastic processes and stochastic differential equations, variational methods, numerical solution to degenerate nonlinear PDEs and to problems in unbounded domains, Galerkin finite element method, finite difference method, and Monte Carlo method.

Martin Scholtus (1984) obtained master degrees in economics (2007) and econometrics (2009), as well as a PhD in economics (2014) from the Erasmus University Rotterdam. His research focuses on high-frequency and algorithmic trading, in particular the performance of high-frequency technical trading strategies, the behavior of algorithmic traders around macroeconomic announcements, and their role in initial trading for newly listed stocks. Part of his work has been published in the *Journal of Banking and Finance*.

Tayyeb Shabbir is concurrently Adjunct Professor of finance, Department of Finance, Wharton School, University of Pennsylvania, Philadelphia, as well as tenured Full Professor of finance and Director of the Institute of Entrepreneurship at the College of Business and Public Policy at the California State University. Dr Shabbir has vast teaching, research, and consulting experience that has been acquired internationally. Previously, Dr Shabbir has served as a faculty member at the economics department of the University of Pennsylvania, Wharton Executive Education program, in the doctoral program at the Pennsylvania State University, University Park, and the LeBow School of Business at Drexel University. His areas of expertise include prediction, management, and prevention of financial crises, global financial flows, entrepreneurial finance, microfinance, and human capital investments. Dr Shabbir has scores of publications and competitive research grants to his credit and has also served as a consultant to the World Bank, UNDP, and the Asian Development Bank. Recently, acclaimed international academic publisher, Edward Elgar, published Dr Shabbir's book about financial crises which was coedited with Professor Lawrence Klein, Nobel Laureate in economics and Benjamin Franklin Professor of finance and economics at the University of Pennsylvania. Dr Shabbir is especially interested in policy-relevant analyses of global economic issues, financial crises, entrepreneurial finance, and financial markets. Dr Shabbir is frequently sought by press for interviews as an expert as well as a keynote speaker in professional meetings. Recently, he served as a CBAPP Consultant to Honda headquarters in Torrance for a training program about finance for Non-Finance Managers. He is also a regular speaker to the visiting Chinese delegations at the CSUDH's College of Extended Education as well as the Society of Government Accountants in South Bay, California.

Yanlin Shi is currently Assistant Professor in statistics at the Research School of Finance, Actuarial Studies and Applied Statistics in The Australian National University (ANU). His dissertation focuses on volatility modeling of high-frequency time series. He has published an article in the Thomson Reuters SSCI journal *North American Journal of Economics and Finance*, and presented papers at several international conferences, such as the 2014 China Meeting of the Econometric Society and the 19th International Congress on Modelling and Simulation, of which the conference proceedings are included in the Thomson Reuters CPCI. He received two masters degrees from ANU in the fields of applied statistics and business with the highest distinction. In 2009 and 2010, he was awarded the ANU Chancellor's Letters of Commendation for Outstanding Academic Achievements.

Abhay K. Singh is a B.Tech graduate with an MBA in finance from the Indian Institute of Information Technology, Gwalior, India and a PhD in finance from Edith Cowan University in Western Australia. He currently works as Postdoctoral Fellow in the School of Business at Edith Cowan University.

Russell Smyth is Professor and Head of the Department of Economics Monash University, Australia. He has published approximately 300 book chapters and journal articles in the fields of economics, law, and political science. His research interests encompass Asian economies, Chinese economic reform and financial economics, among others. From 1998 to 2008, he was Editor of Economic Papers, the policy journal of the Economic Society of Australia and was a member of the Central Council of the Economic Society of Australia. In 2008, he received the Honorary Fellow Award of the Economic Society of Australia. He is currently Associate Editor of Energy Economics and a member of seven editorial boards. There are 4600 citations to his research on Google Scholar.

M.Nihat Solakoglu is currently Assistant Professor in the banking and finance department of Bilkent University in Ankara, Turkey. He received his PhD in economics and masters degree in statistics from North Carolina State University. After graduation, he worked for American Express in the US at international risk and information management departments. His main interests are in applied finance and international finance. His papers have been published in *Applied Economics, Journal of International Financial Markets, Institutions, and Money, Applied Economics Letters*, and *Economic Systems Research*. His current interests are in herding in financial markets, the role of news arrival on return and volatility, the effect of exchange rate risk on trade, and the role of gender diversity on firm performance.

Masayuki Susai is Full Professor of international finance at the Faculty of Economics, Nagasaki University, Japan. He graduated from the Graduate School of Commerce at Waseda University with an MA. His research interests lie in international finance, including market microstructure in international financial markets, intervention in foreign exchange markets, and foreign exchange risk. He has edited two books, titled as *Empirical Study on Asian Financial Markets* (Kyushu Univ. Press) and *Studies on Financial Markets in East Asia* (World Scientific Pub.). His recently published articles appear in the *Proceedings of the Institute of Statistical Mathematics* and the *Annals of the Society for the Economic Studies of Securities*.

Rossen Trendafilov is Assistant Professor of economics in the Economics Department at Truman State University, where he teaches macroeconomics and financial economics. He maintains active academic research in the fields of financial economics, behavioral finance, financial econometrics, market microstructure, algorithmic trading, data mining, Fourier series analysis, wavelet analysis, and fractal analysis. He was a member of a hedge fund administration and also worked as a junior auditor and private consultant in Bulgaria. Professor Trendafilov holds a PhD in economics from Fordham University with a concentration in finance and market microstructure.

Dick van Dijk (1971) is Professor in financial econometrics at the Econometric Institute, Erasmus School of Economics, Erasmus University Rotterdam. His research interests include volatility modeling and forecasting, high-frequency data, asset return predictability, business cycle analysis, and nonlinear time series analysis. On these topics he has published widely in the *International Journal of Forecasting, Journal of Applied Econometrics, Journal of Banking and Finance, Journal of Business and Economic Statistics, Journal of Econometrics,* and *Review of Economics and Statistics,* among others. He coauthored the textbooks *Nonlinear Time Series Models in Empirical Finance* (with Philip Hans Franses; Cambridge University Press, 2000) and *Time Series Models for Business and Economic Forecasting* (with Philip Hans Franses and Anne Opschoor; Cambridge University Press, 2014).

Bonnie F. Van Ness is Otho Smith Professor of finance at the University of Mississippi. Bonnie is also Coeditor of The Financial Review and the department chair of finance. Bonnie received her undergraduate degree from the University of North Alabama, an MBA from the University of Mississippi, and PhD from the University of Memphis. Bonnie's primary research interest is market microstructure and she has published over 50 articles in this area.

Robert A. Van Ness is Bruce Moore Scholar of finance and Coeditor of The Financial Review. Robert received his undergraduate degree from Vanderbilt University, and an MBA and a PhD from the University of Memphis. Robert's primary research interest is market microstructure and he has published over 50 articles in this area.

Bruce Vanstone has over 7 years of experience as a portfolio manager, is Assistant Professor and holds a PhD in computational finance from Bond University in Australia. He has experience in applying statistics, mathematics, advanced technologies and computing to the development of investment processes and systems. A regular publisher and presenter at the international level, his book "Designing Stock Market Trading Systems" is available in most bookstores. His key skills are the development, testing, and benchmarking of quantitative trading and investment systems.

Camillo von Müller (PhD (HSG), MA (JHU), MA (HU)) is an economist at the German Federal Ministry of Finance in Berlin. He obtained a PhD in management/finance at the University of St Gallen, Switzerland, and has been Visiting and Teaching Fellow at Harvard University's Economics Department having also taught at the economics and social science departments at the universities of Zurich, St Gallen, and Leuphana University. Camillo has published widely in the field of management and finance. Prior to joining the Federal Ministry of Finance he has worked and consulted for nonprofit, public, and private sector institutions including Finance Watch in Brussels, the Ministry of Finance and Economics of Baden-Württemberg, and Deutsche Börse.

Yushi Yoshida is Full Professor of economics at the Faculty of Economics of Shiga University in Japan. Before joining Shiga University, he was Full Professor of economics at Kyushu Sangyo University. He obtained his MA and PhD in economics from Osaka University. His research interests lie in the area of international finance, including exchange rate pass-through, foreign exchange intervention, and international financial transmission. He has also written on empirical international trade, including intraindustry trade and extensive margin of exports. His recently published articles appear in the *Asia Pacific Business Review*, *IMF Staff Papers*, *International Review of Economics and Finance*, *North American Journal of Economics and Finance*, and *World Economy*. He is Pass-through Research Group researcher at Research Institute of Economics, Trade, and Industry (RIETI).

Zhaoyong Zhang obtained his PhD in economics from the Catholic University of Leuven (Belgium) in 1991, is currently Associate Professor of economics & finance and Head of Asian Business & Organizational Research Group (ABORG) in the School of Business at Edith Cowan University (ECU) in Australia. Previously, he was Professor of economics & finance at NUCB Graduate School of Commerce and Business in Japan, and Associate Professor and Director of CSTE at National University of Singapore (NUS). He held several visiting professor positions at ECU, Yokohama National University (YNU), ICSEAD (Japan), and KIEP (Korea), and was also Visiting Fellow/Adjunct (Associate) Professor at University of Western Australia, University of South Australia, University of Macau, as well as several universities in China. He also held several consulting positions with international institutions including OECD, IDRC, and Hanns Seidel Foundation (Germany). He has been included in the 2000 Outstanding Intellectuals in the twenty-first century by Cambridge International Biographical Centre in 2008; and also in *Who's Who in the World* in 2007—2012. His major research interests are International Trade and Finance, East Asian Financial Crisis, East Asia Monetary and Economic Integration, Foreign Exchange Policy and Reform in China. Zhaoyong has published 1 book manuscript, 34 chapters in book, and 53 articles in international journals, as well as (co)edited four special issues with the international journals including *Papers in Regional Science* in 2003 and *The World Economy* in 2006 and 2012, respectively.

EDITOR BIOGRAPHY

A native of Montreal, Professor Greg N. Gregoriou obtained his joint Ph.D. in finance at the University of Quebec at Montreal which merges the resources of Montreal's four major universities McGill, Concordia, UQAM, and HEC. Professor Gregoriou is Professor of Finance at State University of New York (Plattsburgh) and has taught a variety of finance courses such as alternative investments, international finance, money and capital markets, portfolio management, and corporate finance. He has also lectured at the University of Vermont, Universidad de Navarra, and at the University of Quebec at Montreal.

Professor Gregoriou has published 50 books, 65 refereed publications in peer-reviewed journals, and 24 book chapters since his arrival at SUNY Plattsburgh in August 2003. Professor Gregoriou's books have been published by McGraw-Hill, John Wiley & Sons, Elsevier-Butterworth/Heinemann, Taylor and Francis/CRC Press, Palgrave-MacMillan, and Risk Books. Four of his books have been translated into Chinese and Russian. His academic articles have appeared in well-known peer-reviewed journals such as the *Review of Asset Pricing Studies, Journal of Portfolio Management, Journal of Futures Markets, European Journal of Operational Research, Annals of Operations Research, Computers and Operations Research*, etc.

Professor Gregoriou is the derivatives editor and editorial board member for the *Journal of Asset Management* as well as editorial board member for the *Journal of Wealth Management, the Journal of Risk Management in Financial Institutions, Market Integrity, IEB International Journal of Finance, and the Brazilian Business Review*. Professor Gregoriou's interests focus on hedge funds, funds of funds, commodity trading advisors, managed futures, venture capital and private equity. He has also been quoted several times in the New York Times, Barron's, the Financial Times of London, Le Temps (Geneva), Les Echos (Paris), and L'Observateur de Monaco. He has done consulting work for numerous Canadian and US investment firms.

He is a part-time lecturer in finance at the School of Continuing Studies at McGill University, an advisory member of the Markets and Services Research Centre at Edith Cowan University in Joondalup (Australia), a senior advisor to the Ferrell Asset Management Group in Singapore, and a research associate with the University of Quebec at Montreal's CDP Capital Chair in Portfolio Management.

ACKNOWLEDGMENTS

We would like to thank the handful of anonymous referees who helped in selecting the papers for this book. We thank Dr J. Scott Bentley, Mckenna Bailey, and Nicky Carter at Elsevier for their suggestions and continuing support throughout this process. In addition I would like to thank both the President of Barclay Hedge Sol Waksman and Beto Carminhato for their helpful comments and suggestions. Neither the editor nor the publisher can guarantee the accuracy of the papers in this book and it is solely the contributors who are individually responsible for their own papers. In addition, we thank eVestment (www.evestment.com) for use of their data and the Pertrac software.

INTRODUCTION

Chapter 1 documents stylized facts of overall trading activity and algorithmic trading activity in the S&P 500 ETF traded on NASDAQ over the period January 6, 2009 up to December 12, 2011. Overall trading activity is characterized by strong periodicity over the day, hour, minute, and second. Algorithmic activity at the top of the order book has no periodicity within the second and is mainly event-based, in particular, around macroeconomic news announcements. About 60% of all orders are canceled within 1 s after entering the order book. The percentage of bid or ask improvements that disappears within 1 s is 80%. Especially in 2009 vanished bid or ask improvements leave a worse order book behind.

Chapter 2 deals with the literature on high-frequency trading (HFT) and discussions on the desirability or otherwise of regulating the practice that are typically based on misconceptions and confusion as well as faulty reasoning. One argument against HFT is that it is a license to print money that is owned by a minority of market participants. The authors argue that there is no reason why HFT is particularly profitable and that the shortness of the holding period is not necessarily conducive to the generation of super profit. They further examine the relation between the holding period and profitability by calculating the profit generated from carry trade operations in the foreign exchange (FX) market with a wide range of holding periods. In this analysis they avoid the confusion between HFT and automated trading and define HFT only in terms of the holding period and the frequency of trading.

Chapter 3 looks at how HFT systems work by exploiting inefficiencies in the pricing process. Before embarking on designing a HFT system, it is important to confirm that the price data for the instrument one intends to trade exhibit inefficiencies at the time frame one intends to exploit. Tests for randomness and market efficiency should be conducted at the required time frame to confirm that the instrument is not efficient at that time frame. The results of these tests also give some direction to the future style of the trading system that is likely to be successful in the required time frame.

Chapter 4 examines the large literature using unit root tests to test for weak form of market efficiency in financial markets. Much of this literature takes account of the low power to reject the unit root null in the presence of structural breaks. However, the literature largely ignores the low power to reject the unit root null in the presence of heteroskedasticity. Heteroskedasticity is particularly problematic in high-frequency financial data. The authors extend the literature by applying a unit root test which accommodates both heteroskedasticity and structural breaks to hourly data for five ASEAN stock indices.

Their results point to the importance of allowing for heteroskedasticity when testing for a random walk in high-frequency financial data.

Chapter 5 examines economies of co-location in standard and low latency trading environments. Existing evidence shows that HFT strategies include the exploitation of technical arbitrage opportunities. The authors discuss limitations to arbitrage opportunities that rest on co-location (Hawk-Dove Game), and models strategic and spatial consequences for money managers such as the technological and geographic segmentation of markets (von Thünen).

Chapter 6 describes the regulatory evolution of HFT with a focus on the European level. It illustrates differences between algorithmic trading and HFT and how the former is a more comprehensive genus of the latter. It also outlines the main HFT strategies, in particular with respect to the concept of liquidity. Finally the chapter takes into consideration the HFT regulatory framework laid down in the recently passed European Directive 2014/65/EU (the so-called "MiFID II").

Chapter 7 shows how HFT has become more commonplace in the last few years, more importantly, it has become more noticeable by the general investing public as well as the policy makers. The growing use of HFT raises some important questions and the author will address the following three: (1) provide an introduction to the nature of HFT and its progression in terms of use in execution of financial investment order flow, (2) implication of HFT for market efficiency specifically in relation to the "Efficient Market Hypothesis" and (3) implications for 'fairness' in the financial markets.

Chapter 8 looks at Michael Lewis' book *Flash Boys* which paints a highly unsympathetic view of HFT. But while Lewis' book has focused public attention on the phenomenon of HFT, he is far from the only critic. In this chapter, the author reviews some of the more common criticisms in light of the extant empirical evidence. These criticisms are mostly found to be lacking in substance. On the whole, HFT has improved market quality by reducing bid/ask spreads, enhancing immediacy, improving price discovery, and making markets more resilient to unexpected shocks. Despite this, a relatively small suite of pathological behaviors merit attention, such as front running, spoofing, and smoking. Addressing these behaviors, however, must recognize that all possible market and regulatory structures have both costs and benefits. The job of the regulator, in essence, is to choose which warts to live with, in order to achieve a satisfactory trade-off of these pluses and minuses.

Chapter 9 explores the history and development of HFT to its current stance of prominence in today's financial markets. The authors review the major types of HFT strategies in use, discuss their possible benefits and potential harms, and examine some of the regulatory responses seen so far.

Chapter 10 examines the key regulatory issues associated with HFT in the Australian equity markets. HFT has significant benefits but is not, however, free from perceived drawbacks. One matter, in particular, predatory trading, has recently attracted regulatory scrutiny in Australia. The author discusses those practices in the context of Australia's market manipulation rules.

Chapter 11 investigates the controversy over HFT and highlights the nexus of global exchanges. They are under pressure from three sets of actors—their customers (firms that trade on their exchanges), their regulator, and government-political officials—in an operating environment transformed by technology firms providing new capabilities for exchanges and their counterparties. The authors compare and contrast major global exchanges in terms of how these actors pressure them with respect to the trade-off between commercial viability and fairness and how the exchanges have responded to these challenges. Because the various actors have different agendas, exchanges face a dilemma. Efforts to accommodate one set of actors may generate opposition from another set. Competition among global exchanges for business encourages them to mobilize regulators and government-political officials to support their efforts to deal with HFT, but many exchanges face regulators who are attempting to control HFT. These relations define the nexus within which global exchanges must operate.

Chapter 12 looks at the empirical work investigating commonality in liquidity, and systematic liquidity risk utilizes various different estimators of systematic liquidity. The authors are the first to compare and contrast such estimators. They distinguish two classes of systematic liquidity estimators that both have many followers in the literature: (1) weighted average estimators based on concurrent liquidity shocks and (2) principal component estimators based on both concurrent and past liquidity shocks. Their results show that the simpler weighted average estimators perform at least as well as the more complex principal components estimators. Their finding is robust across different evaluation criteria and different underlying liquidity measures.

Chapter 13 observes the cancellation/revision rates in the electronic broking system (EBS) FX markets have dramatically increased as FX traders have relied more on algorithm trading in recent years. As an unintended consequence, market orders that were intended to be executed instantly with the best existing quotes in the market have experienced an increased likelihood of not being executed. Across various currency pairs in 2010, the failure rate of market orders was approximately 60 percent. This high rate of market order execution failures cannot be observed in 2003–2004. By fully examining the EBS order-by-order database, the authors provide vivid illustrations of behaviors observed in limit orders and market orders at high frequency. The authors find evidence that market orders in the EBS FX markets fail to be executed because (1) turnover of orders is too fast for a market order to hit a moving target and (2) market orders are not only being used in the traditional sense in which a trader is promised an immediate transaction but also being used for strategic trading.

Chapter 14 shows how the pantheon of modified Sharpe Ratios in the literature could be adjusted by a single factor which identifies trader efficiency via adaptive HFT stock price dynamics and cycle lengths for maximal alpha. The author derives a directing process for HFT trade strategy which jumps positively only when the trader executes a successful trade or stays flat otherwise. The author identifies a simple intuitively appealing summary statistic which can be extrapolated from publicly available data, and which serves as the single factor for modifying annualized Sharpe Ratio to get an efficient Sharpe Ratio.

Chapter 15 examines trading activity (1) before regular trading hours, (2) during regular trading hours, and (3) after regular trading hours on earnings announcement days and nonannouncement days for high-frequency traders and nonhigh-frequency traders. First, the authors show that, although HFT firms initiate more trades on earnings announcement days than on nonannouncement days, the proportion of volume that these trades account for is either constant or marginally lower. HFT firms initiate trades representing a higher proportion of volume during regular trading hours than during before market or after market hours. Second, the authors provide evidence that trades initiated by nonhigh-frequency traders generally contribute more to price discovery than trades initiated by high-frequency traders. For before market open earning announcements, trades initiated by nonhigh-frequency traders contribute more to price discovery than high-frequency traders, for both NYSE- and NASDAQ-listed stocks. However, the authors find that trades initiated by high-frequency traders contribute heavily to price discovery for NYSE-listed stocks during the regular trading hours following an after-hour earnings announcement. Third, the authors show that firm size, trading volume, and a stock's listing exchange influence the price discovery of trades between nonhigh-frequency traders.

Chapter 16 observes that on April 2014, Michael Lewis released the high profile book *Flash Boys* on how investment brokerages colluded with stock exchanges and high-frequency traders to the detriment of other investors and the stability of the market. Accounting educators can incorporate the lessons from the HFT scandal to reinforce the importance of organizational trust, simplicity, and personal ethical responsibility in the face of a culture of legalism, complexity, and herd mentality. The lessons can further be applied toward internal controls and building an ethical tone-at-the-top as part of the 2013 COSO internal control framework.

Chapter 17 presents ways by which HFT can benefit from the identification of information regimes in limit order books. As introduced by Lehmann (2008), in an information regime, all the information are trade related, arrive via order flow and, the fundamental value that underlines the prices does not change, it is simply translated by the size of the executed market order and the backfilling adjustment. During an information regime, the best quotes and the underlying values follow a path defined by the limit order book. This implies that algorithmic trading gains can be strengthened by identifying not only these information regimes but also by forecasting the transition periods between regimes, that signal fundamental changes in assets' prices, trading behavior and, optimal trading strategies. The results of the authors show that the discovery and identification of information regimes essentially uncovers the mechanism by which latent demands are translated into realized prices and volumes and, from here, that they can be used by professional traders.

Chapter 18 investigates the effects of firm-specific announcements during the year 2010 for companies listed on Borsa Istanbul. These announcements were obtained from the Public Disclosure Platform (KAP) which is the first official channel for accessing company related news. Specifically, liquidity dynamics such as time- and quantity-weighted bid and ask prices, spreads, limit order book aggregates and waiting times between buy and sell orders as well as trade dynamics such as volume-weighted average price, price variance, price fluctuation, volumes and numbers of buyer- and seller-initiated trades and inter-trade durations during continuous auction are compared for the period before and after the arrival of particular types of news. The results are examined for the eventual application of HFT strategies.

Chapter 19 features an analysis of the relationship between the volatility of the Dow Jones Industrial Average (DJIA) Index and a sentiment news series using daily data obtained from the Thomson Reuters News Analytics (TRNA) provided by SIRCA (The Securities Industry Research Center of the Asia Pacific). The expansion of online financial news sources, such as the Internet news and social media sources, provides instantaneous access to financial news. Commercial agencies have started developing their own filtered financial news feeds, which are used by investors and traders to support their algorithmic trading strategies. In this paper, the authors use a high-frequency sentiment series, developed by TRNA, to construct a series of daily sentiment scores for DJIA stock index component companies. A variety of forms of this measure, namely basic scores, absolute values of the series, squared values of the series, and the first differences of the series, are used to estimate three standard volatility models, namely GARCH, EGARCH, and GJR. The authors use these alternative daily DJIA market sentiment scores to examine the relationship between financial news sentiment scores and the volatility of the DJIA return series. The authors demonstrate how this calibration of machine-filtered news can improve volatility measures.

Chapter 20 investigates the profitability of technical trading rules applied to high frequency data across two time periods: (1) periods of increased market volatility, and (2) periods of market's upward trend. The analysis utilizes 5-min data for the S&P 500 Index and the VIX from 2011 to 2013. Three variants of four common trading rules are tested (moving averages, filter rules, Bollinger bands, and breakouts). The results suggest that the VIX is not a useful indicator for technical trading profitability at high frequencies regardless of the volatility regime. The S&P 500 Index data are shown to generate profitable trading signals during periods of higher volatility, but not during steady market increases. Overall, the results suggest that technical trading strategies calculated at high frequencies are more profitable when the market is volatile.

Chapter 21 examines the relationship between high-frequency news flow and the states of asset return volatility. To estimate the asset return volatility and smoothing probability, the authors first apply the Markov Regime-Switching GARCH model. Second, the different states of asset return volatility are identified by comparing the previously generated smoothing probability with certain thresholds. Subsequently, they employ discrete choice models to investigate the impact of high-frequency news flow on the volatility states of hourly returns of the constituent stocks in the Dow Jones Composite Average (DJN 65). Their data set for high-frequency news flows is constructed from the new RavenPack Dow Jones News Analytics database that captures over 1200 types of firm-specific and macroeconomic news releases at high frequencies. Estimated results show that the different types of news flows have varying significant effects on the likelihood of volatility states of intraday asset returns.

Chapter 22 investigates the effect of public information arrival on return volatility for Borsa Istanbul (BIST) using intraday, 60-min returns between October 3, 2013 and March 31, 2014. Stock return and return volatility is expected to react to news arrival if such news causes market participants to adjust their portfolios. To measure new information arrival, the authors count the number of daily news headlines for Turkey, the United States and a sample of European countries with close trading ties with Turkey. Furthermore, the authors focus on economic news and particularly on news on real economy and inflation. In addition, along with the BIST100 index, which is the most commonly used market portfolio index, they also utilize Second National Market (SNM) index. Their results show that news arrival influences return volatility negatively, and it has no significant effect on index returns. Moreover, return volatility responds significantly to negative surprises in GDP and inflation announcements. Finally, they do not provide evidence that indicates differences in the usage of information that arrives to the market between BIST100 and SNM investors.

Chapter 23 addresses that the issue that under the Capital Asset Pricing Model assumptions, the market capitalization weighted portfolio is mean–variance efficient. In real world applications it has been shown by various authors that low risk portfolios outperform the market capitalization-weighted portfolio. The authors revisit this anomaly using high-frequency data to construct low risk portfolios for the S&P 500 constituents over the period 2007–2012. The portfolios that they consider are invested in the 100 lowest risk portfolios and apply either equal-, market capitalization, or inverse risk weighting. The authors find that the low risk anomaly is also present when using high-frequency data, and for downside risk measures like semivariance and Cornish–Fisher value at risk. For the portfolios considered, there does not seem to be any statistically or economically significant gain of using high-frequency data.

Chapter 24 examines multifactor stochastic volatility models of the financial time series can have important applications in portfolio management and pricing/hedging of financial instruments. Based on the semi-martingale paradigm, the authors focus on the study and the estimation of the leverage effect, that is defined as the covariance between the price and the volatility process and modeled as a stochastic process. Their estimation procedure is based only on a pre-estimation of the Fourier coefficients of the volatility process. This approach constitutes a novelty in comparison with the nonparametric leverage estimators proposed in the literature, generally based on a pre-estimation of the spot volatility, and it can be directly applied to estimate the leverage effect in the case of irregular trading observations and in the presence of microstructure noise contaminations, i.e., in a high-frequency framework. The finite sample performances of the Fourier estimator of the leverage are tested in numerical simulations and in an empirical application to S&P 500 index futures.

PART 1

Trading Activity

CHAPTER 1

High-Frequency Activity on NASDAQ

Martin Scholtus, Dick van Dijk
Econometric Institute and Tinbergen Institute, Erasmus University Rotterdam, Rotterdam, The Netherlands

Contents

1.1 INTRODUCTION

Electronic trading and the large investments in IT infrastructure have completely transformed the trading process in recent years. The most practical implication of the rise in automated trading is the large increase in trading activity accompanied by an apparent decline in trading efficiency measured by, for example, the order-cancellation rate. Biais et al. (1995) report that in 1991, 48.2% of all orders for 19 stocks traded on Paris Bourse are executions. Since then the percentage of executions appears to be decreasing over time. For example, Lo et al. (2002) find that, for the 100 largest stocks in the S&P 500 over the period 1994–1995, 37.5% of limit orders submitted through ITG (an institutional brokerage firm) are fully executed, while Ellul et al. (2007) document that between April 30, 2001 and May 4, 2001 the percentage of market orders for 148 stocks traded on the NYSE is 35.2%. By June 2008, just 7.7% of all orders submitted to NASDAQ for a set of 394 stocks consists of executions (Hasbrouck and Saar, 2013).

A clear example of how automation affects trading is provided by Boehmer et al. (2005) who investigate the introduction of the NYSE OpenBook system, which makes it possible for traders to observe depth in the order book in real time at each price level. Following the introduction of OpenBook in 2002, the expected time-to-cancellation of limit orders decreased with 24.3%, while the overall order-cancellation rate increased

The Handbook of High Frequency Trading
ISBN 978-0-12-802205-4

by 17.2%.[1] Another recent technological change on the NYSE is the introduction of the hybrid market, designed to automate executions and increase trading speed. However, Hendershott and Moulton (2011) do not find conclusive evidence that the introduction of the hybrid market leads to a change in the ratio of canceled shares to total shares placed.

The large increase in order (or message) activity leads to the dilution of traditional market microstructure concepts and, at the same time, to the introduction of new concepts. Hasbrouck and Saar (2009) introduce the notion of fleeting orders, which are nonmarketable limit orders that are canceled within a short time interval after having been submitted to the exchange. Hasbrouck and Saar (2009) document that, for a sample of 100 NASDAQ listed stocks traded on INET during October 2004, 36.7% (11.5%) of the limit orders are fleeting and get canceled within 2 seconds (100 milliseconds). On the other hand, O'Hara (2010) describes how fleeting orders (but also, for example, flash orders or "match only" orders) lead to a situation where it is no longer clear what can be considered a quote and argues for a reexamination of this basic concept.

The increase in message traffic is a concern for regulators such as the SEC and for exchange venues as well. The SEC's task to investigate illegal practices such as insider trading or market manipulation is highly complicated by the huge amount of message activity generated in different markets and on different exchanges. In order to alleviate the regulatory problems, the SEC required exchanges and national security associations to design and implement a consolidated order tracking system, or audit trail, in October 2012. The continuing increase in message activity also imposes a burden on exchanges as large investments in IT infrastructure are necessary to keep order management systems running smoothly. Apparently, it is hard for exchanges to keep up as on July 2, 2012, NASDAQ introduced a fee for market participants that exceed a (weighted) order-to-trade ratio of 100:1.

This chapter provides an extensive overview of message (or trading) activity in the S&P 500 (SPY) Exchange Traded Fund (ETF) traded on NASDAQ over the period January 6, 2009 up to December 12, 2011. First, we describe message activity over the day, hour, minute, and second, differentiating between overall trading activity and algorithmic trading activity. Second, we zoom in on the millisecond environment. For example, we investigate the percentage of improvements to the best bid and ask quote that disappear within a short period of time (between 10 milliseconds and 1 second) and how frequently this leads to lower bid and higher ask quotes (a missed opportunity). Finally, we zoom in on trading activity around macroeconomic news announcements. We single out the S&P 500 ETF as it is the most liquid instrument traded on NASDAQ over the sample period.

---

[1] Although in the end the NYSE observed a technological shock, Boehmer et al. (2005) point out that the increase (decrease) in cancellation rates (order lifetimes) is because traders try to limit the exposures associated with limit orders, as described by Harris (1996).

The main characteristics of the new trading environment are as follows. First, the activity of algorithmic traders over the day, hour, and minute shows pronounced periodic patterns, similar to overall message intensity. This does not hold within the second for the activity of algorithms that target the top of the order book. In this case, the absence of periodicity suggests that these algorithms are mainly event based. Second, 35.5% (60.6%) of all orders added to the order book are canceled within 100 milliseconds (1 second). The majority of these orders is added at the best bid or ask quote. Third, 34.9% (80.3%) of all quotes that improve upon the best bid or ask quote disappear within 10 milliseconds (1 second). Especially in 2009, vanished improvements to the best bid or ask quote leave a worse order book behind.

The main contribution of this chapter is an extensive overview of (seasonalities in) regular trading activity as well as algorithmic trading activity using order-level data for a highly liquid instrument over a sample period of almost three years. To the best of our knowledge, no such complete descriptive overview exists. Related work includes Prix et al. (2007) and Hasbrouck and Saar (2013). Prix et al. (2007) describe the lifetimes of canceled orders for the DAX 30 stocks traded on Deutsche Börse for one week in 2004 and one week in 2005. They document, among others, peaks in cancellations at order lifetimes of 1, 2, 30, 60, 120, and 180 seconds. Hasbrouck and Saar (2013) use order-level data from NASDAQ for individual stocks in October 2007 and June 2008 and distinguish between traders that act based on a fixed time schedule and traders that are triggered by market events. An analysis of the millisecond environment, similar to what we perform in this chapter, identifies peaks in activity within the second. The peaks are contributed to market participants that trade, due to their geographic locations, with the same speed.

The outline of this chapter is as follows. Section 1.2 provides a description of the NASDAQ data. Section 1.3 discusses the stylized facts of the trading environment, starting with periodicity in overall message activity (Section 1.3.1), followed by a description of algorithmic activity and details of the millisecond environment (Section 1.3.2), and trading activity during news (Section 1.3.3). Section 1.4 provides concluding remarks.

1.2 DATA

We use complete intraday order book information for the State Street S&P 500 ETF traded on NASDAQ over the period from January 6, 2009 up to December 12, 2011. The total number of trading days in the sample period is 741. We exclude four trading days with an early close due to holidays (November 27, 2009, December 24, 2009, November 26, 2010, and November 25, 2011) and the day of the flash crash (May 6, 2010), leading to a sample of 736 days. NASDAQ does not directly provide the full order book, but this is constructed by means of the daily NASDAQ TotalView ITCH files (V4.0 and V4.1). NASDAQ ITCH data does not include orders at other exchanges such as NYSE (Arca), BATS, or NSX. According to the market share, files published on https://www.nasdaqtrader.com/trader.aspx?ID=marketsharedaily, NAS-DAQ's market share in SPY is, on average, 53.2% during our sample period. Hence, although we work with a subset of the trading universe, we capture more than half of the total activity in SPY.

The TotalView ITCH files contain recordings of a direct data feed product offered by NASDAQ. This is exactly the same data as market participants would receive in real time. The data entries in the files are order-level data as well as trade messages, administrative messages, and net order imbalance data. We make use of order-level data and some of the trade and administrative messages. The order-level data consists of messages to add a new order (types A and F) and messages to modify existing orders (types E, C, X, D, and U). Order modifications include execution messages (types E and C, where an E message is an execution against the price of the limit order originally put in and a C message is an execution against a different price at, for example, a cross trade), order cancellations (type X), deletions (type D), and replace messages (type U). The NASDAQ market rules (http://nasdaq.cchwallstreet.com/NASDAQ/Main/) describe how more "advanced" order types are dealt with. For example, immediate or cancel limit orders are returned to the entering participant when nonmarketable and do not enter the order book (rule 4751.g.1).

From the trade messages, we use the match events of nondisplayable orders (message type P). These messages affect the trade volume counts, but not the order book. The administrative messages provide system event messages (including, for example, start and end of system and market hours), information about trading halts, and market participant positions. All messages have a time stamp with potential nanosecond precision. However, nanoseconds are not provided over the full sample period, therefore we use millisecond (ms) precision.

There are two challenges in the construction of the order book. The first challenge is the large amount of data that must be processed. The total size of the TotalView ITCH files for our sample period of close to three years is about 7 terabytes. The second challenge is the large number of search operations required, resulting from the fact that only add order messages (types A and F) have a field with a ticker symbol. Once an order has been added to the order book, it is referred to by means of the order identification number. The only way to determine whether a nonadd order message is relevant to the order book of the S&P 500 ETF is by checking whether the order number is already in the order book. The construction of the order book itself is a straightforward bookkeeping exercise that can be verified because the book, which starts empty at the beginning of system hours, must be empty again at the end of the day.

From June 5, 2009 to August 31, 2009 it was possible to use so-called flash orders on NASDAQ. The flash order functionality makes it possible that, if an order has executed against the orders in the top of the NASDAQ order book, the remainder of the order is shown at the top of the book for a maximum of 500 ms instead of being sent to another exchange. If, after 500 ms, there is still reason to send the order to another exchange, the order is canceled (this is the case when the order is still marketable at another exchange). When there is no reason to send the order to another exchange (the order is nonmarketable at other exchanges), it remains in the order book until canceled by the customer. The three months with flash order functionality are included in the analysis, but could affect our findings concerning fleeting orders. Any results that are potentially affected by the inclusion of flash orders are tested for robustness.

1.3 RESULTS

In Table 1.1 we provide summary statistics regarding the number of messages per type per day for the complete sample period January 6, 2009—December 12, 2011 (panel A) and for the individual calendar years (panels B—E). For the individual message types in Table 1.1, the statistics are calculated on a daily basis and then averaged across all days the message type is supported by NASDAQ.[2]

From Table 1.1, it is clear that SPY is a highly liquid ETF with almost 5.0 million messages per day on average. Throughout the sample period the average daily activity varies somewhat, ranging from 4.8 million messages per day in 2011 up to 5.2 million messages per day in 2010. Given a 6.5 hours trading day from 09:30 a.m. to 04:00 p.m., the average number of messages per second is 212.2. Figure 1.1 provides the empirical distributions of total message activity. Not surprisingly, these differ strongly from a normal distribution. Total message activity is positively skewed and has excess kurtosis. This is most pronounced in 2009 and 2011.

Most of the message activity consists of add order (A and F) and delete order (D) messages, which make up more than 80% of the total message activity. This percentage is quite stable over time, at 82.3%, 81.3%, and 81.7% in the years 2009, 2010, and 2011, respectively. The percentage of messages that are executions (type C, E, or P) is rather modest at 4.39% over the whole sample period. This is substantially lower than the 7.7% reported by Hasbrouck and Saar (2013) for individual stocks in June 2008. The difference can, at least partly, be attributed to the different type of asset and different sample period considered here. We also note that the decline in the percentage of executions since the early 1990s may have stabilized as the decrease from 5.9% in 2009—3.4% in 2010 is followed by an increase to 3.9% in 2011. The percentage of order replacements (U) is considerably lower in 2009 (10.9%) compared to the full sample period (13.4%). This is due to the fact that the U message type was not available during the first 64 trading days in 2009, as it was introduced only in April 2009 (http://www.nasdaqtrader.com/TraderNews.aspx?id=dn2009-010).

---

[2] Results without explicit reference to a figure or table number are provided in an Internet Appendix located at https://goo.gl/ZxCf3H.

Table 1.1 Average message intensity (×1000) per day per message type

	A	C	D	E	F	P	U	X	TOTAL
Panel A: full sample 2009–2011									
Mean	2129.42	10.41	1980.61	195.09	7.92	7.14	607.44	27.48	4965.51
Median	1821.83	6.76	1692.94	161.34	3.04	6.00	588.46	8.18	4452.41
% Of total	42.34	0.19	39.26	4.05	0.15	0.15	13.42	0.45	100.00
Stdev	1147.62	11.08	1073.84	112.83	30.61	4.51	353.84	70.31	2406.50
Panel B: 2009									
Mean	2191.57	15.46	1995.29	251.73	4.28	6.64	372.20	63.49	4900.66
Median	1416.25	8.27	1269.44	201.39	3.07	5.37	291.65	11.45	3494.17
% Of total	43.20	0.26	38.98	5.47	0.09	0.14	10.91	0.95	100.00
Stdev	1643.08	15.40	1531.69	139.95	3.50	4.54	360.47	112.40	3260.96
Panel C: 2009 ex. f.o.									
Mean	2509.76	19.21	2292.27	276.28	4.69	7.33	349.37	78.52	5537.43
Median	1725.63	11.34	1547.52	237.18	3.31	6.23	247.54	45.62	4403.10
% Of total	43.78	0.31	39.65	5.27	0.08	0.14	9.68	1.08	100.00
Stdev	1775.58	16.00	1654.97	152.25	3.89	4.16	400.09	125.00	3512.17
Panel D: 2010									
Mean	2167.19	5.99	2042.90	158.44	2.88	5.51	789.01	8.76	5180.68
Median	2085.82	5.52	1985.18	143.30	2.40	5.20	792.52	7.65	5107.04
% Of total	41.83	0.12	39.38	3.13	0.06	0.11	15.19	0.18	100.00
Stdev	821.84	3.37	783.08	69.98	1.80	2.57	330.04	4.31	1930.73
Panel E: 2011									
Mean	2024.98	9.79	1899.86	174.58	17.01	9.36	661.85	9.63	4807.06
Median	1849.74	6.69	1754.10	150.78	3.53	7.67	638.67	7.64	4460.58
% Of total	41.98	0.19	39.43	3.53	0.31	0.19	14.17	0.21	100.00
Stdev	738.04	8.59	689.92	93.44	52.59	5.15	206.84	10.00	1697.85

Note: This table shows the mean, median, and standard deviation of the number of messages per message type per day (in thousands) for the S\&P 500 ETF traded on NASDAQ over the period January 6, 2009 to December 12, 2011 (panel A). Panels B–E shows the same statistics for individual calendar years. The year 2009 is also provided excluding the 64 days with flash order functionality (2009 ex. f.o.). The percentage of total message activity per day attributed to a certain message type is provided by % of Total. The message types, denoted by capital letters are: A; add order message (no market participant identifier), F; add order message (with market participant identifier), C; order executed message (with price), E; order executed message (without price), D; order delete message, U; order replace message, P; trade of nondisplayable order message.

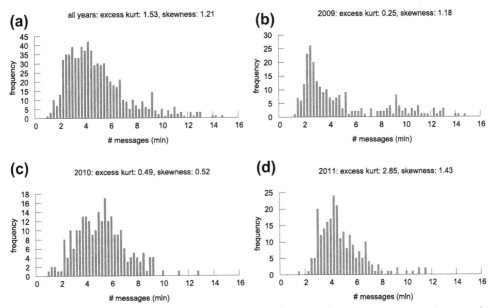

Figure 1.1 *Number of messages per pay.* Distribution of the number of messages per day over the period January 6, 2009 to December 12, 2011 in subplot (a) and separately for the Years 2009, 2010, and 2011 in Subplots (b) to (d).

Figure 1.2 displays the average number of messages per week over time (panel a), as well as the average number of messages per month of the year (b), day of the month (c), and day of the week (d). Figure 1.2(a) provides a more detailed picture of the variation in message activity over time. Comparing this with the underlying S&P 500 index, it appears that message activity is relatively high during periods of declining stock prices, in particular during periods of turmoil such as the first months of 2009 (the latter part of the financial crisis), and April–June 2010 and August 2011 (European sovereign debt crisis). Although the average number of messages per week does not exhibit any clear signs of seasonality, Figure 1.2(b) indicates that total message activity is highest during January–March with approximately six million messages per day on average. Message activity strongly declines toward the end of the year, with an average day in December having only three million messages.[3] Figure 1.2(c) reveals that message activity also declines toward the end of the month, with the final trading days of the month receiving 10–20% less messages than other days on average. Finally, Figure 1.2(d) shows that on

---

[3] Figure 1.2(b) is constructed by averaging the number of messages per day across all days in a certain month instead of averaging the messages per month and then averaging the months over the years. Hence, we account for differences in the average number of trading days in different months and for the fact that our sample only contains the first half of December 2011.

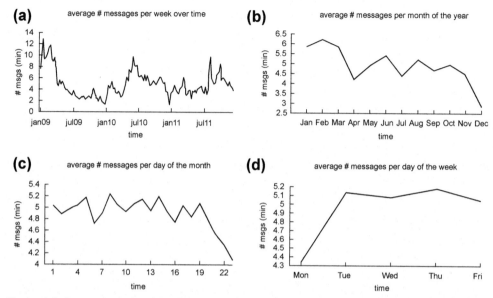

Figure 1.2 *Average message intensity.* Average message intensity per week over time (a), average number of messages per month of the year (b), average number of messages per day of the month (c), and the average number of messages per day of the week (d) over the period January 6, 2009–December 12, 2011.

average Monday has about 20% less messages than the other days of the week, which is consistent with the lower trading volumes (and higher) volatility on Monday observed by Kiymaz and Berument (2003).

1.3.1 Intraday Overall Message Activity

In this section we investigate how the message intensity is distributed over the day, hour, minute, and second. The analysis over the day is performed by (1) calculating the percentage of total daily activity that occurs during each minute of the day for each day in the sample period and (2) averaging the percentage in each minute across all trading days. In order to gain insight in the distribution of message activity over the hour, minute, and second, we consider subintervals of 1 minute (min), 1 second (s), and 1 millisecond (ms), respectively. In all cases, message activity in a given subinterval is expressed as a percentage of total activity during the complete period (of 1 hour, minute, or second). Furthermore, for this analysis we exclude the first 90 minutes and last 60 minutes of the trading day, to avoid undue influence of these specific trading periods (which show by far the highest message activity). Unless there are considerable differences over time, we report the average (relative) message activity over the complete sample period.

Figure 1.3(a) shows the average message activity during the complete trading day. Total message activity follows a pronounced U-shape, which is also found for intraday

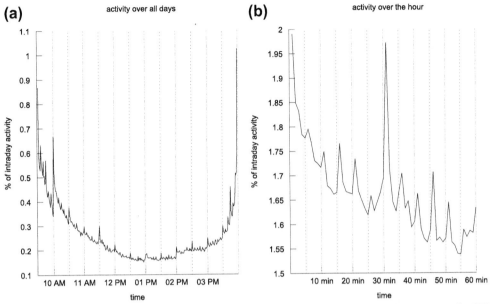

Figure 1.3 *Average message intensity—minute by minute.* Average total message intensity for SPY per minute for each day (a) and per minute of each hour excluding the first 90 and last 60 min of the trading day (b) over the period January 6, 2009–December 12, 2011.

bid—ask spreads and trading volumes (McInish and Wood, 1992; Lehmann and Modest, 1994, among others). At 10:00 a.m., a large peak occurs in message intensity, which is a consequence of macroeconomic news announcements (the spike disappears when we exclude the 354 days with macroeconomic news at 10:00 a.m.). This is no surprise as the S&P 500 ETF is a popular instrument for speculation and hedging with simultaneous activity in both futures and option markets. In addition, Figure 1.3(a) provides a first indication of periodic intraday patterns in message activity, by showing small but regular peaks at full and half hours. This is further investigated by analyzing message intensity over the hour, minute, and second.

The average message activity during the hour is displayed in Figure 1.3(b). Within the hour we find peaks in message intensity just after the hour change, at the half hour change, and quite regularly at 5 min interval changes, but in particular at one and three quarters into the hour.[4] The hourly and half-hourly peaks remain when we exclude the days with macroeconomic news announcements at 10:00 a.m. These spikes in message activity may therefore be attributed to market participants that are triggered by clock

---

[4] Note that activity at minute 16 is an average percentage of activity that occurs during the minute starting at hh:15:00 up to (but not including) hh:16:00.

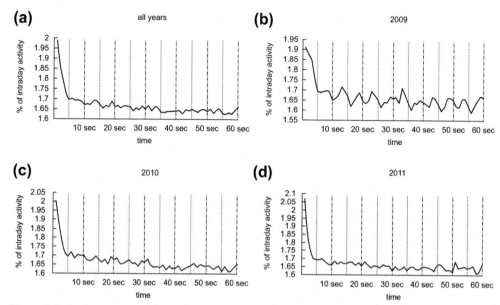

Figure 1.4 *Average message intensity—second by second.* Average total message intensity for SPY per second for each minute excluding the first 90 and last 60 min of the trading day over the period January 6, 2009–December 12, 2011.

activity, or could be explained by other events, such as non-10 a.m. macroeconomic news arrivals (either at whole or half hours), scheduled dark pool crosses, or the close of equity markets in Europe.

The message intensity per second within the minute over the complete sample period, presented in Figure 1.4(a), reveals a peak in intensity when the minute changes, whereas during the rest of the minute small peaks occur that do not match a regular pattern. There are some differences in message intensity over the minute for different calendar years (subplots (b) to (d) in Figure 1.4). Whereas the year 2009 shows periodicity through the minute, message activity in 2010 and 2011 is more centered around the start of the minute. The regularities during the beginning of every minute can also be explained by market participants that trade at a certain fixed frequency or fixed schedule based on clock time.

Figure 1.5 displays the message intensity within the second for the complete sample period (subplot (a)) and the individual years 2009–2011 (subplots (b) through (d)). The first peak within the second provides a good insight in how fast traders act on periodic (clock-time) events. For the years 2009 and 2010, the first peak can be found at 5 ms and 1 ms in the second, respectively. It is remarkable that for the year 2011, the first peak is only found at 19 ms. A potential explanation is that the most advanced (fastest) market participants no longer base their trading on clock time. Unique features of the

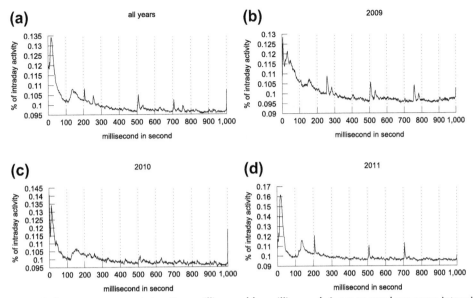

Figure 1.5 *Average message intensity—millisecond by millisecond.* Average total message intensity for SPY per millisecond for each second excluding the first 90 and last 60 min of the trading day over the period January 6, 2009–December 12, 2011.

year 2009 are the high message intensity around 50 ms and the double peaks at 250, 500, and 750 ms. The latter are most likely caused by traders in the same geographic location, but with differences in hardware and complexity of trading algorithms (the more complex an algorithm the more time it takes to provide a trade signal). Activity in 2010 is characterized by a spike at 13 ms and a large increase in activity at the end of the second, whereas peaks in message activity are observed at 200, 500, and 700 ms in 2011. The pattern in Figure 1.5 does not change when the first 5 seconds of each minute (which are characterized by most activity, see Figure 1.4) are excluded.

1.3.2 Algorithmic Activity

Next, we investigate message traffic of algorithmic traders and high-frequency traders. The message entries in the TotalView ITCH files do not include the identity of the market participant submitting the order; hence, we cannot determine directly whether a message originates from algorithmic and high-frequency trading activity. To distinguish between human market participants and computers we therefore make use of the concept of a fleeting order, introduced by Hasbrouck and Saar (2009). A fleeting order is an order added to the order book and removed "very quickly." The removal can be due to the fact that an order is fully canceled or updated (message type U). In turn, an updated order can again be fleeting when it is updated or fully canceled within a short period of time.

We make the concept of fleeting orders operational by defining "very quickly" as within 10, 25, 50, 100, 200, 500 ms, and 1 s. Especially for the first five of these so-called fleet levels, it is extremely unlikely that a human can consistently submit and cancel orders at such high speed. In addition to the aggregate of all fleeting orders, we separately investigate three subgroups, namely those fleeting orders (1) that occur at the best bid or ask quote; (2) that improve upon the best bid or ask quote; or (3) that are "missed opportunities." By the latter category, we mean fleeting orders that are added above the best bid or below the best ask and leave a worse order book when they are removed. Hence, these fleeting orders represent a missed opportunity for other market participants to trade at a more attractive price. Note that all three subgroups of algorithmic trading proxies focus on the top of the order book. These may capture activities of different algorithmic or high-frequency traders than the aggregate fleeting order measure that takes the full order book into account. Furthermore, as we only observe NASDAQ trading activity it is possible that the missed opportunities are executed elsewhere.

Figure 1.6(a) provides the percentage of fleeting orders with respect to the total number of limit orders added to the order book. This shows that fleeting orders account for a substantial part of total message activity. Over the full sample period, the percentage of fleeting orders added to the order book is 18.8% at the 10 ms level, which increases to 35.3% and 60.6% for the 100 ms and 1 s levels. As total message activity consists for 95.2% of the message types A, F, D, and U, 57.7% of total message activity involves fleeting orders at the 100 ms level. This is considerably higher than the numbers provided by Hasbrouck and Saar (2009) who find that 11.5% of nonmarketable limit orders is fleeting at the 100 ms level for individual stocks traded on INET in October 2004. The difference is most likely caused by (1) the fact that we consider a highly liquid ETF instead of individual stocks and (2) because automated trading is much more extensive and prominent in 2009−2011 compared to 2004. This increase in automated trading can, to a large extent be attributed to new regulation, in particular the "Order-Protection-Rule" component of Regulation NMS introduced in 2007. This rule prevents the execution of orders at prices inferior to those displayed at the best bid or ask quotes of other trading centers. Complying with these rules is only possible in a fully electronic trading environment, leading to a boost in automated trading. McInish and Upson (2013) and Ding et al. (2014) discuss the order protection rule and (quantify) its adverse impact on slow liquidity demanders.

The percentage of fleeting orders over the individual years in Figure 1.6(a) indicates that the percentage of fleeting orders increases steadily over time during our sample period, for all fleet levels considered. For example, at the 1 s level, the percentage of fleeting orders increases from 54.7% in 2009 to 65.7% in 2011. It also appears that for "slow" fleeting orders, which remain in the order book for more than 100 ms, the increase occurs gradually and is about the same in 2010 and 2011. For "faster" fleets,

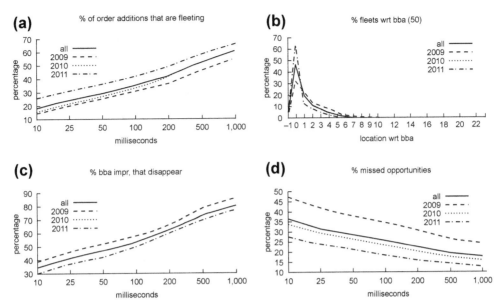

Figure 1.6 *Fleeting order characteristics.* Percentage of add order messages over the period January 6, 2009—December 12, 2011 during normal trading hours that are fleeting orders (a), (b) the distribution of the point of entry of fleeting orders in the order book where 0, −1, and x indicate additions at the best bid or ask quote, before the best bid or ask quote, and x cents behind the best bid or ask quote (with $1 \leq x \leq 23$), respectively. Subplot (c) provides the percentage of all improvements to the best bid or ask quote that disappear (either due to cancellations or executions) within 10 ms up to 1 s, whereas (d) shows the percentage of missed opportunities within 10 ms up to 1 s. A missed opportunity is an add order message, which is an improvement to the best bid or ask quote that, when it is either removed or executed, leaves a worse price in the order book.

which are removed within 100 ms after entering the order book, the percentages for 2009 and 2010 are approximately the same, whereas there is a large increase to 2011.

An overview of the locations where fleeting orders (at the 50 ms level, results are qualitatively similar for other fleet levels) enter the order book is presented in Figure 1.6(b). For the complete sample period, most fleeting orders (46.8%) enter the order book at the best bid or ask quote (location 0). The percentage of fleeting orders added more than five cents away from the best bid or ask is negligible. The same holds for fleeting orders that improve the best bid or ask quote (location −1). This is not surprising given the fact that the overall number of improvements to the best bid or ask is low compared to total message activity. This is because most of the times the bid—ask spread is one cent, leaving no additional room to improve upon. Interestingly, the results for individual years show that fleeting orders increasingly target the top of the order book. The percentage of fleeting orders entering at the best bid or ask quote almost doubles from 32.4% in 2009 to 64.6% in 2011. The results in Figure 1.6(b) are similar when we consider alternative fleet levels. The main difference is that "slower" fleeting orders are less likely to be added at the top of the order book. For example, at the 10 ms, 100 ms, and 1 s levels the percentage of fleeting orders that is added before or at the best bid or ask quote is 48.4%, 47.0%, and 45.4%, respectively.

Next, in Figure 1.6(c), we zoom in on those orders that improve upon the best bid or ask quote. In this case we do not only include fast order cancellations, but also those limit orders that are fully executed within a short time interval after having been submitted to the exchange (fleeting executions). Over the complete sample 34.9% of all quotes that improve upon the best bid or ask disappears within 10 ms. This increases to 53.6% and 80.3% after 100 ms and 1 s. Bid or ask improvements disappear fastest in 2009. For example, within 10 ms 39.0% of quote improvements disappear in 2009, compared to 30.7% in 2011.

Missing an improvement to the best bid or ask quote is problematic only if the remaining entries in the order book are less attractive. Figure 1.6(d) provides the number of missed opportunities, which is defined as the percentage of orders that improve the best bid or ask when entering the order book and leave a worse book when they are removed or executed. Hence, during the time the fleeting order is at the top of the order book no other orders are added at the price level of the fleeting order. We find that at the 10 ms level, 36.3% of the disappeared improvements to the best bid or ask quote lead to a worse order book over the complete sample period. This percentage steadily declines from 47.4% in 2009 to 27.6% in 2011. The percentage of missed opportunities decreases when bid and ask improvements remain longer in the order book. At the 1 s level, for example, 24.3% and 12.8% of improvements to the best bid or ask quote is a missed opportunity in 2009 and 2011.

Combining the above, we find that although 2011 has a higher percentage of fleeting orders compared to 2009, the fleets that improve the best bid and ask quote live longer. In case a quote improvement disappears quickly in 2011, it is less likely (compared to 2009) that this leads to a worse order book. In Figure 1.7 we split the percentage of vanished improvements in fleeting orders and fleeting executions. It appears that the main difference between 2009 and 2011 is a lower percentage of fleeting executions in the latter year. It is possible that due to the lower amount of missed opportunities in 2011, there is less need for immediate execution as the rapid supply of new orders at the improved bid and ask quote is sufficient. Another explanation for the observed differences may be the turbulent market conditions in 2009 compared to 2011. The average (maximum) daily closing value of the VIX (obtained from http://www.cboe.com/micro/vix/historical.aspx) is 31.4 (56.7) in 2009 compared to 22.5 (45.8) and 24.2 (48.0) in 2010 and 2011, respectively.

Figure 1.8 gives an overview of fleeting order intensity at the 50 ms level conditional upon the bid—ask spread. For each day, we count how frequently fleeting orders occur when the bid—ask spread is one to seven cents. We do not take into account larger spreads, because the number of seconds per day that the spread is wider than seven cents

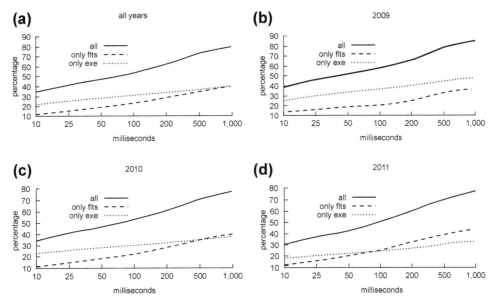

Figure 1.7 *Disappeared bid–ask improvements due to cancellations and executions.* Total percentage of all improvements to the best bid or ask quote that disappear within 10 ms up to 1 s split up into the component resulting from cancellations (only flts) and from executions (only exe). This figure provides more details for subplot (c) in Figure 1.6.

is negligible. The average number of seconds per day that the spread is one to seven cents is: 21,762 (6 h, 2 min, and 42 s), 1551 (25 min and 51 s), 19.5, 8.0, 8.2, 6.0, and 3.8 s, respectively. Although hardly visible, the total number of fleeting orders and the number of fleeting orders at the best bid or ask quote is 6 and 10 times larger when the spread is two cents instead of one cent. Spread levels of three cents or more are rare but lead to a steep increase in all fleeting order variants. This reaction is strongest in 2011. The reaction to large spreads is least pronounced in 2009, which may indicate that in this year algorithms are still more clock-based instead of event-triggered (event-based strategies can be based on order book events such as large spreads or large market orders, but also news events).

Next, in Figure 1.9 we investigate the distribution of fleeting orders (at the 50 ms level) over the day, hour, minute, and second.[5] The distribution of all fleeting orders over the day, hour, and minute closely resembles the patterns obtained for total message intensity, as shown in Figure 1.3, Figure 1.4(a) and Figure 1.5(a). The same holds for fleeting orders that enter at the best bid or ask quote. One exception is that within

---

[5] Algorithmic trading activity over time, per month of the year, per day of the month, and per day of the week for all fleeting orders is highly similar to the findings of overall trading intensity provided in Figure 1.2, except for the fact that algorithmic activity shows a spike in August 2011.

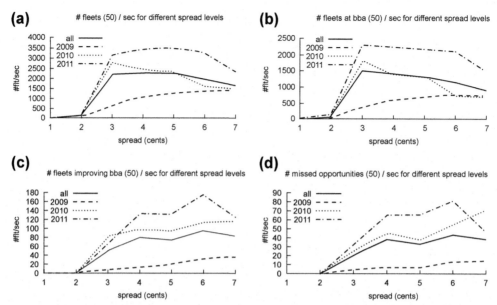

Figure 1.8 *Different types of fleeting orders and bid–ask spread.* Intensity of all fleeting orders (a), fleeting orders at the best bid or ask quote (b) that improve upon the best bid or ask quote (c) and missed opportunities (d) per second (all at the 50 ms level) conditional on the size of the bid–ask spread. For each day, we count how frequently fleeting orders occur when the bid–ask spread is one to seven cents. In order to compare the number of fleeting orders across spread levels we scale by the number of seconds the bid–ask spread is at a specific level.

the second fleeting orders at the best bid and ask quote show less periodicity compared to overall market activity within the second. This especially holds for the years 2009 and 2010. Different patterns emerge when we focus on the fleeting orders that improve upon the best bid or ask quote. Figure 1.10 displays the distribution for this subgroup of fleeting orders, again at the 50 ms level. The fleeting orders that improve upon the best bid or ask are heavily concentrated around 10:00 a.m. (Figure 1.10(a)). This most likely is due to the occurrence of macroeconomic news announcements at that time. After removing the days with macroeconomic news at 10:00 a.m. most of the peak disappears. We return to this issue in more detail in the next section.

Figures 1.10(b) and (c) show algorithmic activity captured by fleeting orders that improve the best bid or ask quote over the hour and minute. Algorithmic activity is more peaked than total message activity, compare Figure 1.3(b) and Figure 1.4(a). This remains the case when we remove the days with macroeconomic news at 10:00 a.m. The pattern of algorithmic activity within the second in Figure 1.10(d) is considerably different from overall market activity, compare Figure 1.5(a). In fact it is hard to distinguish any pattern. When we exclude days with macroeconomic news at 10:00 a.m. or when we consider missed opportunities, the distribution within the second

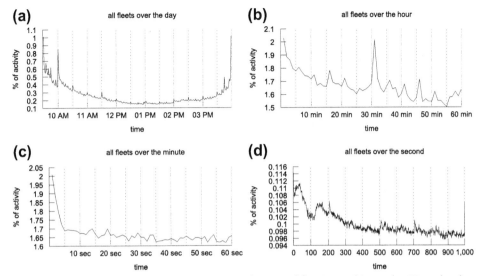

Figure 1.9 *Fleeting orders intraday intensity.* Distribution of fleeting orders at the 50 ms level over the day (a), over the hour (b), over the minute (c), and within the second (d) over the period January 6, 2009–December 12, 2011. Subplots (b), (c), and (d) are constructed excluding the first 90 and last 60 min of the trading day. The percentage of activity is obtained by first calculating the percentage of fleeting orders at the 50 ms level that occurs in each subinterval over the day, followed by averaging overall subintervals in the sample period (e.g., subplot (a) is constructed by (i) calculating the percentage of fleeting orders at the 50 ms level per minute and (ii) averaging every minute of the trading day over the 736 trading days in the sample).

becomes even more erratic. The reverse is true for all fleeting orders (over the full order book), see Figure 1.9(d). Despite the fact that fleeting orders at the top of the order book show periodicity within the hour and minute, the higher spike around macroeconomic news announcements and the absence of regularities within the second suggests that these algorithms may be more advanced and triggered by market events instead of clock-time events.

1.3.3 News Events

In the final part of the analysis, we focus on the question whether algorithmic activity is mostly based on clock time or on market events that (likely) represent the actual arrival of new information. For this purpose, we examine the intensity of fleeting orders around 10:00 a.m., which is the time that new releases of many important US macroeconomic variables are made public. We consider 12 of the most prominent macro news announcements (construction spending, factory orders, business inventories, leading indicators, new home sales, consumer confidence, ISM index, ISM services index, pending home sales, wholesale inventories, Philadelphia FED, existing home sales; source:

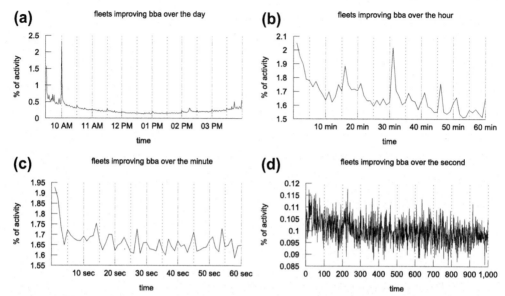

Figure 1.10 *Bid—ask improving fleeting orders intraday intensity.* Distribution of fleeting orders that improve upon the best bid or ask quote at the 50 ms level over the day (a), over the hour (b), over the minute (c), and within the second (d) over the period January 6, 2009—December 12, 2011. Subplots (b), (c), and (d) are constructed excluding the first 90 and last 60 min of the trading day. The percentage of activity is obtained by first calculating the percentage of fleeting orders that improve upon the best bid or ask quote at the 50 ms level that occurs in each subinterval over the day, followed by averaging overall subintervals in the sample period (e.g., subplot (a) is constructed by (i) calculating the percentage of fleeting orders that improve upon the best bid or ask quote at the 50 ms level per minute and (ii) averaging every minute of the trading day over the 736 trading days in the sample).

http://www.econoday.com), which together account for 423 news events on 354 different trading days. The exact news arrival time is, with millisecond precision, obtained from the Thomson Reuters SIRCA global news database.

In Figures 1.11 and 1.12 we plot the number of fleeting orders and fleeting executions at the 50 ms level entering the order book in a short interval of 2 seconds around the time of the news announcement. For days without macroeconomic news, the number of fleeting orders and executions are shown in clock time, aligned at exactly 10:00 a.m. For days with macroeconomic news they are shown in event time, aligned at the exact millisecond the news arrives in the market. Figure 1.11 considers the total number of fleeting orders and executions, whereas Figure 1.12 focuses on the fleeting orders and executions that improve upon the best bid or ask quote.

We observe a clear reaction in the total number of fleeting orders shortly before the SIRCA news arrival time. The magnitude of this reaction is, with almost 1.8 fleeting orders or executions per ms, much stronger in 2011 compared to 2010 or 2009 (about 1.0

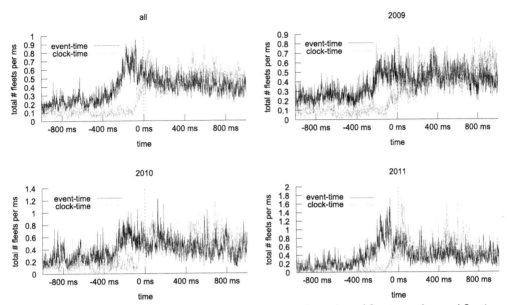

Figure 1.11 *Fleeting orders around 10:00 a.m.* Average total number of fleeting orders and fleeting executions (orders added to the order book and executed quickly) at the 50 ms level per millisecond for 1000 ms around 10:00 a.m. in clock time (dashed line) and event time (solid line) over the period January 6, 2009–December 12, 2011 (a) and, in (b) through (d) over the years 2009, 2010, and 2011, respectively. The clock-time (event time) observations are constructed by means of all days without (with) macroeconomic news at 10:00 a.m. The 0 ms value is 10:00 a.m. for days without news, and the exact SIRCA arrival time of the news in case of macroeconomic news announcements.

and 0.8 fleeting orders per ms, respectively). This supports the suggestion that algorithmic traders may have expanded their arsenal with more event-triggered strategies. Also in clock time we observe reactions around 10:00 a.m., which are most pronounced in 2011. The main difference between the total number of fleeting orders and executions (Figure 1.11) and the number of fleeting orders and executions that improve upon the best bid or ask quote (Figure 1.12) is that the reaction to news is more concentrated (the number of fleeting orders that improve upon the best bid or ask quote return faster to their preannouncement values compared to the total number of fleeting orders).

1.4 CONCLUSION

We analyze the characteristics of overall trading intensity and algorithmic trading intensity by means of order-level data of the S&P 500 ETF traded on NASDAQ over the period January 6, 2009 to December 12, 2011. Overall message activity exhibits a U-shape over the day with a large (macroeconomic news induced) peak at 10:00 a.m. Within the hour, (minute) clear periodic patterns are identified with the largest spikes

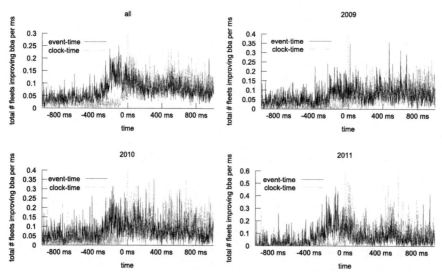

Figure 1.12 *Bid–ask improving fleeting orders around 10:00 a.m.* Average number of fleeting orders and fleeting executions (orders added to the order book and executed quickly) that improve the best bid or ask quote at the 50 ms level per millisecond for 1000 ms around 10:00 a.m. in clock time (dashed line) and event time (solid line) over the period January 6, 2009–December 12, 2011 (a) and, in (b) through (d) over the years 2009, 2010, and 2011, respectively. The clock-time (event-time) observations are constructed by means of all days without (with) macroeconomic news at 10:00 a.m. The 0 ms value is 10:00 a.m. for days without news, and the exact SIRCA arrival time of the news in case of macroeconomic news announcements.

at the change of the hour (minute). The periodicity over the day and hour is consistent over the different years, whereas activity within the minute becomes more concentrated at the minute change in 2010 and 2011. Message intensity within the second changes over the years. The fastest clock-based traders in 2009, 2010, and 2011 act in 5, 1, and 19 ms, respectively.

Algorithmic trading intensity is investigated by means of different variants of fleeting orders (orders added to the order book and removed very quickly) and fleeting executions (orders added to the order book and executed very quickly). Fleeting orders account for a substantial part of limit orders added to the order book. Over the full sample period the percentage nonmarketable limit orders that is fleeting at the 100 ms (1 s) level is 35.5% (60.6%). The importance of fleeting orders is also increasing over time. Most fleeting orders are added at the best bid or ask quote. In 2009, improvements to the best bid or ask quote disappear fastest and have the highest probability of leaving a worse order book once the fleeting quote is removed. Furthermore, in 2009 algorithms react less to large spreads and macroeconomic news compared to 2011, indicating that the average algorithm has become more event-oriented over time. This especially holds for the algorithms that target the top of the order book. The main difference between periodicity in overall message activity and algorithmic activity occurs within the second. Fleeting order measures that focus on the top of the order book show no periodicity over the second. For the fleeting order measure over the full order book, the pattern over the second is similar to that of general (overall) message intensity. A plausible explanation is that advanced algorithms that target the top of the order book are more event-based, whereas the general algorithms over the full order book are influenced by events in clock-time.

ACKNOWLEDGMENTS

The authors would like to thank NASDAQ and the Securities Industry Research Center of Asia—Pacific (SIRCA) on behalf of Thomson Reuters for providing the data for this research.

REFERENCES

Biais, B., Hillion, P., Spatt, C., 1995. An empirical analysis of the limit order book and the order flow in the Paris bourse. J. Finance 50 (5), 1655—1689.

Boehmer, E., Saar, G., Yu, L., 2005. Lifting the veil: an analysis of pre-trade transparency at the NYSE. J. Finance 60 (2), 783—815.

Ding, S., Hanna, J., Hendershott, T., 2014. How slow is the NBBO? A comparison with direct exchange feeds. Financ. Rev. 49 (1), 313—332.

Ellul, A., Holden, C.W., Jain, P., Jennings, R., 2007. Order dynamics: recent evidence from the NYSE. J. Empir. Finance 14 (5), 636—661.

Harris, L.E., (1996). Does a Large Minimum Price Variation Encourage Order Exposure? Unpublished manuscript, University of Southern California.

Hasbrouck, J., Saar, G., 2009. Technology and liquidity provision: the blurring of traditional definitions. J. Financ. Mark. 12 (2), 143—172.

Hasbrouck, J., Saar, G., 2013. Low-latency trading. J. Financ. Mark. 16 (4), 646—679.

Hendershott, T., Moulton, P.C., 2011. Automation, speed, and stock market quality: the NYSE's hybrid. J. Financ. Mark. 14 (4), 568—604.

Kiymaz, H., Berument, H., 2003. The day of the week effect on stock market volatility and volume: international evidence. Rev. Financ. Econ. 12 (4), 363—380.

Lehmann, B.N., Modest, D.M., 1994. Trading and liquidity on the Tokyo stock exchange: a bird's eye view. J. Finance 49 (3), 951—984.

Lo, A.W., MacKinlay, A.C., Zhang, J., 2002. Econometric models of limit-order executions. J. Financ. Econ. 65 (1), 31—71.

McInish, T.H., Upson, J., 2013. The quote exception rule: giving high frequency traders an unintended advantage. Financ. Manag. 42 (3), 481—501.

McInish, T.H., Wood, R.A., 1992. An analysis of intraday patterns in Bid/Ask spreads for NYSE stocks. J. Finance 47 (2), 753—764.

O'Hara, M., 2010. What is a Quote? J. Trading 5 (2), 10—16.

Prix, J., Loistl, O., Huetl, M., 2007. Algorithmic trading patterns in xetra orders. Eur. J. Finance 13 (8), 717—739.

CHAPTER 2

The Profitability of High-Frequency Trading: Is It for Real?

Imad Moosa, Vikash Ramiah
School of Economics, Finance and Marketing, RMIT, Melbourne, VIC, Australia

Contents

2.1 INTRODUCTION

In late June 2014, high-frequency trading (HFT) hit the news again when a lawsuit was filed against Barclays bank on the grounds that the bank had misled its clients by claiming that it was using its "dark pool" to protect them from "predatory high-frequency traders" (Associated Press, 2014). Dark pools are private anonymous trading venues that have become popular destinations for traders who wish to execute large trades without having to worry about high-frequency traders. Barclays promoted its dark pool as a "surveillance" system that would identify and hold accountable "toxic, predatory, and aggressive (high-frequency) traders." However, the New York Attorney General, Eric Schneiderman, announced at a news conference that the service (the dark pool) was "essentially a sham" and that "Barclays has never prohibited any trader from participating in its dark pool, regardless of how predatory or aggressive its behavior was determined to be" (Associated Press, 2014). It has even been reported that the Federal Bureau of Investigation (FBI) is looking into the practice of HFT to determine whether or not those indulging in this practice are breaking the law by having access to nonpublic information (Fiegerman, 2014). While Baumann (2013) uses the term "algorithmic terrorism" to describe the activities of high-frequency traders, the FBI seems to be more worried about the possibility that high-frequency traders may be breaking the insider trading rules.

HFT has been in the news since May 2010 when the practice was blamed for the flash crash of May 2010, an allegation that is not supported by the facts on the ground (for example, Moosa, 2013; Moosa and Ramiah, 2014). It has since become a household expression, particularly following the publication of Michael Lewis's book, *Flash Boys*, in which he argues that high-frequency traders put retail traders at a disadvantage and that, for this reason, retail traders need protection (Lewis, 2014). Durden (2012) describes HFT as a "predatory system which abuses market structure and topology, which virtually constantly engages in such abusive trading practices as the Nanex-branded quote stuffing, as well as layering, spoofing, order book fading, and, last but not least, momentum ignition." It is claimed that high-frequency traders use computers to execute trades in fractions of a second based on complex algorithms in order to take advantage of market conditions and prey on retail traders to make lucrative profit.

In this study, we argue that there is no evidence to indicate that high-frequency traders make extraordinary profit and that there is no theoretical or intuitive reason to believe that trading frequently is a recipe for making a killing. The objective is to examine the proposition that trading frequently is necessarily profitable by testing the hypothesis that profitability is inversely related to the holding period, a proposition that has been put forward by some economists (for example, Aldridge, 2010). One problem here is that of defining HFT and identifying the activities that can be put under the banner of HFT. Our contention is that the profitability of HFT comes primarily from electronic market making, which requires rapid execution of transactions. Otherwise a trader does not necessarily make profit by trading more frequently than others, or equivalently by holding positions for short periods.

2.2 DEFINITION AND CHARACTERISTICS OF HFT

There is no agreement on what HFT is or how it should be defined, which leads to confusion, to the extent that some arguments against HFT are effectively directed at something else. The IOSCO (2011) points out that "defining HFT is difficult and there is no single agreed definition," and that "determining a precise definition may not even be practical for regulatory purposes as it could easily become obsolete or the object of regulatory arbitrage, as HFT may be used in different ways across various markets and asset classes." The IOSCO describes HFT as follows: "it involves the use of sophisticated technological tools for pursuing a number of different strategies, ranging from market making to arbitrage." The IOSCO describes as "an additional complexity in seeking to define HFT" the observation that "it encompasses many players, different organizational and legal arrangements and, most importantly, a wide number of diverse strategies." Likewise, the Securities and Exchange Commission believes that HFT "does not have a settled definition and may encompass a variety of strategies in addition to passive market making" (SEC, 2010).

Philips (2013) echoes the IOSCO and SEC by suggesting that "the definition of HFT varies, depending on whom you ask." However, he describes HFT as follows: "essentially, it's the use of automated strategies to churn through large volumes of orders in fractions of seconds." He then describes HFT as being "about predicting stock prices 30 to 60 seconds into the future and automatically jump in and out of trades," pointing out that "when a stock price changes, a high-frequency trader would trade on the offers humans had entered in the exchange's order book before they could adjust them, and then moments later either buy or sell the shares back to them at the correct price." Baumann (2013) describes HFT as follows: "computer programs send and cancel orders tirelessly in a never-ending campaign to deceive and outrace each other, or sometimes just to slow each other down." He adds that high-frequency traders "might also flood the market with bogus trade orders to throw off competitors, or stealthily liquidate a large stock position in a manner that doesn't provoke a price swing." Baumann's definition sounds very limited in relation to what may be placed under the banner of HFT, perhaps because he is only interested in making one point: that HFT is all about taking advantage of others. Obviously, these descriptions of HFT pertain to more than frequent trading and short holding periods.

Instead of giving an outright definition of HFT, it may be better to describe it by specifying a set of characteristics. Consider, for example, the characteristics specified by the IOSCO (2011) specify the following set of characteristics:

1. It is a highly quantitative tool that employs algorithms along the whole investment chain: analysis of market data, deployment of appropriate trading strategies, minimization of trading costs, and execution of trades.
2. It is characterized by a high-daily portfolio turnover and order to trade ratio (that is, a large number of orders are canceled in comparison to executed trades).
3. It usually involves flat or near-flat positions at the end of the trading day, meaning that little or no risk is carried overnight, with obvious savings on the cost of capital associated with margined positions. Positions are often held for as little as seconds or even fractions of a second.
4. It is mostly employed by proprietary trading firms or desks.
5. It is latency sensitive in the sense that it involves a rapid execution of transactions.

HFT is frequently considered to be equivalent to algorithmic trading, alternatively known as "automated quantitative trading" and "automated program trading." Algorithmic trading may be defined as "the use of computer algorithms to automatically make trading decisions, submit orders, and manage those orders" (Brogaard, 2010). However, while HFT is a type of algorithmic trading, not all forms of algorithmic trading can be described as HFT. The underlying algorithm may be a simple filter or a moving average rule, which may generate buy and sell signals frequently or infrequently. While the term "HFT" is typically associated with computer technology, which is a valid characterization, this does not mean that technology-driven trading is necessarily HFT. Some automated trading strategies may require HFT in cases like electronic market making—this is because the spread between the price at which a market-making algorithm buys shares and the price at which it sells them is as little as one cent, which means that market-making algorithms need to change the quotes they post very quickly as prices and the pattern of orders shift. But market making is not necessarily conducted at a high speed.

Several terms crop up in any discussion of HFT: electronic market making, ticker tape, filter trading, event arbitrage, statistical arbitrage, deterministic arbitrage, momentum ignition, spoofing (layering), front running, quote sniffing, quote dangling, hunt packing, and algo-sniffing. But this is not what the name implies, because HFT literally should be HFT, a practice that involves fast and frequent trading and extremely short holding periods. The other operations, some of which may be illegal, are not necessarily related to HFT. In terms of the frequency of trading, the important factor is the holding period, which can be a fraction of a second but it can be as long (or as short) as a few hours. Hence HFT is basically (an extreme version of) intraday trading, conducted to capture small profit per unit of the asset traded—by doing that thousands of times on big positions, significant profit can accumulate.

2.3 WHAT CONSTITUTES HFT?

Aldridge (2009) argues that most HFT falls within one of the following trading strategies: (1) market making, (2) ticker tape trading, (3) filter trading, (4) event arbitrage, and (5) high-frequency statistical arbitrage. Market making as a HFT strategy involves the placement of a limit order to sell or buy to earn the bid—ask spread. Although, the role of a market maker was traditionally played by specialized firms, a wide range of market participants get involved in this activity at present, thanks mainly to a widespread adoption of direct market access. Ticker tape trading involves the observation of a flow of quotes, which enables traders to extract information that has not yet crossed the news screens. Filter trading involves the monitoring of a large number of stocks for significant or unusual price changes or volume activity. Event arbitrage is about certain recurring events that generate predictable short-term responses in a selected set of securities. Statistical arbitrage comprises strategies that exploit temporary deviations from relatively stable statistical relations among financial prices.

In reality, however, the two activities that constitute HFT are electronic market making and statistical arbitrage, not the range between them as the IOSCO (2011) suggests. The algorithm used for electronic market making posts prices at which the market maker (the high-frequency trader in this case) buys and sells a stock for the purpose of earning the spread between the two prices. The only difference here is that high-speed market makers revise prices very quickly, as fast as the pace at which market conditions change. An execution algorithm is used to take large orders, break them up into smaller slices, and choose the size of those slices and the times at which they are sent to the market in such a way as to minimize slippage (the difference between the expected price of a trade and the price at which the trade is actually executed—it often occurs during periods of higher volatility). A volume participation algorithms is used to calculate the number of shares bought and sold in a given period (for example, the previous minute) and then send in a slice of the institution's overall order whose size is proportional to that number, the rationale being that there will be less slippage when markets are busy than when they are quiet. The most common execution algorithm, known as a volume-weighted average price algorithm, does its slicing in a slightly different way, using data on the volumes of shares traded in the equivalent time periods on previous days.

Statistical arbitrage algorithms are designed to search for temporary deviations from price patterns—for example, deviation from a moving average. A big buy order is likely to cause a short-term increase in price whereas a sell order will lead to a temporary fall in the price. The algorithm in this case produces a buy signal, if the price is x% below the moving average and a sell signal, if the price is x% above the moving average (which sounds like a filter rule). When the price returns to the moving average, profit is realized by buying or selling. Some algorithms search for deviations from the equilibrium conditions (cointegration) linking two or more prices. For statistical arbitrage to qualify as HFT, deviation from the equilibrium condition (or path) must arise frequently, very frequently. The underlying idea here is that deviations occur whenever an order is placed, and since orders are placed very frequently, deviations occur very frequently. But this is not necessarily true because an order must be sufficiently large, relative to the market or the number outstanding shares, to give rise to deviation from the equilibrium condition.

HFT gets its bad name because high-frequency market making may involve algorithms that prey on other algorithms. Some algorithms, for example, can detect the electronic signature of other algorithms—this process is called "algo-sniffing." If an algorithm gives a signal to buy a particular stock, the algo-sniffing algorithm will give a signal to buy the same stock, then sell it for profit. While this practice is indisputably legal, some strategies whereby an algorithm fools other algorithms are dubious, to say the least—an example is "layering" or "spoofing." A spoofer might, for instance, buy a block of shares and then issue a large number of buy orders for the same shares at prices just fractions below the current market price. Other algorithms and human traders would then see far more orders to buy the shares in question than orders to sell them—hence, they are likely to conclude that the price is going to rise. They might then buy the shares themselves, causing the price to rise, in which case the spoofer would cancel the buy orders and sell for profit the shares already held.

Other terms that are associated with HFT and give it a bad reputation include momentum ignition and front running. Momentum ignition refers to a strategy whereby other market participants are induced to trade quickly and cause a rapid price move. By trying to instigate other participants to buy or sell quickly, the instigator of momentum ignition can profit either by taking a preposition or by laddering the book (knowing the price is likely to revert after the initial rapid price move) and trading out afterward. Front running is the act of entering into a trade with advance knowledge of a block transaction that will influence the price of the underlying security. This practice is expressly forbidden by the SEC—traders are not allowed to act on nonpublic information to trade ahead of customers lacking that knowledge because this is tantamount to insider trading.

From a regulatory perspective, any activity that is based on information that is not available to all market participants at any point in time should be illegal. This, however, does not include the private information derived from a research-based trading strategy whether this strategy leads to frequent or infrequent trading. There is indeed nothing wrong with trading frequently.

2.4 THE PROFITABILITY OF HFT

Calls for imposing restrictions on HFT are justified in terms of the claim that HFT is a license to print money, a privilege that is available only to traders who have sophisticated and expensive computer equipment, which represents a barrier to entry that sustains oligopolistic profit. For example, Baron et al. (2012) argue that while high-frequency traders bear some risk, they generate an unusually high average Sharpe ratio. They reject the hypothesis that high-frequency traders do not earn excess returns, as measured both by their gross profit and the Sharpe ratio. While they admit their inability to measure the net return after including the costs of computer systems, labor, overhead, risk management systems, etc., they claim that the magnitude of the profits generated by high-frequency traders suggest that they earn significant net abnormal returns. On the other hand, Kearns et al. (2010) conduct an extensive empirical study to estimate the maximum possible profitability of HFT and arrive at figures that they describe as "surprisingly modest." They demonstrate an upper bound of $21 billion for the entire universe of US equities in 2008 at the longest holding periods, down to $21 million or less for the shortest holding periods. Furthermore, they point out that these numbers are vast overestimates of the profits that could actually be achieved in the real world. To put things into perspective, they compare these figures with "the approximately $50 trillion annual trading volume in the same markets." Other attempts have been made to estimate the total (actual) profits generated by HFT. Iati (2009) arrives at a number of $21 billion or more, Tabb et al. (2009) state a figure of $8.5 billion, and Donefer (2008) suggests a figure of $15—25 billion. However, Schack and Gawronski (2009) argue that all of these numbers are too high, although they do not offer a specific number.

The proclaimed profitability of HFT strategies is attributed to "the ability to process volumes of information, something human traders cannot do." It has been reported that Goldman Sachs earned at least $100 million per day from its trading division, day after day, on 116 out of 194 trading days through the end of September 2009 (Brown, 2010). This sounds dramatic but it does not say anything about what happened on the remaining

78 days (Goldman should have earned profit on those days as well, since it is alleged that HFT generates guaranteed profit). HFT seems to be the answer to why "nearly everyone on Wall Street is wondering how hedge funds and large banks like Goldman Sachs are making so much money so soon after the financial system nearly collapsed" (Duhigg, 2009). But the fact of the matter is that no one knows how much profit is attributed to HFT. It may be true that Goldman Sachs made that much money from its trading division but what we do not know are (1) how much of that is attributed to trading 10,000 times a day as opposed to once a week; and (2) how much is attributed to privileges such as having access to order information a few seconds before the rest of the financial community. It is interesting to note that Goldman Sachs (2009) claims in a note to clients that less than 1% of their revenues come from HFT.

Philips (2013) argues that HFT is in retreat. According to estimates from Rosenblatt Securities, as much as two-thirds of all stock trades in the United States from 2008 to 2011 were executed by high-frequency traders. In 2009, high-frequency traders moved about 3.25 billion shares a day, but in 2012 it was 1.6 billion a day. Average profits have fallen from about one-tenth of a cent per share to one-twentieth of a cent. According to Rosenblatt, the entire HFT industry made about $5 billion in 2009, but in 2012 the number declined to $1 billion. Although these figures sound big, they are not that big if we put them into perspective by comparing them with other profit indicators. For example, JPMorgan Chase earned more than six times as much in the first quarter of 2013. Philips quotes Mark Gorton, the founder of Tower Research Capital (one of the largest and fastest HFT firms) as saying things like "profits have collapsed," "the easy money's gone," and "we're doing more things better than ever before and making less money doing it," Philips also quotes Raj Fernando, chief executive officer and founder of Chopper Trading (a large firm in Chicago that uses high-frequency strategies) complaining that "the margins on trades have gotten to the point where it's not even paying the bills for a lot of firms" and that "no one's laughing while running to the bank now." According to Fernando, an increasing number of high-frequency shops are shutting down and many asked Chopper to buy them before going out of business (the offer was declined in every instance). As more firms flooded the market with their high-speed algorithms, all of them hunting out inefficiencies, it became harder to make money. This observation is consistent with the theory of perfect competition where there are no barriers to entry—abnormal profit disappears. Philips (2013) reports that high-frequency traders have shifted to the use of momentum trading.

Apart from the influx of new entrants into the industry, one reason for the change of fortune is that HFT needs trading volume and price volatility, both of which have dwindled. Trading volumes in US equities are around 6 billion shares a day, roughly the same turnover as in 2006, whereas volatility is about half of what it was a few years ago. Volatility is important if profitability depends on price disparities across assets and exchanges. Volume is important for market making, where profit is derived from narrow bid–offer spreads. Arbitrage trading derives profit from small price differences between related assets. The more prices change, the more likely it is that disparities will arise. As markets have become more tranquil, arbitrage trading has become less profitable.

HFT shops are closing down, not only because profit opportunities have largely vanished but also because HFT is a high-risk activity as confirmed by the story of Knight Capital. Until about 9:30 a.m. on the morning of August 01, 2012, Knight was arguably one of the kings of HFT and the largest trader of US stocks, accounting for 17% of all trading volume in the New York Stock Exchange and about 16% of the NASDAQ listings. When the market opened on August 01, a new algorithm (which Knight had just installed) initiated an aggressive buying of shares at the rate of $2.6 million a second. Each time it bought, the algorithm would raise the price it was offering and other firms were happy to sell at the higher price. By the end of August 02, Knight had spent $440 million in the process of unwinding its trades—that was about 40% of the company's value before the glitch. This episode provides support for the "rogue algorithm" argument for the regulation of HFT, but there is nothing special here. This is just like any operational loss event where a firm incurs losses as a result of technological failure. It has nothing to do with HFT.

What we are mostly concerned with here is the proposition that HFT is profitable only because of the frequency of trading as suggested by Aldridge (2010). There is no reason why trading frequently is more profitable than trading infrequently. High-frequency traders work on algorithms to generate buy and sell signals, but there is no guarantee that these algorithms generate profit. Forecasting financial prices and determining the timing of highs and lows are not easy, even for the brightest quantitative mind. Moosa (2013) argues that the proposition that high-frequency traders are certain winners sounds like suggesting that a gambler who plays on four boxes of a Blackjack table always wins, while a more conservative gambler who plays on one box and skips rounds always loses. This cannot be true because both of these gamblers are subject to the same set of probabilities and the fact that the Blackjack rules favor the casino. Likewise, a high-frequency trader and a long-term trader are subject to the same stochastic behavior of financial prices. While skill is a crucial factor in gambling and financial trading, there is no reason why high-frequency traders are more skillful than long-term traders (tell that to George Soros).

2.5 PROFITABILITY AS A FUNCTION OF THE HOLDING PERIOD

While most commentators argue that HFT is profitable because twisted procedures are used, Aldridge (2010) demonstrates that HFT is profitable for the very reason that it involves short holding periods. Aldridge admits that "hard data on performance of high-frequency strategies is indeed hard to find" and that "hedge funds successfully running high-frequency strategies tend to shun the public limelight." However, she argues that performance at different frequencies can be compared using publicly available data by estimating the maximum potential profitability. She measures risk-adjusted return by calculating "the maximum possible Sharpe ratio for a given trading frequency" as a sample period's average range (High—Low) divided by the sample period's standard deviation of the range, adjusted by square root of the number of observations in a year. She calculates the maximum Sharpe ratios that could be attained at 10-second, 1-minute, 10-minute, 1-hour, and 1-day frequencies in the EUR/USD exchange rate, using data for 30 trading days from February 09, 2009 through March 22, 2009. She finds that as the holding period becomes longer, the standard deviation rises and the maximum annualized Sharpe ratio declines. For example, for 10 s, the standard deviation is 0.01%, producing a Sharpe ratio of 5880, while for one-day trading it is 0.76%, producing a Sharpe ratio of 37.3. Figure 2.1 is a graphical representation of Aldridge's result, showing a positive relation between the holding period and the standard deviation and (consequently) a negative relation between the holding period and the Sharpe ratio. Aldridge suggests an explanation for why HFT produces high Sharpe ratio, arguing that high-frequency traders do not carry overnight positions, which means that they do not incur the overnight cost of carry (proxied by the risk-free rate). This factor alone cannot explain the huge difference between 5580 and 37.

The measure of profitability used by Aldridge is faulty while the underlying arguments are flawed. We should expect nothing other than the standard deviation associated with a 10-second holding period to be lower than that of a 1-minute horizon because financial prices exhibit more variation over longer time periods. By using data on the exchange rate between the US dollar and Australian dollar, Moosa (2013) demonstrates that the standard deviation is lower for shorter holding periods. Because the standard deviation appears in the denominator of the Sharpe ratio, the ratio is typically higher for more frequent trading. Moreover, the numerator of the Sharpe ratio is excess return over and above the risk-free rate—this means that for high-frequency traders to produce higher Sharpe ratios than long-term traders, they must produce significantly higher excess returns.

Furthermore, the range is a measure of (absolute) return only if the trader buys at the lowest price and sells at the highest price, which rarely happens. The trader may sell at a price that is lower than the buy price as a result of the desire to cut losses or to meet liquidity requirements (such as meeting the cost of funding of a leveraged position). In this case, return will be negative.

Kearns et al. (2010) cast doubt on the validity of the results produced by Aldridge, arguing that while she reports per-period returns of 0.04—0.06% at short trading intervals, she is silent on total profits. Specifically, they question the finding that the simulated Sharpe ratio can rise above 5000 at 10 s trading intervals and the labeling of HFT

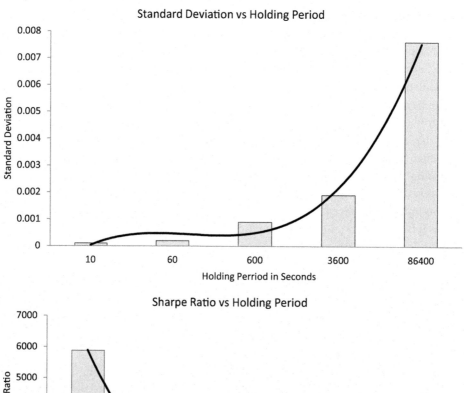

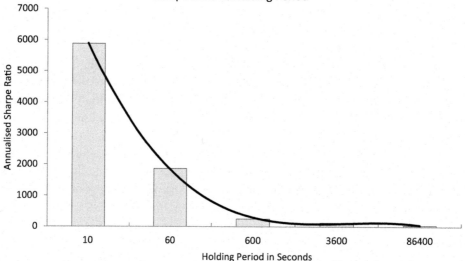

Figure 2.1 The Aldridge results.

strategies as "extremely safe." This is inconsistent with the concept of risk–return trade off and the proposition that "there is no free lunch." They suggest that it is unclear what these numbers mean, given that her simulation assumes an omniscient trader who by definition is never at risk of losing money, and that Sharpe ratios can be driven arbitrarily high under perfect knowledge.

There is simply no logical reason to suggest that trading more frequently is a recipe for guaranteed profit. On the contrary, the practice involves transaction costs, which would reduce profitability. Moosa (2013) demonstrates that high-frequency traders operate on the small ups and downs while long-term traders operate on long-term trends (or cycles). A long-term trader would take a position and sit on it for a long period of time while a high-frequency trader aims to buy low and sell high using the small intraday movements in financial prices. HFT can be more profitable, if the trader has a magical formula that picks the highs and lows but such a formula is unlikely to be available. Dacorogna et al. (2001) give the impression that high-frequency traders have the magical formula, arguing that "their trading technology is so successful that they do not have to do any active marketing and thus do not have to reveal any information to the outside world" and that "this has the effect that only a small group of insiders know about the technology." Two comments are warranted here. The first is that Bernie Madoff told his clients that he had a magical formula and he did not need any active marketing to attract funds—Madoff was not a high-frequency trader. The second is that the monopoly of knowledge on computer technology that high-frequency traders allegedly have is not consistent with the influx of new entrants into the HFT industry that caused a significant drop in profit.

2.6 METHODOLOGY

Intuitively, long holding periods should be more profitable in a rising market and vice versa, which means that HFT is not necessarily profitable. We test the hypothesis on the relation between the profitability of trading in the foreign exchange market and stock market using two different trading strategies conducted over holding periods with varying lengths of the holding period.

The trading strategy in the foreign exchange market is carry trade where a short position is taken on the low-interest currency and a long position is taken on a high-interest currency. Let i_x and i_y be the interest rates on currencies x and y, respectively. Also let S be the spot exchange rate between the two currencies measured as the price of one unit of currency y. If the operation is initiated at time $t-1$ and terminated at time t, the rate of return on carry trade is calculated as follows:

$$\pi_{t-1}^t = \begin{cases} \left(\dot{i}_{t-1}^y - \dot{i}_{t-1}^x\right) + \dot{S}_{t-1}^t & \quad i^y > i^x \\ \left(\dot{i}_{t-1}^x - \dot{i}_{t-1}^y\right) - \dot{S}_{t-1}^t \end{cases} \quad \text{if} \quad \begin{matrix} i^y > i^x \\ i^y < i^x \end{matrix} \qquad [2.1]$$

where $\dot{S}_{t-1}^t$ is the percentage change in the exchange rate between $t-1$ and t, which is calculated as,

$$\dot{S}_{t-1}^t = \frac{S_t}{S_{t-1}} - 1 \qquad [2.2]$$

Equation [2.1] represents the return on carry trade for a holding period of 1. For a holding period of 2, the return on carry trade is

$$
\pi_{t-1}^{t+1} = \begin{cases} \left(i_{t-1}^{y} - i_{t-1}^{x} \right) + \dfrac{S_{t+1}}{S_{t-1}} - 1 \\[12pt] \left(i_{t-1}^{x} - i_{t-1}^{y} \right) - \dfrac{S_{t+1}}{S_{t-1}} - 1 \end{cases} \quad \text{if} \quad \begin{array}{l} i^{y} > i^{x} \\[4pt] i^{y} < i^{x} \end{array} \qquad [2.3]
$$

where the operation is initiated at time $t - 1$ and terminated at time $t + 1$. In general terms, the rate of return on carry trade with a holding period m is

$$
\pi_{t-1}^{t+m-1} = \begin{cases} \left(i_{t-1}^{y} - i_{t-1}^{x} \right) + \dfrac{S_{t+m-1}}{S_{t-1}} - 1 \\[12pt] \left(i_{t-1}^{x} - i_{t-1}^{y} \right) - \dfrac{S_{t+m-1}}{S_{t-1}} - 1 \end{cases} \quad \text{if} \quad \begin{array}{l} i^{y} > i^{x} \\[4pt] i^{y} < i^{x} \end{array} \qquad [2.4]
$$

where the operation is initiated at time $t - 1$ and terminated at time $t + m - 1$.

Suppose, now that we have observations on the interest rates and exchange rates over the period between 0 and n. In this case, we can calculate n observations on the return over a holding period of 1 and $n - m$ observations on the rate of return over a holding period of m, such that $m < n$. In this case, we can calculate the mean and standard deviation of the rate of return with a holding period of m from the observations π_0^m, π_1^{m+1}, π_2^{m+2}, ..., π_{n-m}^n as follows

$$
\overline{\pi}^m = \frac{1}{n - m + 1} \sum_{t=1}^{n-m+1} \pi_{t-1}^{t+m-1} \qquad [2.5]
$$

$$
\sigma(\pi^m) = \sqrt{\frac{1}{n - m} \sum_{t=1}^{n-m+1} \left(\pi_{t-1}^{t+m-1} - \overline{\pi}_m \right)^2} \qquad [2.6]
$$

in which case the Sharpe ratio is defined as

$$
SR = \frac{\overline{\pi}^m}{\sigma(\overline{\pi}_m)} \qquad [2.7]
$$

Once we have calculated these statistics, we will be able to examine the relation between the holding period, on the one hand, and three measures of return: π_{n-m}^n (the end-of-sample return), $\overline{\pi}^m$ (mean return), and SR (risk-adjusted return).

The trading strategy used in the stock market is a moving average rule, using four different lengths of the moving average. If we have observations on stock prices P_1, P_2,...., P_n, then a moving average of length m is defines as

$$
MA(m) = \frac{1}{m} \sum_{t=1}^{m} P_t \qquad [2.8]
$$

A moving average rule works as follows: a buy signal is generated when $MA(m)\text{-}P$ changes from positive to negative whereas a sell signal appears when $MA(m)\text{-}P$ changes from negative to positive. If the buy signal appears at P_t and the sell signal appears at P_{t+k}, the rate of return on the transaction is,

$$r_t^{t+k} = \frac{P_{t+k}}{P_t} - 1 \qquad [2.9]$$

The profitability of the moving average rule is calculated by the accumulated amount obtained at the end of the sample period by investing an initial amount, X_0, at the generated rates of return. For s transactions, with rates of return r_j such that $j = 1, 2, ..., s$, we have,

$$X_n = X_0 \prod_{j=1}^{s} \left(1 + r_j\right) \qquad [2.10]$$

We then compare X_n with the number of transactions. It is intuitive to expect a short moving average to generate a larger number of transactions than a long moving average. If HFT is more profitable than low-frequency trading, then X_n and s should be negatively correlated.

2.7 DATA AND EMPIRICAL RESULTS

We start with the data on the foreign exchange market, which cover four currencies and six exchange rates. Three dollar (USD) exchange rates are those of the euro (EUR), yen (JPY), and the Australian dollar (AUD). The other three are the cross rates involving the nondollar currencies. The data sample, obtained from Datastream, consists of daily observations on exchange rates and the corresponding interest rates covering the period between December 31, 2012 and April 09, 2014.

Figure 2.2 displays the six exchange rates, showing that over the sample period, which should give an idea about the profitability associated with short and long holding periods. Intuitively, we expect short holding periods to be more profitable, if a long position is taken on a depreciating currency. Since these figures do not show straightforward appreciation and depreciation (except perhaps for the USD/JPY and JPY/EUR rates) it is difficult to say, without doing the calculations, which holding period is more profitable.

In Figure 2.3, we see scatter diagrams of the end-of-sample returns against the holding period—the latter ranges between 1 day and 90 days. The returns are annualized by multiplying the percentage change by a factor that is equal to 360 divided by the holding period. If short holding periods are associated with higher returns, the scatter diagrams should show a negative fit, which is not the case, except perhaps for two exchange rates involving the Australian dollar, USD/AUD and AUD/EUR. If we go back to Figure 2.2

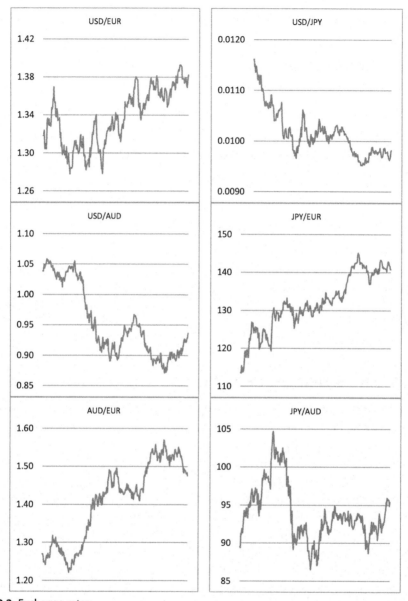

Figure 2.2 Exchange rates.

we observe a declining USD/AUD rate (a depreciating AUD) and a rising AUD/EUR rate (appreciating EUR). Since the interest rate is higher on the AUD than those on the USD and EUR, a long position is always taken on the AUD, which means that in both cases a long position is taken on a depreciating currency. This is why in these two cases, we observe negative correlation between return and the holding period. Therefore, the

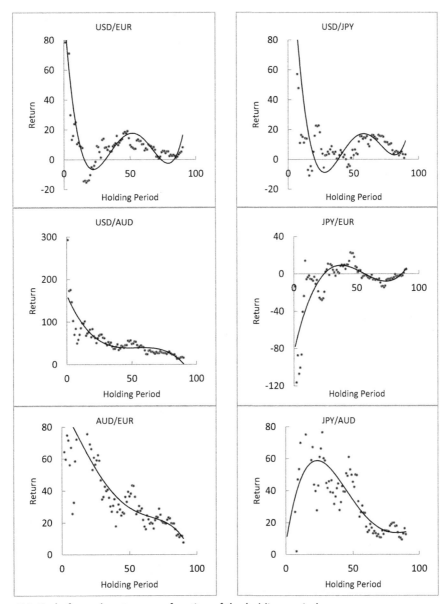

Figure 2.3 End-of-sample return as a function of the holding period.

profitability associated with short holding periods is not the product of the shortness of the holding period, but rather the result of taking a long position on a depreciating currency. We do not observe a regular pattern in the other cases because the exchange rates are up and down. In the case of the JPY/EUR rate, we actually observe mostly positive correlation between return and the holding period because there is a strong upward trend in the exchange rate. In this case, a long position is taken on an appreciating currency (the EUR)—hence the positive correlation.

If we use the mean return as opposed to the end-of-period return, we observe (in Figure 2.4) negative correlation in the three exchange rates involving the AUD—again this is the result of taking a long position on a depreciating currency (the AUD). It is

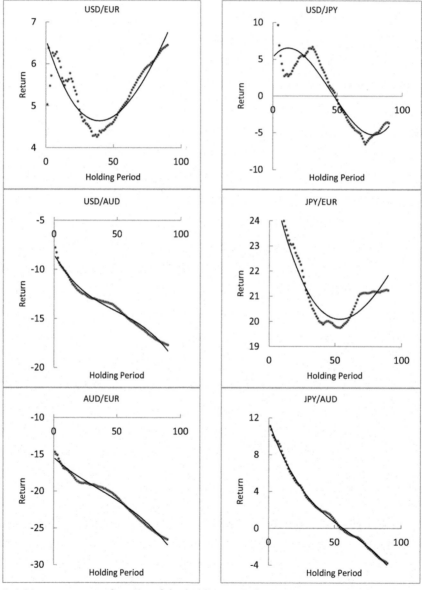

Figure 2.4 Mean return as a function of the holding period.

noteworthy that although the JPY/AUD rate does not show a strong downward trend over the whole sample period, we can observe the rapid depreciation of the AUD during the early part of the period. In Figure 2.5, we observe the relation between the risk-adjusted return, measured by the Sharpe ratio, and the holding period. We observe strong negative correlation in two cases, USD/AUD and AUD/EUR and strong positive

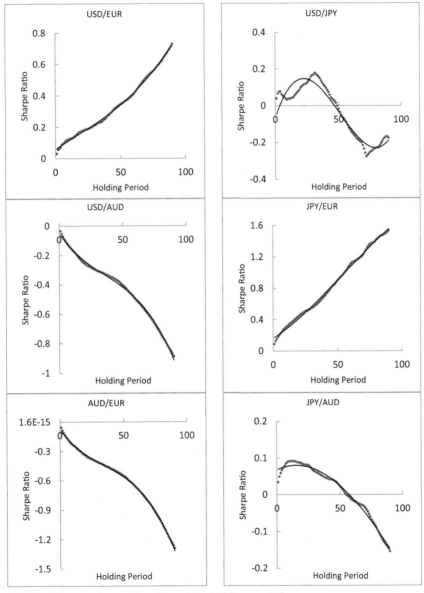

Figure 2.5 The Sharpe ratio as a function of the holding period.

correlation in two cases, USD/EUR and JPY/EUR. Once more, negative correlation arises because a long position is taken on a depreciating currency (AUD) whereas positive correlation arises because a long position is taken on an appreciating currency (EUR). This result is in complete contrast with that of Aldridge (2010) who shows that the Sharpe ratios associated with short holding periods exceed by far those associated with longer holding period.

We now turn to the results obtained by applying a moving average rule to stock market data. Specifically, we use a sample (obtained from Datastream) of daily data on the DJIA covering the period between July 06, 2004 and July 03, 2014. Four moving

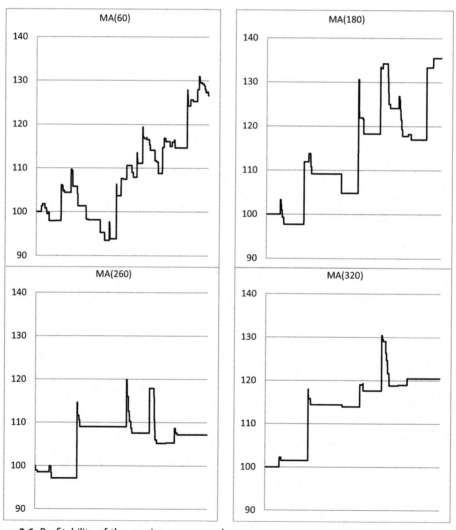

Figure 2.6 Profitability of the moving average rule.

averages are used with lengths of 60, 180, 260, and 320 days. As expected, short moving averages generate more buy and sell signals (therefore more frequent trading) than long moving averages. In this case, the four moving averages generate 81, 39, 27, and 18 transactions, respectively. In Figure 2.6, we observe the profitability of the four moving averages measured by investing an initial capital of 100 at the rates of return generated by applying the moving average rule. If more frequent trading is more profitable than less frequent trading we should find that short moving averages are more profitable than long moving averages. It turns out that this is not the case as shown in Figures 2.6 and 2.7. While the 60-day moving average is more profitable than the 260-day and

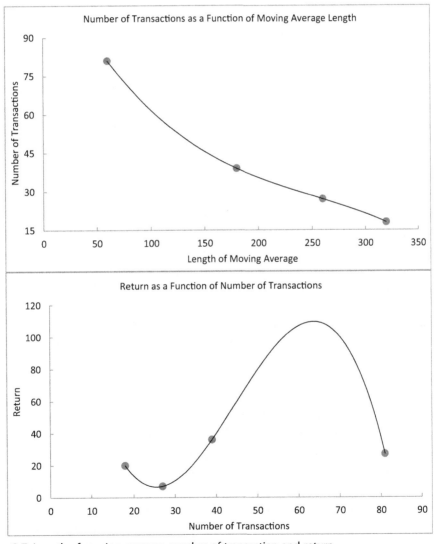

Figure 2.7 Length of moving average, number of transaction and return.

320-day moving averages, the most profitable is the 180-day moving average. The profitability of the moving average rule is not related to the length of the moving average per se, but rather to the use of the appropriate moving average to the underlying price series. As far as we know, this problem has no analytical solution.

2.8 CONCLUSION

HFT is not as profitable as it is typically portrayed to be—even if it is, this cannot be attributed just to the length of the holding period. At one time, HFT was profitable but only because of electronic market making and the use of algorithms that prey on other algorithms or on the orders placed by down-to-earth traders. The facts on the ground demonstrate that this profitability has dwindled because of the influx of market participants into the HFT industry. More importantly, however, we demonstrated that there is no association between profitability and the length of the holding period and the frequency of trading. Depending on the behavior of the underlying financial price, long holding periods and less frequent trading may be more profitable than short holding periods and more frequent trading. It seems, therefore, that the alleged profitability of HFT is grossly exaggerated.

REFERENCES

Aldridge, I., 2009. High-Frequency Trading: A Practical Guide to Algorithmic Strategies and Trading Systems. Wiley, New York.

Aldridge, I., July 26, 2010. How Profitable Are High-Frequency Strategies? http://www.huffingtonpost.com/irene-aldridge/how-profitable-are-high-f_b_659466.html (accessed 14.1.2013).

Associated Press, June 27, 2014. New York Sues Barclays over High-Frequency Trading. http://mashable.com/2014/06/26/new-york-sues-barclays-high-frequency-trading/.

Baron, M., Brogaard, J., Kirilenk, A., 2012. The Trading Profits of High Frequency Traders. Working Paper. http://www.bankofcanada.ca/wp-content/uploads/2012/11/Brogaard-Jonathan.pdf.

Baumann, N., January/February 2013. Too Fast to Fail: Is High-Speed Trading the Next Wall Street Disaster?. Mother Jones. http://www.motherjones.com/politics/2013/02/high-frequency-trading-danger-risk-wall-street.

Brogaard, J.A., 2010. High-Frequency Trading and its Impact on Market Quality. Working Paper. Kellog School of Management. http://www.futuresindustry.org/ptg/downloads/HFT_Trading.pdf.

Brown, E., April 21, 2010. Computerized Front Running, Another Goldman-Dominated Fraud. Counterpunch. http://www.counterpunch.org/2010/04/23/computerized-front-running/11/1/2013.

Dacorogna, M.M., Gençay, R., Müller, U., Olsen, R.B., Pictet, O.V., 2001. An Introduction to High-Frequency Finance. Academic Press, San Diego, CA.

Donefer, B., May 2008. Risk Management and Electronic Trading (FIX Protocol Conference).

Duhigg, C., July 23, 2009. Stock Traders Find Speed Pays, in Milliseconds, New York Times. http://www.nytimes.com/2009/07/24/business/24trading.html?_r=0.

Durden, T., December 14, 2012. Momentum Ignition - The Market's Parasitic 'Stop Hunt' Phenomenon Explained. http://www.zerohedge.com/news/2012-12-14/momentum-ignition-markets-parasitic-stop-hunt-phenomenon-explained.

Fiegerman, S., April 02, 2014. WTF Is HFT? What You Should Know about High-Frequency Trading. http://mashable.com/2014/04/01/high-frequency-trading-explainer/.

Goldman, S., August 2009. Goldman Sachs Practices Relating to High Frequency Shares Trading. Note to Clients.

Iati, R., July 2009. The Real Story of Trading Software Espionage (Advanced Trading).

IOSCO, July 2011. Regulatory Issues Raised by the Impact of Technological Changes on Market Integrity and Efficiency. http://www.finance-watch.org/wp-content/uploads/2012/05/3.-IOSCO-on-HFT-20-October-2011.pdf.

Kearns, M., Kulesza, A., Nevmyvka, Y., 2010. Empirical Limitations on High Frequency Trading Profitability. http://ssrn.com/abstract=1678758.

Lewis, M., 2014. Flash Boys. Norton, New York.

Moosa, I.A., 2013. The regulation of high frequency trading: a pragmatic view. J. Bank. Regul. 1–17.

Moosa, I.A., Ramiah, V., 2014. The regulation of high-frequency trading: an Asian perspective. In: Chuen, D.L.K., Gregoriou, G.N. (Eds.), Handbook of Asian Finance: REITs, Trading, and Fund Performance, vol. 2. Academic Press, Oxford.

Philips, M., June 06, 2013. How the Robots Lost: High-Frequency Trading's Rise and Fall. http://www.businessweek.com/articles/2013-06-06/how-the-robots-lost-high-frequency-tradings-rise-and-fall.

Schack, J., Gawronski, J., September 2009. An in-depth look at high-frequency trading. Rosenblatt Secur. Res. Rep. http://rblt.com/newsletter_details.aspx?id=84.

SEC, January 14, 2010. Concept Release on Equity Market structure. www.sec.gov/rules/concept/2010/34-61358.pdf.

Tabb, L., Iati, R., Sussman, A., 2009. US Equity High Frequency Trading: Strategies, Sizing and Market Structure (TABB Group Report).

CHAPTER 3

Data Characteristics for High-Frequency Trading Systems

Bruce Vanstone, Tobias Hahn
Bond University, Gold Coast, QLD, Australia

Contents

3.1 INTRODUCTION

A necessary condition to developing a successful high-frequency trading system is to understand the time-series characteristics of the instrument you intend to trade. Successful high-frequency trading systems exploit inefficiencies in the pricing process. It is important to confirm that the instrument you intend to trade exhibits these inefficiencies at the chosen time frame you intend to operate in. There are a number of possible inefficiencies that need to be considered and tested for, and these inefficiencies may be present only in specific time frames. Indeed, as Aldridge points out, "the profitability of a trading strategy is bound by the chosen trading frequency" (2010).

The primary tests for inefficiencies revolve around tests for market efficiency, tests for randomness (and the nature of deviations from it), and tests for serial dependence. Each of these tests is important as each helps to determine the extent to which the data contains predictable opportunities. A consistently profitable trading strategy cannot be found, if returns are truly random. Market efficiency describes a market where prices impound all available information instantaneously. In an inefficient market, information may not be reflected promptly, or prices may under/over react to the arrival of new information,

The Handbook of High Frequency Trading
ISBN 978-0-12-802205-4
47

creating trading opportunities. Serial dependence indicates a persistent behavior in returns, indicating potential opportunities for trading approaches like momentum, or reversal trading. Failing to test underlying data for these inefficiencies may result in creating trading systems, which trade against the underlying character of the time series, increasing your risk or lowering your overall chance of success. It may also lead to missed opportunities.

This chapter explains these tests further, and demonstrates how to perform the tests and interpret the results. Five different intraday frequencies of the Euro-US Dollar exchange rate (EURUSD) data from 2000 to 2013 are used for the examples and explanations.

3.2 LITERATURE REVIEW

According to Sewell (2011), when studying high-frequency data it is important to understand the stylized facts associated with the market and time frame of interest. Research into stylized facts for high-frequency foreign exchange (FX) data by Dacorogna et al. (2001) shows that the well-accepted empirical regularities of daily and weekly data often do not hold for intraday data. An understanding of the stylized facts associated with the time series being studied allows for the sensible specification of the tests that should be performed on that data, and the expected outcomes from those tests.

This chapter reviews and describes the main tests necessary to determine whether a time series of high-frequency price data contains persistent trading opportunities. The chapter also demonstrates the application and interpretation of the tests using high-frequency EURUSD data, so it is appropriate to briefly review the characteristics of FX spot markets, from which this data is sourced.

3.2.1 The FX Markets

The primary purpose of FX markets is to allow participants to easily convert one currency into another at an agreed rate. According to Aldridge (2010), the main players in these markets are long-term investors, corporations, and high-frequency traders. Long-term investors seek to profit from global macro changes, corporations traditionally use these markets to hedge international payments against adverse currency moves, and high-frequency traders seek to profit from small intraday price changes.

The FX spot markets provide excellent opportunities for high-frequency traders. For the main currencies, the spot markets are very large, have high liquidity, low transaction costs, and trade 24 h a day, 5 days a week. The Bank for International Settlements (2010) reports the daily turnover of the FX markets to be in excess of $4 trillion. As the FX markets are effectively currency crosses, long and short positions can be taken with equal ease. The currency pair that is most heavily traded is the EURUSD, which accounts for around 28% of the spot market. As it is the trading process that impounds information into prices, this liquid instrument should be highly efficient.

3.2.2 Testing for Market Efficiency

Market efficiency is typically conducted as a test of the random walk hypothesis. The most commonly conducted test for the random walk is the variance ratio test of Lo and MacKinlay (1988). The variance ratio test is based on the property that the variance of increments of a random walk is linear in its data interval. The principle of the test is that if price changes measured at one frequency are random, then price changes at a lower frequency should also be random, and that those variances should be deterministically related.

The variance ratio is reported as the ratio of the variance of the q-fold overlapping return horizon to q times the variance of the return series, where q is the period chosen to create overlapping return horizons. The variance ratio test assesses the null hypothesis that a univariate time series is a random walk. For a random walk series, the variance ratio would be 1. A variance ratio less than 1 implies the series is mean reverting, while a variance ratio greater than 1 implies the series is mean-averting. Aldridge (2010) shows that high-frequency FX spot data decreases in efficiency with increases in data sampling frequency.

3.2.3 Testing for Randomness

The most commonly used test for randomness is the nonparametric runs test. According to Bradley (1968), the runs test measures the probability of a series of consecutive positive or negative returns, known as "runs." A sequence of positive (negative) returns can be of any length, and when the return changes sign, it starts a new run. The runs tests, then, measures whether the number of runs is abnormally high or low. An abnormally low number of runs would mean that there were not very many changes of sign, implying that there was a higher likelihood of clustering—that is, successive returns being of the same sign (either positive or negative). An abnormally high number of runs would mean there were a larger than expected number of changes of sign, implying that there was a higher likelihood of a successor return being of the opposite sign. A runs test is a test of the null hypothesis that the sequence of the return signs is random. Rejection of the runs test implies that the number of runs is not random (indicating either an abnormally low or high number of runs). This is of interest from a trading perspective, as it helps give some expected forecast of the next consecutive return sign.

3.2.4 Testing for Serial Dependence

Autocorrelation (ACF) is a measure of serial dependence (1978). It describes the correlation between a return series and itself at different points in time, known as the lag. For a stochastic process y_t, autocorrelation measures the correlation between y_t and y_{t+k} where $k = 0..K$, (K is the number of lags required). Partial autocorrelation (PACF) measures the correlation between y_t and y_{t+k} adjusted for the effects of the intermediate observations.

It is common to plot autocorrelation over a range of lags with the upper and lower confidence bounds, and also to plot the partial autocorrelation at the same time. Positive serial autocorrelation implies that positive returns at time t are likely to be followed by positive returns at time $t + 1$. Negative serial autocorrelations imply that positive returns at time t are more likely to be followed by negative returns at time $t + 1$.

Autocorrelation is tested using the Ljung—Box test (1978), which assesses the null hypothesis that a series of residuals exhibits no autocorrelation for a fixed number of lags, L, against the alternative that some autocorrelation coefficient (k), $k = 1, ..., L$, is nonzero. From a trading perspective, autocorrelation is important because it indicates whether there are persistent momentum or reversal relationships present in the data. In this sense, positive serial autocorrelations indicate momentum style strategies may be appropriate, while negative serial autocorrelations indicate reversal style strategies may be appropriate.

There is existing evidence that confirms the stylized fact of negative first-order auto-correlation in high-frequency FX markets, see Cont (2001), Dacorogna et al. (2001) and Zhou (1996). Negative autocorrelation is also reported in other high-frequency markets, for example, Italian Stock Index Futures for periods smaller than 20 min by Bianco and Reno (2006). The autocorrelation test and the runs test deal with related concepts; the main difference between them from a trading perspective is that the runs test deals with sign only and the autocorrelation test considers both sign and magnitude.

3.3 METHODOLOGY

Data for the EURUSD instrument covering the period 1st January 2000 to 31st December 2013 was obtained from SIRCA (2014). The data was obtained in 1-min, 5-min, 10-min, 15-min, and 1 hourly frequencies, partitioned annually. Partitioning the data annually allows for some consideration of the different states of the global economy, and obtaining data in a range of sampling frequencies allows for a study of the degree and type of inefficiencies at each sample frequency.

Table 3.1 provides an overall summary of the (log) returns data. Figure 3.1 shows this data graphically for the 1 h frequency.

3.4 ANALYSIS OF DATA

3.4.1 Tests for Market Efficiency

Table 3.2 shows the results of the variance ratio test for market efficiency for each frequency, partitioned annually. Each cell contains the test statistic, its probability, and the variance ratio (vratio), which is the ratio of the twofold overlapping return horizon to 2 times the variance of the return series. Cells that are lightly shaded are those combinations where the variance ratio test fails to accept that the series is a random walk at a 95% level of confidence, and therefore, market efficiency is rejected.

Variance ratios less than 1 imply the series is mean reverting. In every year and frequency combination except one (2002, hourly) where market efficiency is rejected,

Table 3.1 Summary of EURUSD returns data obtained from SIRCA

Year	1 min	5 min	10 min	15 min	1 h
2000	$\mu = -0.000000$ $\sigma = 0.000308$	$\mu = -0.000001$ $\sigma = 0.000556$	$\mu = -0.000002$ $\sigma = 0.000754$	$\mu = -0.000003$ $\sigma = 0.000894$	$\mu = -0.000010$ $\sigma = 0.001598$
2001	$\mu = -0.000000$ $\sigma = 0.000287$	$\mu = -0.000001$ $\sigma = 0.000494$	$\mu = -0.000002$ $\sigma = 0.000659$	$\mu = -0.000002$ $\sigma = 0.000779$	$\mu = -0.000009$ $\sigma = 0.001464$
2002	$\mu = 0.000000$ $\sigma = 0.000291$	$\mu = 0.000002$ $\sigma = 0.000511$	$\mu = 0.000004$ $\sigma = 0.000687$	$\mu = 0.000006$ $\sigma = 0.000822$	$\mu = 0.000024$ $\sigma = 0.001615$
2003	$\mu = 0.000001$ $\sigma = 0.000213$	$\mu = 0.000002$ $\sigma = 0.000400$	$\mu = 0.000005$ $\sigma = 0.000546$	$\mu = 0.000007$ $\sigma = 0.000659$	$\mu = 0.000027$ $\sigma = 0.001272$
2004	$\mu = 0.000000$ $\sigma = 0.000208$	$\mu = 0.000001$ $\sigma = 0.000399$	$\mu = 0.000002$ $\sigma = 0.000554$	$\mu = 0.000003$ $\sigma = 0.000670$	$\mu = 0.000012$ $\sigma = 0.001319$
2005	$\mu = -0.000000$ $\sigma = 0.000189$	$\mu = -0.000002$ $\sigma = 0.000358$	$\mu = -0.000003$ $\sigma = 0.000489$	$\mu = -0.000005$ $\sigma = 0.000595$	$\mu = -0.000021$ $\sigma = 0.001160$
2006	$\mu = 0.000000$ $\sigma = 0.000178$	$\mu = 0.000001$ $\sigma = 0.000317$	$\mu = 0.000003$ $\sigma = 0.000427$	$\mu = 0.000004$ $\sigma = 0.000515$	$\mu = 0.000017$ $\sigma = 0.000990$
2007	$\mu = 0.000000$ $\sigma = 0.000138$	$\mu = 0.000001$ $\sigma = 0.000253$	$\mu = 0.000003$ $\sigma = 0.000339$	$\mu = 0.000004$ $\sigma = 0.000406$	$\mu = 0.000016$ $\sigma = 0.000773$
2008	$\mu = -0.000000$ $\sigma = 0.000245$	$\mu = -0.000001$ $\sigma = 0.000531$	$\mu = -0.000001$ $\sigma = 0.000749$	$\mu = -0.000002$ $\sigma = 0.000909$	$\mu = -0.000007$ $\sigma = 0.001792$
2009	$\mu = 0.000000$ $\sigma = 0.000240$	$\mu = 0.000000$ $\sigma = 0.000490$	$\mu = 0.000001$ $\sigma = 0.000681$	$\mu = 0.000001$ $\sigma = 0.000825$	$\mu = 0.000004$ $\sigma = 0.001608$
2010	$\mu = -0.000000$ $\sigma = 0.000222$	$\mu = -0.000001$ $\sigma = 0.000443$	$\mu = -0.000002$ $\sigma = 0.000610$	$\mu = -0.000003$ $\sigma = 0.000734$	$\mu = -0.000010$ $\sigma = 0.001443$
2011	$\mu = -0.000000$ $\sigma = 0.000222$	$\mu = -0.000000$ $\sigma = 0.000446$	$\mu = -0.000001$ $\sigma = 0.000618$	$\mu = -0.000001$ $\sigma = 0.000741$	$\mu = -0.000005$ $\sigma = 0.001462$
2012	$\mu = 0.000000$ $\sigma = 0.000171$	$\mu = 0.000000$ $\sigma = 0.000332$	$\mu = 0.000000$ $\sigma = 0.000456$	$\mu = 0.000001$ $\sigma = 0.000548$	$\mu = 0.000003$ $\sigma = 0.001046$
2013	$\mu = 0.000000$ $\sigma = 0.000156$	$\mu = 0.000001$ $\sigma = 0.000310$	$\mu = 0.000001$ $\sigma = 0.000428$	$\mu = 0.000002$ $\sigma = 0.000519$	$\mu = 0.000006$ $\sigma = 0.001016$

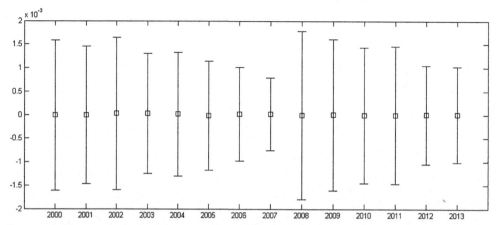

Figure 3.1 *Mean and standard deviation plot of EURUSD hourly data.*

the variance ratio is less than 1. Indeed, out of the 70 different combinations of year and frequency, only 4 combinations have a variance ratio greater than 1, and these are all in the hourly frequency.

Table 3.2 shows that frequencies of 5 min and higher fail the test for market efficiency every year; the 10 min frequency fails the test for market efficiency every year except 2008; and the 15 min frequency fails the test for market efficiency every year except 2012 and 2013. The observations in Table 3.2 are consistent with Aldridge's observation (2010) that high-frequency FX spot data decreases in efficiency with increases in data sampling frequency. The inefficiencies identified suggest that the 15 minutely (and higher frequency) observations contain significant arbitrage opportunities, and that these opportunities increase with any increase in data sampling frequency.

3.4.2 Test for Randomness

Table 3.3 shows the results of the runs test for randomness for each frequency, partitioned annually. Each cell contains the number of runs, its probability, and the z score, which is the number of standard deviations the result is away from the mean. Cells that are lightly shaded are those combinations where the runs test fails to accept that the series is random at a 95% level of confidence, which implies there is a degree of predictability.

Table 3.3 shows that every year and frequency combination fails the test for randomness. There are two ways the test could be failed—there could be too many runs or too few. The nature of the test failure is determined by the sign of the z score. A negative z score implies a fewer number of runs than would normally be expected, which implies clustering, and therefore, that a change in return sign is more likely followed by returns of the same sign. A positive z score implies more runs than would normally be expected, implying that a change in return sign is more likely to be followed by a return of a different sign.

Table 3.2 Tests for market efficiency

Year	1 min	5 min	10 min	15 min	1 h
2000	−35.6003 (0.0000) vratio: 0.8329	−5.2925 (0.0000) vratio: 0.9292	−4.9814 (0.0000) vratio: 0.9092	−3.6050 (0.0003) vratio: 0.8983	0.1680 (0.8666) vratio: 1.0034
2001	−38.4051 (0.0000) vratio: 0.7812	−16.3279 (0.0000) vratio: 0.9042	−10.0936 (0.0000) vratio: 0.9171	−6.1495 (0.0000) vratio: 0.9412	−2.0384 (0.0415) v ratio: 0.9650
2002	−89.8542 (0.0000) vratio: 0.8014	−23.9127 (0.0000) vratio: 0.9089	−9.4301 (0.0000) vratio: 0.9527	−3.9767 (0.0001) vratio: 0.9750	2.2646 (0.0235) vratio: 1.0619
2003	−52.9525 (0.0000) vratio: 0.8562	−10.5748 (0.0000) vratio: 0.9401	−6.7498 (0.0000) vratio: 0.9504	−4.9481 (0.0000) vratio: 0.9553	0.7465 (0.4554) vratio: 1.0126
2004	−28.4602 (0.0000) vratio: 0.8572	−5.4056 (0.0000) vratio: 0.9476	−3.9913 (0.0001) vratio: 0.9515	−3.2397 (0.0012) vratio: 0.9576	−0.2972 (0.7663) vratio: 0.9951
2005	−48.4372 (0.0000) vratio: 0.8354	−9.4877 (0.0000) vratio: 0.9428	−5.0542 (0.0000) vratio: 0.9526	−4.0425 (0.0001) vratio: 0.9477	0.3912 (0.6956) vratio: 1.0082
2006	−67.8169 (0.0000) vratio: 0.7853	−12.8277 (0.0000) vratio: 0.9155	−6.9205 (0.0000) vratio: 0.9375	−4.1143 (0.0000) vratio: 0.9515	−0.5172 (0.6050) vratio: 0.9915
2007	−61.8716 (0.0000) vratio: 0.8108	−14.7939 (0.0000) vratio: 0.9090	−8.4357 (0.0000) vratio: 0.9309	−5.9467 (0.0000) vratio: 0.9447	−0.2134 (0.8310) vratio: 0.9963
2008	−6.7902 (0.0000) vratio: 0.9755	−2.6871 (0.0072) vratio: 0.9806	−1.9066 (0.0566) vratio: 0.9794	−2.5791 (0.0099) vratio: 0.9701	−0.6205 (0.5349) vratio: 0.9857
2009	−24.6005 (0.0000) vratio: 0.9237	−5.3430 (0.0000) vratio: 0.9675	−2.6539 (0.0080) vratio: 0.9765	−2.0907 (0.0366) vratio: 0.9767	−1.2317 (0.2181) vratio: 0.9787
2010	−30.1022 (0.0000) vratio: 0.8988	−8.0021 (0.0000) vratio: 0.9572	−5.2787 (0.0000) vratio: 0.9623	−2.1437 (0.0321) vratio: 0.9810	−0.6281 (0.5299) vratio: 0.9897
2011	−25.9139 (0.0000) vratio: 0.8989	−8.5113 (0.0000) vratio: 0.9545	−5.3850 (0.0000) vratio: 0.9585	−2.3398 (0.0193) vratio: 0.9782	−0.4769 (0.6334) vratio: 0.9924
2012	−46.4718 (0.0000) vratio: 0.8615	−8.4867 (0.0000) vratio: 0.9462	−2.8869 (0.0039) vratio: 0.9732	−0.9150 (0.3602) vratio: 0.9904	−1.3056 (0.1917) vratio: 0.9789
2013	−32.9627 (0.0000) vratio: 0.8851	−7.4765 (0.0000) vratio: 0.9505	−2.3479 (0.0189) vratio: 0.9579	−1.7827 (0.0746) vratio: 0.9660	−1.6012 (0.1093) vratio: 0.9582

Table 3.3 Tests for randomness

Year	1 min	5 min	10 min	15 min	1 h
2000	149261 (0.0000) $z = 102.28$	35463 (0.0000) $z = 29.73$	18683 (0.0000) $z = 20.13$	12614 (0.0000) $z = 14.15$	3321 (0.0000) $z = 4.40$
2001	160158 (0.0000) $z = 120.15$	35519 (0.0000) $z = 35.69$	18419 (0.0000) $z = 22.36$	12380 (0.0000) $z = 15.24$	3279 (0.0000) $z = 5.42$
2002	179779 (0.0000) $z = 137.01$	38671 (0.0000) $z = 45.47$	19433 (0.0000) $z = 25.10$	13269 (0.0000) $z = 19.68$	3360 (0.0000) $z = 4.89$
2003	165526 (0.0000) $z = 98.77$	35767 (0.0000) $z = 24.58$	18385 (0.0000) $z = 13.86$	12631 (0.0000) $z = 12.19$	3291 (0.0003) $z = 3.65$
2004	176667 (0.0000) $z = 106.05$	36811 (0.0000) $z = 26.21$	19032 (0.0000) $z = 17.26$	12770 (0.0000) $z = 12.63$	3374 (0.0000) $z = 5.81$
2005	178681 (0.0000) $z = 115.24$	36891 (0.0000) $z = 27.64$	18955 (0.0000) $z = 16.27$	12814 (0.0000) $z = 12.59$	3244 (0.0017) $z = 3.14$
2006	183062 (0.0000) $z = 140.23$	37125 (0.0000) $z = 35.45$	19187 (0.0000) $z = 22.38$	12902 (0.0000) $z = 16.50$	3358 (0.0000) $z = 6.94$
2007	170189 (0.0000) $z = 130.91$	35953 (0.0000) $z = 33.29$	18601 (0.0000) $z = 20.87$	12479 (0.0000) $z = 14.42$	3264 (0.0000) $z = 5.95$
2008	165520 (0.0000) $z = 52.45$	36146 (0.0000) $z = 12.67$	18779 (0.0000) $z = 9.66$	12716 (0.0000) $z = 8.09$	3320 (0.0001) $z = 3.92$
2009	166032 (0.0000) $z = 63.89$	36770 (0.0000) $z = 15.46$	18955 (0.0000) $z = 10.56$	12877 (0.0000) $z = 9.59$	3346 (0.0000) $z = 4.70$
2010	168393 (0.0000) $z = 78.68$	36960 (0.0000) $z = 17.93$	18911 (0.0000) $z = 10.91$	12810 (0.0000) $z = 8.79$	3343 (0.0000) $z = 4.08$
2011	181528 (0.0000) $z = 83.62$	37834 (0.0000) $z = 22.86$	19158 (0.0000) $z = 13.42$	12906 (0.0000) $z = 10.18$	3316 (0.0001) $z = 3.91$
2012	176054 (0.0000) $z = 120.22$	36628 (0.0000) $z = 28.82$	18758 (0.0000) $z = 17.63$	12746 (0.0000) $z = 13.80$	3344 (0.0000) $z = 6.29$
2013	163820 (0.0000) $z = 118.10$	35813 (0.0000) $z = 32.90$	18487 (0.0000) $z = 20.52$	12570 (0.0000) $z = 15.59$	3251 (0.0000) $z = 5.08$

Table 3.3 shows there are far more runs than would normally be expected, which implies there is a higher likelihood of a subsequent return being of the opposite sign to its predecessor. This result is consistent with the variance ratio tests above, and provides further evidence that the data is mean reverting. From a trading perspective, this information indicates that reversal style strategies are probably more appropriate than momentum style strategies.

3.4.3 Tests for Serial Dependence

Table 3.4 shows the results of the autocorrelation tests for each frequency, partitioned annually. Each column contains the number of lags used in the test and the probability that the series of residuals exhibits no autocorrelation for that number of lags. The number of lags is typically chosen such that the longest cyclical component is included and such that the maximum length at a higher frequency is equal to a single period at a chosen lower sampling frequency. In this test, the residuals are the difference between the time series and its mean. Cells that are lightly shaded are those combinations where the Ljung–Box Q-test fails to accept that the series contains no autocorrelation at a 95% level of confidence.

Table 3.4 shows that frequencies of 15 min and higher consistently fail the test for autocorrelation every year, and the autocorrelation test is failed in more than half of the hourly combinations. The autocorrelation test can fail due to positive or negative autocorrelation, which is easily assessed visually. As an example, Figure 3.2 shows the ACF and PACF results for the six lags tested in the 10-minutely ACF/PACF test in 2007. The first lag value (marked with a dot) is clearly outside the confidence limits

Table 3.4 Tests for serial dependence

Year	1 min (lags = 60)	5 min (lags = 12)	10 min (lags = 6)	15 min (lags = 4)	1 h (lags = 24)
2000	p = 0.0000	p = 0.0000	p = 0.0000	p = 0.0000	p = 0.0124
2001	p = 0.0000	p = 0.0000	p = 0.0000	p = 0.0000	p = 0.0448
2002	p = 0.0000	p = 0.0000	p = 0.0000	p = 0.0000	p = 0.0000
2003	p = 0.0000	p = 0.0000	p = 0.0000	p = 0.0000	p = 0.1806
2004	p = 0.0000	p = 0.0000	p = 0.0000	p = 0.0000	p = 0.6125
2005	p = 0.0000	p = 0.0000	p = 0.0000	p = 0.0000	p = 0.2996
2006	p = 0.0000	p = 0.0000	p = 0.0000	p = 0.0000	p = 0.2729
2007	p = 0.0000	p = 0.0000	p = 0.0000	p = 0.0000	p = 0.3916
2008	p = 0.0000	p = 0.0000	p = 0.0000	p = 0.0000	p = 0.0043
2009	p = 0.0000	p = 0.0000	p = 0.0001	p = 0.0000	p = 0.0019
2010	p = 0.0000	p = 0.0000	p = 0.0000	p = 0.0183	p = 0.0043
2011	p = 0.0000	p = 0.0000	p = 0.0000	p = 0.0012	p = 0.0029
2012	p = 0.0000	p = 0.0000	p = 0.0000	p = 0.0354	p = 0.0180
2013	p = 0.0000	p = 0.0000	p = 0.0000	p = 0.0000	p = 0.1038

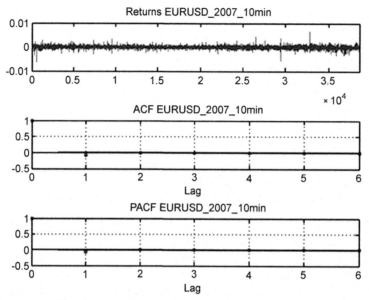

Figure 3.2 *Autocorrelation of 10-min returns in 2007.*

(shown by thin black lines close to zero on the horizontal-axis), and is below the confidence limit, hence it is negative autocorrelation.

Negative autocorrelation implies that positive returns are more likely to be followed by negative returns rather than by more positive returns. This result is consistent with the results and conclusions already drawn from the market efficiency tests and randomness tests previously performed. From a trading perspective, this result implies that reversal style strategies should be more appropriate than momentum style strategies.

3.5 CONCLUSION

Returns data from the EURUSD currency pair have been tested in the 1-min, 5-min, 10-min, 15-min, and 1 hourly time frame for each of the prior 14 years, 2000—2013.

At the 1-min and 5-min frequencies, each year has failed the tests for market efficiency, randomness and serial dependence. At the 10-min frequency, the market efficiency test was failed for every year except 2008, and the tests for randomness and serial dependence were failed every year. At the 15-min frequency, every year has failed the tests for randomness and serial dependence, and only 2 years out of the last 14 (2012, 2013) could not reject market efficiency. At the hourly frequency, every year failed the tests for randomness, and more than half of the years failed the test for serial dependence. In every case where a test failed, the test result indicated the underlying time-series had mean reverting characteristics. Although this would be expected in very high-frequency data, especially tick data, due to market microstructure effects, the observation holds at lower frequencies.

From the results presented in this chapter, high-frequency traders aiming to create trading systems for use within the intraday EURUSD pair should consider basing their trading signals on a mean-reverting model. Traders wishing to pursue this path should conduct their system development within a well-defined methodology, such as that proposed for developing stock market trading systems by Vanstone and Finnie (2009).

Finally, it should be noted that while the tests performed in this chapter may, and at certain frequencies in some data sets will, reveal a linear relationship in the time series being studied, absence of a linear relationship does not, however, imply randomness. Rather, it indicates that the return series (or the data more generally) may either be random or the underlying dynamics may be nonlinear. There is some evidence of nonlinearity in FX markets, see Christoffersen and Diebold (2006), Hsieh (1989) and Brooks (1996).

ACKNOWLEDGMENTS

The data used in this research was supplied by the Securities Industry Research Center of Asia–Pacific (SIRCA) on behalf or Reuters and the ASX.

REFERENCES

Aldridge, I., 2010. High-Frequency Trading. Wiley, New Jersey.

Bianco, S., Reno, R., 2006. Dynamics of intraday serial correlation in the italian futures market. J. Futures Mark. 26 (1), 61–84.

BIS, 2010. Triennial Central Bank Survey: Foreign Exchange and Derivatives Market Activity in April: Preliminary Results. September, 1–21.

Bradley, J.V., 1968. Distribution-Free Statistical Tests. Prentice-Hall, New Jersey.

Brooks, C., 1996. Testing for non-linearity in daily sterling exchange rates. Appl. Financ. Econ. 6 (4), 307–317.

Christoffersen, P.F., Diebold, F.X., 2006. Financial asset returns, direction-of-change forecasting, and volatility dynamics. Manag. Sci. 52 (8), 1273.

Cont, R., 2001. Empirical properties of asset returns: stylized facts and statistical issues. Quant. Finance 1 (2), 223–236.

Dacorogna, M.M., Gencay, R., Müller, U.A., Olsen, R.B., Pictet, O., 2001. An Introduction to High-frequency Finance. Academic Press, San Diego, CA.

Hsieh, D.A., 1989. Testing for non-linear dependence in daily foreign exchange rates. J. Bus. 62 (3), 339–368.

Lo, A.W., MacKinlay, C., 1988. Stock market prices do not follow random walks: evidence from a simple specification test. Rev. Financ. Stud. 1, 41–66.

Ljung, G.M., Box, G.E.P., 1978. On a measure of Lack of Fit in time series Models. Biometrika 65 (2), 297–303.

SIRCA., 2014. Thomson Reuters Tick History. www.sirca.org.au.

Sewell, M., 2011. Characterization of Financial Time Series. UCL Research Note RN/11/01.

Vanstone, B., Finnie, G., 2009. An empirical methodology for developing Stockmarket trading systems using artificial neural networks. Expert Syst. Appl. 36 (3), 6668–6680.

Zhou, B., 1996. High-frequency data and volatility in foreign-exchange rates. J. Bus. Econ. Stat. 14 (1), 45–52.

CHAPTER 4

The Relevance of Heteroskedasticity and Structural Breaks when Testing for a Random Walk with High-Frequency Financial Data: Evidence from ASEAN Stock Markets

Hooi Hooi Lean[1], Vinod Mishra[2], Russell Smyth[3]

[1]Economics Program, School of Social Sciences, Universiti Sains Malaysia, Penang, Malaysia; [2]Department of Economics, Monash University — Berwick Campus, Berwick, VIC, Australia; [3]Department of Economics, Monash University, Clayton, VIC, Australia

Contents

4.1 INTRODUCTION

Beginning with the seminal contributions of Samuelson (1965) and Fama (1970), there is a large literature, which tests for weak form of the efficient market hypothesis (EMH) in financial markets (see Lim and Brooks, 2011 for a review). Interest in the EMH reflects the fact that it has important implications for financial markets (Malkiel, 2003). First, the EMH is important for predicting whether investors can earn profits through trading stocks. If markets are efficient, then prices fully reflect all the information present in the market and, hence, there is no scope for making profits using either technical analysis or fundamental analysis of financial markets. Thus, if financial markets are efficient, then an expert will not do any better than a layman holding a randomly selected portfolio of individual stocks (with a comparable level of risk). On the other hand, if markets are not efficient, the potential exists for investors to predict future price movements based on historical price changes. Second, the EMH has implications for the efficient allocation of resources. One of the main roles of a stock market is to efficiently allocate resources by converting savings into investments. If markets are efficient, then the stock market

The Handbook of High Frequency Trading
ISBN 978-0-12-802205-4

will allocate savings to the most efficient investment. However, if markets are not efficient, and prices do not reflect all information in the market, then the efficiency of this resource allocation mechanism becomes questionable. This, in turn, justifies an increased role for regulators to protect the investments of individual investors.

A number of methods have been employed to test the EMH in financial markets (see Lim and Brooks, 2011 for a review). One of the most popular methods to test the EMH in financial markets has been to test for a unit root in stock prices. If stock prices contain a unit root, or exhibit a random walk, shocks to stock prices will result in a permanent departure from the long-run equilibrium, making it impossible to predict future price movements based on information about past prices. However, if stock prices are stationary, they will revert to their long run mean following a shock, making it possible to forecast future price movements using past data.

The early studies testing the EMH used conventional unit root tests without structural breaks. The problem with conventional unit root tests is that they have low power to reject the unit root null in the presence of one or more structural breaks (Perron, 1989). More recent studies of the EMH take account of the low power to reject the unit root null in the presence of one or two structural breaks (see e.g., Chaudhuri and Wu, 2003, 2004; Lee et al., 2012; Narayan and Smyth, 2004, 2005, 2007, 2006). The findings from these studies have been mixed. As Guidi and Gupta (2013, p. 266) conclude after an extended review of the literature: "It is evident … that a mix of different results has been achieved by using different methods, different datasets and different time periods." One potential reason for the mixed results is that while the literature has allowed for structural breaks, thus far, it has largely ignored the low power to reject the unit root null in the presence of heteroskedasticity (Narayan and Liu, 2013). Heteroskedasticity is particularly problematic in high-frequency financial data.

We extend the literature by applying a unit root test that accommodates both heteroskedasticity and structural breaks to high-frequency financial data for ASEAN stock price indices. Specifically, we apply the Narayan and Liu (2013) generalized autoregressive conditional heteroskedasticity (GARCH) unit root test to hourly data for an ASEAN five (Indonesia, Malaysia, Philippines, Singapore, and Thailand) over the period January 2011 to March 2014. There have only been two previous applications of the Narayan and Liu (2013) test to high-frequency financial data (Narayan and Liu, 2013; Mishra et al., 2014), but neither employ hourly data. Mishra et al. (2014) employ monthly data for Indian stock prices over the period January 1995 to December 2013. Narayan and Liu (2013) use monthly stock price data for the New York Stock Exchange for the period January 1980 to December 2007.

We focus on ASEAN markets for several reasons. First, ASEAN as a region is becoming increasingly important on the world economic stage (Lean and Smyth, 2014). This undoubtedly reflects its population base—ASEAN has a combined population of 580 million people (World Bank, 2012)—and that ASEAN is moving toward becoming a single market. The target is for ASEAN to establish the ASEAN Economic Community (AEC) by December 31, 2015.[1] As part of this process, ASEAN is moving toward the creation of a single supranational stock market via ASEAN Trading Link.[2] Second, stock markets in ASEAN have grown significantly in recent times and are regarded as one of the main contributors to economic development in the region (Hsieh and Nieh, 2010; Niblock et al., 2014). In particular, the percentage of stock market capitalization to GDP in Singapore, Malaysia, and Indonesia exceeded 100% at the end of 2010, while in the Philippines and Thailand the corresponding figure was 80% (Niblock et al., 2014). Third, while the ASEAN financial markets were badly hit by the Asian financial crisis in the late 1990s, more recently, ASEAN stock markets have impressed investors with their resilience to the global financial crisis (Niblock et al., 2014).

A subset of the literature that has applied unit root tests to test the EMH has focused on ASEAN financial markets (see e.g., Chancharat et al., 2009; Guidi and Gupta, 2013; Hamid et al., 2010; Lean and Smyth, 2007, 2014; Munir and Mansur, 2009; Munir et al., 2012). Consistent with the broader literature, these studies have reached mixed results as to whether ASEAN stock price indices exhibit a random walk. We extend this literature by applying the GARCH unit root test, which is particularly well-equipped to test the EMH with high-frequency financial data, and focus on hourly data.

To illustrate our argument that it is important to take account of heteroskedasticity when testing the EMH in high-frequency financial data, we first apply conventional unit root tests with, and without, structural breaks that do not take account of heteroskedasticity. We find that ASEAN stock prices are characterized by a random walk. We then apply the Narayan and Liu (2013) test, which allows for heteroskedasticity and structural breaks and find evidence of mean reversion for four of the five series. Our results point to the importance of allowing for heteroskedasticity when testing for a random walk in high-frequency financial data.

4.2 METHOD

In order to provide a benchmark, we commence through applying the Augmented Dickey Fuller (ADF) and Phillips Perron (PP) unit root tests as well as the Kwiatkowski et al. (1992, KPSS) stationarity test. Each test is well known so we do not reproduce the

---

[1] Officially ASEAN remains committed to establishing the AEC by 2015, but increasingly regard December 31, 2015 as a target and not as a deadline. ASEAN releases scorecards as to the progress of implementing the AEC Blueprint — the document outlining the targets, sectors and proposed measures covered under the AEC initiative. The scorecards produce a statistic referred to as the "implementation rate," which is the ratio of measures that are fully implemented to total number of measures targeted. A news article published in February 2014 (Kyodo News, 2014) quotes ASEAN officials that place this figure at 72% and notes that the overall progress has declined since 2013.

[2] More information about the creation and background of ASEAN Trading link can be obtained from the joint Web site of ASEAN stock markets (http://www.aseanexchanges.org/Default.aspx).

details here. A problem with the conventional ADF and Phillips—Perron unit root tests is their low power to reject the unit root null in the presence of one or more structural breaks (Perron, 1989), while ignoring one or more structural breaks biases the KPSS test in favor of rejecting the null of stationarity (Lee et al., 1997).

We next apply the Lee and Strazicich (2003) lagrange multiplier (LM) unit root test with two breaks and the Narayan and Popp (2010) unit root test with two breaks. We apply both the LM unit root test Model AA (two breaks in the intercept) and Model CC (two breaks in the intercept and trend) and Narayan and Popp (2010) Model 1 (two breaks in the intercept) and Model 2 (two breaks in the intercept and trend). As with the conventional tests without structural breaks, both tests are well known so we do not reproduce the details of the tests here. Suffice to say, these tests have been shown to have better power and size than their main alternatives. The LM unit root test with two breaks developed by Lee and Strazicich (2003) represents a methodological improvement over the Dickey—Fuller-type endogenous two break unit root test proposed by Lumsdaine and Papell (1997), which has the limitation that the critical values are derived while assuming no breaks under the null hypothesis. Meanwhile, Narayan and Popp (2013) show that the Narayan and Popp (2010) test has better size and higher power, and identifies the breaks more accurately, than either the Lumsdaine and Papell (1997) or Lee and Strazicich (2003) tests.

The GARCH unit root with two structural breaks, proposed by Narayan and Liu (2013), has the advantage that it models heteroskedasticity and structural breaks simultaneously. Since Narayan and Liu (2013) is not yet published and there are only limited applications of this test in the literature, we set out the method here. Narayan and Liu (2013) relax the assumption of independent and identically distributed errors and propose a GARCH (1,1) unit root model that accommodates two endogenous structural breaks in the intercept in the presence of heteroskedastic errors. The test considers a GARCH (1,1) unit root model of the following form:

$$y_t = \alpha_0 + \pi y_{t-1} + D_1 B_{1t} + D_2 B_{2t} + \varepsilon_t \tag{4.1}$$

Here, $B_{it} = 1$ for $t > T_{Bi}$ otherwise $B_{it} = 0$, T_{Bi} are structural break points, where $i = 1, 2$. D_1 and D_2 are break dummy coefficients. ε_t follows the first-order GARCH (1,1) model of the form:

$$\varepsilon_t = \eta_t \sqrt{h_t}, h_t = \kappa + \alpha \varepsilon_{t-1}^2 + \beta h_{t-1} \tag{4.2}$$

Here, $\kappa > 0$, $\alpha \geq 0$, $\beta \geq 0$ and η_t is a sequence of independently and identically distributed random variables with zero mean and unit variance. To estimate these equations, Narayan and Liu (2013) use joint maximum likelihood (ML) estimation. Since break dates (T_{Bi}) are unknown and have to be substituted by their estimates, a sequential procedure is used to derive estimates of the break dates. The unit root null is tested with the ML t-ratio for π with a heteroskedastic-consistent covariance matrix.

4.3 DATA

The sample consists of hourly data for the specific ASEAN five (Malaysia, Indonesia, Philippines, Singapore, and Thailand) over the period January 2011 to March 2014. For Indonesia and the Philippines, we have 39 months of data. For the others we have 30 months of data. The five indices are Jakarta Stock Exchange Composite (JSX), Bursa Malaysia Kuala Lumpur Composite Index (KLSE), the Philippine Stock Exchange Composite Index (PCI), Singapore Straits Times Index (STI), and Stock Exchange of Thailand Index (SETI). The specific ASEAN stock price indices that we used were determined by the availability of hourly data. The time zone is GMT, mean 3:00 = 11:00 in Kuala Lumpur. We reject months if average ticks per active day is less than five in a month and the number of active days is less than 10 in a month. The source of the data is the database of Olsen Financial Technologies.

The time series of each stock price index and returns are presented in Figure 4.1. Figure 4.1 suggests that the stock price indices in each of the five ASEAN countries have generally rebounded strongly following the global financial crisis. Table 4.1 presents descriptive statistics on the returns for each stock index. Over the period, the Philippines experienced the largest variation in hourly returns, followed by Thailand. Of particular note for our purposes are the results of the ARCH LM test. The null hypothesis of no arch effect is rejected at the 1% level for all the indices, indicating the presence of significant time varying volatility in hourly returns.

4.4 RESULTS

We commenced through conducting the ADF and Phillips—Perron unit root tests as well as the KPSS stationarity test with and without a trend. The results are presented in Table 4.2. At the 5% level or better each test suggests the same conclusion; namely that each of the five stock price indices contains a random walk.

While the results of these tests provide a benchmark, one cannot read too much into these findings given that each of the tests is biased in the presence of structural breaks (Perron, 1989; Lee et al., 1997) and the ADF test is biased in the presence of conditional heteroskedasticity (Kim and Schmidt, 1993). Thus, we proceed to present the results for the Narayan and Popp (2010) and Lee and Strazicich (2003) tests. Both of these tests allow for two structural breaks in the stock price indices.

The results of the Narayan and Popp (2010) unit root test with two structural breaks are reported in Table 4.3. The results of both Model 1 (intercept only) and Model 2 (intercept and trend) suggest that at the 5% level each stock price index contains a random walk. The results of the Lee and Strazicich (2003) LM unit root test with two breaks in the intercept (Model AA) are presented in Table 4.4. The corresponding results for two breaks in the intercept and trend (Model CC) are presented in Table 4.5. At the

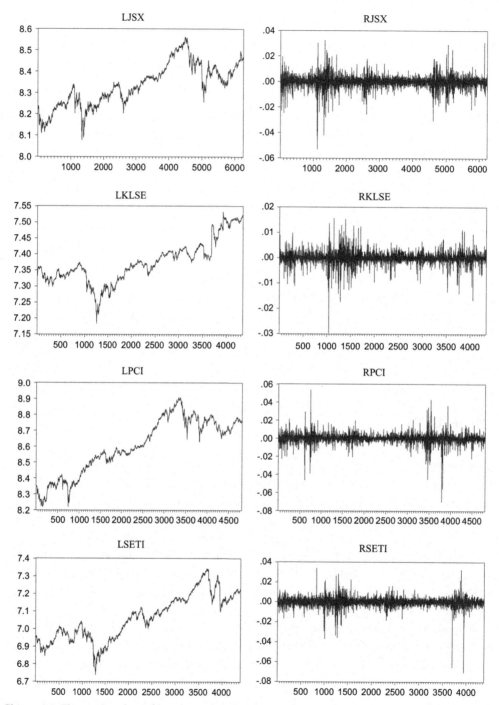

Figure 4.1 *Time series plots of hourly stock index and return.*

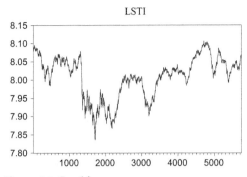
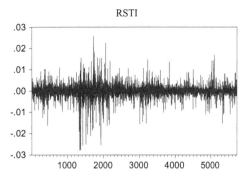

Figure 4.1 Cont'd.

Table 4.1 Descriptive statistics

Index	No. of observation	Min	Max	Skewness	ARCH (8) lagrange multiplier test
JSX	6243	−0.053	0.032	−1.096	64.578★★★
KLSE	4335	−0.030	0.016	−0.983	51.824★★★
PCI	4798	−0.070	0.054	−1.128	26.148★★★
SETI	4376	−0.070	0.034	−2.190	8.271★★★
STI	5730	−0.028	0.026	−1.008	2.182★★

Note: ★★ and ★★★ denotes statistical significance at the 5% and 1% levels, respectively.
JSX, Jakarta Stock Exchange Composite; KLSE, Bursa Malaysia Kuala Lumpur Composite Index; PCI, Philippine Stock Exchange Composite Index; STI, Singapore Straits Times Index; SETI, Stock Exchange of Thailand Index.

5% level or better, both Model AA and Model CC suggest that each of the five stock price indices contain a random walk.

Hence, on the basis of the traditional unit root and stationarity tests, as well as two of the best known and often used unit root tests with two structural breaks, the five ASEAN stock price indices are characterized by a random walk at the 5% level. This is the case irrespective of whether one includes a trend in the specification.

Table 4.2 Traditional unit root tests

Index	Intercept			Intercept and trend		
	ADF test	PP test	KPSS test	ADF test	PP test	KPSS test
JSX	−1.579	−1.736	7.230★★★	−2.903	−3.163★	0.753★★★
KLSE	−0.435	−0.593	5.986★★★	−2.213	−2.391	1.039★★★
PCI	−1.240	−1.279	7.649★★★	−1.877	−2.043	1.220★★★
SETI	−1.020	−1.129	6.905★★★	−2.662	−2.817	0.566★★★
STI	−1.927	−2.157	1.914★★★	−2.201	−2.407	1.331★★★

Note: ★ and ★★★ denotes statistical significance at the 10% and 1% levels, respectively.
JSX, Jakarta Stock Exchange Composite; KLSE, Bursa Malaysia Kuala Lumpur Composite Index; PCI, Philippine Stock Exchange Composite Index; STI, Singapore Straits Times Index; SETI, Stock Exchange of Thailand Index.

Table 4.3 Results of Narayan–Popp two breaks unit root test

Series	M1				M2			
	t-stat	TB$_1$	TB$_2$	k	t-stat	TB$_1$	TB$_2$	k
JSX	−3.4961	2011/09/21, 10:00	2011/09/26, 10:00	7	−4.9004★	2011/09/21, 10:00	2013/06/11, 02:00	6
KLSE	−3.8637	2011/08/08, 09:00	2011/09/30, 09:00	6	−4.9272★	2011/08/08, 09:00	2011/09/30, 09:00	6
PCI	−3.3026	2013/08/16, 08:00	2013/08/27, 08:00	6	−4.1669	2013/08/16, 08:00	2013/08/27, 08:00	7
SETI	−3.1192	2011/08/08, 10:00	2011/09/30, 10:00	7	−3.7044	2011/08/08, 10:00	2011/09/30, 10:00	7
STI	−3.7139	2011/08/04, 09:00	2011/10/05, 10:00	2	−3.7881	2011/08/04, 09:00	2011/10/05, 10:00	2

Notes: M1 is Narayan and Popp's Model 1. M2 is Narayan and Popp's Model 2. TB is the date of the structural break; K is the lag length; ★ denotes statistical significance at the 10% level respectively.

JSX, Jakarta Stock Exchange Composite; KLSE, Bursa Malaysia Kuala Lumpur Composite Index; PCI, Philippine Stock Exchange Composite Index; STI, Singapore Straits Times Index; SETI, Stock Exchange of Thailand Index.

Table 4.4 Results of lagrange multiplier test with two breaks in the intercept (model AA)

Series	TB_1	TB_2	K	S_{t-1}	B_{t1}	B_{t2}
JSX	2013/06/11, 02:00	2013/08/20, 03:00	7	−0.0035★ (−3.6978)	−0.0302★★★ (−7.9145)	−0.0216★★★ (−5.6495)
KLSE	2011/08/08, 02:00	2011/08/08, 09:00	6	−0.0043 (−3.2058)	−0.0136★★★ (−5.2303)	−0.0304★★★ (−11.6520)
PCI	2013/08/16, 08:00	2013/08/27, 08:00	8	−0.0028 (−2.8514)	−0.0695★★★ (−15.7418)	−0.0538★★★ (−12.1133)
SETI	2011/08/08, 10:00	2013/02/28, 10:00	7	−0.0027 (−2.7650)	−0.0360★★★ (−8.7207)	−0.0655★★★ (−15.9071)
STI	2011/08/05, 10:00	2011/08/10, 10:00	5	−0.0019 (−2.4523)	−0.0275★★★ (−10.0532)	−0.0275★★★ (−10.0645)

Notes: Critical values for the LM test at 10%, 5%, and 1% significance levels = −3.504, −3.842, and −4.545, respectively. Critical values for the dummy variables denoting the break dates follow the standard asymptotic distribution. ★(★★)★★★ denote statistical significance at the 10%, 5%, and 1% levels, respectively. TB is the break date; K is the lag length; S_{t-1} is the LM test statistic; B_{t1} is the coefficient on the first break in the intercept; B_{t2} is the coefficient on the second break in the intercept.
JSX, Jakarta Stock Exchange Composite; KLSE, Bursa Malaysia Kuala Lumpur Composite Index; PCI, Philippine Stock Exchange Composite Index; STI, Singapore Straits Times Index; SETI, Stock Exchange of Thailand Index.

The results for the Narayan and Liu (2013) GARCH unit root test with two breaks in the intercept are presented in Table 4.6. In contrast to the findings for the Lee and Strazicich (2003) and Narayan and Popp (2010) unit root tests, there is evidence of mean reversion in four of the five indices at the 5% level. Specifically, the Narayan and Liu (2013) test suggests that the stock market indices in Malaysia, Philippines, Singapore, and Thailand are mean reverting, while the stock price index in Indonesia is characterized by a random walk. That the Narayan and Liu (2013) test rejects the unit root null for 80% of the countries is consistent with the argument in Narayan and Liu (2013) that the GARCH unit root test with two structural breaks is superior in terms of rejecting the unit root null compared with the Lee and Strazicich (2003) and Narayan and Popp (2010) unit root tests because Narayan and Liu (2013) take account of both structural breaks and heteroskedasticity. Given that each of the five stock price indices are heteroskedastic (see Table 4.1), we conclude that the findings for the Narayan and Liu (2013) test are to be preferred.

4.5 DISCUSSION

A characteristic of high-frequency financial data is heteroskedasticity. A large literature has emerged that tests the EMH in financial markets employing stationarity and unit root tests. This literature has recognized the importance of allowing for structural breaks, but has largely ignored the relevance of heteroskedasticity. The purpose of this study has been to show the importance of addressing heteroskedasticity, in addition

Table 4.5 Results of lagrange multiplier test with two breaks in the intercept and slope (model CC)

Series	TB_1	TB_2	K	S_{t-1}	B_{t1}	B_{t2}	D_{t1}	D_{t2}
JSX	2013/02/26, 05:00	2013/08/19, 05:00	7	−0.0069 (−5.2262)	−0.0001 (−0.0135)	0.0012 (0.3053)	0.0007*** (3.4155)	−0.0006*** (−2.7265)
KLSE	2011/08/04, 09:00	2013/08/12, 03:00	6	−0.0086 (−4.4871)	−0.0112*** (−4.2408)	0.0006 (0.1913)	−0.0004*** (−2.9202)	0.0003*** (2.4237)
PCI	2013/01/10, 02:00	2013/05/31, 08:00	8	−0.0102* (−5.3638)	−0.0091** (−1.9854)	−0.0272*** (−5.9554)	0.0010*** (3.7986)	−0.0011*** (−4.1877)
SETI	2011/09/21, 05:00	2013/02/28, 10:00	7	−0.0069 (−4.3655)	−0.0013 (−0.3202)	−0.0653*** (−15.7263)	−0.0003 (−1.7028)	−0.0002 (−0.9138)
STI	2011/08/04, 08:00	2012/01/25, 10:00	4	−0.0049 (−3.8673)	−0.0009 (−0.3176)	−0.0007 (−0.2589)	−0.0004*** (−2.7075)	0.0005*** (3.5730)

Critical values for the LM test

λ_2	0.4			0.6			0.8		
λ_1	1%	5%	10%	1%	5%	10%	1%	5%	10%
0.2	−6.16	−5.59	−5.27	−6.41	−5.74	−5.32	−6.33	−5.71	−5.33
0.4	−	−	−	−6.45	−5.67	−5.31	−6.42	−5.65	−5.32
0.6	−	−	−	−	−	−	−6.32	−5.73	−5.32

Notes: λ_j denotes the location of breaks. Critical values for the dummy variables denoting the break dates follow the standard asymptotic distribution. *(**)*** denote statistical significance at the 10%, 5% and 1% levels respectively. TB is the break date; K is the lag length; S_{t-1} is the LM test statistic; B_{t1} is the coefficient on the first break in the intercept; B_{t2} is the coefficient on the second break in the intercept; D_{t1} is the coefficient on the first break in the slope; D_{t2} is the coefficient on the second break in the slope.

JSX, Jakarta Stock Exchange Composite; KLSE, Bursa Malaysia Kuala Lumpur Composite Index; PCI, Philippine Stock Exchange Composite Index; STI, Singapore Straits Times Index; SETI, Stock Exchange of Thailand Index.

Table 4.6 Results for Narayan and Liu (2013) GARCH unit root test with two structural breaks in intercept

Series	Test statistic	TB_1	TB_2
JSX	−3.115	2011/12/15, 08:00	2012/12/20, 09:00
KLSE	−6.191**	2012/12/24, 04:00	2013/09/04, 04:00
PCI	−5.119**	2011/12/29, 02:00	2012/11/19, 08:00
SETI	−4.396**	2012/01/17, 03:00	2012/11/21, 08:00
STI	−3.962**	2012/11/21, 08:00	2013/02/25, 10:00

Notes: The test was performed under the assumption of two breaks in intercept and slope of the series. The 5% critical for the unit root test statistics are obtained from Narayan and Liu (2013). Narayan and Liu (2013) provide critical values for 5% level of significance only. ** indicates rejection of null of unit root at 5% level of significance.
JSX, Jakarta Stock Exchange Composite; KLSE, Bursa Malaysia Kuala Lumpur Composite Index; PCI, Philippine Stock Exchange Composite Index; STI, Singapore Straits Times Index; SETI, Stock Exchange of Thailand Index.

to structural breaks, when applying unit root tests to high-frequency financial data. To illustrate our argument, we have applied three types of unit root tests to high-frequency financial data for five ASEAN countries. These tests are: (1) unit root and stationarity tests, which do not allow for either structural breaks or heteroskedasticity; (2) unit root tests that accommodate structural breaks, but not heteroskedasticity; and (3) the Narayan and Liu (2013) test that allows for two structural breaks and accommodates heteroskedasticity. While the tests in (1) and (2) suggest that all five ASEAN financial markets are characterized by a random walk, the Narayan and Liu (2013) test finds that 80% of the markets are mean reverting. Given that each of the five series is heteroskedastic, this result suggests that the tests, which fail to allow for heteroskedasticity are producing biased estimates.

The results reported here are consistent with those reported in Mishra et al. (2014). Those authors failed to reject the unit root null for the two main Indian stock price indices when the Lee and Strazicich (2003) and Narayan and Popp (2010) unit root tests were applied to monthly data, but found mean reversion with the Narayan and Liu (2013) test. While the findings of previous studies for Asian markets are mixed, the results here are consistent with the conclusion in Guidi and Gupta (2013) that Asian stock markets are characterized by a certain degree of predictability, when–high frequency data is used. Guidi and Gupta (2013) based their conclusions on daily data. The results reported here suggest this conclusion is also true with hourly data.

Some authors have argued that support for the EMH depends on the level of equity market development. For example, Kim and Shamsuddin (2008) suggest that more developed markets are likely to be characterized by a random walk, while less-developed markets are mean reverting. Comparing the results for Singapore with the less-developed markets in this study, there is no support for this conjecture. Instead, the different findings across tests are being driven by the presence of heteroskedasticity in the data, irrespective of the level of equity development.

Overall, our results suggest that with hourly data financial markets in Indonesia are efficient, but financial markets in Malaysia, Philippines, Singapore, and Thailand revert to their mean over time. Our findings have important implications for investors in ASEAN's growing markets. Specifically, our results suggest that in Malaysia, Philippines, Singapore, and Thailand, it is possible for investors to make profits through the application of technical analysis to hourly data, but in Indonesia it is not possible to forecast future price movements based on technical analysis of hourly data.

The Asian financial crisis resulted in calls for tighter regulation of Asian financial markets (see e.g., Wade, 1998). While Asian financial markets were relatively resilient to the global financial crisis, this event led to a further round of calls for tighter financial regulation (see e.g., Kawai et al., 2013). The issue is particularly relevant in ASEAN markets given that legal enforcement and property rights are relatively weak and share prices are often volatile (Niblock et al., 2014).

Our findings also have implications for regulation of high-frequency trading across the ASEAN markets. In those markets that are not efficient—Malaysia, Philippines, Singapore, and Thailand—our results suggest that there is a bigger role for regulatory mechanisms to protect individual investors. However, in Indonesia, our results suggest that prices will fully reflect information in the market on an hourly basis and allocation of resources will be efficient. The implication that there is less need to regulate the Indonesian market, at least when high-frequency data is considered, differs from authors such as Jaswadi (2013) who have argued for greater regulation of the Indonesian stock market to protect investors from financial scandals.

4.6 CONCLUSION

We conclude with a brief discussion of the location of the breaks. The breaks obtained by Narayan and Liu (2013), which are plotted in Figure 4.2, can be classified into three distinct time periods. The first time-period is December 2011—January 2012 (JSX, SETI); the second time period is November—December 2012 (JSX, KLSE, PCI, SETI, and STI) and the third time period is early to mid 2013 (STI and KLSE).

The first break date corresponds to the global stock market downturn following the European debt crisis and downgrade of US sovereign debt by Standard and Poor's in August 2011. Although Narayan and Liu (2013) detect breaks in some series in late 2011/early 2012, the other tests used in the analysis detect some time around mid-late 2011 (August/September/October) as the first break date in most of the series. The plunge in Asian stock markets in response to the economic crisis in Europe and the United States is argued by some analysts to be a confirmation of the fact that ASEAN equity markets are still very much integrated with their developed counterparts.

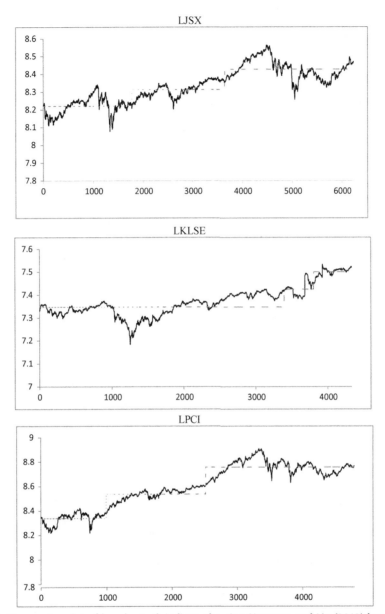

Figure 4.2 *Time series plot of hourly stock indices, showing Narayan and Liu (2013) breaks.*

The second time period associated with breaks in the data is November—December 2012, which seems to be more related to developments in ASEAN than global events. The most probable cause of breaks in this period is the launch of the ASEAN Trading Link in September 2012. The six ASEAN stock exchanges joined to create a virtual

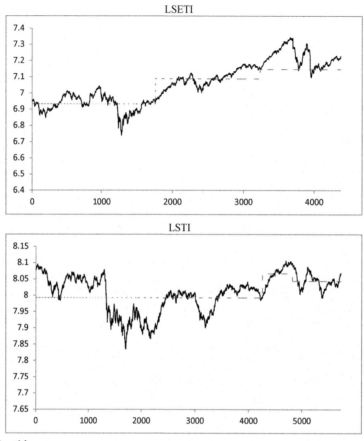

Figure 4.2 Cont'd.

market for securities trading accessible across all the six ASEAN exchanges. Bursa Malaysia and the Singapore Exchange joined Trading Link on the launch day in September, while Stock Exchange of Thailand joined in October 2012. The ASEAN stock markets were upbeat following the launch of ASEAN Trading Link in late 2012. The integration of all six ASEAN stock markets is expected to be complete by 2015.

The third set of breaks in the Narayan and Liu (2013) test (as well as other tests) correspond to the period June–September 2013 when stock market prices first fell in response to the Fed's announcement in June 2013 that it was winding down its asset repurchase program by 2014 and then rose in September 2013 when the Fed announced postponement of its earlier decision on winding down its asset repurchase program. This period was very volatile for equity markets across the world.

REFERENCES

Chancharat, S., Kamalian, A.R., Valadkhani, A., 2009. Random walk and multiple structural breaks in the Thai stock market. Empir. Econ. Lett. 8 (5), 501–506.

Chaudhuri, K., Wu, Y., 2003. Random-walk versus breaking trend in stock prices: evidence from emerging markets. J. Bank. Finance 27 (4), 575.

Chaudhuri, K., Wu, Y., 2004. Mean reversion in stock prices: evidence from emerging markets. Manag. Finance 30 (2), 22–31.

Fama, E.F., 1970. Efficient capital markets: a review of theory and empirical work. J. Finance 25 (2), 383–417.

Guidi, F., Gupta, R., 2013. Market efficiency in the ASEAN region: evidence from multivariate and cointegration tests. Appl. Financ. Econ. 23 (4), 265–274.

Hamid, K., Suleman, M.T., Shah, S.Z.A., Akash, R.S.I., 2010. Testing the weak form of the efficient market hypothesis: evidence from Asia Pacific markets. Int. Res. J. Finance Econ. 58 (3), 121–133.

Hsieh, J., Nieh, C.C., 2010. An overview of asian equity markets. Asian Pac. Econ. Lit. 24, 19–51.

Jaswadi, J., 2013. Corporate Governance and Accounting Irregularities: Evidence from the Two-Tier Board Structure in Indonesia. DBA Thesis. Victoria University, Melbourne, Australia.

Kawai, M., Mayes, D.G., Morgan, P.J., 2013. Implications of the global financial crisis for financial reform and regulation in Asia. Edward Elgar, Cheltenham, UK.

Kim, J.H., Shamsuddin, A., 2008. Are asian stock markets efficient? Evidence from new multiple variance ratio tests. J. Empir. Finance 15 (3), 518–532.

Kim, K., Schmidt, P., 1993. Unit root tests with conditional heteroskedasticity. J. Econ. 59 (3), 287–300.

Kwiatkowski, D., Phillips, P.C.B., Schmidt, P., Shin, Y., 1992. Testing the null hypothesis of stationarity against the alternative of a unit root. J. Econ. 54 (1/2/3), 159–178.

Kyodo News, February 27, 2014. ASEAN Reaffirms 2015 Goal for Economic Community. Kyodo News. http://english.kyodonews.jp/news/2014/02/276368.html (last accessed 01.04.14).

Lean, H.H., Smyth, R., 2007. Do asian stock markets follow a random-walk? Evidence from LM unit root tests with one and two structural breaks. Rev. Pac. Basin Finan. Mark. Policies 10 (1), 15–31.

Lean, H.H., Smyth, R., 2014. Stock market co-movement in ASEAN and China. In: Arouri, M., Boubaker, S., Nguyen, D.K. (Eds.), Emerging Markets and the Global Economy. Elsevier, Amsterdam.

Lee, C.-C., Lee, J.D., Lee, C.C., 2012. Stock prices and the efficient market hypothesis: evidence from a panel stationary test with structural breaks. Jpn. World Econ. 22 (2), 49–58.

Lee, J., Huang, C.J., Shin, Y., 1997. On stationarity tests in the presence of structural breaks. Econ. Lett. 55 (1), 165–172.

Lee, J., Strazicich, M.C., 2003. Minimum lagrange multiplier unit root test with two structural breaks. Rev. Econ. Statistics 85 (4), 1082–1089.

Lim, K.-P., Brooks, R., 2011. The revolution of stock market efficiency over time: a survey of the empirical literature. J. Econ. Surv. 25 (1), 69–108.

Lumsdaine, R.L., Papell, D.H., 1997. Multiple trend breaks and the unit-root hypothesis. Rev. Econ. Statistics 79 (2), 212–218.

Malkiel, B.G., 2003. The efficient market hypothesis and its critics. J. Econ. Perspect. 17 (1), 59–82.

Mishra, A., Mishra, V., Smyth, R., 2014. The random walk on the indian stock market. Emerg. Mark. Finance Trade (in press).

Munir, Q., Ching, K.S., Furouka, F., Mansur, K., 2012. The efficient market hypothesis revisited: evidence from five small open ASEAN stock markets. Singap. Econ. Rev. 57 (3), 1–12.

Munir, Q., Mansur, K., 2009. Is the malaysian stock market efficient? Evidence from threshold unit root tests. Econ. Bull. 29 (2), 1359–1370.

Narayan, P.K., Liu, R., 2013. New Evidence on the Weak-Form Efficient Market Hypothesis. Working Paper. Centre for Financial Econometrics, Deakin University.

Narayan, P.K., Popp, S., 2010. A new unit root test with two structural breaks in level and slope at unknown time. J. Appl. Statistics 37 (9), 1425–1438.

Narayan, P.K., Popp, S., 2013. Size and power properties of structural break unit root tests. Appl. Econ. 45 (6), 721–728.

Narayan, P.K., Smyth, R., 2004. Is South Korea's stock market efficient? Appl. Econ. Lett. 11 (11), 707–710.

Narayan, P.K., Smyth, R., 2005. Are OECD stock prices characterised by a random-walk? evidence from sequential trend break and panel data models. Appl. Financ. Econ. 15 (8), 547–556.

Narayan, P., Smyth, R., 2006. Random walk versus multiple trend breaks in stock prices: evidence from fifteen European markets. Appl. Financ. Econ. Lett. 2 (1), 1–7.

Narayan, P.K., Smyth, R., 2007. Mean reversion versus random-walk in G7 stock prices: evidence from multiple trend break unit root tests. J. Int. Mark. Finan. Inst. Money 17 (2), 152–166.

Niblock, S.J., Heng, P., Sloan, K., 2014. Regional stock markets and the economic development of Southeast Asia. Asian Pac. Econ. Lit. 28 (1), 47–59.

Perron, P., 1989. The great crash, the oil Price shock, and the unit root hypothesis. Econometrica 57 (6), 1361–1401.

Samuelson, P.A., 1965. Proof that properly anticipated prices fluctuate randomly. Ind. Manag. Rev. 6 (2), 41–49.

Wade, R., 1998. The asian debt and development crisis of 1997-?: causes and consequences. World Dev. 26 (8), 1535–1553.

World Bank, 2012. World Development Indicators. World Bank, Washington DC.

CHAPTER 5

Game Theoretical Aspects of Colocation in High-Speed Financial Markets

Camillo von Müller
CLVS-HSG University of St. Gallen, St. Gallen, Switzerland

Contents

5.1 INTRODUCTION

Geography matters in financial markets. In his book "Flash Boys" financial journalist Michael Lewis (2014) develops a scheme in which high-frequency traders front-run markets by using "fiber-optic cables that link superfast computers to brokers … [so as to] … intercept and buy outstanding orders" that are then sold back to their originators at a higher price (Ross, 2014). "The mother of all schemes," in Lewis' book, "is an 827-mile cable running through mountains and under rivers from Chicago to New Jersey that reduces the journey of data from 17 to 13 milliseconds. A transatlantic cable still under construction will give a 5.2 millisecond advantage to those looking to profit from the spread trade between New York and London" (Ross, 2014).

The Handbook of High Frequency Trading
ISBN 978-0-12-802205-4

The economics and technology described by Lewis may read like (science) fiction. They are, however, reality: "In 2010, Spread Networks completed construction of a new high-speed fiber optic cable connecting financial markets in New York and Chicago. ... Construction costs were estimated at $300 million ... [reducing] ... [r]ound-trip communication time between New York and Chicago... from 16 milliseconds to 13 milliseconds" (Budish et al., 2013, p. 1). Other examples of recent investments into latency reducing technology and infrastructure, include the "microwave connection between London and Frankfurt [that] was turned on ... [in] October (2012) by Perseus Telecom ... [so as to] cut about 40% off the time taken to complete a trade compared with traditional fibre-optic networks" as the company claims (BBC, 2013). Throughout 2014, "an array of laser devices" shall be set up and be put into operation, "linking the New York Stock Exchange's data center in Mahwah, N.J., with the Nasdaq Stock Market's data center in another New Jersey community, Carteret" (The Wall Street Journal, 2014).

While trading firms and exchanges are currently heavily investing to speed up signal transmission between remotely connected trading hubs around the globe, the quest for latency reduction is also driving firms ever closer to the data centers of trading hubs, such as the NYSE Liquidity Hub in Mahwah, (NJ.) or the "340,000 square foot facility" Equinex in Secaucus (NJ, Miller, 2014). Given this brief list of evidence, Michael Lewis (2014) depicts an accurate picture of how High-Frequency Trading (HFT) is not only changing financial markets but also shaping financial geography today.

5.2 LITERATURE AND STRUCTURE OF THE CHAPTER

Why should money managers care about the analysis by Lewis (2014)? In order to answer this question, the current chapter analyses colocation as latency reducing technology that high-frequency traders employ to minimize latencies of HFT even further (cf. Shorter and Miller, 2014; Hasbrouck and Saar, 2013). While various market effects of latency reduction in context of HFT (e.g., Wah and Wellman, 2013; Miao, 2014) and spatial optimization (Wissner-Gross and Freer, 2010; Laughlin et al., 2013) exist that influence markets and market quality, a basic rationale for colocation is that it promises additional profits and other benefits to colocating firms (Brogaard et al., 2013). At the same time, asymmetries in latency reduction can imply costs to traders who do not speed up their IT infrastructures thus trading at higher latencies (e.g., Ahmed et al., 2009). The current analysis adds to afore-listed literature by focusing on colocation from a strategic viewpoint. It uses empirical evidence from a recent study of Budish et al. (2013), who demonstrate the existence of technical arbitrage opportunities within contexts of Continuous Limit Order Books (CLOBs). In a second step, it derives a theoretical perspective based on the empirical insights on technical arbitrage in context of HFT that allows for discussing the strategic choices money managers are left with when deciding on spatial location and latency reduction. Taking the current regulatory and institutional environment as a given, the chapter does not discuss ethical or societal considerations of latency reduction (e.g., Angel and McCabe, 2013, Pagnotta and Philippon, 2011).

The argument proceeds as follows. In the subsequent section, I will review some general aspects of information asymmetries and order matching before discussing how these aspects matter in context of latency reduction and colocation (Section 5.3). Having thus described the general terminological and conceptual background of the argument, I will summarize current empirical findings on the existence of technical arbitrage opportunities due to HFT (Section 5.4). In Section 5.5, I will model basic strategic aspects that follow from the characteristics of technical arbitrage in context of HFT, namely zero sum payoffs, and the relative nature of costs and benefits in this context. Section 5.6 discusses strategic decisions on whether or not to invest into HFT technologies through the lenses of evolutionary games, while also reviewing spatial aspects that follow from technical market fragmentation. In Section 5.7, I examine the limitations before I will summarize its main findings in the form of five propositions to money managers.

5.3 COLOCATION AND LATENCY REDUCTION

Historic and current developments in financial infrastructure development underline the general relevance of latency-reducing technologies for financial markets. In order to understand ongoing challenges to money managers it is, however, important to become aware of recent shifts within the industry that are characterized by the intertwining of gigatrends such as increases in bandwidth communication and the global synchronization of asset price movements and nanotrends such as decreases in the transmission latencies and tick size.

5.3.1 Information Asymmetries and Order Matching

In a famous passage, thirteenth-century scholiast Thomas Aquinas observed that a wheat seller who "carries wheat to a place where wheat fetches a high price, knowing that many will come after him carrying wheat … [so that] if the buyers knew this they would give a lower price … need not give the buyer this information" (in: McGee, 1990, p. 16). For, "the seller, since he sells his goods at the price actually offered him, does not seem to act contrary to justice through not stating what is going to happen" (ibid.). What reads merely like a problem of medieval moral philosophy is in fact a question that is directly connected to technological aspects of ultra-low latency trading in contemporary financial markets. This becomes clear when we focus on the abstract mechanics that underlie the setting described by Thomas. The latter boil down to the question of what happens if markets are such that the sell-offers (buy-offers) are matched systematically with buy-offers (sell-offers) that lag behind in the process of information updating? As Budish, Cranton and Shim (2013) demonstrate, this question is relevant in contemporary financial markets. They show that even if markets are efficient in that information updates are incorporated by all parties instantaneously and at the same time, differences in latency—i.e., "the time it takes to access and respond to market information" (Wah and Wellman, 2013, p. 856)—can imply that some firms cannot withdraw old orders fast enough. As their outstanding orders lag behind, the latter are matched with orders that reflect new updates in information.

The question of how to treat information asymmetries in context of order matching requests a moral solution (c.f. the quote by Thomas above), and leads to considerations on regulation (e.g., von Müller, 2012), and optimal market design (Budish et al., 2013). However, it is also of relevance to spatial decisions in financial markets. The present chapter will focus on this issue with a special emphasis on consequences for money managers.

5.3.2 Current Trends in Latency Reduction

Historically, the quest for updating and placing updated orders faster than others has been an integral part of financial markets: "From 1847 through 1851, Paul Reuter employed carrier pigeons between Brussels and Aachen to bridge a gap in telegraph stations on the route connecting Berlin to Paris, thereby providing a low-latency data feed for market-moving events ... In 1865, the financier James Fisk completed a purpose-built telegraph line to Halifax in order to signal a fast steamship to cross the Atlantic with instructions to short Confederate bonds at the close of the U.S. Civil War ... One of Thomas A. Edison's best known inventions was the stock ticker, which transmitted market pricing information using the then newly practical transmission of information by telegraph" (Laughlin et al., 2013, p. 1).

Advantages in computational power and signal transmission have been main drivers of latency reduction over the past years. For example, with regard to point-to-point connections between major trading hubs in the United States "the cutting-edge method used to communicate financial information from Chicago to New Jersey has recently progressed through three distinct stages. ... [A]s of April, 2010, the fastest communication route connecting the Chicago futures markets to the New Jersey equity markets was through fiber optic lines that allowed equity prices to respond within 7.25–7.95 ms of a price change in Chicago ... In August of 2010, Spread Networks introduced a new fiber optic line that ... reduced Chicago–New Jersey latency to approximately 6.65 ms. Beginning in approximately March of 2011 ... a further progressive ($\sim$2 ms) decline ... [due to the] deployment of custom-built microwave communications networks ... reduce[d] the inter-market latency ... to fall in the 4.2–5.2 ms range" (Laughlin et al., 2013, p. 2).

The continuous development of latency reducing technologies from pigeon post and steamships to fiber optics and laser networks underlines the dependence of financial markets and their geography on technological evolution. While some fundamental questions remain unchanged (as has been shown by quoting Thomas Aquinas' reflections on the incorporation of information updates in markets), recent technological developments also imply new challenges to financial markets and their participants.

5.3.3 Colocation as a Specific Form of Latency Reduction

Aspects of geographical concentration are a fundamental characteristic in the evolution of modern financial markets (cf. Kindleberger, 1974; Preda, 2009). The rationale for colocation in context of HFT stems from the fact that "[r]ecent advances in high-frequency financial trading have brought typical trading latencies below 500 μS, at which point light propagation delays due to geographical separation information sources become relevant for trading strategies and coordination (e.g., it takes 67 ms, over 100 times) longer for light to travel between antipodal points along the Earth's surface" (Wissner-Gross and Freer, 2010, pp. 056,104−1). In other words, "[t]he speed of trading has entered the special relativistic regime, in which speed-of-light related delays are a significant factor" (Laughlin et al., 2013, p. 1).

That is, latency reduction no longer depends exclusively on investments into latency-reducing technologies but also on optimal spatial location of the servers of a trading firm in proximity to the servers of a given trading platform (colocation), respectively at the optimal location between the servers of multiple trading platforms (cf. Wissner-Gross and Freer, 2010) depending on the kind of trading strategy a firm employs. A basic economic rationale of colocation consists of advantages in relative speed. Depending on the specifics of their technological and legal arrangements with colocation service providers, colocating firms enjoy early information access or latency advantages in order execution due to server proximity (or access to high-speed data freeways that move remote trading hubs closer together as they decrease latencies in the communication between the latter). The nature and benefits of these advantages will be discussed in the following section on the basis of existing empirical evidence.

5.4 EMPIRICAL EVIDENCE: TECHNICAL ARBITRAGE THROUGH LATENCY REDUCTION

Before discussing strategic choices of colocation, I will review basic mechanics of technical arbitrage due to latency reduction in form of HFT investments and/or colocation. In a second step, I will summarize the main findings by Budish et al. (2013), which demonstrate the existence of arbitrage opportunities in this context.

5.4.1 Price, Adjustments, Epps Effect, and Arbitrage

Fama (1970) famously observed that "in an efficient market prices 'fully reflect' available information" (384). According to this observation traders incorporate private information into prices through trading (Hachmeister, 2007, p. 35). "When they buy an asset they push up prices, while prices decrease when they sell. As a consequence their trading activity reflects their beliefs about fundamental values and prices consequentially become more informative" (ibid., p. 36).

In his classical argument, Bagehot (1971) differentiates between informed traders who possess information that is not yet reflected in prices, and uninformed traders who do not yet possess information that is not yet reflected in markets (Hachmeister, 2007, p. 35). Although, Bagehot (1971) was "the first to introduce information as a trading motive" systematically (Bagehot, 1971), insight on the nonsynchronic nature of price adjustments in markets can be traced back as far as to the thirteenth century as demonstrates the quote above by Thomas Aquinas.

Thomas' argument is an intuitive depiction on how the temporal information asymmetries matter for processes of price adjustments in inefficient markets: As long as above-mentioned wheat merchant reaches the "place where wheat fetches a high price" (see above) earlier than his competitors, and—more importantly—earlier than the information on the additional supply of wheat that is to be expected upon the arrival of the other wheat merchants, market prices will remain unchanged. Price adjustments will occur only upon the sequential arrival of the other sellers (or the announcement thereof). That is, the wheat of the first seller to arrive at the market will fetch higher prices than the wheat of the second seller etc.

Thomas' insight is relevant to contemporary financial markets as shows the following intellectual exercise: If the process described by Thomas was to be duplicated and would thus take place at two geographically separated places (let us say in Paris, where Thomas had conducted his studies, and Naples, where Thomas had lived for his final years) but on the same day, the same amount of wheat would be sold from the same number of sequentially arriving merchants to an identical number of buyers in Naples and Paris. Under this condition, opening prices (at which the first amount of wheat is being sold) and closing prices (at which the last bushel of wheat is being sold) would be identical in Paris and Naples. Hence, if measured on a daily basis, the correlation value for wheat markets in Naples and Paris would be 1. However, if measured at shorter time intervals (let us say on an hourly basis) correlation values for changes in wheat prices in Paris and Naples would be much lower (unless the wheat merchants in Paris and Naples would arrive at the exact same times at each market respectively). Epps (1979) was the first to provide empirical evidence for the sequential nature of price adjustments and its relevance in financial markets. Relying on the argument that the correlation of changes in prices of different common stocks of a day or longer "tend to be particularly high for firms in the same industry," he demonstrated that "[c]orrelations among price changes in common stocks of companies in one industry … decrease with the length of the interval for which the price changes are measured" (p.291). Figure 5.1 summarizes the

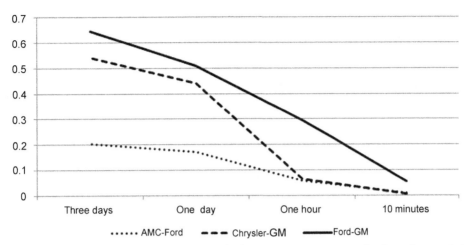

Figure 5.1 Correlations of changes in log price for four stocks during intervals of 10 minutes—3 days representation of select data from Epps (1979).

descriptive statistics provided by Epps (1979) on the breakdown of equity market correlations in decreasing time intervals.[1]

There are several explanations for why market data behaves as observed by Epps (1979). A potential reason is "non-synchronous trading across markets, which causes fresh observations of price not to arise simultaneously across markets, but to be separated by ... certain time intervals" (Large, 2007). This situation is identical to the hypothetical discussion of wheat prices in Paris and Naples described above. Other explanations refer to the fact that "financial markets, which are often the most liquid, incorporate information onto their prices faster than others, called the lagers. As a result, when dealing with two assets that exhibit a so-called lead—lag relationship, there will be only partial correlation at timescales shorter than the characteristic lead—lag time" (Huth and Abergel, 2011, p.189—190). In noncomputerized market environments, lead—lag relationships can also be explained through the fact that "information needs a human timescale to be processed" (Huth and Abergel, 2011, p. 189—190).

Epps (1979) observations matter as they imply opportunities for traders by leveraging the lead—lag effect systematically. This would be possible by making use of the Ford-GM

---

[1] Epps (1979) also provides correlation values for intervals of 20 min, 40 min, 2 h, 3 h, and 2 days, as well as correlation values for the stock price changes of AMC-Chrysler, AMC-GM, Chrysler-Ford. These data are not shown in Figure 5.1 for reasons of graphical representations and readability. The omission does not change the general results. Epps (1979) chose the "stocks of [what were in 1979] the four major automakers in the United States as source of data ... which [at that time] essentially constitute[d] the domestic auto industry," since these were "not highly diversified, [so that] their yields during long intervals were expected to be highly correlated. ... Prices of each stock were recorded at 10-minute intervals during each of the 125 trading days in the first six months of 1971" (Epps, 1979, p. 291).

correlations shown in Figure 5.1. Figure 5.1 illustrates basic mechanics that analogously apply to the issue of HFT latency arbitrage - only in much shorter time intervals. At a 10 min interval, price jumps in Ford show no reaction in GM. However, at intervals of 3 days "[t]his creates a temporary profit opportunity ... available to whichever acts the fastest" (Budish et al., 2013, p. 2). For example, a simplistic and straight forward strategy depending on the direction of the price jump could be to sell GM (if it goes up) and use the proceeds to buy Ford before the lag closes and Ford will be up, too. It is to note, however, that it is easy to postulate these mechanics from an ex-post basis. When looking for systematic correlation lags that allow predictions into the future, one should note that the "lead–lag relationships between daily returns of stocks" that Epps (1979) observed in the 1970s on the New York Stock Exchange have "vanished in less than 20 years" (Tóth and Kertész, 2006, p. 507). While this can be interpreted as a sign of increased efficiency in financial markets, it also means that technical arbitrage opportunities have vanished on human timescale. However, at a higher breakdown of intervals, Epps (1979) observations can still be made out in today's electronic markets as will be discussed in the next sections.

5.4.2 Technical Arbitrage Opportunities and HFT

Budish et al. (2013) provide empirical evidence for the existence of arbitrage opportunities through HFT in current markets. They base their observations on data of "the two largest securities that track the S&P 500 index, the iShares SPDR S&P 500 exchange traded fund ... [henceforth ticker SPY, or SPY], and the E-mini Future ... [henceforth ticker ES, or ES]" (Budish et al., 2013, p. 1) from January 1, 2005–December 31, 2011 (excluding 3 months because of data issues). As a key finding, they show that "CLOBs do not actually work in continuous time" (Budish et al. (2014) as "market correlations completely break down" at narrow time intervals (ibid.), which opens up "frequent opportunities of technical arbitrage." Budish, Cranton and Shim (2013) demonstrate that these opportunities exist as the "correlation between ES and SPY is nearly 1 at long-enough intervals ... but almost completely breaks down at high-frequency time intervals," while decreasing even further so that "[t]he 10 millisecond correlation is just 0.1016, and the 1 ms correlation is just 0.0080" (p.1). Table 5.1 summarizes observations of Budish et al. (2013) on the correlation breakdown in ES and SPY.

The data in Table 5.1 represents "an extreme version of ... [the] phenomenon discovered by Epps (1979)." Yet, it is more than just "a theoretical curiosity" (Budish et al., 2013, p. 2) since it implies profit opportunities have the potential to shape the HFT industry and its geography. In order to grasp the implications of the empirical proof on the existence of technical arbitrage opportunities in low-latency environments as it is provided by Budish et al. (2013), I will first review the basic mechanics of their model. The practical relevance of the environment described by Budish et al. (2013) becomes apparent when considering that "limit order books match buyers and sellers in more than half of the world's financial markets" (Gould et al. 2013, p. 1709). In their analysis,

Table 5.1 Correlation breakdown in ES and SPY

Location:	NY	Chi	Mid
1 ms	0.0209	0.0023	0.0080
10 ms	0.1819	0.0441	0.1016
1 sec	0.6913	0.6868	0.6893
10 sec	0.9079	0.9073	0.9076
1 min	0.9799	0.9798	0.9798
10 min	0.9975	0.9975	0.9975

The table shows correlations calculated by Budish et al. (2013) for the return of the E-mini S&P 500 future (ES) and SPDR S&P 500 EF (SPY) bid-ask midpoints as a function of the return time interval, reported as a median over all trading days in 2011. Correlations are shown for simple returns for traders situated in New York (NY), Chicago (Chi), and at equidistance between the two cities (Mid).
(Source: Budish, Cranton and Shim, 2013, p. 14).

Budish et al. (2013) show that HFT traders can exploit arbitrage opportunities due to correlation breakdowns between ES and SPY. The latter occur through instantaneous changes in the relation between market prices of ES/SPY that happen every so often, e.g., when ES goes up in one instant and SPY will follow only an instant later.[2] In this situation, trading firms will adjust their quotes, as it will be less profitable to sell SPY and more profitable to sell ES.

Budish et al. (2013) demonstrate that the time lags between the instants at which trading firms send off their updated quotes, and the instants at which old quotes are withdrawn from the CLOB, open up arbitrage opportunities for traders whose updated signals can overtake the update signals of others. "[A]t the exact same time [at which trading firms send updates on their orders], other trading firms send a message to the CLOB attempting to snipe the stale quotes before they are adjusted" and "since the CLOB processes messages in serial that is, one at a time it is possible that a message to snipe a stale quote will get processed before the message to adjust the stale quote" (Budish et al., 2014). In this situation, the CLOB matches orders that are based upon information from before the update, with orders that are based upon updated information. The result is comparable to the Thomistic analysis of information discrepancies in wheat markets described above: traders whose quotes are updated faster than others benefit from being able to place sell (buy) orders based on old information that are matched with buy (sell) orders based upon old information due to differences in the latencies of order transmission.

In how far are technical arbitrage opportunities relevant in current markets? Budish et al. (2013) "estimate ... the annual value of the ES—SPY arbitrage opportunity" arriving at average values "of around $75 mm per year, fluctuating as high as $151 mm

---

[2] Budish et al. (2014) describe the evolution of ES prices of SPY in form of a compound Poisson jump process.

in 2008 … and as low as \$35 mm in 2005" (p.26). Given the fact that Budish et al. (2013) base their calculation on a single arbitrage strategy while additional strategies are available, they reason that their estimate of the annual ES-SPY arbitrage value is a lower bound of the total value of technical arbitrage opportunities in the market segment under discussion. Also, the computed value focuses on just two instruments traded at two different exchanges, leaving aside other highly correlated assets at other exchanges.

5.5 MODELING STRATEGIC CHOICES ON COLOCATION

The analysis of Budish et al. (2013) shows that within current markets, opportunities of technical arbitrage exist that render investments into latency reduction technologies attractive. The current section will discuss strategic choices on colocation as specific form of latency reduction in HFT-environments.

5.5.1 The Rationale for Colocation

In the scenario described by Budish et al. (2013), there are N trading firms. Due to the sequential nature of how CLOBs are processing orders, each firm runs the risk of getting sniped by the other (N−1) firms. That is, the probability of each firm getting sniped is $\frac{N-1}{N}$ (Budish et al., 2014). According to this rationale, latency reductions through HFT delivers payoffs to firms not only as they increase the likelihood of profiting from arbitrage opportunities by "sniping" the orders of other firms. In the CLOB-environment described by Budish et al. (2013) and Budish et al. (2014), latency reduction reduces a firm's risk of being sniped by other firms as the number of firms on a trading platform (N) typically includes firms that do not reduce latencies (N∗) and firms that reduce latencies through HFT (N∗∗) so that $N = N* + N**$ and $\frac{N-1}{N} > \frac{N**-1}{N**}$ as long as N∗ and N∗∗ > 0.

Since location decisions promise additional latency reductions in HFT environments as it has been discussed above, firms benefit from these reductions as they increase arbitrage opportunities through sniping while reducing the probability of being sniped. Figure 5.2 depicts the mechanics of the arbitrage game described by Budish et al. (2013) as rationale for latency reduction through HFT investments and colocation.

The empirical data and technological environment discussed in this section underlines the relative nature of the benefits accruing from latency reduction. Systematic technical arbitrage opportunities vanish if all firms would trade at exact latencies. Hence, expected payoffs of investments into latency-reducing technologies (including colocation) depend on the question if and to what extent other firms will be able to reduce latencies at the same rate. The nature of these contingencies will be discussed at more detail below before resulting consequences for money managers shall be examined.

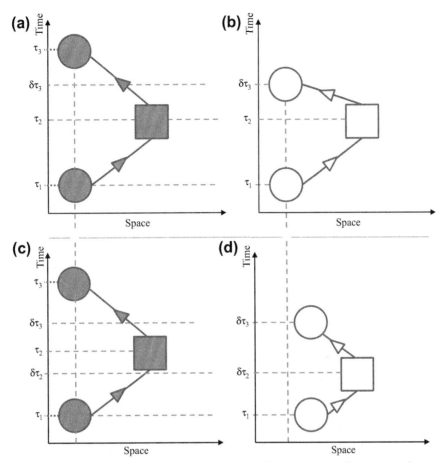

Figure 5.2 *Order transmission and latency reductions.* Circles represent trading venues that send updates on price information and receive orders in response to/from trading firms (squares). Figures 2 (a) and 2 (c) show firms that communicate at given latencies. Figures 2 (b) and 2(d) represent firms that communicate at relatively lower latencies. Note that firms in 2 (a) and 2 (b) are at equidistances to the respective trading venues as they are located at identical points on the X-axis. Due to technological advantages that decrease transmission latencies, orders by Firm (b) reach the trading platform earlier than orders of Firm (a). Firm (d) is colocated within the immediate proximity to the server thus sending off signals to the server at lower latency than Firm (c). *(Wissner-Gross and Freer, 2010, p. 056104-2.)*

5.5.2 Prisoner's Dilemma

There are several ways how to model strategic choices of HFT firms that aim at leveraging arbitrage opportunities due to latency advantages. The present section will discuss these choices in form of the well-known Prisoner's Dilemma (PD) and as Hawk–Dove Game (cf. Budish et al., 2013: von Müller, 2012).

First, it will be shown that the systematic exploitation of technical arbitrage opportunities through latency reduction is a dominant strategy if there are only two firms that compete for latency advantages. Under this outcome, colocating is the "choice ... preferred, irrespective of which choice the other ... [firm] makes" (Schelling, 1973, p. 385.). In the current PD-model markets consist exclusively of two firms that maximize their identical profit functions by trading on the basis of technologies that are identical in the initial state. Each firm has to decide whether or not to update its technology through colocation so as to lower latencies in its communication with the trading platform relative to the other firm. If only one firm colocates, it benefits from the arbitrage opportunities that have been discussed above, i.e., the firm that colocates will be able to trade at latencies that are sufficiently low for updating its orders before the orders of the other firm can be replaced by new orders. The first firm will thus be able to incorporate all benefits from latency reduction into its profit function. In this situation, the value of arbitrage opportunities to the colocating firm is such that $P_{C; NC} = (V) > 0$.

Consistent with the argument by Budish et al. (2013), the noncolocating firm is the firm to be "sniped," i.e., it bears the full costs of being located at a larger distance to the server. Whatever the first firm gains through latency reduction (e.g., by being able to sell at higher prices), is a loss to the second firm (e.g., by having to buy at prices that do not reflect the information update). Hence, the costs of noncolocation are reciprocal to the positive value of the arbitrage profits that accrue to the colocating firm. In this situation the value of the payoffs that accrue to the noncolocating firm can be written as $P_{NC; C} = [-(V)]$.

Firms colocate if the costs of colocation are such that $(C) < (V)$ so that net benefits (v) from colocating are $[(V)-(C)] = (v) > 0$. If both firms exercise trades at equal latencies, the value of arbitrage opportunities (V) is zero, which is also the payoff value $P_{NC; NC}$ to each of the two firms if neither firm colocates. However, if both firms colocate, each firm earns negative payoffs due to the costs of colocation at $P_{C; C} = [-(C)]$. This leads to the "characteristic ranking" of payoffs in the PD, where $P_{C; NC} > P_{NC; NC} > P_{C; C} > P_{NC; C}$. Table 5.2 summarizes the payoffs to each firm.

The matrix illustrates the relative nature of arbitrage gains due to latency advantages. As the matrix shows, under current conditions, "[a]ny given firm would clearly be best off, if it would be the sole agent ... [that colocates as this] ... situation would allow the firm to exploit the technology at full capacity by trading at lower latencies than the other firm. ... [For in] ... this situation, the ... [co-locating] firm would capture the full benefits of the technology enjoying total payoffs minus costs of ... [co-location] ... In reverse, ... a firm is worst off, if it is the only agent that does not ... [co-locate]. In this case, its competitor can exploit ... [advantages due to server proximity] at full capacity by trading at lower latencies than the firm itself" (von Müller, 2012). For the noncolocating firm, this outcome implies negative payoffs.

The matrix further illustrates that each of the two firms does not only have a dominant preference with respect to its own choices but also with regard to "the other's choice preferring the other firm to not co-locate" (c.f. von Müller, 2012).

Table 5.2 Prisoner's dilemma of latency reduction

		Firm B	
		Co-locate	Do Not Co-locate
Firm A	Co-locate	-(C); -(C)	(v); -(V)
	Do Not Co-locate	-(V); (v)	0;0

The above-described scenario rests on a static comparison assuming a world in which a firm chooses to colocate independently of what its competitors do. To make the model more realistic, further dimensions can be added by assuming that (1) there are more than 2 firms; (2) due to the relative nature of arbitrage due to colocation, a firm's choices are contingent on the choices of other firms; (3) the model is dynamic in that an equilibrium is to be reached by the sequential choices of firms.

5.5.3 Hawk–Dove Game

The above-described modification can be summarized in the form of a Hawk–Dove Game (Bowles, 2004, p. 78). In this game, n firms have to decide on how to share existing profits from arbitrage opportunities that they enjoy with respect to the rest of the market due to colocation (in the following, I will discuss the case for n = 2. Note that analogous mechanics apply for n > 2). A firm receives net benefits $P_{C;\ NC} = [(V) - (C)] = (v)$ that result from arbitrage opportunities if it is situated closer to the server of the exchange platform than the other firm. In this situation, the value of payoffs $P_{NC;\ C}$ accruing to the non-colocating firm is zero. If both firms behave as "doves," (i.e., abstain from colocation), each firm shares the benefits accruing from arbitrage opportunities with the respective other firm at a value of $P_{NC;\ NC} = v/n$. However, if both firms colocate, each firm does not only face the costs of adoption (C) but also its share of the additional costs (c) created by the extra demand in colocation services (we can think of (c) as additional costs due to additional compensation that providers of colocation services are able to impose on colocating firms in inefficient markets where (C′) no longer represents the marginal benefits of colocation). In this situation, the payoffs to each firm are $P_{C;\ C} = \frac{(v-c)}{n}$ (Note that

Table 5.3 A Hawk—Dove game of latency reduction

		Firm B	
		Co-locate	Do Not Co-locate
Firm A	Co-locate	$[(v) - (c)]/2;$ $[(v-c)]/2$	$(v); 0$
	Do Not Co-locate	$0; (v)$	$v/2; v/2$

the loss minimizing boundary of $(v)-(c) = 0$ does not apply in this situation due to market inefficiencies). This leads to the characteristic payoff ranking of the Hawk—Dove Game in which $P_{C; NC} > P_{NC; NC} > P_{NC; C} > P_{C; C}$ (Doebeli and Hauert, 2004). Table 5.3 summarizes the strategic choices and the respective payoffs to the two firms.

The matrix in Table 5.3 differs from the matrix in Table 5.2 as it describes a situation that is characterized by contingent strategies. Rather, in the current game, a firm's behavior depends on the strategic moves of the other party (cf. Doebeli and Hauert, 2004). The implications of this will be discussed in the next sections.

5.6 DISCUSSION: EVOLUTIONARY OPTIMIZATION AND SPATIAL DYNAMICS

The fact that the payoffs of a firm are contingent on the decisions of other firms has consequences for the determination of firms' spatial behaviors, i.e., their decisions of whether to colocate or not. The subsequent section will discuss the strategic and spatial behavior of firms so as to be able to identify consequences for money managers and other investing firms under the various assumptions presented in this chapter in the last section.

5.6.1 Optimal Behavior of Colocating Firms—an Analytic Approach

The matrix in Table 5.3 describes a situation in which it can be profitable for firms to colocate, depending on what other firms do. There are two "corner solutions" that mark the extreme values of payoffs accruing to a given colocating firm (hawk): if the firm is only trading with other noncolocating firms (i.e., firms that trade at higher latencies), the firm will benefit fully from existing latency advantages due to to arbitrage

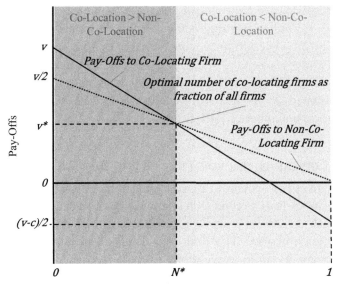

Figure 5.3 *A evolutionary equilibrium of the optimal number of latency-reducing firms. (Bowles, 2004, p. 80.)*

opportunities in this situation at value (v). However, if markets are such that the colocating firm interacts only with other colocating firms, the firm will not be able to benefit from latency advantages. In this situation, it will render zero profits from colocation while having to pay for colocation services, i.e., its payoffs are $\frac{(v-c)}{2}$. Vice versa, a firm that is not colocating (dove) may either trade only with other noncolocating firms earning profits of $v/2$, or with other colocating firms earning zero profits. Figure 5.3 represents a graphic summary of the extreme values of the benefits that accrue to colocating and noncolocating firms under given circumstances. It also represents a graphical solution to the problem of determining an evolutionary equilibrium of the optimal frequency of colocating firms.[3] Firms will colocate as long as it is profitable to do so, i.e., as long as the benefits of colocation outweigh the costs of trading with other colocated firms. In terms of the graphic solution represented in Figure 5.3, the optimal number of colocating firms as a fraction of the total number of firms depends on the expected costs of the profits that accrue to "hawks" and "doves," if no other firm is colocating (the zero value of the X-axis), and if all other firms are colocating (at the end of X-axis where X = 1).

The rationale underlying the Hawk–Dove framework as depiction of firms' choices on latency reduction is backed by the fact that profits in the HFT industry have been declining over the last few years. The year, 2009 was "considered a peak year for industry

---

[3] For a formal presentation of the Hawk–Dove Game please refer to Bowles (2004, pp. 78–81).

profits" that are estimated to have ranged "from $7.2 billion to $25 billion" (Laughlin et al., 2013, p. 1). According to current estimates, HFT industry revenues declined "to $1.8 billion in 2012" while "[o]ther estimates suggest 2012 profits of no more than $1.25 for the industry as a whole" (ibid.). Declining profits may partially be explained by decreasing trading volumes and partially by increases in competition (ibid.). They can also be interpreted as evidence for limitations of HFT markets, which put a limit to the optimal relative number of HFT firms.

5.6.2 Spatial Consequences; von Thünen and beyond

The relative nature of the benefits of latency reduction as discussed above and the fact that location decisions have become a relevant factor due to continuous increases in the speed at which computers process orders (also discussed above) implies that HFT firms make specific use of space. That is, firms that aim at generating profits from latency reduction will choose locations in proximity to the servers and data centers of trading venues and/or in proximity of knots in the infrastructure that connects different trading venues. Figure 5.4 schematically depicts spatial decisions by HFT firms by representing market demand for spatial server proximity as combined result of varying demand functions. As the Hawk–Dove game indicates, the relative advantages that accrue from latency-reducing investments to firms implies that HFT firms form a subset of firms in

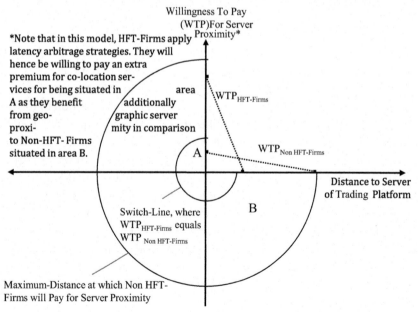

Figure 5.4 A von Thünen model of spatial decisions of latency-reducing firms. *(Fujita, Krugman and Venables, 2001, p. 6.)*

the market. Consequentially, Figure 5.4 differentiates between HFT firms that have a higher willingness to pay for server proximity and non-HFT-firms that have a lower willingness to pay for server proximity. Note that all other things being equal, overall reductions in the profitability of HFT investments (e.g., through increased competition as a consequence of further latency reduction among HFT firms) reduce the willingness to pay for server proximity from WTP_{HFT} to WTP'_{HFT} in Figure 5.4. At the same time, if relative latency advantages increase in comparison to firms that do not employ HFT technologies, firms that base their profits on latency advantages can be situated further away from the server of trading hubs and still earn profits, hence, the slope of the demand curve of HFT firms.

Figure 5.4 is an illustration of how latency-reduction fragments markets not only in terms of technology but also in terms of geography (cf. Pagnotta and Philippon, 2011). The resulting consequences for money managers will be discussed in the subsequent section.

5.7 CONCLUSION, LIMITATIONS, AND IMPLICATIONS FOR MONEY MANAGERS

The present chapter discussed the issue of spatial market fragmentation as a consequence of latency reductions through HFT that bring relative advantages to those who are situated the closest to the servers of trading hubs such as exchanges and other platforms. As colocation is a specific form of latency reduction, it promises benefits that are equal to advantages discussed in other contexts, namely the exploitation of technical arbitrage opportunities. The relativistic nature of benefits that accrue from this kind of strategy, as well as the fact that arbitrage entails zero sum outcomes, has specific implications for trading firms that have to decide of whether to invest into latency reductions or not. These consequences have been discussed on a theoretical basis within two game theoretical settings confirming existing empirical evidence on the fragmentation of markets as a consequence of arbitrage generating latency reductions. A dynamic equilibrium has been identified in which the number of firms that invest into latency reduction is limited by the fact that increases in the relative number of latency reducing firms decrease expected profits. Due to the nature of the costs and benefits of colocation that have been discussed, this situation is reflected by geographical market fragmentation that can be illustrated straight-forwardly in the form of a von-Thünen model.

The empirics of the current discussion are based on existing evidence (Budish et al., 2013) on the existence of technical arbitrage opportunities due to latency reduction. Limitations persist as other rationales for latency reduction are not part of the discussion in this chapter. Also, the discussion of strategic and spatial choices in the form of a Hawk–Dove Game and the von Thünen model remains theoretical as it does not attribute any concrete empirical values to the outcomes that are presented but interprets given data such as the reduction of profits in the HFT industry as indicator for own conclusions. However, given the data from Budish et al. (2013) as well as in light of aforedescribed observations on the diminishing profitability of HFT, the theoretical discussion allows for drawing five essential consequences for money managers in form of subsequent propositions:

PROPOSITION #1: As it is been shown above, the fact that colocation implies relative advantages that depend on the decisions of other firms as well, the optimal number of latency-reducing firms in a given market is limited. That is, investing into latency reduction is neither necessarily an optimal nor a dominant strategy.

PROPOSITION #2: Firms that do not invest into latency reductions run an increased probability of being "sniped" if they are competing with HFT firms. This implies that their orders will be executed at suboptimal quotes. If HFT firms have sufficient market power, non-HFT-firms have to incorporate the probabilities of being sniped as additional costs into their profit functions.

PROPOSITION #3: If demand for server proximity is driven by the rationale of latency reduction, there is—within the given assumptions and in light of the evidence on current technological standards discussed above—no rational for non-HFT firms to undergo costs so as to locate nearby trading hubs and their servers.

PROPOSITION #4: A potential explanation for recent decreases in the profits of latency-reducing firms is the fact that HFT has gained increasing market shares over the last years and that HFT markets are limited in size. If the point should be on the horizon, where HFT market saturation will be reached, HFT firms should adopt their strategies from exploration to competition.

PROPOSITION #5: As time intervals are continuously narrowing at which correlation breakdowns open up opportunities of technical arbitrage, profits generated through investments into HFT technologies are short term per definition (unless HFT technologies are updated cost-free by the providing firms). This implies that profits of HFT investments will have to be such that they refinance variable and fixed costs.

Given the empirical and theoretical evidence discussed in this chapter, it looks like low-latency trading will sooner rather than later become a mundane operation in financial markets. "[H]ow … [it] will evolve in the future depends on a number of factors, including those in the regulatory space not addressed here (Laughlin et al., 2013, p. 17)." Whatever the outcome will be, financial geography will be shaped rather more than less by technological advancements in the future.

REFERENCES

Ahmed, M., Chai, A., Ding, X., Jiang, Y., Sun, Y., 2009. Statistical Arbitrage in High Frequency Trading Based on Limit Order Book Dynamics. URL. http://web.stanford.edu/class/msande444/2009/2009Projects/2009-2/MSE444.pdf. retrieved on 07-30-2014.

Angel, J.J., McCabe, D., 2013. Fairness in financial markets: the case of high frequency trading. J. Bus. Ethics 112 (3), 585–595.

Bagehot, W., 1971. The only game in town. Financ. Anal. J. 7 (2), 12—14.

BBC, 2013. Financial Traders Turn to Lasers for Faster Deals. Published by BBC on BBC.com. May 2, URL. www.bbc.com/news/technology-22380611. Retrieved on 07-30-2014.

Bowles, S., 2004. Microeconomics. Behavior, Institutions, and Evolution. Russel Sage Foundation, New York (NY) et al.

Brogaard, J., Hendershott, T., Riordan, R., 2013. High Frequency Trading and Price Discovery. European Central Bank. Working Paper Series No 1602.

Budish, E., Cramton, P., Shim, J., 2013. The High-frequency Trading Arms Race: Frequent Batch Auctions as a Market Response. Fama-Miller. Working Paper; Chicago Booth Research Paper, 14(03). Available at SSRN: http://ssrn.com/abstract=2388265 or http://dx.doi.org/10.2139/ssrn.2388265.

Budish, E., Cramton, P., Shim, J., 2014. The High-frequency Trading Arms Race: Frequent Batch Auctions as a Market Response. Published on Faculty webpage of Eric Budish. Seminar Slides, URL. http://faculty.chicagobooth.edu/eric.budish/research/HFT-FrequentBatchAuctions-Slides.pdf. Retrieved on 07-30-2014.

Epps, T., 1979. Comovements in stock prices in the very short run. J. Am. Stat. Assoc. 74 (336), 291—298.

Fama, E.F., 1970. Efficient capital markets: a review of theory and empirical work. J. Finance 25 (2), 383—417.

Fujita, M., Krugman, P., Venables, A.J., 2001. The Spatial Economy. Cities, Regions, and International Trade. The MIT Press, Cambridge (MA) and London (UK).

Gould, M.D., Portera, M.A., Williams, S., McDonald, M., Fenn, D.J., Howison, S.D., 2013. Limit Order Books. Quantitative Finance 13 (11), 1709—1742.

Hachmeister, A., 2007. Informed Traders as Liquidity Providers. Evidence from the German Equity Market. Deutscher Universitätsverlag, Wiesbaden.

Hasbrouck, J., Saar, G., 2013. Low-latency trading. Journal of Financial Markets 16, 646—679.

Hauert, C., Doebeli, M., 2004. Spatial structure often inhibits the evolution of cooperation in the snowdrift game. Letters to nature. Nature 428, 643—646.

Huth, N., Abergel, F., 2011. High frequency correlation modelling. In: Abergel, F., Chakrabarti, B.K., Chakraborti, A., Mitra, M. (Eds.), Econophysics of Order-driven Markets. Springer Verlag Italia, Milan, pp. 189—202.

Kindleberger, C.P., 1974. The Formation of Financial Centers: A Study in Comparative Economic History. Princeton University, Princeton (NJ).

Large, J., 2007. Accounting for the Epps Effect. Realized Covariation, Cointegration and Common Factors. Published as draft version on web.stanford.edu/group/SITE/.../Large_Epps8.pdf. Working Paper, URL. http://web.stanford.edu/group/SITE/archive/SITE_2007/segment_3/Large_Epps8.pdf. Retrieved on 07-30-2014.

Laughlin, G., Aguirre, A., Grundfest, J., 2013. Information Transmission between Financial Markets in Chicago and New York. Available at SSRN: http://ssrn.com/abstract=2227519 or http://dx.doi.org/10.2139/ssrn.2227519. Stanford Law and Economics Olin Working Paper No. 442, Rock Center for Corporate Governance at Stanford University. Working Paper No. 137.

Lewis, M., 2014. Flash Boys. A Wall Street Revolt. Norton & Company, New York, NY.

McGee, R.W., 1990. Thomas Aquinas. A Pioneer in the Field of Law and Economics. Western State University Law Review 18 (1), 471—483 retrieved from. http://ssrn.com/abstract=713924 on 07-30-2014.

Miao, G.J., 2014. High frequency and dynamic Pairs trading based on statistical arbitrage using a two-stage correlation and cointegration approach. Int. J. Econ. Financ. 6 (3), 96—110.

Miller, R., 2014. The Data Centers Powering High Frequency Trading. Published on Datacenterknowledge.com. © by iNET Interactive. URL. http://www.datacenterknowledge.com/archives/2014/03/31/data-centers-powering-hft-trend/. Retrieved on 07-30-2014.

von Müller, C., 2012. Regulating high frequency trading: a micro-level analysis of spatial behavior, optimal choices, and pareto-efficiency in high speed markets. University of St. Gallen Law & Economics Working Paper No. 2012-04. Available at SSRN: http://ssrn.com/abstract=2000119 or http://dx.doi.org/10.2139/ssrn.2000119 on 07-30-2014.

Pagnotta, E., Philippon, T., 2011. Competing on Speed. NBER Working Paper 17652, URL. http://www.nber.org/papers/w17652. Retrieved on 07-30-2014.

Preda, A., 2009. Framing Finance. The Boundaries of Markets and Modern Capitalism. The University of Chicago Press, Chicago (IL) and London (UK).

Ross, A., 2014. Flash Boys by Michael Lewis. Review. Guardian News and Media Limited, The Guardian, May 16, URL. http://www.theguardian.com/books/2014/may/16/flash-boys-michael-lewis-review. Retrieved on 07-30-2014.

Schelling, T., 1973. Hockey helmets, concealed weapons, and daylight saving: a study of binary choices with externalities. The Journal of Conflict Resolution 17 (3), 381−428.

Shorter, G., Miller, R.S., 2014. High-frequency trading: background, concerns, and regulatory developments. In: CRS Report Prepared for Members and Committees of Congress. Congressional Research Service, pp. 7−5700.

The Wall Street Journal, February 11, 2014. High-speed Stock Traders Turn to Laser Beams. Published on webpages of wsj.com, © Dow Jones & Company Inc.. URL. http://online.wsj.com. Retrieved on 07-30-2014.

Tóth, B., Kertész, J., 2006. Increasing market efficiency: evolution of cross-correlations of stock returns. Phys. A 360, 505−515.

Wah, E., Wellman, M.P., 2013. Latency arbitrage, market fragmentation, and efficiency: a two-market model. In: Proceedings of the 14th ACM Conference on Electronic Commerce, June 2013, pp. 855−872. Conference Proceedings published by the ACM.

Wissner-Gross, A.D., Freer, C.E., 2010. Relativistic statistical arbitrage. Phys. Rev. E 82, 056104-1−0561941-7.

CHAPTER 6

Describing and Regulating High-Frequency Trading: A European Perspective

Giuseppe Ciallella
Law and Economics, LUISS Guido Carli, Rome, Italy

Contents

6.1 INTRODUCTION

This chapter aims at providing an overview on the regulatory conception of high-frequency trading (HFT), describing its evolution, its early definitions, and eventually its regulation at the European level. It proceeds as follows. Sections 6.2–6.4 analyze HFT drivers and strategies. The main differences between HFT and Algorithmic Trading (AT) are also considered, in order to define characteristics of each of them. Section 6.5 summarizes these characteristics and provides a summary table. Sections 6.6 and 6.7 explore two much-discussed aspects of HFT—its role with respect to liquidity and flash crashes. Finally, Section 6.8 describes the HFT regulatory framework recently passed at the European level in the context of the MiFID II review.

6.2 HFT DESCRIPTION AND DRIVERS

HFT is a heterogeneous concept. It includes a multifaceted group of self-sufficient trading techniques, which nevertheless share some structural characteristics. It is an evolving concept, because it concerns some technological advances, which struggle to stabilize. It might be argued that HFT's intrinsic nature constantly requires technological progress to be achieved. HFT is also a fragmented bottom-up phenomenon. This means that it primarily takes place at the micro level and subsequently it informs the market-place, although to some extent it is recognized to be an example of unintended regula-tory consequences—to that extent, it may be better described as a top-down induced phenomenon. For these reasons and because it is a recent development, (at least in a legal timescale) HFT is naturally elusive and difficult to define.[1]

Although it could be a somewhat arbitrary exercise to identify a closed set of causes with respect to a social phenomenon, from a broad perspective HFT may be traced back to two main drivers: technological developments and competition. Competition has a twofold meaning with respect to HFT, since it refers to both regulatory changes, which have reshaped trading market infrastructure turning it into a competitive environment and also to the nature of the HFT industry, which is inherently competitive.

With respect to regulatory changes, competition refers to the rules implemented dur-ing the last two decades primarily in the United States and then in the EU to enhance competitive pressure on the incumbent stock exchanges with the purpose of bringing efficiency on trading markets. At present, it is certain that this top-down imposed exercise has contributed to generate a wide process of demutualization of the incumbent exchanges, together with an increasing number of alternative trading venues, all of them in competition with each other.[2]

It is less certain that it has also generated efficiency. To some extent, HFT embodies the efficiency of this highly fragmented, highly competitive marketplace because it en-sures, inter alia, synchronization of prices on the different venues trading the same finan-cial instruments (statistical arbitrage). Further, HFT is currently among the major sources of revenues for exchanges, which fiercely contend each other in this profitable industry.[3]

---

[1] Among the growing literature about HFT, only some works describe it from a general point of view. For a regulatory perspective see e.g., Lattemann et al. (2012), Clark (2011), Goldsmith (2012), Yoon (2010), and McGowan (2010). For an economic perspective see e.g., Gomber et al. (2011), Brogaard (November 2010), Hasbrouck and Saar (September 2011), Biais and Woolley (March 2011), Jovanovic and Menkveld (October 2011), and Foresight Government Office for Science (2011) . Other accounts are Arnuk and Salluzzi (2012), and Aldridge (2011) who primarily provide a technical analysis on the functioning of the algorithms, Lehalle and Burgot (April 2010).

[2] For the EU regulatory changes that have caused HFT to emerge see, e.g., Ferrarini and Moloney (2012) who examine more in general the overall effect of MiFID I also in relation with OTC and dark trading, and the proposed MiFID II. For a comprehensive analysis of MiFID I see, e.g., Moloney (2008), pp. 337–378, 761–913, Ferrarini and Wymeersch (eds), *Investor Protection in Europe: Corporate Law Making, The MiFID and Beyond* (OUP 2006). For the US see, e.g., Coldby and Sirri (2010), more in general see Loss et al. (2004). The demutualization process in the United States is considered by Karamel (2002), for the EU see, e.g., Ferran (2004), pp. 236–266. For a seminal work about exchange regulation see Lee (2000). The economic causes behind the fragmentation of today's equity markets are considered by Fioravanti and Gentile (July 2011).

[3] See Finance Watch (April 2012), pp. 27–38, where is affirmed that "exchanges and alternative trading platforms have developed a dedicated range of special services for HFT firms. These lucrative services represent a substantial share of their revenue." For the size of the HFT industry see, e.g., Arnuk and Salluzzi (2012), p. 19, who report that HFT firms generate between $8 billion and $21 billion a year in profits. IBIS World estimates that HFT industry revenue has increased at an average annual rate of 11.6% to about $28.1 billion, including a 6.2% increase in 2012 http://www.ibisworld.com/industry/high frequency-trading.html accessed on the 10th of August 2012.

Technology and competition are mutually reinforcing drivers. Alternative Trading Systems (ATS) were among the impulses that led to the adoption of regulatory changes both in the United States and in the EU.[4] Regulation ATS for the United States and MiFID for the EU can be considered those regulatory measures that caused a technological race among market participants and trading venues, and then the HFT industry to sharply escalate.

It is then important to investigate to what extent HFT industry is compatible with interests of other market participants, in particular to understand some of the economic effects caused by HFT on listed companies, because HFT is widespread in the equity market.[5]

The event that brought HFT into the spotlight was the Flash Crash on the 6th of May 2010 (Section 6.7 below). From then on, regulators have started to investigate this phenomenon focusing on microstructural dynamics.[6] At present, however, little attention has been paid to the consequences that HFT might have for securities regulation and listed companies on a border perspective.

6.3 HIGH FREQUENCY TRADING VERSUS ALGORITHMIC TRADING

HFT is generally considered a subset of the more comprehensive genus AT, because both employ computers implementing algorithms during the trading process. However, there are some features that dramatically differentiate them from each other. These are both structural and operational, since AT and HFT employ different infrastructures, and take and implement trading decisions in a different fashion, ultimately because of their diverse objectives.[7]

AT can be broadly defined as the execution of human trading decisions by the means of algorithms, whereas HFT represents a "real-time computer-generated decision-making

---

[4] The regulatory impetus of the EU has also been characterized by some peculiarities consisting in the FSAP's ambitions in terms of harmonization and promotion of market finance, see Moloney (2010), pp. 16–50.

[5] Gomber et al. (2011), pp. 72–73, Appendix I, summarize data regarding HFT market sizing from industry data, academic studies and from the responses to the CESR Call for Evidence on Micro-structural Issues of the European Equity Markets. From their findings, it is possible to infer that HFT activity in Europe is between 30% and 50% of the equity market (considering either number of transactions or value traded). In the United States, HFT activity is widely recognized to be above 70% of the market. Considerable is the pace at which HFT is growing, in both Europe and the United States, see Nanex (January 2012a).

[6] See SEC (January 2010), CFTC-SEC (September 2010). In the EU see CESR (July 2010), pp. 39–43, the recent MiFID II proposed Directive, COM (2011) 656 final, rec. (44), and ESMA (24 February 2012), which is the first EU measure that considers, inter alia, organizational requirements for Regulated Markets, MTFs and investment firms with respect to orders, market access and market manipulation related to automated trading. See also AFM, "High frequency trading: the application of advanced trading technology in the European marketplace" Report (November 2010), FSA, *The FSA's markets regulatory* agenda (May 2010) 19–25, BIS (September 2011).

[7] Trading decision, in the context of this work, encompasses buy and sell intentions (orders), transactions (orders executions), holding periods, and the exercise of rights attached to financial instrument traded.

in financial trading, without human interference and based on automated order generation and order management."[8]

At the European level, one of the first "official" definition of HFT has been provided by the European Securities Markets Authority, whose Stakeholder Group has pointed out that "(HFT) usually involves trading in a very short time span with small price differences, with a predominant focus on highly-liquid instruments and aims at ending the day with closed positions. HFT players are usually different from the typical investor since they have no real interest in the underlying they trade in. The most significant strategic advantage for HFT players is related to their velocity. Usually, HFT involves no conventional or traditional traders but rather mathematically and/or technically oriented staff."[9]

It has also agreed on the relationship between AT and HFT, pointing out that "Automated trading, also known as AT, can be defined as the use of computer programs to enter trading orders where the computer algorithmic decides on aspects of execution of the order such as timing, quantity and price of the order. A specific type of automated or AT is known as high frequency trading […] HFT is typically not a strategy in itself but corresponds to trading activities that employ sophisticated, algorithmic technologies to interpret signals from the market and, in response, implement trading strategies that generally involve the high frequency generation of orders and a low latency transmission of these orders to the market."[10]

AT and HFT are usually referable to different market participants. AT is mainly used to execute large orders and therefore is generally linked to the activity of institutional investors. HFT usually refers to proprietary trading units of investment firms, quantitative hedge funds, and proprietary trading firms.[11]

Even though both AT and HFT use direct market access,[12] they employ different infrastructures because speed really matters only for high-frequency traders. Indeed, the latter usually colocate their computers into trading venues in order to minimize the distance between them and the data source, thereby being able to start the data elaboration process as soon as possible. Further they process data, which is not only received faster than publicly available data, it is also different. Trading venues often provide private data feeds to

---

[8] Lattemann et al. (2012), p. 93.
[9] ESMA, Securities Markets and Stakeholder Group Position Paper, ESMA/2011/SMSG/12 (October 2011).
[10] Ibid.
[11] For an extensive description of the different players involved in AT and HFT see, e.g., Arnuk and Salluzzi (2012) passim.
[12] At the European level Direct Market Access ("DMA") and Sponsored Access ("SA") have been both recently defined, see ESMA (24 February 2012), p. 4−5, which clarifies that DMA is "An arrangement through which an investment firm that is a member/participant or user of a trading platform permits specified clients (including eligible counterparties) to transmit orders electronically to the investment firm's internal electronic trading systems for automatic on-ward transmission under the investment firm's trading ID to a specified trading platform" whereas SA is the same type of arrangement, without the orders being routed through the investment firm's internal electronic trading systems, see also Gomber et al. (2011), p. 9.

high-frequency traders, which in addition to trades and quotes contain information about order modifications, order cancellations, order identification numbers, and other administrative messages. This is obviously very controversial since the access to this information does not require any investment in technology or market research.[13] Also HFT employs the most advanced high-speed computers to process data as quickly as possible. For these reasons, orders generated and transmitted by HFT are usually called *low-latency orders*.

To illustrate the importance of low latency in the high-frequency world, it might be worth reminding the reader of the recent discovery of "Project Express," the first new transatlantic cable in nearly 10 years. It has caused sensation that the length of the cable will be around 10% shorter than its predecessor, enabling data to make the journey in less than 60 ms, a saving of 5 ms on the current one-way trip. The cable is dedicated to the HFT industry and will not be available to traditional investors.[14] Even though this fact may be surprising, in the high-frequency world it is ancient history. Already on the way is a project to microwave trading orders to avoid physical obstacles and further increase speed.[15] Next step is to locate trading machines in well-defined points between two trading venues, thereby becoming the first able to discover correlations used in statistical arbitrage strategies. For instance, this implies that computers could be located in the middle of the Atlantic Ocean in order to instantly recognize correlations between the trading venues based in the United States and those based in the UK.[16]

Differently from HFT, AT does not imply low-latency reception and the ultrafast processing of data (which means taking high-speed trading decisions) and low-latency transmission of orders (which leads to low-latency execution of trading decisions). AT is used to implement trading strategies characterized by holding periods of days, weeks, months, or more. AT usually aims at minimizing the market impact of large orders (parent orders), slicing them into several smaller orders (child orders) and spreading the latter out across time or venues, according to a preset benchmark, which can vary according to the strategy chosen to execute the order. In particular, AT execution strategies may look for dark liquidity or for a particular price, may be neutral and slowly execute the order, or may be aggressive and seek to execute it as quickly as possible.[17] However, even when AT decisions are aggressively executed, low-latency does not matter as it

---

[13] Arnuk and Salluzzi (2012), pp. 101–103, 111–124.

[14] Finance Watch (2012), p. 29.

[15] Financial Times http://video.ft.com/ft-trading-room.

[16] See Weiner-Gross and Freer (2010) and the related talk given by one of the author's available at http://vimeo.com/44494574.

[17] For a description of AT types, strategies and algorithms see Arnuk and Salluzzi (2012), pp. 143–145, where are mentioned algorithms calibrated for Volume Weighted Average Price, Time Weighted Average Price, Percentage of Volume (POV), Close-Targeting, Arrival-Targeting, Dark Liquidity and anti-HFT. Gomber et al. (2011), pp. 21–24, distinguish among three generations of execution algorithms plus the fourth generation of newsreader execution algorithms. For a detailed explanation of the parameters used by algorithmic traders, see Gsell (2006).

matters for HFT because the characteristics of AT (i.e., reasonable time horizons, large positions) inform trading strategies, trading decisions and execution strategies. For instance, if the time horizon of a trading strategy executed using AT is more than one month, the execution time does not necessarily need to be in the range of micro seconds. On the contrary, high-frequency traders, because of their strategies, take trading decisions characterized by extremely short time horizons. High-frequency traders need to be instantly aware of any data that could be relevant in their time horizon, need to process data as fast as possible and then generate low-latency orders, which furthermore need to continue high-speed calibration during execution.[18]

6.4 STRATEGIES OF HFT

HFT can be described such an automated trading decision making process, characterized by highly-frequent orders and low-latency. This section deals with the description of trading strategies usually adopted by high-frequency traders that are the reasons that cause them to take a particular trading decision.

ESMA Securities Market and Stakeholders Group observed that "Trading strategies of HFT can be both non-directional (quasi market-making and arbitrage) and directional (mean-reverting, trend-following). They usually involve the execution of trades on own account (rather than for a client) and positions usually being closed out at the end of the day."[19] In this respect, it is important to note that market participants leveraging HFT belong to different institutions with different business models; therefore, there are many hybrid trading strategies with different features. However, HFT often relates to well-known traditional trading strategies that are implemented by the means of the most advanced technology, thus it is still possible to give a short description of probably the most prominent types of HFT strategies, together with some other debated practices.[20]

Electronic liquidity provision strategies encompass spread capturing and rebate-driven strategies. The former is a quasimarket making activity and allow HFT to earn the spread between bid and ask limits, while the latter is based on fee structures adopted by trading venues to incentivize liquidity providers by granting rebates or reduced transactions fees.[21]

High-frequency traders implementing statistical arbitrage strategies (i.e., market neutral, cross asset, cross market and exchange traded fund arbitrage) operate in the same way as their traditional counterparties but they leverage state-of-the-art technology to profit from small and short-lived discrepancies.

---

[18] AT is also analyzed in Hendershott and Jordan (2013).
[19] ESMA (24 February 2012), p. 2.
[20] The following is based on Gomber et al. (2011), pp. 24–31.
[21] For the relation between HFT market making and fragmentation, see Menkveld (August 2011). For HFT market making activity in general see, e.g., Jovanovic and Menkveld (October 2011) passim.

Liquidity detection includes HFT strategies that try to discern patterns of other market participants and accordingly adjust their actions. The focus in this case is on the detection of large orders usually implemented by AT.[22]

ESMA has clarified that some HFT practices are potential cases of market manipulation and that European trading platforms should adopt specific organizational requirements to identify them. The practices under accusation are:

- Ping Orders—entering small orders in order to ascertain the level of hidden orders and particularly used to assess what is resting on a dark platform.
- Quote Stuffing—entering large numbers of orders and/or cancellations/updates to orders so as to create uncertainty for other participants, slowing down their process and to camouflage their own strategy.[23]
- Momentum Ignition—entry of orders or a series of orders intended to start or exacerbate a trend, and to encourage other participants to accelerate or extend the trend in order to create an opportunity to unwind/open a position at a favorable price.
- Layering and Spoofing—submitting multiple orders often away from the touch on one side of the order book with the intention of executing a trade on the other side of the order book. Once that trade has taken place, the manipulative orders will be removed.

Some other practices have been criticized in the United States for their potential effect on the National Best Bid and Offer (NBBO) rule. For instance, latency arbitrage strategies, which are techniques exclusively based on the privileged position of colocated market participants, are currently under the spotlight because latency arbitrageurs are said to be able to profit from their speed.[24] Another example is the practice of flashing orders, which seems to be potentially harmful for the fairness of the marketplace in general, other than in contrast with the NBBO. When this practice is in place, a market order that cannot be executed against available liquidity at the marketplace where it is issued, it is flashed within this market instead of directly being routed away to the NBBO. Since these flashes last only fractions of a second, only HFT firms are able to intercept them.[25]

It also has to be noted that it should not be accepted the oft-repeated assertion that HFT strategies, to the extent that embody established trading strategies, can be assessed independently form the way in which they are implemented that is through ultramodern

---

[22] Hirschey, "Do High Frequency Traders Anticipate Buying and Selling Pressure?" Job Market Paper (20 December 2011) <https://www2.bc.edu/~taillard/Seminar_spring_2012_files/Hirschey.pdf>, 25, finds that HFT forecasts price changes caused by buying and selling pressure from traditional asset managers and causes information to become incorporated into prices more quickly, but also notes that in doing so it captures some of the informed traders' profits and consequently decreases their incentive to become informed. HFT anticipates and trades ahead of liquidity, it increases price impacts and consequently traditional asset managers' transaction costs. For the US see also note 24 below.

[23] Eggington et al. (March 2012), find that this practice impacts 74% of a sample of US listed equities and those stocks experienced decreased liquidity, higher trading costs, and increased short-term volatility.

[24] McInish and Upson (November 2011) estimate that latency differences allow fast traders to earn more than $281 million per year at the expense of slow traders.

[25] Sandler (2011).

computers. Indeed, the logic behind this assertion does not hold. An oversimplification may be helpful to explain this criticism. It is well known that many phenomena change when they are observed at different frequency. For instance, consider that radio waves, microwaves, X-rays, and gamma radiation are manifestation of the same physic phenomenon that is electromagnetic radiation. However, as the frequency increases, the energy of the radiation increases. Would anyone argue that microwaves and X-rays should be equally regulated?

6.5 CHARACTERISTICS OF AT AND HFT

The description drawn so far about the structural and operational differences between HFT and AT enables one to infer the characteristics of both these phenomena, together with their common features. Table 6.1 below summarizes such characteristics.

6.6 ABOUT THE CONCEPT OF LIQUIDITY

Liquidity is a twofold concept. When it represents the relationship of financial assets to cash is considered as an adjective of another substance. However, sometimes it also represents a quantity because it is measured in its aggregate form; thus, in this respect, liquidity is considered a noun.[26]

For a market to be liquid it is essential, among other things, to be composed by a wide range of market participants characterized by heterogeneous objectives and methods. On the contrary, a market in which there is widespread homogenization (similar time horizons, similar access to information, similar market valuations and similar infrastructures) is likely to be illiquid because buyers are not broadly balanced by sellers, especially in times of stress. Thus, the liquidity of a market rests not so much on its size (market capitalization and turnover) as in the diversity of its participants. Liquidity is often mistaken with trade volume, even though the latter is approximately the product of liquidity multiplied by velocity. More specifically, liquidity is the result of the balance between *systemic liquidity* provided by risk absorbers under times of market stress and *search liquidity* provided by risk traders during normal times.[27]

The absence of heterogeneity during normal times risks to increase strategic behavior and generate a market awash with liquidity, because during these periods risk traders are desperately looking for assets that may become the focus of speculation, in the sense that

---

[26] Eatwell and Milgate (2011), p. 21.
[27] Ibid., 21−22, 25, 29−30, 41−47.

Table 6.1 Characteristics between structural and operational differences between high-frequency trading (HFT) and algorithmic trading (AT)

Common characteristics
1. Predesigned trading strategies
2. Automated order execution
3. Without human intervention
4. Use of direct market access
5. Used by professional trade
6. Observing real-time market data

Characteristics of HFT	**Characteristics of AT**
1. Automated trading decisions	1. Agent trading
2. Proprietary trading	2. Minimize impact for large orders
3. Very high number of orders	3. Holding periods days/week/months
4. Rapid order cancellation	4. Goal is to achieve a benchmark
5. Very short holding periods	5. Working an order through time
6. Extracting low margins per trade	6. Working an order across markets
7. Profit from quasi market making	
8. Flat position at the end of the day	
9. Focus on high liquid instruments	
10. Low-latency requirement	
11. Use of colocation services	
12. Use of individual data feeds	

they can be purchased as financial placements instead of their intrinsic value.[28] The combination of this tendency and the continuing expansion of market participants purchasing power (often provided by financial innovation) are widely considered the classic elements of instability.[29]

6.7 HFT AND FLASH CRASHES

The dynamics described in relation to the concept of liquidity were originally analyzed observing events whose speed was determined by the interaction between human market participants. However, the same dynamics are useful to analyze the current equity market, whose "rhythm" is mainly the consequence of the interaction between high-speed traders. More specifically, the concept of liquidity as described above could be a valid key to understand unprecedented events like the "Flash Crash," which happened on the US

---

[28] Turner (February 2011), pp. 23–24 demonstrates how the overall level of financial activities is not positively correlated with financial stability, equality and social value; id., Turner (2009), pp. 39–51. See also O'Hara (May 2004), pp. 2–3, for the observation that liquidity can enhance collective action problems in listed companies.

[29] Kindleberger and Aliber (2011) passim.

exchanges on the 6th of May 2010. In that occasion, the Dow Jones experienced its largest ever intraday fall and some of the world's biggest company's shares appeared to be in a race to zero.[30]

High-frequency share traders provide *search liquidity*. Haldane, commenting on the Flash Crash, noticed that "HFT liquidity, evident in sharply lower peacetime bid-ask spreads, may be illusory. In wartime, it disappears. [...] HFT proved fickle under stress, as flood turned to drought."[31] The equity market also needs low-frequency share traders, which are able to provide *systemic liquidity*, because high-frequency share traders are not designed to face extreme events. High-frequency share traders have similar time horizons, similar access to information, perform similar market valuations, and use similar infrastructures. Therefore, a market populated to a considerable extent by this type of trader is likely to be homogeneous and illiquid (see Section 6.6 above). Further, the concentration of liquidity providers, as in markets dominated by high-frequency traders, could itself decrease the value of liquidity.[32] Even the measurement of liquidity in normal times can be problematic in markets with strong HFT activity.[33]

The Flash Crash is not an isolated fracture. Other crashes are increasingly linked to the HFT activity. Single flash crashes have been observed in many stocks.[34] Recently, NYSE experienced another relevant computer-driven crash and had to review the trading activities of 148 stocks and canceled transactions in six of them.[35]

Instability is represented also by thousands of mini-flash crashes that have been observed in the equity market during the last few years in correlation with the rise of

---

[30] Haldane (2011). On the flash crash see also CFTC-SEC (see note 6 above), which having identified the cause of the Flash Crash in a combined selling pressure ("hot-potato effect") from a mutual fund sell algorithm, HFTs and other traders, have accordingly advised the SEC to implement circuit breakers for the largest and most liquid stocks. For a different interpretation on the events that triggered the Flash Crash see Nanex (October 2010), which assign a central role to HFT. Nanex has also published empirical evidence to prove that the circuit breakers implemented by the SEC would not have avoided the Flash Crash, see Nanex (February 2011b). Other accounts of the Flash Crash are Kirilenko et al. (May 26, 2011); Easley et al. (2011). For a law perspective see, e.g., Angstadt (2011), Rose (2011).

[31] Haldane (2011), pp. 8–9.

[32] Sornette and Von der Becke (August 2011) at 8, where is reported that the HFT make up 2% of approximately 20,000 trading firms in the United States and account for about 60–70% of trading volume.

[33] Kim and Murphy (July 2011).

[34] Sornette and Van der Becke (August 2011), pp. 12–14, report single flash crashes of Progress Energy, Apple (then followed by other tech stocks) and also other crashes in the commodity market and currency market. Arnuk and Salluzzi (2012), p. 189, report "a particular ironic example" of the flash crashes happened when BATS Global Market attempted to go public on its own exchange.

[35] This event, happened on the 1st of August 2012, has been traced back to the activity of Knight Capital, an electronic market maker whose shares plunged in heavy volume in New York after the problem was revealed. Apparently Knight released their test software (which they use to monitor their market making activity) into NYSE's live system, see Nanex (August 2012b).

HFT activity.[36] In this regard, it has been shown how the self-similarity, which characterizes the ever smaller transactions in today's equity market is among the causes of increased volatility on short times. This microviolent excursion compounds market makers' difficult position and, if not prompted contained in reasonable intervals, obliges them to widen the bid—ask spread up to a level at which leaving the market becomes the only possible option.[37]

On October 2, 2012, Nanex detected a single algorithm implementing a new form of quote stuffing to which was referable to more than 4% of the US stock quotes.[38]

It is important to understand whether or not the current marketplace is able to guarantee the heterogeneity that is essential to enhance market stability and investor confidence, thereby encouraging the flows of capital to move toward issuers. On the contrary, trading volume (*search liquidity*) generated by high-frequency share traders is not enough. HFT alone may increase instability in the equity market and potentially evolve in a source of systemic risk.

6.8 MiFID II AND HFT REGULATION IN THE EU

At the European level, the recently passed Directive 2014/65/EU on markets in financial instruments (the so-called "MiFID II") has laid down a harmonized framework for HFT, which will apply to every European member state. Even if this piece of legislation will need extensive implementation at both the European and the national level, it is already possible to draw some preliminary observations in relation to the HFT regulatory framework.[39]

---

[36] Nanex (February 2011a). See also Johnson et al. (February 2012) that looking at many stocks on multiple exchanges in the period 2006—2011 find that there were about 18,500 fractures or Black Swan events in which markets crash for micro-periods (less than 1.5 s). Further, they study the distribution of these events by size and consider if this distribution changes when looking at events taking place on different timescales. The data suggests that for times shorter than 0.8 s, where human interaction is not possible, the distribution begins to depart from the power law, and approaches a new, unknown distribution. The concept of Black Swan has been developed by Taleb (2010) passim. See also Golub and Keane (2011).

[37] Smith (2010). Filimonov and Sornette (2012), looking at two specific events, on 27 April and 6 May 2010, where markets moved suddenly and in a dramatic way (the first caused by S&P downgrading Greece's debt rating, the second is, of course, the Flash Crash) find that while the first event of 27 April showed absolutely no change in the fraction of market activity due to internal dynamics, given the apparently clear origin of this event in external information, the 6 May Flash Crash shows a sudden spike in the internal dynamics and reflect the rise of computer trading, as computers interact with one another in lots of complex feedback loops. The authors envision their technique as a device for measuring the amount of "reflexivity" in the market, referring to the term used by George Soros to describe how (human) perceptions and misperceptions interact in the market to drive changes. In the author's opinion financial markets are "always wrong" and this influences the real value of fundamentals, Soros, "Reflexivity in Financial Markets" *The new paradigm for financial markets* (Public Affairs 2008) 65—99.

[38] Nanex (October 2012).

[39] See Directive 2014/65/EU of the European Parliament and of the Council of 15 May 2014, on markets in financial instruments.

It is worth noting how the European legislator has highlighted the different features of AT and HFT. In particular, "AT" has been defined as "trading in financial instruments where a computer algorithm automatically determines individual parameters of orders such as whether to initiate the order, the timing, price or quantity of the order or how to manage the order after its submission, with limited or no human intervention, and does not include any system that is only used for the purpose of routing orders to one or more trading venues or for the processing of orders involving no determination of any trading parameters or for the confirmation of orders or the post-trade processing of executed transactions." The definition of HFT given by the European legislator accepts the view that HFT is a subset of AT and at the same time points out that HFT "means an AT technique characterized by: (1) infrastructure intended to minimize network and other types of latencies, including at least one of the following facilities for algorithmic order entry: colocation, proximity hosting or high-speed direct electronic access; (2) system-determination of order initiation, generation, routing, or execution without human intervention for individual trades or orders; and (3) high message intraday rates, which constitute orders, quotes, or cancellations."[40]

The European legislator has also recognized some of the risks potentially associated with AT and HFT and has decided to intervene in respect of several contentious issues. First, in the EU any person engaging in HFT will fall within the scope of MiFID II, even if dealing on own account.[41]

Second, from an organizational perspective, investment firms that engage in AT must have in place effective controls to ensure trading systems' resiliency. Such firms need to implement appropriate trading thresholds and limits to prevent the sending of erroneous orders that may cause a disorderly market or market abuse. Investment firms involved in AT have also to implement continuity arrangements to deal with any failure of their trading systems. Finally, firms have to notify competent authorities if they engage in AT and following this notification competent authorities may require firms to provide, on a regular or *ad-hoc* basis, a description of the nature of their AT strategies, details of the trading parameters or limits to which systems are subject, and other relevant information. A specific provision has been established for HFT firms, since the latter have to store accurate and time-sequenced records of all placed orders, including cancellations, executed orders and quotations on trading venues, and have to make them available to competent authorities upon request.[42]

---

[40] Article 4 (1), No. 39–40, Directive 2014/65/EU.
[41] See Article 2 (1), letters (d) and (j), Directive 2014/65/EU.
[42] See Article 17 (1–3), Directive 2014/65/EU.

Third, investment firms that engage in AT to pursue a market making strategy must carry this activity continuously—except under exceptional circumstances—with the result of providing liquidity on a regular and predictable basis to trading venues and also have to enter into a binding written agreement with them.[43]

Fourth and last, European Regulated Markets have to put in place effective systems and procedures to carry out testing of algorithms and to limit the ratio of unexecuted orders, to be able to slow down the flow of orders if there is a risk of the system capacity being reached. With respect to fee structures, Regulated Markets have also to limit the minimum tick size that may be executed and have to ensure that their fee structures, including execution fees, ancillary fees, and any rebates that are transparent, fair, and nondiscriminatory and that they do not create incentives to place, modify, or cancel orders or to execute transactions in a way which contributes to disorderly trading conditions or market abuse. In particular, Regulated Markets have to impose market-making obligations in individual shares in exchange for any rebate that is granted, adjust fees for canceled orders according to the length of time for which the order was maintained and have to calibrate the fees to each financial instrument to which they apply. Depending on national implementing measures, regulated markets may also have to impose a higher fee for placing an order that is subsequently canceled, to impose a higher fee on participants placing a high ratio of canceled orders and on those operating a high-frequency AT technique, in order to reflect the additional burden on system capacity. Regulated Markets need also to be able to identify, by means of flagging from members or participants, orders generated by AT, the different algorithms used for the creation of orders and the relevant persons initiating those orders and make that information available to competent authorities.[44]

---

[43] See Article 17 (4), Directive 2014/65/EU. The concept of "liquid market" has also been defined as "a market for a financial instrument or a class of financial instruments, where there are ready and willing buyers and sellers on a continuous basis, assessed in accordance with the following criteria, taking into consideration the specific market structures of the particular financial instrument or of the particular class of financial instruments: (1) the average frequency and size of transactions over a range of market conditions, having regard to the nature and life cycle of products within the class of financial instrument; (2) the number and type of market participants, including the ratio of market participants to traded instruments in a particular product; and (3) the average size of spreads, where available."

[44] See Article 17 (1—3), Directive 2014/65/EU. Under MiFID II "regulated markets" are the most heavily regulated type of trading venue that falls within the scope of the directive, the other three are "systematic internalizer," "multilateral trading facility," and "organized trading facility." The latter is new with respect to MiFID I and is meant to be a residual and all-encompassing category in which almost every exchange systems falls, see Article 4(1) No. 19—23, Directive 2014/65/EU.

REFERENCES

Aldridge, I., 2011. High Frequency Trading Models: Technology, Algorithms and Implementation. John Wiley and Sons, Hoboken, NJ.

Angstadt, J.M., 2011. What will be the legacy of the 'Flash crash'? Developments in the US equities market regulation. Cap. Mark. Law J. 25 (1), 80.

Arnuk, S., Salluzzi, J., 2012. Broken Markets. FT Press, London.

Biais, B., Woolley, P., March 2011. High Frequency Trading. Working Paper. http://idei.fr/doc/conf/pwri/biais_pwri_0311.pdf.

BIS, September 2011. High-frequency Trading in the Foreign Exchange Market. Report by the Markets Committee, Basel, Switzerland.

Brogaard, J.A., November 2010. High Frequency Trading and its Impact on Market Quality. Working Paper. http://www.fsa.gov.uk.

CESR, July 2010. Technical Advice to the Commission in the Context of the MiFID Review and Responses to the European Commission Request for Additional Information. Frankfurt, Germany.

CFTC-SEC, September 2010. Findings Regarding the Market Events of May 6, 2010. Reports of the Staffs of the CFTC and SEC to the Joint Advisory Committee on Emerging Issues. Washington, D.C.

Clark, E., 2011. The legal tortoise and the high frequency hare: the Challenge for regulators. Aust. J. Corp. Law 25 (1), 274.

Coldby, R.L.D., Sirri, E.R., 2010. Consolidation and competition in the US equity markets. Cap. Mark. Law J. 5 (1), 169.

Easley, D., Lopez de Prado, M.M., O'Hara, M., 2011. The microstructure of the 'Flash crash': flow toxicity, liquidity crashes and the probability of informed trading. Portf. Manag. 37 (2), 118. http://ssrn.com/abstract=169504.

Eatwell, J., Milgate, M., 2011. The Rise and Fall of Keynesian Economics. Oxford University Press, Oxford.

Eggington, J., Van Ness, B.F., Van Ness, R.A., March 2012. Quote Stuffing. Working Paper. http://ssrn.com/abstract=1958281.

ESMA, 24 February 2012. Guidelines on Systems and Controls in an Automated Trading Environment for Trading Platforms, Investment Firms and Competent Authorities. ESMA/2012/122.

Ferran, E., 2004. Building a EU Securities Market. Cambridge University Press, Cambridge.

Ferrarini, G., Moloney, N., 2012. Reshaping order execution and the role of interest groups under MiFID II. Eur. Bus. Organ. Law Rev. 13 (2), 557–597.

Filimonov, V., Sornette, D., 2012. Quantifying reflexivity in financial markets: towards a prediction of flash crashes. Phys. Rev. 85 (2), 1.

Finance Watch, April 2012. Investing Not Betting – Making Financial Markets Serve Society. Position Paper on MiFID II/MiFIR.

Fioravanti, S.F., Gentile, M., July 2011. The Impact of Market Fragmentation on European Stock Exchanges. CONSOB, Rome, Italy. Working Papers No. 69.

Foresight Government Office for Science, 2011. The Future of Computer Trading in Financial Markets. Working Paper. www.bis.gov.uk/foresight/our-work/projects/current-projects/computer-trading.

Goldsmith, B., 2012. Regulatory challenges with respect to high-frequency-trading. JIBLR 27 (1), 19.

Golub, A., Keane, J., 2011. Mini Flash Crashes. Working Paper. https://fp7.portals.mbs.ac.uk/Portals/59/docs.

Gomber, P., Arndt, B., Lutat, M., Uhle, T., 2011. High-frequency Trading. Working Paper Commissioned by Deutsche Börse Groupe. http://ssrn.com/abstract=1858626.

Gsell, M., 2006. Is algorithmic trading distinctively different? Assessing its behaviour in comparison to informed, momentum and noise traders. In: Proceedings of the International Conference on Business & Finance 2006, Discussion-paper 15.

Haldane, G., 2011. The Race to Zero. Bank of England Speeches, London, UK. http://www.bankofengland.co.uk.

Hasbrouck, J., Saar, G., September 2011. Low-latency Trading. Johnson School Research Paper Series No. 35-2010. http://ssrn.com/abstract=1695460.

Hendershott, T., Riordan, R., 2013. Algorithmic trading and the market for liquidity. J. Financ. Quant. Anal. 48 (4), 1001–1024.

Johnson, N., Guannan, Z., Hunsader, E., Meng, J., Ravindar, A., Carran, S., Tivnan, B., February 2012. Financial Black Swan Driven by Ultra-fast Machine Ecology. Working Paper. http://arxiv.org/abs/1202.1448.

Jovanovic, B., Menkveld, A.J., October 2011. Middlemen in Limit-order Markets. Working Paper. http://ssrn.com/abstract=1624329.

Karamel, S., 2002. Turning seats into shares: causes and implications of demutualization of stock and future exchanges. Hast. Law J. 53 (3), 367.

Kim, S., Murphy, D., July 2011. The Impact of High-frequency Trading on Stock Market Liquidity Measures. Working Paper. http://www.kellogg.northwestern.edu.

Kindleberger, P., Aliber, R., 2011. Manias, Panics and Crashes: A History of Financial Crisis, sixth ed. Palgrave, New York.

Kirilenko, A., Kyle, A., Samandi, M., Tuzun, T., May 26, 2011. The Flash Crash: The Impact of High Frequency Trading on an Electronic Market. Working Paper. http://ssrn.com/abstract=1686004.

Lattemann, C., Loos, P., Gomolka, J., Burghof, H.-P., Breuer, A., Gomber, P., Krogmann, M., Nagel, J., Riess, R., Riordan, R., Zajonz, R., 2012. High frequency trading – costs and benefits in securities trading and its necessity of regulations. Bus. Inf. Syst. Eng. 4 (2), 93–105.

Lee, R., 2000. What Is an Exchange: Automation, Management, and Regulation of Financial Markets. Oxford University Press, Oxford, UK.

Lehalle, C.-A., Burgot, R., April 2010. Navigating liquidity 4. Working Paper, Cheuvreux Credit Agricole Group Research. https://www.cheuvreux.com.

Loss, L., Seligman, J., Paredes, T., 2004. Fundamentals of Securities Regulation, fifth ed. Wolters Kluwer, New York, NY.

McGowan, 2010. The rise of computerized high frequency trading: use and controversy. Duke Law Technol. Rev. 16 (2), 1–24. http://dltr.law.duke.edu.

McInish, T., Upson, J., November 2011. Strategic Liquidity Supply in a Market with Fast and Slow Traders. Working Paper. http://ssrn.com/abstract=192499.

Menkveld, A.J., August 2011. High Frequency Trading and the New-market Makers. Working Paper, AFA 2012. http://ssrn.com/abstract=1722924.

Moloney, N., 2008. EC Securities Regulation. Oxford University Press, Oxford.

Moloney, N., 2010. How to Protect Investors: Lessons from the EC and the UK. Cambridge University Press, Cambridge.

Nanex, February 2011a. Flash Equity Failures in 2006, 2007, 2008, 2009, 2010 and 2011. Working Paper. http://www.nanex.net/FlashCrashEquities/FlashCrashAnalysis_Equities.html.

Nanex, October 2010. May 6, 2010 Flash Crash. Working Paper. http://www.nanex.net/FlashCrashFinal.

Nanex, February 2011b. New SEC Limit Up/Down Proposal Would Have Made Flash Crash Worse. Working Paper. http://www.nanex.net/research/LimitUpDown/LUD.Simulated.html.

Nanex, January 2012a. The Rise of the HFT Machines. Working Paper. http://www.nanex.net/aqck/2804.HTML.

Nanex, August 2012b. New Quote Stuffing Algo. Working Paper. http://www.nanex.net/aqck2/3525.html.

O'Hara, M., 2004. Liquidity and Financial Market Stability. Working Paper, NBB No. 55.

Rose, C., 2011. The flash crash of may 2010: accident or market manipulation? J. Bus. Econ. Res. 9 (1), 85.

Sandler, A.J., 2011. The Invisible Power of the Machines: Revisiting the Proposed Flash Order Ban in the Wake of the Flash. Crash. Duke Law and Technology Review (003): 1.

SEC, January 2010. Concept Release on Equity Market Structure. Washington, D.C. No. 34–61358.

Smith, R., 2010. Is High-frequency Trading Inducing Changes in Market Microstructure and Dynamics? Working Paper. http://ssrn.com/abstract=1632077.

Sornette, D., Von der Becke, S., August 2011. Crashes and High Frequency Trading. Working Paper, Swiss Institute Research Paper No. 11–63. http://ssrn.com/abstract=1976249.

Taleb, N., 2010. The Black Swan: The Impact of the Highly Improbable, second ed. Random House, New York, NY.

Turner, A., February 2011. Reforming Finance: Are We Being Radical Enough? Working Paper, Clare Distinguished Lecture in Economics and Public Policy. http://www.fsa.gov.uk/library.

Turner, A., 2009. The Turner Review. Working Paper, Financial Services Authority Discussion Paper DP09/2. http://www.fsa.gov.uk/library/corporate/turner.

Weiner-Gross, A.D., Freer, C.E., 2010. Relativistic statistical arbitrage. Phys. Rev. 82 (5), 56–104.

Yoon, H., 2010. Trading in a Flash: implication of high-frequency trading for securities regulators worldwide. Emory Int. Law Rev. 24 (2), 913–948.

PART 2

Evolution and the Future

CHAPTER 7

High-Frequency Trading: Implications for Market Efficiency and Fairness

Tayyeb Shabbir

Department of Finance, CBAPP, California State University Dominguez Hills, Carson, CA; Department of Finance, Wharton School, University of Pennsylvania, Philadelphia, PA, USA

Contents

7.1 INTRODUCTION

High-frequency trading (HFT) is a relatively recent phenomenon which is characterized by the use of propriety trading algorithms which are executed with the help of superfast computers to make a profit on the basis of informational speed advantage measured in milliseconds; rapid entry and exit from the order stream may fetch a small fractional profit but the large volume turns that into substantial sums for the HF traders. This phenomenon speaks to the heart of the avowed objective of financial markets namely the allocation of capital to the most productive use done in a credible, transparent, and efficient manner through a process of price discovery and its signaling. To date, the HFT has usually been active in the arena of securities transactions where the HFT computer may even be located in as close a physical proximity to the securities exchange as possible to gain the crucial time advantage, however, it is also spreading to other financial markets such as currency markets.

As the use of HFT becomes more commonplace, it has spurred heated debate in the academe as well as the public policy and regulatory arenas. The growing use

The Handbook of High Frequency Trading
ISBN 978-0-12-802205-4

of HFT raises some really important questions and this chapter will address the following three: (1) provide an introduction to the nature of HFT and its progression in terms of use in execution of financial investment order flow with particular reference to the securities markets, (2) implication of HFT for market efficiency specifically in relation to the "efficient market hypothesis" but also including a discussion in the context of liquidity, price volatility, propensity for precipitating sudden and severe market crises, and finally (3) implications of HFT for "fairness" in the financial markets.

The rest of the chapter is organized as follows: Section 7.2 presents the nature of HFT and recent trends, Section 7.3 describes some salient issues related to HFT, Section 7.4 explains HFT and "fairness," and Section 7.5 consists of concluding remarks.

7.2 NATURE OF HFT AND RECENT TRENDS

HFT comprises of algorithmic-based trading with the help of superfast computers. HFT uses trading strategies carried out by computers to move in and out of positions in milliseconds or nanoseconds. This explains the motivation behind trading firms' efforts to establish the fastest connections between trading hubs like New York, Chicago, and London. One such firm has built an 825-mile-long, $300-million fiber-optic cable between Wall Street and the Chicago Mercantile Exchange. According to an estimate, HF traders spent over $2 billion on infrastructure in the year 2010. Also, HF traders try to colocate maximum possible physical proximity to the exchanges for execution time advantage.

It is estimated that as of 2009, HFT accounted for 60—73% of all US equity trading volume, with that number falling to approximately 50% in 2012. The growth in HFT is somewhat slow; however, the size of HFT is still very significant. Also, while stabilizing its growth in stock market, HFT trading is spreading to other financial markets such as currency markets.

HFT is characterized by traders moving in and out of short-term positions aiming to capture sometimes just a fraction of a cent in profit on each trade; however, volumes of trade are typically very high. HFT firms do not rely on leverage to any great extent; instead they accumulate positions or hold their portfolios over ultra-short time periods often not longer than overnight. HFT firms typically compete against other HFT firms, rather than long-term or fundamental investors.

The two primary activities that HFT firms are involved in are (1) market-making and (2) statistical arbitrage which are discussed later in this chapter along with some other features of the HFT that cause concerns about efficiency and fairness.

7.3 SOME SALIENT ISSUES RELATED TO HFT

This section will discuss a few of the important phenomena related to HFT such as its implications for market efficiency, provision of market liquidity, price volatility, propensity for precipitating crises, and its possible social cost in terms of possible "rent seeking" behavior.

7.3.1 Market Efficiency

A primary tenet of the familiar (semistrong) efficient market hypothesis due to Fama (1965) in essence maintains that no abnormal (market beating) returns are possible in the securities market since any past information and future known information will be already incorporated in the stock price and any new or surprise information will be rapidly reflected in the stock market prices. What is the evidence in terms of HFT relative to market efficiency in the above sense? Are there systematic advantages due to HFT? The evidence is mixed though it indicates certain persistent advantages in favor of the HFT. Such advantages may be due to (1) ability of HFT firms to front run the anticipated order flow ahead of the non-HFT firms and (1) early access to the relevant financial information. Let us consider these two items in turn.

1. Front running of order flow

   Hirschey (2013) reports that HFT firms are able to correctly anticipate actions of the non-HFT firms in the securities market. In fact, due to this phenomenon, the HFT firms are able to reap significant advantage in returns by quickly buying stocks that non-HFT firms intend to buy which the latter then continue to purchase, or short stocks that the non-HFT firms intend to sell which the latter then continue to sell thus conferring this return advantage to the HFT firms.

2. Early access

   HFT firms can enjoy early access by purchasing financially relevant information such as earnings' releases, Philadelphia FED economic reports, and ADP monthly reports directly from companies such as Business Wire who normally supply this information first to media companies such as Bloomberg and Yahoo who in turn make them available to the average investor. This is an obvious advantage and it was in full display during an episode when a cosmetic retailer, ULTA's price dropped suddenly on December 5, 2013 in the midst of front running of sell orders in the light of missed analyst's estimates per company earnings announcement at 150 ms after 4:00 p.m. (Patterson (2014)). This information was accessible to HFT firms within 50 ms and was not announced by media companies until another 92 ms (Bloomberg) before it could reach the general investors. Due to this early access advantage, HFT firms were able to obtain this crucial information first and act on it which resulted in about $ 800,000 worth of company stock being sold. Though procedurally not illegal, paying distributors to get direct access to information can create huge negative externalities possibly causing a complete loss of confidence in the stock market.

7.3.2 Price Discovery Process and HFT

The role of HFT in the price discovery process or equivalently its effect on the overall quality of the market functioning is a widely debated issue. On one hand, HFT can contribute to increased liquidity in the market by compressing the bid-ask spreads. Such increased liquidity in the market provides fundamentals-based investors with an opportunity to adjust their investments according to the news on companies' fundamentals. This fosters a movement of stock prices toward their respective fundamental value. On the other hand, HFT firms trade solely on the basis of short-term oriented statistics and pay no heed to the fundamentals—they are not in the market with a view to "buy and hold" rather they are there for "here and now." This focus of the HFT on (ultra) short-term returns can potentially move stock prices away from their fundamental value. Experts on both sides of the debate have thoroughly researched the topic with evidence being mixed.

While Hudson et al. (2014), Brogaard et al. (2014), and O'Hara and Ye (2011) provide evidence that HFT actually facilitates the price discovery process in the market, Zhang (2010) and Froot et al. (1992) demonstrate that on account of their relative emphasis on the short-term horizon, the HFT firms hamper the price discovery process in the market. In fact, the HFT activities may be making the markets "too efficient" (overshooting fundamental values) and may need to be restrained (Zhang (2010)).

This study shows that in the short run, HFT activity causes stock prices to move excessively in the direction of the news about fundamentals making it detrimental for the price discovery process. This is so since HFT investors and fundamental investors act independently of each other. For instance, after positive fundamental news about a stock is released, HFT firms rapidly buy the stock causing its price to rise. Subsequently, fundamental investors buy the stock too which causes the stock price to rise more than the news about the fundamentals warranted thus leading to "overshooting." Another reason for this phenomenon could be that HFT firms try to front run fundamental investors by anticipating the general direction of the subsequent trades. These firms will buy/sell stock before the fundamental investors can do so and when they (fundamental investors) eventually execute their trades it causes price to move excessively.

7.3.3 Price Volatility

Another factor closely related to the efficiency of markets is stock volatility—it pertains to the quality of the price discovery process. According to EMH, discussed above, the prices of stocks incorporate all available information. If a stock experiences large swings in prices in short time durations then it is highly probable that certain exogenous factors are causing the variation in prices. This indicates a market inefficiency such that stock prices are not just a reflection of fundamental information available to the market participants.

Besides being a reflection of market inefficiency, stock volatility is also an undesirable feature for risk-averse investors since high stock volatility increases the perceived risk attached to a firm's stock resulting in raising the firm's cost of capital.

Researchers have differing opinions about the effect of HFT on stock price volatility. A few experts believe that since the market-making activities of HFT firms actually increase the liquidity available in the market, this would enable the fundamental investors to place trades without increasing stock price volatility. On the other hand, however, since algorithms developed by fundamental investors often use trading volume as a proxy for liquidity, they place large trade orders when HFT firms place a large number of orders. This often leads to large swings in stock prices. Front running of orders by HFT may also contribute to increased volatility of securities' prices. Zhang (2010) empirically tested the hypothesis that HFT firms actually cause an increase in stock price volatility. Using regression analysis, this study found a statistically significant determinant of higher volatility of the order of 11.2%.

7.3.4 HFT, "Flash Crash," and Dark Pools

The HFT are also prone to the kinds of dramatic and apparently inexplicable price swings such as the one witnessed during the so-called "Flash Crash" of May 6, 2010 where within few moments equity worth $1 trillion dollars was completely wiped off from the market following a sudden drop in the E-mini future contracts' spread over the other stocks. Even more strangely, the market bounced back immediately after the large drop. However, the round trip was exhausting and full of systemic danger. Investigations revealed that a few large orders placed using high-powered computers caused the exchange to break down.

With their apparent penchant for speed coupled with anonymity, the HFT are also active in the arena of the so-called "dark pools" this ominous-sounding term refers to private exchanges or forums for trading securities as alternative to regular exchanges. These dark pools are not accessible by the investing public. Their general lack of transparency makes them vulnerable to possible conflicts of interest between their owners and predatory trading practices by HFT.

7.4 HFT AND "FAIRNESS"

There has been much recent concern over the fairness of HFT practices. As discussed in Angel and McCabe (2013), in order to address the issue of fairness in relation to HFT, there are three natural questions one needs to ask: (1) what constitutes HFT, (2) what are the criteria to be used to judge fairness, and (3) how fair are the HFT practices?

The HFT practices comprise of a multitude of practices which range from clearly legitimate and beneficial to the markets and society at large to certain rather dubious ones which can be relatively more easily recognized as "unfair." Among the former group are primarily such functions as market-making, arbitrage, reaction to news, and order discovery strategies of HFT while in the latter group are practices such as order front running, order triggering strategies, spoofing, wash sales, and quote stuffing. Following is a brief description of the strategies from each group.

7.4.1 What constitutes HFT?

a. Group I functions of HFT
- Market-making. Since, generally speaking, the time of arrival of buy orders and sell orders in the market is asynchronous; an investor who wants to trade immediately may not find an acceptable price. By acting as market-makers, i.e., participants willing to buy and sell immediately at the bid and ask price respectively ("spread") HFT provide a beneficial service while making a profit for them. Improved and keener competition (helped in the case of HFT by speedier computers and enhanced technology) among the market-makers reduces the spread between the bid and ask prices to a competitive level. The reduced bid–ask spreads benefit investors by reducing their cost of trading as well as increases the number of shares that an investor can trade at any given time without impacting the market price. This provision of liquidity service by HFT is a positive.
- Arbitrage. This is the age old practice of buy low and sell high to make a profit while in the process aid the market in price discovery and maintain an equilibrium or "fair" price. The HFT can be involved in two kinds of arbitrage—keep the relative prices of bundled financial instruments and its components such as an exchange-traded fund and constituent stocks or "statistical arbitrage" which involves a pair of securities which on average co-move in a strong, predictable manner.
- News reaction strategies. Market prices will normally react to the new information—prices going up with favorable news and conversely. Traditionally markets have invested substantial resources in acquiring and process such information. HFT will tend to perform this function more quickly and efficiently given the high-speed computer technology and software ("algorithms") that are at its disposal.
- Order discovery strategies. In order to benefit from the expected knowledge, traditionally investors have always tried to discern the pattern and sequencing of the relatively large institutional traders who typically and generally place large buy and sell orders. So as not to influence the market price to their determinant, the institutional traders try to break down a large order into smaller chunks and

"feed" it to the market in a stealth way if possible. HFT via various strategies try to discern this information ("sniff out?") by analyzing the order flow patterns. These constitute beneficial practices as they speed up the market's adjustment process to the new equilibrium price of securities.

b. Group II functions of HFT

— Order triggering. One common type of order triggering strategy employed by HFT is referred to as "bear raid" which involves placing a large short sale order for the purpose of pushing down price of the security. When other market participants observe this, they follow suit and place large sale orders believing that the trader who placed the initial order had some sort of fundamental information about the stock. Once the stock price drops to a certain point, the HF trader covers the short position and makes a profit generally using high-speed computers to identify areas in which this strategy will be particularly useful.

— Spoofing. In this strategy, a HFT firm may employ amounts of efforts to trick other market participants into reducing their offer prices. For example, if an investor wants to buy additional shares of a firm whose shares he/she already owns, such an investor tries to trick the seller into reducing the offer price. Suppose that the bid price is $5.50 and ask price is $5.52, our investor places a large sell order of this security at $5.51. Seeing that other sellers are offering their stock at a lower price, the original seller also drops price to $5.51. Meanwhile, the said investor cancels the sell orders and buys the stock at a favorably reduced price of $5.51.

— Wash sales. This strategy is an effort by a HFT firm to simultaneously submit buy and sell orders in a given stock in an effort to create sense of deeper market activity to increase the price of its target stock(s).

— Quote stuffing. Akin to a "denial of service" attack by a hacker on a financial payment service firm, in this strategy, a HF trader places a large number of orders and then cancels them immediately which results in slowing down the stock exchange system and hence cause delays in the orders placed by other market participants.

7.4.2 What are the criteria to be used to judge fairness?

There are myriad criteria that may be used to judge fairness. However, borrowing Angel and McCabe (2013)'s description of the seven part criteria proposed by Shefrin and Statman (1993), we will identify fairness in the financial markets in terms of the following seven dimensions.

a. Freedom from coercion. Participants are not free to participate or not participate in a transaction.

b. Freedom from misrepresentation. Fraud is not involved.

c. Equal information. All participants have access to the same information, so there is no insider trading.

d. Equal processing power. There is no disparity in the ability of participants to process information.

e. Freedom from impulse. Participants are protected from their own irrational impulses, for example, cooling-off periods that allow customers to cancel a transaction expost.

f. Efficient prices. Prices reflect all the information—past as well as anticipatory-available in the market.

g. Equal bargaining power. There is no gross disparity or asymmetry in the power relationships among the participants.

7.4.3 How fair are the HFT practices?

It is fairly obvious that the practices mentioned in Group II above such as order triggering and quote stuffing cannot be condoned by any defensible market efficiency or ethical standard. Thus it is easy to reject them as not fair. As a matter of fact, a major part of the public outcry and even professional criticism of the HFT practices refers to these practices. Thus these practices are ripe for regulatory reform.

Regarding the Group I phenomenon, the discussion needs to be more nuanced as people in academia and technical experts as well as policy-makers have differing opinions about the fairness of some aspects of the Group I HFT strategies/effects.

Invoking the Shefrin and Statman (1993) set of fairness criteria noted above, Angel and McCabe (2013) clearly exonerates HFT with respect to "freedom from coercion" (Criteria 1) and with regards to "freedom from misrepresentation" (Criteria 2) and surprisingly enough with respect to inequality of bargaining power of the colocated HFT firms. However, they are relatively more circumspect regarding the equal information and related equal processing power criteria. Angel and McCabe (2013) main defense seems to be that if you purchase colocation and better computing prowess in a free market, more power is gained by you. They use the analogy of firms hiring better talented employees relative to their competition and ask the question is that unfair? While desire to invest in better computing power may be relatively more palatable to many critics, the colocation issue is not that simple. Presumably, colocation assignments are made on the basis of "first come first serve" and all of the prime (and often idiosyncratically unique) spots will go early, the first-mover advantage imposes an externality which is not comparable to the analogy of hiring talent. The colocation advantage translates into five-millionth of an advantage in speed or order execution relative to a firm located a mile away from the physical location of the exchange. This is an eternity in the world of nanosecond executions of trades. The aspect of a negative externality that this practice poses to the system as a whole is ignored. It may be akin to supporting abandoning any campaign finance reforms and in fact promoting access to political influence and advantage at the voting booth while ignoring the overbearing negative externality such a "pay to play" scheme imposes.

Again, from the perspective of efficient prices (Criteria 6) too, the HFT is given a pass on the premise that this advantage of HFT is relevant only for the other institutional investors and HFT trades who are engaged in the same kind of arbitrage and market-making activities.

Regarding another important issue related to fairness, i.e., does HFT hurts the quality of price discovery process by leading to increased price volatility, Angel and McCabe (2013), while conceding this to be an empirical question, cite Brogaard (2010) to refute the fact supported by other more recent studies (such as Zhang (2010)) that demonstrate support for the hypothesis that HFT results in greater price volatility. Further, recent empirical evidence (some of it mentioned earlier in the chapter) illustrates that HFT activities not only increase volatility, but they may hamper the price discovery process all together. Besides, as the ULTA stock example showed that by having an early access to information, HFT firms are able to sell their position before other market participants can act and hence cause a significant loss to other market participants.

In general, it appears that Angel and McCabe (2013) take a somewhat rosier view of the performance and fairness issue of HFT; it is in part that the "bad stuff" is already placed in Group II as indefensible and these comments only apply to functions of HFT placed in Group II—so there is a bit of self-selection issue.

In any event, it is evident from more recent empirical studies that HFT may be a worthwhile innovation, however, it may not be ready for primetime without substantial reforms or modifications.

7.5 CONCLUDING REMARKS

HFT has grown in use in the last decade or so and lately it has raised a significant amount of controversy and debate both in the academic as well as policy arenas regarding the nature and impact of this practice.

HFT can contribute to relatively enhanced liquidity and price discovery under the right circumstances. It is an innovation which needs to be properly modified, reformed, and thus harnessed. It has significant cons which can be distracting such as relative opaqueness of its transactions, "too high" a speed of order execution which may contribute to stock price volatility and its propensity to precipitate sudden, sharp rather inexplicable swings in stock prices such as the "Flash Crash" of May 6, 2010. There are important questions about fairness and procedural as well as substantive nature of HFT that need to be addressed. It is pertinent to consider reforms aimed at "normalizing" the ("excessive") speed of trading (perhaps via a Tobin Tax type of transaction tax to slow down the excessive speed and the resulting prospective volatility), need for access of information for regulatory monitoring (via something like SEC's Consolidated Audit Trail ("CAT") which will oversee the activities of 4400 brokers in 13 equity exchanges and 10 options markets). Regulatory agencies are now beginning to take steps in the right direction.

In summary, HFT is a viable and an important innovation and as such, it needs to be monitored and, if necessary, reformed to accentuate its pros and curb its cons. It is not the high-speed computers and algorithms that are evil per se but the use they may be put to.

REFERENCES

Angel, J.J., McCabe, D., 2013. Fairness in financial markets: the case of high frequency trading. J. Bus. Ethics 112 (4), 585–595.

Brogaard, J., 2010. High frequency trading and its impact on market quality. In: 5th Annual Conference on Empirical Legal Studies Paper. http://www.futuresindustry.org/ptg/downloads/HFT_Trading.pdf.

Brogaard, J., Hendershott, T., Riordan, R., 2014. High-Frequency Trading and Price Discovery. The Review of Financial Studies: Retrieved online. http://rfs.oxfordjournals.org/content/early/2014/06/13/rfs.hhu032.abstract.

Fama, E.F., 1965. The behavior of stock-market prices. J. Bus. 38, 34–105.

Froot, K.J., Scharfstein, D.S., Stein, J.C., 1992. Herd on the street: informational inefficiencies in a market with short-term speculation. J. Finance 57 (4), 1461–1484.

Hirschey, N., 2013. Do High Frequency Traders Anticipate Buying and Selling Pressure? http://papers.ssrn.com/sol3/papers.cfm?abstract_id=2238516&download=yes.

Hudson, R., Gebka, B., Manahov, V., 2014. Does high frequency trading affect technical analysis and market efficiency? and if so, how? J. Int. Finan. Markets Inst. Money 28 (2), 131–157.

O'Hara, M., Ye, M., 2011. Is market fragmentation harming market quality? J. Finan. Econ. 100 (3), 459–474.

Patterson, S., 2014. Speed Traders Get an Edge. http://online.wsj.com/news/articles/SB10001424052702304450904579367050946606562.

Shefrin, S., Statman, M., 1993. Ethics, fairness and efficiency in financial markets. Finan. Anal. J. 49 (6), 21–29.

Zhang, F., 2010. High-Frequency Trading, Stock Volatility, and Price Discovery. http://papers.ssrn.com/sol3/papers.cfm?abstract_id=1691679.

CHAPTER 8

Revisioning Revisionism: A Glance at HFT's Critics

Jeffrey G. MacIntosh
University of Toronto, Faculty of Law, Toronto, ON, Canada

Contents

8.1 INTRODUCTION: HIGH-FREQUENCY TRADING UNDER SIEGE

Without question, Michael Lewis' book "Flash Boys" has brought high-frequency trading (HFT) into the popular spotlight, and in a far from favorable hue. Lewis' much-ballyhooed claim that markets are "rigged for the benefit of insiders" (Lewis, 2014)—and that high-frequency traders (HFTRs) are the principal cause—has been widely (and often

The Handbook of High Frequency Trading
ISBN 978-0-12-802205-4

uncritically) reported in a broad spectrum of news media (e.g., Value Walk, 2014; Baram, 2014; Massoudi and Alloway, 2014; Maslin, 2014; Ross, 2014; Parker, 2014). One need go no further than the book's dust jacket to find the startling proclamation that:

> …post-financial crisis, the markets have become not more free but less, and more controlled by the big Wall Street banks… The light that Lewis shines into the darkest corners of the financial world may not be good for your blood pressure, because if you have any contact with the market, even a retirement account, this story is happening to you (Lewis, 2014).

Although much of the book deals with alleged front running of institutional orders by HFTRs, as the above quotation suggests, Lewis portrays HFTRs as opportunistic parasites that abuse both institutional and retail traders.

In a wide-ranging promotional tour, Lewis focused more on the purported harm to retail investors. As reported by Newsweek (Philips, 2013),

> In his first two TV appearances, Lewis stuck to a simple pitch: Speed traders have rigged the stock market, and the biggest losers are average, middle-class retail investors—exactly the kind of people who watch 60 Minutes and the Today show. It's "the guy sitting at his E-Trade account," Lewis told Matt Lauer. The way Lewis sees it, speed traders prey on retail investors by "trading against people who don't know the market."

In this chapter, I review not only Lewis' claims but also those of other critics of HFT, in light of the extant empirical evidence. This evidence suggests that HFT has brought very palpable benefits to securities markets. These include tightened bid/ask spreads, improved price discovery, enhanced immediacy, and, in at least some studies, reduced intraday volatility. Unlike traditional market makers, HFTRs thrive in volatile markets. Far from being fickle summer soldiers who abruptly withdraw their liquidity when markets swing sharply downward, HFTRs tend to hang in even in times of market peril.

The bounty of these changes has been reaped by both institutional and retail traders. The result is that securities markets are more transactionally efficient than ever before. Heightened transactional efficiency means, in turn, that securities markets are more allocatively efficient. This is a very far cry from the message in Flash Boys. Before reviewing the empirical evidence, however, I take a wider look at the context in which the Lewis controversy arose, and the broad array of public and private criticisms that have been leveled at HFT in the past several years. I then review some of the more frequent criticisms of HFTRs, and respond to these criticisms in view of the empirical evidence.

8.2 THE LEWIS DEBATE IN CONTEXT

8.2.1 Dodd—Frank

While Lewis' book has been the focal point of recent discussion about financial markets, what is sometimes overlooked is that, whether by fortuity or design, Flash Boys was planted in an unusually fertile political and popular medium. Following the near-financial and economic meltdown of the Credit Crisis, popular suspicion of and hostility to "Wall Street"[1] has been running high. The Credit Crisis and attendant public anger directed at Wall Street actors were the proximate cause of Congress' 2010 adoption of sweeping reforms to financial regulation. These are embodied in the Dodd—Frank Wall Street Reform and Consumer Protection Act (U.S. Congress, 2010).

These reforms make it abundantly clear that concern about the position of the retail investor did not originate with Flash Boys. Dodd-Frank, for example, mandates the creation by the Securities and Exchange Commission (SEC) of an "Office of the Investor Advocate" to (*inter alia*) "assist retail investors in resolving significant problems such investors may have with the Commission or with self-regulatory organizations."[2] Dodd—Frank also requires the SEC to create an ombudsman to "act as a liaison between the Commission and any retail investor in resolving problems that retail investors may have with the Commission or with self-regulatory Organizations."[3] It further mandates the creation of a "Bureau of Consumer Financial Protection" within the Federal Reserve Bank, "for the purpose of ensuring that all consumers have access to markets for consumer financial products and services and that markets for consumer financial products and services are fair, transparent, and competitive."[4] These reforms reflect popular rumblings that go back many years about what is popularly perceived to be the increasing parlous state of the retail investor.

8.2.2 Technical Problems and Public Confidence in Securities Markets

A variety of technical problems in trading markets have also served to focus public attention on a variety of risks associated with computerized trading. Of these, the Flash Crash is perhaps the most dramatic and the most widely reported. In May 2010, a faulty algorithm was used by a large mutual fund to effect the liquidation of a $4.1 billion block of E-Mini S&P 500 contracts. The intense downward price pressure created by the continual flood of sell orders into the market negatively impacted the price of the E-Mini S&P 500, a stock market index futures contract traded on the Chicago Mercantile Exchange's Globex electronic trading platform. As the underlying value of the contract is the S&P index, as the E-Mini fell, so did all the stocks comprising the index. While HFTRs (and others) were initially liquidity suppliers that purchased some of the E-Mini contracts being sold by the mutual fund, liquidity dried up as the price of the contract continued to plunge, and market makers found themselves unable to find

---

[1] I use the phrase "Wall Street" in the popular manner; that is, as a synecdoche for the U.S. financial industry as a whole. Many HFTRs, of course, are neither located on or near Wall Street nor affiliated with Wall Street incumbents, a subject discussed further below.

[2] Dodd-Frank, Title IX ("Investor Protections and Improvements to the Regulation of Securities"), s.915, amending Section 4 of the Securities Exchange Act of 1934 (15 U.S.C. 78d).

[3] Dodd—Frank, Title IX ("Investor Protections and Improvements to the Regulation of Securities"), s.919D.

[4] Dodd—Frank, Title X ("Bureau of Consumer Financial Protection"), s.1021.

buyers to lay off their positions. The resulting withdrawal of liquidity caused the Dow Jones Index to plunge nearly 600 points in 5 minutes—although within 20 minutes following a trading halt, the Dow had recovered most of the 600 point loss.

In the early months of 2012, three technical glitches garnered much public attention. In March, BATS (Better Alternative Trading Systems), the third largest exchange in the United States, withdrew its initial public offering (IPO), which had been slated to trade over the BATS exchange, after a software error caused the newly listed stock (priced at $16 per share) to trade for as little as $0.01 per share. (Oran et al., 2012; Schaefer, 2012). In May, a software glitch at Knight Capital, then the largest trader in U.S. equities, resulted in the firm losing $440 million in 45 minutes of trading (Popper, 2012a). In August, Nasdaq computers were unable to cope with the volume of orders associated with the Facebook IPO, resulting in a reported loss of $350 million for UBS and $35.4 million for Knight Capital (Clark, 2012). Nasdaq was subsequently fined $10 million by the SEC for violations of securities laws arising out of the technical problems (SEC, 2013b).

A rash of technical problems also occurred in 2013. In April, the Chicago Board Options Exchange was closed for three and a half hours as a result of a software malfunction (Frankel and Saphir, 2013). Then, in the space of a single week, three major computer malfunctions occurred—two of them on the same day. On Monday August 19, a programming error at Goldman Sachs resulted in a flood of mispriced orders being sent into the options market (Gammeltoft and Griffin, 2013). The error affected several hundred thousand option contracts and may have cost Goldman Sachs as much as $100 million (Lopez, 2013a; CNBC, 2013). On Thursday of the same week, the ARCA electronic exchange (owned and operated by the New York Stock Exchange (NYSE) found itself unable for a period of 9 minutes to report trades on Nasdaq stocks with ticker symbols with alphabetical designations coming after TACT (Norris, 2013). More seriously, later that day, a software failure in Nasdaq's Securities Information Processor (which collects bid/ask and trading information with respect to all Nasdaq stocks and makes this information available for a fee to all market participants) resulted in the suspension from trading of all Nasdaq stocks for 3 hours (Norris, 2013).

Press reports of these events paint a picture of a growing lack of confidence in U.S. financial markets. The Goldman error, for example, prompted Bloomberg News to state "a programming error at Goldman Sachs Group Inc. caused unintended stock-option orders to flood American exchanges this morning, roiling markets and shaking confidence in electronic trading infrastructure" (Gammeltoft and Griffin, 2013). The Chicago Board Options Exchange problems prompted Reuters to state that "these events have shaken investors' confidence about whether markets can be fair and orderly given how dominated they now are by complex, computer-driven systems" (Frankel and Saphir, 2013). Similarly, following the Knight meltdown, an article in the New York Times stated that "the event was the latest to draw attention to the potentially destabilizing effect of the computerized trading that has increasingly dominated the nation's stock markets" (Popper, 2012a).

8.2.3 New York Attorney General Eric Schneiderman Goes on the Attack

In addition to these unsettling technical problems, Lewis' book was preceded by aggressive anti-HFT rhetoric on the part of New York State Attorney General Eric Schneiderman, who appears to have cast his lot with those who see nothing positive about HFT. In 2013, he was quoted (Lopez, 2013b) as saying:

When blinding speed is coupled with early access to data, it gives small groups of traders the power to manipulate market movements in their own favor before anyone else knows what's happening… They suck the value out of market-moving information before it even goes public. That's 'Insider Trading 2.0,' and it should be a huge concern to anyone who cares about the markets and the free flow of capital on which our economy depends.

Similarly, in an interview on CBS, Schneiderman stated "what's improper is front-running the market…using any special advantage or edge with your speed to have an unfair advantage over anyone else" (Cochrane, 2014).

Schneiderman's antipathy to "early access to data" includes the provision of company-specific or marketwide fundamental information to paying customers on a privileged basis. A number of developments in 2013 appear to have resulted from this concern. Reuters, for example, agreed to cease allowing paying customers advance access to its widely watched data on analyst and consumer sentiment (Freifeld, 2014). Business Wire stopped selling advance access to news releases (Alden, 2014a). Similarly, Black-Rock ceased surveying financial analysts with respect to their views about various companies before those views were made public (Alden, 2014a).

Schneiderman's suspicion of HFT, however, goes well beyond the provision of various sorts of fundamental information to paying customers on a privileged basis. He has also vigorously questioned the practice of colocation and other connection-related advantages (such as the provision to paying customers of broadband connections and high-speed switches) available to HFTRs and other paying customers of various trading venues. As the above quotes suggest, Schneiderman has gone as far as intimating that, in his view, these practices may constitute illegal insider trading (Levine, 2014b; Freifeld, 2014).

In response, one observer (Levine, 2014b) writes:

New York Attorney General Eric Schneiderman…pretty clearly believes that high-frequency trading is bad. He thinks the whole thing is "Insider Trading 2.0." So his goal seems to be to eradicate it entirely, by going after direct feeds from exchanges and co-location and even just the continuous trading of stocks. In Schneiderman's ideal world, speed would simply be eliminated as a trading advantage.

Other commentators have interpreted Schneiderman's statements in a similar light (e.g., Alden, 2014a).

8.2.4 Department of Justice, Federal Bureau of Investigation, and Commodity Futures Trading Commission Concerns

Schneiderman is not the only governmental authority with an interest in HFT. The publication of Flash Boys almost immediately triggered an announcement by the U.S. Justice

Department that it was investigating HFT with a view to determining whether insider trading laws were being broken (ElBoghdady, 2014). Even prior to publication (and Schneiderman's public statements questioning the legality of HFT), the Federal Bureau of Investigation (FBI) had begun an investigation into whether various practices associated with HFT constitute illegal insider trading (Geiger and Hurtado, 2014). After publication of the book, the FBI stepped up its efforts by making a public plea for insiders at HFT firms to act as whistleblowers and bring wrongful conduct of their employers to the attention of the FBI (Geiger and Hurtado, 2014).

Also prior to Lewis' book, in September of 2013, the Commodity Futures Trading Commission (CFTC) published a concept release that examines the systemic risks associated with HFT and possible policy responses (CFTC, 2013). More recently, following the publication of Flash Boys, the CFTC held public hearings with the specific purpose of responding to Lewis' allegations (CFTC, 2014). The CFTC has also announced that it intends to examine trading inducements given to traders such as volume discounts and "early adopter" rebates (Leising, 2014).[5]

8.2.5 Senate Hearings

Unquestionably, however, Lewis' book has resulted in a marked increase in public awareness and scrutiny of HFT. There is perhaps no better evidence of this than the public hearings held by various Senate committees into HFT. The Senate Permanent Subcommittee on Investigations held a hearing in June on whether conflicts of interest created by payment for order flow and maker-taker pricing impair a broker's duty of best execution to its clients (Senate Permanent Subcommittee on Investigations, 2014; Alden, 2014c). Only a day later, the Senate Committee on Banking, Housing, and Urban Affairs held a hearing into the impact of HFT on the U.S. economy (Senate Committee on Banking, Housing, and Urban Affairs, 2014a) and a further hearing in July entitled "The Role of Regulation in Shaping Equity Market Structure and Electronic Trading" (Senate Committee on Banking, Housing, and Urban Affairs, 2014b; Gandel, 2014). Even the Senate Committee on Agriculture, Nutrition and Forestry (which oversees the CFTC) was moved to hold a hearing in May 2014 into the role of high-frequency and automated trading in futures markets (Senate Committee on Agriculture, Nutrition and Forestry, 2014). These rapid political responses to the Lewis furor are indicative of the political *gravitas* of the HFT debate.

The publication of Flash Boys even affected financial markets. Virtu Financial, one of the largest HFTRs, announced that it was canceling its IPO (Alden, 2014b). The stock of

---

[5] The futures exchanges that are supervised by the CFTC do not have "maker/taker" pricing like equity exchanges. However, they do offer other incentives such as tiered pricing based on volume and programs to reward early adopters of new futures contracts.

KCG Holdings (a company that is the result of a merger between HFT industry giants Knight and Getco) fell 3.3 percent, while the shares of Nasdaq OMX fell 3 percent (Alden and de la Merced, 2014). Similarly, the shares of the IntercontinentalExchange Group, owner of the New York Stock Exchange, fell by 2.4 percent (Alden and de la Merced, 2014). Clearly, the Michael Lewis furor led the market to believe that rough waters were ahead for both HFTRs and trading venues that host HFTRs.

8.2.6 Flash Boys in the SEC: A Chilly Reception

Lewis' views have received a notably chilly reception at the SEC. In a direct refutation of Lewis' most widely quoted claim, Chairman Mary Jo White testified before Congress that "the markets are not rigged...[they] are the strongest and most reliable in the world" (Rubenstein, 2014). Similarly, in a public speech in June 2014 (Remarks of Chair Mary Jo White, 2014), White stated:

> All of these market quality metrics show that the current market structure is not fundamentally broken, let alone rigged. To the contrary, the equity markets are strong and generally continue to serve well the interests of both retail and institutional investors.

White has also stated that the SEC was already engaged in a review of trading practices prior to the publication of Flash Boys and that the Lewis book raises no new issues for the SEC (Remarks of Chair Mary Jo White, 2014; Davidoff, 2014; Knutson, 2014). She has endorsed the view that HFT has generally benefitted retail investors by lowering spreads and creating other price advantages (Knutson, 2014).

Despite this broad endorsement, however, White has also stated her belief that some HFTRs engage in improper practices (Remarks of Chair Mary Jo White, 2014; Knutson, 2014). Recent news reports indicate that the SEC has targeted some HFT firms for a review of their business practices (McCrank, 2014). White has also indicated that the SEC will put a number of aspects of market structure that advantage HFTRs under the microscope, in an attempt to determine whether "specific elements of the computer-driven trading environment [are] working against investors rather than for them" (Remarks of Chair Mary Jo White, 2014). This includes whether "low-latency tools, even though they are available to investors through brokers, tend to advantage certain types of proprietary trading strategies that may detract from the interests of investors." On the same theme, White has indicated her willingness to consider allowing trading venues to trade via batch auctions rather than continuous processing of incoming orders. A batch auction would marry bid and ask quotes at discrete intervals, treating as equally ranked all incoming orders arriving in the interim (Budish et al., 2013). While not entirely eliminating the advantage of the fast trader, the purported advantage of a batch auction would be to render speed advantages of far lesser significance.

White has also wondered if "the SEC's own rules, such as the trade-through rule of Regulation NMS, have contributed to excessive fragmentation across all types of venues," and has somewhat cryptically mused that perhaps trading venues "could also include affirmative or negative trading obligations for high-frequency trading firms that employ the fastest, most sophisticated trading tools" (Remarks of Chair Mary Jo White, 2014). This suggests that the SEC is prepared to consider allowing trading venues to impose continuous market making obligations on HFTRs similar to the obligation imposed on designated market makers.

All these statements will be of concern to HFTRs. Low-latency trading, continuous trading, the trade-through rule, and the absence of an affirmative market making obligation are all central to the HFT business model.

White has also stated "an area of particular focus is the use of aggressive, destabilizing trading strategies in vulnerable market conditions", albeit without specifically identifying any such allegedly destabilizing practices (Remarks of Chair Mary Jo White, 2014). To this end, White has instructed SEC staff to prepare an "antidisruptive trading rule." She has also instructed SEC staff to develop rules subjecting all proprietary traders (including HFTRs) to registration requirements, facilitating oversight and discipline by the SEC and the Financial Oversight and Regulatory Authority (the financial services industry self-regulatory organization).

More generally, White has indicated her concern about systemic risks associated with computerized trading, stating (Remarks of Chair Mary Jo White, 2014):

> ...one of the most serious concerns about today's equity markets is the risk of instability and disruption. Technology can and has greatly increased the efficiency of our markets, but it can also allow severe problems to develop very quickly—just consider some of the systems events of the last few years at exchanges and brokers.

Accordingly, White has indicated that she has "instructed the staff to prepare recommendations for the Commission to improve firms' risk management of trading algorithms and to enhance regulatory oversight over their use" (Remarks of Chair Mary Jo White, 2014).

Among the recent changes put in place by the SEC to address systemic risks is the "limit up-limit down" rule (LULD) applicable to all national market system (NMS) stocks. The LULD system suspends trading in individual securities if prices depart from the arithmetic mean of a stock's transaction price (as measured in the preceding 5 min) by more than a specified amount ranging from 5 to 20 percent (SEC, 2012). LULD, which replaced a single stock circuit breaker program put in place in June of 2010 following the Flash Crash, requires all trading centers "to establish, maintain and enforce written policies and procedures that are reasonably designed to comply with the limit up-limit down and trading pause requirements."

In 2010, the Commission also adopted Rule 15c3-5 under the Securities Exchange Act of 1934 to reduce risks associated with the provision of "direct access" by brokers and dealers (SEC, 2010c). The rule requires broker/dealers to adopt financial risk management controls and supervisory procedures in respect of direct access arrangements. The SEC is also in the process of finalizing "Regulation Systems Compliance and Integrity" (Regulation SCI), which will impose system integrity requirements on various market actors' computer systems (including all trading venues that host HFTRs) (SEC, 2013a).

In addition to these formalized measures, the SEC has used its suasive powers to convince the stock exchanges to adopt measures designed to ensure the robustness and resilience of the Securities Information Process (SIP) consolidated data feeds (Hope, 2014).

8.2.7 Summary

While Michael Lewis' Flash Boys is perhaps the most vigorous and highly publicized assault on HFT, it was by no means the first. Rather, the book was well timed to capitalize on currents of suspicion, hostility, and misunderstanding that were already circulating in the industry and in various public and political arenas. Various governmental entities, including the FBI and New York Attorney General Eric Schneider, were already investigating HFTRs for potential breaches of law. Attorney General Schneider has been particularly prominent in the anti-HFT camp, apparently allying himself with those who see nothing whatever positive about HFT.

By contrast, the Chair of the SEC has stated that the overall contribution of HFT to financial markets is a positive one, and has committed to an empirically based review of HFTR practices. Despite this, she has indicated a number of concerns about certain (largely unspecified) HFTR behaviors, and a willingness to review various features of market structure and operation that are central to HFTRs' business models. Only time will tell whether changes to the regulatory regime will significantly alter or imperil those models.

In what follows, I address some of the key complaints against HFTRs—both those made by Lewis and by others—in light of the empirical record. This shows that, in the main, as SEC Chair Mary Jo White has stated, HFT has been beneficial to both institutional and retail investors. Markets have become more efficient, brokerage costs have fallen, price discovery has improved, and bid/ask spreads have dramatically narrowed. Nonetheless, some HFT practices may well detract from market quality. This includes front running (the primary focus of the Lewis book). It also includes "spoofing (or "layering")," in which large numbers of bids or asks are flooded into the market (away from the inside quote. This is designed to frighten naive traders into believing that an order imbalance exists, prompting them to soften their bid or ask quotes. It also includes "smoking," where the HFTR sends quotes to market that offer price improvement over the national best bid and offer (NBBO), with the intention of inducing other traders to send market orders. Before these orders can be executed against the HFTR's quotes, however, they are quickly withdrawn, resulting in the market orders being executed against less favorable bid or ask quotes posted by the HFTR. Another reputed illicit practice is "quote stuffing", in which the HFTR submits and immediately cancels a very large number of orders purely to slow down or confuse other traders and/or illicitly move the market price.

The regulatory challenge is to find ways of preventing or at least minimizing the damage caused by these abusive tactics while not jeopardizing the manifest benefits that HFT has brought into the market.

8.3 AN HFT TABLEAU: PERCEPTION VERSUS REALITY

8.3.1 HFT and the "Wall Street" Myth

Michael Lewis and many in the popular press identify HFTRs as "Wall Street" players. Indeed, as noted as the outset, the dust jacket of the Lewis book states that as a result of HFT, "the markets have become not more free but *less*, and more controlled by the big Wall Street banks" (Lewis, 2014).

The identification of HFT with "Wall Street" is misleading. Many of the most successful HFTRs are found outside New York. Tradebot, an early entrant onto the HFT landscape, (and still one of the largest and most prosperous HFTRs) is headquartered in Kansas City, Missouri. Industry titans GETCO and Knight Capital were respectively operated out of Chicago and Jersey City, New Jersey. Their merged successor, KCG, is operated out of Jersey City. Another industry titan, Citadel, is located in Chicago. Virtu Financial and Hudson River Trading are two of the few industry giants located in New York.

Nor are most other HFTRs affiliated with traditional Wall Street actors. According to the TABB Group's Robert Iati (cited in Golub, 2011), there are between 10 and 20 broker/dealer proprietary desks engaged in HFT, and fewer than 20 hedge funds. By contrast, there are somewhere between 100 and 300 independent proprietary HFTRs. As Scott Paterson's book *Dark Pools* (Paterson, 2012) makes plain, HFT did not emerge under the aegis of traditional Wall Street actors. Rather, it was born and nurtured as a virtual counterculture to the Wall Street establishment, with a view to breaking the stranglehold of the extant *dramatis personae* on the business of trading securities. While some of HFT's founding fathers were situated in New York, they are nonetheless singularly ill suited to the "Wall Street" cognomen.

Ironically, given how they are portrayed by Lewis and others, HFTRs are competitors of traditional Wall Street incumbents, and they have poached significant trading revenue from the latter. They have been instrumental in introducing vigorous competition to the business of trading securities—competition that was largely absent in the days when Nasdaq and the NYSE had virtual monopolies in the trading of listed stocks.

While the identification of HFT with Wall Street may thus be a convenient synecdoche for writers such as Michael Lewis and many in the popular media, it is nonetheless one that is quite misleading.

8.3.2 Are HFTRs Modern-Day Robber Barons?

Michael Lewis and many in the popular media have characterized HFTRs as modern-day robber barons whose presence in securities markets has seriously impaired the returns of retail and institutional investors. But consider that the aggregate revenue in 2013 of all HFT operators in the United States was on the order of $2 billion (MacSweeney, 2013b). In the same year, in excess of $21-trillion worth of stocks was traded. This means that HFT revenue was about 1/100 of 1% of the total value of stock traded.

When measured against profits, the figures are even more modest. Based on 2012 HFT industry profits of $1.25 billion (Popper, 2012b), profits were less than 1/150 of 1% of the total value of stock traded. By way of comparison, each of Wells Fargo and JPMorgan Chase earned more in a single quarter of 2012 than the U.S. HFT industry in the entire year (Popper, 2012b).

In fact, HFT revenue and profits are dwarfed by the benefits that HFTRs have brought into the market. As noted below, there is a general consensus that HFT has significantly lowered bid/ask spreads—one of the most important components of trading cost. A conservative estimate of the size of that benefit can be achieved by assuming that the presence of HFT has reduced the average spread on traded stocks by just $0.01 per share. There are about 1.75 trillion shares traded in the United States each year at an average price of $12 per share, and HFTRs are involved in about half of those trades (Brogaard, 2010; Remarks of Chair Mary Jo White, 2014; MacSweeney, 2013; Popper, 2012b). Thus, the aggregate benefit of tighter bid/ask spreads to investors is on the order of $9 billion per year—nearly an order of magnitude greater than HFT industry profits for all of 2013. An average reduction in the bid/ask spread of $0.02 per share would yield an $18 billion saving, and so on. This does not account for other benefits brought to the market by HFT, such as enhanced immediacy, improved price discovery, and (at least in some studies) reduced intraday volatility.

Thus, while Michael Lewis portrays HFTRs as fat cats who take little risk to earn a Sultan's ransom, the reality is quite different. Figure 8.1 indicates the declining market share and revenue of HFTRs in the trading of equities in the United States and Europe. In addition, the period from 2009 to 2013 was characterized by falling profits, layoffs, consolidation, and withdrawals from the industry (Popper, 2012b; FTSE Global Markets, 2012; MacSweeney, 2013a; Phillips, 2013).

US HFT industry profits reached their apogee in 2009 at approximately $5 billion, on a revenue of $7.2 billion (MacSweeney, 2013b; Overholt, 2014; Rodier, 2013). By 2012, Rosenblatt Securities estimates that total HFT profits were not >$1.25 billion (Overholt, 2014; Rodier, 2013). This was down 35% from 2011% to 64% below the record profits of 2009. In 2013, the figures were even more modest, with an aggregate revenue of $2 billion and profits of $1 billion (Overholt, 2014).

Further evidence of the falling fortunes of the HFT industry may be found in the profits of some of its largest players. For example, in the course of effecting a merger with Knight Capital Group in 2012, Getco reported that its profit for the first 9 months of 2012 was down by 82% from a year earlier (from $134.8 million to $24.6 million) even though revenue was down by only half that amount (Knight Holdco, Inc., 2013).

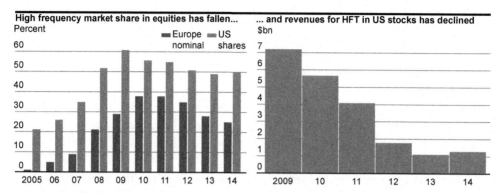

Figure 8.1 High frequency trading (HFT). *(Source: High-Frequency Trading, compiled from data from TABB Group, available at http://www.ft.com/intl/cms/s/0/ac3bdb3a-badf-11e3-8b15-00144feabdc0. html#axzz38xzhidAm.)*

What has caused the reduction in HFT profits? Two key factors are lower trading volumes and diminished volatility (Jarnecic and Snape, 2010, 2014; Brogaard, 2010; MacSweeney, 2013a; Wang, 2013). But in addition, economic rents earned by the relatively small number of early players have now largely been competed away. HFT is a young industry that has matured rapidly. In an industry of this character, one would expect early entrants to earn supracompetitive rents, for at least two reasons. One is the lack of competition. Another is the inevitable lag between the deployment of high-speed HFT strategies and a combination of strategic trading responses and technology upgrades by other traders (particularly buy-side institutions). To the extent that front running or order anticipation increase institutional trading costs, for example, a variety of commercial vendors now sell both technology and trading strategies to institutions to disguise their trading behavior. In addition, some institutional players have moved their trading into dark pools, in which HFTRs play a lesser role. The combination of new HFT entrants and enhanced competition has inevitably reduced or eliminated economic rents. Strategic and technological responses by non-HFTRs have also been a factor in diminishing aggregate industry profits.

It is also noteworthy that HFT profits do not always come at the expense of other types of traders. Baron et al. (2012) find that 32.8% of the profits earned by aggressive HFTRs (defined as those for whom >60% of their trades are liquidity taking) come at the expense of "mixed" HFTRs (for whom 20−60% of their trades are liquidity taking). Aggressive HFTRs make a further 11.6% of their profits from passive HFTRs (for whom <20% of their trades are liquidity taking). Thus, in total, aggressive HFTRs make 44.4% of their profits *from other HFTRs*. Baron et al. also find that passive HFTRs lose significantly to both aggressive HFTRs and mixed HFTRs, and mixed HFTRs lose to aggressive HFTRs. HFTRs' profits are thus not all earned at the expense of natural traders.

In the early part of 2014, New York Attorney General Schneider and others made much of Virtu Financial's disclosure (for purposes of its ultimately aborted IPO) that the firm suffered only one losing day in 1238 days of trading (Perlberg, 2014; Durden, 2014; Levine, 2014a). The inference that has been drawn by some is that HFT is virtually a risk-free industry, and that it is impossible to imagine how this could be the case without illegal behavior or other skullduggery.

Consider the following, however. It is possible to have positive net operating revenues on each and every day of operations while nonetheless failing to earn one's cost of capital. Many firms that ultimately go bankrupt have consistently positive operating revenues prior to their bankruptcies, and many more limp along skirting the margins of profitability. In fact, the capital outlays necessary to become and remain competitive in HFT have increased substantially (MacSweeney, 2013b). While this would require higher revenues to maintain profitability, as noted, revenues have shrunk substantially.

In addition, Virtu's disclosure comprises a single data point (i.e. only one firm), which no one should assume is representative of the industry as a whole. Indeed, there is ample reason to believe that Virtu's fortunes are nonrepresentative. For one thing, Virtu is one of the most successful firms in the industry. For another, Baron et al. (2012) find that HFTR profits are highly heterogeneous (with new entrants having a higher propensity to underperform and exit, and the fastest HFTRs realizing the greatest profits). They also find that HFTR profits tend to be concentrated in a relatively small number of aggressive HFTRs.

Finally, HFTRs offer a service—liquidity—for which they charge. It is true that, in dynamic markets, not every round-trip trade can be expected to be a winner. Nonetheless, over a very high volume of trades, we would expect a sophisticated and successful firm such as Virtu to have an overwhelming number of trading days with positive, as opposed to negative revenue, just as we would expect of a successful firm in any industry (Levine, 2014a). In short, the data regarding HFT profitability are starkly inconsistent with the picture painted by Lewis and others in public statements and in the popular press.

8.3.3 Is HFT Speed Purely Value Destructive?

Lewis and others rather single-mindedly characterize the HFTR's drive for speed as a device to front run institutional investors or pick off the stale quotes of slower investors, creating no social value. This is erroneous. The most significant activity of HFTRs is market making (Brogaard, 2010; Hagströmerm and Norden, 2013; Menkveld, 2013; IIROC, 2011; Gomber et al., 2011). Market making is an important liquidity function in any securities market, since not all buyers or sellers are present in the market at any given time. Traditional market makers (e.g., NYSE specialists) continuously post bid and ask prices at which they are willing to transact. In this manner, they bridge the temporal gap between the arrival of buyers and sellers. When sellers are present, the market maker buys—and then subsequently resells the securities when buyers arrive (restoring its inventory in that security to its target level). Conversely, when buyers are present, the market maker sells, and subsequently repurchases the same securities from sellers who happen to be on the scene (again, restoring its target inventory to the desired level). The market maker's compensation for offering this liquidity service is the difference between the bid/ask spread, that is, the price at which it buys the securities, and the price at which it sells.

Unlike traditional market makers, HFTRs functioning as market makers are under no obligation to create a continuous market. This is in fact a principal reason why HFTRs are able to quote much tighter bid/ask spreads than do traditional market makers. So long as a bid or ask quotation is outstanding, it effectively cedes an option to trade to all other market participants. As the price of the security underlying the option is subject to change, it has value. The longer an option is outstanding, the greater the value.

The option value varies with a number of other parameters. Greater volatility increases option value (since the likelihood that the trading price will be different from the option price, at any given point in time, increases). The thinner the trading in the security in question, the greater the option value (since the market maker must anticipate a longer average time interval between any purchase/sale or sale/purchase round trip, exposing it to the risk that the price will change in the interval). The greater the degree of informed trading in a given security, the greater the option value, since the market maker's quote is exposed to a greater risk of being "picked off" by a trader with superior knowledge (i.e., the market maker experiences a higher level of adverse selection risk).

Since traditional market makers have an obligation to continuously post bid and ask prices, their options are continually outstanding and have great value to other market participants. Such market makers are able to profit only if they receive compensation for the grant value of the option. This is achieved by posting a relatively wide bid/ask spread. As a result, traditional market makers make money by executing a relatively small number of trades at relatively wide bid/ask spreads.

By contrast, HFTRs functioning as market makers are under no obligation to continuously make a market. They may thus trade or not trade depending on whether the conditions are favorable for generating positive revenue. One device for minimizing option value (and adverse selection risk) is embodied in the high order-to-trade ratio commonly observed of HFTRs, and the rapid rate at which nonexecuted orders are canceled (frequently replaced by updated quotes). If a posted quote is not immediately hit by another trader, that by itself conveys information about the state of market demand, including hidden liquidity—such as that embodied in iceberg orders or pendant liquidity waiting on the sidelines. In addition, HFTRs continually keep abreast of the latest fundamental information and quickly revise their quotes accordingly.

HFTRs also reduce the option value of their quotes by minimizing the time that it takes to effect a round-trip transaction in any given security (i.e., a purchase/sale or a sale/purchase), and by keeping their orders small (KCG, for example, will rarely be on the order book for more than 100 shares per order).

Particularly in volatile markets and those in which there is an elevated risk of informed trading, all these devices allow HFTRs to trade at tight bid/ask spreads that are much smaller than those posted by traditional market makers. HFTRs profit by executing a very large number of small transactions at very low bid/ask spreads (in addition to collecting the liquidity rebates offered by many trading venues).

HFTRs also minimize the option value of their quotes by avoiding markets in which securities are thinly traded. These markets continue to be the province of traditional market makers. They further reduce their risk by "going home flat" at the end of the trading day; that is, holding neither a long nor a short position. This contrasts with traditional market makers, whose target inventory will typically be positive, in order to minimize the transaction costs of accommodating purchasers as they arrive across the transom. This exposes the traditional market maker to the risk of overnight changes in the value of its inventory securities. Once again, this forces the market maker to widen its bid/ask spread in order to be compensated for bearing the additional risk.

Speed is also essential to HFTRs that perform statistical arbitrage or that trade on fundamental information, since being at the top of the order book—and hence the first to exploit the profit opportunity—is the difference between making and losing money. This use of trading speed enhances price discovery and makes markets more efficient.

Speed can be used in socially counterproductive ways. Front running of institutional orders, for example, and the use of low-latency trading purely to pick off other traders' stale quotes can be value destructive. Nonetheless, evidence suggests that, in the main, HFT speed has been used to lower bid/ask spreads, and enhance both immediacy and price discovery. To the extent that some HFTRs employ predatory strategies that harm other traders and subtract from market efficiency, regulators should devise strategies to identify and weed out such trading practices, in such a manner as to preserve the many benefits that HFT has brought to securities markets.

8.3.4 HFT and Institutional Execution Costs

Even aside from Michael Lewis' onslaught on HFT, buy-side institutional traders frequently complain that HFTRs increase their costs of trading large blocks. These complaints are many and diverse, but include at least the following:

8.3.4.1 Do HFTRs Increase Price Slippage when Institutional Blocks are Traded?

It is often argued that the presence of HFTRs in securities markets has increased price slippage associated with trading large blocks, and that quoted bid/ask spreads are therefore not an accurate measure of block trading costs. Institutional traders typically break block trades into a large number of small orders executed over a period of time (sometimes as much as several days) and over a variety of different trading venues. This is done in order to hide the block trade from the market, since market awareness that a block trade is being executed will often cause the price to move against the block trader. But even when this is done, sophisticated HFTRs "sniffer" algorithms employ historical analysis of institutional trading patterns to deduce when an institutional block trade is underway, and respond by lowering their bid prices and increasing their ask prices. For this reason, quoted bid/ask spreads are not representative of actual institutional execution costs.

8.3.4.2 Do HFTRs Increase Adverse Selection Costs?

Institutions complain (and academic studies tend to affirm) that HFTRs are often "informed" traders who are able to use their superior information to pick off institutional (and other) quotes that are inconsistent with the best pricing information available. Informed HFTRs are often styled "aggressive" HFTRs, since they are not typically passive, but active traders who are capable of making money off other traders' comparatively uninformed quotes.

8.3.4.3 Latency Arbitrage

Like many terms pertinent to HFT, the term "latency arbitrage" does not seem to bear one consistent usage. It has been used to refer to the type of "front running" or "quote matching" described by Michael Lewis in Flash Boys. The term has also been used to refer to the practice of capitalizing on the difference between the latency of a direct colocated data feed and the slightly slower consolidated (or "SIP"[6]) feeds available for a fee to all members of the public.

Front running, one type of latency arbitrage, capitalizes on two trading artifacts. First, institutional block trades often move the price of a given stock. Second, an institutional order will reach a nearby trading venue prior to reaching more geographically distant venues. To effectuate a front running strategy, the HFTR detects the initiation of the block trade from the order that arrives at the geographically proximate venue. It then dispatches its own trading orders, on the same side of the market as the institution, to more geographically distant venues, hoping to place its own orders prior to those of the institutional trader and ultimately satisfy the institutional trader's orders at a slightly better price.

For example, if an institutional order to buy at $30.00 is sent to venue 1 and the more geographically distant venue 2, and received first at venue 1, the HFTR will detect that an institutional trade is in progress when it observes the order arrive at venue 1. The HFTR will then outrace the institutional order to venue 2, quickly purchasing all the stock for sale (or as much as it thinks will satisfy the institutional order) at $30.01. When the institutional order arrives at venue 2, there will be no stock for sale at $30.00 nor $30.01—but the HFTR (having scooped up available stock) will be quite

---

[6] SIP stands for Securities Information Processor, which is a consolidated data feed collected by a designated entity and distributed on demand (for a fee) to various end users such as buy-side institutions. The Nasdaq currently runs the SIP for Nasdaq-listed securities, the NYSE for securities listed on the NYSE and American Stock Exchange (AMEX), and the NYSE for the options market.

willing to sell the stock that it has purchased to the institution at $30.02, making a profit of $0.01 per share on its round trip trade (Arnuk and Saluzzi, 2009).

The sort of speed that enables this kind of arbitrage to occur derives from two technological advantages. One is the purchase of a direct data feed in the same building as each trading venue's matching engine (i.e., "colocation") to minimize the time it takes for message traffic to travel from the HFTR's servers to each venue's matching engine, and vice versa.

Another is the use of leased fiber optic cables to spirit message traffic at high rates between trading venues. Thus, for example, in 2010, Spread Networks spent $300 million to construct a straight line fiber optic cable running from Chicago to New York, all in service of saving a mere 1.4 ms off round-trip message latency (Adler, 2012). That 1.4 ms was enough to allow Spread's customers to outrace other trader's orders and message traffic passing between the two cities. Remarkably, however, the Spread Networks cable may already be tottering on the brink of obsolescence; various other companies are building or have built faster radio and microwave communications networks (although unlike fiber optic cable, these are subject to weather disturbances).

Latency arbitrage is also used to refer to the practice of capitalizing on the difference between the latency of a direct colocated data feed and that of the slightly slower SIP feeds. In this sense, it has sometimes been analogized to the ability of the colocated trader to peer several milliseconds into the future, since the colocated trader will effectively be able to see the NBBO several milliseconds before that information is made available to other traders (Wah and Wellman, 2013).

In general, latency arbitrage tends to be value reducing as it generates adverse selection costs for non-HFTRs without any material enhancement to market quality (Wah and Wellman, 2013).

8.3.4.4 Order Anticipation

More benignly, HFTRs that use algorithms to detect institutional trades may widen their bid/ask quotes or reduce or withdraw liquidity in anticipation that the block trade will move the market price. HFTRs that do not do so will suffer losses if the price does indeed move in response to the trade. Such anticipatory adjustments thus enable HFTRs to quote tighter bid/ask spreads when block traders are not in the market.

Order anticipation could also involve dealing on the same side of the market as the institutional trader. Unlike in the case of front running, however, the HFTR's trading is not simply an attempt to beat the institution to the altar at geographically distant venues. Rather, the HFTR deduces that *future* orders from the institution are likely to be placed with various venues, and may therefore establish a position in that stock (long or short) to capitalize on the price movement created by the institutional order. In either case, order anticipation is not a form of latency arbitrage, since it does not simply capitalize on superior speed in beating the institution to one or more trading venues.

8.3.4.5 The Growth of Dark Pools

One result of the perception by many institutions (whether right or wrong) that they cannot get a fair shake in public markets is the rapid growth of dark pools, in which HFTRs have relatively modest participation. As SEC Chairman Mary Jo White has recently noted, however, many of these pools operate with little transparency. Further, their growth raises serious issues related to price discovery (Remarks of Chair Mary Jo White, 2014). Future SEC regulatory action with respect to dark pools may have the effect (whether intended or unintended) of stifling further growth.

8.3.4.6 Vanishing Liquidity

The phrase "vanishing liquidity" (or "illusory liquidity") has been used to refer to a number of phenomena. One of these is the withdrawal of liquidity and/or the widening of bid/ask spreads after HFTRs detect an institutional order in the market. Another is the high HFTR ratio of orders to trades, with the bulk of submitted orders being canceled before being executed. Yet another is the lack of market depth at or near the inside quote, making the quoted bid/ask spread unrepresentative of effective and realized spreads.

8.3.4.7 An Empirical Weighing

Kim and Murphy find that while the average size of a block trade has not changed significantly over time, the average size of all trades (both block and non-block) has become much smaller (Kim and Murphy, 2013). They attribute this to a variety of factors, including the decimalization of the minimum bid/ask spread, the reduction of trading costs, and the increased use of algorithmic trading. In addition, however, they suggest that institutional traders are increasingly splitting their trades into smaller trances in order to avoid detection of their trades by other traders (such as HFTRs). They find that using the quoted bid/ask spread as a measure of liquidity understates actual trading costs by as much as 40%.

Nonetheless, HFTRs have been shown to substantially reduce quoted bid/ask spreads. For example, Menkveld (2013) finds that the entry of the first HFTR into the Dutch market reduced bid/ask spreads by 50%. Malinova et al. (2013) find that the imposition of a fee on message traffic that disproportionately affected HFTRs resulted in a measurable and economically significant widening in bid/ask spreads for retail traders. Hasbrouck and Saar (2013) find that low-latency trading decreases spreads, increases displayed depth in the limit order book, and reduces short-term volatility. Hendershott et al. (2011) find that, particularly for large stocks, algorithmic trading narrows spreads and reduces adverse selection costs. Similarly, Jovanovic and Menkveld (2012) find that informed HFTRs reduce adverse selection risk for uninformed traders by quickly and continuously updating their quotes to reflect new information, lessening the risk that these traders will post uninformed quotes that are picked off by later-arriving informed traders. Brogaard (2010) finds that HFTRs provide the inside quote 50% of the time.

Brogaard et al. (2014a) find that HFTRs improve price discovery by trading in the direction of permanent price changes, and also trade against transitory price changes, moderating the price impact of large trades. These are merely representative of the many studies that suggest that HFTRs have improved market quality in various ways.

In addition, while the empirical record with respect to front running is slender, Brogaard (2010) finds no evidence of front running. Even Themis Trading, perhaps the most impassioned industry critic of HFT, suggests that front running constitutes <20% of all HFT (Arnuk and Saluzzi, 2009). Moreover, HFTRs that front run institutional orders are likely to be active (or "aggressive") rather than passive traders. However, most studies show that passive trading predominates (e.g., Jovanovic and Menkveld, 2012).

But in any case, even if we concede that some HFTRs increase institutional costs of execution some of the time, it is an empirical question whether the positive effects of HFT on institutional execution costs outweigh the negatives. The evidence suggests that the positives dominate.

Figure 8.2 shows that, between 2009 and 2014, overall institutional costs of execution fell. Indeed, extending the data back to 2003—close to the dawn of the HFT age—institutional execution costs have experienced a secular decline. Implementation costs were 63 basis points in Q3 of 2003. However, by Q1 of 2006, such costs had fallen to 44 basis points. By Q4 of 2013, they were 40 basis points (Remarks of Chair Mary Jo White, 2014). Importantly, these figures measure implementation cost, which takes into account price slippage between the initiation of an institutional trade and its conclusion. This evidence is inconsistent with the view that the presence of HFT in securities markets has resulted in an increase in institutional execution costs.

Brogaard et al. (2014b) examine the implementation costs of institutional investors trading over the London Stock Exchange. They find that institutional execution costs have been falling since 2003, with an interruption associated with the 2008 financial crisis. They also find no evidence that HFT activity has resulted in an increase in institutional execution costs.

Above, three different interpretations were suggested of the phrase "vanishing" or "illusory" liquidity. The first (that detection of an institutional trade results in widening of the bid/ask spread, and/or withdrawal of liquidity from the market) is a rational response by a market maker to the possibility that the block trader is informed, and/or that the block trade will result in transitory price pressure that will expose the market maker to the risk of losses at the hands of other traders if it does not update its quotes. It is not only HFTRs that widen their bid/ask spreads in these circumstances; traditional market makers will react in a similar manner. Thus, this version of "vanishing liquidity" is no more an indictment of HFT than it is of traditional market makers.

The second usage of the phrase "vanishing" or "illusory" liquidity refers to the large number of HFTR quotes that are canceled before being executed (often within a fraction of a second of being submitted) and hence the high HFTR ratio of orders to trades. Again, however, as already discussed, there is nothing sinister about this (with the

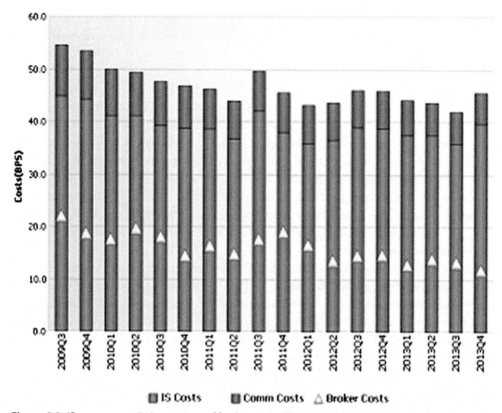

Figure 8.2 IS costs, commission costs, and broker costs. *(Source: ITG Peer Analysis Global Cost Review, Q4 2013, available at http://itg.com/marketing/ITG_GlobalCostReview_Q42013_20140509.pdf. Note: All values are in basis points (BPS). "IS Costs" means "the difference, or slippage, between the arrival price and the execution price for a trade." "Total Cost" means "the sum of Average Commission" (BPS) and IS Cost (BPS). "Broker Costs" means "the difference, or slippage, between the broker arrival price and the execution price for a trade.")*

exception of those relatively rare situations in which the HFTR seeks to manipulate securities prices through devices such as "spoofing" (or "layering"), which present a unique and easily auditable trading pattern). HFTRs are able to quote very tight bid/ask spreads precisely because their nimble trading reduces adverse selection risk to a minimum. Since every outstanding order constitutes an option for other market traders, the quick cancellation of orders (which are often updated to reflect new information as it arrives) substantially reduces the option value of HFTR quotes.

As noted above, a third meaning of "vanishing" or "illusory" liquidity is the lack of market depth at or near the inside quote, making the quoted NBBO unrepresentative of true market liquidity. However, as Figure 8.3 demonstrates, over the period of time during which HFTRs have become active participants in capital markets, displayed market

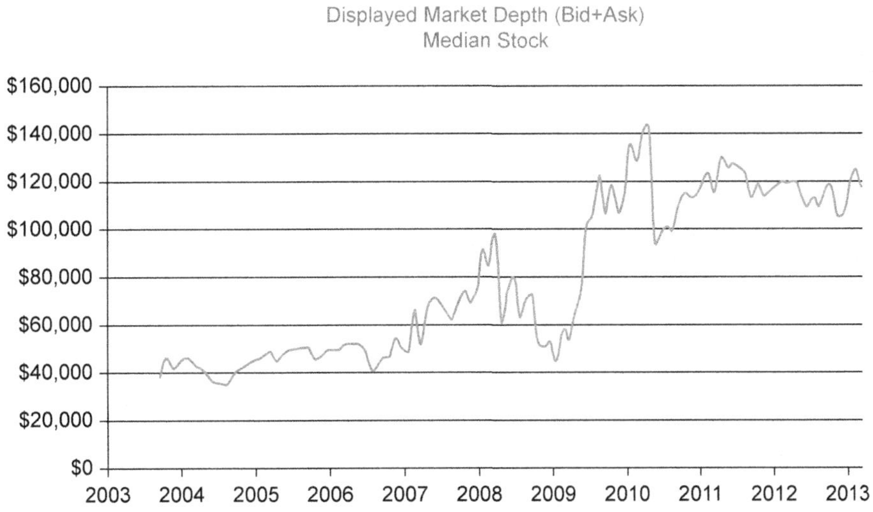

Displayed Market Depth (Bid+Ask)
Median Stock

Figure 8.3 Displayed market depth (Bid + Ask) median stock. *(Source: James J. Angel, Lawrence E. Harris, Chester S. Spratt, "Equity Trading in the twenty-first Century: An update" (using NYSE TAQ data), availabile at http://www.q-group.org/wp-content/uploads/2014/01/Equity-Trading-in-the-21st-Century-An-Update-FINAL1.pdf.)*

depth has increased substantially. Thus, none of the three interpretations of vanishing or illusory liquidity appears to embody a valid criticism of HFT.

There is more evidence that institutional traders are not the hapless victims of HFT that many have asserted. Baron et al. (2012) find that only 7.7% of the total profits of aggressive (liquidity consuming) HFTRs and 2.9% of the profits of mixed HFTRs (i.e., sometimes liquidity making, sometimes liquidity consuming) are earned at the expense of large institutional traders (although 37.2% of aggressive HFTR profits come at the expense of "opportunistic" traders, defined as "brokerage firms, hedgers, small institutional investors, hedge funds, and other hard-to-identify traders").

Further, while passive HFTRs made the lion's share of their profits from trades with opportunistic traders, this is hardly a case of HFTRs abusing other market participants. For one thing, the profits made by passive HFTRs were quite modest in dollar terms (and only just slightly >2% of the profits made by aggressive HFTRs). For another, opportunistic traders are described by Baron et al. as "medium-sized traders who either take large directional positions (but are not large enough to be classified as Fundamental [i.e., institutional] traders) or who move in and out of positions throughout the day but with significantly larger fluctuations and persistence in their positions than HFTs and Non-HFT Market Makers." They are therefore a class of liquidity-demanding traders who are willing to pay for the market making services offered by passive HFTRs. In other words, the profits of passive HFTRs are not made at the expense of these traders, but by virtue of furnishing them with a valuable service.

8.3.5 HFT and Retail Investors

As noted in Part I, one of Michael Lewis' assertions is that the biggest losers from HFT activity are retail investors. The truth is very different. Indeed, retail investors have been the biggest winners from HFT participation in securities markets. This is true despite the fact that HFTRs use their speed and superior information to "pick off" stale quotes posted by uninformed retail investors (i.e., execute against standing retail quotes that are no longer consistent with the best information about the true value of a stock). As in the case of institutional investors, it is the big picture that matters.

Thus, for example, Baron et al. (2012) suggest that the adverse selection cost that traders experience as a result of the presence of aggressive HFTRs (those for whom >60% of their trades are liquidity taking) is small. For trades in the E-mini S&P 500, the average loss per contract was only $0.36. Based on a per contract value of $50,000, this represents a mere 0.0007% of the value of the contract. While retail traders fare worse than the average trader, their average loss is only 1.7 times that realized by the average trader, or about 0.001% of the value of the contract. This is one or two orders of magnitude smaller than the benefit realized by retail and institutional traders as a result of reductions in bid/ask spreads occasioned by the presence of HFTRs. Interestingly, the Baron et al. study also found that retail traders suffered very similar losses when trading with non-HFTRs, a result that suggests that if HFTRs were removed from the capital markets, retail investors' adverse selection risk would not be very materially different than at present.

It should also be noted that, for retail investors, quoted spreads are much closer to the real cost of trading than for institutional investors. Retail orders are sufficiently small to escape the danger of being front run. Thus, they do not suffer from price slippage in the manner of institutional block orders. The increased depth of the limit order book associated with HFT also means that retail investors can take advantage of heightened immediacy.

The decline in retail participation in securities markets in recent years has sometimes been laid at the feet of HFTRs, not only on the basis suggested by Lewis but also because of an asserted popular perception that HFTRs have destabilized securities markets (Zweig, 2012). The Flash Crash of May 6, 2010, is often mentioned in this regard. However, so far as the Flash Crash is concerned, the argument relies on faulty assumptions. One is that the Flash Crash was the result of HFT. This is false. The Flash Crash was triggered by a runaway algorithm employed by a large mutual fund to effect the liquidation of a $4.1 billion block of E-mini S&P 500 contracts. While many HFTRs ultimately withdrew liquidity as the market plunged (Kirelenko et al., 2011), the withdrawal of liquidity is only an indictment of HFT if HFTRs withdrew liquidity at a faster rate than traditional market makers. This can easily be doubted. While traditional market makers are under an obligation to "trade against the market" in order to stabilize the market price, the obligation is not open-ended, nor does it extend to the market maker's entire capital. Indeed, while market intermediaries as a group lost money in the market collapse of October 1987, it has been widely reported that as markets plunged, many market makers simply stopped answering their telephones in order to evade their market making responsibilities to their clients and to the marketplace (Pisani, 2010; Stewart and Hertzberg, 1987).

In addition, it is not clear that even if market makers put their entire capital at risk, they would collectively have sufficient capital to arrest a substantial plunge. The Flash Crash of 2010, for example, trimmed 6% off the Dow Jones Index (and a corresponding amount off the S&P Index and its underlying stocks). If we use a rough figure of $19 trillion for the total capitalization of U.S. public markets (World Bank, 2014), a 6% drop in value represents $1.14 trillion. Even if only 10% of this value was actually at risk, it does not seem realistic to think that traditional market makers would have been willing or able to put sufficient capital at risk to stop such a dramatic slide.

Another questionable assumption is that there is a causal connection (as opposed to a mere correlation) between the Flash Crash (and other technical glitches) and the declining participation of retail investors in capital markets. A more plausible explanation is poor investor returns. Large outflows from mutual funds began in 2008—after the Credit Crisis caused markets to plunge (Zweig, 2012). In fact, the upward surge of markets in 2013 caused a strong rebound in retail participation in the United States (Cox, 2013), Japan (Inagaki, 2013), and Canada (Pelletier, 2014). This rebound occurred despite the occurrence (as recounted above) of multiple technical glitches in markets in 2012 and 2013. By contrast, in India, where retail-heavy small and medium-sized enterprises continue to deliver poor returns, the slump in retail participation has only deepened (Kriplani, 2013; Mascarenhas, 2013).

8.3.6 HFT and Market Crashes

Another frequent criticism of HFT is that HFTRs withdraw liquidity from the market whenever the going gets rough, such as in the May 2010 Flash Crash (e.g., Finger, 2013). This view runs contrary to the evidence. A number of studies (Brogaard, 2010; Brogaard et al., 2014a; Groth, 2011) find that HFTRs do not withdraw when markets are under stress or highly volatile. Similarly, in a study of the European flash crash of August 25, 2011 (on facts that are startlingly reminiscent of the U.S. Flash Crash of 2010), Eurex Exchange found that HFTRs not only continued to supply liquidity but also supplied 30—50 percent of the quotes at the best bid and offer (Automated Trader Magazine, 2013). Indeed, HFTRs thrive in volatile markets, not only because bid/ask spreads are wider but also because their high-speed trading allows them to minimize the high degree of adverse selection risk attendant upon a volatile market.

8.4 CONCLUSION

Critics, of whom Michael Lewis is only the latest, have made a number of assertions regarding HFTRs that do not stand up to the facts. The description of HFTRs as "Wall Street" actors may be a convenient synecdoche, but it is not an accurate description either of the origins of HFT or of the current industry make-up. HFTRs have in fact poached profits from traditional Wall Street actors and have been spectacularly successful in introducing a measure of competition in stock trading that can hardly be described as a congenial development for Wall Street incumbents.

Similarly, the notion that HFTRs siphon billions upon billions of dollars out of financial markets is erroneous. The entire profit earned by the HFT industry in all of 2012 was less than that earned by each of Wells Fargo and Morgan Chase in a single quarter, and somewhere in the vicinity of 1/150 of 1% of the total value of stock traded in 2013. That profit, by any conservative estimate, is far exceeded by the benefits that HFTRs have brought into the marketplace.

The speed with which HFTRs trade is depicted by Michael Lewis as little more than a way to steal from investors. In fact, speed is the tool that enables HFTRs to quote extremely tight bid/ask spreads, by reducing to a minimum the option value of its quotes (and by the same token, the adverse selection component of trading cost). The predominant undertaking of HFTRs is market making, which creates rather than destroys value. Other principal undertakings, such as statistical arbitrage and trading on fundamental information, improve price discovery and make securities markets more efficient.

The theme of Flash Boys is that HFTRs prosper by front running buy-side institutional traders, a charge that has also been made by others. The empirical record, however, is not consistent with this view. Academic studies suggest that front running is not a predominant activity of HFTRs. Even Themis Trading, perhaps the most articulate of the anti-HFT crowd, suggests that front running constitutes <20% of all HFT. In fact, the percentage is probably much smaller. Front running HFTRs will almost certainly trade "aggressively"; i.e., on the active side of the trade. However, the majority of HFTRs trade on the passive side of a transaction.

The empirical record is thus not consistent with the view that front running or other HFTR behaviors, taken singly or collectively, have increased institutional execution costs. Evidence from the United States and the United Kingdom is more consistent with the view that HFTRs have diminished institutional execution costs, which have on the whole declined in the 2003–2014 period.

In like manner, the assertion by Lewis and others that HFT is inimical to the interest of the retail trader is quite mistaken. Even though retail traders are far slower than HFTRs and subject to being adversely selected, the cost of this adverse selection is small compared to the many benefits (such as reduced bid/ask spreads) that HFTRs have brought into the marketplace.

Except as noted below, HFTRs do not exacerbate the likelihood of market crashes. As against the charge that HFTRs liquidity dries up when markets are under stress, studies show that HFTRs thrive in volatile markets, and do not generally withdraw liquidity (the U.S. Flash Crash of May 2010 being an apparent exception caused by an unusual set of circumstances, including the sudden and unexpected routing of high volumes of order flow from internalizers into the public market, creating insuperable pressure on market makers).

While the net benefits that HFTRs have brought into financial markets have been positive, there are some negatives. The chief among these is the heightened systemic risks that have resulted from vastly increased message traffic. From the height of the tech bubble in 1999—2013, the number of quotes pumped into securities markets increased by more than three orders of magnitude (from 1000 quotes per second to 2,000,000 quotes per second) (Finger, 2013). The market fragmentation that HFT has helped to bring about has created an enormously complex web of electronic tentacles binding trading venues, traders, data collectors, regulators, back-office service providers, data backup facilities, phone networks, fiber optic networks, colocation facilities, and the like. This explosion in systems complexity has put unprecedented demands on an inter-locking array of hardware, software, and physical and human components.

Luckily, regulators are paying attention. A host of regulatory actions aimed at man-aging systemic risks have been adopted or are in the pipeline at the SEC, CFTC, and elsewhere.

In addition, some HFTRs have adopted tactics, such as front running, spoofing, quote stuffing and smoking, that subtract from market quality and abuse other investors. The job of the regulators is to address these particular behaviors without jettisoning the mani-fold advantages that HFTRs have brought into the marketplace.

While colocation is an integral element of some of these abuses, it is not at all clear that there is any easy solution. If colocation were to be banned, HFTRs would undoubt-edly respond by purchasing expensive real estate in close proximity to various trading venues. This would only subtract from market quality. For one thing, it is likely that at least some of the added costs would be passed on to investors. For another, the vastly increased costs of achieving physical proximity would necessarily result in functional colocation being made available to a much smaller number of well-heeled actors. In addi-tion, trading venues currently give all colocated customers equal lengths of cable, to ensure that no one colocated customer has an advantage over any other. Creating data parity would be far more difficult to do if high-frequency servers were located outside each trading venue. As a result, the best-capitalized firms would likely realize a speed advantage over their competitors, raising entry barriers and stifling competition.

Another controversial aspect of the current market structure is maker/taker pricing, in which a trading venue pays liquidity rebates to the passive side of a trade and an access fee to the active side. Such liquidity rebates facilitate HFTRs market making by encouraging

HFTRs to line the limit order books of various trading venues with passive limit orders. Maker/taker pricing lowers the cost of market making and almost certainly tightens bid/ask spreads. It also compensates the maker of liquidity for the option value represented by the posting of passive limit orders. Unfortunately, it also creates a variance between the broker's duty of best execution and her financial well-being. The source of the conflict lies in the fact that client charges do not vary with the broker's cost of trading at different venues. Thus, a broker has an incentive to internalize order flow via a proprietary dark pool, or to route active order flow (such as retail orders) to a trading venue that has lower (or no) access fees, an internalizer that purchases the broker's retail order flow, or a trading venue with taker/maker pricing, even if this does not result in best execution for the client. There is a corresponding incentive to route passive order flow to the trading venue that offers the highest liquidity rebate—again regardless of the quality of execution for the client. Battilio et al. (2013) present evidence that these conflicts of interest do in fact impair fulfillment of the broker's duty of best execution.

Regulators should nonetheless be cautious about eliminating maker/taker pricing. By compensating the maker of liquidity for the option value of its quotes, it allows HFTRs to quote tighter spreads. By attracting HFTR order flow, such pricing has allowed small trading venues, more nimble and responsive to shifts in market demand and technology than their larger competitors, to compete against industry incumbents. This competition has been of benefit to all investors.

Moreover, as Tabb (2014) points out, maker/taker pricing is far from unique in distorting order routing decisions. Other sources of conflict include trading venue pricing tiers (whereby large volume traders are the beneficiaries of lower trading fees, incentivizing large operators to route their order flow to a single venue), order internalization (where owners of internalizer platforms have an incentive to internalize their own order flow rather than exposing it to the public market), payment for order flow (where retail brokers have an incentive to route order flow to the internalizer that pays them the highest fee), "and soft-dollar relationships in which commission dollars are used to pay for brokerage services, typically including trading tools, research, and corporate access." Any review of maker/taker pricing should include a review of all these potentially distortionary practices, keeping in mind that a first best solution is rarely possible; that is, all potential market structures yield both positives and negatives. A broad range of regulatory solutions must therefore be canvassed with a view to finding the best possible trade-off within inevitable practical and institutional constraints.

Yet another conflict of interest arises when broker/dealers who generate order flow have an ownership interest in a particular trading venue. These broker/dealers have an incentive to route order flow to that venue, even if this does not achieve best execution, in order to enhance the value of their ownership stake. Such behavior is capable of harming a client's interests, and, by routing order flow (and hence profits) away from competitor trading venues, can be used as an anticompetitive device.

Another problematic aspect of HFT is the much-discussed "arms race," in which HFTRs compete for greater and greater speed with declining, and ultimately negative social utility. Budish et al. (2013) argue that, because of "relativistic" limitations (i.e., the finite speed of message traffic between geographically disparate locations), arbitrage opportunities are robust to competition. For this reason, the arms race has no natural end point. Budish et al. suggest that holding "batch auctions" at discrete intervals, such as 5 or 10 ms, and in which all quotes arriving within the interim receive the same priority, will largely naturally cap the speed advantage of HFTRs and end the arms race. The SEC has signaled that it is currently exploring this option.

In the end, HFT is here to stay. Business models may morph as regulators change the parameters of the game, but HFT is not going away. From the time when carrier pigeons were the state of the art in spiriting information from one place to another, through a variety of successive technologies such as overland and undersea cables, the telegraph, the telephone, the internet, and now hyperfast information processors with artificial intelligence capability allied to communications networks whose latencies are measured in microseconds, speed means profit. The name of the game is to ensure that this speed is used in productive and not destructive ways. The evidence is consistent with the view that this is a very attainable goal.

REFERENCES

Adler, J., August 3, 2012. Raging Bulls: How Wall Street Got Addicted to Light-Speed Trading. Wired. http://www.wired.com/2012/08/ff_wallstreet_trading/all/.

Alden, W., March 18, 2014a. Inquiry into High-Speed Trading Widens. The New York Times. http://dealbook.nytimes.com/2014/03/18/schneiderman-announces-inquiry-into-services-for-high-speed-traders/?_php=true&_type=blogs&_r=0.

Alden, W., April 17, 2014b. Virtu Financial Said to Shelve I.P.O. Plans. The New York Times. http://dealbook.nytimes.com/2014/04/17/virtu-financial-said-to-shelve-i-p-o-plans/?_php=true&_type=blogs&_r=0.

Alden, W., June 16, 2014c. Senate Hearing on Fairness of High-Speed Stock Trading Could Get Heated. The New York Times. http://dealbook.nytimes.com/2014/06/16/senate-panel-to-scrutinize-possible-conflicts-in-the-stock-market/?_php=true&_type=blogs&_r=0.

Alden, W., de la Merced, M.J., April 4, 2014. High-Frequency Trading Firm Virtu Is Said to Delay I.P.O. The New York Times. http://dealbook.nytimes.com/2014/04/02/virtu-high-frequency-trading-firm-is-said-to-delay-i-p-o/?_php=true&_type=blogs&_r=0.

Arnuk, S., Saluzzi, J., December 4, 2009. Latency Arbitrage: The Real Power Behind Predatory High Frequency Trading. Themis Trading. http://www.themistrading.com/article_files/0000/0519/THEMIS_TRADING_White_Paper_-_Latency_Arbitrage_-_December_4__2009.pdf.

Automated Trader Magazine, 2013. Eurex Exchange Releases Results of Proprietary Research. Automated Trader Magazine 30. http://www.automatedtrader.net/magazine/33/Issue-29-Q2-2013.

Baram, M., March 27, 2014. Michael Lewis Exposes High-Frequency Trading: "You're Enabling People to Screw Their Customers". Value Walk. http://www.valuewalk.com/2014/03/michael-lewis-exposes-high-frequency-trading-youre-enabling-people-screw-customers.

Baron, M., Brogaard, J., Kirilenko, A., 2012. The Trading Profits of High Frequency Traders. Working Paper. University of Chicago, Chicago, Illinois.

Battilio, R., Corwin, S., Jennings, R., 2013. Can Brokers Have It All? On the Relation between Make Take Fees and Limit Order Execution Quality. Working Paper. Notre Dame, Notre Dame, Indiana.

Brogaard, J., 2010. High Frequency Trading and Its Impact on Market Quality. Working Paper. Northwestern University, Evanston, Illinois.

Brogaard, J., Hendershott, T., Riordan, R., 2014a. High-frequency trading and price discovery. Rev. Financ. Stud. 27 (8), 2267–2306.

Brogaard, J., Hendershott, T., Hunt, S., Ysusi, C., 2014b. High-frequency trading and the execution costs of institutional investors. Financ. Rev. 49, 345–369.

Budish, E., Crampton, P., Shim, J., 2013. The High-Frequency Trading Arms Race: Frequent Batch Auctions as a Market Design Response. Working Paper. University of Chicago, Chicago, Illinois.

CFTC Press Release 6928-14, May 28, 2014. CFTC's Technology Advisory Committee to Meet on June 3, 2014. CFTC. www.cftc.gov/PressRoom/PressReleases/pr6938-14.

CFTC, September 12, 2013. Concept release on risk controls and system safeguards for automated trading environments; proposed rule. Fed. Regist. 78 (177), 56541–56574.

Clark, C., 2012. How to Keep Markets Safe in the Era of High-Speed Trading. Working Paper #303. The Federal Reserve Bank of Chicago, Chicago, Illinois.

CNBC, August 20, 2013. Goldman Trading Glitch Could Cost More Than $100 Million. CNBC. http://www.cnbc.com/id/100976404.

Cochrane, A., March 31, 2014. New York State AG Schneiderman: Some High-Frequency Trading Practices "May Be Illegal". CBS News. http://www.cbsnews.com/news/new-york-state-ag-eric-schneiderman-some-high-frequency-trading-practices-may-be-illegal.

Cox, J., December 9, 2013. Retail and Big-Money Crowd Heading in Opposite Directions. CNBC NetNet. http://www.cnbc.com/id/101258193.

Davidoff, S.M., February 11, 2014. S.E.C.'s Review of Trading Will See Some of Its Own Work. The New York Times. http://dealbook.nytimes.com/2014/02/11/s-e-c-s-review-of-stock-trading-will-see-some-of-its-own-work/.

Durden, T., March 3, 2014. The Holy Grail of Trading Has Been Found: HFT Firm Reveals 1 Losing Trading Day in 1238 Days of Trading. HSBC Global Banking. http://www.zerohedge.com/news/2014-03-10/holy-grail-trading-has-been-found-hft-firm-reveals-1-losing-trading-day-1238-days-tr.

ElBoghdady, D., April 4, 2014. Justice Dept. Investigating High-Frequency Traders. The Washington Post. http://www.washingtonpost.com/business/economy/justice-department-investigating-high-frequency-traders/2014/04/04/e77d1cb4-bc00-11e3-9c3c-311301e2167d_story.html.

Finger, R., September 30, 2013. High Frequency Trading: Is It a Dark Force Against Ordinary Human Traders and Investors? Forbes. http://www.forbes.com/sites/richardfinger/2013/09/30/high-frequency-trading-is-it-a-dark-force-against-ordinary-human-traders-and-investors/.

Frankel, D., Saphir, A., April 25, 2013. CBOE Dark for Much of Day Due to Software Glitch. Reuters. http://www.reuters.com/article/2013/04/26/us-cboe-delay-idUSBRE93O0XV20130426.

Freifeld, K., March 18, 2014. New York's Schneiderman Seeks Curbs on High-Frequency Traders. Reuters. http://www.reuters.com/article/2014/03/18/us-highfrequency-nyag-idUSBREA2H0K120140318.

FTSE Global Markets, November 26, 2012. A Head Start for HFT, or a Downward Spiral? FTSE Global Markets, 66. http://www.ftseglobalmarkets.com/issues/issue-66-november-2012/a-headstart-for-hft-or-a-downward-spiral.html.

Gammeltoft, N., Griffin, D., August 20, 2013. Goldman Sachs Said to Send Stock-Option Orders by Mistake. Bloomberg. http://www.bloomberg.com/news/2013-08-20/goldman-says-exchanges-working-to-resolve-options-order-mishap.html.

Gandel, S., July 9, 2014. Senate Panel Backs High Frequency Trading, and Gets Nowhere. Fortune. http://fortune.com/2014/07/09/high-frequency-trading-senate/.

Geiger, K., Hurtado, P., April 1, 2014. FBI Seeks Help from High-Frequency Traders to Find Abuses. Bloomberg. http://www.bloomberg.com/news/2014-03-31/fbi-said-to-probe-high-speed-traders-over-abuse-of-information.html.

Golub, A., 2011. Overview of High Frequency Trading. Traders place: Clenow Futures Intelligence Report. Manchester Business School, Manchester, UK.

Gomber, P., Arndt, B., Lutat, M., Uhle, T., 2011. High-Frequency Trading. Working Paper (commissioned by Deutsche Borse Group). Goethe University, Frankfurt am Main.

Groth, S., 2011. Does Algorithmic Trading Increase Volatility? Empirical Evidence from the Fully-electronic Trading Platform Xetra. Working Paper. Goethe University, Frankfurt am Main, Germany.

Hagströmerm, B., Norden, L.L., 2013. The Diversity of High-frequency Traders. Working Paper. Stockholm University, Stockholm, Sweden.

Hasbrouck, J., Saar, G., 2013. Low-Latency Trading. Working Paper. Cornell University, Ithaca, New York.

Hendershott, T., Jones, C.M., Menkveld, A.J., 2011. Does algorithmic trading improve liquidity? J. Finance 66 (1), 1–33.

Hope, B., January 14, 2014. Nasdaq Cancels Deal to Operate Data Feed. The Wall Street Journal. http://online.wsj.com/news/articles/SB10001424052702304549504579320754286900452.

IIROC (Investment Industry Regulatory Organization of Canada), 2011. The HOT Study: Phases I and II of IIROC's Study of High Frequency Trading Activity on Canadian Equity Marketplaces. IIROC, Toronto, Ontario.

Inagaki, K., April 6, 2013. Investors Take Plunge: Japan's Mrs. Watanabe Decides It's Time to Buy Stocks. The Wall Street Journal. http://online.wsj.com/news/articles/SB10001424127887323916304578404141851559674.

Jarnecic, E., Snape, M., 2010. An Analysis of Trades by High Frequency Participants on the London Stock Exchange. Working Paper. University of Sydney, Sydney, Australia.

Jarnecic, E., Snape, M., 2014. The provision of liquidity by high-frequency participants. Financ. Rev. 49, 371–394.

Jovanovic, B., Menkveld, A.J., 2012. Middlemen in Limit Order Markets. Working Paper. New York University, New York.

Knight Holdco, Inc., February 12, 2013. Form S4 Registration Statement. http://www.sec.gov/Archives/edgar/data/1569391/000119312513053260/d484578ds4.htm.

Kim, S., Murphy, D., 2013. The Impact of High-Frequency Trading on Stock Market Liquidity Measures. Working Paper. Northwestern University, Evanston, Illinois.

Kirilenko, A., Kyle, A.S., Samadi, M., Tuzun, T., 2011. The Flash Crash: The Impact of High Frequency Trading on an Electronic Market. Working Paper. University of Maryland, College Park, MN, CFTC, Washington, DC.

Knutson, T., April 10, 2014. White: No Changes in SEC's High-Frequency Trading Stance. Financial Advisor. http://www.fa-mag.com/news/white-no-changes-in-sec-s-high-frequency-trading-stance-17581.html?section=.

Kriplani, J., October 21, 2013. Retail Volumes in Cash Segment of Equity Markets Dip 20% in 2013. The Financial Express. http://www.financialexpress.com/news/retail-volumes-in-cash-segment-of-equity-markets-dip-20-in-2013/1183882.

Leising, M., May 30, 2014. High-Speed Trading Perks Said to Be Focus of CFTC Review. Bloomberg. http://www.bloomberg.com/news/2014-05-29/hft-perks-are-focus-of-cftc-review-source-says.html.

Levine, M., March 20, 2014b. Why Do High Frequency Traders Never Lose Money? Bloomberg View. http://www.bloombergview.com/articles/2014-03-20/why-do-high-frequency-traders-never-lose-money.

Levine, M., June 5, 2014. SEC Will Keep Thinking About High Frequency Trading. Bloomberg View. http://www.bloombergview.com/articles/2014-06-05/sec-will-keep-thinking-about-high-frequency-trading.

Lewis, Michael, 2014. Flash Boys. W.W. Norton & Company, New York, NY.

Lopez, L., August 21, 2013a. Goldman Sachs' Massive Trading Error Bears a Scary Resemblance to the One That Brought Down Knight Capital. Business Insider. http://www.businessinsider.com/goldman-knight-capital-trading-errors-2013-8.

Lopez, L., September 24, 2013b. New York's Attorney General Has Declared War on Cheating High-Frequency Traders. Business Insider. http://www.businessinsider.com/schneiderman-targets-hft-front-running-2013-9.

MacSweeney, G., March 18, 2013a. HFT Profits Shrinking? The Data Doesn't Lie. Information Week Wall Street and Technology. http://www.wallstreetandtech.com/trading-technology/hft-profits-shrinking-the-data-doesnt-lie/a/d-id/1267900?

MacSweeney, G., April 2013b. Isn't This Getting a Little…Nuts? Information Week Wall Street Technology. http://www.wallstreetandtech.com/messages.asp?piddl_msgthreadid=13289&piddl_msgid=218036.

Malinova, K., Park, A., Riordan, R., 2013. Do Retail Traders Suffer from High Frequency Traders? University of Toronto, Toronto, Ontario. Working Paper.

Mascarenhas, R., October 21, 2013. Retail Participation at 10-Year Low: Investors Keep Off Rally, Seek Safety in NSCs, Bonds. The Economic Times. http://articles.economictimes.indiatimes.com/2013-10-21/news/43250490_1_retail-investors-small-investors-destimoney-securities.

Maslin, J., March 31, 2014. Hobbling Wall Street Cowboys. The New York Times. http://www.nytimes.com/2014/04/01/books/flash-boys-by-michael-lewis-a-tale-of-high-speed-trading.html?_r=0.

Massoudi, A., Alloway, T., March 31, 2014. "Flash Boys" Starts Wall St Soul Searching. Financial Times. http://www.ft.com/intl/cms/s/0/6f514f02-b684-11e3-b230-00144feabdc0.html.

McCrank, J., July 17, 2014. Exclusive: SEC Targets 10 Firms in High Frequency Trading Probe—SEC Document. Reuters. http://tabbforum.com/news/sec-targets-10-firms-in-high-frequency-trading-probe-sec-document?utm_source=TabbFORUM+Alerts&utm_campaign=b6d61fc1d2-UA-12160392-1&utm_medium=email&utm_term=0_29f4b8f8f1-b6d61fc1d2-275994673.

Menkveld, A.J., 2013. High frequency trading and the new market makers. J. Financ. Mark. 16, 712—740.

Norris, F., August 22, 2013. In Markets' Tuned-Up Machinery, Stubborn Ghosts Remain. The New York Times. http://dealbook.nytimes.com/2013/08/22/in-markets-tuned-up-machinery-stubborn-ghosts-remain/?_php=true&_type=blogs&_r=0.

Oran, O., Spicer, J., Mikolajczak, C., Mollenkamp, C., March 24, 2012. BATS Exchange Withdraws IPO After Stumbles. Reuters. http://www.reuters.com/article/2012/03/24/us-bats-trading-idUSBRE82M0W020120324.

Overholt, K., January 1, 2014. High-Frequency Trading: Friend or Foe? On Point Investment Management Blog. http://blogs.advent.com/on-point/2013/01/14/high-frequency-trading-friend-or-foe/.

Parker, T., April 04, 2014. Has High Frequency Trading Ruined the Stock Market for the Rest of Us? Investopedia. http://www.investopedia.com/financial-edge/0113/has-high-frequency-trading-ruined-the-stock-market-for-the-rest-of-us.aspx.

Paterson, S., 2012. Dark Pools: The Rise of the Machine Traders and the Rigging of the U.S. Stock Market. Crown Business, New York, NY.

Pelletier, M., March 24, 2014. Should Retail Investors Continue Plowing into Stocks or Follow the Smart Money? The Financial Post. http://business.financialpost.com/2014/03/24/should-you-plow-into-stocks-or-follow-the-smart-money/.

Perlberg, S., March 11, 2014. Everyone's Talking About the High-Frequency Trading Firm That Just Had 1 Day of Trading Losses in 1238 Days. Business Insider. http://www.businessinsider.com/virtu-hft-only-one-losing-day-2014-3.

Phillips, M., June 6, 2013. How the Robots Lost: High-Frequency Trading's Rise and Fall. Bloomberg Businessweek Technology. http://www.businessweek.com/articles/2013-06-06/how-the-robots-lost-high-frequency-tradings-rise-and-fall.

Pisani, B., September 13, 2010. Man vs. Machine: How Stock Trading Got So Complex. CNBC. http://www.cnbc.com/id/38978686#.

Popper, N., August 2, 2012a. Knight Capital Says Trading Glitch Cost It $440 Million. The New York Times. http://dealbook.nytimes.com/2012/08/02/knight-capital-says-trading-mishap-cost-it-440-million/?_php=true&_type=blogs&_r=0.

Popper, N., October 14, 2012b. High-Speed Trading No Longer Hurtling Forward. The New York Times. http://www.ftseglobalmarkets.com/issues/issue-66-november-2012/a-headstart-for-hft-or-a-down-ward-spiral.html.

Remarks of Chair Mary Jo White, June 5, 2014. Sandler O'Neill & Partners, L.P. In: Global Exchange and Brokerage Conference, New York, NY. http://www.sec.gov/News/Speech/Detail/Speech/1370542004312#.U8lFjhZIni4.

Rodier, M., April 9, 2013. Struggling HFT Firms Focus on New Technologies. Information Week Wall-Street and Technology. http://www.wallstreetandtech.com/it-infrastructure/struggling-hft-firms-focus-on-new-techno/240152559.

Ross, A., May 16, 2014. Flash Boys by Michael Lewis—Review. The Guardian. http://www.theguardian. com/books/2014/may/16/flash-boys-michael-lewis-review.

Rubenstein, A., April 30, 2014. Thank You, Michael Lewis. CNBC Commentary. http://archive.today/ FfyQm.

Schaefer, S., March 23, 2012. Bad Day for BATS: IPO Canceled, Snafu Causes Apple Halt. Forbes. http:// www.forbes.com/sites/steveschaefer/2012/03/23/bad-day-for-bats-ipo-falls-flat-snafu-causes-apple-halt/.

SEC Release 34-67091, May 31, 2012. Joint Industry Plans; Order Approving, on a Pilot Basis, the National Market System Plan to Address Extraordinary Market Volatility by BATS Exchange, Inc., BATS Y-Exchange, Inc., Chicago Board Options Exchange, Incorporated, Chicago Stock Exchange, Inc., EDGA Exchange, Inc., EDGX Exchange, Inc., Financial Industry Regulatory Authority, Inc., NAS-DAQ OMX BX, Inc., NASDAQ OMX PHLX LLC, the Nasdaq Stock Market LLC, National Stock Exchange, Inc., New York Stock Exchange LLC, NYSE MKT LLC, and NYSE Arca, Inc. SEC. http:// www.sec.gov/rules/sro/nms/2012/34-67091.pdf.

SEC Release 34-63241, November 3, 2010c. Risk Management Controls for Brokers or Dealers with Market Access. http://www.sec.gov/rules/final/2010/34-63241.pdf.

SEC Release 34-69077, March 8, 2013b. Regulation System Compliance and Integrity. SEC. http://www. sec.gov/rules/proposed/2013/34-69077.pdf.

SEC Press Release 2013-95, May 29, 2013. SEC Charges NASDAQ for Failures During Facebook IPO. SEC. http://www.sec.gov/News/PressRelease/Detail/PressRelease/1365171575032#.U8XhYxZIni4.

Senate Committee on Agriculture, Nutrition and Forestry, May 13, 2014. High Frequency and Automated Trading in Futures Markets. Senate Committee on Agriculture, Nutrition and Forestry. http://www.ag. senate.gov/hearings/high-frequency-and-automated-trading-in-futures-markets.

Senate Committee on Banking, Housing, and Urban Affairs, June 18, 2014a. High Frequency Trading's Impact on the Economy. Senate Committee on Banking, Housing, and Urban Affairs. http://www. banking.senate.gov/public/index.cfm?FuseAction=Hearings.Hearing&Hearing_ID=2ab3ead5-3ee1-422d-a0ce-a8c599fac03d.

Senate Committee on Banking, Housing, and Urban Affairs, July 8, 2014b. The Role of Regulation in Shaping Equity Market Structure and Electronic Trading. Senate Committee on Banking, Housing, and Urban Affairs. http://www.banking.senate.gov/public/index.cfm?FuseAction=Hearings.Hearing&Hearing_ID =2e98337f-d5c5-490f-80e7-6c1c81af7243.

Senate Permanent Subcommittee on Investigations, June 17, 2014. Conflicts of Interest, Investor Loss of Confidence, and High Speed Trading in U.S. Stock Markets. Permanent Subcommittee on Investiga-tions. http://www.hsgac.gov/subcommittees/investigations/hearings/conflicts-of-interest-investor-loss-of-confidence-and-high-speed-trading-in-us-stock-markets.

Stewart, J.B., Hertzberg, D., November 20, 1987. How the Stock Market Almost Disintegrated a Day After the Crash. The Wall Street Journal. http://online.wsj.com/news/articles/SB119256599114260941.

Tabb, L., June 20, 2014. Can the Markets Function Without Maker-Taker? TABB Forum. http:// tabbforum.com/opinions/can-the-markets-function-without-maker-taker.

The World Bank, 2014. Market Capitalization of Listed Companies (Current US$). The World Bank. http://data.worldbank.org/indicator/CM.MKT.LCAP.CD.

U.S. Congress, 2010. Dodd-Frank Wall Street Reform and Consumer Protection Act. Pub. L. No. 111-203, § 929-Z, 124 Stat. 1376, 1871 (2010) (codified at 15 U.S.C. § 78o) [Bluebook R. 12.4].

Value Walk, March 30, 2014. Stock Market Rigged, Says Michael Lewis in New Book and in an Interview on 60 Minutes. Value Walk. http://www.valuewalk.com/2014/03/michael-lewis-60-minutes.

Wah, E., Wellman, M.P., 2013. Latency arbitrage, market fragmentation, and efficiency: a two-model. In: Proceedings of the Fourteenth ACM Conference on Electronic Commerce. ACM New York, New York, NY.

Wang, L., April 15, 2013. Getco Profit Drops 90% as Equity Volumes Slump. Bloomberg. http://www. bloomberg.com/news/2013-04-15/getco-profit-drops-90-to-16-2-million-as-equity-volumes-slump. html.

Zweig, J., August 2, 2012. When Will Retail Investors Call It Quits? The Wall Street Journal. http://online. wsj.com/news/articles/SB10000872396390443545504577563511537138938.

CHAPTER 9

High-Frequency Trading: Past, Present, and Future

François-Serge Lhabitant[1], Greg N. Gregoriou[2]

[1]CEO and CIO, Kedge Capital, Jersey; EDHEC Business School, Nice, France; [2]State University of New York (Plattsburgh), NY, USA

Contents

9.1 INTRODUCTION

The advent of fast and affordable computers has encouraged the development of program trading in the 1980s and later on, electronic trading and algorithmic trading in the 1990s. Initially, the focus was the optimal execution of large orders through electronic platforms, primarily by splitting them automatically into smaller ones and bringing them to the market in a way designed to minimize price impact. Progressively, with technological advances in market access, narrowing spreads, increased processing speed, regulatory changes, and the availability of large tick-by-tick data sets, the focus has gradually shifted to higher-frequency trading (HFT). Today, HFT represents the majority of trading volumes on exchanges. Its strategies typically consists in moving in and out of extremely short-term positions to capture fraction of pennies in profit on every trade, with a view that extremely large volumes of transactions can compensate the low margin per trade.

Concerns about HFT have increased following the Flash Crash of May 6, 2010, when the Dow Jones Industrial Average (DJIA) lost almost 1000 points in intraday trading, and the publication of a controversial book by Michael Lewis on that topic, which makes the claim that this practice is harmful for smaller investors. However, this discussion is not new and has been going on in the securities industry for almost a decade. High frequency

The Handbook of High Frequency Trading
ISBN 978-0-12-802205-4

(HF) traders claim that their activity enhances liquidity, increases pricing efficiency, reduces transaction costs, and lowers market volatility. Opponents are worried about their potential impact on systemic risk, fairness, and transparency, particularly when venturing into dark pools and over-the-counter markets, and their ability to manipulate stock prices. Most regulators have stepped in and are now scrutinizing and regulating—although with very different approaches depending on the region. In this chapter, we offer a review of the evolution of HFT, discuss its current status, and examine its possible future.

9.2 THE ORIGINS OF HFT

In its early days, HFT—or maybe we should call it *higher-frequency trading*—was not about round-trip execution times expressed in milliseconds. It was about using modern technology to gain information, analyze it, and act upon it before the rest of the financial market. The first important milestone in this direction was the creation of the National Association of Securities Dealers Automated Quotations (NASDAQ) in 1971, as it allowed the quotation of 2500 over-the-counter stocks on what was initially a simple computer bulletin board. The second one was the introduction of the Designated Order Turnaround system (DOT) on the New York Stock Exchange (NYSE) in 1976, followed by the Super-DOT in 1984. With these systems, small orders for listed securities were no longer phoned down to a floor trader and processed manually but were sent directly to a specialist on the trading floor. Computer automation allowed for faster execution, better reporting, and facilitated the dissemination of information. It also opened the door of program trading and electronic trading to large institutional traders such as investment banks.

Electronic trading received a big boost in the 1990s with the emergence of electronic communication networks (ECNs). ECNs allowed individual investors to subscribe to the system and enter orders electronically into the network via a custom computer terminal. Orders were matched internally (outside of regular exchanges) and executed whenever possible. If no match was found, orders were sent to the exchange for execution as soon as they became the best price. ECNs dramatically lowered execution speed and lowered transaction costs, two prerequisites for the development of sophisticated automated execution strategies and algorithmic trading by investment banks, as well as by some pension funds, mutual funds, and other buy-side investors.

Ultimately, support for electronic and HFT came from regulators, more specifically from three important decisions taken by the Securities and Exchange Commission (SEC). In 1998, the SEC passed the Regulation Alternative Trading Systems (Reg. ATS), which resulted in the proliferation of alternative electronic trading platforms competing against the more traditional markets such as the NYSE and the NASDAQ. As a result, the same security can trade across multiple venues, creating opportunities for arbitrage. In 2001, the SEC ordered securities markets to decimalize—that is, to quote stock

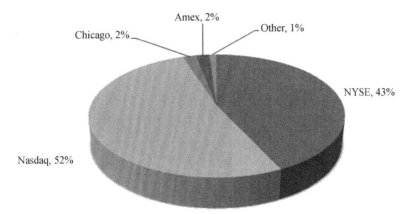

Figure 9.1 *The US Market Structure (market share by exchange) in 1997.*

prices in decimals instead of increments of $1/16 or $1/8 of a dollar, or $0.0625. In most cases, competition immediately tightened spreads between bids and asks to a penny, implying trading in and immediately out was not as costly as it used to be.[1] Finally, in 2005, to promote competition among exchanges and allow for greater access, the SEC pushed through Regulation National Market System (Reg. NMS), which applied equally to all markets with no distinction between exchanges and security associations like the NASDAQ. Reg. NMS required in particular "that market orders be posted electronically and immediately executed at the best price nationally" (see Shorter and Miller (2014)). As a result, any trader could profit from any small price difference of a security between two different exchanges, provided he/she was fast enough to act versus his/her peers.

The result is illustrated in Figures 9.1 and 9.2. In a couple of years, markets became competitive and fragmented, with more than 13 exchanges, 50 dark pools,[2] and alternate electronic trading systems. In a sense, the SEC thought that replacing Wall Street by computers was a great idea. What it probably did not expect is that it also sown the seeds for the development of HFT as we know it today.

9.3 HFT TODAY

Financial regulators, market participants, and most operators seem to have a strong opinion on HFT. Despite this, a common definition of what HFT is exactly seems to be difficult to find. This is not very surprising because HFT is not a simple trading strategy or

---

[1] Note that the situation is somehow different in some European markets, where the tick size may depend on the stock price level.

[2] A dark pool is a private forum only open to sophisticated traders for buying and selling securities. Unlike in a stock exchange, the size and price of the orders are not revealed to other participants. Note that despite their name, all dark pools are broker-dealers registered with the SEC and the Financial Industry Regulatory Authority (FINRA).

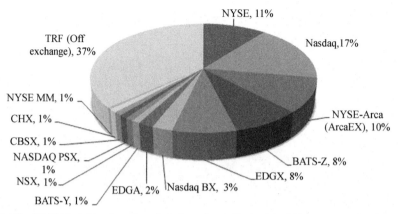

Figure 9.2 *The US Market Structure (market share by exchange) in 2014.*

a monolithic phenomenon, but rather the use of the latest technological advances in market access, market data access, and order routing to optimize the profitability of a diverse range of *established* trading strategies. Most of the time, these HFT strategies have only one thing in common, the need to be competitively fast in order to address profit opportunities. Moreover, they are protean in nature and keep updating their algorithms on a continuous basis, which explain some of the suspicion and hostility they are facing.

9.3.1 The Regulators Perspective

While the SEC (2010) has not formally defined HF traders, it describes them as "professional traders acting in a proprietary capacity that engage in strategies that generate a large number of trades on a daily basis." This definition is both broad and subjective, but since HFT is a moving target, it is difficult to be more specific. Fortunately, Commissioner O'Malia has suggested in his letter to the Technology Advisory Committee of the SEC in 2011, a list of seven characteristics often seen at HFT. It includes: (1) "the use of extraordinarily high-speed order submission/cancellation/modification systems with speeds in excess of 5 milliseconds or generally very close to minimal latency of a trade; (2) the use of computer programs or algorithms for automated decision making where order initiation, generating, routing, and execution are determined by the system without human direction for each individual trade or order; (3) the use of co-location services, direct market access, or individual data feeds offered by exchanges and others to minimize network and other types of latencies; (4) very short time-frames for establishing and liquidating positions; (5) high daily portfolio turnover and/or a high order-to-trade ratio intraday; (6) the submission of numerous orders that are canceled immediately or within milliseconds after submission; and (7) ending the trading day in as close to a flat position as possible (not carrying significant, un-hedged positions overnight" (CFTC,

2011, pp. 1–2). Note that having only one of these characteristics is sufficient for a firm to be classified as a HF trader by the SEC.

In Europe, the European Securities and Markets Authority (ESMA) has recently opened its consultation on the review of the Markets in Financial Instrument Directive (MiFID II). In its Article 4.1.40, it defines HFT by the following characteristics: "(1) an infrastructure intended to minimize network and other types of latencies, including at least one of the following facilities for algorithmic order entry: colocation, proximity hosting, or high-speed direct electronic access; (2) system-determination of order initiation, generation, routing, or execution without human intervention for individual trades or orders; and (3) high message[3] intraday rates which constitute orders, quotes, or cancellations." Interestingly, the ESMA also indicates that trading volumes should be estimated over a 12-month rolling period, and that 2 messages per second (75,000 messages per day) or more would be considered as a HFT activity.

9.3.2 Key Strategies

Classifying HFT strategies according to the nature of market participants running them, e.g., electronic broker-dealers, proprietary trading firms, quantitative hedge funds, etc., is difficult. HF traders form a relatively mixed group, with no clear mapping between institutions and strategies. In our opinion, any strategy classification should therefore be done from a functional rather than from an institutional perspective. In the following, we will make a distinction between three main types of HFT strategies: market-making, arbitrage, and predatory strategies.

9.3.2.1 Market-Making/Electronic Liquid Provision

Market-makers provide liquidity by posting simultaneously limit-orders (quotes) on both sides of the mid-price. Their goal is to earn the bid–ask spread over a large number of trades, and in some instances, to capture the rebates offered by some exchange.[4]

For a human, market-making is not as simple as it sounds. A good market-maker needs to constantly place new orders and cancel existing orders as prices move, and keep buying and selling while at the same time avoiding ending up with a large deviation from his preferred inventory position (see for instance Garman (1976) or Amihud and Mendelson (1986)). As new information arrives, market-makers bear the risk of trading

---

[3] A "message" means any content that requires independent processing, e.g., entering a new order, changing an existing order, canceling an order, etc. As a result, an "immediate or cancel" order is counted as two messages.

[4] Several exchanges have moved away from their traditional model—charging a small fee to both buyers and sellers. They now charge a relatively high fee to liquidity takers and rebate most of it to liquidity suppliers. Liquidity suppliers are buyers or sellers whose standing limit-orders provide the option to trade. Liquidity takers use that option to trade by submitting only marketable orders. Note that since January 2014, these rebates are currently under serious review as regulators believe they can distort price discovery, diminish liquidity, and cost long-term investors (see for instance Harris (2013)).

with a better-informed market participant and losing money as a result. To reduce this risk, they must (1) receive with minimum delay all relevant new information, including about orders submissions or cancellations; (2) process that information as quickly as possible; and (3) revise the bids/offers they have provided to the exchange accordingly, before others take advantage of an outdated quote. Machines obviously have speed, cost, and accuracy advantages over humans in each of those activities. Since a higher revision frequency lowers the risk of liquidity provision and adverse selection, this opens the door to algorithmic market-making and ultimately, to HF market-making. The latter can be seen as a technological "arms race" that often boils down more to relative speed rather than better algorithms. For instance, HF market-makers pay trading venues hefty fees to "co-locate," that is, to place their servers in the same building; they invest in faster optical fiber cables or even in series of microwave towers.

Market-makers, including HF market-makers, often claim their actions are positive because they act as liquidity providers, which reduces bid—ask spreads as well as market volatility. In our opinion, this is not always true. First, an algorithm—as well as a human—may sometimes need to take liquidity out of markets in order to reduce its inventory risk. Second, while traditional market-makers such as designated market-makers at the NYSE or designated sponsors at the Frankfurt Stock Exchange have the obligation to post competitive prices *at all times*, HF market-makers frequently do not face such constraints. They can withdraw their quotes at any time. In particular, they are not obliged to provide liquidity during periods of market stress, such as a flash crash (see for instance Easley et al. (2011)). This could seriously exacerbate price volatility at the worst possible time. Third, traditional market-makers view the order flow but cannot front run their customer orders (they have a "negative obligation"). By contrast, HF market-makers can follow the trend—or in fact, front run the trend—and amplify market movements during periods of market stress.

9.3.2.2 Relative Value Arbitrage

Relative value arbitrage (RVA) regroups a large number of trading strategies that generally aim to profit from short-lived discrepancies in the valuation of related securities, usually through a market-neutral strategy and by capitalizing on some form of reversion to the mean. HF traders use computers to systematically scan markets, detect these opportunities, and exploit them. They act in the same way as their traditional counterparts, but have progressively replaced them because they were cheaper and faster.

As an illustration, equity pairs trading and statistical arbitrage are two of the oldest relative value arbitrage strategies. In pairs trading, the rationale is that pairs of related stocks see their (normalized) price difference fluctuate around a long-term spread. When the current spread deviates from its historical mean and reaches a certain threshold (normally measured in standard deviations terms), a long-short or short-long position is established and maintained until the spread has reversed back enough to its long-term mean. In statistical arbitrage, the idea is to consider not just a pair of stocks, but actually tens or hundreds of stocks, whose prices are expected to be related in the long run but may diverge in the short run. Similarly, the arbitrage can be between a basket of equities and a corresponding exchange-traded fund, a stock and its American depositary receipt, or between an index and its futures contract, etc. Whenever the prices diverge sufficiently, they buy the cheapest and sell short the most expensive, bringing the prices of the two instruments back into line. While the strategy seems simple, its implementation is actually more complex. First, one needs to take into account bid and ask prices rather than the last traded price to assess the existence of the arbitrage. Second, knowledge of the order flow allows one to play optimally the arbitrage in size. Third, speed is a key advantage, and if one HFT is able to trade faster than its peers, it will capture all the arbitrage and leave nothing for slower traders. Also, note that contrarily to the SEC definition mentioned before, and contrarily to market-makers, these HFT tend to close the day with high inventories.

Relative value arbitrage strategies are generally considered as useful—even when run at higher frequencies—because they fight discrepancies and improve price discovery and market efficiency.

9.3.2.3 Predatory Strategies

HF traders active in predatory strategies (also known as "latency arbitrage") essentially attempt to use their superior speed to take advantage of other market participants—and in particular slower human traders—or exploit structural vulnerabilities in the market or in the exchange. Here are a few examples:

- "Quote stuffing" involves sending large amounts of nonexecutable orders to the market (orders well outside the current bid and offer) and almost immediately canceling them. The goal is to create order congestion and slow down some of the competitors. Obviously, the originators of stuffing know exactly when it will occur and do not need to consider the orders they generate, while their competitors are uninformed and will analyze them. The competitive advantage may just be a few milliseconds, but this represents a lot for HF traders. In some malevolent cases, a HF trader may attempt to slow down the entire exchange by quote stuffing, for instance to have more time to capitalize on cross-exchange price differences.

- "Spoofing" (also known as "layering" or "painting the tape") involves placing orders with no intention to buy or sell, but simply to create a false sense of the actual supply and demand, induce other market participants to react and "push" the book away in the benefit of the spoofing trader. For instance, if the HF trader's true intention is to buy, he will initially place a small bona-fide limit order to buy below the best bid, followed by a sequence of limit non-bona-fide sell orders above the best ask, potentially for very large amounts. Scared by the possibility of considerable selling interest, naive market participants will start selling, increasing the probability of filling the small buy order. The HF trader will then immediately cancel all his large sell orders, and possibly start anew the spoof in reverse.

- "Smoking" involves posting alluring limit-orders to attract slower traders' market orders, and then rapidly changing them to less generous terms. Since market orders are only executed at the best market price, smokers hope to execute profitably against the incoming flow of slow traders' market orders. The key for the success of that strategy is the speed at which an order can be entered and then canceled.
- "Liquidity detection" or "order anticipation" strategies attempt to detect the trading patterns of other market participants and adjust orders accordingly. For instance, a HF trader may keep sending out small orders ("pinging" or "sniffing") to decipher whether large orders exist in a matching engine or even in the order book, and then trade ahead of those buyers or sellers. Historically quite effective, this strategy has now declined in importance.
- "Momentum ignition" consists in entering orders or a series of orders, possibly combined with spreading false rumors in the marketplace, in an attempt to trigger a number of other participants to trade quickly and ignite a rapid price move up or down.

Most of the time, predatory strategies imply rapid trades, short holding periods, and in some instances entering and canceling a large number of orders with no real economic benefit in terms of price discovery or market liquidity. They are therefore heavily criticized. Note that some of them are very close to market manipulation and could be deemed illegal, but it is in practice difficult to distinguish manipulative and legitimate patterns of trading, particularly when done at a high frequency.

9.4 HFT GOING FORWARD

Since the publication of Michael Lewis' book "Flash Boys"—which almost exclusively focuses on the rogue element of HFT—and his claims about faster traders rigging the stock market for average investors, HFT has received lots of attention. In particular, it has been criticized for a series of potential risks and externalities—most of which, to be honest, are not novel and did exist before, when some traders were just faster than others. Let us quote some of them:

- market manipulation and parasitic trading, with no real economic benefit in terms of price discovery or market liquidity.
- unfairness to less technologically sophisticated investors, in particular retail and long-term orientated investors. Items like colocation, direct data feeds from exchanges and flash order trading[5] are obviously not available to all and provide a crucial advantage to their beneficiaries. However, one could compare them to the old-days

---

[5] When an exchange has an order that cannot be immediately executed at the best price nationwide, instead of sending it to another exchange, it can "flash" it to its customers for a few milliseconds. Anyone that is fast enough can execute that order at the best price nationwide. This allows traders to execute orders without revealing them to the market by making them visible in the limit order book.

market "specialists" who had special trading floor privileges, physical speed, and prox-imity advantages over "ordinary" traders.

- shoddy algorithms could go out of control, cause a serious market failure, and move prices away from fundamental values. Examples of such situations include the near-collapse of Knight Capital in August 2012 and possibly the Flash Crash of 2010, when the Dow Jones lost 1000 points in 5 min, followed by an equally dramatic re-covery. In a sense, these are the electronic version of the old and manual "fat finger" trades.[6]
- overburdening of market infrastructure. Despite their small number, HF traders ac-count for more than half of the daily trading volumes in the US. Should they continue to grow, their activity will strain exchanges, increase latency, and create sys-tem instability.
- increasing volatility during stressed periods. However, this statement is still very controversial in academic research, and some critics claim the opposite (see SEC (2014) for a comprehensive discussion).

On the other side, HF traders have increased competition between exchanges and brokers, which resulted in lower transaction costs, higher market quality, enhanced trade execution and liquidity, and reduced volatility in most circumstances. These are real *observed* benefits, not potential ones, and have been shared across all market participants including retail ones. Moreover, in principle, a market should be more efficient when prices reflect information sooner, and HF traders contribute to this.

Banning HF traders, as suggested by some, or capping their activity, is unlikely to be the solution. It makes more sense in our opinion to monitor, investigate, and ultimately regulate it, as for any new innovation. Unfortunately, regulators do not seem to be work-ing collaboratively, which results in different regulations and opens the door to regulatory arbitrage. In Germany, for instance, HF traders must obtain a federal license and maintain an appropriate order-to-executed-trade ratio; they are subject to excessive system usage fees and all algorithmically generated orders must be flagged. By contrast, Italy does not regulate HF traders, but has introduced a 0.02% tax on the counter-value of orders auto-matically generated by an algorithm, including revocations or changes to the original order. At the European level, EU politicians have agreed on an updated set of rules as part of the MiFID II. These require all HFT firms to be authorized and regulated, to have in place sufficient risk controls, to disclose the details of their algorithmic trading strategies to their national supervisor, and to provide liquidity with no interruption when pursuing a market-making strategy. Regulated markets should also be able to temporarily halt trading if there is a significant price movement in a financial instrument

---

[6] The May 2010 Flash Crash was originally attributed to high-frequency traders. However, a six-month joint SEC-CFTC investigation identified the sale of 76,000 E-mini S&P 500 futures contracts by a large institutional investor as the initial motivator.

during a short period. The implications of these new rules on the ground remain to be seen.

9.5 HEDGE FUNDS

Although many believe that hedge funds are the main culprits when it comes to HFT, reality is that a majority of the trading volume arises from specialized HFT boutiques (48%) followed by investment banks (46%), and only the rest (6%) from hedge funds (see Psomadelis and Powell (2011)). Nevertheless, hedge funds involved in HFT are often put in the spotlight by the financial press.

One of the hedge fund groups that has been in the news for its high returns in HFT is the Citadel Group run by Ken Griffin. Its HFT strategy posted a net return of 300% since its inception in 2007, and jumped about 31 percent in 2008 (Burton, 2014)—a much better result than the average hedge fund (−19%), the S&P 500 (−37%) or even Citadel's Kensington and Wellington flagship funds (−55%). However, it should be noted that this fund progressively migrated from a pure HFT strategy in 2008 to a more diversified portfolio today, which includes in particular market-neutral long-short equity strategies. Another well-known and often quoted actor is Renaissance Technologies and its Medallion Fund, which only uses computer-based rapid trading algorithms and has annualized 35% annual net return after fees over 11 years, including an annual compound return 62.8% in the 3 years preceding the 2010 Flash Crash report by the Bank of England.

Beyond these famous examples, one should be cautious when associating HFT and hedge funds. In his book, Michael Lewis discusses the IEX exchange and some of its founders and owners, which include hedge funds Greenlight Capital, Pershing Square Capital Management, Brandes Investment Partners, Scoggin Capital Management, Senator Investment Group, and Third Point Partners. Considered by many as a dark pool, IEX is an alternative trading system (ATS) that matches buyers and sellers of stocks. IEX's matching engine is based in New Jersey, where its optical fibers provide faster trading. However, IEX's goal is to create a fair and transparent market that is be protected from HF predatory trading. IEX actually fights predatory trading by imposing 350 milliseconds of latency, prohibiting colocation, refusing to give special access to data, and not offering any rebates for taking or making liquidity (it only charges a flat 9/100th of a cent per share). Although it is still small from a trading volume perspective, the IEX is growing quickly and has already surpassed four of the 13 American exchanges.

More recently, numerous due diligence firms such as Cliffwater LLC are making sure for their clients that their reports identify if the hedge fund in question uses HFT. However, one argument by both Jaffe (2014) and Conway (2014) suggests that the performance of hedge funds over the last 10 years has dropped at the same time when HFT has increased. In terms of cyber security one HFT hedge fund called BAE was recently attacked on June 2014 by hackers slowing down their trading speed and rerouting their data to another site thus affecting its profitability (Strohm, 2014). In essence, these HFT systems have become so sophisticated generating high profits that large hedge funds will no doubt attract cyber criminals, one more headache for HFT firms and hedge funds.

9.6 CONCLUSION

As acknowledged by IOSCO (2011), "high frequency trading is not a single strategy but it is rather a set of technological arrangements and tools employed in a wide number of strategies, each one having a different market impact and hence raising different regulatory issues." As a consequence, it is a difficult domain to analyze—but it must be analyzed and monitored in order to understand how it operates, and more importantly, how it is evolving.

Technology has been and continues to be a key driver of innovation, growth, and development in financial markets. In our opinion, HF traders are here to stay, but probably not under the same shape or form. They are likely to become faster. The HF traders of today are likely to be the dinosaurs of tomorrow, and the fossils of the day after tomorrow. Their decline has already started. According to the Tabb group, HFT profits have declined from $7.2 billion in 2009 to $1.1 billion in 2013; and HFT volumes went from 61% in 2009 to 49% in 2013 and from 38% to 25% in the European Union. The survival of the fastest seems to be once more verified.

REFERENCES

Amihud, Y., Mendelson, H., 1986. Asset pricing and the bid-ask spread. J. Financ. Econ. 17 (2), 223–249.

Burton, K., April 11, 2014. Citadel Fund Said to Quadruple with High Frequency Trades. Bloomberg. Available at http://www.bloomberg.com/news/2014-04-11/citadel-fund-said-to-quadruple-with-high-frequency-trades.html.

CFTC, 2011. Letter to the Technical Advisory Committee. SEC, Washington, D.C.

Conway, B., May 9, 2014. Hedge Funds as the Real High-Frequency Trading Losers. Barron's.

Easley, D., De Prado, M.L., O'Hara,, M., 2011. The microstructure of the 'flash crash': flow toxicity, liquidity crashes and the probability of informed trading. Journal of Portfolio Management 37 (2), 118–128.

Garman, M.B., 1976. Market microstructure. J. Financ. Econ. 3 (3), 257–275.

Harris, L., 2013. Maker-taker pricing effects on market quotations. Working Paper. USC Marshall School of Business, Los Angeles, CA.

IOSCO, 2011. Regulatory issues raised by the impact of technological changes on market integrity and efficiency. In: Consultation Report, July 2011. International Organization of Securities Commissions, Madrid, Spain.

Jaffe, C., May 5, 2014. High-frequency Trading Hurts Hedge Funds-Not You, MarketWatch.

Psomadelis, W., Powell, S.B., 2011. Special Report: High Frequency Trading—Credible Research Tells the Real Story. http://www.schroderstalkingpoint.com/tp/thelongview?id=a0j50000000uyzwAAA.

SEC, 2010. Concept Release on Equity Market Structure. Working Paper. Securities and Exchange Commission, Washington, D.C.

SEC, 2014. Equity Market Structure Literature Review, Part II: High Frequency Trading. Working paper. Securities and Exchange Commission, Washington, D.C.

Shorter, G., Miller, R.S., 2014. High-frequency Trading: Background, Concerns, and Regulatory Developments. Congressional Research Service, Working Paper 7–5700.

Strohm, C., June 19, 2014. Hedge-fund Hackers Disrupting Trades for Profits, BAE Says. Available at http://www.bloomberg.com/news/2014-06-19/hackers-sought-monetary-gain-in-hedge-fund-attack-bae-says.html.

CHAPTER 10

High-Frequency Trading and Its Regulation in the Australian Equity Markets

Paul U. Ali
Melbourne Law School, Parkville, Melbourne, VIC, Australia

Contents

10.1 INTRODUCTION

Australia has recently introduced regulations specifically directed at high frequency trading (HFT), in response to the growth in HFT activity in the Australian securities markets and to address concerns as to the risks that HFT might pose to the integrity of those markets.

HFT is a subset of algorithmic trading, a broad term that encompasses trading activity where orders to buy and sell securities are generated via computer in accordance with automated or preprogrammed trading instructions. The Australian Securities and Investments Commission (ASIC)—the government body that regulates Australia's securities markets—has explicitly adopted the description of HFT published by the Technical Committee of the International Organization of Securities Commissions, a description that is worth setting out in full (IOSCO, 2011):

> [HFT] is frequently equated to algorithmic trading. However, whilst HFT is a type of algorithmic trading, not all forms of algorithmic trading can be described as high frequency. Algorithmic trading predates HFT and has been extensively used as a tool to determine some or all aspects of trade execution like timing, price, quantity and venue. Algorithmic trading is used by many intermediaries for their own proprietary trading or offered to their clients and has also become a standard feature in many buy-side firms, mainly with the purpose of devising execution strategies that minimize price impact or to rebalance large portfolios of securities as market conditions change.

A number of common features and trading characteristics related to HFT can be identified:
- It involves the use of sophisticated technological tools for pursuing a number of different strategies, ranging from market making to arbitrage.

The Handbook of High Frequency Trading
ISBN 978-0-12-802205-4
167

- It is a highly quantitative tool that employs algorithms along the whole investment chain: analysis of market data, deployment of appropriate trading strategies, minimization of trading costs, and execution of trades.
- It is characterized by a high daily-portfolio turnover and order-to-trade ratio (i.e., a large number of orders are canceled in comparison to trades executed).
- It usually involves flat or near-flat positions at the end of the trading day, meaning that little or no risk is carried overnight, with obvious savings on the cost of capital associated with margined positions. Positions are often held for as little as seconds or even fractions of a second.
- It is mostly employed by proprietary trading firms or desks.
- It is latency sensitive. The implementation and execution of successful HFT strategies depend crucially on the ability to be faster than competitors and to take advantage of services such as direct electronic access and colocation.

However, while some of the entities that engaged in HFT in the Australian market demonstrated the above characteristics, ASIC, following a recent survey of Australian HFT, found that (ASIC, 2013b):

- HFT entities in Australia exhibit only moderate order-to-trade ratios (the number of times orders are amended or canceled relative to the number of orders executed) compared to HFT entities in overseas markets. Most of these entities had order-to-trade ratios below 4:1. ASIC, moreover, found that these levels of order-to-trade ratios were not dissimilar to the levels associated with algorithmic trading generally in Australia.
- Only a very small minority of HFT entities held positions for less than 2 min (1.2%), while the majority of these entities (51%) held positions for 30 min or less.

Nonetheless, HFT in Australia, in common with HFT in other markets, is characterized by rapid turnover. ASIC also found that (ASIC, 2013b) just under two-thirds (65%) of all HFT in Australia was intraday trading. In addition, while only a very small proportion of participants in the Australian market could be described as engaging in HFT (less than 0.1%), those participants accounted for a significant portion of total turnover by value (27%) and total trades (32%) of securities represented in the S&P/ASX 200 Index (ASIC, 2013b).

10.2 REGULATORY RESPONSE

ASIC's response to HFT is the product of ASIC's ongoing consultation process—which commenced in November 2010—relating to market structure issues. As part of this process, ASIC established two task forces in July 2012 to examine HFT and the related issue of dark liquidity specifically. In March 2013, the task forces published their findings and recommendations in two documents: a Consultation Paper (ASIC, 2013a) and a Report (ASIC, 2013b). Then, in August 2013, ASIC published its responses to the submissions it had received from the public in relation to the Consultation Paper (ASIC, 2013c). This was accompanied by the publication of market integrity rules for HFT and a Guide to those rules (ASIC, 2013d).

The key regulatory responses to HFT are:

- Market operators must have controls in place to filter out anomalous orders for securities (to prevent buy orders above a maximum threshold or sell orders below a minimum thresholds, with these thresholds determined by reference to prevailing market conditions for the relevant security, historical trading patterns for the security, and the tick size or index multiplier for the security).

- Market operators must have controls in place to prevent orders for securities being executed when there is an extreme price movement for the relevant security (the extreme price range for a security is all prices, which are greater than the number of the cents or percentage away from the reference price for that security, with the extreme price range determined by ASIC by reference to the price at which, in ASIC's opinion, a transaction in the security is likely to have an impact on market integrity and the reference price determined by the auction on the market operator's market for the relevant security on the relevant trading day).

- Market participants must, when considering whether a false or misleading market in securities has been created, explicitly take into account the frequency with which orders for securities have been placed by a person, the volume of securities that are the subject of each order placed by a person and the extent to which a person amends or cancels an order relative to the number of orders executed for that person.

10.3 CONCLUSION

The regulatory response to HFT in Australia summarized above reflects ASIC's view that "public concerns over HFT appear to have been overstated" and that the strategies employed by entities engaged in HFT in Australia are not unique to HFT but are, in fact, "commonly adopted by many other algorithmic traders, including the institutions" (ASIC, 2013e).

This relatively benign view of HFT is shared by regulators in other markets, for example, the Bank of England. Researchers from the Bank of England recently concluded that (Benos and Sagade, 2012):

In terms of their impact on market quality … there are instances where HFTs contribute significantly more to both price discovery and to noise than the rest of the traders … HFTs' trading is, overall, informationally more efficient than that of the rest of the traders in the sense that they have a higher ratio of information to noise contribution. Nevertheless, the overall welfare implications of HFT are unclear; these will depend on how the marginal benefit of information at some times compares with the marginal cost of excess volatility at other times, including in periods of market stress.

Other researchers have taken a more emphatic view of the benefits of HFT and those opinions—given the relatively small amount of published scholarly research on HFT—were influential in shaping ASIC's response to HFT in Australia. ASIC noted that most research had found that HFT improved price efficiency and liquidity and thus contributed positively to the quality of securities markets (ASIC, 2013b). ASIC, in this regard, explicitly cited the following research (ASIC, 2013b): Hendershott and Riordan (2009); Brogaard (2010); Hasbrouck and Saar (2010); Hendershott et al. (2011); Brogaard et al. (2012); Menkveld (2012); and Hendershott and Riordan (2013). Accordingly, while the regulatory response in Australia to HFT recognizes that HFT is not synonymous with algorithmic trading, it essentially treats HFT as no different to algorithmic trading.

REFERENCES

Australian Securities and Investments Commission (ASIC), 2013. Dark Liquidity and High-frequency Trading: Proposals. Consultation Paper 202. ASIC, Sydney, Australia.

Australian Securities and Investments Commission (ASIC), 2013. Dark Liquidity and High-frequency Trading. ASIC, Sydney, Australia. Report 331.

Australian Securities and Investments Commission (ASIC), 2013. Response to Submissions on CP 202 Dark Liquidity and High-frequency Trading: Proposals. Report 364. ASIC, Sydney, Australia.

Australian Securities and Investments Commission (ASIC), 2013. Guidance on ASIC Market Integrity Rules for Competition in Exchange Markets. ASIC, Sydney, Australia. Regulatory Guide 223.

Australian Securities and Investments Commission (ASIC), 2013. ASIC Reports on Dark Liquidity and High-frequency Trading. Media Release 13–052. ASIC, Sydney, Australia.

Benos, E., Sagade, S., 2012. High-frequency Trading Behaviour and its Impact on Market Quality: Evidence from the UK Equity Market. Working Paper 469. Bank of England, London, UK.

Brogaard, J., 2010. High Frequency Trading and its Impact on Market Quality. Working Paper. Kellogg School of Management, Northwestern University, Chicago, USA.

Brogaard, J., Hendershott, T., Riordan, R., 2012. High Frequency Trading and Price Discovery. Working Paper. University of Washington, Seattle, USA.

Hasbrouck, J., Saar, G., 2010. Low-latency Trading. Working Paper. New York University, New York, USA.

Hendershott, T., Jones, C.M., Menkveld, A.J., 2011. Does algorithmic trading improve market liquidity? J. Finance 66 (1), 1–33.

Hendershott, T., Riordan, R., 2009. Algorithmic Trading and Information. Working Paper. Haas School of Business, University of California, Berkeley, USA.

Hendershott, T., Riordan, R., 2013. Algorithmic trading and the market for liquidity. J. Financial Quantitative Analysis 48 (4), 1001–1024.

International Organization of Securities Commissions (IOSCO), 2011. Regulatory Issues Raised by the Impact of Technological Changes on Market Integrity and Efficiency. Consultation Report CR02/11. Technical Committee, IOSCO, Madrid, Spain.

Menkveld, A.J., 2012. High Frequency Trading and the New-market Makers. Working Paper. VU University Amsterdam, Amsterdam, The Netherlands.

CHAPTER 11

Global Exchanges in the HFT Nexus

David R. Meyer[1], George Guernsey[2]
[1]Olin Business School, Washington University in St. Louis, St. Louis, MO, USA; [2]Managing Partner, Insight Mapping, St. Louis, MO, USA

Contents

11.1 INTRODUCTION

The controversy over high-frequency trading (HFT), defined as the use of computerized rapid trading systems based on complex algorithms that draw on public and nonpublic information, spans the global world of trading on exchanges. Although this controversy has brewed for several years, Michael Lewis' (2014) *Flash Boys* stoked it, raising the attention of government. The Senate Banking Committee and House Financial Services Committee of the United States Congress are looking into the controversy (US Congress Week, 2014). The European Securities and Markets Authority (ESMA) issued a report that called for more research to examine the risks and benefits of HFT (Cave, 2014).

Governments, regulators, and exchanges take divergent approaches to the controversy, and this is exemplified across countries outside of highly developed United States and Western Europe (Mellow, 2014). In Russia, the Moscow Exchange openly welcomes HFT firms. Roman Sulzhyk, head of the exchange's derivatives market, said, "We have traditionally been very accessible to the algo [algorithm] community." He claimed that HFT volume accounted for over half of the exchange's trading. Brazil's exchange, BM&FBOVESPA, headquartered in Sao Paulo, likewise is positive about HFT.

The Handbook of High Frequency Trading
ISBN 978-0-12-802205-4

According to Mario Palhares, the exchange's operations officer, its "controls have guaranteed the stability of our market." In contrast, China's regulators impose a stamp duty and prohibit selling stock the same day it is purchased (Mellow, 2014).

Debate about HFT invariably views positive and negative features as outcomes of contemporary technology, including high-speed, high-capacity servers and computers, sophisticated software algorithms, and advanced telecommunications—fiber optic lines and microwave systems (Agarwal, 2012). The positive argument is that HFT provides greater liquidity, lower costs, and smaller differences between bid and ask prices. The negative side claims HFT leads to front-running and market manipulation (Cave, 2014; Mellow, 2014).

Although the HFT controversy has become heated recently, technological changes based on computers and telecommunications have impacted trading since at least the late 1960s when computers were first incorporated into record keeping and trading (Agarwal, 2012; Mihm, 2013). This process accelerated during the 1970s, and a major step was incorporation of NASDAQ in 1971 as the world's first electronic stock market. During the 1980s, computerized program trading commenced, and during the 1990s, electronic trading advanced considerably with the introduction of electronic communications networks that allowed trading financial securities outside regular exchanges (Agarwal, 2012). Recent advances in telecommunications for sending trading data involve use of microwave signals that travel almost as fast as the speed of light; whereas data sent over fiber optic lines move at just over two-thirds the speed of light (As Fast as Light, 2014).

Controversy over HFT, which has developed since the late 1960s, is rooted in computer technology and advances in telecommunications. Nevertheless, positive and negative features that are telecommunications technology related and that impact exchanges actually date from the advent of the telegraph. For the first time in human history, messages no longer had to accompany physical movement of goods and people (Pred, 1980). Beginning in the 1840s, the spread of the telegraph in North America and Europe and its international expansion during the subsequent two decades, both overland and undersea, allowed traders on exchanges to receive price and other relevant data within hours domestically and within a day or so globally (DuBoff, 1983; Wenzlhuemer, 2009). Because telegraph networks were created as businesses, telegraph firms targeted major financial, trade, and industrial centers that would generate the most traffic. As the greatest world finance-trade center, London occupied the hub of the global telegraph network (Wenzlhuemer, 2009, 2012).

Changes in trading Asian goods vividly illustrate the impact of the telegraph on exchanges (Meyer, 2000). By 1871, telegraph connection had crossed Russia to Vladivostok and moved undersea along the coast of China, passing through Shanghai and on to Hong Kong. Another telegraphic connection crossed Europe, passed through the Red Sea, and connected to Bombay, Singapore, and finally, Hong Kong (Farnie, 1969).

Instead of price data about cotton, rice, and tea in Asia reaching the London Exchange by sailing ships and steamers, the telegraph allowed this data and other relevant information to reach the London Exchange in, at most, two days (Farnie, 1969; Wenzlhuemer, 2009, 2012). This resulted in sharp declines in differences between bid—ask prices, improved liquidity as more brokers entered trading, and increased competition. Great trading houses such as Jardine, Matheson & Company, which dominated Asian trade based on large, fixed infrastructure of shipping, warehouses, offices, and staff, lost out to fast-paced, smaller brokerage houses (Lockwood, 1971; Marriner, 1961). At the same time, brokers in major business centers such as London and Shanghai had quicker access to price quotes and sophisticated market information (Wenzlhuemer, 2009, 2012). Thus they could front run and manipulate markets relative to traders situated at lesser business centers.

The HFT controversy, therefore, is an old concern for global exchanges. The interface between telecommunications and technology, which constitute the basis of HFT goes back 150 years, and changes in that interface have impacted trading on exchanges episodically over that time span. This suggests that a focus on general principles of how exchanges operate in a larger context constitutes a more useful approach to the HFT controversy. Next, we set out a conceptualization of the nexus of an exchange and identify two pairs of relations. Then, we compare and contrast exchanges, mostly focused on stock exchanges, in terms of how they operate in that nexus.

11.2 THE NEXUS OF AN EXCHANGE

We propose that an exchange operates in a nexus of customers, regulator, and government—political officials in an operating environment transformed by technology firms providing new capabilities for exchanges and their counterparties (Figure 11.1). Exchanges may be privately owned, publicly owned, or be a private—public partnership. Regardless of the ownership structure, exchanges attend to customers' needs, including public or private institutional investors, brokerage firms, trading firms, private individuals, and the like. They provide revenue that covers operations and profit, if the exchange is privately owned. While some exchanges may monopolize trading selected domestic securities, other global firms' securities trade on multiple exchanges. Exchanges also create products for trading such as specialized derivatives. Consequently, global exchanges compete with each other for trading revenue, reinforcing the aim of exchanges to attend to their customers' needs. The relationship between an exchange and its customers, therefore, is portrayed as a two-way arrow in Figure 11.1.

The regulator of an exchange directly impacts its operation through setting rules (procedures) for trading, customer characteristics (minimum net worth, for example), taxes/fees for trading, safety triggers on trading, and so on. This relation between regulator and exchange is indicated by a one-way arrow from regulator to exchange (Figure 11.1).

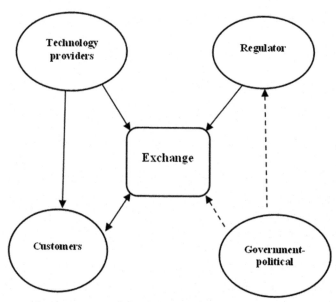

Figure 11.1 An exchange occupies a nexus of customers, regulator, and government—political officials in an operating environment transformed by technology firms providing new capabilities for exchanges and their counterparties.

Nevertheless, the exchange also has some impact on the regulator because it can support
competition with other exchanges for customers, thus benefiting the domestic economy.

While the regulator directly impacts an exchange, government—political officials
exert influence through public or private pressure that may take the form of threats to
take action. Officials can directly pressure the exchange by passing laws that deal with
legal/illegal behavior in financial transactions; the regulator must implement these
laws. Thus, the impact of government—political officials on both regulator and an exchange is shown as a dashed line in Figure 11.1. While some actions may be seen as direct,
much of the influence of the government—political officials is indirect. At the same time,
government—political officials have an incentive to support their exchanges because they
provide prestige and business for the country, and successful exchanges enhance the
wealth of the global business center where the exchange(s) locate.

Technology providers supply software, algorithms, and equipment (servers, high-
speed fiber optics, and microwave) to the exchange and to customers; these relations
are shown as one-way arrows in Figure 11.1. Although not indicated on the diagram,
we could add data providers but these are not included to simplify the relations. Sometimes, data providers are accused of giving traders preferential access to tradable information, which HFT firms use to run their software and algorithms. Thus, a regulator may
attempt to control these providers.

Our analysis of this nexus focuses on its two core components. First, we compare and contrast the relationships between exchanges and their customers, including how these relationships impact the way exchanges deal with the risks of HFT. Second, we compare and contrast the relationship between regulators (including the influences of government—political officials) and exchanges and how these relationships impact approaches to issues of fairness and transparency. Technology providers will not be examined directly, but we will bring them into the discussion as enablers of HFT for customers and exchanges.

11.3 EXCHANGES AND THEIR CUSTOMERS

11.3.1 The Views of Customers

Customers possess divergent views about the value of HFT and this poses a dilemma for exchanges (Figure 11.1). One set of customers views HFT as a positive contributor to markets. According to David Gonski, head of the multibillion-dollar Future Fund based in Australia, HFT now is a regular component of trading on exchanges to which customers must adapt. At the same time they must understand it in order to work with it appropriately (Hutchens, 2013). Gary Head, UBS Australia's cohead of equities, claims that the concerns over HFT are overblown. Still, he recognized that traders who engage more in the market such as through sending greater numbers of "messages" about trades require more supervision and should pay more of the regulatory costs (Liondis, 2013).

The claim that HFT has positive benefits does not rest solely on opinion; research supports that claim (Bell and Searles, 2014). A review of about 30 studies of HFT concluded that it added liquidity to markets, lowered trading costs, and reduced the spread between bid and ask prices (Columbia Business School, 2013). Other research that surveyed capital market participants concluded they generally believed HFT will become more important because of the financial incentives and greater efficiency, which derive from that trading. Rather than regulators discouraging its use, market players said the focus should be to make it safer (High-Frequency Trading Continues, 2013). In sum, this view of HFT claims that positive aspects should be retained, while negative spillovers are reduced or eliminated (Harris, 2013).

Opponents of HFT propose a variety of actions to deal with it. At the extreme level some advocate an outright ban on HFT. Anton Tagliaferro, investment director of Investors Mutual, said, "I just don't like all this interference from high frequency traders and hedge funds, which can cause extra volatility in the market and interfere with genuine investment decisions in the market" (Liondis, 2013). Average investors are viewed as the victims of HFT, a point of view expressed by Ian Curry, Chairman of the Australian Shareholders' Association. The HFT traders get unfair access to market-sensitive information before other investors (Lowe, 2013). This leads to one of the major criticisms of these types of traders; they engage in front running, which then undermines investor confidence (Harris, 2013).

Investor funds that collaborate in expressing views, such as the Industry Super Network in Australia, have proposed slowing down trading to reduce the advantage of HFT and adding transaction taxes to inhibit these traders (Shapiro and Durbin, 2014; Yeates, 2013). Advantages HFT firms possess require substantial capital investment in algorithmic software, large computers, and colocation near exchanges to achieve low latency (short time between receipt and processing of information). Only the largest brokers can afford these investments, which further concentrates trading in the hands of HFT firms, exacerbating problems for smaller customers (Prasad, 2013). According to the Stockbrokers Association of Australia, competition from HFT firms also has driven down commissions on trading to "unprecedented low levels," thus reducing profits of brokerage firms (Moullakis, 2014).

11.3.2 Exchanges Compete for Customers

Divergent views of customers about the value of HFT poses challenges to exchanges because they compete for customer business (Figure 11.1). Advances in telecommunications technology and increasing globalization of capital markets intensify this competition among exchanges. These trends motivated exchanges to switch to for-profit entities so they could invest in technology and respond to growing competition. Consequently, exchanges view high-frequency traders as targets for business and providing colocation is a means to generate revenue (Russell and Waitzer, 2012).

Several Asian exchanges have implemented plans aimed at attracting HFT firms to participate in their exchanges. Dato Tajuddin Atan, Bursa Malaysia's chief executive, claims: "Markets are about liquidity. As they say, liquidity begets liquidity. And these [high frequency traders] are providers of liquidity." The chief executive of the trading business for Bursa Malaysia, Chong Kim Seng, was blunter; he argued that if the exchange did not cater to HFTs, it would lose liquidity (Grant, 2012a). Nonetheless, as of late 2012, Bursa Malaysia had little HFT (Grant, 2012b). Web searches of HFT activity on the exchange since that time failed to find evidence that the exchange's competitive position had changed.

In India competition to attract HFT firms heated up when MCX-SX opened for business in 2013 as the third Indian exchange, along with the older BSE (Bombay Stock Exchange) and NSE (National Stock Exchange). India's major public and private sector banks and financial institutions own the majority of MCX-SX, signifying that it has broad support from political and economic leaders (Crabtree and Stafford, 2013; MCX-SX, 2014). The three exchanges are making substantial investments in technology to appeal to HFT firms because they want to increase their business and enhance their liquidity (Mohan and Laskar, 2013; Puaar, 2014). They offer colocation for servers so

HFT firms can achieve low latency for their algorithms (Kumar, 2014). India is also home to Omnesys, a major supplier of order management systems and algorithmic trading platforms for HFT firms (Shrikant Pandit, 2013). Nevertheless, technology experts outside India claim the country's exchanges still lag the so-called Western exchanges based on their speed for handling trading (Shah, 2013).

The Japan Exchange (JPX), a 2013 merger of Tokyo Stock Exchange and Osaka Securities Exchange, aims to increase its competitiveness by raising trading volume and diversifying products. It is improving its Arrowhead trading system to expand electronic trading and attract HFT firms (Puaar, 2013). JPX is shrinking the increment in which stock prices may move to as small as 0.1 yen, which is believed will attract institutional investors using HFT (Japan Exchange to Set, 2013). Technology firms provide support systems for the exchange's effort to appeal to HFT. Cyan, a supplier of packet-optical transport platforms and software-defined solutions for carriers and data center providers, and KVH (Tokyo), supplier of integrated communications and information technology solutions, formed a joint venture to improve data transmission among the major metropolitan centers in Japan (Cyan Partners with KVH, 2013). This directly supports the operation of Japan's HFT firms.

The same technology firms supply support for HFT business on multiple exchanges, thus equalizing competition among exchanges for this business. KVH also partners with Koscom, a financial information technology solutions provider, to supply proximity hosting services for the Korea Exchange's derivative trading customers (Frequency Trading Needs, 2012). The hosting services offer HFT firms high-speed, low-latency trading from Koscom's new data center in Busan, Korea. These services connect from Busan to the major financial centers of Tokyo, Singapore, Hong Kong, Sydney, and Chicago.

Australia features a variant on competition for HFT. The dominant Australian Securities Exchange (ASX) tries to acquire new revenue sources by adding a wide range of specialized products (ASX on the Hunt, 2014). Its chief executive, Elmer Kupper, argues that HFT on the ASX is not a problem as it is elsewhere, such as the United States (Wilkins, 2014). In contrast to ASX, the Asia Pacific Stock Exchange (APX), which commenced formal trading in 2014, initially will specialize in Chinese and other Asian companies that are not listed on ASX. As a competitive differentiator, APX will introduce short pauses in trading to hinder HFT, thus appealing to Chinese retail investors (Drummond, 2014; New Australian Bourse, 2013).

The emergence of electronic global exchanges that operate in multiple regions and are backed by leading financial institutions has intensified competition among exchanges. Chi-X Global operates market centers in Canada, Japan, and Australia and is backed by Nomura (majority owner), Bank of America Merrill Lynch, Goldman Sachs, Morgan Stanley, UBS, J.P. Morgan Chase, among others (Haines, 2014a). These Chi-X exchanges aggressively develop and implement technology-driven platforms that appeal to HFT firms, as well as other traders. They offer greater liquidity, shorter queue times, lower trading fees, and price improvement opportunities to their customers (Haines, 2013a, 2013b, 2014b).

BATS Global Markets, another multiregion exchange operator, has its global head-quarters in Kansas City, Missouri, and offices in New York and London. It focuses on the United States and on Europe through its BATS Chi-X Europe (BATS, 2014). The U.S. Securities and Exchange Commission (SEC) approved BATS Global's merger with Direct Edge Holdings in January 2014. Affiliates of Citadel, Goldman Sachs, Institutional Securities Exchange, J.P. Morgan Chase, and KCG Holdings controlled Direct Edge (BATS Global Markets, 2014). These are some of the same firms that back Chi-X, indicating that trading firms operate across multiple exchanges through overlapping ownership stakes. Nevertheless, these exchanges compete for HFT customers, as exemplified in Europe. BATS Chi-X Europe introduced interoperable features across market venues to attract more traders (Randall, 2014; Stafford, 2014).

While exchanges compete to attract high-frequency traders, they remain cognizant that their platforms must not disadvantage customers, both those who use HFT and those not using it. India's NSE sets a predetermined throttle rate (speed at which firms can send orders) to ensure that an algorithm that may have errors or one which deliberately is set at too high of a speed is prevented from trading. This is part of the exchange's risk management strategy (Algorithmic Trading, 2012). The APX's introduction of short pauses in trading to reduce HFT is an attempt to protect traders who do not use these algorithms (Drummond, 2014). In testimony to the U.S. Senate Banking Committee, BATS Global Markets CEO Joe Ratterman (2014) stated that exchanges should aim to disseminate data through the public securities information processor as quickly as possible to address perceptions of lack of fairness in trading. He added that exchanges should handle potential conflicts of interest, which arise from payments for order flow and should improve transparency over how they route institutional orders.

Exchanges, however, operate in a larger political economy; thus, they can rarely avoid regulation by government. Not only do regulators directly oversee exchanges, but also these same regulators are subject to government—political officials who can directly and indirectly attempt to influence regulators and exchanges (Figure 11.1).

11.4 REGULATORS AND EXCHANGES

Political pressure on regulators and exchanges to do something about HFT can be as blatant as the Senate Banking Committee and the House Financial Services Committee of the United States Congress holding hearings on the controversy (US Congress Week, 2014). A less direct, but equally forceful view of a political leader, can raise anxiety among market participants such as the statement by Najib Razak, Malaysia's Prime Minister: "with the opening up of markets and the emergence of high-frequency trading, the potential for regional shocks to spread fast, far and wide is greater than ever" (Grant, 2012b). Alternatively, pressure on exchanges can be as blunt as a regulator filing a suit against the operator of an exchange. This is the approach of New York Attorney General, Eric Schneiderman, who sued Barclays regarding the character of its "dark pool" (Dey, 2014). At the same time, operators of exchanges are highly sensitive to negative repercussions from political pressure. Thus, CEO Joe Ratterman of BATS Global Markets, an exchange operator, which allows HFT firms to trade, agreed to testify to the U.S. Senate Banking Committee (Ratterman, 2014).

Approaches of regulators to how exchanges should deal with HFT vary significantly across political economies, and regulators views on HFT have changed over time. Some regulators see relatively little problem with HFT, whereas others, often pressured by government—political officials, decided to impose measures to limit HFT. At times, limitations appear as direct laws passed by the government. The fact that much research on HFT fails to provide support for the most negative accusations, whereas results often show improved liquidity, lower costs, and smaller bid—ask spreads, poses a dilemma for regulators who are subject to their respective government—political officials (Bell and Searles, 2014).

11.4.1 Canada Proceeds Cautiously

Regulators in Canada take a research-driven approach to HFT. The 10 provinces and three territories of Canada are responsible for securities regulation, and they collaborate in the umbrella organization, Canadian Securities Administrators (CSA) (2014a). In 2001, the CSA established a framework for exchanges and other marketplaces to compete and formalized these into rules. The objectives were to achieve transparency, immediacy (quick execution of trade), price discovery, fairness, market integrity, and lower transaction costs. In 2014, after extensive research, the CSA published a lengthy document requesting comments on proposed changes to the rules of trading (Canadian Securities Administrators, 2014b).

The CSA works closely with the Investment Industry Regulatory Organization of Canada (IIROC), a self-regulating group, which likewise is engaged in extensive research on trading in Canada and the impact of HFT (IIROC, 2014). It published "The HOT Study" to set the stage for more detailed analyses (IIROC, 2012). The final research stage to be completed by the end of 2014 is being carried out by two project teams led by prominent researchers who study HFT, including algorithmic, as well as related market issues (Archer and Yee, 2014). Based on IIROC's research, it is estimated that HFT accounts for 15% of volume, 24% of value, and 35% of trades on exchanges (Pinnington, 2013). Thus, HFT is moderately important in Canada, but not at such a high level as to require drastic action; consequently, Canada's regulators may be justified in taking a measured approach.

The Ontario Securities Commission that is responsible for regulating securities trading in the province, including on the major exchanges in Toronto, is awaiting results of the IIROC study before deciding on regulations for HFT (Duarte and Lam, 2014). This cautious approach to regulation recognizes the sharp disputes over whether HFT offers positive or negative benefits to markets. As Ian Russell, CEO of the Investment Industry Association of Canada, argued in a letter to industry executives, "As a starting point, let me state categorically that the Canadian equity markets are definitely not rigged" (Langton, 2014). While he concedes that there may be important issues that need addressing, his organization supports the careful research approach of Canadian regulators.

11.4.2 India Aims to Increase Regulation of HFT

While Canada awaits conclusions of research before changing its current regulations, India's regulators have steadily raised their rhetoric about the need for regulation of HFT on exchanges. This trend has some basis in the growing share of trading accounted for by high-frequency traders, perhaps to as much as one-fourth, but this is about the same level as Canada's and remains less than half the United States' share (Democratize Trade, 2013; Trader, 2014). One reason given for more limited HFT on Indian exchanges is that the government imposes a transaction tax on trading (What is Securities Transaction Tax, 2013). As of late 2009, the Securities and Exchange Board of India (SEBI), the regulator of exchanges, paid little attention to commencement of colocation facilities for trading servers of firms near the NSE and the BSE (Democratize Trade, 2013). Such colocation gave firms advantages in trading ahead of other firms not colocated at exchanges.

By early 2012, India's regulator had intensified its attention to HFT. It issued detailed guidelines for how exchanges should deal with algorithmic trading (SEBI Issues Rules, 2012). Exchanges were to institute risk management procedures for monitoring price and quantity checks and sudden surges in price, and were to install mechanisms to shut down dysfunctional algorithms. These guidelines, however, did not seem onerous according to Rajesh Baheti, Managing Director of Crosseas Capital Services, a proprietary trader. He said: "At the outset, the regulatory guidelines deal with systemic risk management and do not seem to infringe on a broker's intellectual property, which is great" (SEBI Issues Rules, 2012).

Nonetheless, this regulatory effort did not quell concerns about HFT. By the latter part of 2012, the Intermediaries and Investor Welfare Association of India filed suit in Delhi High Court alleging that SEBI and the nation's finance ministry were not protecting retail investors from algorithmic traders and from those operating at colocation servers; the Association aimed to ban HFT (Henderson, 2012). Coincidentally, SEBI's International Advisory Board met, and SEBI released a statement saying: "The pros and cons of high frequency trading (HFT)/algo trading on capital formation, efficiency of secondary markets and fairness to market participants were intensely deliberated" (Prasad, 2012).

The attempt of SEBI to deal more effectively with HFT escalated in mid-2013, when it proposed an amendment to its governing act to centralize regulation of securities markets under its umbrella. The chairman of SEBI, U.K. Sinha, said that it needs to deal with algorithmic and HFT and ensure that risk management systems work better (SEBI Seeks Sweeping Powers, 2013). In 2014, SEBI latched on to the colocation controversy, stimulated by discussion of that topic in Lewis (2014) book, *Flash Crash*. The regulator proposed that exchanges set up two queues for HFT, one for colocated traders and one for those not near the exchange, in order to improve fairness and prevent some traders from being crowded out of trades (Shah, 2014a).

The exchanges, however, may find this proposal will incur financial losses on them. According to Hirander Misra, CEO of Global Markets Exchange Group, "People will stop co-locating." He added that "Co-location is mainly for time priority. It gives liquidity to markets with high number of passive orders. If you say orders that come first may not go first, then people will stop using it. Separate order queues will close down co-location" (Shah, 2014a). Attempts to reduce colocation benefits may further harm markets, if a study of futures contracts on the ASX receives confirmation by additional research. The study showed that colocation enhanced market liquidity through a decrease in bid—ask spreads and increased efficiency of traders in making markets (Frino et al., 2014). The Indian regulator's attempt to increase controls on HFT, therefore, may harm their own exchanges and have unintended consequences of decreased market liquidity.

11.4.3 Australia's Regulator Aims for Balance

Estimates of the relative importance of HFT in Australia suggest that it amounts to less than one-fourth of all trading, placing it approximately at the level of Canada and India (Liondis, 2012; Pinnington, 2013; Smith, 2014). Nevertheless, the Australian Securities and Investments Commission (ASIC), the country's exchange regulator, takes a different approach than India's SEBI. Australia's regulator makes statements that vary from concern about HFT risks and fairness to saying that there are few problems on the country's exchange, and, at the same time, issuing regulations to control HFT and improve its operations.

By 2012, similar to Indian regulators' increased attention to HFT, Greg Medcraft, Chairman of ASIC, told a meeting of the Asian and Oceanian Stock Exchanges Federation that his commission was concerned about HFT and algorithmic trading, as well as the emergence of "dark pools" because they were raising risks to markets (Liondis, 2012). Early in 2013, ASIC (2013a) released a report on dark pools and high-frequency traders. It concluded that dark pools degraded market quality, and this should be addressed through minimum-size thresholds for trading, consideration of reducing tick sizes, and greater transparency of operators across dark pools. At the same time, the study found relatively few problems with HFT itself and, likewise, argued that colocation did not introduce any important degree of unfairness into market trading. Nevertheless, ASIC (2013b) did not back away from regulation; it published a detailed regulatory guide for market operators and participants.

The efforts of ASIC to find a balance continued into 2014. Between early April and early May, the regulator made opposing claims. In early April, ASIC testified to a financial services inquiry chaired by former Commonwealth Bank chief executive, David Murray, that investors are concerned that markets are "rigged." The regulator threatened to introduce curbs on HFT speed, using pauses in trading (Durkin et al., 2014). At the same inquiry the Industry Super Network in Australia claimed that high-frequency traders were costing large investors about AUD$2 billion per year and proposed adding transaction taxes to inhibit these traders, thus providing fuel to efforts to have ASIC clamp down on HFT (Shapiro and Durbin, 2014).

Within a month ASIC rebuffed claims that HFT was a serious problem on Australia's exchanges (Spits, 2014). The regulator argued that HFT is a much smaller proportion of trading than in the United States and that ASIC has taken an active approach to install safeguards to protect investors. In a statement, it said: "ASIC's lack of hysteria regarding high-frequency trading should not be mistaken for complacency" (Lee, 2014). Nevertheless, some groups representing the buy side, such as Industry Super Australia, continue to claim that HFT poses risks to markets. On the other hand, a major buy-side investment firm took a less negative perspective. Rodney Comegys, head of investments for Vanguard's Asia—Pacific business, based in Melbourne, said: "HFT plays a role in modern Australian equity markets and as a result, interacting with it cannot be avoided entirely. It is important to recognize that not all HFT activity has a negative impact on long-term investors" (Lee, 2014).

Elmer Kupper, chief executive of the Australian Securities Exchange (ASX), repeatedly backs ASIC's view that HFT is not a problem on the country's exchanges (Smith, 2014). At a stockbroker's conference in Melbourne he said, "Here, the behavior of HFT is more aligned with the broader market. And as a result, we have few concerns at the moment" (Wilkins, 2014). However, ASX attempts to be sensitive to the dual claim of ASIC that HFT is not a serious problem, yet safeguards for that trading should be installed. ASX is providing transaction data to the first comprehensive study of the impact of HFT on Australia's financial markets. Funding comes from a variety of sources, including AUD$300,000 from the Australian Research Council, thus counteracting claims that the research will be self-serving for the HFT community. The team is led by three of the leading financial researchers at Macquarie Graduate School of Management (Wood and Gibbens, 2014).

ASIC continues to aim for a balanced approach to HFT. Following its March 2013 report on dark pools and high-frequency traders (ASIC, 2013a), it implemented rule

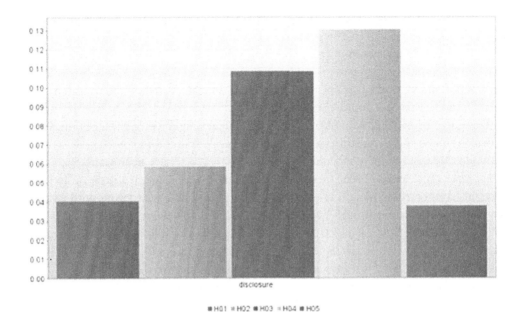

Figure 11.2 Relative proportion of articles on Australia combining transparency and HFT for five six-month periods from January 1, 2012, to June 30, 2014. *(Insight Mapping.)*

changes dealing with dark pools, which went into effect in May 2013. These changes dealt with HFT-related issues of market quality, queue jumping, and liquidity. ASIC then commissioned a study of the impact of the rule changes; it issued a report in mid-2014 claiming the rule changes achieved their desired purpose. At the same time, the regulator said it "will continue to monitor market developments" (ASIC, 2014).

The balance Australia's regulator aims to achieve between maintaining benefits of HFT and assuring investors that exchanges operate in a fair and transparent manner is an ongoing process. Evidence regarding the relative importance of transparency for HFT in Australia reveals that this issue has become increasingly important in the business press since 2012 (Figure 11.2).

Most of the exchanges want to support HFT because it generates profits, yet their customers also include investors who believe they are harmed by HFT. ASIC, therefore, must continually respond to government—political officials who support the aggrieved investors; that response impacts its approach to exchanges.

11.4.4 The United Kingdom and Europe Follow Different Regulatory Paths

While Australia's ASIC aims for a balanced approach to HFT regulation, neither the United Kingdom (UK) nor Europe follow such an approach; and, their efforts follow diametrically opposite paths. The UK's regulator, the Financial Conduct Authority (FCA), focuses on risks to markets when evaluating HFT. Exchanges need to develop procedures to mitigate systemic risks, and they should use a "risk-based and proactive approach to monitoring customers" (Henderson, 2013b). The FCA spokesperson said this was not aimed at any particular market players such as high-frequency traders, and the FCA did not favor a punitive approach.

The CEO of FCA, Martin Wheatley, formerly an employee of the London Stock Exchange, stated that regulation of HFT cannot be the same on all exchanges around the world. He opposes hasty reaction to fears of HFT, which have been stoked by Lewis (2014) *Flash Boys*. Instead, Wheatley said: "We do not want to be in a position [where] acting in haste precedes repenting at leisure. Innovation will always bring with it some risk. Sometimes too much risk" (Watkins, 2014). He emphasizes benefits of HFT and will maintain the UK's risk-based approach. This means establishing procedures such as testing algorithms prior to deployment and building in circuit breakers, otherwise known as "kill switches," on exchanges and within trading firms (Hall, 2014).

In contrast to the UK, where government–political officials have tended to be more restrained in dealing with HFT, Germany's parliament entered the debate in earnest. It passed rules to restrict HFT, including suspending stock trading when large price fluctuations occur, pauses in completion of trades, imposition of higher costs on HFT firms, and registration with the Federal Financial Supervisory Authority (BaFin). The latter requirement seemed to imply that foreign firms trading in Germany would need to establish an expensive local presence (Busemann, 2013; German States, 2013; Henderson, 2013a; Lock-Up Period, 2013). HFT firms claimed this requirement would encourage firms to exit German exchanges, undermining their liquidity (Henderson, 2013a). These exits may be intensified because exchanges are required to have algorithmic traders identify their models and to impose special fees for HFT firms making large amounts of trades (Schuster, 2013).

Germany's "High Frequency Trading" law, which went into effect in 2014, requires each algorithmic order sent to a German exchange to reference the decision-making process behind the order. Traders claimed the law would have significant negative consequences: it would substantially raise compliance costs because algorithms are complex; and it would hinder traders' capacity to respond to changing markets (Parsons, 2014). The German Bourse, however, argued that HFT regulation in Germany would not impede trading on its exchange, because it already fulfilled all of the requirements (Gould, 2014). The discrepancy between views of HFT firms and the German Bourse on the impact of the regulation contrasts with the more agreeable relations between exchanges and their HFT customers in Australia and the UK.

European Commission regulators are focused on increased control of HFT, partly at the behest of government–political officials who advocate taxing that trading. Evidence regarding the relative importance of transaction taxes for HFT in Europe reveals that this

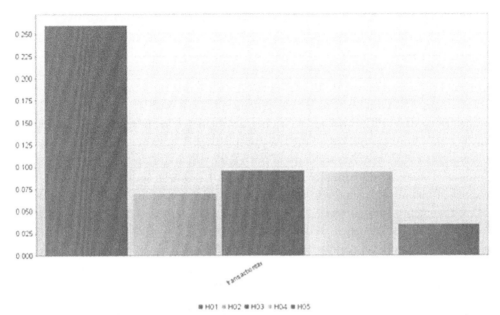

Figure 11.3 Relative proportion of articles on Europe combining transaction tax and HFT for five six-month periods from January 1, 2012, to June 30, 2014. *(Insight Mapping.)*

issue was especially important in early 2012. Since that time it has remained modestly important in the business press (Figure 11.3). The Commission adopted a financial transaction tax to reduce the amount of HFT and to raise revenue, perhaps as much as €30 billion to €35 billion annually (Financial Transaction Tax, 2013). The size of the projected revenue raises the question whether the European Commission was engaged in a punitive approach to HFT. As of early 2013, 11 of the 28 European Union countries had agreed to adopt the tax. France passed a tax the previous year that explicitly targeted HFT, as well as trading in sovereign credit default swaps (Horobin, 2012). Then, coincidental with the European Union's new tax, the finance commission of the French Senate made amendments to a bank reform bill to hinder HFT (Lejoux, 2013).

The financial transaction tax continues to be debated, not least because it is set at a punitive level, but equally important, it generates distortions and unintended consequences. HFT firms may avoid the tax by relocating their operations to another of the large number of exchanges around the world. This tax avoidance approach means that the large revenue estimates may be unrealistic, as was shown in lower tax revenue than anticipated in France and Italy. Furthermore, taxes are a cost of doing business and will increase trading firms' cost of capital, thus lowering investment. Finally, taxes will be passed on to consumers, which means the financial transaction tax is essentially a tax on investors (Vella, 2014).

The tax approach of the European Commission is part of its broader effort to rein in HFT, influenced by the view that HFT is bad for markets. That approach is being taken under an umbrella law called the Markets in Financial Instruments Directive (MiFID), which governs trading of every security in Europe (Stafford, 2013). The current effort to control HFT is part of MiFID II, and it provides the framework for the ESMA to regulate exchanges. The target date for implementation is 2016 (MiFID II Takes Step, 2014).

The sweep of MiFID II has led to numerous challenges from trading firms, and this partially results from complexity of the law's proposals (EC1 Partners Ltd, 2014). Some of the key items reflect broader concerns about HFT, which are discussed in a European Commission working document related to MiFID II. One proposal contains limits on the speed of trading and data feeds, which market participants argue will hinder liquidity. Not well recognized is that some HFT firms serve as market makers. Another proposal discusses how high-frequency traders should agree to limit their efforts to use faster speeds, but this raises anticompetitive issues. Finally, batch auctions are proposed, but these would not work throughout the day because trading typically declines in the middle of the day (Cave and Puaar, 2014).

The European Commission and its regulatory agency, the ESMA, face a dilemma. Their approach to HFT seems motivated by a punitive philosophy, which leads them to propose regulations that are at variance with the way HFT operates to provide liquidity to markets, reduce bid—ask spreads, and lower costs of trading. They also appear uncertain how to deal with ongoing technological innovations in trading (Shah, 2014b). These efforts of the European Commission and ESMA place them at odds with regulators in the United Kingdom and the Netherlands who claimed that solid evidence did not exist to support the approach of the Commission and ESMA (Puaar, 2012). A consistent theme of opponents of the European approach is that if regulations covering HFT are too onerous, this trading will decline in Europe and move to more welcoming environments because exchanges now are highly competitive entities.

11.4.5 Growing Threats to HFT in the United States

While punitive actions against HFT are progressing in Europe, the United States appeared focused on rhetorical and legal actions, accompanied more recently by targeted regulations that restrict HFT trading. Nonetheless, challenges to HFT seem to be growing. Regulators initiated a wide-ranging examination of computer trading following the May 2010 "flash crash." By 2012, federal regulators had turned their attention to HFT; questions of fairness became the topic of debate. High-frequency traders presumably had unfair advantages because they traded faster than less sophisticated traders, and they received tradable information prior to other investors. The SEC, therefore, commenced an examination of computer-driven trading platforms of electronic exchanges that attracted HFT firms (Patterson and Eaglesham, 2012).

Similar to Canada's regulators and Australia's ASIC, the SEC has increasingly taken a research-driven approach to HFT. Early in 2013, the regulator launched its Market Information Data Analytics System (MIDAS), which it acquired from Tradeworx, a HFT firm and technology vendor (SEC Launches, 2013; SEC to Report, 2013). Each trading day, the MIDAS system collects about 1 billion records time-stamped to the microsecond from proprietary data feeds of 13 equity exchanges in the United States. These provide data for research into HFT and other issues (MIDAS, 2014). Later in 2013, the SEC launched its Market Structure Data and Analysis Web site (SEC Launches, 2013; Market Structure, 2014). It makes nonproprietary data available for analysis, and posts research from its staff covering trading, including a recent literature review of HFT (Staff of the Division of Trading and Markets, 2014).

By late 2013, the SEC began to challenge self-regulation of exchanges in the United States. In a speech, Chair Mary Jo White said: "the current nature of exchange competition and the self-regulatory model should be fully evaluated in light of the evolving market structure and trading practices" (Ackerman et al., 2013). Not only was this challenge aimed at individual exchanges, but it was also directed at their self-funded watchdog, the Financial Industry Regulatory Authority (FINRA). Thus, centralization of regulation under one agency, namely, the SEC, was now up for debate. Opponents of HFT supported this push for greater regulation. They latched on to typical accusations that HFT firms acquired early access to tradable information, which enables front running, and that the exchanges provided facilities for colocation of servers, which gave HFT firms speed advantages (Massoudi, 2013).

Increased efforts to rein in HFT are being pursued on various fronts. The New York State Attorney General, Eric Schneiderman, continues to attack HFT firms and the exchanges that enable their activity. His moves vary from getting data providers to stop giving early news to HFT firms to attacking these firms for colocating their servers with exchanges, which he terms, "insider trading 2.0" (Alden, 2014). The SEC has joined the Commodity Futures Trading Commission to investigate ties between HFT traders and exchanges, and it was revealed that the Federal Bureau of Investigation is probing high-speed traders (Ackerman, 2014).

The SEC's new commissioner, Kara Stein, has added maker–taker pricing, the mechanism of exchanges providing rebates to brokers who boost liquidity, to the agency's "so-called" reform agenda. Yet, even exchanges that cater to HFT firms disagree over whether it is harmful or supportive of fair market prices. Calls to study its impacts, as well as to look at alternatives, are coming from various constituencies (Henderson, 2014; Patterson and Ackerman, 2014).

Even as Australia's ASIC continues to monitor and regulate dark pools, the controversy over these trading venues has intensified in the United States. The major exchanges have opposed dark pools saying they hurt market quality; on the other hand, they are losing trading revenue (McCrank, 2013). The SEC has taken their concerns into account;

it continues to study these trading venues (U.S. Securities and Exchange Commission, 2014). The controversy over them has moved beyond discussion to regulatory action. The financial industry's self-funded regulator, FINRA, levied an $800,000 fine on a unit of Goldman Sachs for executing trades at an inferior price (Lynch, 2014b). At the same time, Schneiderman, the New York State Attorney General, filed a lawsuit against Barclays alleging that the bank allowed high-frequency traders unfair advantages in its dark pool, even as the bank said it did not do so. Concurrently, the SEC is looking into the same issue at Barclays (Baram, 2014; Dey, 2014). Schneiderman, the SEC, and FINRA also are looking at the dark pool-HFT question at Swiss bank UBS (Shotter et al., 2014).

In early June 2014, SEC Chair Mary Jo White unleashed a major set of proposals to revamp trading on exchanges. She said: "I am recommending additional measures to further promote market stability and fairness, enhance market transparency and disclosures and build more effective markets for smaller companies" (Michaels, 2014a). Many of the proposals directly or indirectly deal with HFT, including limiting short-term trading during times of market stress, requiring proprietary traders to register as broker dealers, requiring better risk management of algorithms, adding micro-time stamps to data feeds, and having dark pools provide more information about how they handle orders of institutional clients (Lynch, 2014a).

In the speech White added conciliatory comments, saying: "I am receptive to more flexible, competitive solutions that could be adopted by trading venues." Still, she then added a thrust to the core of HFT: "These could include frequent batch auctions or other mechanisms designed to minimize speed advantages" (US SEC's, 2014). White, however, did not advocate ending the maker—taker system of rebates, which have been banned in Australia, and proposed rules about dark pool trading seem to lag efforts to control it in Australia and Canada (Michaels, 2014b). Nevertheless, the proposals reflect a shift by U.S. regulators to imposing more controls on HFT. Because these efforts are coming at a time of heightened negative commentary about such trading, this adds to uncertainty about how far regulators will go.

11.5 CONCLUSION

Recently, the controversy over HFT on exchanges has reached a crescendo, in part motivated by publication of Lewis (2014) *Flash Boys*. Nevertheless, disagreement exists over the positive and negative features of HFT. Not only do exchanges differ in their view of this trading, but also regulators, customers, and government—political officials disagree. At the root of the controversy is the claim that HFT firms possess an advantage over other traders, thus violating principles of fairness. Yet, advantages in trading based on exploitation of telecommunications and other technologies have roots that date to the spread of the telegraph in the nineteenth century. We propose a means to evaluate HFT by viewing exchanges as operating in a nexus that links them to customers, regulator, and government—political officials—in an operating environment transformed by technology firms providing new capabilities for exchanges and their counterparties (Figure 11.1).

Customers disagree over the use of HFT. Some claim it adds liquidity to markets, lowers trading costs, and reduces the bid—ask spread, thus enhancing market efficiency. Others argue that high-frequency traders cause market volatility, engage in front running, and operate in a nontransparent manner, thus raising costs and risks for investors. Because most exchanges are profit-driven institutions that compete with other exchanges, they must balance divergent views of customers regarding HFT. Many exchanges are receptive to high-frequency traders because they generate revenue. Exchanges implement technological improvements to accommodate the needs of HFT and offer various services, including colocation of servers. Even exchanges that are receptive to HFT make efforts to manage this trading in ways that do not harm customers who do not use HFT algorithms, but their success in doing so remains disputed.

Regulators of exchanges have the most direct impact on their operations, but government—political officials also enter the debate. Relations between regulators and exchanges diverge significantly among countries. At one extreme, Canada has followed a research-driven path to identify the impact of HFT on exchanges. In contrast, India's regulator has increased its attention to HFT as it shifted from a relatively benign approach to one which involves greater regulation. Australia's regulator has continued to argue for balance in control of HFT. Approaches of regulators in the United Kingdom (UK) and Europe stand apart from those in Canada, India, and Australia. The UK's regulator follows a risk-based approach that evaluates HFT from the standpoint of market risk. In contrast, continental Europe has taken a more punitive approach to HFT, based on a belief that negative features of that trading outweigh any positive features; therefore, HFT must be controlled. In the United States, regulators are embarking on more research even as they threaten greater controls on HFT.

11.5.1 Implications

Our analysis suggests the following implications of HFT for exchanges. First, HFT undermines the business model of traditional exchanges; thus, many of them have merged. Among numerous examples are: The New York Stock Exchange, Euronext, and ICE to form NYSE Euronext, the Toronto Stock Exchange and Montreal Exchange to form TMX Group, and the Tokyo Stock Exchange and Osaka Securities Exchange to form the JPX. Competition with traditional exchanges comes from a plethora of new electronic exchanges worldwide. Some of these operate in multiregional markets, such as BATS Global and Chi-X. Because many HFT firms trade on these new electronic exchanges, this shifts trading volume off traditional exchanges, thus reducing their revenue. At the same time, these exchanges must make substantial investments in technology to serve HFT firms; yet, traditional exchanges retain many customers who do not use HFT. Consequently, customer interests on exchanges are not aligned. This forces traditional exchanges to set priorities and, perhaps, underserve some market segments. Nevertheless, the new electronic exchanges face similar issues: heavy investment in trading systems that support HFT and miss-alignment of customer interests.

Second, HFT creates significant technical challenges for exchanges. Firms test their algorithms for logical errors and for decision-making processes that may run out of control, but until algorithms run under actual trading conditions it is unknown if they may cause a crisis, including even a trading crash. Thus, exchanges are exposed to customer errors that potentially may be catastrophic, perhaps imposing financial losses on the exchange. However, when government–political officials, regulators, and customers who do not use HFT demand controls on high-speed trading, the efficiency of algorithmic trading may be impaired. This may reduce liquidity, increase bid–ask spreads, and raise transaction costs for everyone, even those not using HFT. Implementation of controls may have unintended consequences; greater complexity of running HFT algorithms may make trading systems more unstable.

Third, the HFT controversy reduces the ability of exchanges to control trading. In some countries, one regulator already controls all of the exchanges. In other countries where each exchange controls trading, the proliferation of exchanges leads to demands from government–political officials and regulators to set up one regulator for all of the exchanges. This shifts rule making from private exchanges to governments and regulators with a wider scope. Once regulation is removed from exchanges, reporting and trading restrictions may raise costs for exchanges and customers. This shrinks profit margins for exchanges and reduces their competitiveness vis-à-vis exchanges in other countries that are less tightly regulated. Exchanges with stricter regulations, therefore, face difficulty responding to rapid changes in trading markets and product innovations.

Finally, calls for greater transparency in HFT collide with the demands by many customers to disguise their trading strategies to avoid being front run by other traders. One of the reasons dark pools are favored by some traders is that they provide places to trade without revealing their strategies to competitors. Demands by some regulators that they be given algorithms of HFT firms raise the specter that competitors will discover these trading models and processes. Corrupt regulators are not unknown.

These four implications of HFT for exchanges suggest that the nexus within which they operate will continue to be a contested arena.

ACKNOWLEDGMENTS

Much of the evidence in this chapter on high frequency trading was provided by Insight Mapping, a global strategic consulting firm headquartered in London and St. Louis (Missouri).

REFERENCES

Ackerman, A., April 1, 2014. SEC and CFTC are looking into ties between high-speed traders and major exchanges. Wall Str. J.

Ackerman, A., Patterson, S., Bunge, J., October 4, 2013. SEC issues warning to exchange police. Wall Str. J. Asia.

Agarwal, A., 2012. High Frequency Trading: Evolution and Future. Capgemini, London, UK.

Alden, W., March 20, 2014. Level playing field. N. Y. Times.

Algorithmic trading: curbing the risks involved. Mint, February 14, 2012.

Archer, K., Yee, J., April 23, 2014. IIROC Announces Academics for HFT Impact Analysis. Investment Industry Regulatory Organization of Canada (News Release).

As fast as light: a matter of milliseconds. Aust. Financ. Rev., March 14, 2014.

ASIC, March 2013a. Dark Liquidity and High-Frequency Trading. Report 331. Australian Securities and Investments Commission.

ASIC, August 2013b. Guidance on ASIC Market Integrity Rules for Competition in Exchange Markets. Regulatory Guide 223. Australian Securities and Investments Commission.

ASIC, May 2014. Review of Recent Rule Changes Affecting Dark Liquidity. Report 394. Australian Securities and Investments Commission.

ASX on the hunt for revenue. Aust. Financ. Rev., March 3, 2014.

Baram, M., July 24, 2014. SEC step up probe of Barclays over "dark pool" trading. Int. Bus. Times.

BATS, 2014. http://bats.com (accessed 16.07.14).

BATS global markets direct edge receive SEC approval to merge. Bus. Wire, January 31, 2014.

Bell, H.A., Searles, H., 2014. An Analysis of Global HFT Regulation: Motivations, Market Failures, and Alternative Outcomes. Working Paper No. 14–11 (April). Mercatus Center, George Mason University, Fairfax, VA.

Busemann, H.E., March 22, 2013. German Bundesrat approves HFT clampdown rules. HedgeWorld News.

Canadian Securities Administrators, 2014a. https://www.securities-administrators.ca/ (accessed 19.07.14).

Canadian Securities Administrators, May 15, 2014b. CSA Notice and Request for Comment, Proposed Amendments to National Instrument 23-101, Trading Rules. https://www.securities-administrators.ca/aboutcsa.aspx?id=1239 (accessed 19.07.14).

Cave, T., March 13, 2014. ESMA demand spotlight on high-speed trading; European watchdog reveals greater scrutiny into HFT. Financ. News.

Cave, T., Puaar, A., May 29 , 2014. High-speed traders face slowing effects of regulatory hurdles. Financ. News.

Columbia Business School, March 20, 2013. High-frequency trading: is it good or bad for markets. India Bank. News.

Crabtree, J., Stafford, P., February 10, 2013. New bourse launched in India. Financ. Times.

Cyan partners with KVH to deliver point-to-point 100 gigabit ethernet service in Japan. Opt. Netw. Dly., March 15, 2013.

Democratise trade. Financ. Chron., May 5, 2013.

Dey, I., June 29, 2014. Senior Barclays trader sidelined after "dark pools" lawsuit. The Sunday Times, Bus.

Drummond, S., March 10, 2014. Asia Pacific exchange lists first ventures. Aust. Financ. Rev.

Duarte, E., Lam, E., June 13, 2014. Predatory trading rules considered in Canada. Bloomberg.

DuBoff, R.B., 1983. The telegraph and the structure of markets in the United States, 1845–1890. Res. Econ. Hist. 8, 253–277.

Durkin, P., Shapiro, J., Kehoe, J., April 7, 2014. ASIC poised to clamp down on HFT. Aust. Financ. Rev.

EC1 partners Ltd: ESMA gets an earful from industry 10 July 2014, July 11, 2014. News Bites-Private Companies.

Farnie, D.A., 1969. East and West of Suez: The Suez Canal in History, 1854-1956. Clarendon Press, Oxford, UK.

Financial transaction tax tabled by European commission. Bank. Newslink, February 15, 2013.

Frequency trading needs of global traders. Exch. News Direct, February 27, 2012.

Frino, A., Mollica, V., Webb, R.I., 2014. The impact of co-location of securities exchanges' and traders' computer servers on market liquidity. J. Futur. Mark. 34 (1), 20−33.

German states approve tougher HFT rules. Boersen-Zeitung, March 25, 2013.

Gould, J., April 29, 2014. Deutsche Boerse sees no threat from high frequency trade debate. HedgeWorld News.

Grant, J., February 13, 2012a. Superfast trading heads to Malaysia. Financ. Times.

Grant, J., October 2, 2012b. Malaysian PM warns on high speed trade. Financ. Times.

Haines, B., September 17, 2013a. Chi-X Canada Introduces Retail Market Data Program. Chi-X Global.

Haines, B., November 12, 2013b. Chi-X Australia Sets Firm Record Market Share on Second Anniversary. Chi-X Global.

Haines, B., January 7, 2014a. J. P. Morgan Joins Chi-X Global Ownership Consortium. Chi-X Global.

Haines, B., February13, 2014b. Chi-X Japan appoints Makoto Nagahori as President and COO. Chi-X Global.

Hall, C., June 6, 2014. FCA chief backs HFT, downplays UK measures. The Trade.

Harris, L., March 1, 2013. What to do about high-frequency trading. Financial Analysts J.

Henderson, R., September 1, 2012. Asia-Pacific watchdogs consider range of HFT curbs. The Trade.

Henderson, R., April 12, 2013a. German HFT law licencing issue could spark liquidity rush. The Trade.

Henderson, R., May 9, 2013b. FCA seeks consistent "proactive" oversight by UK venues. The Trade.

Henderson, R., February 12, 2014. Maker-taker rises up SEC reform agenda. The Trade.

High-frequency trading continues to grow, despite regulatory initiatives, reveals GreySpark. Exch. News Direct, March 21, 2013.

Horobin, W., February 9, 2012. France details financial tax proposal. Financ. News.

Hutchens, G., March 26, 2013. Learn to live with risks of high-tech trading, says Gonski. Canberra Times.

IIROC, 2012. The HOT Study: Phases I and II of IIROC's Study of High Frequency Trading Activity on Canadian Equity Marketplaces. Investment Industry Regulatory Organization of Canada, Toronto, Canada (released 12 December).

IIROC, 2014. http://www.iiroc.ca/ (accessed 17.07.14).

Japan exchange to set stock prices in Y0.1 increments. Nikkei Rep., March 29, 2013.

Kumar, R., 2014. High Frequency Trading and Colocation. http://rksv.in/2014/02/high-frequency-trading/ (posted 18 February).

Langton, J., June 2, 2014. Canadian markets not "rigged", Russell says. Investment Executive. Ind. News.

Lee, J., May 7, 2014. ASIC calm over HFT impact but Australian buy-side lobby groups disagree. Asia Risk.

Lejoux, C., March 14 , 2013. French senate wants to crack down on high-frequency trading. La Trib.

Lewis, M., 2014. Flash Boys. Norton, New York, NY.

Liondis, G., March 30 , 2012. High-speed trading troubles ASIC. Aust. Financ. Rev.

Liondis, G., March 7, 2013. Market split on HFT levy. Aust. Financ. Rev.

Lock-up period must be included in HFT law. Süddeutsche Ztg., March 1, 2013.

Lockwood, S.C., 1971. Augustine Heard and Company, 1858−1862: American Merchants in China. Harvard University Press, Cambridge, MA.

Lowe, M., March 12, 2013. A leading share market analyst about to speak in Launceston is calling for action. The Exam. Newsp.

Lynch, S.N., June 5, 2014a. US SEC chair outlines major proposed equity market reforms. Reuters News.

Lynch, S.N., July 1, 2014b. Goldman Sachs fined over trade rule violations in dark pool. Reuters News.

Market Structure Data and Analysis, 2014. U.S. Securities and Exchange Commission. http://www.sec.gov/marketstructure/#.U9VKXPldX7M (accessed 27.07.14).

Marriner, S., 1961. Rathbones of Liverpool, 1845-73. Liverpool University Press, Liverpool, UK.

Massoudi, A., October 17, 2013. Regulators set to round on data providers. Financ. Times.

McCrank, J., April 16, 2013. U.S. stock exchanges call for new rules on "dark pools". Reuters News.

MCX-SX, 2014. About MCX-SX. http://www.mcx-sx.com/about-us.aspx (accessed 15.07.14).

Mellow, C., June 9, 2014. High frequency trading gets a mixed reception in emerging markets. Institutional Invest. Mag.

Meyer, D.R., 2000. Hong Kong as a Global Metropolis. Cambridge University Press, Cambridge, UK.

Michaels, D., June 6, 2014a. High-speed trading rules coming in SEC initiative, White says. Traders Mag.

Michaels, D., June 12, 2014b. No high-frequency crackdown in SEC blueprint for tighter control. Traders Mag.

MIDAS, 2014. Market information data analytics system. U.S. Securities and Exchange Commission. http://www.sec.gov/marketstructure/midas.html#.U9VDCfldX7M (accessed 27.07.14).

MiFID II takes step but faces many hurdles. Euromoney Institutional Invest., March 6, 2014.

Mihm, S., August 22, 2013. How computers took over trading. Bloomberg.

Mohan, V., Laskar, A., March 12, 2013. India's stock exchanges take their battle to new frontiers. Mint.

Moullakis, J., April 1, 2014. Brokers call for controls on shadow sector. Aust. Financ. Rev.

New Australian bourse eyes on Chinese firms, investors of long-term growth, December 23, 2013. Xinhua News Agency.

Parsons, J., March 12, 2014. Algo flagging looms large in Germany. Euromoney Institutional Invest.

Patterson, S., Ackerman, A., April 16, 2014. Move to curb trading fees gains steam. Wall Str. J.

Patterson, S., Eaglesham, J., March 23, 2012. SEC probes rapid trading. Wall Str. J.

Pinnington, V., November 21, 2013. Market quality in a rapidly changing environment. In: Presentation Notes at the OSC-IIROC Conference.

Prasad, R.R., November 5, 2012. SEBI weighs ways to rein in high-speed stock trading. Financ. Chron.

Prasad, R.R., March 29, 2013. Small brokers in peril. Financ. Chron.

Pred, A.R., 1980. Urban Growth and City-Systems in the United States, 1840–1860. Harvard University Press, Cambridge, MA.

Puaar, A., April 24, 2012. Europe's HFT curbs slammed by regulators. The Trade.

Puaar, A., March 27, 2013. JPX charts course for growth. The Trade.

Puaar, A., July 15, 2014. Bombay bourse targets HFT firms after tech revamp. Financ. Times.

Pandit, S., March 11, 2013. Managing director, omnesys. India Infoline News Serv.

Randall, H., July 14, 2014. BATS Chi-X Europe extends interoperable clearing to include exchange traded funds. BATS Chi-X Eur.

Ratterman, J., July 8, 2014. Testimony of Joe Ratterman. U.S. Senate Banking Committee. http://www.batsglobalmarkets.com/ (accessed 16.07.14).

Russell, I.C.W., Waitzer, E., March 2, 2012. Should exchanges retain regulatory role in a new age. Natl. Post. Financ. Post.

Schuster, G., May 15 , 2013. New regulatory requirements for algorithmic and high frequency trading. Mondaq Bus. Brief.

SEBI issues rules for algorithmic trading. Economic Times, March 31, 2012.

SEBI seeks sweeping powers. MintAsia (India), May 31, 2013.

SEC Launches Market Structure Data and Analysis Website, 2013. U.S. Securities and Exchange Commission. Press Release 2013-217. http://www.sec.gov/News/PressRelease/Detail/PressRelease/1370539865877#.U9VAjPldX7M (accessed 27.07.14).

SEC to report high-speed trader research. Securities Technology Monitor, October 1, 2013.

Shah, P., March 12, 2013. BSE to cut trading time by 97%. Bus. Stand.

Shah, P., April 11, 2014a. SEBI wants bourses to provide a level playing field for HFT traders. Econ. Times.

Shah, S., May 13, 2014b. Finding the perfect HFT-regulatory balance. Traders Mag.

Shapiro, J., Durbin, P., April 7, 2014. High-speed trading costs investors $2b, say industry super funds. Syd. Morning Her. Business Day.

Shotter, J., Schäfer, D., Ross, A., July 29, 2014. UBS, Deutsche drawn into "dark pool" probes. Financ. Times.

Smith, M., April 1, 2014. The ASX is not "rigged". Investor.

Spits, J., April 29, 2014. ASIC claim HFT not cause for concern in Australia. Money Manag.

Staff of the Division of Trading and Markets, March 18, 2014. Equity Market Structure Literature Review. Part II: High Frequency Trading. U.S. Securities and Exchange Commission.

Stafford, P., October 22, 2013. Europe agrees on high-speed trading regulation. Financ. Times.

Stafford, P., April 3, 2014. BATS Chi-X bids to win back Europe market share. Financ. Times.

Trader, T., March 21, 2014. NY attorney general cracks down on HFT exchange co-location. EnterpriseTech. DataCenter Edition.

US Congress week: hill to ponder high frequency trading, Fed. Mark. News Int., July 7, 2014.

US SEC's HFT shocker reverberates on street. Mark. News Int. Wash. Bur., June 10, 2014.

U.S. Securities and Exchange Commission, 2014. http://secsearch.sec.gov/search?utf8=%E2%9C%93& affiliate=secsearch&query=dark+pool (accessed 27.07.14).

Vella, J., February 26, 2014. The "Robin Hood Tax" is neither simple nor the right solution. Tax Watch. http://taxwatch.org.au/the-robin-hood-tax-is-neither-simple-nor-the-right-solution/ (accessed 21.07.14).

Watkins, J., June 5, 2014. Regulating HFT "no easy task", says FCA's Wheatley. Euromoney Institutional Invest.

Wenzlhuemer, R., 2009. London in the global telecommunications network of the nineteenth century. New. Glob. Stud. 3 (1), 1–32.

Wenzlhuemer, R., 2012. Connecting the Nineteenth-Century World: The Telegraph and Globalization. Cambridge University Press, Cambridge, UK.

What is securities transaction tax. India Infoline News Serv., March 1, 2013.

Wilkins, G., May 29, 2014. ASX chief not concerned about high frequency trading. Syd. Morning Her.

Wood, M., Gibbens, M., July 3, 2014. MGSM Embarks on Landmark Research into the Impact of High Frequency Trading. Macquarie Graduate School of Management. Market Wired.

Yeates, C., February 15, 2013. Plan to slow high-speed trades. Syd. Morning Her.

PART 3

Liquidity and Execution

CHAPTER 12

Liquidity: Systematic Liquidity, Commonality, and High-Frequency Trading

Richard G. Anderson[1], Jane M. Binner[2], Björn Hagströmer[3], Birger Nilsson[4]

[1]School of Business and Entrepreneurship, Lindenwood University, St Charles, MO, USA; [2]Department of Accounting and Finance, Birmingham Business School, University of Birmingham, Birmingham, UK; [3]School of Business, Stockholm University, Stockholm, Sweden; [4]Department of Economics, Lund University, Sweden

Contents

12.1 INTRODUCTION

Financial market liquidity—that is, the ability to convert quickly a financial asset into medium of exchange, at low cost, and without significant loss in value—plays an essential role in the banking system and the macroeconomy. It is now well understood that a sharp decrease in liquidity, due to an equally sharp increase in perceived counterparty risk, was one of the root causes of the 2007–2009 worldwide financial crisis. Warning signals, during 2007, included BNP Paribas and Bear, Sterns and Co. restricting customers' rights to withdraw putatively liquid funds from mutual funds schemes because no market valuations existed for the longer-term assets held by these funds. The September 2008 failure of Lehman Brothers brought forth a full-scale liquidity crisis as many (and perhaps most) financial intermediaries ceased to trust counterparties except those offering UK gilts or US Treasury securities as collateral.

Modern financial economics stresses that the economy's key source of liquidity is maturity intermediation: Financial firms of many types provide liquidity by issuing short-maturity financial liabilities while simultaneously purchasing longer-maturity instrument issued by others. In "normal" times, this process occurs quietly, and liquidity

The Handbook of High Frequency Trading
ISBN 978-0-12-802205-4

is measured by the transaction cost of completing each trade. In extraordinary times, a collapse of asset trading may create a liquidity crisis, the effects of which can only be attenuated by massive central bank intervention.

A challenging aspect of understanding market liquidity is to understand the relationship between unanticipated changes in market return and liquidity and in individual securities' returns and liquidity, a set of correlations often referred to as *liquidity risk*. When investors are assumed to seek to smooth consumption and, perhaps, are risk averse, liquidity risk will affect asset prices. Investors, for example, are likely to pay a premium for assets that retain liquidity when the market becomes less liquid, and to pay a premium for assets whose liquidity tends to be relatively insensitive (compared to other securities) to changes in the market rate of return (Acharya and Pedersen, 2005; Hagstromer et al., 2014; Anderson et al., 2013). Further, unanticipated changes in the liquidity of individual securities tend to be correlated: one security suddenly becoming less liquid provides information to liquidity demanders and suppliers in related securities (e.g., Cespa and Foucault, 2013). This covariance generates commonality in liquidity (across securities), a phenomenon we explore in detail below.

An important aspect of the financial crisis has been central banks' lack of powerful tools to stimulate economic growth: zero short-term interest rates and "quantitative easing" policies largely have been ineffective. Some analysts have speculated that, in part, this is due to liquidity risk premia that increased sharply during the crisis and are only slowly retreating to more normal levels.

12.2 HIGH-FREQUENCY TRADING AND LIQUIDITY

There is a continuing debate regarding whether high-frequency trading (HFT) firms provide "liquidity" to markets. Perhaps the defining characteristic of HFT is speed: faster computer servers, faster networks, and colocation of traders' servers as close as possible to the exchanges matching engines (the machines that actually record trades).[1] Advocates

---

[1] Levitt (2000) surveys the development of the current automated U.S. national equity market system beginning with the 1975 Congressional mandate that the SEC create such a system with "maximum reliance on computer and communications technologies." He notes that price transparency was the first task because prior to 1975 no exchange was required to make prices public. In 1998, the SEC passed Regulation ATS (alternative trading system) which provided a regulatory structure for electronic communication networks (ECN) that chose to be regulated as ATS rather than exchanges. In 2000, the SEC approved repeal of NYSE Rule 390 that essentially restricted the trading of NYSE-listed stocks to the NYSE. Finally, the 2007 implementation of RegNMS (national market system) removed most remaining regulatory barriers to a multiexchange national electronic trading system. Leinweber (2002) notes that by 1991, the NYSE electronic DOT system handled two-thirds of the exchange's orders; by 2001, it was 90% of orders and 50% of volume. Angel et al. (2010) note that the NYSE's share of trading in its listed stocks, following the repeal of Rule 390, fell from 80% in January 2003 to 25.8% in December 2009. Martin (2007) provides an interesting snapshot of the state of high-speed trading in 2007.

for HFTs argue that their very large numbers of outstanding orders at any moment and their increasing share of trading is de facto evidence that HFTs provide liquidity.[2] Critics argue that HFT firms' outstanding orders are "phantom liquidity" because such orders are actionable only when their portfolio holdings are those suggested by their risk models (that is, HFTs are "in equilibrium"), that large numbers of orders are placed frequently, and that the orders often quickly vanish ("in a flash") from the market.

Academic researchers have reached mixed conclusions on the impact of HFTs. The theoretical literature in general regards the speed advantage of HFTs (fast traders) as an informational advantage: a fast trader can access and react to public news (including just-posted quotes and just-completed trades) before slow traders do. News is defined very broadly, including news on fundamentals, news on order flows, and news about related securities. An important watershed in the theoretical literature lies in what fast traders do with their informational advantage. One set of models assume that fast traders use their advantage to trade actively before the liquidity suppliers have had time to react (Biais et al., 2014; Cartea and Penalva, 2012; Foucault et al., 2013; Martinez and Rosu, 2013). These models conclude that fast trading may have negative influence on liquidity, as liquidity suppliers are deterred by the fast arbitrageurs. Another set of models assumes that the liquidity suppliers are relatively fast, and that they use their speed advantage to revise their outstanding quotes according to the latest news, before anyone can pick them off (Jovanovic and Menkveld, 2012; Hoffmann, 2014; Aït-Sahalia and Saglam, 2013). Their conclusions on market quality are in general positive, because the liquidity suppliers can afford to quote larger volumes at tighter spreads if their exposure to short-term informed traders is smaller.

The empirical literature also finds mixed results on the impact of HFTs on market quality and liquidity. Many studies support the conjecture that HFT activity benefits market liquidity (see, e.g., Hendershott et al., 2011; Menkveld, 2013; Hasbrouck and Saar, 2013; Brogaard et al., 2014a). There is also an empirical support for the proposition that HFT leads to improvements in market efficiency and price discovery (Brogaard et al., 2014b) and reductions in price volatility (Hagströmer and Nordén, 2013). The latter result is however contrasted by Boehmer et al. (2014), who find that the introduction of colocation services leads to increased short-term volatility.

Critics point to that the observation that the apparent liquidity provided by HFTs vanishes when buyers seek to act on it. They argue that HFT quotes (nonmarketable orders),

---

[2] The share of equity market trading due to algorithmic trading, including HFTs, is not known precisely. Estimates range from more than half to as high as 80%. See White (2014), footnote 9, and references cited therein. In their detailed survey, Angel et al. (2010) note that average daily U.S. equity trading volume increased more than threefold between 2003 and 2009, that "the market share of the NYSE in its listed stocks fell from 80% of all volume in January 2003—25.8% in December 2009," and that high-frequency and algorithmic trading "grew to dominate trading volumes," but they offer no estimates of the proportion of that volume due to HFTs.

for small blocks of shares, are designed to capture information under the Securities and Exchange Commission (SEC) RegNMS (national market system), not to provide true liquidity to the market. As evidence, they cite the frequency with which HFTs rebalance by canceling quotes (putative liquidity providers) and become sellers, that is, demanders of liquidity. Patterson (2012) notes that during 2009, more than 90% of orders issued by HFT firms were canceled within seconds of being issued. The academic evidence on liquidity improvements following HFT activity extend to trade-based liquidity measures (such as effective spreads (ESs)), that account for this possibility. Brogaard et al. (2014a) show that the liquidity improvement associated with a colocation upgrade indeed reaches slow traders. Malinova et al. (2013) show that the liquidity costs incurred by institutional and retail traders increased after a regulatory event at the Canadian market that limited HFT activity. Both studies conclude that slow traders do benefit from HFT activities.

That bid—ask spreads are tighter now than 20 years ago is undisputed, but the execution of large positions may still be more expensive. Trading costs include broker fees and commissions, the bid—ask spread, and the market impact of the trade. During the late 1990s, bid—ask spreads often were 1/8 wide (12.5 cents) and trades were large. By 2010, spreads and commissions were small but slower fundamental investors risked higher-than-anticipated trading costs if better-informed HFTs picked off early market signals and absorbed market liquidity in the shares of interest. This conjecture finds empirical support in Hirschey (2013), who shows that HFTs engage in anticipatory trading. Such behavior forces institutional investors to employ algorithms that break up large trades in many child orders, aiming to reduce their value-weighted average execution price.

A popular recent book is Michael Lewis's *Flash Boys: A Wall Street Revolt* (2014). The book is the story of the founding of IEX, a brokerage that does not sell its limit-order book to high-frequency traders and does not permit queue jumping, that is, it does not permit high-frequency traders to use trading data to front-run actions by other traders. The mechanism is devilishly simple: introduce a delay into the network such that all customers receive data on completed transactions at the same time. Trading ahead of the elephants and whales thus is impossible.

Another concern around HFTs and the modern market structure in general, is that the trading system has become more vulnerable to extraordinary events. Such concerns date back to the disappearance of liquidity during the market crash on October 19, 1987. According to Lewis (2014), most trading at the time (perhaps in excess of 85%) was done by specialists at the NYSE and brokers on NASDAQ: liquidity vanished (at least for small- and mid-sized customers) as specialists and brokers simply did not pick up their telephone calls. Angel et al. (2010) label the event a failure due to the interaction of automated exchange trading systems built on the concept of portfolio insurance: the result in a down market was a cascade of liquidity withdrawals. Market liquidity vanished.

More than 20 years later, when market making had become largely computerized, the "Flash Crash" began at 2:32 pm ET on May 6, 2010. Within a half hour, prices on a number of interconnected US equity markets fell sharply and rebounded. The final CFTC-SEC (2010) report, academic studies (e g., Kirilenko et al., 2014; Menkveld and Yueshen, 2013), and the popular discussion by Patterson (2012) largely agree on the sequence of events. A large fundamental investor (Waddell & Reed of Kansas City), using an automated system, initiated selling 75,000 S&P E-Mini contracts worth approximately $4 billion on the Chicago Mercantile Exchange (CME). Although the sale was consistent with a defensible hedging strategy and ordinary market practice, markets were nervous due to adverse economic and political news from Europe. Initially, few fundamental investors purchased the contracts; instead, the contracts were largely purchased by intermediaries, including HFTs. As inventories increased and resting orders for the securities faltered HFTs began selling, generating a massive increase in volume. The fundamental investor's algorithm, instructed to not allow its sales pace to exceed 9% of market volume, dutifully increased its sales as volume increased, accentuating the price decline.[3] A feedback loop began. The CFTC (Commodity Futures Trading Commission)-SEC report notes that buy-side resting orders were essentially exhausted by 2:45:28 pm when the CME's Stop Logic Functionality halted trading for 5 s. When trading resumed, low prices attracted buying by fundamental investors. Menkveld and Yueshen (2013) note that, during the downward cascade, cumulative volume response grew to more than six times the initial order sizes and the long-run cumulative price response was 19 times higher than the typical long-run response.

The evidence is clear that HFTs did not cause but did contribute to the Crash. Academic studies (e.g., Kirilenko et al., 2014) have discussed indirect market mechanisms through which HFT activity might reduce market liquidity and increase financial fragility. HFTs "engage in immediacy absorption activity just ahead of any slower immediacy-seeking market participant. This immediacy absorption activity makes prices move against all slower customers who seek immediacy and, thus, imposes an immediacy absorption cost on all slower traders, including traditional market makers. This activity increases the cost of maintaining continuous market presence and makes market makers choose to maintain risk exposures that are too small to offset temporary liquidity imbalances." (Kirilenko et al., 2014). Essentially, by accelerating price adjustments, HFTs can narrow margins for traditional market makers below those required to remain as market makers.

On October 1, 2010, the CME Group (2010) also issued a brief report. It concluded that "fundamentally negative financial, economic and political events in Europe and

---

[3] The CFTC-SEC report states that the selling algorithm focused solely on market volume and not at all on price. Menkveld and Yueshen (2013) offer evidence that the algorithm was somewhat sensitive to price, tending to slow sales when prices were falling and accelerate them when prices were rising.

elsewhere contributed to investor uncertainty and impacted participation and liquidity in all market segments" but that its systems worked correctly, including credit controls, order quantity limitations, stop and market order protection points, price banding procedures, and stop logic functionality. The CME, agreeing with facts in the CFTC-SEC report, notes that the 75,000 contracts were small relative to the seller's $75 billion investment portfolio and to the day's total E-Mini volume of 5.7 million contracts. Further, more than half of the contracts were sold as the market rallied, not as it declined. Although these CME defensive comments are perfectly reasonable, the Crash nonetheless illustrates that cascades fueled by interactions among HFTs and their algorithms can be a risk to financial stability.

12.3 AN EMPIRICAL STUDY OF EQUITY MARKET LIQUIDITY

Absent extraordinary data access, studying the determinants of market liquidity via measures such as implementation shortfall, order book depth, and individual firm trading patterns is not possible for academic researchers.[4] In this section, we used publicly available data to address a related question: To what extent are high-frequency changes in the liquidity of individual U.S. equities correlated with each other? And, if such correlation exists, does there exist a statistical measure of market-wide liquidity that well captures both period-to-period changes in individual securities' liquidity and their cross-section correlations?

The finance literature refers to the concept of market-wide liquidity as "systematic liquidity" and to comovement among the measured liquidities of individual stocks as "commonality." Commonality in liquidity has been well established for many asset classes (stocks, bonds, options, and foreign exchange), for all dimensions of liquidity (tightness, depth, and resiliency, as categorized in the seminal paper by Kyle (1985)), and for geographical regions around the world. Further, both the liquidity of individual assets and commonality has been shown to affect asset prices.

Measuring (statistically) liquidity commonality is a two-stage problem. First, a suitable liquidity measure must be chosen for individual securities—here, we consider eight alternatives. Second, an estimator for systematic liquidity must be chosen—here, we consider five alternatives. Our five systematic liquidity estimators lie in two classes: (1) weighted average estimators, each based only on current period (concurrent) data for individual securities, and (2) principal components (PCA) estimators based on both concurrent and prior period data. The former class is attractive due to its simplicity and ease of period-to-period updating—but, statistically, estimators in the latter class utilize more of the

---

[4] We note that both Kirilenko et al. (2014) and Menkveld and Yueshen (2013) rely on proprietary data not available to other researchers. Leinweber (2002), an interesting study of implementation shortfall, similarly relies on proprietary data.

information contained in the data set. PCA-based estimators are derived to maximize the explanatory power on total variation in liquidity by utilizing the information in the covariance matrix of the shocks. The weighted average estimators, on the other hand, do not have objective functions, but they are appreciated for their simplicity and their analogy to the market return factor.

So as to explore time variation in commonality, we generalize previously published estimators in two aspects. First, we allow for short-term trends in all our evaluations. Second, we allow time variation in the covariance matrix used for PCA estimation. Specifically, we introduce a "short-term" PCA estimator calculated over a rolling fixed-width estimation window. The short-term PCA performs better than previously applied versions of PCA throughout our evaluations, indicating that the covariance matrix of liquidity shocks is indeed time varying.

In our horse race, which class of estimators wins the flag? Our results suggest that the class of less-complex weighted average estimators performs at least as well at identifying systematic liquidity and commonality as the class of more complex principal component estimators (even when time variation in the covariance matrix is permitted). This finding is robust across our eight measures of liquidity. Commonality is a risk factor potentially important in asset pricing: investors should be willing to pay a premium for stocks that remain relatively more liquid when the market is becoming less liquid.[5] The importance of our findings for studies of equity returns is a topic of ongoing research.

12.3.1 Measures of Liquidity for Individual Stocks

Let $L^1, L^2, L^3, L^4, L^5, L^6, L^7, L^8$ denote measured levels of individual stock liquidity, where the each superscript denotes a different measure. Each L^j is a matrix, with the row and column indexes denoting firms and time periods (months), respectively. L^1 is quoted spread (QS), the monthly average ratio of the quoted bid—ask spread and its midpoint, observed at each trade. L^2 is ES, the absolute difference between trade price and quoted bid—ask spread midpoint prevailing at the time of the trade, divided by the midpoint of the same bid—ask spread, and averaged across all trades in the month. L^3 is turnover (TO), the ratio of monthly volume traded and shares outstanding, adjusted for the number of trading days in the month. L^4 is the illiquidity ratio introduced by Amihud (2002), ILLIQ, the ratio of absolute daily returns and daily dollar volume averaged across days in the month, adjusted for the trend increase in asset prices (e.g., Acharya and Pedersen, 2005). L^5, L^6, L^7, L^8 are the price impact coefficients defined by Sadka (2006) and Korajczyk and Sadka (2008) that describe adverse selection costs (permanent variable and fixed costs, Ψ and λ, respectively) and inventory costs (transitory variable and fixed

---

[5] Consumption smoothing, for example, suggests this type of behavior.

costs, $\tilde{\Psi}$ and $\tilde{\lambda}$, respectively).[6] Specifically, these coefficients are obtained by Ordinary Least Squares estimation of the equation

$$\Delta p_{k,t} = \alpha_t + \Psi_t \varepsilon_{\Psi,k,t} + \lambda_t \varepsilon_{\lambda,k,t} + \tilde{\Psi}_t \Delta D_{k,t} + \tilde{\lambda}_t \Delta \left(D_{k,t} V_{k,t} \right) + \gamma_{k,t}$$

where $\Delta p_{k,t}$ is the price change associated with trade k in month t, $\varepsilon_{\Psi,k}$ is the unanticipated direction of order flows, $\varepsilon_{\lambda,k}$ is the unanticipated order flow volume, $\Delta D_{k,t}$ is the change in the direction of order flow, $\Delta(D_{k,t}V_{k,t})$ is the change in the signed order volume, and $\gamma_{k,t}$ is a measure of the public information flow at the time of trade, k. Coefficients are estimated each month for each stock and are scaled by the end-of-month stock price, and winsorized at the first and 99th percentile to limit the influence of outliers.

Our statistical analysis utilizes liquidity innovations ("shocks"). Levels of liquidity for individual stocks tend to be highly persistent period to period, and hence readily forecastable: innovations, essentially, are the period-by-period forecast errors that move market prices and returns (phrased equivalently, the innovation is that portion of today's liquidity level that was not anticipated last period). Commonality seeks to understand the covariances among such shocks: How closely do innovations to the liquidity of individual stocks move with innovations to market liquidity?

Absent a well-agreed upon structural model for liquidity, we assume that levels of liquidity for individual stocks are projected forward using an extrapolative model

$$E_{t-1}L_t^j = \sum_{s=1}^{S} w_{t-s} L_{t-s}^j,$$

where $E_{t-1}L_t^j$ is the expectation for period t conditional on information available through the end of period $t-1$. We assume the weights decay exponentially as

$$w_{t-1} = \frac{1-d}{1-d_j^s} \quad \text{and} \quad w_{t-s} = d_j^{s-1} w_{t-1}$$

where d_j is a decay parameter specific to liquidity measure j, $0 \le d_j < 1$, and $\sum_{s=0}^{S} w_{t-s} = 1$. Values of d_j are those that maximize Root Mean Square Forecast Error in our full data sample: 0.225, 0.425, 0.757, 0.425, 0.825, 0.775, 0.600, and 0.825 for measures $L^1, L^2, L^3, L^4, L^5, L^6, L^7, L^8$, respectively.

12.3.2 Estimators for Systematic Liquidity and Commonality

The finance literature most often assumes that systematic liquidity and individual stocks' liquidities—both levels and innovations—are connected in a linear fashion. Let Ω be a

---

[6] To avoid the influence of outliers, each liquidity measure is winsorized by setting values lower (higher) than the first (99th) percentile in each time period equal to the first (99th) percentile.

matrix of innovations (one-period forecast errors, or "shocks") in individual firm's liquidity, with row and column indexes representing firms and dates, respectively. We assert that Ω can be described by an approximate static latent factor model (Chamberlain and Rothschild, 1983), $\Omega = Bf + \varepsilon$, where the common component is Bf (the product of the factor loadings and the systematic factors f) and the idiosyncratic component is ε.

Our weighted average estimators of systematic liquidity, which we denote as f^{ave}, are row vectors containing weighted averages of the columns of Ω. Weights of unity yield the equal-weighted measure, f^{ave}_{eq}; weights proportional to the firm's market value among stocks included during that 60-month estimation window yield the value-weighted measure, f^{ave}_{va}; and weights proportional to each stock's variability in the liquidity shocks calculated over the same 60-month window as used in the regression yield the variance-weighted measure, f^{ave}_{vw}. Previous studies have concluded that the properties of the equal-weighted and value-weighted versions are similar (Chordia et al., 2000, Chordia et al., 2001; Acharya and Pedersen, 2005; Kamara et al., 2008). Further, Acharya and Pedersen (2005) argue that the equal-weighted estimator is preferable as large liquid companies can be overrepresented in the value-weighted average. Hence, below we do not further consider the value-weighted average.

Our principal component-based estimators exploit the nonzero cross-section covariances among the measured liquidity measures for individual stocks. Specifically, we use the first principal component of the innovation covariance matrix as the systematic liquidity estimator, that is, $f^{pca} = \Gamma\Omega$ where Γ is the eigenvector that corresponds to the largest eigenvalue of the cross-sectional covariance matrix of Ω.[7] As noted above, we also relax the restriction, commonplace in previous studies, that the cross-sectional liquidity covariance structure is time invariant. Evidence suggests, for example, that commonality is stronger when stock prices are falling (Coughenour and Saad, 2004; Domowitz et al., 2005), and that it changes through time (Kamara et al., 2008; Karolyi et al., 2009). Allowing time variation also increases the robustness of our experiments to possible structural breaks in the time series. Our method is to introduce a rolling estimation window, reestimating f^{pca} window-by-window. We therefore have three PCA-based estimators that differ in their data span: f^{pca}_a uses a rolling, fixed-width, 60-period window ("short-term PCA"); f^{pca}_b uses an expanding, variable width window that begins with 36 observations and ends with the entire data sample ("long-term PCA"); and f^{pca}_c uses a single fixed-width window that contains the complete time series of data ("full-sample PCA").[8]

We choose a 60-month rolling window width for the rolling short-term PCA estimator but the choice of window width is subject to a trade-off between asymptotic

---

[7] We do not calculate this directly in our empirical application, but rather utilize asymptotic PCA, an asymptotically equivalent algorithm that is computationally more economical. See Connor and Korajczyk (1986).

[8] The long-term PCA estimator also is used by Chen (2007).

unbiasedness and consistency. Absent autocorrelation in the idiosyncratic component, a PCA estimator is consistent as the number of firms approaches infinity, independent of the number of time periods (Stock and Watson, 2002). When the error terms are auto-correlated, however, consistency further requires that the number of time periods approaches infinity. Applying the LM test (Breusch, 1978; Godfrey, 1978) with four lags, we are unable to reject the null hypothesis of no residual autocorrelation in 98% of our 60-month-wide estimation windows.

12.4 DATA

Our data set is the NYSE's Trades and Quote (TAQ) database, covering the years 1993–2007. We end our sample in 2007, the year when RegNMS was implemented, so as to avoid the volume-boosting effects of HFT. Due to the large size of the TAQ database, we limit our sample to firms that were in the S&P 500 index at the end of 2007.[9] During our sample period, the NYSE was the primary listing for most S&P 500 stocks, with approximately 100 on the Amex and a few on the NASDAQ. To be included in the S&P 500 index, NYSE and Amex firms' shares were required to have minimum monthly TOs of 30%; firms on the Amex were required to have 60% TO. It is well known that trading rules on these exchanges during our sample period both differed from each other and changed through time; hence, measures of the levels of individual stock liquidity are not directly comparable across exchanges. However, our estimation of systematic liquidity utilizes innovations, not levels, and is focused on covariation, not levels, permitting us to statistically pool liquidity measures across exchanges.

Liquidity estimation using TAQ data requires extensive data processing. Accepted data cleaning practices, as discussed below, were developed prior to HFT; their appropriateness in more recent data influenced by HFT remains a topic for future research.[10] We include stocks from the NYSE, Nasdaq, Amex, and the electronic platforms Nasdaq-ADF and Arca. We exclude trades marked to be erroneous or to have special conditions, and trades executed at very high (>$15,000) or very low (<$0.5) prices. Spreads are excluded if they are negative, larger than $5, or when they exceed 25% of their midpoint. Simultaneous trades (trades recorded in the same second) are aggregated by summing the volumes and by calculating the volume-weighted trade price; to the extent that HFT

---

[9] By including only firms with data for all periods, we acknowledge a potential survivorship bias toward large, profitable—and hence more liquid—firms.

[10] A consequence of the SEC's 2007 implementation of RegNMS was that equities began trading on multiple exchanges, with trades and quotes on all exchanges and alternative trading systems (ATS) reported via Securities Information Processors to a consolidated national database. As of June 2014, there were 11 public exchanges and perhaps 40 ATS. SEC rules require that reporting feeds to the national market system database have performance comparable to direct feeds from the exchanges to HFTs; see White (2014).

affects the later years of our sample, we trust this minimizes the effect. Where simultaneous quotes exist, the last observation in each second is used. We filter the trades for outliers using the algorithm suggested by Brownlees and Gallo (2006), excluding any trade observation that deviates more than three standard deviations from its local mean. Matching of trades and quotes is done using a one second delay, following the findings of Henker and Wang (2006). For cases in which the trade price is more than 10% higher (lower) than the ask(bid) price, the quote observation is deleted. Measured individual stock liquidities are aggregated to a monthly frequency.

12.5 STATISTICAL RESULTS

We noted above that the existence of commonality and systematic liquidity implies, statistically, the existence of a common factor model. Do different estimators of systematic liquidity capture the same common factor? Our statistical analysis focuses on the regression

$$l_{i,t} = \alpha_i^l + \beta_i^i f_t + u_{i,t}$$

where $l_{i,t}$ denotes stock-specific liquidity innovations, f_t the (latent) systematic liquidity innovation, and $u_{i,t}$ captures stock-specific effects. Two popular metrics of degree of commonality are common in the literature: R^2 and β^l. Both metrics are typically reported as cross-sectional averages of regressions run on all stocks; here, β^l denotes that average. As a measure of explanatory power, R^2 is straightforward to compare across systematic liquidity estimators and liquidity measures. To compare β^l across estimators, we normalize the mean and variance of the systematic liquidity estimators. Finally, as previously noted, we seek to capture time variation in liquidity commonality by use of a rolling, fixed-width (60-month) estimation window in the regressions that yield β^l. To be included in a regression, a stock must have at least 30 (monthly) observations during the 60-month rolling window.

Table 12.1 displays summary statistics (panel A) and correlations (panel B) for our eight liquidity-level measures. Measures L^1, L^2, L^3, L^4 have only positive values by construction, while the distributions of the measures L^5, L^6, L^7, L^8 contain both positive and negative values. The transitory variable cost, $\tilde{\lambda}$, is also negative on average, perhaps because variable inventory costs decrease as a proportion of total costs as volume increases. (In our results, the two variable cost series have a strong negative correlation, -0.72).

The values of our price impact coefficients are smaller than those found by Sadka (2006) in a similar study, perhaps because overall liquidity is higher in our sample than in his: we study larger firms and a later time period. Overall, our estimates are comparable to previous studies: fixed inventory costs are much higher than adverse selection costs by a factor of 10, and variable trading costs are dominated by adverse selection costs. Turnover and the variable inventory cost are measures of liquidity; both in general

Table 12.1 Descriptive statistics of liquidity measures

Panel A: Summary statistics

	Mean	Median	Std deviation	Max	Min
L^1 (QS)	0.37	0.26	0.41	9.99	0.02
L^2 (ES)	0.11	0.07	0.14	3.50	0.01
L^3 (TO)	10.49	7.70	11.41	556.58	0.122
L^4 (ILLIQ)	0.10	0.02	0.70	47.77	0.00
L^5 (Ψ)	0.006	0.004	0.014	0.779	−0.591
L^6 (λ)	0.37	0.16	1.38	63.98	−53.42
L^7 ($\tilde{\Psi}$)	0.06	0.03	0.12	3.96	−0.58
L^8 ($\tilde{\lambda}$)	−0.12	−0.02	0.84	71.89	−46.58

Panel B: Time-series correlations

	L^1	L^2	L^3	L^4	L^5	L^6	L^7	L^8
L^1 (QS)	1							
L^2 (ES)	0.74	1						
L^3 (TO)	−0.24	−0.16	1					
L^4 (ILLIQ)	0.58	0.45	−0.36	1				
L^5 (Ψ)	0.06	0.04	−0.1	0.19	1			
L^6 (λ)	0.19	0.13	−0.26	0.28	−0.13	1		
L^7 ($\tilde{\Psi}$)	0.52	0.53	−0.21	0.44	0.01	0.23	1	
L^8 ($\tilde{\lambda}$)	−0.18	−0.14	0.22	−0.22	0.11	−0.72	−0.25	1

Notes:
1. L^1, L^2, L^3, L^5, L^7 are measured in percent.
2. L^4, L^6, L^8 are rescaled via multiplication by 10^6.

negatively correlated with other liquidity measures. Other measures are measuring *illiquidity*. As expected, the two bid-ask spread measures are highly correlated: the expected spread measures the half-spread while the quoted spread measures the full spread. A high occurrence of trading inside the spread is indicated by the expected spread being less than half the size of the quoted spread. The spreads also are highly correlated with Amihud's illiquidity ratio (ILLIQ) and the fixed inventory costs.

Table 12.2 reports our analysis of correlation among systematic liquidity estimators. Overall, the correlations shown in Table 12.2 provide significant evidence against our implicit null hypothesis that all estimators are equivalent. Because systematic liquidity varies from period to period, we explore both time-series and cross-section correlation within as well as across classes of systematic liquidity estimators. Figures shown in the table are time-series averages of correlations calculated using a 60-month-wide moving window.

First, the two weighted average estimators, f_{EQ}^{ave} and f_{VW}^{ave}, are highly correlated (>0.7) for all liquidity measures despite the estimators' different weighting schemes, perhaps indicating similar variation in liquidity shocks across stocks. Second, for the PCA-based estimators, we find perfect correlation between the long-term and full-sample versions, f_b^{pc} and f_c^{pc}, for all liquidity measures except TO. We would expect these two estimators to converge over time and to become perfectly correlated at time T, but that they are (almost) perfectly correlated from the beginning is surprising. A hypothesis is that these measures' covariances are constant over time; unfortunately, the low correlations to short-term PCA (between 0.2 and 0.5) suggest rejecting the hypothesis. An alternative hypothesis is that early observations are dominating the covariance estimation. For the first few months of our sample, short-term PCA is perfectly correlated with full-sample PCA, but the correlation falls sharply as the early observations exit the estimation window of short-term PCA. The causes of this behavior remain a subject of future research.

Turning to correlations across classes of estimators, we see that the variance-weighted average is highly correlated with the short-term PCA. Significant correlation is to be expected since both use the same covariance matrix. They differ because the variance-weighted average only utilizes the main diagonal, while PCA utilizes all elements; the high correlation signals the influence of the diagonal elements. Correlations of the short-term PCA with the equal-weighted average are lower, hovering near 0.6. Only weak correlation is found between the weighted averages and the PCA (long-term and full-sample). This reflects the fact that the weighted averages are oriented toward the short term, only using current information.

We conclude with a regression-based summary of how the differences in our systematic liquidity measures and estimators. Table 12.3, panel A, explores the explanatory power of the regression introduced above, $l_{i,t} = \alpha_i^l + \beta_i^i f_t + u_{i,t}$, where the reported coefficients are averaged first across stocks and then over time (that is, each time-series observation is a cross-sectional average), and panel B shows estimated sensitivities

Table 12.2 Correlation between systematic liquidity estimators, for eight liquidity measures

	L^1 (QS)	L^2 (ES)	L^3 (TO)	L^4 (ILLIQ)	L^5 (Ψ)	L^6 (λ)	L^7 ($\tilde{\Psi}$)	L^8 ($\tilde{\lambda}$)
$f^{ave}_{ew}, f^{ave}_{vw}$	0.89	0.94	0.94	0.85	0.91	0.83	0.91	0.73
f^{pca}_a, f^{pca}_b	0.41	0.14	0.93	0.45	0.36	0.34	0.52	0.50
f^{pca}_a, f^{pca}_c	0.40	0.14	0.71	0.45	0.36	0.35	0.52	0.50
f^{pca}_b, f^{pca}_c	1.00	1.00	0.78	1.00	1.00	1.00	1.00	1.00
f^{ave}_{ew}, f^{pca}_a	0.48	0.76	0.67	0.76	0.63	0.60	0.62	0.52
f^{ave}_{ew}, f^{pca}_b	0.29	0.30	0.63	0.52	0.44	0.22	0.53	0.37
f^{ave}_{ew}, f^{pca}_c	0.28	0.30	0.71	0.52	0.44	0.22	0.53	0.37
f^{ave}_{vw}, f^{pca}_a	0.75	0.85	0.75	0.96	0.77	0.81	0.78	0.90
f^{ave}_{vw}, f^{pca}_b	0.38	0.27	0.73	0.46	0.37	0.33	0.53	0.48
f^{ave}_{vw}, f^{pca}_c	0.37	0.27	0.78	0.46	0.37	0.34	0.53	0.48

Note: In this table, L^i denotes the innovation to the liquidity measure, not its level.

Table 12.3 Commonality in liquidity

	L^1 (QS)	L^2 (ES)	L^3 (TO)	L^4 (ILLIQ)	L^5 (Ψ)	L^6 (λ)	L^7 ($\tilde{\Psi}$)	L^8 ($\tilde{\lambda}$)
Panel A: R^2								
f_{ew}^{ave}	0.253	0.338	0.153	0.151	0.095	0.145	0.273	0.081
f_{vw}^{ave}	0.0186	0.292	0.131	0.081	0.086	0.108	0.208	0.050
f_a^{ave}	0.105	0.244	0.099	0.071	0.079	0.085	0.156	0.047
f_b^{ave}	0.062	0.071	0.088	0.059	0.055	0.030	0.114	0.038
f_c^{ave}	0.059	0.071	0.089	0.059	0.055	0.030	0.114	0.038
Panel B: $\hat{\beta}^t$								
f_{ew}^{ave}	0.00051	0.00030	0.00046	0.0213	0.000017	0.0128	0.00012	0.0051
f_{vw}^{ave}	0.00047	0.00035	0.00044	0.0205	0.000017	0.0115	0.00013	0.0048
f_a^{ave}	0.00038	0.00040	0.00037	0.0207	0.000020	0.0116	0.00028	0.0055
f_b^{ave}	0.00029	0.00026	0.00035	0.0179	0.00016	0.0075	0.00019	0.0048
f_c^{ave}	0.00029	0.00026	0.00036	0.0179	0.000016	0.0075	0.00019	0.0048

Note: In the table, L^i denotes the innovation to the liquidity measure, not its level.

to systematic liquidity, averaged also first over stocks and then over time. Panel A suggests there is a clear tendency of the equal-weighted average f_{ev}^{ave} to outperform other systematic liquidity estimators: about 25%, 19%, and 11% of the variation in quoted spreads is explained by the equal-weighted, variance-weighted average, and short-term PCA, respectively. Although the magnitudes of the differences vary across liquidity measures, the ranking of the estimators is consistent: across liquidity measures, the long term and static versions of PCA, f_b^{pca} and f_c^{pca}, consistently perform worse than the other estimators.

Why does the equal-weighted average, arguably the simplest of the five, outperform? Recalling the objective functions of the PCA estimators, it is obvious that average R^2 is not what PCA is designed to maximize. Algebraically, principal component analysis seeks to find an alternative basis in which to represent a matrix: because it is a linear operator, the complete set of principal components (in the new basis) fully describes the original matrix (in its basis). Statistically, the first principal component seeks to explain as large a proportion as possible of the data set's variance subject to certain orthogonality conditions. Hence, intuition might predict that PCA-based estimators must always be "best." The variance-weighted average, by construction, seeks to explain total variance in liquidity, not covariances. It can be argued that the R^2 measure reported here for the equal-weighted average is biased upward although we are not aware of a study that has explored such bias.

Our second metric of commonality (Table 12.3, panel B) is the sensitivity of individual stock liquidity to systematic liquidity shocks, β^i. The differences across estimators are smaller than those found for R^2. For five liquidity measures, the highest numbers are recorded for the equal-weighted average but for ESs and transitory costs the short-term PCA is superior. The long-term PCA estimators are still consistently outperformed by the other estimators, but the difference is much smaller than before. The average $\widehat{\beta}^t$ metric shares many of the shortcomings discussed for average R^2 above. Still, the importance of these measures lies in that we know that individual liquidity is priced (Amihud et al., 2005), so the more liquidity variation that can be explained, the better we can understand asset prices. The conclusion of our commonality investigation should hence be that the equal-weighted average is doing well relative to other estimators, but to say which estimator is most useful in asset pricing, we need an application that investigates the problem more directly. One obvious method is a Fama French-style high vs low portfolio analysis based on $\widehat{\beta}^t$. We leave this as a topic for future research.

12.6 CONCLUDING THOUGHTS

Liquidity is a fundamental topic in modern finance. While many analysts have discussed the relationship between liquidity and HFT, the research at this time is inconclusive. Yet, sudden changes in the liquidity of individual stocks can convey information about potential changes in the liquidity of correlated stocks and, perhaps, of the market as whole—the so-called systematic liquidity and commonality. We have examined a broad set of alternative commonality estimators based on eight alternative measures of individual stock liquidity.

While principal components remain the natural choice of systematic liquidity estimators, our study suggests that weighted average estimators are at least as good as principal component-based estimators, regardless of liquidity measure and evaluation criterion. Applying our results to explain equity returns is a topic for future research.

REFERENCES

Acharya, V., Pedersen, L., 2005. Asset pricing with liquidity risk. J. Financ. Econ. 77 (2), 375—410.
Aït-Sahalia, Y., Saglam, M., 2013. High Frequency Traders: Taking Advantage of Speed. Working paper. Department of Economics, Princeton University, Princeton, NJ.
Amihud, Y., 2002. Illiquidity and stock returns: cross-section and time-series effects. J. Financ. Mark. 5, 31—56.
Amihud, Y., Pedersen, L., Mendelson, H., 2005. Liquidity and asset prices. Found. Trends Finance 1 (4), 269—364.
Anderson, R., Binner, J., Hagströmer, B., Nilsson, B., 2013. Does Commonality in Illiquidity Matter to Investors? Working Paper 2013-020A Research Division, Federal Reserve Bank of St. Louis.
Angel, J., Harris, L., Spatt, C., 2010. Equity Trading in the 21st Century. Working Paper FBE 09—10. Marshall School of Business, University of Southern California, Los Angeles, CA.
Biais, B., Foucault, T., Moinas, S., March 2014. Equilibrium Fast Trading. Working Paper 968/2013. HEC Paris.
Boehmer, E., Fong, K., Wu, J., June 2014. International Evidence on Algorithmic Trading. Working Paper. Lee Chian School of Business, Singapore Management University, Singapore.

Breusch, T., 1978. Testing for autocorrelation in dynamic linear models. Aust. Econ. Pap. 17 (31), 334–335.

Brogaard, J., Hagströmer, B., Nordén, L., Riordan, R., 2014a. Trading Fast and Slow: Colocation and Market Quality. Working Paper. Foster School of Business, University of Washington, Seattle, WA.

Brogaard, J., Hendershott, T., Riordan, R., 2014b. High frequency trading and price discovery. Rev. Financ. Stud. 27 (8), 2267–2306.

Brownlees, C., Gallo, G., 2006. Financial econometric analysis at ultra-high frequency: data handling concerns. Comput. Stat. Data Anal. 51 (4), 2232–2245.

Cartea, A., Penalva, J., 2012. Where is the value in high frequency trading? Q. J. Finance 2 (3), 1–46.

Cespa, G., Foucault, T., 2013. Illiquidity Contagion and liquidity Crashes. Working Paper. Cass Business School, London, UK., and HEC Paris.

Chamberlain, G., Rothschild, M., 1983. Arbitrage, factor structure, and mean variance analysis on large asset markets. Econometrica 51 (5), 1281–1304.

Chen, J., 2007. Understanding Equity Returns (Ph.D. thesis). Columbia University, New York.

Chordia, T., Roll, R., Subrahmanyam, A., 2000. Commonality in liquidity. J. Financ. Econ. 56 (1), 3–28.

Chordia, T., Roll, R., Subrahmanyam, A., 2001. Market liquidity and trading activity. J. Finance 56 (2), 501–530.

CME Group, October 2010. CME Group Statement on the Joint CFTC/SEC Report Regarding the Events of May 6. CME Group, Chicago.

Connor, G., Korajczyk, R., 1986. Performance measurement with the arbitrage pricing theory: a new framework for analysis. J. Financ. Econ. 15 (3), 373–394.

Coughenour, J., Saad, M., 2004. Common market makers and commonality in liquidity. J. Financ. Econ. 73 (1), 37–69.

Domowitz, I., Hansch, O., Wang, X., 2005. Liquidity commonality and return co-movement. J. Financ. Mark. 8 (4), 351–376.

Foucault, T., Hombert, J., Rosu, I., May 2013. News Trading and Speed. Working Paper. HEC Paris.

Godfrey, L., 1978. Testing against general autoregressive and moving average error models when the regressors include lagged dependent variables. Econometrica 46 (6), 1293–1301.

Hagströmer, B., Hansson, B., Nilsson, B., 2013. The components of the illiquidity premium: an empirical analysis of U.S. Stocks 1927–2010. J. Bank. Finance, 37 (11), 4476–4487.

Hagströmer, B., Nordén, L., 2013. The diversity of high-frequency traders. J. Financ. Mark. 16 (4), 741–770.

Hasbrouck, J., Saar, G., 2013. Low-latency trading. J. Financ. Mark. 16 (4), 646–679.

Hendershott, T., Jones, C., Menkveld, A., 2011. Does algorithmic trading improve liquidity? J. Finance 66 (1), 1–33.

Henker, T., Wang, J., 2006. On the importance of timing specifications in market microstructure research. J. Financ. Mark. 9 (2), 162–179.

Hirschey, N., April 2013. Do High-frequency Traders Anticipate Buying and Selling Pressure? Working paper London Business School.

Hoffmann, P., 2014. A dynamic limit order market with fast and slow traders. J. Financ. Econ. 113 (1), 156–169.

Jovanovic, B., Menkveld, A., November 2012. Middlemen in Limit-order Markets. Working Paper. Department of Economics, New York University.

Kamara, A., Lou, X., Sadka, R., 2008. The divergence of liquidity commonality in the cross-section of stocks. J. Financ. Econ. 89 (3), 444–466.

Karolyi, G., Lee, K.-H., van Dijk, M., 2009. Commonality in Returns, Liquidity, and Turnover Around the World. Working Paper. Fisher College of Business, Ohio State University.

Kirilenko, A., Kyle, A., Samadi, M., Tuzun, T., May 2014. The Flash Crash: The Impact of High Frequency Trading on an Electronic Market. Working paper. MIT Sloan School of Management.

Korajczyk, R., Sadka, R., 2008. Pricing the commonality across alternative measures of liquidity. J. Financ. Econ. 87 (1), 45–72.

Kyle, A., 1985. Continuous auctions and insider trading. Econometrica 53 (6), 1315–1336.

Leinweber, D., 2002. Using Information from Trading in Trading and Portfolio Management: Ten Years Later. Working paper. California Institute of Technology, Pasadena, CA.

Levitt, A., 2000. Testimony Concerning Preserving and Strengthening the National Market System for Securities in the United States. Before the U.S. Senate Committee on Banking, Housing, and Urban Affairs, Washington, D.C.

Lewis, M., 2014. Flash Boys. W.W. Norton and Company, New York, NY.

Malinova, K., Park, A., Riordan, R., 2013. Do Retail Traders Suffer from High Frequency Traders? Working paper University of Toronto.

Martin, R., April 2007. Business at light speed. Inf. Week 23, 43–47.

Martinez, V., Rosu, I., 2013. High Frequency Traders, News and Volatility. Working Paper. HEC Paris.

Menkveld, A., 2013. High frequency trading and the new-market makers. J. Financ. Mark. 16 (4), 712–740.

Menkveld, A., Yueshen, B., December 2013. Anatomy of the Flash Crash. Working Paper. Tinbergen Institute and Duisenberg School of Finance, VU University, Amsterdam.

Patterson, S., 2012. Dark Pools: The Rise of the Machine Traders and the Rigging of the U.S. Stock Market. Random House.

Sadka, R., 2006. Momentum and post-earnings announcement-drift anomalies: the role of liquidity risk. J. Financ. Econ. 80 (2), 309–349.

Stock, J., Watson, M., 2002. Forecasting using principal components from a large number of predictors. J. Am. Stat. Assoc. 97 (460), 1167–1179.

U.S. Commodity Futures Trading Commission and U.S. Securities & Exchange Commission, 2010. Findings Regarding the Market Events of May 6, 2010. Report of the Staffs of the CFTC and SEC to the Joint Advisory Committee on Emerging Regulatory Issues.

White, M., June 2014. Enhancing our equity market structure. Presented at Sandler O'Neill & Partners, L.P., Global Exchange and Brokerage Conference, New York.

CHAPTER 13

We Missed It Again! Why Do So Many Market Orders in High-Frequency FX Trading Fail to be Executed?

Masayuki Susai[1], Yushi Yoshida[2]
[1]Nagasaki University, Nagasaki, Japan; [2]Shiga University, Hikone, Japan

Contents

13.1 INTRODUCTION

Due to the ever-increasing speed of information processing technology, financial markets have undergone drastic changes, especially in terms of high-frequency trading. FX markets are the largest, fastest, thickest markets of all financial markets. The daily average turnovers of spot FX markets exceed one trillion US dollars according to the Bank for International Settlements (2010). However, the Electronic Broking System (EBS), one of the two major FX electronic dealing platforms, has only in recent years begun providing the automated interface. Algorithmic trading in the EBS FX spot markets was negligible in 2004 but has experienced rapid growth.[1] Chaboud et al. (2014) show that algorithmic trading at the end of 2007 was involved in approximately 60%

---

[1] Algorithmic trading is a part of the trading strategies of financial institutions and thus is private information they are not required to reveal. Algorithmic trading is approximated in Hendershott et al. (2011) by the number of electronic messages sent per minute at the NYSE. From February 2001 to December 2005, electronic messages per minute for the largest quintile capital stocks increased from 35 to 250 messages. Following Chaboud et al. (2014), we define program trading as human trading assisted by a computer program to signal to trade and algorithmic trading as computers directly placing orders.

215

of all trading in the USD/EUR and JPY/USD markets and was even higher (80%) in the cross-rate of the JPY/EUR market.

The two major FX market systems, both of which are electronic limit order markets, are provided by Reuters and the EBS. Because of the scale of the economy and network externalities, trading in currency pairs naturally concentrates on only one of the two systems, rather than being equally divided between two platforms. USD/EUR and JPY/USD are mostly traded in the EBS whereas GBP/USD is mainly traded in the Reuters system. In this study, we investigate high-frequency trading in the FX markets by using the unique EBS data set, including all submissions and cancellations/revisions of limit and market orders. Instead of covering the long-term sample, we focus on the nine most actively traded currency pairs on 1 day in September of 2010. These FX spot markets are EUR/USD, USD/JPY, EUR/JPY, USD/CHF, EUR/CHF, AUD/USD, GBP/USD, USD/CAD, and EUR/GBP. Despite the restriction on the sample, the data set still has over 2 million orders (Table 13.1).

We examine market-order behaviors at high frequency by utilizing the unique EBS FX spot market. Mancini, Ranaldo, and Wrampelmeyer (2013) also use the EBS data set to investigate the liquidity risk in FX markets. In a different FX platform, Nolte and Voev (2011) examine the OANDA FX Trade market, involving relatively smaller retail markets. Why focus on market orders? The trading behaviors underlying limit and market orders were considered to be different in the literature, reflecting whether traders possess private information on the traded financial asset. Traditional theoretical models have regarded a limit order strategy as passive, whereas informed traders use market orders as observed in Glosten (1994) and Seppi (1997). However, recent models of Foucault (1999), Foucault et al. (2005), and Rosu (2009) assume that informed traders use both limit and market orders. A number of empirical studies including Biais et al. (1995) and Ranaldo (2004) investigate limit orders, but studies on market orders, especially in the FX markets, are rather limited. In this study, we particularly focus on market orders in the EBS spot markets.

High rates of cancellation/revision of limit orders are widely observed in both stock markets and FX markets by Biais et al. (1995), Harris and Hasbrouck (1996), Hasbrouck and Saar (2002), Hollifield et al. (2004), Yeo (2005), and Susai and Yoshida (2014b). In this study, we find that market orders in the FX markets frequently fail to be executed. Technically, a market order in the EBS FX spot market is an "immediate or cancel" (IOC) order with the specified quote rate, aimed at the primary target. In general, market orders miss the target if (1) the targeted quote disappears due to cancellation/revision of limit orders or (2) the targeted quote is hit by competing traders milliseconds earlier.[2]

---

[2] A "trader" in FX markets is traditionally called a "dealer." For the sake of convenience, we use "trader" for both stock markets and FX markets throughout the rest of the chapter.

Table 13.1 The number of orders by order type (September 8, 2010)

Currency pair	No. of data	QS	QD	HS	HAD	No. of successful market orders	Missed market orders	DSM
EUR/USD	1,221,649	544,172	544,208	42,354	42,354	17,610	58%	48,566
USD/JPY	674,295	307,283	307,315	19,199	19,199	7340	62%	21,302
EUR/JPY	570,268	269,632	269,641	11,423	11,423	4607	60%	8152
USD/CHF	345,569	162,385	162,377	7485	7485	3379	55%	5837
EUR/CHF	476,336	228,364	228,372	6863	6863	3263	52%	5877
AUD/USD	704,344	347,360	347,359	4176	4176	1019	76%	1278
GBP/USD	429,522	210,149	210,151	3654	3654	1105	70%	1915
USD/CAD	190,946	91,611	91,613	3398	3398	681	80%	927
EUR/GBP	728,576	362,688	362,690	1198	1198	509	58%	808

The first column represents pairs of currencies. The second column shows the number of all messages including QS, QD, HS, HAD, and DSM. QS (QD) indicates the submission (termination) of limit orders. HS (HAD) indicates the submission (termination) of market orders. DSM indicates transactions.

Therefore, the likelihood of missing the target becomes especially high in a high-frequency trading environment. In addition, we also find that market orders frequently aim at the price off the best quote. For example, a buy market order is submitted with a targeted price below the best bid quote. This market-order strategy is only rational in terms of the expected return because the probability of transaction is small but still nonzero when the market is so volatile that the best bid may come below the targeted price or a new limit offer order may come at the targeted price just a millisecond prior to market-order submission.

The remaining part of this study is structured as follows. Section 13.2 describes in detail the structure of the EBS FX spot markets and provides evidence for market-order failure. Section 13.3 investigates the failure rate of hourly aggregated market orders, provides vivid illustrations of behaviors of limit orders and market orders at high frequency, and tests whether high rates of market-order failure are due to the strategy to postmarket orders consecutively. Section 13.4 offers conclusions.

13.2 THE STRUCTURE OF THE EBS FX MARKET

The EBS FX spot market is essentially a limit order market supplemented with market orders. Market orders are aggressive "IOC" orders, whereas limit orders are considered to be passive orders. The "work the balance" functionality of the EBS FX platform automatically converts an aggressive IOC order into a passive limit order when it misses its primary target. A limit order can be submitted with "shown" amount of volume along with "hidden" volume.[3]

The unique EBS all-order data set records whenever a limit order is submitted (denoted as QS), a limit order is revised/canceled/executed (QD), a market order is submitted (HS), a market order is executed/missed (HAD), and a transaction takes place (DSM). Each QS or HS is recorded with an individual trader-order 20-digit ID, time stamp at millisecond, order side, quote, and location (London, New York, or Tokyo). At a later time, a corresponding QD (HAD) is recorded with the same 20-digit ID, millisecond time stamp, and volume transacted (remained). DSM records the volume transacted along two trader-order IDs. Example flows of limit and market orders in the EBS market are depicted in Figure 13.1. A transaction occurs if two limit orders from both sides are submitted at matching price levels or if an existing limit order is hit by a counter-side market order. The best bid and ask quote is visible to all participants but the volume amount of orders within the book are only visible to market participants subject to any

---

[3] See Chaboud, Chernenko, and Wright (2007) and Chaboud et al. (2014) for a detailed description of the workings of the EBS FX market. Buti and Rindi (2013) investigate limit order strategies including "reserve" orders in which volume is invisible to other market participants.

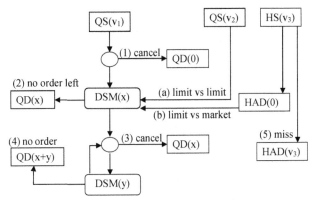

Figure 13.1 *Records of limit and market orders on the EBS spot market.* QS indicates the start of the limit order with the volume *v*. QD indicates the end of the limit order with the accumulated transaction volume in parenthesis. DSM indicates a transaction with the volume. (1) All volume of a limit order is canceled. (2) All volume of order is executed by counterparty order, (*v* = *x*). Counterparty may be either (a) limit order or (b) market order. (3) A limit order is canceled after a part of the order volume is executed (*v* > *x*). (4) All-order volume is executed by two consecutive transactions (*v* = *x* + *y*). HS indicates the start of the market order with the volume *v*. HAD indicates the result of market order with the remaining volume. (5) Therefore, the remaining volume is the same as the ordered volume when a market order misses the target.

product specific restrictions, i.e., availability of credit lines and visibility of order book depth.

To observe the degree of the speed in high-frequency trading in FX markets, we calculate two measures of limit order flows. The first measure is "duration," as used in Manganelli (2005), which is the time elapsed between the preceding limit order submission and a new limit order submission. Even in a timescale measured in milliseconds, simultaneous submissions are occasionally observed and these are recorded as 0 ms duration. The second measure is "lifetime," as suggested by Susai and Yoshida (2014a,b). Lifetime measures the length of time of an individual limit order from submission to termination, the latter caused by cancellation, revision, or transaction.

Duration and lifetime are shown for the EUR/USD, i.e., the most heavily traded FX market, in Figure 13.2. Both measures similarly show the peak in the very short intervals and decline monotonically afterward. For duration, the shortest interval, i.e., less than or equal to 0.1 s, consists of 79.9% of all limit orders. Duration decays exponentially and the number of corresponding orders in a 0.1-s bin are fewer than 100 after 4.5 s. For lifetime, the peak is at the interval (0.2,0.3) and consists of 23.3%. It is surprising that only 27.9% of limit orders stay active in the market after 10 s.

The limitation of this unique data set should be noted. Because of confidentiality of client information, traders' identities are not revealed. For this reason, the end of limit order denoted by QD cannot distinguish between quote revisions and cancellations.

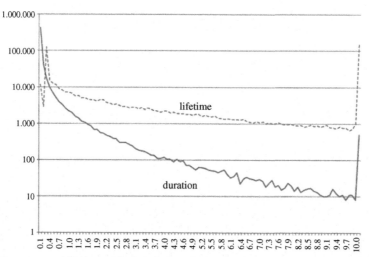

Figure 13.2 *Duration and lifetime of limit orders in the EUR/USD market on September 8, 2010.* All of the limit orders in the EUR/USD spot market from September 7 (Tuesday) at 21:00:00 (GMT) to September 8 (Wednesday) at 20:59:59 (GMT) are considered. The number of data points is 544,171 for duration and slightly less at 544,079 for lifetime due to some limit orders not exiting the market at the end of the sample period. The length of duration and lifetime in terms of seconds is shown on the horizontal axis. The width of a bin is 0.1–10 s, and the last bin aggregates orders with duration or lifetime over 10 s. The vertical axis is shown in the log scale.

Even for quote revisions, the first order and the revised order are given two different 20-digit IDs, and thus we have no way to connect these two orders. This indistinctness blurs the behavioral characteristics of limit orders, but not the market orders we focus on in this study. Revisions and cancellations are distinguishable in the data set provided by some stock exchanges, e.g., the Australian Securities Exchange investigated by Fong and Liu (2010).

Table 13.1 provides the number of limit (QS and QD) and market orders (HS and HAD) for nine pairs of currencies along with the number of successful market orders. We should note that GBP/USD is mostly traded on Reuters (Chaboud et al., 2007). The number of transactions between two limit orders can be calculated by subtracting the number of successful market orders from DSM in Table 13.1. The primary transaction tool varies among FX markets. The proportion of limit–limit (limit–market) transactions is 63.7 (36.3)% in the EUR/USD market whereas that of limit–limit (limit–market) transactions is 20.3 (79.7)% in the AUD/USD market.

Inconsistent with the perception of market orders that transaction execution is guaranteed, the failure of market orders is pervasive. Surprisingly, the rate of market-order failure is above 50% for any pair of currencies. The lowest failure rate of 52% is observed in the EUR/CHF market, and the highest failure rate is 80% in the USD/CAD market. These high rates are partly because market order in the

Table 13.2 The number of orders by order type (September 30, 2003)

Currency pair	No. of data	QS	QD	HS	HAD	No. of successful market orders	Missed market orders	DSM
EUR/USD	254,933	91,591	91,633	13,306	13,306	9532	28%	45,102
USD/JPY	151,368	53,173	53,179	10,001	9999	7224	28%	25,019
USD/CHF	47,498	17,148	17,152	3794	3794	2580	32%	5610
EUR/JPY	36,391	13,572	13,567	2794	2794	1926	31%	3664
EUR/CHF	28,726	10,130	10,119	2092	2092	1754	16%	4293
GBP/USD	13,729	6241	6239	450	450	316	30%	349
EUR/GBP	11,594	5547	5547	169	169	133	21%	162

EBS market is "IOC" or "fill or kill" order. We will discuss this feature in the next section.

However, in 2003, when algorithmic trading in the EBS FX market was still in the incipient stage, the rates of market-order failure were much lower, ranging from 16% in the EUR/CHF to 32% in the USD/CHF (Table 13.2). The comparison of 2003 and 2010 leads us to suspect that high-frequency trading is the cause of the recent rise in market-order failure rates. We will investigate this hypothesis both by formal testing and by scrutinizing each order episodes in the next section.

13.3 AGGRESSIVE IOC ORDERS

In the following, we investigate the failure rate of hourly aggregated market orders in 13.3.1, provide vivid illustrations of behaviors with limit orders and market orders at high frequency in 13.3.2, and test whether high rate of market-order failure is due to the strategy to postmarket orders consecutively in 13.3.3.

13.3.1 Hourly Decomposition of Market-Order Failures

Table 13.3 shows the failure rate of market orders at hourly intervals for six pairs of currencies along the number of market orders in parenthesis.[4] The magnitude of the failure rate tends to be smaller during the hours in which the flow of market orders is relatively small. For example, at the hourly interval starting from 21:00 (GMT), the failure rate is below 30% for all six pairs of currencies. By contrast, the failure rates are approximately 60% for the most heavily traded hours. Because market orders compete with each other for the current best quote, liquidity at the best quote can dry up fast when the market-order flow is greater. Consequently, an incoming market order is more likely to fail at hitting the primary target. At the slower pace of the market, a market order can hit the intended price without failure.

To test whether this interpretation is correct, we calculated the correlation between market-order failure rate and the number of market order flows at hourly intervals. We find high correlations between failure rate and order flows for EUR/USD, USD/JPY, and EUR/CHF. The correlations are 0.63, 0.58, 0.34, 0.47, 0.70, and 0.29 for EUR/USD, USD/JPY, EUR/JPY, USD/CHF, EUR/CHF, and AUD/USD, respectively.[5] These high correlations support the explanation that market-order failure is partly forced

---

[4] We further break down market orders by order side (buy or sell) and by geographical location (America, Europe, Asia), but these breakdowns do not reveal additional heterogeneity in failure rates. The results from the geographical breakdown are provided in the Appendix.

[5] The failure rates are also correlated strongly between these pairs of currencies. The strongest correlation (0.87) is found between EUR/USD and USD/JPY.

Table 13.3 The rates of missed market orders (September 8, 2010)

Hour	EUR/USD	USD/JPY	EUR/JPY	USD/CHF	EUR/CHF	AUD/USD
21:00	0.14 (79)	0.27 (30)	0.08 (12)	0.17 (18)	0.09 (11)	0.25 (4)
22:00	0.41 (160)	0.31 (83)	0.28 (36)	0.30 (30)	0.28 (25)	0.74 (38)
23:00	0.33 (157)	0.47 (136)	0.27 (37)	0.57 (14)	0.33 (12)	0.80 (66)
0:00	0.30 (422)	0.56 (563)	0.50 (153)	0.27 (45)	0.20 (15)	0.82 (120)
1:00	0.39 (504)	0.45 (710)	0.42 (284)	0.38 (63)	0.35 (74)	0.59 (118)
2:00	0.38 (172)	0.49 (407)	0.45 (76)	0.61 (31)	0.36 (25)	0.82 (114)
3:00	0.37 (386)	0.52 (864)	0.35 (305)	0.36 (45)	0.37 (49)	0.77 (176)
4:00	0.43 (298)	0.51 (405)	0.34 (116)	0.54 (37)	0.24 (25)	0.83 (157)
5:00	0.49 (515)	0.56 (358)	0.52 (101)	0.35 (78)	0.50 (82)	0.74 (232)
6:00	0.57 (1798)	0.57 (778)	0.61 (557)	0.60 (561)	0.63 (565)	0.64 (236)
7:00	0.57 (3824)	0.61 (1705)	0.67 (1539)	0.55 (956)	0.50 (1201)	0.76 (247)
8:00	0.55 (3566)	0.62 (1812)	0.66 (1573)	0.55 (795)	0.59 (879)	0.70 (223)
9:00	0.49 (1636)	0.63 (1089)	0.63 (555)	0.56 (259)	0.60 (542)	0.71 (235)
10:00	0.52 (2762)	0.58 (993)	0.60 (804)	0.63 (425)	0.50 (483)	0.79 (204)
11:00	0.53 (1998)	0.61 (521)	0.54 (360)	0.57 (324)	0.55 (405)	0.78 (175)
12:00	0.60 (3277)	0.67 (1277)	0.64 (423)	0.58 (626)	0.51 (517)	0.78 (384)
13:00	0.64 (6530)	0.64 (2207)	0.56 (1406)	0.55 (1264)	0.50 (981)	0.76 (523)
14:00	0.65 (6555)	0.69 (1996)	0.62 (1232)	0.52 (754)	0.54 (597)	0.78 (370)
15:00	0.62 (3239)	0.69 (1125)	0.64 (749)	0.58 (461)	0.47 (198)	0.72 (95)
16:00	0.67 (1519)	0.67 (506)	0.55 (287)	0.53 (180)	0.38 (64)	0.84 (57)
17:00	0.63 (1305)	0.71 (854)	0.54 (334)	0.48 (180)	0.17 (35)	0.71 (65)
18:00	0.62 (884)	0.61 (437)	0.58 (331)	0.52 (217)	0.36 (47)	0.81 (205)
19:00	0.62 (593)	0.68 (229)	0.59 (129)	0.56 (89)	0.06 (18)	0.79 (115)
20:00	0.40 (175)	0.48 (114)	0.25 (24)	0.33 (33)	0.23 (13)	0.65 (17)

Figures are the ratios of missed market orders to all market orders in the specific GMT hour. Figures in parenthesis are the number of market orders submitted in the corresponding hour.

by the surge of high-frequency trading in the FX markets, which in turn causes the market conditions to be more competitive.

13.3.2 Episodes

In this subsection, we pick up two specific episodes of market-order failure in the AUD/USD market. We provide all limit orders in the short sample period surrounding each episode, and we vividly demonstrate under what market conditions a market order fails to be executed.

Episode 1. approximately 00:00:00 (GMT) on September 8, 2010 (AUD/USD)

Approximately 00:00:00 (GMT) for AUD/USD, we find two market orders successfully hit the primary targets. The first transaction took place at 23:57:01.1410 when a market sell order hits the best bid quote of 0.91218 AUD/USD. This transaction is indicated as a circle at the leftmost part of Figure 13.3. After this successful market order, 29 consecutive market sell orders missed the targets. The targeted prices are shown in Figure 13.3 as diamonds. The 31st market sell order at 0.91130 AUD/USD finally hits the intended target, again indicated by a circle.

Were these missed market orders too slow to grab the disappearing target? We can exclude the possibility of the best quote being hit by another competing market order because all 29 market orders missed the target. The only remaining possible explanation is that the best bid quote is canceled just before the market order is submitted. Close examination of the EBS order data set reveals that the answer is "no." Figure 13.4 shows that the most recent limit offer orders just before the third market order (a big diamond in Figure 13.3) is submitted.

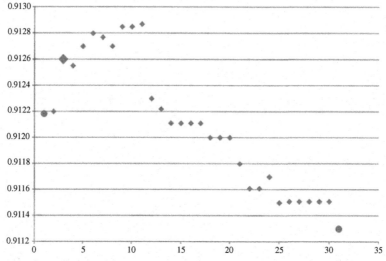

Figure 13.3 *Market sell orders.* The circle (diamond) dots represent market orders with successful (missed) transactions. The first market order was posted at 23:57:01.410 and the 31st order was posted at 00:10:43.025. These two market orders were successful and there were 29 missed market orders between these two. Note the horizontal axis does not represent the real timeline.

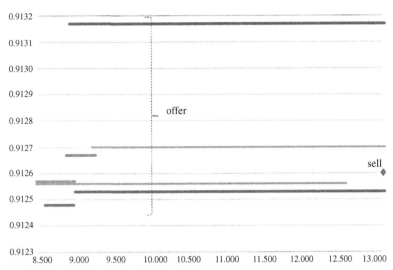

Figure 13.4 *Line segments are offer limit orders with ends corresponding to entering and exiting time.* On the vertical axis, quoting prices are shown. Times on the horizontal line are seconds at GMT 0 h and 0 min. The diamond dot is a market sell order and corresponds to the third order in Figure 13.3.

The sample in Figure 13.4 begins at 00:00:08.500 (GMT) and ends at 00:00:13.230 (GMT), just 0.005 s after the third market order enters the market. Each horizontal line segment represents a limit order. Four limit offer orders were canceled prior to the entry of this particular market order, whereas three limit offer orders remained active when the market order was submitted. The lowest offer quote is at 0.91253. Notwithstanding the market sell order is above the best bid quote, the market order is entered with a price higher than the existing offer price. Even if a bid quote were to be posted at the price of the market order, price priority would have yielded to the limit order with the lowest offer quote.

How can this market-order submission be rational? In comparison with limit order, market order in the traditional sense is aimed at the counterside best quote and is considered to have an advantage in certainty of execution. Limit order, on the other hand, is associated with "nonexecution risk" and "free-option risk," i.e., a quote left in the market to be hit by a counterside informed trader as discussed in Fong and Liu (2010). Prior to the introduction of algorithmic trading in the FX markets failures of market orders are relatively rare, as shown in Table 13.2 for 2003. However, with the advent of algorithmic trading and its rapid adoption by a growing number of financial institutions worldwide, the primary target, i.e., counterside best quote, is as constantly moving and disappearing as a flickering light bulb. Then, the role of market order evolved from "certainty of execution" to an order "with nonexecution risk, but without free-option risk." Therefore, market order (IOC) is used strategically for seeking a better price. To conclude, the current use of market order is interpreted as an extreme form of limit order in the sense that the cancellation time-lag, i.e., lapsed time between submission and cancellation, approaches zero and therefore, free-option risk vanishes.

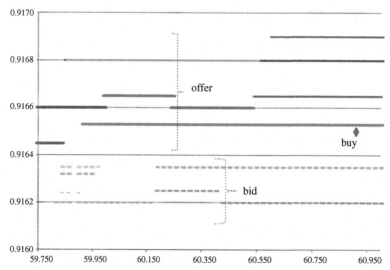

Figure 13.5 *Solid (dotted) line segments are offer (bid) limit orders with ends corresponding to entering and exiting time.* On the vertical axis, quoting prices are shown. The horizontal axis begins at 12:59:59.750 (GMT) and ends at 13:00:01.000 (GMT). The diamond dot is a market-buy order.

Episode 2 approximately 13:00:00(GMT) on September 8, 2010 (AUD/USD)

Another episode at approximately 13:00:00 (GMT) for AUD/USD is shown in Figure 13.5. The subsample begins at 12:59:59.750 (GMT) and ends at 13:00:01.000 (GMT), just 101 ms after the market-buy order (denoted as a diamond) missed a transaction. The market order is submitted at 13:00:00.899 (GMT) at the buying price of 0.91650 AUD/USD. Seven dotted lines denote the most recent limit-bid orders, and the market-buy quote is higher than competing limit-bid quotes, differentiating this episode from the case in episode 1.

The counterside limit offer orders are denoted by nine solid lines. Two orders overlap in both time and quote; therefore, graphically there are only eight solid lines apparent. The best offer quote active at the submission of the market order was 0.91653, 0.00003 ticks above the market-order quote. The prior best offer quote of 0.91645, 0.00005 ticks below the market-order quote, disappeared just 1.063 s earlier. This market quote was more likely to hit the target, were another limit offer order placed aggressively to undercut the prevailing best quote. Then again, the market order in this episode is used strategically to seek a better price.

13.3.3 Runs Tests

In previous sections, we provided evidence that market orders are not used in the traditional manner for an immediate execution, but are used strategically for seeking a deal for a better price. Consequently, a trader needs to keep submitting a series of market orders consecutively until he/she hits a counterside limit order. This in turn causes market orders of one side to appear in a cluster. To test this hypothesis, we apply the well-known nonparametric runs test of Wald and Wolfowitz (1940) to market orders. The Wald—Wolfowitz runs test consists of counting the number of buy orders (m), sell orders (n), and the number of runs (U), which is a sequence of the same side orders. For example, {buy, sell, sell, buy, buy, sell} contains four runs: {buy}, {sell, sell}, {buy, buy}, and {sell}. Wald and Wolfowitz (1940) show that the distribution of Z converges uniformly to the standard normal distribution.

$$Z = \frac{U - E(U)}{\sqrt{Var(U)}},$$

where $E(U) = \frac{2mn}{m+n} + 1$ and $Var(U) = \frac{2mn(2mn-m-n)}{(m+n)^2(m+n-1)}$.

The results for the runs tests are shown for EUR/JPY in Table 13.4 and for AUD/USD in Table 13.5. In conformity with Section 13.3.1, the runs tests are repeated for each hourly

Table 13.4 Runs tests for order sides of all market orders (EUR/JPY, September 8, 2010)

Hour	No. of market orders	No. of SELL orders	No. of BUY orders	Mean	Variance	Runs	Runs test
21:00	12	2	10	4.33	0.71	5	0.786
22:00	36	24	12	17.00	6.86	14	0.126
23:00	37	15	22	18.84	8.34	11	0.003[a]
0:00	153	103	50	68.32	29.37	31	0.000[a]
1:00	284	149	135	142.65	70.40	76	0.000[a]
2:00	76	31	45	37.71	17.48	24	0.001[a]
3:00	305	150	155	153.46	75.96	93	0.000[a]
4:00	116	52	64	58.38	28.13	45	0.006
5:00	101	43	58	50.39	23.90	22	0.000[a]
6:00	557	289	268	279.10	138.60	80	0.000[a]
7:00	1539	861	678	759.62	373.70	212	0.000[a]
8:00	1573	705	868	779.05	384.60	201	0.000[a]
9:00	555	270	285	278.30	138.30	82	0.000[a]
10:00	804	422	382	402.00	199.76	138	0.000[a]
11:00	360	160	200	178.78	87.54	67	0.000[a]
12:00	423	230	193	210.88	103.89	67	0.000[a]
13:00	1406	644	762	699.05	346.32	234	0.000[a]
14:00	1232	534	698	606.08	296.93	183	0.000[a]
15:00	749	421	328	369.73	181.27	144	0.000[a]
16:00	287	118	169	139.97	67.04	81	0.000[a]
17:00	334	134	200	161.48	76.86	69	0.000[a]
18:00	331	174	157	166.06	82.06	51	0.000[a]
19:00	129	91	38	54.61	22.04	30	0.000[a]
20:00	24	12	12	13.00	5.74	4	0.000[a]

[a]indicates the null hypothesis of random submissions from BUY side and SELL side is rejected at the 1% significance level for two-sided test.

Table 13.5 Runs tests for order sides of all market orders (AUD/USD, September 8, 2010)

Hour	No. of market orders	No. of SELL orders	No. of BUY orders	Mean	Variance	Runs	Runs test
21:00	4	2	2	3.00	0.67	2	0.110
22:00	38	20	18	19.95	9.19	8	0.000[a]
23:00	66	48	18	27.18	10.14	15	0.000[a]
0:00	120	68	52	59.93	28.69	40	0.000[a]
1:00	118	71	47	57.56	26.86	36	0.000[a]
2:00	114	53	61	57.72	27.97	27	0.000[a]
3:00	176	125	51	73.44	29.57	33	0.000[a]
4:00	157	37	120	57.56	20.14	25	0.000[a]
5:00	232	108	124	116.45	57.20	39	0.000[a]
6:00	236	100	136	116.25	56.04	55	0.000[a]
7:00	247	123	124	124.50	61.50	64	0.000[a]
8:00	223	135	88	107.55	50.66	58	0.000[a]
9:00	235	51	184	80.86	26.92	43	0.000[a]
10:00	204	79	125	97.81	45.69	42	0.000[a]
11:00	175	70	105	85.00	40.07	38	0.000[a]
12:00	384	201	183	192.58	95.33	80	0.000[a]
13:00	523	275	248	261.80	129.80	121	0.000[a]
14:00	370	165	205	183.84	90.10	75	0.000[a]
15:00	95	41	54	47.61	22.62	21	0.000[a]
16:00	57	19	38	26.33	11.01	19	0.014
17:00	65	33	32	33.49	15.99	18	0.000[a]
18:00	205	64	141	89.04	37.56	38	0.000[a]
19:00	115	39	76	52.55	22.86	16	0.000[a]
20:00	17	8	9	9.47	3.96	4	0.003[a]

[a]indicates the null hypothesis of random submissions from BUY side and SELL side is rejected at the 1% significance level for two-sided test.

interval. The null hypothesis is that market orders of each side, i.e., buy and sell, arrive in the FX markets randomly. The number of runs will be lower than the mean if market orders come consecutively from the same side, and this corresponds with the case of the strategic use of market orders. On the other hand, the number of runs will exceed the mean if market orders arrive alternately from each side. In most of the hourly intervals for both pairs of currencies, we find that the rejection of the null applies to the former case.

For the EUR/JPY market, the null of random side cannot be rejected for the early 2 h when the market is relatively inactive. Another such case is found at 4:00 (GMT) when traders in America and Europe are inactive. It is 13:00 in the Japanese local time, 5:00 in the British local time, and 0:00 in the US Eastern time. Similarly for the AUD/USD market, the null of random side cannot be rejected for the early hours of 21:00 (GMT) and

16:00 (GMT) where Japan (Australia) is at 1:00 (2:00) in the local time. For the remaining hours, the null is rejected, indicating evidence for the strategic use of market orders.

From microanalysis of individual market-order episodes in the previous section, we suspected the strategic use of consecutive market orders by the same individual trader. If a trader opts to use consecutive market orders to obtain the most beneficial quote, the same side orders follow one another until the trader finally gets his/her desired transaction. This strategic behavior is assumed to influence the runs tests to reject the null. A simple way to check robustness is to apply the runs tests to the subsample of successful market orders. All market orders used strategically are thus removed from the sample. With this restricted sample, we expect the runs tests to be less likely to be rejected. The results of the runs test for successful market orders are shown in Tables 13.6 and 13.7. Supporting our intuition, the cases for not rejecting the null increase to 10 (from 3) for the EUR/JPY market and to 19 (from 2) for the AUD/USD market. Reversing the argument, we find evidence that consecutive market orders are used strategically by traders in the EBS FX markets, possibly by algorithmic trading.

This finding does not apply to the same degree to other pairs of currencies. Table 13.8 shows the runs test results for EUR/USD, USD/JPY, USD/CHF, and EUR/CHF. The cases for not rejecting the null increase for all pairs of currencies when subsamples of only successful market orders are used, but the increases in these markets are relatively less drastic.

13.4 CONCLUSION

We examined market orders in the electronic limit order market of FX. Our data set is unique in the sense that each limit order submission can be matched with its termination and each market order is checked whether the transaction is successfully executed. Unexpectedly, given the standard view of market orders, the failure rates of market orders are high for a number of pairs of currencies in the recent period.

By examining the microlevel of order submissions and a simple test of consecutive orders, we demonstrated that market orders in the EBS FX markets fail to be executed because (1) turnover of orders is too fast for a market order to hit a moving target and (2) market orders are not only used in the traditional sense in which a trader is promised of immediate transaction but also in strategic trading for a better price.[6] The result is all because of the rise of high-frequency trading and algorithmic trading in the FX markets.

---

[6] Numerous strategies of algorithmic trading are available for FX traders (Dalton, 2012), for example, time slicers, sweepers, iceberg, opportunistic, participators among others including combinations and modified versions of above strategies mentioned.

Table 13.6 Runs tests for order sides of successful market orders (EUR/JPY, September 8, 2010)

Hour	No. of successful market orders	No. of SELL orders	No. of BUY orders	Mean	Variance	Runs	Runs test
21:00	11	2	9	4.27	0.74	5	0.800
22:00	26	18	8	12.08	4.46	12	0.485
23:00	27	12	15	14.33	6.32	11	0.093
0:00	76	44	32	38.05	17.81	25	0.001[a]
1:00	164	86	78	82.80	40.55	58	0.000[a]
2:00	42	21	21	22.00	10.24	22	0.500
3:00	197	104	93	99.19	48.69	81	0.005[a]
4:00	77	34	43	38.97	18.47	37	0.323
5:00	48	21	27	24.63	11.37	22	0.218
6:00	215	104	111	108.39	53.38	72	0.000[a]
7:00	503	253	250	252.49	125.49	176	0.000[a]
8:00	528	260	268	264.94	131.69	163	0.000[a]
9:00	203	102	101	102.50	50.50	72	0.000[a]
10:00	324	159	165	162.94	80.69	112	0.000[a]
11:00	165	75	90	82.82	40.32	59	0.000[a]
12:00	152	89	63	74.78	35.56	60	0.007
13:00	615	282	333	306.39	151.39	206	0.000[a]
14:00	473	206	267	233.57	114.10	155	0.000[a]
15:00	268	135	133	134.99	66.74	130	0.271
16:00	130	55	75	64.46	30.73	56	0.063
17:00	154	70	84	77.36	37.61	53	0.000[a]
18:00	138	75	63	69.48	33.73	47	0.000[a]
19:00	53	38	15	22.51	8.48	27	0.938
20:00	18	7	11	9.56	3.80	4	0.002[a]

[a]indicates the null hypothesis of random submissions from BUY side and SELL side is rejected at the 1% significance level for two-sided test.

Table 13.7 Runs tests for order sides of successful market orders (AUD/USD, September 8, 2010)

Hour	No. of successful market orders	No. of SELL orders	No. of BUY orders	Mean	Variance	Runs	Runs test
21:00	3	2	1	2.33	0.22	2	0.240
22:00	10	7	3	5.20	1.49	5	0.435
23:00	13	8	5	7.15	2.64	8	0.699
0:00	22	8	14	11.18	4.45	11	0.466
1:00	48	31	17	22.96	9.79	18	0.057
2:00	21	9	12	11.29	4.78	9	0.148
3:00	40	30	10	16.00	5.38	15	0.333
4:00	26	10	16	13.31	5.57	11	0.164
5:00	60	36	24	29.80	13.57	18	0.001[a]
6:00	85	38	47	43.02	20.52	29	0.001[a]
7:00	60	37	23	29.37	13.16	23	0.040
8:00	66	44	22	30.33	12.79	20	0.002[a]
9:00	69	19	50	28.54	10.75	23	0.046
10:00	43	19	24	22.21	10.21	20	0.245
11:00	39	17	22	20.18	9.18	14	0.021
12:00	86	41	45	43.91	21.15	24	0.000[a]
13:00	124	74	50	60.68	28.47	47	0.005
14:00	80	31	49	38.98	17.77	38	0.409
15:00	27	9	18	13.00	5.08	6	0.001[a]
16:00	9	2	7	4.11	0.82	4	0.451
17:00	19	10	9	10.47	4.46	10	0.411
18:00	39	14	25	18.95	8.01	13	0.018
19:00	24	11	13	12.92	5.66	10	0.110
20:00	6	2	4	3.67	0.89	2	0.039

[a]indicates the null hypothesis of random submissions from BUY side and SELL side is rejected at the 1% significance level for two-sided test.

Table 13.8 Runs test for order sides for other currency pairs, September 8, 2010

	EUR/USD		USD/JPY		USD/CHF		EUR/CHF	
Hour	All	Success	All	Success	All	Success	All	Success
21:00	0.020	0.059	0.137	0.669	0.095	0.251	0.013	0.025
22:00	0.000[a]	0.000[a]	0.000[a]	0.000[a]	0.000[a]	0.000[a]	0.087	0.331
23:00	0.000[a]	0.028	0.000[a]	0.005	0.069	0.181	0.673	0.718
0:00	0.000[a]	0.000[a]	0.000[a]	0.004[a]	0.000[a]	0.000[a]	0.537	0.895
1:00	0.000[a]	0.000[a]	0.000[a]	0.000[a]	0.000[a]	0.016	0.003[a]	0.194
2:00	0.000[a]	0.006	0.000[a]	0.000[a]	0.000[a]	0.054	0.033	0.323
3:00	0.000[a]	0.000[a]	0.000[a]	0.000[a]	0.001[a]	0.002[a]	0.000[a]	0.011
4:00	0.000[a]	0.001[a]	0.000[a]	0.023	0.054	0.406	0.022	0.136
5:00	0.000[a]	0.001[a]	0.000[a]	0.008	0.000[a]	0.004[a]	0.000[a]	0.010
6:00	0.000[a]	0.000[a]	0.000[a]	0.000[a]	0.000[a]	0.003[a]	0.000[a]	0.000[a]
7:00	0.000[a]	0.000[a]	0.000[a]	0.000[a]	0.000[a]	0.000[a]	0.000[a]	0.000[a]
8:00	0.000[a]	0.000[a]	0.000[a]	0.000[a]	0.000[a]	0.000[a]	0.000[a]	0.000[a]
9:00	0.000[a]	0.000[a]	0.000[a]	0.000[a]	0.000[a]	0.129	0.000[a]	0.000[a]
10:00	0.000[a]	0.000[a]	0.000[a]	0.000[a]	0.000[a]	0.000[a]	0.000[a]	0.000[a]
11:00	0.000[a]	0.000[a]	0.000[a]	0.000[a]	0.000[a]	0.000[a]	0.000[a]	0.028
12:00	0.000[a]	0.000[a]	0.000[a]	0.000[a]	0.000[a]	0.000[a]	0.000[a]	0.004[a]
13:00	0.000[a]	0.000[a]	0.000[a]	0.000[a]	0.000[a]	0.000[a]	0.000[a]	0.000[a]
14:00	0.000[a]	0.000[a]	0.000[a]	0.000[a]	0.000[a]	0.000[a]	0.000[a]	0.000[a]
15:00	0.000[a]	0.000[a]	0.000[a]	0.000[a]	0.000[a]	0.000[a]	0.000[a]	0.121
16:00	0.000[a]	0.000[a]	0.000[a]	0.000[a]	0.000[a]	0.002[a]	0.211	0.974
17:00	0.000[a]	0.000[a]	0.000[a]	0.000[a]	0.000[a]	0.000[a]	0.002[a]	0.009
18:00	0.000[a]	0.000[a]	0.000[a]	0.000[a]	0.000[a]	0.013	0.001[a]	0.164
19:00	0.000[a]	0.000[a]	0.000[a]	0.003[a]	0.000[a]	0.210	0.436	0.466
20:00	0.000[a]	0.625	0.000[a]	0.058	0.000[a]	0.015	0.625	0.800
Random	1	4	1	5	3	9	9	16

[a]indicates the null hypothesis of random submissions from BUY side and SELL side is rejected at the 1% significance level for two-sided test. The bottom row (Random) shows the number of hourly intervals not rejecting the null hypothesis that orders are submitted randomly from both sides, i.e., sell and buy.

The role of market order evolved from "certainty of execution" to an order "with nonexecution risk, but without free-option risk." Therefore, market order (IOC) is used strategically for seeking a better price. To conclude, the current use of market order is interpreted as an extreme form of limit order in the sense that cancellation time-lag, i.e., the lapsed time between submission and cancellation, approaches zero, and therefore free-option risk vanishes away. Building a theoretical model on the strategic use of market orders would be a valuable contribution to the literature.

Appendix 1 The rates of missed market orders (AUD/USD, September 8, 2010)

Hour	London	New York	Tokyo	Total
21:00	0.00 (1)	0.50 (2)	0.00 (1)	0.25 (4)
22:00	0.60 (10)	0.88 (25)	0.00 (3)	0.74 (38)
23:00	0.75 (24)	0.88 (40)	0.00 (2)	0.80 (66)
0:00	0.86 (50)	0.84 (56)	0.57 (14)	0.82 (120)
1:00	0.61 (46)	0.73 (51)	0.24 (21)	0.59 (118)
2:00	0.74 (34)	0.88 (72)	0.63 (8)	0.82 (114)
3:00	0.77 (44)	0.78 (120)	0.67 (12)	0.77 (176)
4:00	0.82 (38)	0.91 (104)	0.33 (15)	0.83 (157)
5:00	0.78 (63)	0.79 (143)	0.38 (26)	0.74 (232)
6:00	0.45 (89)	0.77 (130)	0.65 (17)	0.64 (236)
7:00	0.74 (103)	0.78 (138)	0.67 (6)	0.76 (247)
8:00	0.71 (112)	0.68 (101)	0.90 (10)	0.70 (223)
9:00	0.65 (123)	0.76 (99)	0.85 (13)	0.71 (235)
10:00	0.71 (86)	0.83 (103)	0.93 (15)	0.79 (204)
11:00	0.80 (86)	0.73 (82)	1.00 (7)	0.78 (175)
12:00	0.74 (147)	0.79 (226)	1.00 (11)	0.78 (384)
13:00	0.86 (167)	0.72 (356)		0.76 (523)
14:00	0.83 (113)	0.76 (257)		0.78 (370)
15:00	0.82 (38)	0.65 (57)		0.72 (95)
16:00	1.00 (23)	0.74 (34)		0.84 (57)
17:00	0.79 (19)	0.67 (46)		0.71 (65)
18:00	0.86 (43)	0.80 (162)		0.81 (205)
19:00	0.55 (11)	0.82 (104)		0.79 (115)
20:00	0.80 (5)	0.58 (12)		0.65 (17)

Figures are the ratios of missed market orders to all market orders in the specific GMT hour. Figures in the parenthesis are the number of market orders submitted in the corresponding hour. The missed rates are shown by the area where the order submissions are originated.

Appendix 2 The rates of missed market orders (EUR/JPY, September 8, 2010)

Hour	London	New York	Tokyo	Total
21:00	0.00 (1)	0.00 (9)	0.50 (2)	0.08 (12)
22:00	0.50 (6)	0.29 (14)	0.19 (16)	0.28 (36)
23:00	0.71 (7)	0.20 (15)	0.13 (15)	0.27 (37)
0:00	0.78 (37)	0.54 (74)	0.19 (42)	0.50 (153)
1:00	0.58 (55)	0.51 (123)	0.24 (106)	0.42 (284)
2:00	0.56 (16)	0.60 (35)	0.16 (25)	0.45 (76)
3:00	0.76 (41)	0.42 (151)	0.12 (113)	0.35 (305)
4:00	0.67 (24)	0.38 (53)	0.08 (39)	0.34 (116)
5:00	0.74 (34)	0.57 (44)	0.13 (23)	0.52 (101)
6:00	0.67 (282)	0.62 (193)	0.43 (82)	0.61 (557)
7:00	0.63 (722)	0.73 (668)	0.62 (149)	0.67 (1539)
8:00	0.65 (748)	0.69 (639)	0.66 (186)	0.66 (1573)
9:00	0.63 (258)	0.63 (239)	0.67 (58)	0.63 (555)
10:00	0.54 (361)	0.63 (393)	0.74 (50)	0.60 (804)
11:00	0.52 (195)	0.57 (162)	0.67 (3)	0.54 (360)

Continued

Appendix 2 The rates of missed market orders (EUR/JPY, September 8, 2010)—cont'd

Hour	London	New York	Tokyo	Total
12:00	0.52 (174)	0.73 (246)	0.67 (3)	0.64 (423)
13:00	0.54 (541)	0.58 (856)	0.78 (9)	0.56 (1406)
14:00	0.59 (534)	0.64 (697)	0.00 (1)	0.62 (1232)
15:00	0.68 (367)	0.61 (382)		0.64 (749)
16:00	0.71 (117)	0.44 (170)		0.55 (287)
17:00	0.62 (97)	0.51 (237)		0.54 (334)
18:00	0.69 (96)	0.54 (235)		0.58 (331)
19:00	0.83 (41)	0.48 (88)		0.59 (129)
20:00	1.00 (1)	0.22 (23)		0.25 (24)

Figures are the ratios of missed market orders to all market orders in the specific GMT hour. Figures in the parenthesis are the number of market orders submitted in the corresponding hour. The missed rates are shown by the area where the order submissions are originated.

ACKNOWLEDGMENTS

Susuai acknowledges financial support from the Japan Society for the Promotion of Science KAKENHI Grant Number 26285070. Yoshida acknowledges financial support from the Japan Society for the Promotion of Science KAKENHI Grant Number 26380295.

REFERENCES

Bank for International Settlements, 2010. Triennial Central Bank Survey: Report on Global Foreign Exchange Market Activity in 2010, BIS.

Biais, B., Hillion, P., Spatt, C., 1995. An empirical analysis of the limit order book and the order flow in the Paris bourse. J. Finance 50 (5), 1655–1689.

Buti, S., Rindi, B., 2013. Undisclosed orders and optimal submission strategies in a limit order market. J. Financ. Econ. 109 (3), 797–812.

Chaboud, A., Chernenko, S., Wright, J., 2007. Trading Activity and Exchange Rates in High-frequency EBS Data. International Finance Discussion Papers, 903. Board of Governors of the Federal Reserve System, Washington, D.C.

Chaboud, A., Chiquoine, B., Hjalmarsson, E., Vega, C., 2014. Rise of the machines: algorithmic trading in the foreign exchange market. J. Finance 69 (5), 2045–2084.

Dalton, J.E., 2012. Algorithm execution in foreign exchange. In: James, J., Marsh, I.W., Sarno, L. (Eds.), Handbook of Exchange Rates. John Wiley & Sons, Hoboken, NJ.

Fong, K.Y.L., Liu, W.M., 2010. Limit order revisions. J. Bank. Financ. 34 (8), 1873–1885.

Foucault, T., 1999. Order flow composition and trading costs in a dynamic limit order market. J. Financ. Mark. 2 (2), 99–134.

Foucault, T., Kadan, O., Kandel, E., 2005. Limit order book as a market for liquidity. Rev. Financ. Stud. 18 (4), 1171–1217.

Glosten, L., 1994. Is the electronic open limit order book inevitable? J. Financ. 49, 1127–1161.

Harris, L., Hasbouck, J., 1996. Market vs. Limit orders: the SuperDOT evidence on order submission strategy. J. Financ. Quant. Anal. 31 (2), 213–231.

Hasbrouck, J., Saar, G., 2002. Limit Orders and Volatility in a Hybrid Market: The Island ECN. Working paper. New York University, NY.

Hendershott, T., Jones, C.M., Menkveld, A.J., 2011. Does algorithmic trading improve liquidity? J. Finance 66 (1), 1–33.

Hollifield, B., Miller, R.A., Sandås, P., 2004. Empirical analysis of limit order markets. Rev. Econ. Stud. 71 (4), 1027–1063.

Mancini, L., Ranaldo, A., Wrampelmeyer, J., 2013. Liquidity in the foreign exchange market: measurement, commonality, and risk premiums. J. Finance 68 (5), 1805–1841.

Manganelli, S., 2005. Duration, volume and volatility impact of trades. J. Financ. Mark. 8 (4), 377–399.

Nolte, I., Voev, V., 2011. Trading dynamics in the foreign exchange market: a latent factor panel intensity approach. J. Financ. Econ. 9 (4), 685–716.

Ranaldo, A., 2004. Order aggressiveness in limit order book markets. J. Financ. Mark. 7 (1), 53–74.

Rosu, I., 2009. A dynamic model of the limit order book. Rev. Financial Stud. 22 (11), 4601–4641.

Seppi, D., 1997. Liquidity provision with limit orders and a strategic specialist. Rev. Financ. Stud. 10 (1), 103–150.

Susai, M., Yoshida, Y., 2014a. Algorithm trading in Asian currency FX markets. In: Chuen, D.L.K., Gregoriou, G.N. (Eds.), Handbook of Asian Finance, vol. 2. Academic Press, San Diego, CA.

Susai, M., Yoshida, Y., 2014b. Life-time of Limit Orders in the EBS Foreign Exchange Market. MPRA Paper. University Library of Munich.

Wald, A., Wolfowitz, J., 1940. On a test whether two samples are from the same population. Ann. Math. Statistics 11 (2), 147–162.

Yeo, W.Y., 2005. Cancellations of Limit Order. Working paper. National University of Singapore.

CHAPTER 14

Efficient Performance Evaluation for High-Frequency Traders

Godfrey Charles-Cadogan
School of Economics, UCT, Rondebosch, Cape Town, South Africa

Contents

Computers enact code that might have some strategic reasoning built into it but they are basically just running hard-wired rules. High frequency traders have pressure to keep their code short, there's a limit to how much they can process, and all they can do is give a quick response to a stimulus. That changes how we should perceive the market and makes dealing with rules of thumb and evolutionary knowledge a more suitable model for information processing by computers in markets than de novo reasoning. HFT in particular works that way. Stimulus response means something happens, you look it up in a table and then you act on it

Doyne Farmer, 2013.

14.1 INTRODUCTION

If we consider the following heuristic example involving two traders A and B whose performances are evaluated for returns measured over a given period, say, monthly. Let $SR_p^A(12) = SR_p^A\sqrt{12}$ and $SR_p^B(12) = SR_p^B\sqrt{12}$ be the annualized Sharpe ratio (ASR)[1] and σ_p^A and σ_p^B be the volatility of the portfolios managed by A and B, respectively. Suppose that $SR_p^A = SR_p^B$ and $\sigma_p^A = \sigma_p^B$. Other things equal, extant portfolio performance evaluation theory, based on those statistics concludes that the performance of each trader is the same. However, suppose trader A traded for 9 months of the year

---

[1] If $E[R_p]$, σ_p, r_f are the expected returns, volatility, i.e., standard deviation, and risk-free rate for a portfolio, the ex ante Sharpe ratio for the portfolio is $SR_p = (E[R_p] - r_f)\backslash\sigma_p$. The annualized SR is $SR_p(T) = SR_p\sqrt{T}$ for T trading periods in a year, i.e., $T = 252$ if portfolio returns are measured daily.

The Handbook of High Frequency Trading
ISBN 978-0-12-802205-4

237

while trader B traded for 4 months of the year. If each trader is in the same style class, faces the same universe of assets and transaction costs, then trader B is more efficient than trader A because he/she attains the same SR at lower cost when his/her *trading time* is compared to that of trader A. Specifically, the ratio $\frac{SR_p^B/\sqrt{4}}{SR_p^A/\sqrt{9}} = 1.5$ implies that trader B is 1.5 times more efficient than trader A because his/her *trading times* are lower than those of trader A, even though the annualized *clock time* is 12 for each trader. Replacing SR_p^A and SR_p^B by $\widetilde{SR}_p^A = SR_p^A/\sqrt{9}$ and $\widetilde{SR}_p^B = SR_p^B/\sqrt{4}$ provides a more accurate assessment of the traders' performance. In which case $\widetilde{SR}_p^A(12) = \widetilde{SR}_p^A\sqrt{12} = SR_p^A\sqrt{12/9}$ and $\widetilde{SR}_p^B(12) = \widetilde{SR}_p^B\sqrt{12} = SR_p^B\sqrt{12/4}$. This is functionally equivalent to replacing the volatility of the respective portfolios by $\tilde{\sigma}_p^A = \sigma_p^A\sqrt{9}$ and $\tilde{\sigma}_p^B = \sigma_p^B\sqrt{4}$. So $\tilde{\sigma}_p^A$ and $\tilde{\sigma}_p^B$ are subordinate to $\sigma_p^i\sqrt{12}$, $i = A, B$. Thus, trading times should be included as an adjustment factor in volatility estimates for portfolio performance evaluation. This example implies a 100% hit rate for A and B. In practice, the hit rate is lower so the SR will have to be adjusted to account for that. This chapter proposes a mechanism for doing so.

The significance of our proposed mechanism lies in the fact that portfolio performance evaluation is one of the most actively researched areas in financial economics. For instance, Elton et al. (2014) reference 141 articles that span 6 pages on this topic. Aldridge (2013) tabulation of the pantheon of modified SRs in the literature spans two pages. However, much of the portfolio performance evaluation literature is based on equilibrium asset pricing models and factor models developed in static or low-frequency environments. Recently, some analysts extended portfolio performance evaluation to high-frequency trading (HFT) by using performance evaluation metrics like ASR (Sharpe, 1966), which was designed to evaluate single period mutual fund performance. For example, studies by Baron et al. (2014); Clark-Joseph (2013); Menkveld (2013); and Aldridge (2013, 2014) report *average* ASR[2] numbers for HFTers ranging from 4.3 to 5000. Ironically, if returns are normally distributed, then the SR statistic has a noncentral normal distribution, so those numbers imply that there is virtually zero probability that *any* HFT portfolio could exceed the average.[3] This implies that ASR is an inappropriate statistic for evaluating HFT even if returns have fat tails. None of the aforementioned papers used *trading time* as a directing process to compute

---

[2] A Sharpe ratio (SR) is annualized by computing the SR for daily returns and multiplying it by a factor of $\sqrt{252}$ under the assumption of 252 trading days in a year. In general, if there are T periods in the year relative to the period for which the SR is computed the ASR is SR multiplied by a factor of $\sqrt{T}$.

[3] $SR = (E[R_p] - r_f)/\sigma_p = [(E[R_p] - \mu_{R_p})/\sigma_p] + [(\mu_{R_p} - r_f)/\sigma_p] \Rightarrow SR \sim Z + \delta_{r_f}$ where Z is standard normal and δ_{r_f} is a noncentrality parameter.

the ASRs they use to evaluate HFT. However, Baron et al. (2014, p. 20) reports that the ASR for passive HFTers (5.85) in their sample is higher than that for aggressive HFTers (4.29) who trade more. In the context of our example, this implies that passive HFT is more efficient than aggressive HFT.[4] We show later in the chapter that those rankings and conclusions change once our efficient SR is applied.

An important paper by Lo (2002) used the delta method[5] and generalized method of moments (GMM) to illustrate how Sharpe ratios (SRs) are biased by violation of normality and serial correlation in returns. While the former may not be as severe for observations that are not in the tail, the latter is more severe—especially for HFT. For instance, Aldridge (2014) studies runs in HFT data as predictors of flash crashes while Egginton et al. (2014) studies quote stuffing as a source of these runs. According to Egginton et al., p. 1 "[q]uote stuffing is a practice where a large number of orders to buy or sell securities are placed and then canceled almost immediately." This practice may be related to the concept of pinging.[6] Clarke-Joseph (2013) studies how exploratory trading by HFTers segment the market into aggressive and passive traders that induce runs in HFT data. And Baron et al. (2014) study the distribution of ASRs across trader types. In fact, in Figure 14.1 Jonathan Mackinlay demonstrates how spectral analysis of alpha signals determines trading cycles that HFTers use to trade.[7] Mackinlay describes the plot as "[t]he spectral density of the combined alpha signals across twelve pairs of stocks. It is clear that the strongest signals occur in the shorter frequencies with cycles of up to several hundred seconds." So, by definition, HFT is based on exploiting market microstructure with low latency[8] trades where trading rules, not fundamentals, are the order of the day (Farmer, 2013; Mackinlay, 2014).

Recently, Bailey and De Prado (2014) introduced a deflated SR concept that is tangentially related to the heuristic example in the introduction. However, their model is concerned with backtesting trading strategies with big data to correct for selection bias and non-Normality of returns. They identified the *number of trials* required to achieve

---

[4] Aldridge (2013, p. 43) defines aggressive traders as those who place limit orders close to the prevailing market price while passive traders place limit orders further away from the prevailing market price.

[5] Refer to Lehmann (1999, p. 295) for exposition of this concept.

[6] "Ping" is a computer network utility that measures the round trip time for a host to receive and respond to a message. If the host is flooded with such requests then the host system may be overwhelmed so it diverts resources to respond to the ping requests. See Zubulake and Lee (2011, pp. 42–43) for its strategic use by HFTers to detect dark pool trades.

[7] See Jonathan Mackinlay (May 22, 2011) "Alpha spectral analysis." Available at http://jonathankinlay.com/index.php/2011/05/alpha-spectral-analysis/. Hasbrouck and Sofianos (1993, pp. 1588–1591) provide and excellent summary of the econometric procedures involved.

[8] Latency is an engineering concept. In the context of HFT it refers to the time interval between the execution and exchange response to an order. "Obviously," pinging or "quote stuffing" is a means of keeping track of latency, which could fluctuate based on the time the exchange takes to respond. For example, if it is "busy" response time will be slower. Thus, latency is an important factor in mitigating slippage (Narang, 2013, 94). Mertens (2002) proffered a correction to the critical asymptotic variance in Lo (2002).

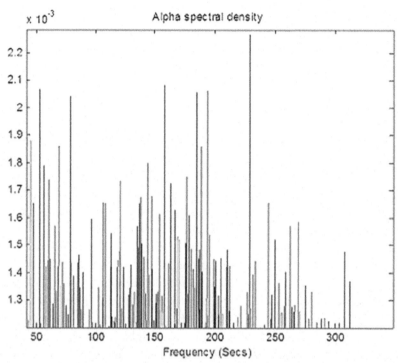

Figure 14.1 Spectral decomposition of HFT alpha signals. *(Jonathan Mackinlay (May 22, 2011) "Alpha spectral analysis," available at http://jonathankinlay.com/index/php/2011/05/alpha-spectral-analysis/.)*

a given SR as a critical element in constructing a deflator for SRs. An earlier paper by Gregoriou and Gueyie (2003) addressed issues like the one presented in the introduction. However, they were concerned with extreme values that affect portfolio returns but which may not be captured by ASR. They proposed a modified value-at-risk factor in lieu of the standard deviation to account for skewness and kurtosis in hedge fund returns. In contrast, our model identifies a subordinator induced by HFTers trading strategy as a deflator. Ironically, Sharpe (1994) states "[t]he Sharpe Ratio is not independent of the time period over which it is measured. This is true for both ex ante and ex post measures."

The heuristic example in the introductory paragraph suggests that using ASR to evaluate HFT is biased and inefficient because the clock time used for reporting data is different from the trading times of HFTers. Specifically, a trading time variable should be used to compute an efficient standard deviation[9] for HFT. To do so, one has to identify high-frequency stock price dynamics in order to derive a suitable metric for HFT

---

[9] The efficiency concept for comparing standard deviations was introduced by Cramer (1946, p. 481) in the context of maximum likelihood estimates. Our notion of efficiency is consistent with the notion of Blackwell efficient procedures (Blackwell, 1947).

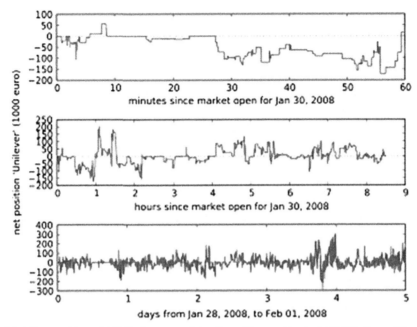

Figure 14.2 Net position of HFT in large stock by time. *(Source: Menkveld (2013, Figure 3.)*

portfolio performance evaluation. Figure 14.2 is reproduced from Menkveld (2013, Figure 3, p. 721). According to Menkveld it is a "[r]aw data plot [of] high frequency trader net position by frequency. This figure plots, for the median week in the sample, the high frequency trader's net position in Unilever, the median stock in the large stock group. It plots the series for essentially three frequencies: minutes, hours, and days". The plots show that the patterns of HFT positions change dramatically when the underlying frequency is changed from minutes to hours to days. Somewhat surprisingly, despite the explosion of research on high-frequency trading (refer to Jones (2013) for a recent review), the literature is silent on mathematical models of underlying high-frequency stock price for the depiction in Figure 14.2. To be sure, continuous asset pricing models (Merton, 1992) proliferate the mathematical finance and financial economics literature. However, those models are normative. They are not asset pricing models adapted to market microstructure. To the best of our knowledge, the HFT stock price formula proposed by Cadogan (2012) is the only high-frequency stock price formula derived from an asymptotic theory of a trading rule.[10] Thus, we will employ analytics from Cadogan's HFT stock price formula to derive a suitable metric for HFT portfolio performance evaluation.

---

[10] According to some observers it is the first stock price formula to come along since Gordon (1959) growth formula. See Faille, C. (2012) "High Frequency Trading Inspires A Formula" available at http://allaboutalpha.com/blog/2012/01/11/high-frequency-trading-inspires-a-formula/.

14.2 THE MODEL

The SR is a summary statistic based on the mean and standard deviation of the difference between portfolio returns (R_p) and returns on a benchmark usually taken as the risk-free rate r_f. Sharpe (1994) emphasized two important characteristic of the ratio, which we summarize as follows.

Assumption 1. The SR is not independent of the time period over which it is measured.

Assumption 2. The differential return on the portfolio is based on a zero investment strategy.

In this chapter we assume that Assumption 2 holds and examine the implications of Assumption 1 for SR computation.

Let σ_p be the volatility, i.e., standard deviation, of a portfolio and $E[R_p]$ be the expected return. The *ex ante* Sharpe ratio SR_p for returns computed for a given single period, i.e., daily, monthly, or annual is represented by the formula

$$SR_p = \frac{E[R_p] - R_f}{\sigma_p} \tag{14.1}$$

Sharpe (1994) provides a heuristic example in which he extended the "one period mean and standard deviation of the differential mean" to T periods by assuming that $\sigma_p(T) = \sigma_p T$ so that the "T-period" Sharpe ratio $SR_p(T)$ is now represented by

$$SR_p(T) = \frac{E[R_p] - R_f}{\sigma_p} \sqrt{T} = SR_p \sqrt{T} \tag{14.2}$$

As already mentioned in the introduction, and presented with more details here, several analysts have used that formula to annualize SR computed for daily returns by multiplying by the factor $\sqrt{252}$ based on the assumption of 252 trading days in a year. For example, the Baron et al. (2014, p. 3) study of HFT returns report that "[t]he median HFT firm demonstrates unusually high and persistent risk-adjusted performance with an *annualized* Sharpe ratio of 4.3." They used a formula like the one in (14.2) for $SR_i = SR_p\sqrt{252}$. Clark-Joseph (2013, p. 15) study reports that 30 HFT firms he studied "earned a combined average of $1.51 million per trading day during the sample period. Individual HFTs' *annualized* Sharpe ratios are in the neighborhood of 10 to 11." Menkveld (2013, Table 2, p. 727) reports an ASR of 7.6 for the anonymous HFTers engaged in cross-market trading in his study. Aldridge (2014) reported ASRs for which "the maximum possible annualized Sharpe ratio for EUR/USD trading strategies with daily position rebalancing was 37.3, while EUR/USD trading strategies that held positions for 10 seconds could potentially score Sharpe ratios well over 5000 (five thousand) mark."

14.2.1 The Call for an Efficient Sharpe Ratio

The heuristic example in the introduction calls for an efficient SR (ESR), which is based on a concept of efficiency in mathematical statistics where it is a procedure that uses a subset of a set of sufficient statistics deemed Blackwell (1947) efficient. It implies that we could modify Sharpe's T period volatility adjustment in (14.2) with a volatility measure of type $\tilde{\sigma}_p(T(t)) = \sigma_p\sqrt{T(t)}$ where $T(t)$ is a *trading time*. In the sequel we show that the latter is a random time for high-frequency trades. The concept of trading time is not new to the financial economics literature. For instance, seminal papers by Clark (1973) and more recently Carr and Wu (2004) provide evidence that clock time and trading times differ and matter for asset pricing and risk management. Clark found that finite variance distributions subordinate to the normal distribution fit cotton futures prices data better than the normal distribution. Carr and Wu claim that a time changed Levy process addresses: (1) asset prices jump, leading to non-normal return innovations; (2) stochastic volatility; and (3) correlation of returns and their volatilities. However, those papers were not applied to HFT environments. Each of the authors above used subordinate processes (which we define next) in their analyses. And we do the same in this chapter.

Definition (Subordinate process).[11] *Let $S(t,\omega)$ be a Markov process with continuous transition probabilities Q_t and $T(t,\omega)$ be a process with nonnegative independent increments. Then $S(T(t),\omega)$ is a Markovian process with transition probabilities P_t, given by a linear combination of Q_t. The process $S(T(t),\omega)$ is said to be subordinate to $S(t,\omega)$ using the random or operational time $T(t,\omega)$. The process $T(t,\omega)$ is called a subordinator or directing process.*

If returns are approximately normally generated, the mean and standard deviation of a sample of returns generated by a portfolio manager are sufficient statistics (DeGroot, 1970) for characterizing the sample distribution she induced by her decision-making. In other words, the portfolio manager generates a distribution of returns that is subordinate to the underlying distribution for the universe of asset returns available to her. Therefore, one might expect her trading time to be based on the sufficient statistics as well. The intuition behind this argument is as follows.

Assume for the sake of argument that a stock price follows a Brownian motion $B_t(\omega)$. Thus, $(0,t)$ are sufficient statistics since Brownian motion has a normal distribution with mean 0 and variance t. Define the running maximum as $M_t(\omega) = \max_{\{0 \le s \le t\}} B_t(\omega)$. Let $\tau_b(\omega) = \inf\{t > 0 | B_t(\omega) > b\}$ be the first time the stock price exceeds the level b. Figure 14.3 depicts a typical sample path for $M_t(\omega)$. For example, the horizontal axis could be measured in milliseconds (ms). Cursory inspection shows that $M_t(\omega)$ jumps

---

[11] This definition is adapted from Feller (1970, p. 347). Technical details in the sequel assume that (Ω, F, P) is a probability measure space where Ω is the set of all possible states, F is the σ-field of all possible subsets generated from Ω, and P is a probability measure on Ω such that $P(\Omega) = 1$. A state is represented by $\omega \in \Omega$. Refer to Øksendal (2003, pp. 7–8) for further details.

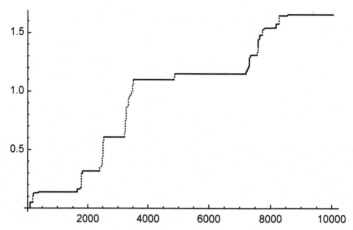

Figure 14.3 Sample path for running maximum of Brownian motion $M_t(\omega) = max_{\{0 \le s \le t\}} B_t(\omega)$. *(http://math.stackexchange.com/questions/109873/maximum-of-a-brownian-motion-and-its-integral.)*

shortly after 0 at around 0.25 ms, then remains flat until it jumps again around 2 ms and so on. So the running total on the vertical axis is smaller than that on the horizontal axis. It can be shown (Karatsas and Shreve (1991, p. 96)) that

$$P\{\tau_b(\omega) < t\} = P\{M_t(\omega) > b\} = \frac{2}{\sqrt{2\pi}} \int_{\frac{b}{\sqrt{t}}}^{\infty} e^{-x^2} dx = \sqrt{2}(1 - \Phi(b\sqrt{2/t})) \quad [14.3]$$

where $\Phi(b\sqrt{2/t})$ is the cumulative normal distribution probability estimate in the right (or left) tail starting at $b\sqrt{2/t}$. If either b is small or t is large or both, then the probability in (14.3) is close to 1. In other words, the subordinate time $\tau_b(\omega)$ when the stock price exceeds level b is less than the clock time t at which the stock price movement is recorded almost surely. Moreover, it can be shown (Karatzas and Shreve, 1991) that the subordinate (time–changed) process $M_{\tau_b(\omega)}$ is also a Brownian motion characterized by sufficient statistics $(0, \tau_b(\omega)) \subset (0, t)$. In the context of Figure 14.3, $M_{\tau_b(\omega)}$ would tend to lie above $M_t(\omega)$ almost surely since it is a running maximum that only jumps for values greater than b. So the sufficient statistics for the subordinate process is a *subset* of the sufficient statistics from the supervening process. Specifically, the SR for evaluating the stock price performance is based on the mean and standard deviation of the stock (Sharpe, 1994). So the SR for the subordinate process for the stock is based on a *subset* of the sufficient statistics for the stock. We summarize this argument with the following.

Proposition 1. (Sufficient statistics for ESR). The ESR for a portfolio depends on a *subset* of the sufficient statistics of the stocks that comprise that portfolio.

In the sequel $T(t,\omega)$ is a subordinate trading time analogous to $\tau_b(\omega)$ in the heuristic example above. So the volatility for an underlying HFT portfolio $S_p(t,\omega)$ is given by $\tilde{\sigma}_p(t,\omega) = \sigma_p\sqrt{T(t,\omega)}$ where σ_p is the corresponding single period volatility. We assume the stock price formula adapted to high-frequency trading strategies is the one introduced in Cadogan (2012, p. 18) as follows:

$$S_p(t,\omega) = S_p(t_0)\exp\left(\int_{t_0}^{t} \underbrace{\sigma_X(u,\omega)}_{\text{volatility}} \underbrace{\beta_X(u,\omega)}_{\text{exposure}} \underbrace{dB_X(u,\omega)}_{\text{news}}\right) \quad [14.4]$$

where X is a hedge factor, σ_x is its volatility, β_x is exposure to the hedge factor, and $B_x(u,\omega)$ is a background driving Gaussian process motivated by news about the hedge factor. After discretizing (14.4) over dyadic partition $\Pi^{(n)}$ for the interval [0,1] say, Cadogan (2012, p. 26) derived diagnostics for the SR for HFT, which implies the following empirical SR processes for HFT:

$$SR_{HFT}(t,\omega) = \underbrace{\left(\frac{\bar{r}_{HFT}(t,\omega) - r_f}{\tilde{s}_{HFT}(t,\omega)}\right)}_{\text{ex post Sharpe ratio}} \quad [14.5]$$

$$r_{HFT}(t,\omega) = \sigma_X(t,\omega)\beta_X(t,\omega)\tilde{\varepsilon}_X(t,\omega)\exp(-\bar{r}_{HFT}(t,\omega)),$$

$$\bar{r}_{HFT}(T,\omega) = T^{-1}\sum_{j=0}^{T-1} r_{HFT}(t_j,\omega), \quad \tilde{s}^2_{HFT}(T,\omega) = T^{-1}\sum_{j=0}^{T-1}\left(r_{HFT}(t_j,\omega) - \bar{r}_{HFT}(T,\omega)\right)^2$$

$$[14.6]$$

The right-hand side of $r_{HFT}(t,\omega)$ in (14.6) is a decomposition of HFT returns by hedge factor and news. Menkveld (2013, Table 3, p. 728) reports ASRs (with Lo (2002) serial correlation correction) that depend on Capital Asset Pricing Model (CAPM) betas.[12] However, the SR formula above depends on the beta for HFTers hedge factor exposure. Furthermore, Menkveld's estimated ASR jumps by a factor of about 3 from 7.62 for daily returns to 23.43 for returns computed every half hour. So ASR is sensitive to the frequency of measurement. In contrast, some of the past HFT returns in the summand in (14.5) are negative. Moreover, the exponential term is positive but not monotonic so it cannot be used in lieu of the correction factor T in (14.2). Thus, we need to construct a subordinator from HFT returns to supplant T.

[12] This was conveyed to the author in private communications with Albert Menkveld since it was not apparent in his paper.

14.2.2 Construction of Subordinate Trading Time for HFT

Let $\tau_j^{(n)}(\omega)$ be a stopping time for HFTers over dyadic intervals[13] for $[0,1]$ such that

$$\tau_j^{(n)}(\omega) = \inf\left\{t_j^{(n)}\middle|r_{\text{HFT}}\left(t_j^{(n)},\omega\right)\in E\right\}, \quad E = \left\{r_{\text{HFT}}\left(t_j^{(n)},\omega\right)\middle|r_{\text{HFT}}\left(t_j^{(n)},\omega\right) > r_f\right\}$$

[14.7]

where E is the set of all HFT returns that exceed the risk-free rate. In practice, r_f is often taken as 0 in the HFT literature. Let $T\left(t_0^{(n)},\ldots,t_{2^n-1}^{(n)},1;\omega\right)$ be a subordinator, i.e., directing process, for HFT returns defined as follows:

$$T\left(t_0^{(n)},\ldots,t_{2^n-1}^{(n)},1;\omega\right) = \sum_{j=0}^{2^n-1} r_{\text{HFT}}\left(t_j^{(n)},\omega\right)I_{\left\{r_{\text{HFT}}\left(t_j^{(n)},\omega\right)\in E\right\}}$$

[14.8]

$$r_{\tau_j}(\omega) = r_{\text{HFT}}\left(t_j^{(n)},\omega\right)I_{\left\{r_{\text{HFT}}\left(t_j^{(n)}\right)\in E\right\}}$$

[14.9]

We claim that $T(\cdot)$ is an efficiency measure. It jumps only when the HFTer executes a successful trade in the set of returns E that exceeds the risk-free rate. Let $T_A\left(t_0^{(n)},\ldots,t_{2^n-1}^{(n)},1;\omega\right)$ and $T_B\left(t_0^{(n)},\ldots,t_{2^n-1}^{(n)},1;\omega\right)$ be the directing process for two HFTers A and B with the same empirical Sharpe ratio $SR_{\text{HFT}}(T)$, and let $T_B(\cdot) > T_A(\cdot)$ and

$$SR_{\text{HFT}}(T) = \frac{\bar{r}_{\text{HFT}}(T,\omega) - r_f}{s_{\text{HFT}}(T,\omega)}$$

[14.10]

The ESR relationship is

$$ESR_{\text{HFT}}^B(T|T_B(\cdot)) = SR_{\text{HFT}}(T)\sqrt{T_B(\cdot)} > ESR_{\text{HFT}}^A(T|T_A(\cdot))$$
$$= SR_{\text{HFT}}(T)\sqrt{T_A(\cdot)}$$

[14.11]

Thus, trader B is more efficient because he/she executes more successful trades in the same window when compared to trader A. Under extant modifications of the SR there is no way to tell which of two traders is more efficient. According to the seemingly complex looking formula in (14.6) the subordinator is simply the sum of positive returns. Most important, in the context of Proposition 1 *it is a subset of the sufficient statistics that characterize the underlying stock price.* This conveys information not only about how many successful trades there were but it incorporates the cumulative returns for

---

[13] Refer to Øksendal (2003, pp. 23–24) for treatment of $t_j^{(n)} \leq t < t_{j+1}^{(n)}$ where $t_j^{(n)} = j.2^{-(n)}$, $j = 0,\ldots,2^{(n)}$.

successful trades in the SR formula. Since the returns will be less than 1 almost surely, the subordinator is less than T. That is

$$\Pr\left\{ T > T\left(t_0^{(n)}, \ldots, t_{2^n-1}^{(n)}, 1; \omega\right) \right\} = 1 - \eta \qquad [14.12]$$

for some small $0 < \eta < 1$. Probabilistically,

$$P\{T(t_0^{(n)}, \ldots, t_{2^n}^{(n)}-1, 1; \omega) = T(\mathbf{r}(\tau, \omega))\} = 1, \; \mathbf{r}(\tau, \omega) = (r_{\tau_0}(\omega), \ldots, r_{\tau_{2^n}-1}(\omega)),$$

$$T(\mathbf{r}(\tau, \omega)) = \sum_{j=0}^{2^n-1} r_{\tau_j}(\omega)$$

$$[14.13]$$

Note that $r_{\tau_j}(\omega) = 0$ when $r_{\mathrm{HFT}}(t_j^{(n)}, \omega) \notin E$. If $r_{\tau_j}(\omega)$ is independent for $j = 0, \ldots, 2^{(n)} - 1$, then $T(\mathbf{r}(\tau, \omega))$ is a Levy process characterized by the jumps $r_{\tau_j}(\omega)$ (Karatzas and Shreve, 1991, p. 405). In other words, the *joint distribution* of $\mathbf{r}(\tau, \omega)$ is in the class of Levy distributions. Assuming that $r(t, \omega)$ is drawn from a stable distribution with index α so $r(t, \omega) = t^{\frac{1}{\alpha}} r(1, \omega)$, the exponential term in $r_{\mathrm{HFT}}(t, \omega)$ in (14.6) implies that

$$SR_{\mathrm{HFT}}(T) \sim O_p\left(\exp\left(T^{-1+\frac{1}{\alpha}}\right)\right) \qquad (14.14)$$

where $O_p(\cdot)$ means that the growth of the respective variable is bounded by the term inside the bracket. For internal consistency in our model, this requires that for some function $\gamma(t)$ the growth of $SR_{\mathrm{HFT}}(t)$ must be consistent with $T(\mathbf{r}(\tau, \omega))$. In which case we write

$$\exp(\gamma(t)\bar{r}_{\mathrm{HFT}}(t, \omega)) = T(\mathbf{r}(\tau, \omega)) \Rightarrow \gamma(t)\bar{r}_{\mathrm{HFT}}(t, \omega) = \ln(T(\mathbf{r}(\tau, \omega))) \qquad (14.15)$$

$$\Rightarrow \bar{r}_{\mathrm{HFT}}(t, \omega) \approx 2\gamma(t)^{-1}\left(\ln(r_{\tau_0}) + r_{\tau_0}^{-1}\sum_{j=1}^{2^n-1} r_{\tau_j}\right) \qquad (14.16)$$

where the right-hand side of (14.15) was derived from a first-order approximation of $\ln(T(\mathbf{r}(\tau, \omega)))$ in (14.13), and the summand is $\left[\sum_{j=1}^{2^n-1}\tau_j(\omega)\right]^{\frac{1}{\alpha}}r(1, \omega)$. Feller (1970, Eq. (1.8), p. 171). Evidently, $\gamma(t)$ is a slow varying normalizing factor. Perhaps more important (14.15) establishes a nexus between our sufficient statistics for ESR and the sufficient statistics for $(\bar{r}_{\mathrm{HFT}}(t, \omega), \bar{s}_{\mathrm{HFT}}(t, \omega))$ SR in accord with Proposition 1.

HFT data is characterized by runs so we would expect returns to be correlated. Even so, Billingsley (1956, Thm. 5.2, p. 263) implies that if $\{r_{\tau_j}(\omega)\}_{j=0}^{2^{(n)}-1}$ is an m-dependent sequence, i.e., there are independent runs in the data separated by periods of length greater than m, and if $T(\mathbf{r}(\tau, \omega))$ is suitably normed, then the invariance principle holds. That is, $T(\mathbf{r}(\tau, \omega))$ will be an approximate Levy process with positive jumps. We summarize this with the following.

Lemma 1. (*Subordinator*). The subordinator $T(\mathbf{r}(\tau,\omega))$ is an approximate Levy process.

Based on the foregoing arguments we proved the following.

Proposition 2. (*Efficient Sharpe ratio*). Let SR_p be the Sharpe ratio computed for a given frequency for measuring portfolio returns, and $SR_p(T) = SR_p T$ be the corresponding "annualized" Sharpe ratio for the portfolio at frequency T different from the underlying frequency of measurement. The ESR for the portfolio is given by

$$ESR_p(T|T(\mathbf{r}(\tau,\omega))) = SR_p\sqrt{\frac{T}{T(\mathbf{r}(\tau,\omega))}}, \quad T(\mathbf{r}(\tau,\omega)) > 0 \qquad (14.17)$$

almost surely, where the subset of cumulative returns for successful trades $T(\mathbf{r}(\tau,\omega)) = \sum_{i=1}^{N} r_{\tau_j}(\omega)$ is a sufficient statistic for ESR, and $\Pr\{T > T(\mathbf{r}(\tau,\omega))\} = 1 - \eta$ for some small $\eta > 0$.

Remark: Notice how the inclusion of $T(\mathbf{r}(\tau,\omega))$ in the denominator in (14.17) mitigates against the exponential growth of SR in (14.14).

14.2.3 Application of ESR to HFT Risk and Return Data

In this section we apply the formula in Proposition 2 to published data on risk and return for the sample of HFT firms in Baron et al. (2014), hereinafter referenced as BBK. Table 14.1 provides rough estimates for the ESR extrapolated from BBK (2014, Tables 1 and 3). Our ESR numbers in column 10 are strikingly lower than the ASR numbers reported by BBK in column 9. For instance, in BBK the reported ASRs for aggressive, median, and passive HFTs are 4.26, 5.26, and 5.85, respectively. Our corresponding ESR estimates are 1.15, 2.88, and 1.43, respectively. Those numbers are more in line with Aldridge (2010) observation that "[r]eal-life Sharpe ratios for well-executed daily strategies tend to fall in the 1–2 range".

Perhaps more important, is the change in rank order of HFTs when the BBK ASR statistics are used compared to our ESR statistics. Our ESR ranks median HFTers above passive and aggressive whereas BBK ranks median HFTers between passive and aggressive. Lo (2002, p. 45) also found that after his serial correlation correction was applied to ASR the ranking of hedge funds in his sample changed dramatically. According to our ESR for HFT numbers, in the context of Lo (2002, Table 4) correlation adjusted SR for hedge funds, aggressive, median, and passive HFTers are comparable to hedge funds that employ multistrategy, convertible option arbitrage, and fund-of-fund strategies, respectively. Additionally, in the context of Gregoriou and Gueyie (2003, Exhibit 2, pp. 80–81) our imputed ESR numbers are consistent with the SRs for the top 10 and middle 10 hedge funds in their samples even though the average SR for those funds were much lower than that for the HFT's here.

Table 14.1 Efficient Sharpe ratio (ESR) estimates for HFT

HFTer	N	$\bar{r}_p^{ann}$	σ_p^{ann}	$CS(\bar{r}_p^d)$	%Vol	$PS(\bar{r}_p^d)$	$T(r)$	ASR	ESR
Aggressive	18	91.08	170.55	22,952.16	15.22	3493.32	13.86	4.29	1.15
Median	39	27.42	45.61	6909.84	30.28	2092.30	8.30	5.26	2.88
Passive	28	23.13	22.24	5828.76	8.87	517.01	2.05	5.85	1.43

Data on high-frequency trader type (HFTer), sample size N, average annualized returns $\bar{r}_p^{ann}$, average annualized volatility σ_p^{ann}, daily % of market volume traded (% Vol), and annualized Sharpe ratio (ASR) are taken from Baron et al. (2014, Tables 1 and 3). $CS(\bar{r}_p^d)$ is the cumulative average daily returns $252 \star \bar{r}_p^{ann}$ assuming annualized returns $252 \star \bar{r}_p^{ann}$ were compute as in Campbell et al. (1997, Eqn (1.4.4), p. 10), $PS(\bar{r}_p^d)$ is a partial sum %Vol★$CS(\bar{r}_p^d)$, the directing process $T(r)$ is $PS(\bar{r}_p^d)/252$ and ESR $=$ ASR $\times$ $\{T(\mathbf{r})\}^{-1/2}$.

One obvious shortcoming of our analysis is we do not have granular data that allow us to compute the partial sum of positive returns on HFT trades. However, we believe that given our data limitations, the critical partial sum statistic PS $\left(\bar{r}_p^d\right) = \%\mathrm{Vol}\star\mathrm{CS}(\bar{r}_p^d)$ is a reasonable *instrumental variable* in view of Carrion (2013, p. 689) use of volume to evaluate HFT performance.

14.3 CONCLUSION

In this chapter we introduce an intuitively appealing ESR formula adapted to high-frequency trading. It takes into account the number of successful trades executed by a trader—which is a subset of the sufficient statistics used to compute *SRs*. Specifically, the correction factor is the cumulative total returns for successful trades. Other correction factors in the literature are based on extension of sample moments that invariably include at least a subset of our correction factor. The upshot of our ESR formula is it shows that the spectacular ASR estimates reported in the emerging literature on high-frequency trading are functionally equivalent to *SRs* for hedge funds or other traditional investment vehicles after our single correction factor is applied. Our model warns against the use of naïve ASRs for performance evaluation of HFTers without correction factors of the type introduced here. Our ESR formula can be applied to publicly available data on risk and return provided that suitable instruments for estimating the partial sum for positive returns in the underlying portfolio can be identified.

ACKNOWLEDGMENTS

I thank Oliver Martin for his comments on an earlier draft of this chapter I thank Jonathan Mackinlay for granting me permission to use his chart.

REFERENCES

Aldridge, I., 2013. High Frequency Trading: A Practical Guide to Algorithmic Strategies and Trading Systems. John Wiley & Sons, Hoboken, NJ.

Aldridge, I., 2014. High-frequency runs and flash-crash predictability. J. Portfolio Manag. 4 (3), 113—123.

Aldridge, I., July 26, 2010. How Profitable Are High Frequency Traders?. Huffington Post Business Section. Available at. Last visited 10/24/2014. http://www.huffingtonpost.com/irene-aldridge/how-profitable-are-high-f_b_659466.html.

Bailey, D.H., de Prado, M.L., 2014. The deflated sharpe ratio: correcting for selection bias, backtest overfitting and non-normality. J. Portfolio Manag. Forthcom. Available at: http://ssrn.com/abstract=2460551.

Baron, M., Brogaard, J., Kirilenko, A.A., 2014. Risk and Return in High Frequency Trading. Available at SSRN: http://ssrn.com/abstract=2433118; http://dx.doi.org/10.2139/ssrn.2433118.

Billingsley, P., 1956. The invariance principle for dependent random variables. Trans. Amer. Math. Soc. 83 (1), 250—268.

Blackwell, D., 1947. Conditional expectation and unbiased sequential estimation. Ann. Math. Statistic 18 (1), 105—110.

Cadogan, G., 2012. Trading Rules over Fundamentals: A Stock Price Formula for High Frequency Trading, Bubbles and Crashes. Available at SSRN: http://ssrn.com/abstract=1977561; http://dx.doi.org/10.2139/ssrn.1977561.

Campbell, J.Y., Lo, A.W., MacKinlay, A.C., 1997. The Econometrics of Financ. Markets. Princeton University Press, Princeton, NJ.

Carr, P., Wu, L., 2004. Time-changed Lévy processes and option pricing. J. Financ. Econ. 71 (1), 113–141.

Carrion, A., 2013. Very fast money: high-frequency trading on the NASDAQ. J. Financ. Mark. 16 (4), 680–711.

Clark, P.A., 1973. A subordinated stochastic process model with finite variance for speculative prices. Econometrica 41 (1), 135–155.

Clark-Joseph, A.D., 2013. Exploratory Trading. Working Paper. Harvard University.

Cramer, H., 1946. Methods of Mathematical Statistics. Princeton University Press, Princeton, NJ.

DeGroot, M., 1970. Optimal Statistical Decisions. McGraw-Hill, New York, NY.

Egginton, J., Van Ness, B.F., Van Ness, R.A., 2014. Quote Stuffing. Working Paper. Available at: http://ssrn.com/abstract=1958281.

Elton, E.J., Gruber, M.J., Brown, S.J., Goetzmann, W.N., 2014. Modern Portfolio Theory and Investment Analysis. John Wiley and Sons, Hoboken, NJ.

Farmer, D., 2013. Interview in the Trading Mesh, High Frequency Review Feburary 21, 2013. Available at: http://www.thetradingmesh.com/pg/blog/mike/read/72400/beyond-economics-prof-doyne-farmer-on-how-computers-are-changing-the-way-trading-is-analysed.

Feller, W., 1970. An Introduction to Probability Theory and its Applications. Vol. II. John Wilye and Sons, New York, NY.

Gordon, M.J., 1959. Dividends, earnings, and stock prices. Rev. Econ. Statistics 41 (2), 99–105.

Gregoriou, G.N., Gueyie, J.-P., 2003. Risk-adjusted performance of funds of hedge funds using a modified sharpe ratio. J. Altern. Investments 6 (3), 77–83.

Hasbrouck, J., Sofianos, G., 1993. The trades of market makers: an empirical analysis of NYSE Specialists. J. Finance 48 (50), 1565–1593.

Jones, C.M., 2013. What Do We Know about High-frequency Trading?. Columbia Business School Working Paper. Available at: http://ssrn.com/abstract=2236201.

Karatzas, I., Shreve, S., 1991. Brownian Motion and Stochastic Calculus. Springer-Verlag, New York, NY.

Lehmann, E.L., 1999. Elements of Large Sample Theory. Springer, New York,NY.

Lo, A.W., 2002. The statistics of sharpe ratios. Financ. Analysts J. 58 (4), 36–52.

Mackinlay, J., 2014. Pattern Trading. Quantitative Research and Trading Blog. Available at: http://jonathankinlay.com/index.php/2014/07/pattern-trading/.

Menkveld, A.J., 2013. High frequency trading and the new market makers. J. Financ. Mark. 16 (4), 712–740.

Mertens, E., 2002. Variance of the IID Estimator. Working Paper. University of Basel, Switzerland.

Merton, R.C., 1992. Continuous-time Finance. Blackwell Publishing, Boston, MA.

Narang, R., 2013. Inside the Black Box: A Simple Guide to Quantitative and High Frequency Trading. John Wiley & Sons, New York, NY.

Øksendal, B., 2003. Stochastic Differential Equations: An Introduction with Applications. Springer-Verlag, New York, NY.

Sharpe, W., 1994. The sharpe ratio. J. Portfolio Manag. 21 (1), 49–58.

Sharpe, W.F., 1966. Mutual fund performance. J. Bus. 39 (1), 119–138.

Zubulake, P., Lee, S., 2011. The High Frequency Game Changer: How Automated Trading Strategies Have Revolutionized the Market. John Wiley & Sons, Hoboken, NJ.

PART 4

Impact of News Releases

CHAPTER 15

Do High Frequency Traders Care about Earnings Announcements? An Analysis of Trading Activity before, during, and after Regular Trading Hours

Brittany Cole, Jonathan Daigle, Bonnie F. Van Ness, Robert A. Van Ness
University of Mississippi, School of Business, University, MS, USA

Contents

15.1 INTRODUCTION

Research shows that high frequency traders (HFTs) add to price discovery (Brogaard et al. (2014); Viljoen et al. (2014)) and behave as market makers (Menkveld, 2013). Current research on HFTs focuses primarily on regular trading hours (RTHs), but not on trading before the market opens or after the market closes. Jiang et al. (2012) show that most earnings announcement are made after the market closes. In addition, they show a significant portion of the price change and price discovery occurs after earnings releases, both in the period prior to the market opening and in the after-hours trading sessions. We seek to blend the two above-mentioned streams of research by examining how high frequency trading firms trade on information-rich days (earnings announcements days). We compare the aggressiveness of HFTs on earnings announcement days and nonannouncement days and detail the price contribution of HFTs on these days. We document the timing of HFTs' trades (before the open of trading, during the normal trading day and after the market closes). Last, we study the factors that influence price discovery for both HFTs and non-HFTs.

Many factors motivate our interest in studying the trading activity of HFTs outside of normal trading hours on high information days. Hendershott and Riordan (2013) show that algorithmic traders react more quickly to news than do human traders. Since many earnings announcements do not occur during RTHs, we are interested to see if HFTs react quickly to earnings announcements in after-market hours and before open trading. If it is true that HFTs end the day with zero inventory, does their trading day end with the normal close of trading or does it creep into the evening? Understanding the trading behavior of HFTs, including how and when they trade, is crucial to the debate regarding the role HFTs play in markets.

Initially, we focus on whether HFTs are more likely to initiate trades on earnings announcement days or non-earnings announcement days. We find that HFTs initiate fewer trades on earnings announcement days. In addition, we investigate if HFTs trade differently in before and after market trading than they do in RTHs. We find that HFTs initiate a higher proportion of RTHs' trades than either before or after market trades. We also determine that non-HFTs' trades provide more information to the market than HFTs' trades. Lastly, we investigate factors that influence price discovery of both high frequency and non-high frequency trades. Firm size, trading volume, and the firm's listing exchange affect the price contribution of non-HFTs' trades, but we do not find evidence that the same factors influence the weighted price contribution of HFTs.

15.2 HIGH FREQUENCY TRADING

High frequency trading is the term used for trading that uses computer algorithms to rapidly submit and cancel orders. High frequency trading results not only in many trades, but also in many canceled orders. High frequency trading is controversial. Some suggest that this type of computerized trading (rapidly submitting and immediately canceling many orders) does not influence long-term prices, but that it improves liquidity (see Hasbrouck and Saar (2013); Hendershott et al. (2011)). Others question if HFTs adversely impact markets; see Goldstein et al. (2014) and Menkveld (2014) for more on this discussion.

High frequency trading strategies generally fall into four categories (described in Aldridge (2010); Goldstein et al. (2014)): (1) automated liquidity provision, which involves buying and selling securities across exchanges to remove order imbalances; (2) market microstructure trading, which utilizes trading to predict future buys and sales; (3) event arbitrage, which involves determining the direction of the market's reaction to news and subsequently trading ahead of the market to profit from this prediction; and (4) statistical trading, which involves finding price discrepancies between securities (such as futures and options or interrelated securities) and trading on the price discrepancies.

High frequency trading is prevalent in markets, and it can be extremely profitable (see Baron et al. (2012)). Brogaard (2010) reports an HFT participation rate of 73.7% for a sample of NASDAQ stocks while Cardela et al. (2014) document high frequency trading in foreign exchange markets and derivative markets.

High frequency trading can have detrimental effects for financial markets. Gai et al. (2012) study the changes made to NASDAQ's trading architecture to increase trading speed and find that canceled orders increase along with the increase in trading speed, thereby reducing the liquidity on NASDAQ. Egginton et al. (2014) identify intense episodic spikes in quoting activity, termed quote stuffing, using a minimum increase of 20 standard deviations in mean quotes-per-minute. The authors find that more than 70% of US exchange listed stocks experience at least one quote stuffing event in 2010. Also, quote stuffing is associated with a deterioration of market quality. Specifically, quote stuffing leads to an increase in canceled orders, an increase in trading costs, a decrease in order size, and a decrease in duration. Angel (2014) discusses the fairness of and regulatory concerns regarding the speed of trading, and concludes that market architects should be cautious when increasing trading speed.

High frequency trading is being watched and discussed by market regulators. The SEC and CFTC released a joint report after the 2010 flash crash (the sudden drop and subsequent rebound of the Dow Jones Industrial average of about 1000 points on Thursday, May 6, 2010). The report documents high HFT activity during the flash crash (more than 50% of volume). The agencies did not conclude that HFTs caused the flash crash; although, HFTs were identified as net sellers during the event. Other regulators and regulatory bodies are scrutinizing high frequency trading. In 2012, the United Kingdom government called for a study to analyze computer generated trading in their markets and determine how computer generated trading might evolve over the next 10 years (this study is called Foresight). Financial Industry Regulatory Authority (FINRA) identified high frequency trading as an enforcement priority in 2014 and the United States Senate held hearings on June 17, 2014, related to high frequency trading in US markets.

15.3 RELATED LITERATURE

Recent work details a shift in the timing of earnings announcements. Michaely et al. (2014) show that five percent of earnings are reported during RTHs in 2002, down sharply from the 45% of earnings announcements made during RTHs in the late 1990s. Jiang et al. (2012) use this decline in RTH announcements to motivate a study about when investors trade (before the market opens or after the market closes) and how investors contribute to price discovery following earnings announcements. Jiang et al. (2012) show that trading volume increases on announcement days, and also document a smaller average trade size during the before and after market trading sessions. They also study price formation in relation to the earnings announcement time and show that the timing of the announcement matters for price discovery. Specifically, 36% of weighted price contribution occurs from the announcement time to the opening trade for earnings announcements made before the market open. For after market announcements, 60% of price discovery occurs before the opening trade on the day following the announcement.

HFTs play a dominant role in financial markets. According to the Securities and Exchange Commission, HFTs contribute 50% or more of total trading volume. The SEC (2010) indicates, "by any measure, HFT is a dominant component of the current market structure and is likely to affect nearly all aspects of its performance." Brogaard et al. (2014) show HFTs trade on the information content from macroeconomic announcements. Zhang (2013) finds that HFTs are more adept at analyzing hard information, such as S&P 500 futures return shocks and VIX return shocks, than soft information, such as textual news data. Using what we know about HFTs, we take the Jiang et al. (2012) earnings announcement analysis a step further and show not only when investors trade, but also who (HFTs or non-HFTs) is trading after hours. Our data allow us to distinguish between trades by high frequency trading firms and non-HFTs, which facilitates our documentation of who participates in after-hours trading.

Our contribution to the literature is threefold. First, we highlight differences between trading activity of HFTs and non-HFTs on earnings announcement days and nonannouncement days. Second, we show who (HFTs and non-HFTs) is trading and when they are trading on announcement days. Third, we measure the price contribution of HFTs' and non-HFTs' trades during after-hours trading on announcement days compared to nonannouncement days.

15.4 DATA

Our data consists of trades in 120 stocks (60 NYSE-listed and 60 NASDAQ-listed) from the NASDAQ HFT Database. The sample includes 2008 and 2009. Each trade includes a time stamp in milliseconds, stock ticker, trade size (in shares), a buy/sell indicator, and trade price of transactions that occur on NASDAQ. Additionally, the data indicates whether the trade is initiated by a high frequency trading firm or non-HFT, and also whether the other side (the liquidity providing side) of the trade is a high frequency firm or not. HFT firms are identified by an H while non-HFTs are identified by an N. There are four trade types in the sample, with the first letter being the trade initiator (or liquidity demander) and the second letter being the liquidity provider: HH, HN, NH, and NN.

We use COMPUSTAT to collect earnings announcement dates and Thomson Reuters StreetEvents to collect earnings announcement times. We designate a before market open (BMO) announcement as one that occurs from 4:00 am to 9:29 am Eastern Standard Time (EST). RTH announcements occur between 9:30 am and 4:00 pm EST, and after market close (AMC) announcements occur between 4:01 pm and 8:00 pm EST. Table 15.1 details the distribution of earnings announcements with identifiable times during our sample period. Our sample contains 836 announcements. A total of

Table 15.1 Number of earnings announcements by time and day and announcements by time of day, by year

Panel A: Number of earnings announcements by time of day

Time of announcement	NYSE-listed	NASDAQ-listed	Total
7:00–9:29 am (BMO)	156	83	239
9:30 am to 4:00 pm (RTH)	190	138	328
4:01–8:00 pm (AMC)	71	198	269
Total	417	419	836

Panel B: Announcements by time of day, by year

	NYSE-listed		NASDAQ-listed	
	2008	2009	2008	2009
BMO	75	81	39	44
RTH	99	91	65	73
AMC	33	38	98	100
Total	207	210	202	217

Panel A provides details regarding earnings announcements for our 120 stocks by time of announcement and exchange-listing. The majority of before market open (BMO) announcements are for NYSE-listed stocks, while the majority of after market close (AMC) announcements are for NASDAQ-listed stocks. Stocks from both exchanges have a large number of regular trading hours (RTH) announcements. Panel B shows the number of earnings announcements during each of our two sample years by exchange listing.

239 announcements occur before the market opens. A total of 328 of these announcements occur during RTHs. A total of 269 announcements are made after the market closes. We also split the announcements by exchange-listing. Most earnings announcements for NYSE-listed stocks occur either before the market opens (156) or during RTHs (190). The announcement distribution is slightly different for NASDAQ-listed stocks, with the majority of earnings announcements occurring during RTHs (138) and after the market close (198). Similar patterns are evident when we look at the earnings announcements for each exchange by year.

We separate our data into BMO, RTH, and AMC samples. The BMO announcement sample consists of announcement day trading data prior to the market open for the stocks making BMO announcements. The BMO nonannouncement sample consists of trading data prior to the market open for all nonannouncement trading days for the stocks from the BMO announcement sample. The RTH samples are retained in a similar manner, consisting only of trading data from RTHs for stocks making earnings announcements during RTHs. The AMC announcement sample consists of announcement day trades after the market close for stocks making AMC announcements, and the AMC nonannouncement sample contains after-hours trading data for all nonannouncement days for the stocks with AMC announcements.

15.5 RESULTS

First, we focus on highlighting differences in earnings announcement days and nonearnings announcements days. Table 15.2 reports the comparisons of volume for our three time segments by trade type: BMO, RTH, and AMC. Volume is listed by trader type: HH, HN, NH, and NN. The first letter identifies the liquidity demander (trade initiator), and the second letter identifies the liquidity supplier. H signifies a high frequency trading firm and N signifies a non-HFT, so an HN trade is one where a high frequency trading firm is the liquidity demander and a non-HFT is the liquidity provider. Panel A reports the average announcement day volume in the preopen period for stocks with earnings announcements before the trading day begins and the nonannouncement days' trading

Table 15.2 Comparison between average trading volume on earnings announcement days and nonannouncement days for stocks having earnings announcements before the market open (BMO), during regular trading hours (RTH) and after market close (AMC), by trade type

	Announcement	Nonannouncement	Difference	T-Stat
Panel A: BMO earnings announcements				
HH	1736	145	1591	1.51
HN	12,126	702	11,424★	1.76
NH	31,891	904	30,987	1.49
NN	222,627	8,283	214,343★	1.73
Panel B: RTH announcements				
HH	152,937	98,281	54,656★★	2.60
HN	308,194	188,667	119,526★★★	4.00
NH	436,701	204,770	231,932★★	2.16
NN	520,890	246,012	274,878★★★	3.54
Panel C: AMC earnings announcements				
HH	51,641	233	51,409★★	2.62
HN	177,595	1,191	176,404★★★	3.01
NH	142,192	1,230	140,962★★★	2.98
NN	605,420	8,183	597,238★★★	3.51

We identify four trade types: HH, HN, NH, and NN. The first letter identifies the trade initiator (liquidity demander) and the second letter identifies the liquidity supplier. H signifies a high frequency trading firm and N signifies a non-high frequency trader, so an HN trade is one where a high frequency trading firm is the liquidity demander and a non-high frequency trader is the liquidity provider. Panel A reports the average announcement day volume in the preopen period for stocks with earnings announcements before the trading day begins and the nonannouncement days' trading activity for these same stocks in the BMO period. Panel B shows the average announcement day volume during RTHs for stocks with earnings announcements during RTHs and the nonannouncement days' trading activity for these same stocks during RTHs. Panel C contains the average announcement day volume in the after-hours period for stocks with earnings announcements after the close of trading and the nonannouncement days' trading activity for these same stocks in the after-hours period. Panel A utilizes trades that occur on NASDAQ before regular market hours (4:00 am–9:29 am). Panel B uses trades that occur on NASDAQ during regular NASDAQ trading hours (9:30 am–4:00 pm). Panel C includes trades that take place on NASDAQ in after-hours trading (4:01 pm–8:00 pm). Significance is indicated at the 1%, 5%, and 10% levels with ★★★,★★★, and ★.

activity for these same stocks in the BMO period. Panel B shows the average announcement day volume during RTHs for stocks with earnings announcements during RTHs and the nonannouncement days' trading activity for these same stocks during RTHs. Panel C contains the average announcement day volume in the after-hours period for stocks with earnings announcements after the close of trading and the nonannouncement days' trading activity for these same stocks in the after hours period.

Volume is significantly higher for all trade types on earnings announcements days compared to nonannouncement days for announcements made during RTHs and in the period after the market closes. We show that both HFT and non-HFT traders are active during before market and after market trading. However, HFTs are not as active as non-HFTs. While average volume of all trade types increases when firms announce earnings in the after-market period, the average volume exchanged between non-HFTs after the market closes is about one and one half times the average volume of the other trade types combined. While after-hours activity is higher on days with earnings announcements, non-HFT initiated trades (NH and NN) account for substantially more volume on announcement days. Specifically, non-HFT initiated volume is about three times greater than HFT initiated volume. Trades between HFTs (HH) account for the smallest portion of after-hours volume on both announcement days and nonannouncement days. Volume is marginally higher for trades with non-HFTs as liquidity provider on announcement days for BMO announcements, but there is no statistical difference between announcement day volume and nonannouncement day volume in the preopen period for trades where HFTs provide the liquidity.

We formally compare the proportion of volume on announcement days with the proportion of volume on nonannouncement days for the four trade types. Table 15.3 details the percentage volume of each trade type in the three announcement periods. Panel A lists the proportion of volume for each of the trade types in the BMO period for stocks that make announcements in the preopen as well as the proportion of volume in the preopen on nonannouncement days for these same stocks. Panels B and C show similar proportions for stocks with announcements made during RTHs and AMC, respectively. The three panels show that non-HFT trades account for the majority of the volume in our sample stocks in BMO, RTH, and AMC trading, and that the proportion of NN volume increases only with after-market close announcements. The increase in NNHH's proportion of after-market volume on AMC announcement days is nearly offset by the decrease in the proportion of NH volume on these days. Although high frequency trading firms initiate more trades on earnings announcement days than on nonannouncement days, the proportion of volume that these trades account for is either constant or marginally lower. Overall, Table 15.2 shows that volume increases considerably (for most trader types) in the trading period when a firm announces earnings, and Table 15.3 shows that most trader types participate in reasonably similar proportions of the increased volume on announcement days as on nonannouncement days.

Table 15.3 Comparison between proportional trading volume on earnings announcement days and nonannouncement days for stocks having earnings announcements before the market open (BMO), during regular trading hours (RTH) and after market close (AMC), by trade type

	Announcement	Nonannouncement	Difference	T-Stat
Panel A: BMO announcements				
HH	0.45%	1.63%	−1.18%★★	−2.54
HN	8.26%	13.67%	−5.41★	−1.74
NH	10.66%	7.79%	2.87%	1.13
NN	80.64%	76.91%	3.73%	0.79
Panel B: RTH announcements				
HH	6.37%	6.62%	−0.25%	−0.72
HN	25.21%	27.52%	−2.31%★★★	−4.00
NH	15.27%.	13.47%	1.80%★★★	3.95
NN	53.14%	52.39%	0.21%	0.81
Panel C: AMC announcements				
HH	2.11%	2.74%	−0.63%	−1.04
HN	10.43%	10.59%	−0.16%	−0.11
NH	9.03%	16.89%	−7.86★★★	−3.79
NN	78.43%	69.77%	8.66%★★	2.46

We identify four trade types: HH, HN, NH, and NN. The first letter identifies the trade initiator (liquidity demander) and the second letter identifies the liquidity supplier. H signifies a high frequency trading firm and N signifies a non-high frequency trader, so an HN trade is one where a high frequency trading firm is the liquidity demander and a non-high frequency trader is the liquidity provider. Panel A reports the average announcement day proportional volume in the preopen period for stocks with earnings announcements before the trading day begins and the nonannouncement days' proportional volume for these same stocks in the BMO period. Panel B shows the average announcement day proportional volume during RTHs for stocks with earnings announcements during RTHs and the nonannouncement days' proportional volume for these same stocks during RTHs. Panel C contains the average announcement day proportional volume in the after-hours period for stocks with earnings announcements after the close of trading and the nonannouncement days' proportional volume for these same stocks in the after-hours period. Panel A utilizes trades that occur on NASDAQ before regular market hours (4:00 am–9:29 am). Panel B uses trades that occur on NASDAQ during regular NASDAQ trading hours (9:30 am–4:00 pm). Panel C includes trades that take place on NASDAQ in after-hours trading (4:01 pm–8:00 pm). Significance is indicated at the 1%, 5%, and 10% levels with ★★★,★★, and ★.

We further investigate who is trading and when they are trading by comparing the average number of trades on earnings announcement days and nonannouncement days. Table 15.4 shows our comparison of trader types. Panel A reports the average number of trades on announcement day in the preopen period for stocks with earnings announcements before the trading day begins and the nonannouncement days' average number of trades for these same stocks in the BMO period. Panel B shows the average number of trades on announcement day during RTHs for stocks with earnings announcements during RTHs and the nonannouncement days' average number of trades for these same stocks during RTHs. Panel C contains the average number of trades on announcement day in the after-hours period for stocks with earnings announcements after the close of trading and the nonannouncement days' average number of trades

Table 15.4 Comparison between the average number of trades on earnings announcement days and nonannouncement days for stocks having earnings announcements before the market open (BMO), during regular trading hours (RTH) and after market close (AMC), by trade type

	Announcement	Nonannouncement	Difference	T-Stat
Panel A: BMO earnings announcements				
HH	11.28	0.85	10.43	1.58
HN	50.35	2.70	47.65★	1.76
NH	163.51	4.13	159.38	1.46
NN	297.21	18.98	278.23★★	2.10
Panel B: RTH announcements				
HH	1147.03	765.05	381.98★★★	3.24
HN	2074.85	1399.59	675.26★★★	4.90
NH	2315.67	1197.93	1117.73★★★	3.15
NN	2519.60	1445.17	1074.43★★★	5.05
Panel C: AMC earnings announcements				
HH	396.61	1.16	395.44★★	2.50
HN	788.07	4.49	783.58★★	2.71
NH	952.20	4.69	947.51★★★	2.85
NN	1504.44	26.70	1477.74★★★	3.60

We identify four trade types: HH, HN, NH, and NN. The first letter identifies the trade initiator (liquidity demander) and the second letter identifies the liquidity supplier. H signifies a high frequency trading firm and N signifies a non-high frequency trader, so an HN trade is one where a high frequency trading firm is the liquidity demander and a non-high frequency trader is the liquidity provider. Panel A reports the average number of trades on announcement day in the preopen period for stocks with earnings announcements before the trading day begins and the nonannouncement days' average number of trades for these same stocks in the BMO period. Panel B shows the average number of trades on announcement day during RTHs for stocks with earnings announcements during RTHs and the nonannouncement days' average number of trades for these same stocks during RTHs. Panel C contains the average number of trades on announcement day in the after-hours period for stocks with earnings announcements after the close of trading and the nonannouncement days' average number of trades for these same stocks in the after-hours period. Panel A utilizes trades that occur on NASDAQ before regular market hours (4:00 am–9:29 am). Panel B uses trades that occur on NASDAQ during regular NASDAQ trading hours (9:30 am–4:00 pm). Panel C includes trades that take place on NASDAQ in after hours trading (4:01 pm–8:00 pm). Significance is indicated at the 1%, 5%, and 10% levels with ★★★,★★★, and ★.

for these same stocks in the after-hours period. We note few trades involving HFTs (HH, HN, and NH) take place outside RTHs on nonannouncement days. All trade types experience an increase in the number of trades outside RTHs on earnings announcement day, with the exception of before market trades with liquidity provided by HFTs. The increases are especially large for stocks with after-market earnings announcements. The figures in Panel C lead us to believe that HFTs' normal day ends with the close of trading; however, it appears that the algorithms continue trading into the evenings on earnings announcement days when there is more non-HFTs with which to transact.

We analyze trading volume and number of trades around earnings announcements in RTHs and outside of regular hours, and we show who (which trader type) is transacting.

We now focus on price discovery weighted price contribution (WPC) around earnings announcements. The data used in our WPC analyses differs. We retain the trades from the time of the BMO announcement until the end of RTHs and then divide this data into BMO and RTH segments. If the announcement is made after the market close, we retain the trading data from the time of the announcement until market close the following trading day. This data is divided into three segments: AMC on the announcement day and BMO and RTH on the following day. Using the segments following the announcement will help us observe when price discovery takes place, and if traders react immediately when the announcement is made outside RTHs. We also run our analysis separately for NYSE- and NASDAQ-listed stocks.

We detail WPC in relation to when the earnings announcement occurs in Table 15.5. Panel A shows WPC for before market announcements. The majority of price discovery occurs during the RTHs following BMO announcements. Only 11% of the price contribution can be attributed to trades taking place from the BMO announcement time to the start of regular trading, and 89% of price contribution occurs during the subsequent RTHs. Non-HFT initiated trades account for the majority of WPC following the BMO announcement in both the preopen period and RTHs. HFT initiated trades either detract or provide no WPC on the day of a BMO earnings announcement.

We also split the announcements into NYSE- and NASDAQ-listed stocks. Overall, no WPC is provided from the BMO announcement to the opening trade on NASDAQ for our sample of NYSE-listed stocks. Of the four trade types, only trades between non-HFTs (HH) contribute positively to WPC (9%) before the open. This positive price contribution in the preopen period is more than offset by negative or zero WPC for the other three types. Price contribution for NYSE-listed stocks with BMO announcements takes place in non-HFT initiated trades during RTHs following the announcement. NH trades, non-HFT initiated trades with HFT liquidity suppliers, provide the most to price discovery for these stocks during RTHs, followed by NN trades, which are trades between non-HFTs.

WPC for NASDAQ-listed stocks with BMO earnings announcements is segmented between the preopen time subsequent to the announcement (21%) and the RTHs of the same trading day (79%). The positive price contribution in the preopen comes from trades between non-HFTs (21%) and HN trades (6%). All trade types, except trades between HFTs, contribute positively to price discovery during RTHs for stocks with BMO earnings announcements.

We focus on the after market announcements in Panel B. 19% of WPC for all stocks with after hours earnings announcements occurs from the time of the announcement to 6:30 pm. Similar to BMO announcements, the majority of the outside-regular-trading-hours price discovery on NASDAQ comes from non-HFT initiated trades. NN trades contribute 10%, while NH trades contribute 30%. HFT initiated trades detract from WPC from the AMC announcement to 6:30 pm. The same is true during the before

Table 15.5 Weighted price contribution (WPC) for earnings announcement days for stocks having earnings announcements before the market open (BMO) and after market close (AMC), by trade type

Panel A: WPC for BMO announcements

| | All stocks | | NYSE-listed | | NASDAQ-listed | |
	Announcement to 9:29	9:30 to 4:00	Announcement to 9:29	9:30 to 4:00	Announcement to 9:29	9:30 to 4:00
Full Sample	11.0%	89.0%	-2.0%	102.0%	21.0%	79.0%
HH	-1.0%	-23.0%	0.0%	-44.0%	-5.0%	-11.0%
HN	-1.0%	-12.0%	-4.0%	-20.0%	6.0%	14.0%
NH	-5.0%	69.0%	-7.0%	104.0%	-1.0%	30.0%
NN	18.0%	55.0%	9.0%	62.0%	21.0%	46.0%

Panel B: WPC for AMC announcements

| | All stocks | | | NYSE-listed | | | NASDAQ-listed | | |
	Announcement to 6:30	7:00 to 9:29	9:30 to 4:00	Announcement to 6:30	7:00 to 9:29	9:30 to 4:00	Announcement to 6:30	7:00 to 9:29	9:30 to 4:00
Full Sample	19.0%	-1.0%	82.0%	26.0%	19.0%	55.0%	16.0%	-18.0%	102.0%
HH	-6.0%	-3.0%	-32.0%	0.0%	-6.0%	71.0%	-3.0%	0.0%	-59.0%
HN	-15.0%	-24.0%	25.0%	-4.0%	-8.0%	31.0%	-16.0%	-20.0%	32.0%
NH	30.0%	6.0%	-6.0%	-3.0%	-7.0%	-96.0%	41.0%	8.0%	61.0%
NN	10.0%	20.0%	95.0%	33.0%	40.0%	49.0%	-6.0%	-6.0%	68.0%

We identify four trade types: HH, HN, NH, and NN. The first letter identifies the trade initiator (liquidity demander) and the second letter identifies the liquidity supplier. H signifies a high frequency trading firm and N signifies a non-high frequency trader, so an HN trade is one where a high frequency trading firm is the liquidity demander and a non-high frequency trader is the liquidity provider. Panel A includes BMO earnings announcements and Panel B includes AMC earnings announcements. We measure the WPC from the time of the preopen announcement until the market opens and then during the RTHs (Panel A). WPC is calculated on announcement day for all stocks making an announcement during the period as well as by exchange listing. Panel B reports WPC for stocks with AMC announcements. We calculate WPS from the time of announcement until the end of after-hours trading on announcement day and during before market trading and during RTHs the following day. The BMO period is from 4:00 am–9:29 am and the AMC period is from 4:01 pm–6:30 pm.

market trading period following the AMC announcement. HFT initiated trades detract from price discovery while non-HFT initiated trades contribute positively. The majority of price discovery for AMC announcements of NASDAQ-listed stocks (82%) occurs during the following day's RTHs. During the RTHs following the AMC announcement, HN trades and NN trades positively contribute to WPC.

We also separate the NYSE- and NASDAQ-listed stocks with after market announcements. The story for NYSE-listed stocks with AMC announcements is slightly different. While a majority of the WPC on NASDAQ for these NYSE-listed stocks occurs during the following days' RTHs, a substantial amount occurs both in after hours (26%) and subsequent before open (19%) trading. Trades between non-HFTs appear to provide the most WPC in AMC and BMO segments of NASDAQ trading. NASDAQ trades between HFTs provide the most WPC (71%) in the RTHs on the day following the announcement for NYSE-listed stocks. Trades between non-HFTs also contribute substantially (49%) as do HN trades (31%). NH trades contribute negatively during the RTHs following the AMC announcement. Overall, for our sample of NYSE-listed stocks with earnings announcements in the preopen, it appears that HFT initiated trades provide the most WPC in the RTHs following the announcement and non-HFTs provide the most WPC in the after-hours and preopen segments following the announcement.

The WPC for NASDAQ-listed stocks with AMC earnings announcements is similar to that for the full sample of AMC announcements. 16% of the WPC takes place in after hours trading. As in the full sample, trades between HFTs do not positively contribute to price discovery in any of the three periods following the announcement. Only NH trades contribute positively to price discovery in after-hours trading for NASDAQ-listed stocks with AMC earnings announcements. The other trader types have negative WPC, lowering the price contribution for period from the announcement time to 6:30 pm to 16%. Although NH trades have positive price contribution in the preopen period following the AMC announcement, the preopen period has an overall negative WPC. All trades types, with the exception of trades between HFTs, have positive WPC in the RTHs of the day following the NASDAQ-listed stock's AMC earnings announcement.

Overall, non-HFT initiated trades appear to be the most informative on the NASDAQ market both during and outside RTHs for stocks with earnings announcements in the preopen or after-market periods. NASDAQ-listed stocks (and the overall sample) with preopen announcements experience positive WPC in the preopen segment; however, all BMO announcements have more price discovery during the regular trading day following the preopen announcement. Stocks that trade on NASDAQ and have earnings announcements after the close of trading have positive price contribution in the after-hours. The contributing trades are non-HFT initiated, with non-HFTs supplying the liquidity for NYSE-listed stock trades and HFTs supplying the liquidity for the

NASDAQ-listed stock trades. HFT initiated trades do not appear to positively contribute to price formation on NASDAQ in after-hours market subsequent to earnings announcements. Only NYSE-listed stocks experience overall positive WPC in preopen trading following an after-hours announcement.

Jiang et al. (2012) examine the relation between WPC and stock characteristics when studying earnings announcements and after-hours trading. We follow a similar method to Jiang et al. (2012) cross-sectional regression analysis for our entire sample and for each of the four trade types. The dependent variable in column 1 is the WPC per stock, and the dependent variable in columns 2–5 is the WPC by stock and trade type. Volume is the natural log of average daily volume for each stock (column 1) and the natural log of the average daily volume for each stock per trade type (columns 2–5). We use 21 trading days before the announcement to compute average volume. Firm size is the natural log of the average market cap of each stock over 21 days before the announcement day. We include N_Announcements, the number of firms that make announcements during the same outside-regular-market-hours segments as our BMO and AMC sample stocks, as Hirshleifer et al. (2009) find lower price reaction and trading volume on days when multiple firms announce earnings. AMC_DV is a dummy variable equal to one if the announcement is an AMC announcement. We also include NYSE_DV, a dummy variable equal to one for NYSE-listed stocks. As explained in Jiang et al. (2012), Masulis and Shivakumar (2002) show NASDAQ stocks' prices adjust faster to seasoned equity offers than did NYSE/AMEX stocks. It follows that differences in price adjustment may exist between NYSE and NASDAQ stocks when earnings announcements are made (and thus, information is shared with the market).

Table 15.6 provides the estimations of our WPC regression analysis. For the full sample of BMO and AMC announcements, volume negatively influences WPC, while firm size positively influences the WPC. These relations between volume (size) and WPC are opposite that found in Jiang et al. (2012). While it is reasonable to assume that, holding all else constant, a trade in a stock with higher volume will carry less weight than a trade in a stock with little volume, we are puzzled as to the positive relation between WPC and firm size. The coefficient of the AMC announcement indicator variable is positive and the coefficient of the NYSE-listing indicator variable is negative. Both coefficients are of the same sign as in Jiang et al. (2012), which indicates that earnings announcements made after the market closes have higher price impact while stocks listed on the NYSE have a slower price adjustment process. We also control for the number of earnings announcements during the same trading sessions and we find no evidence that announcements made during the same time period distracts. Only the regression estimation for the NN trade type is meaningful, and the results from this estimation are similar to that of the full sample. We conclude that WPC for NN trades is influenced by trading volume, firm size and exchange listing.

Table 15.6 Regression estimates for cross-sectional regressions of weighted price contribution (WPC) on stock characteristics

	1	2	3	4	5
	Full sample	HH	HN	NH	NN
Intercept	−0.107	−0.025	−0.0161	0.015	−0.057
	(−5.61)★★★	(−0.89)	(−0.62)	(0.73)	(−2.96)★★★
Volume	−0.013	−0.001	−0.000	0.001	−0.013
	(−7.07)★★★	(−0.92)	(−0.33)	(0.77)	(−5.28)★★★
Firm size	0.014	0.001	0.001	−0.001	0.011
	(7.77)★★★	(0.92)	(0.64)	(−0.81)	(5.64)★★★
N_Announce-ments	−0.000	0.000	0.000	0.001	−0.001
	(−0.19)	(0.07)	(0.50)	(0.78)	(−1.24)
AMC_DV	0.010	0.000	0.003	−0.001	0.007
	(3.00)★★★	(0.10)	(0.67)	(−0.37)	(1.88)★
NYSE_DV	−0.019	−0.002	−0.007	0.003	−0.016
	(−5.35)★★★	(−0.46)	(−1.59)	(1.06)	(−3.67)★★★
R-square	0.1560	0.0023	0.0122	0.0055	0.0786
F value	17.52★★★	0.22	1.17	0.52	8.09★★★
Number of observations	480	480	480	480	480

The dependent variable in Model 1 is WPC per stock. The dependent variable in Models 2−5 is the WPC by stock by trader type. We identify four trade types: HH, HN, NH, and NN. The first letter identifies the trade initiator (liquidity demander) and the second letter identifies the liquidity supplier. H signifies a high frequency trading firm and N signifies a non-high frequency trader, so an HN trade is one where a high frequency trading firm is the liquidity demander and a non-high frequency trader is the liquidity provider. Volume is the natural log of average daily stock volume (column 1), and the natural log of the average daily volume stock volume per trader type (columns 2−5) 21 days before the announcement. Firm size is the natural log of the average market cap of each stock over the 21 days before the announcement day. N_Announcements is the number of firms that make announcements during the same outside-regular-market−hours as our BMO and AMC sample stocks. The AMC_DV is a dummy variable equal to one if the announcement is an AMC announcement. The NYSE_DV is a dummy variable equal to one for NYSE stocks. T statistics are in parentheses. Significance is indicated at the 1%, 5%, and 10% levels with ★★★, ★★, and ★.

15.6 CONCLUSION

Market participants are questioning the benefits of HFTs in financial markets. In this study, we attempt to answer several questions about the role of HFTs in markets. First, we focus on the roles of high frequency trading firms and non-HFTs during before-market trading hours, RTHs, and after-market trading hours on earnings announcements days and nonearnings announcements day. We analyze these participants trading volume and number of trades in the three segments of the extended trading day. Second, we determine if HFTs contribute to price discovery when firms announce earnings outside of RTHs. Third, we seek to identify factors that may influence price discovery of HFTs' and non-HFTs' trades.

Overall, we find that trades between non-HFTs make up the largest proportion of volume in our sample on both earnings announcement days and nonannouncement days and during our three trading segments—BMO, RTHs, and AMC. We observe few changes between announcement day and nonannouncement day proportions of volume for trade types. The proportion of after-hours trades between non-HFTs increases when firms announce earnings after the market close, while the proportion of trades initiated by non-HFTs with HFTs as liquidity providers decreases. HFTs do not appear to be extremely active outside of RTHs, even stepping away from the market on earnings announcement days. We document that, generally, non-HFT initiated trades contribute the most to price discovery, both inside and outside regular market hours following a pre-open or after-hours earnings announcement. Further, we find that HFT initiated trades provide little or no price discovery in preopen or after hours trading following a BMO or AMC earnings announcement. Lastly, we show that three factors appear to influence the weighted price discovery of trades between non-HFTs: firm size, trading volume, and listing exchange.

REFERENCES

Aldridge, I., 2010. High Frequency Trading: A Practical Guide to Algorithmic Strategies and Trading Systems. John Wiley and Sons, Inc., Hoboken, NJ.

Angel, J., 2014. When finance meets physics: the impact of the speed of light on financial markets and their regulation. Financ. Rev. 49 (2), 271–281.

Baron, M., Brogaard, J., Kirilenko, A., 2012. The Trading Profits of High Frequency Traders. Working paper. University of Washington.

Brogaard, J., 2010. High-Frequency Trading and Its Impact of Market Quality. Working paper. Northwestern University.

Brogaard, J., Hendershott, T., Riordan, R., 2014. High Frequency Trading and Price Discovery. Forthcoming, Review of Financial Studies 27 (8), 2267–2306.

Cardela, L., Hao, J., Kalcheva, I., Ma, Y., 2014. Computerization of the equity, foreign exchange, derivatives, and fixed-income markets. Financ. Rev. 49 (2), 231–243.

Egginton, J., Van Ness, B., Van Ness, R., 2014. Quote Stuffing. Working paper. University of Mississippi.

Gai, J., Yao, C., Ye, M., 2012. The Externalities of High-Frequency Trading. Working paper. University of Illinois.

Goldstein, M., Kumar, P., Graves, F., 2014. Computerized and high-frequency trading. Financ. Rev. 49 (2), 177–202.

Hasbrouck, J., Saar, G., 2013. Low-latency trading. J. Financ. Mark. 16 (4), 646–679.

Hendershott, T., Riordan, R., 2013. Algorithmic trading and the market for liquidity. J. Financ. Quant. Anal. 48 (4), 1001–1024.

Hendershott, T., Jones, C., Menkveld, A., 2011. Does algorithmic trading improve liquidity? J. Finance 66 (1), 1–33.

Hirshleifer, D., Lim, S., Teoh, S., 2009. Driven to distraction: extraneous events and underreaction to earnings new. J. Finance 64 (5), 2289–2325.

Jiang, C., Likitapiwat, T., McInish, T., 2012. Information content of earnings announcements: evidence from after hours trading. J. Financ. Quant. Anal. 47 (6), 1303–1330.

Masulis, R., Shivakumar, L., 2002. Does market structure affect the immediacy of stock price responses to news? Journal of Financial and Quantitative Analysis 37 (4), 617–648.

Menkveld, A., 2013. High frequency trading and the new market makers. J. Financ. Mark. 16 (4), 712−740.

Menkveld, A., 2014. High-frequency traders and market structure. Financ. Rev. 49 (2), 333−344.

Michaely, R., Rubin, A., Vedrashko, A., 2014. Corporate Governance and the Timing of Earnings Announcements. Review of Finance 18 (6), 2003−2044.

Securities and Exchange Commission, 2010. Concept Release on Equity Market Structure. Release No. 34−61358, File No. S7-02-10.

Viljoen, T., Westerholm, P., Zheng, H., 2014. Algorithmic trading, liquidity, and price discovery: AN intraday analysis of the SPI 200 futures. Financ. Rev. 49 (2), 245−270.

Zhang, S., 2013. Need for Speed: An Empirical Analysis of Hard and Soft Information in a High Frequency World. Working paper. Manchester Business School, Manchester, UK.

CHAPTER 16

Why Accountants Should Care about High Frequency Trading

Dov Fischer
Brooklyn College, School of Business, Brooklyn, NY, USA

Contents

16.1 INTRODUCTION

The high frequency trading (HFT) scandal has captured the attention of the press, regulators, and legislators. It is a story of how since the mid 2000s stock brokerages and exchanges colluded with a select group of traders to the detriment of other market participants. Essentially, high frequency traders got an early peek at market orders before they were executed, which allowed them to game the system to their advantage. It would seem that such practices are beyond the ethical pale, but they in fact were and remain legal.

In April 2014, best-selling author Michael Lewis released a high profile book "Flash Boys" on how investment brokerages for almost a decade colluded with stock exchanges and high-frequency traders to the detriment of other investors and the stability of the market as a whole (Lewis, 2014a). The book was extensively covered by the *New York Times, 60 Minutes*, and the *Charlie Rose Show*, among others (Charlie Rose Show, 2014). The extensive media attention prompted the attention of the US Senate's Permanent Subcommittee on Investigations and the Securities & Exchange Commission (SEC) (White, 2014).

Accounting professors, like all educators, naturally seek to stimulate student interest by relating their subject matter to current events. However, unlike most other business scandals of the past two decades, the HFT scandal at first blush seems to be purely a finance matter with no accounting implications. Accounting educators may therefore initially shy away from discussing the HFT scandal with their students. After all, class time is limited and one does not want to appear to be wasting it on tangential topics.

The Handbook of High Frequency Trading
ISBN 978-0-12-802205-4

This chapter puts these inhibitions to rest. The HFT scandal highlights the very issues that have bedeviled the accounting profession with scandals for at least two decades. The issues are organizational trust, system complexity, and individual responsibility for ethical actions.

16.1.1 Organizational Trust

Americans have lost faith in the stock market. US stock ownership is at record lows (CBS News 60 Minutes, 2014). In the wake of the scandals beginning with Enron over a decade ago investors have similarly lost faith the usefulness of financial statements (IFAC, 2003). The accounting educator can use the HFT scandal to initiate and stimulate a conversation about the importance of trust in ensuring the proper functioning of organizations and society.

The "60 Minutes" episode on the HFT scandal provides a good introduction to this crisis of trust. After watching the "60 Minutes" episode, ask your students "What is the most important asset that accountants have?" The class conversation should evolve to identifying the importance of public trust in the profession and in the economic institutions whose financial performance we report.

High frequency traders and their enablers did not necessarily violate any laws currently on the books, but they did contribute to the further erosion of public trust in economic institutions. In order for members of the public to place trust in social and economic institutions, those institutions must exhibit benevolence, integrity, and ability/competence (Mayer et al., 1995). Unfortunately, the large stock exchanges and brokerages failed to live up to high standards of benevolence and integrity when they placed the interests of a few high frequency traders ahead of smaller, less sophisticated customers.

16.1.2 System Complexity

For the accounting profession, the implosion of Enron in 2001 was a cataclysmic event that shook the profession's confidence in its ability and competence. In the early 1970s the accounting profession went through one of its periodic soul-searching episodes. The product of the soul searching was a conceptual framework that was supposed to provide a theoretical underpinning for technical accounting standards. The most important feature of the conceptual framework was the notion that the purpose of accounting information is to provide investors with useful information for decision making (FASB, 2010).

One reason Enron's management was able to pull off such an elaborate hoax (it was at one time number 7 on the *Fortune* 500) was the inordinate complexity that has crept into balance sheets (Fortune, 2001). The Enron debacle indicated the general opacity and complexity that has gradually crept into financial statements. This is particularly true for companies that carry large amounts of off-balance sheet items (FASB. 2006).

In his *60 Minutes* interview, Michael Lewis made the following statements about HFT: "*If it wasn't complicated, it wouldn't be allowed to happen. The complexity disguises what is happening. If it's so complicated you can't understand it, then you can't question it.*"

Financial statements, particularly those of financial services companies, are so complex that investors and regulators fail to flag accounting practices that would never be allowed for simple retail businesses. For example, banks are allowed to *net* their derivative assets and against derivative liabilities outstanding with the same counterparties (Fischer, 2013a). This makes bank balance sheets look less leveraged than they would look if such netting were not allowed. As for bank regulators, they have attempted to introduce a simple leverage ratio, but banks protested so vigorously that the Basel Committee watered down the proposed requirements (Basel Committee, 2013, 2014; Ember, 2014; Fischer, 2013b).

16.1.3 Individual Responsibility

Lewis's "Flash Boys" is such a compelling story because, in addition to the familiar Wall Street villains who care nothing about the small trader, the book also features an unlikely hero in the person of Brad Katsuyama. This mild mannered Asian-Canadian seems the most unlikely person to shake up Wall Street. He was only 23 years old in 2002 when the Royal Bank of Canada sent him to New York to head the bank's American trading desk.

Upon his arrival in New York, Katsuyama found that the trading systems did not operate as expected. When the bank tried to enter an order on behalf of a client, the bid and ask quotes indicated on the trading screen would instantly disappear. He discovered that high frequency traders had an insider's preview of orders arriving at exchanges. As a result they were able to trade before his clients' orders were executed, thus altering the ability of his clients to trade on fair terms. Katsuyama teamed up with another immigrant, Irish-born Ronan Ryan, to help him understand how HFTs were rigging the system. Once they understood how the system was broken, they went about educating investors at considerable risk to their professional careers and financial security.

The following passage from Lewis (2014b) shows how even the most sophisticated investors began to lose trust in brokerages and the exchanges. These investors, who included famous hedge-fund managers, were befuddled by the market's immense complexity in how orders were processed and filled:

Eventually Brad Katsuyama came to realize that the most sophisticated investors didn't know what was going on in their own market. Not the big mutual funds, Fidelity and Vanguard. Not the big money-management firms like T. Rowe Price and Capital Group. Not even the most sophisticated hedge funds. The legendary investor David Einhorn, for instance, was shocked; so was Dan Loeb, another prominent hedge-fund manager. Bill Ackman runs a famous hedge fund, Pershing Square that often buys large chunks of companies. In the two years before

Katsuyama turned up in his office to explain what was happening, Ackman had started to sus-pect that people might be using the information about his trades to trade ahead of him. "I felt that there was a leak every time," Ackman says. "I thought maybe it was the prime broker. It wasn't the kind of leak that I thought." A salesman at RBC who marketed Thor recalls one big investor calling to say, "You know, I thought I knew what I did for a living, but apparently not, because I had no idea this was going on."

Katsuyama and Ryan between them met with roughly 500 professional stock-market investors who controlled many trillions of dollars in assets. Most of them had the same reaction: They knew something was very wrong, but they didn't know what, and now that they knew, they were outraged. Vincent Daniel, a partner at Seawolf, took a long look at this unlikely pair—an Asian-Canadian guy from a bank no one cared about and an Irish guy who was doing a fair impression of a Dublin handyman—who just told him the most incredible true story he had ever heard and said, "Your biggest competitive advantage is that you don't want to [expletive] me."

Trust on Wall Street was still—just—possible.

16.2 INTERNAL CONTROLS AND TONE AT THE TOP

The phrase "tone at the top" is a corporate governance concept that originated from the accounting profession's subfield of internal controls. The HFT scandal holds specific les-sons to the study of internal controls, corporate governance, and an ethical tone at the top. In 2013, the Committee of Sponsoring Organizations (COSO; the accounting con-sortium dedicated to internal controls) released an updated framework for internal con-trols. The COSO framework is surprising in that it seems less like an accounting/auditing framework than a corporate governance framework. COSO recognizes that the basis for effective internal controls over financial reporting, operations, and compliance is an envi-ronment with an ethical "tone at the top" (COSO, 2013).

The COSO framework has 17 principles and five components. The first component is the Control Environment, and the first principle deals with a commitment to ethics and integrity. Table 16.1 lists the first two principles associated with Control Environment. The very first principle is a commitment to ethics and integrity, and the second principle deals with appropriate supervision by directors and upper management. Table 16.1 de-scribes some of the key terms of the Control Environment, two of its five principles, and some specific lessons from the HFT scandal.

The implications of the HFT scandal for companies applying the COSO internal con-trol framework do not end with the Control Environment. The implications extend to the other four components of internal controls as listed in Table 16.2—Risk Assessment, Con-trol Activities, Information and Communication, and Monitoring. To get a handle on Risk Assessment, companies must first work to minimize system complexity, since it is impossible to assess the risk of an immensely complex system understood by no one.

Table 16.1 COSO's control environment

Key terms	Principles 1 and 2	Lessons from the HFT scandal
• Integrity • Ethics • Board of directors • Independence • Oversight • Authority • Responsibility • Competence • Accountability	1. The organization demonstrates a commitment to **integrity** and **ethical** values. 2. The **board of directors** demonstrates **independence** of management and exercises **oversight** of the development and performance of internal control.	1. Brokerages should place the interests of their **customers first**, even when the law allows the brokerage to take advantage of customers. 2. The boards of directors of brokerages and exchanges should **question management** when events like the 2010 Flash Crash occur.

Table 16.2 COSO components of internal control

Control environment:		
• Integrity • Ethics • Board of directors	• Independence • Oversight • Authorities	• Responsibilities • Competency • Accountability

Risk assessment:		
• Specific (operations, reporting, compliance) objectives	• Identify risk • Analyze risk	• Fraud • Assess changes in environment

Control activities:		
• Relate to risks	• General controls over technology	• Policies and procedures

Information and communication:
Note: This component should not be confused with the reporting objective. Rather, the component relates to information required to enable internal controls to function.

Monitoring activities:		
• Ongoing evaluations	• Separate evaluations	• Address deficiencies

Without appropriate Risk Assessment any Control Activities actually implemented become meaningless or worse, since these Control Activities provide a false sense of risk management. Finally, an overly complex system makes it impossible to effectively

Communicate and Monitor the internal controls in place. Complexity is therefore a severe threat to the proper functioning of internal controls. The HFT scandal brought out the same lesson: Complexity leads to erosion of trust.

16.3 CONCLUSION

The HFT scandal has peeled away yet another layer of the already eroded public trust in financial institutions and in government agencies such as the SEC to effectively regulate those institutions. It was only in June 2014 that SEC chair Mary Jo White announced an initiative aimed at "Addressing High Frequency Trading and Promoting Fairness". The same alarm at the lack of fairness was also a prominent concern in the investigation launched by Senators Carl Levin and John McCain (US Senate Permanent Subcommittee, June 2014).

Although at first blush the HFT scandal seems unrelated to the myriad of recent accounting scandals, they are symptomatic of the same problems that have plagued the accounting profession going back to the Enron debacle and earlier. First, the focus on "what's legal" rather than what "what's ethical and fair" has eroded the public's trust in financial information and the institutions and professions that stand behind that information. Second, trading systems and financial reporting systems have become overly complex, making it impossible to monitor or even to understand them. Third, the HFT drama as it unfolds in Lewis's "Flash Boys" provides a rare *positive* example of what it would take to save the accounting and finance professions and institutions. It would take *individual* responsibility to ensure that their organizations conform to principles that promote trust. Those principles are benevolence, integrity, and ability.

ACKNOWLEDGMENT

Support for this project was provided by a PSC-CUNY Award, jointly funded by The Professional Staff Congress and The City University of New York.

REFERENCES

Basel Committee on Bank Supervision, June 2013. Consultative Document: Revised Basel III Leverage Ratio Framework and Disclosure Requirements. Bank for International Settlements, Basel Switzerland. Accessed at: http://www.bis.org/publ/bcbs251.pdf.

Basel Committee on Bank Supervision, January 2014. Basel III Leverage Ratio Framework and Disclosure Requirements. Bank for International Settlements, Basel. Accessed at: http://www.bis.org/publ/bcbs270.pdf.

CBS News 60 Minutes by S. Croft, March 30, 2014. Is the U.S. Stock Market Rigged? Accessed at: http://www.cbsnews.com/news/is-the-us-stock-market-rigged/.

Charlie Rose Show, March 31, 2014. Flash Boys: A Wall Street Revolt. Michael Lewis discusses his latest book. WNET New York, NY, USA. Accessed at: http://www.charlierose.com/watch/60368500.

Committee of Sponsoring Organizations of the Treadway Commission (COSO, 2013. Internal Control — Integrated Framework. AICPA, New York, NY, USA. Access Executive Summary at: http://www.coso.org/documents/990025P_Executive_Summary_final_may20_e.pdf.

Ember, S., March 20, 2014. Questioning the Leverage Ratio. New York Times DealBook Blog. Accessed at: http://dealbook.nytimes.com/2014/03/20/morning-agenda-questioning-the-leverage-ratio/?_php=true&_type=blogs&_r=0.

Financial Accounting Standards Board (FASB), February 16, 2006. FASB Responds to SEC Study on Off-balance Sheet Arrangements, Reaffirming Commitment to Address and Improve Outdates, Complex Standards. News Release. Financial Accounting Foundation, Norwalk, CT, USA. Accessed at: http://www.fasb.org/news/nr021606a.shtml.

Financial Accounting Standards Board (FASB, 2010. Concept Statement No. 8 — Conceptual Framework for Financial Reporting. Financial Accounting Foundation, Norwalk, CT, USA. Accessed at. http://www.fasb.org/cs/ContentServer?site=FASB&c=Document_C&pagename=FASB%2FDocument_C%2FDocumentPage&cid=1176157498129.

Fischer, D., 2013a. The hidden effects of derivatives on bank balance sheets. CPA J. 83 (9), 67—69.

Fischer, D., 2013b. Aftermath of Financial Crisis for the Big-6 U.S. Banks: Basel III Proposals on Credit Derivatives, Effects and Reactions. Working Paper. Brooklyn College, Brooklyn, NY. Accessed at: http://ssrn.com/abstract=2356718.

Fortune, 2001. Fortune 500: A Database of 50 Years of Fortune's List of America's Largest Corporations. Time Inc., New York, NY, USA. Accessed at: http://money.cnn.com/magazines/fortune/fortune500_archive/snapshots/2001/478.html.

International Federation of Accountants (IFAC, 2003. Rebuilding Public Confidence in Financial Reporting: An International Perspective. International Federation of Accountants, New York, USA. Accessed at: http://www.ifac.org/sites/default/files/publications/files/rebuilding-public-confidenc.pdf.

Lewis, M., 2014a. Flash Boys: A Wall Street Revolt. W.W. Norton, New York, NY.

Lewis, M., 2014b. The Wolf Hunters of Wall Street: An Adaptation from 'Flash Boys: A Wall Street Revolt'. The New York Times Magazine. Accessed at: http://www.nytimes.com/2014/04/06/magazine/flash-boys-michael-lewis.html.

Mayer, R.C., Davis, J.H., Schoorman, F.D., 1995. An integrative model of organizational trust. Acad. Manag. Rev. 20 (2), 709—734.

US Senate Permanent Subcommittee on Investigations, 2014. Conflicts of Interest, Investor Loss of Confidence, and High Speed Trading in U.S. Stock Markets. U.S. Senate Committee on Homeland Security & Governmental Affairs, Washington, D.C., USA. Accessed at: http://www.hsgac.senate.gov/subcommittees/investigations/hearings/conflicts-of-interest-investor-loss-of-confidence-and-high-speed-trading-in-us-stock-markets.

White, M.J., 2014. Enhancing Our Equity Market Structure. U.S. Securities and Exchange Commission. http://www.sec.gov/News/Speech/Detail/Speech/1370542004312#.U9AcvPldVqV.

CHAPTER 17

High-Frequency Trading under Information Regimes

Erick Rengifo[1], Rossen Trendafilov[2]
[1]Fordham University, Bronx, NY, USA; [2]Department of Economics, Truman State University, Kirksville, MO, USA

Contents

17.1 INTRODUCTION

Market microstructure literature and quantitative modeling focus on the information conveyed by trade executions and placement of market orders that are seen as information driven (Easley et al., 2008). On the other hand, models that deal with complete limit order books are not widely analyzed, even though their importance is stressed by cornerstone papers written by Glosten (1994), Lehmann (2008).

One of the main reasons for limited applications of limit order book models is that complete limit order book data sets are not readily available to the academic and research community. With the development of information and computer technology, the cost of obtaining large data sets has been considerably decreased. However, obtaining limit order data, which has been preprocessed and is ready for analysis, can be quite challenging and sometimes cumbersome. In this chapter we use a high-quality and readily available data set provided by BATS Global Markets, Inc. (BATS) and processed by Dynamic Trading Data.

Besides the issue of data availability, cost, quality, and readiness, huge limit order book data sets impose enormous challenges not only on the researcher but also on the

The Handbook of High Frequency Trading
ISBN 978-0-12-802205-4

technology to handle them. The complete limit order book (supply and demand side) is tracked at a millisecond (one-thousandth of a second) frequency. Complete limit order books can have more than 100 steps (combinations of price and quantity) at each moment in time. Moreover, with the implementation of algorithmic trading performed by computers, the volume of high-frequency trades have skyrocketed, dramatically increasing both the volume and the noise of the intraday data. As reported by Guo et al. (2014) high-frequency trading firms in the United States only represent 2% of the total number of firms operating today, but account for 73% of all equity orders volume. Further noted by Easley et al. (2008) and Kirkpatrick and Dahlquist (2010), the effects of increased volume due to high-frequency trading executed by computers has drawn the criticism from regular market participants who argue that algorithmic trading distorts the information typically provided by trading volume. It is well known the algorithmic trading also introduces noise in the price formation processes and that is responsible for what is now known as flash crashes.[1]

Such technological and strategic trading developments create considerable challenges for professional traders making it harder for them to distinguish between information and noise. All these reasons together have made the use of complete limit order books modeling very scarce.

Another obvious reason why working with complete limit order books is hard is that when a trader forms his expectations about the assets' future value, he has to condition his decision on all the available information that can affect the future unobservable value of a given financial instrument. This information set includes the information content of the past and current limit order book, other past trading data, and future expectations about the order flows. Once more, the high dimensionality of the data poses a tremendous challenge for theoretical modeling and empirical applications. It is under this circumstance that it is important to find ways to reduce the noise present in the limit order books and to reduce the dimensionality of the data in order to be able to obtain some valuable information from these limit order books.

Related to the previous comments and as noted by Cont and Kukanov (2013), in the literature on optimal order placement, researchers avoid such problems by the use of restricted execution costs represented by idealized limit order book shapes. For example, Obizhaeva and Wang (2012) adopt linear price impact function, while Alfonsi et al. (2010) and Predoiu et al. (2011) allow for more general shape of the book and nonlinear price impacts. We argue that by making those assumptions one ignores the fact that the actual shape of the limit order book, at each point of time, carries specific information about the price impact, liquidity, and the market sentiment, which can be used in the trading process.

---

[1] The flash crash of May 6, 2010, is considered the biggest point decline (998.5 points) in the history of Dow Jones (Easley et al., 2010).

In this chapter we introduce a technique to identify information regimes that can help to reduce limit order books' noise, with minimal loss of information, and that can provide more effective ways to analyze the data and to set possible trading strategies.

The notion of information regimes was first presented by Glosten (1994), who developed a static model that was later generalized by Lehmann (2008). Lehmann (2008) provided for the formal definition and the dynamic behavior of the information regimes. According to him when all the information is trade related and arrives via order flow, the fundamental value that underlines the price schedule does not change and it is simply translated by the size of the executed market order and the process of replenishing (backfilling) some of the limit orders against which the market order was executed. Moreover, during an information regime the best quotes follow a path outlined by the regime's time-one limit order book. This implies that given the size of the incoming market order and the depth of the book, the future best quotes can be adequately estimated.

Changes of information regimes within a given day are shown to alter the provision of liquidity to the market with consequences for asset prices, trading behavior, and optimal trading strategies. The discovery and identification of information regimes essentially un-covers the mechanism by which latent demands are translated into realized prices and volumes and, from here, that they can be used by professional traders.

The identification of information regimes is described in detail in Trendafilov and Rengifo (2013). Their model is based on wavelet decomposition and frequency analysis of limit order books. The identification of the regimes is interesting not only from a theo-retical point of view but also for practical applications. For the empirical applications though, it is needed to implement a mathematical model that allows forecasting of regimen changes in order to formulate a trading strategy. In this chapter we present a nat-ural candidate for econometric modeling and forecasting of the changes in the regimes by the use of a Markov Switching Model.

The chapter proceeds in the following way: in Section 17.2 we describe the data used in the chapter, in Section 17.3 we present the theoretical model of information regimes, the procedure to identify them, and a Markov switching model for forecasting the dy-namics among them. In the same section we present the results we obtain by applying the suggested methodology and describe in detail its use in a trading strategy setting. In Section 17.4 we suggest two high-frequency trading strategies. Finally, Section 17.5 presents the conclusions and suggestions for future lines of research.

17.2 DATA

The date used considers the full limit order book schedules (price and volume for the ask and bid sides) for Agilent Technologies (A), S&P 500, and Market Vectors Gold Miners ETF (GDX). We used slightly different dates for each of them, July 1 and 2, 2013, for A;

July 1, 2013, for S&P 500; and July 1, 2013, for (GDX). All of them traded on BATS BYX exchange.

The BATS exchanges allow for reserve orders, discretionary orders, and hidden orders along the usual limit orders. The core trading hours are from 9.30 am to 4.00 pm. As usual, we have trimmed 10 min from the beginning and the end of the trading day to avoid the opening and closing auction contamination typically present at those times.

The minimum lot size is one share and it supports any tick size up to six decimal places. The precision of the data is in milliseconds. As mentioned before, the limit order book data set was compiled from raw data and provided in a ready-to-use format by dynamic market data.

17.3 METHODOLOGY AND RESULTS

For clarity of presentation and implementation of the methodology used in this chapter, in this section we not only briefly describe the underlying theory of information regimes, the way by which we identify them and a brief description of Markov chain models that allow us to observe the changes on regimes, but also present its implementation using the data described in the previous section.

For extended discussion on information regimes and the way they can be identified we refer the reader to Glosten (1994), Lehmann (2008), and Trendafilov and Rengifo (2013).

17.3.1 Information Regimes

According to Glosten (1994), the possibility of trades triggered by information lead to upward sloping offer schedules, meaning that it is more costly to execute large orders versus small ones. In his framework it is assumed that traders are risk neutral, are drawn from a large population, and are price takers. The assumptions lead to zero expected profit equilibrium. In the discrete prices case, the submitted bids and offers are related to, respectively, lower tail and upper tail conditional expectations, due to the discriminatory nature of the limit order book and adverse selection.

To better understand this, let us remember that limit order traders know neither the size of incoming market orders nor when they will occur. This implies that the limit orders could not be executed (execution risk) or they could be adversely picked off if they are bypassed by the security value before the trader has a chance to cancel. This last situation causes regret since the limit order seller (buyer) could have executed at a better price. According to Glosten (1994), these two risks are reflected in the quoted prices. In the limit order book the asset is priced based on the expected full information value of the asset, conditional on the incoming market order of a size just sufficient or larger to trigger execution. This is described as upper (lower) tail conditional expectations.

Limit order traders cannot condition on the quantity of the next market order (Q) when they place their orders. They know that the limit order to sell at price $P(q)$ is hit when the total trade size is at least as large as the cumulated depth of the book up to that price ($q(P)$). For example, consider the offer side in the limit order book and let $P(q)$ be the price of the last limit order executed, where q represents the cumulated volume of the book up to that price. If m is the marginal valuation of incoming order, then $\underline{m}$ is the value of m for which the last limit order executed is the one at $P(q)$. In order for the agent not to regret his price, when his order is the last one executed, he prices at

$$P(q) \geq E\big[X\big|m = \underline{m}(q)\big] \tag{17.1}$$

where X is the full information value. However, since his order may not be the last one, he needs to take this into account and his price has to be at least as large as $E[X|m \geq \underline{m}(q)]$. This means that any agent submitting a market order with valuation $m \geq \underline{m}(q)$ will purchase more than q ($Q > q$). Thus, the competitive equilibrium condition is

$$P(q) = E\big[X\big|m \geq \underline{m}(q)\big] \tag{17.2}$$

Based on these results, Lehmann (2008) explains the dynamics of the limit order book through time. Lehmann (2008) begins providing an analogy for the fundamental theorem of asset pricing in order driven markets. The theorem states that in the absence of arbitrage, assets' prices follow a martingale process. The hypothesis of a free arbitrage market is a source of significant restrictions on asset prices. The complication, in the case of order driven markets, is the absence of short sales needed in the definition of arbitrage opportunities of the first and second types. Limit orders cannot be sold short (shorted). However, the payoff of a zero net investment portfolio can be interpreted as the payoff from a marginal change in an existing portfolio that is long in all of the assets. Therefore, the analogue to arbitrage in an order driven market involves the ability to cancel and replace limit orders freely.

In his work, Lehmann (2008) places three assumptions that will help us explain what is next:

1. Assumption 1: Let $V_t(q)$ denote the asset value if a market order of size q arrives at time t. $V_t(q)$ is both strictly increasing in q and common knowledge among market participants.
2. Assumption 2: $sgn_q[P_t(q) - V_t(q)] > 0, \forall q \in Q_t$ where sgn_q is the sign of its argument. And $Q_t \subseteq \mathbb{R}\$$, which is countable if there is lot size.
3. Assumption 3: A market order can only arrive and be executed against the book after all limit order traders are satisfied with their order placements.

The last assumption is plausible if market orders arrive according to a continuous time jump process, allowing the limit order traders to refresh the book and, if the traders who determine the marginal behavior of the book are active and perfectly competitive.

The price priority and the above assumptions imply that $P_t(q + sgn_q dq) - P_t(q)$ and $P_t(q + sgn_q dq) - V_t(q)$ have the same sign and

$$P_t(q + sgn_q dq) - P_t(q) = \lambda_t(q)[P_t(q + sgn_q dq) - V_t(q)] \tag{17.3}$$

with $\lambda_t(q) > 0$. Figure 17.1 presents a graphical representation of this last relationship. In this figure we have assumed a linear underlying value for easiness of explanation.

By rearranging Eqn (17.3), Lehmann (2008) derives the following pricing rule:

$$P_t(q) = \lambda_t(q) V_t(q) + [1 - \lambda_t(q)] P_t(q + sgn_q dq) \tag{17.4}$$

In this equation, $\lambda_t(q)$ is supported by the risk neutral probabilities $\psi_t = \Pr(Q_t = q | \mathbb{T}_{t-1})$, where $\mathbb{T}_{t-1}$ is the information set at time $t - 1$, q is the cumulative volume of the book, and Q_t is the size of the market order. From there, $\lambda_t(q)$ represents the conditional probability that the market order $Q_t = q$ given that $Q_t \geq q$:

$$\lambda_t(q) = \Pr[Q_t = q | sgn_q \times Q_t|, \mathbb{T}_{t-1}] = \frac{\psi_t(q)}{\int_{sgn_q u \geq |u|} \psi_t(u) du} \tag{17.5}$$

If the three assumptions mentioned before hold, Lehmann's first proposition states that, there is positive pricing rule supported by a set of unique state prices $\psi_t(q) > 0, \forall q \in Q_t$ if and only if there are no arbitrage opportunities. Contained in the proposition is the implication that any upward sloping marginal price schedule can

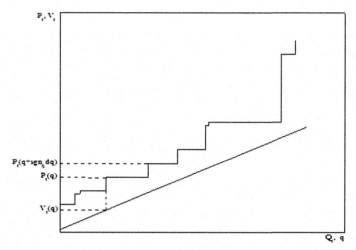

Figure 17.1 Limit order book versus asset value. This figure shows the offer (ask) side of the limit order book and an underlying asset value (assumed to be linear). $P_t(q + sgn_q dq) - P_t(q) = \lambda_t[P_t(q + sgn_q dq) - V_t(q)]$ with $0 < \lambda_t(q) < 1$.

be rationalized as being arbitrage free in the sense of the proposition. Lehmann (2005) shows that, the risk neutral probabilities implicit in $P_t(q_t)$ can be obtained from

$$\psi_t(q) = \lambda_t(q) \exp\left\{ -\int_0^q \lambda_t(u)\,du \right\} \tag{17.6}$$

The value of the asset right after the execution of a market order of size Q_{t-1} is $V_{t-1}(Q_{t-1})$. The asset value before the arrival of the next market order is approximately equal to the midquote:

$$P_t(0) = V_{t-1}(Q_{t-1}) + v_t(0); \quad E_\psi[v_t(0)|Q_{t-1}, \mathbb{T}_{t-2}] = 0 \tag{17.7}$$

One scenario of interest in this chapter, that Lehmann discusses, is when both the order flow dependent asset values and state prices depend only on the cumulative signed order flow. In that case, when a market buy order of size Q_{t-1} arrives at $t-1$, if it does not exhaust the depth on the offer side, it will walk up the book until it reaches $P_{t-1}(Q_{t-1})$ and the asset value after the trade is $V_{t-1}(Q_{t-1})$. The highest unexecuted offer at $P_{t-1}(Q_{t-1})$ will be the new best offer. The original best bid will be Q_{t-1} shares away from the new best bid, because it will take a market order of that size to reach it. Order state prices and values stay unchanged when no additional information arrives at the market, besides the execution of the market order. Thus,

$$V_t = V_{t-1}\left(q + sgn_q Q_{t-1}\right)$$
$$\psi_t = \psi_{t-1}\left(q + sgn_q Q_{t-1}\right) \tag{17.8}$$

This means that the state prices and values are simply translated by the size of the market order. This is because the risk that a market order of (Q_{t-1}) shares at time $t-1$ will be followed by one for q shares, is the same as a market order with size $(q + Q_{t-1})$ will arrive at $t-1$ under the restriction that there is no new information besides the market order. Note that the assumption that all the information is related to trade is frequent in dynamic market microstructure models.

Limit order traders, knowing that there is no new information coming to the market, will then backfill the portion of the book that was cleared by the market order with bid prices at which they will be willing to buy up to (Q_{t-1}) shares. The backfilled best bids are weighted average of the prior best bid and offer, and prior offer at $(q + Q_{t-1})$ shares. Another way to look at (Q_{t-1}) is that it could be considered as net order flow from some earlier time to time $t-1$, with the assumption that the only information arrived with market orders. Based on that, Lehmann defines an information regime or epoch as a period during which it is common knowledge that asset values and state prices in different order flow states satisfy the following:

$$V_{t-1} \equiv E_\psi\left[\tilde{V}\big|Q_{t-1} = q + q',\, \mathbb{I}_{t-2}\right] = E_\psi\left[\tilde{V}\big|Q_t = q',\, Q_{t-1}\right.$$
$$\left. = q,\, \mathbb{I}_{t-2}\right] \equiv V_t\left(q'\big|Q_{t-1} = q\right) \tag{17.9}$$

$$\psi_{t-1}\left(q + q'\right) \equiv E_\psi\left[1_{Q_{t-1}=q+q'}\big|\mathbb{I}_{t-2}\right] = E_\psi\left[1_{Q_t=q'}\big|Q_{t-1} = q,\, \mathbb{I}_{t-2}\right]$$
$$= \psi_t\left(q'\big|Q_{t-1} = q\right) \tag{17.10}$$

where $\mathbb{I}$ is the information set, $\mathbb{I}_{t-2} = \{Q_{t-2}, ..., Q_2, Q_1, \mathbb{I}_0\}$, and $\{q, q', q + q'\} \in Q_t$. Equations (17.9) and (17.10) tell us that there is no change in the fundamental value and the risk neutral probabilities after execution of market order $Q_{t-1} = q$, when trade happens in the same information regime.

During an information regime it can be imagined that there is just a single market order represented by the amount of cumulative signed volume that walks up and down the same (time one) limit order book that does not change its shape. In such case the price at any moment can be determined by a point on this limit order book and, the point itself can be identified by the cumulative volume. In that sense the movement up and down the book is the same for the purposes of determining prices when all information arrives through the market orders during an information regime.

Moreover, given the easiness of creating algorithmic trading strategies over an information regime, it is plausible to assume that traders can cancel and replace limit orders according to their preferences before the arrival of the next market order.

Note that the regime is defined by the same underlying value, which depends on the actions of both limit and market order submissions. The shape of the book represents the upper tail expectations of that value on the ask side (lower tail expectations on the bid side). However, and as we will show later, there is some time between the change of the value and the adjustment of the expectations that translates in the change in the shape and the depth of the book during which limit orders are exposed and can be adversely picked off. For that reason the recognition of the regime is important for the optimal placement of the limit orders and to avoid the limit orders being picked off.

17.3.2 Regime Identification

In this section we briefly describe the methodology used for regime identification. A detailed description of the procedure as well as for deciding on the choice of wavelet and the lag to compare between limit order books is discussed in Trendafilov and Rengifo (2013). The identification procedure compares the shape of two books. In this chapter we use the word lag to express the distance between books that are compared. For example, lag one implies that we are comparing the first book with the second, the second with the third and so on. A lag of five implies that we compare the first book with the sixth, the second with the seventh, and so on.

The basic idea of the procedure is to find the wavelet family that is capable of identifying the maximum number of regimes of a given size (number of books in the regime) by comparing book shapes. Trendafilov and Rengifo (2013) selected the Daubechies 6 wavelet with 16 lags. In this chapter and for the particular data set at hand, we use Daubechies 20 wavelet with one lag. In this choice we impose the restriction that a regime should have at least 30 books in it. The reason for this restriction is to allow for statistical test on the books that belong to the same regime. This condition, however, can be relaxed for the application of the proposed trading strategy.

First of all note that the study is conducted in limit order book time. Note that even though a limit order book exists in each millisecond (clock time) not all of them change in each and every of these milliseconds. There are many consecutive books that are identical. By looking only at the books when they change (limit order book time) we avoid data inflation of identical books and speed up our calculations. It is also important to note that we preserve the time stamp of each limit order book for other type of analysis.

According to the methodology presented in Trendafilov and Rengifo (2013), the identification of information regimes is performed in three steps:

1. Alignment of the limit order books,
2. Frequency decomposition by discrete wavelet transform, and
3. Comparison of the distributions of the detail wavelet coefficients by frequency via two-sample Kolmogorov–Smirnov test.

We proceed to describe in detail the first and third step and suggest the reader to read the details of the second step in the methodology presented in Trendafilov and Rengifo (2013).

17.3.2.1 Limit Order Book Alignment

In Figure 17.2 we plot the bid (left panel) and ask (right panel) side of 5000 consecutive limit order books that belong to a single day (the total number of books in this particular day is 36,310). The books are graphed as they are presented (best quotes at the very beginning of the book) to the traders. Observing this figure we can see that we end up with a lot of (apparently) different curves. Moreover, as presented in this figure it is hard to identify any intradaily regimes at which the exchange may be operating.

In an information regime, the market orders and the best quotes move up and down over the fundamental values and price schedules, which are simply translated by the changes in the cumulative volume. Thus, in order to have a regime, the books should be in such order that the underlying value is

$$V_t(q) = V_{t-1}(q + Q_{t-1}) \tag{17.11}$$

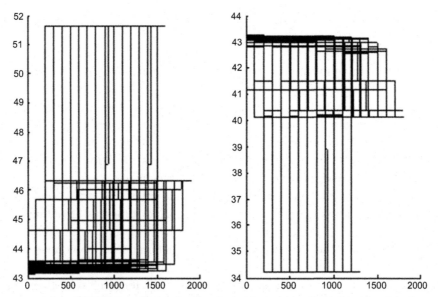

Figure 17.2 *Ask and bid limit order books.* This figure shows the offer (ask) side of the limit order book on the right and the bid on the left, where the best quotes are on the right side of both graphs. There are 5000 books plotted.

According to this definition the limit order books in a particular regime should basically be overlapping. An empirical fact is that most of the activity in the limit order book happens close to the best quote of the book where new orders and cancelations are submitted. Also, another important fact to note is that the orders that are at the end (or very close to the end) of the book stay unchanged for a period of time. In a sense they are left, not canceled by the traders who posted them.

This means that, at least for part of the day the backward part of the book does not change. What changes is the portion of the book that includes the best quote and the portion that is relatively close to the best quote. This observation allows us to align the limit order books in such way that we can more easily identify regimes. Thus, instead of arranging the books from best quote to the end (forward), we proceed in the reverse direction (backward), arranging and plotting them from the last part of the book and proceeding toward the best quote. In this case the very back of the book has cumulative volume zero and the best quote has the maximum cumulative volume, which is exactly the opposite from the forward (usual) case. The left side of Figure 17.3 depicts the backward aligning and plotting.

Both panels in Figure 17.3 plot the same limit order books, with the only difference of where the plot starts. On the left panel of Figure 17.3 one can visually see 112 limit order books arranged as proposed (backward). As such, one can see how these 112 different limit order books appeared to be clustered in single bunch. This panel presents

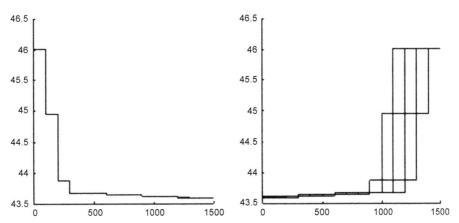

Figure 17.3 *Aligned and unaligned ask limit order books.* This figure shows the offer (ask) side of the limit order book. On the left panel the books are arranged using the backward procedure, where the best quotes are at the end of the books. On the right side the books are arranged in the traditional way (forward), where best quotes are at the beginning of the books. There are 112 books plotted in this figure.

a (apparently) completely different figure than the one presented on the right panel, where the books are not aligned following the procedure we suggest (forward).

17.3.2.2 *Frequency Decomposition by Discrete Wavelet Transform*

Once the books are aligned we proceed to identify the regimes. The procedure involves comparing the shapes of consecutive books to see whether they differ significantly. In order to do that, we select the parts of the two books that are completely overlapping and that are close to the best quote of the book. In this study we compare books that are one after the other, i.e., lag used is one.

To compare the overlapping parts we decompose the books by frequency and compare the contents of each these frequencies. We use wavelet approach to achieve this. Wavelets are localized wave forms, which have amplitude that starts at zero, increases, and then dies out. It can be pictured as a brief oscillation like the one that might be seen on a heart monitor. Wavelets are similar to Fourier series and Fourier transform in that they can be used to analyze the frequency content of a time series. However, unlike Fourier series and Fourier transform, which identify the global properties of time series, wavelet functions are precisely localized in time and frequency and, are very well suited for pattern recognition. The wavelet function separates the data into different frequency components that allows the study of each component with a resolution matched to its scale. When the wavelets interact with time series, the result is a set of detailed wavelet coefficients at each frequency, which we use in the procedure presented in the next section.

The wavelet transform provides efficient and complete representation of the time series. In this chapter we apply the discrete wavelet transform because it is fast to compute and because the size of the transformed data has the same size as the original data,[2] a major consideration when working with large data sets.

17.3.2.3 Two-Sample Kolmogorov–Smirnov Test

As soon as we are interested in finding books that can potentially belong to a same regime, in this next step, we compare the distributions of the wavelet detail coefficients by frequency for two n–lagged–spaced limit order books. It is a question of choice for the researcher to decide to compare books one right after the other, or to skip several and to compare, for example, the first to eleventh, then the second to the twelfth, and so on. For the procedure and graphs presented in this section, we have selected Daubechies 20 wavelet and to use one lag to compare books. The one lag means that we compare one book with the immediately next one.

In order to perform the book comparisons, we compare the distribution of the coefficients in the highest frequency, then the second highest, and so on. To perform these comparisons, we use the two-sample Kolmogorov–Smirnov test that allows us to compare the distributions of the coefficients and to determine if they could belong to the same regime.

Recall that we are interested in finding books that can potentially belong to a same regime. This implies that we are looking for books with similar shapes. In the methodology proposed, the wavelet coefficients in the higher frequencies capture more of the general shape of the book and not the details, exactly what we are looking for. If the coefficients come from the same distribution, this implies that certain frequencies of both books carry the same amount of the variability of the series. Further, this will suggest that the books have same or very similar shape and thus, in our context, this will imply that they are in the same regime. It is for that in the empirical application we focus only at the wavelet coefficients of the two highest frequencies. The distributions of the wavelet coefficients of the lower frequencies have fewer observations due to the nature of the discrete wavelet transform and to the lower cumulative volumes of the data set at hand. Thus, empirically they are not very useful.

In order to understand the procedure described in this section, we present the steps followed. The procedure is summarized below:

1. Obtain the detail coefficients by applying fast discrete wavelet transform.
2. Compare the distributions of the wavelet coefficients frequency by frequency for each two books that are n observations away from each other (n lags in this case n = 1).

---

[2] In the case of the continuous wavelet transformation the size of the transformed data is considerably larger than the original data.

3. Assign 1 if the results of the Kolmogorov–Smirnov test indicate different distributions, 0 otherwise. In this case there is a vector of 0s and 1s for each frequency.
4. The result is a 0 or 1 for each frequency for each pair of books that are compared.
5. Lastly, we impose a minimum size of at least 31 (more than 30) books for a regime. Even though there are a number of shorter regimes we required to have more than 30 observations, so that statistical procedures can be performed on the series while in a regime. However, for the proposed trading strategy the regime length can be more flexible and such restriction is not necessary.

Based on the last step of the procedure, any regime shorter than 31 books is eliminated and considered as part of a transition period. A visual representation of regimes can be seen on Figure 17.4. In this figure, the shaded areas represent the regimes and the white areas the transition periods (periods of no identified regimes). The horizontal axis shows how the regimes are distributed and the numbers represent the books

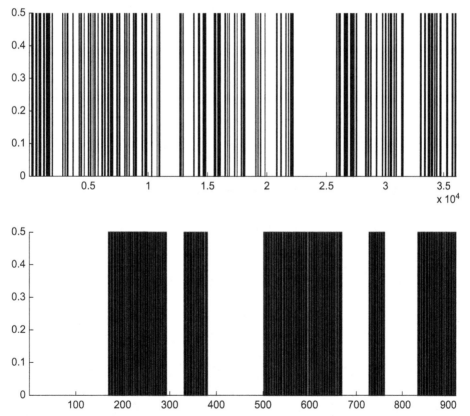

Figure 17.4 *Regime and transition periods.* This figure shows the regimes as shaded areas and the transition periods as white areas. The top panel presents all the regimes for one day. The bottom one shows five of these regimes identified following our proposed procedure.

presented (remember we are in limit order book time). The vertical axis does not have any specific meaning.

The upper panel of the figure presents the way the regimes and the transitions are distributed through a given day (July 1, 2013, for Agilent Technologies) in limit order book time. During this day we have identified 177 regimes. The lower panel of the figure presents a microscopic view, presenting only the first five regimes in that day.

Figure 17.5 presents two consecutive regimes, identified by the above procedure. The new regime (regime two) is plotted below the old regime (regime 1).

In Figure 17.5 we can see that a change of information regime within a given day alters the provision of liquidity to the market. The two regimes provide two different price impact functions for the incoming market orders and as such impact the asset prices and the behavior of the market participants.

17.3.3 Markov Switching Model

The change in the regimes, signaled by the bid or the ask side, can be captured by the absolute difference in the Kolmogorov–Smirnov statistic at the highest frequency of the detailed wavelet coefficients. The Kolmogorov–Smirnov statistic is the maximum distance between the empirical cumulative distribution functions of the two samples (in our case the samples are the distributions of the wavelet coefficients of two consecutive books). When the Kolmogorov–Smirnov statistic is high, the distributions of the wavelet coefficients are different, implying that the two limit order books have

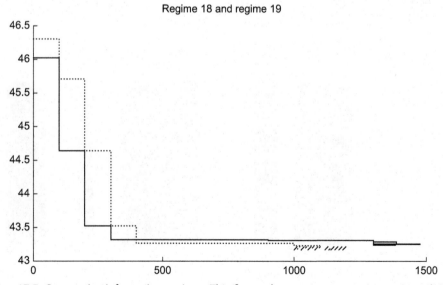

Figure 17.5 Consecutive information regimes. This figure shows two consecutive regimes (18 and 19). The transition period books are not plotted.

different shapes and thus, belong to different regimes. Moreover, it is important to note that we observe high volatility in the Kolmogorov—Smirnov statistic during periods of transition and, lower volatility during periods within regimes (see Figure 17.6). In order to observe the change of regimes on both bid and ask sides with a single measure we take the absolute difference in the Kolmogorov Smirnov statistics from the bid and the ask side.

Similarly to the behavior of the individual Kolmogorov—Smirnov statistics on the bid and the ask sides, the absolute difference between them is more volatile during transition periods and exhibits less volatility during a regime. As mentioned before, we just focus on the highest frequency of wavelet coefficients, because most of the changes in the shape of the book are captured there.

Figure 17.6 is similar to Figure 17.4. It presents the first five regimes for the day. We have plotted the absolute difference in the Kolmogorov—Smirnov statistics over the regimes and the transition periods. From the figure we can observe that during the regimes the volatility is low and during the transitions the volatility is high. In this case the vertical axis measures the absolute difference in the Kolmogorov—Smirnov statistic.

We use this observation provided by the regimes identified by the procedure described before; we propose Markov switching model with two states to allow us

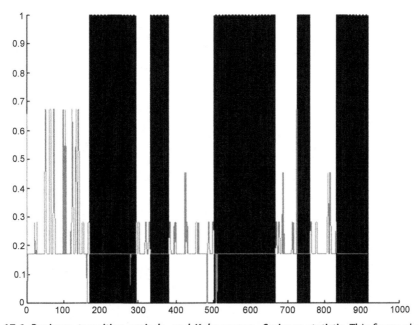

Figure 17.6 *Regimes, transition periods, and Kolmogorov—Smirnov statistic.* This figure shows the regimes as shaded areas while transition periods are presented in white. The gray line represents the absolute difference in the Kolmogorov—Smirnov statistic.

identify the probabilities of being either in a regime or in a transition. The Markov switching model that we use is the one described by Brooks (2014):

$$y_t = \mu_1 + \epsilon_t \quad \text{for state } 1, \text{ where } \epsilon_t \approx N\left(0, \sigma_1^2\right) \tag{17.12}$$

$$y_t = \mu_2 + \epsilon_t \quad \text{for state } 2, \text{ where } \epsilon_t \approx N\left(0, \sigma_2^2\right) \tag{17.13}$$

where y_t is the Kolmogorov–Smirnov statistic, μ_1 is the constant, and ϵ_t is the error term.

The solution to the model provides a matrix of transition probabilities π, which are estimated over the whole period, and a vector Θ_t of current state probabilities. For given π and Θ_t the probability that the next limit order book will continue being on the current regime or in transition period can be written as

$$\Theta_{t+1} = \Theta_t \pi \tag{17.14}$$

In Figure 17.7 we present the results of this model and the one step ahead state probabilities for the same regimes presented in Figure 17.6. Again, the black bars represent the regimes and the white spaces the transition periods. The horizontal axis shows the number of limit order books. In this case the vertical axis represents probabilities. The top panel shows one step ahead state probabilities ($\Theta_{t+1} = \Theta_t \pi$) for the limit order book to belong to a given regime, and the bottom panel depicts the one step ahead probability to be in a transition period. As it can be seen during a regime (over the black bars) both probabilities are not only very stable but also around 1. Observe also that during the transition periods (white spaces) the probabilities estimated with the Markov switching model fluctuate constantly as soon as they are setting probabilities of turbulent periods (as described by transition periods). As one can see, the one step ahead state probabilities signal very well the existence of information regimes.

As seen in Figure 17.6, the difference in the Kolmogorov–Smirnov statistic is more volatile and large in magnitude during transition regimes and that this measure is quite stable during the regimes. Thus, due to the clearly marked difference in the behavior of the absolute difference in the Kolmogorov–Smirnov statistic in these two different periods (regime and transition), the Markov switching model is able to correctly identify virtually all regimes of more than 30 books.

We do use the Markov switching model to estimate the probability that a next period book will still be part of a given regime or will start a period of transition. This finding is important from a trading perspective due to the fact that if the probabilities of staying in the same regime are high, traders will know that the trading is happening under a predetermined set of books that belong to the same regime. As such, the price volume relationship of a market order (price impact) can be estimated before the actual book adjusts. This information is enough to decide the best strategies to execute orders by using the information provided by the regime.

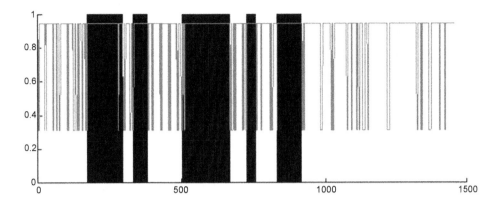

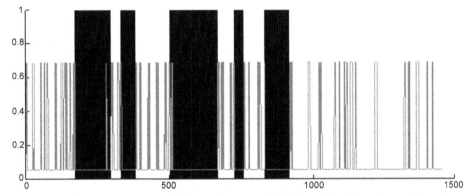

Figure 17.7 *Regimes, transition periods, and state probabilities.* This figure shows the regimes as shaded areas; the white areas represent the transition regimes. The gray lines represent the one step ahead state probability to be in a regime (top panel) and to be in a transition period (bottom panel).

Table 17.1 presents the estimated constant transition probabilities for the estimated Markov switching model.

The top of the table shows the probabilities that correspond to the first five regimes observed during July 1, 2013. The regimes were depicted above in Figures 17.6 and 17.7. The probability of staying in a regime, given that the book is in regime, is 0.693, while the probability of going from regime to transition period is 0.307. On the other side, the probability of the next book to be in a transitional period given that it is actually in transition period is 0.505, and the probability for the book currently in a transition period to move into a regime is 0.495. The second part of the table shows the estimated transition probabilities for the whole day. From these results we can appreciate two useful pieces of information. First, given the variability of books' shapes (as capture by the Kolmogorov–Smirnov statistic) during transition periods, the best probability estimates of being again in the transition period or in a regime is approximately 50%, meaning that there is no

Table 17.1 Transitional probabilities matrix

	First five regimes	
	Information regime	**Transition period**
Information regime	0.692	0.307
Transition period	0.495	0.505
Entire day		
	1	2
Information regime	0.632	0.368
Transition period	0.355	0.645

This table shows the transitional probabilities for Markov switching model. The top panel presents the probabilities for the first five regimes of the day (corresponding to Figures 17.6 and 17.7). The bottom panel presents the transitional probabilities for the entire day (July 1, 2013) corresponding to Agilent Technologies (A).

certainty about the future. This result is coherent with the basic idea that during transition periods the markets are adjusting as a reaction to (possible) new information coming to the market and the fact that there are no instantaneous agreements among the different market participants regarding the new limit order regime shape. Second, the transition probabilities remain quite stable when we compare the results from the first five regimes with the regimes during the whole day. It is important to note we have observed this result in instances when there were no substantial changes of the books during a particular day. However, this is not the case when something dramatic happens with the stock under analysis.

17.4 HIGH-FREQUENCY TRADING STRATEGIES

In this section we propose a simple strategy for optimal placement of limit orders. As we are going to describe later, this strategy will be valid for setting relatively small limit orders in the limit order book. We also present at the end of this section a possible strategy to enter and cancel orders based on the regime idea that is a research topic for an interested reader.

The strategy determines the best tier of the book at which to place the order for a given execution probability and what the maximum size of the order should be assuming that there is no desire to change the actual state (regime) of the book. The discussion that follows is applied to the ask (offer) side of the limit order book.

17.4.1 Limit Order Position and Size

We start by rewriting Eqn (17.4) and solving for $\lambda_t(q)$:

$$\lambda_t(q) = \frac{P_t(q + sgn_q dq) - P_t(q)}{P_t(q + sgn_q dq) - V_t(q)} \tag{17.15}$$

Substituting this in Eqn (17.6) in order to obtain the probability that a given $P_t(q)$ will be reached:

$$\psi_t(q) = \frac{P_t(q + sgn_q dq) - P_t(q)}{P_t(q + sgn_q dq) - V_t(q)} \exp\left\{ -\int_0^q \frac{P_t(u + sgn_q du) - P_t(u)}{P_t(u + sgn_q du) - V_t(u)} du \right\} \quad (17.16)$$

As soon as in reality there is minimum lot size and minimum tick size we rewrite Eqn (17.16) as a discrete case:

$$\psi_t(q) = \frac{P_t(q + sgn_q \Delta q) - P_t(q)}{P_t(q + sgn_q \Delta q) - V_t(q)} \exp\left\{ -\sum_0^q \frac{P_t(u + sgn_q \Delta u) - P_t(u)}{P_t(u + sgn_q \Delta u) - V_t(u)} \right\} \quad (17.17)$$

With the price schedules presented in the limit order books, the assumption of being in a specific information regime and the corresponding probabilities that a given $P_t(q)$ will be reached, the trader can determine the best position of his order in the limit order book, for a given probability of execution, i.e., the trader can choose the highest price in the limit order book where he could submit his limit order that at the same time satisfies his desired execution probability (the probability that a market order will reach his order).

The probability of a limit order to be executed in the next period will be given by $\psi_t(q)\Theta_t\pi$, which is the probability of a market order just big enough to clear the limit order ($\psi_t(q)$) given the probability of the next limit order book to continue in the same regime ($\Theta_t\pi$).

There are two issues that need to be solved before the strategy can be implemented. First, the unobserved $V_t(u)$ needs to be estimated, and second, the fact that the limit order will be submitted after the regime has been identified. Moreover, we need to assume that the trader does not want to change the regime with his order. The trader understands that if a large limit order is added at once to the book and if, moreover, the limit order is close to the best quote, this will potentially change the shape of the book and the limit order book will possibly move to a transition period, where the other traders will reconsider their positions, accordingly.[3] However, if the order is small enough that its impact on the shape of the book is insignificant, then we can be sure that the book will stay in its current regime. Obviously, the probabilities for the tiers after the addition of the order will change. We use this set of assumptions in order to determine what the maximum size of limit order should be.

A final observation is that we need to note that if the trader wants to be sure that the order will bear certain probability of execution, he would need to submit it at the end of a given tier. He would not send it at the next tier because he will lose time priority since his

---

[3] This is something frequently observed in the market. And note that this can happen not necessarily based on the knowledge of new relevant information.

order will go to the end of this next tier; not undercut the next tier by posting a new order a tick above (hoping for a better execution price) because the other traders can simply set their orders at the end of the desired tier (effectively undercutting him). Thus, he needs to locate his order (exactly) at the end of the tier that satisfies his desired execution probability.

In order to implement this strategy, we make the following assumption about $V_t(q)$ following Lehmann (2008). As he noted, in cases when the spread between the best quotes is small, the midquote is approximately equal to the underlying value at that tier (or cumulative volume) of the book. After an execution of market order, which consumes part of the limit order, the new midquote will represent the approximate value at the new tier of the book. Using this approximation, some of the $V_t(q)$ can be adequately modeled, for the limit orders that are not only close to the best quote but also whose spread (the difference between the prices at given tiers with the best order on the opposite side of the book) is small. The $V_t(q)$ calculated for limit orders that are far away from the best quote will be understated (see Figure 17.8).

To obtain the underlying value via midquotes for the higher tiers of the book (far away from the best quote), the midquote can be calculated as the difference between the price of the specific tier and the best quote of the opposite side. For example, the bid best quote and the prices at increasing tiers on the ask side will provide midquotes to approximate the underlying value under the ask schedule. The approximation will become less and less accurate as one moves further up the book.

With a help of these strictly increasing function (complying with Lehmann's first assumption) we could empirically fit $V_t(q)$ at cumulative volumes (q) that are not only

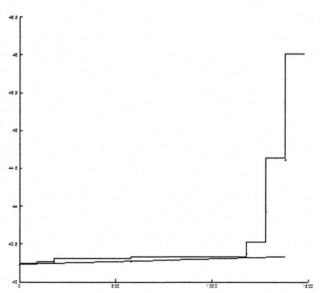

Figure 17.8 Limit order book versus asset value—empirical estimation. This figure shows a single ask limit order book (book id 2837). The dots represent points of underlying value at the beginning of each tier estimated as midquotes based on the described procedure. The straight line is a fitted line on the first four tiers to determine the underlying values that comply with the requirements provided in the section. It is used as a linear approximation of the underlying value.

close to the best quote but also whose spread (the difference between the prices at given tiers with the best order on the opposite side of the book) is small. These are satisfied by the first four tiers of the book presented in Figure 17.8.[4]

With these data at hand, we present a practical example where we show the way the procedure stated in this section works. In the case when the increase in (q) is equal to the minimum lot, Eqn (17.17) becomes

$$\psi_t(q) = \frac{P_t(q + sgn_q\Delta q) - P_t(q)}{P_t(q + sgn_q\Delta q) - V_t(q)} \exp\left\{ -\frac{P_t(q + sgn_q\Delta q) - P_t(q)}{P_t(q + sgn_q\Delta q) - V_t(q)} \right\} \qquad (17.18)$$

Since the limit order book is a step function, Eqn (17.18) can be applied only when we move from one tier of the book to the next (one step to the next). In the other cases (inside a given tier) the numerator will be equal to 0, since the price is the same for different quantities in that specific tier. Note, however, that this observation does not harm our procedure since new limit orders can only be added at the end of a given tier (time priority) and that the probabilities estimated using Eqn (17.18) are exactly the probabilities in which we are interested (the probability that a market order of size Q will arrive and consume exactly a cumulative volume of q). This probability of execution also represents the best approximation of a limit order that is posted at the end of that tier.

In Figure 17.8 the underlying value is estimated at the beginning of each tier (that corresponds to the end of the previous tier). We assume a linear value function, which in this example is fitted on the first four estimated values for the reasons explained before. We thus disregard the last part of this book (after the fourth tier) in order to determine the location of the limit order given a predetermined probability of execution.

Once we have the underlying value, we can calculate $\psi_t(q)$ at the end of each tier using Eqn (17.18). The results are presented in Table 17.2.

The probability that market order of size 89 (which is the size of the entire tier one in the limit order book presented in Figure 17.8) will arrive, given the information provided by the book that belongs to a specific information regime, is 0.3670. In this table we also observe that the probabilities of having larger and larger market orders decrease.

Once we have determined where the trader should locate his limit order (given his desired execution probability), the issue we address is the way to find the maximum size of the limit order at the maximum $P_t(q)$ for a given $\psi_t(q)$. As mentioned before, we assume that the trader has no intentions of causing a regime change. Under this additional restriction, the determination of the maximum quantity to post at the selected tier

---

[4] Observe that after tier four the assumption that the spread (the difference between the prices at given tiers with the best order on the opposite side of the book) is small, is not satisfied. Thus, the approximation suggested by Lehmann is no longer valid. One can see that the book becomes quite steep toward the end, making the linear fit to violate the fundamental assumption that the underlying value cannot cross the limit order book. As such, the approximations after the fourth tier are (at least) underestimating the true fundamental value of the stock.

Table 17.2 Estimated probabilities of execution

Tier (t)	1	2	3
Probability that a market order of size Q will arrive and consume exactly a cumulative volume of q ($\psi_t(q)$)	0.367	0.357	0.250
Price at a given cumulative volume ($P_t(q)$)	43.24	43.26	43.31
Cumulative volume up to tier t (q_t)	89	89	400
Market order size (Q)	89	178	578

This shows the risk neutral probabilities ($\psi_t(q)$) implicit in the limit order book that a market order of size Q_t will arrive and consume exactly a cumulative volume of q.

can be obtained applying the procedure stated in the previous sections where we proposed the methodology to compare the shapes of the books.

The actual book can be compared to what the book would look like if additional limit orders were added at a given tier. As the size of the limit order increased, by the minimum lot allowed by the exchange, at one point the Kolmogorov–Smirnov test will reject that the two books have the same shape. At this point and as soon as the trader does not want the books to change regimes, we should have as a result, the maximum number of shares that the new limit order should have.

For example, if the trader has identified that he would like to add an order to the second tier, i.e., his probability of execution is around 0.3565 (probability that a market order will not bypass his total volume available at that tier), he could compare the actual book to what the book would be if he adds one more share at the second tier. If the Kolmogorov–Smirnov test fails to reject that the books are from the same regime, the operation is repeated with two additional shares. The procedure is repeated until the books are significantly different as indicated by the proposed tests.

Applying the procedure on the above book yields that no more than 99 shares can be added to the second tier, i.e., the second tier can end up having 188 shares (the 89 already in place plus the 99 the trader would add), before the shape of the book is altered significantly. The resulting two books are displayed in Figure 17.9.

Obviously, the probabilities of exercise for the other market participants will be affected. In order to see the impact of these additional 99 shares added to the 89 already existing shares in the second tier, we reapply the above procedure on the new book and present the results in Table 17.3.

As it can be seen the probability that a market order will arrive and that it will consume up to the second tier increased. Intuitively, this can be explained by the following, assuming that we have a market order that walks up the book and passes the second tier. Let us assume that the market order size was equal to 250 shares.

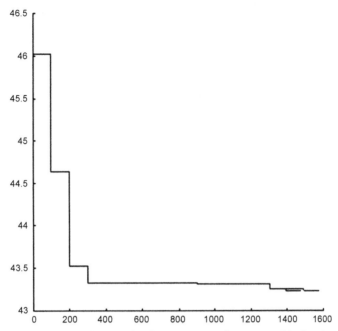

Figure 17.9 *Limit order book and optimal order position and size—empirical estimation.* This figure shows the original book and the new book when 99 shares have been added to the second tier.

Table 17.3 Estimated probabilities of execution with optimal order position and size

Tier (t)	1	2	3
Probability that a market order of size Q will arrive and consume exactly a cumulative volume of q ($\psi_t(q)$)	0.363	0.361	0.251
Price at a given cumulative volume ($P_t(q)$)	43.24	43.26	43.31
Cumulative volume up to tier t (q_t)	89	188	400
Market order size (Q)	89	277	677

This shows the risk neutral probabilities implicit in the limit order book that a market order of size Q_t will arrive.

In the original situation, if a market order of size 200 arrived to the market (consumed up to tier two plus part of tier three), the price impact of this order should have been $10,816.82 (89 × $43.24 + 89 × $43.26 + 72 × $43.31). In the new book 89 shares will sell at $43.24 and the remaining 161 shares (of which 72 are from our hypothetical trader) will sell at $43.26. Thus, the total market impact of this trade now equals $10,813.22, which is lower. This situation increases the probability of a market order coming to the market to consume up to a given cumulative volume.

17.4.2 Strategy for Entry and Exit

A final strategy for minimizing the price impact of a market order during a regime can also be formulated based on the cumulative volume of the limit order book. The cumulative volume reflects all the changes in the limit order book. During a regime these changes happen at the best quote of the book, and during a transition period the changes can also appear at higher tiers. Recall that the cumulative volume could increase during an information regime due to the fact that more favorable quotes (in terms of prices) could be added, reducing the price impact of the transactions (see the example above). Thus, by forecasting the cumulative volume in a given regime a trader can decide when to execute a market order that minimizes his price impact. We left this strategy for future research.

17.5 CONCLUSION

In this chapter we propose a methodology to first determine information regimes and later to estimate the transition probabilities of changing or staying in a given regime or transition period. The identification of the information regimes and the determination of the transition probabilities allow us to use information content in the whole book that can be used to set up possible trading strategies and provide an empirical and practical application to the theoretical model proposed by Lehmann. With the exception of Lehmann (2008) and Trendafilov and Rengifo (2013), previous research does not explore information regimes, and to the best of our knowledge, no other empirical study on the subject is available.

Comparing the results of this chapter with the ones obtained in Trendafilov and Rengifo (2013) shows that, even though the market microstructure that underlies the two data sets are completely different (Xetra vs Bats) and that the frequencies of observing the limit order books are also different (one with a book per second vs a book per millisecond), the methodology is capable of fully identifying information regimes in both cases and for all securities involved. This provides support for the robustness of the procedure and empirically supports Lehmann's theoretical model.

Our research further complements the existing literature with a novel trading strategy that can be utilized in high-frequency environment. We present a model that can be used by traders to determine the position of their limit orders at a specific book's tier that maximizes the price at which his order should be located given a particular probability of execution and the willingness not to change current information regime of the limit order book.

Finally, we propose the idea of an enter/exit strategy that can be potentially developed as a future research area.

REFERENCES

Alfonsi, A., Antje, F., Schied, A., 2010. Optimal execution strategies in limit order books with general shape functions. Quant. Finance 10 (2), 143—157.

Brooks, C., 2014. Introductory Econometrics for Finance. Cambridge University Press, UK.

Cont, R., Kukanov, A., 2013. Optimal Order Placement in Limit Order Markets. Working Paper. Imperial College, London.

Easley, D., Engle, R.F., O'Hara, M., Wu, L., 2008. Time-varying arrival rates of informed and uninformed trades. J. Financial Econ. 6 (2), 171—207.

Easley, D., Lopez de Prado, M., O'Hara, M., 2010. The microstructure of the 'Flash crash': flow toxicity, liquidity crashes and the probability of informed trading. J. Portfolio Manag. 37 (2), 118—128.

Glosten, L.R., 1994. Is the electronic open limit order book inevitable? J. Finance 49 (4), 1127—1161.

Guo, X., de Larrard, A., Ruan, Z., 2014. Optimal Placement in a Limit Order Book. Working Paper. University of California, Berkeley, CA.

Kirkpatrick II, C.D., Dahlquist, J., 2010. Technical Analysis: The Complete Resource for Financial Market Technicians. FT Press. (Upper Saddle River, NJ).

Lehmann, B., 2008. Arbitrage-free Limit Order Books and the Pricing of Order Flow Risk. Working Paper. NBER, Cambridge, MA.

Lehmann, B., 2005. Notes for a Contingent Claims Theory of Limit Order Markets. Working Paper. NBER, Cambridge, MA.

Obizhaeva, A.A., Wang, J., 2012. Optimal trading strategy and supply/demand dynamics. J. Financial Mark. 16 (1), 1—32.

Predoiu, S., Shaikhet, G., Shreve, S., 2011. Optimal execution in a general one-sided limit-order book. SIAM J. Financial Math. 2 (1), 183—212.

Trendafilov, R., Rengifo, E.W., 2013. Regime Identification in Limit Order Books. Working Paper. Fordham University, New York, NY.

CHAPTER 18

Effects of Firm-Specific Public Announcements on Market Dynamics: Implications for High-Frequency Traders

Erdinç Akyıldırım[1], Albert Altarovici[2], Cumhur Ekinci[3]
[1]Akdeniz University, Faculty of Economics and Administrative Sciences, Antalya, Turkey; [2]ETH Zürich, Department of Mathematics, Zürich, Switzerland; [3]ITU Isletme Fakultesi - Macka, Istanbul, Turkey

Contents

18.1 INTRODUCTION

Information and more specifically news have long been acknowledged to have a significant effect on price formation and on various dynamics of financial markets. Market participants' knowledge and understanding of market conditions are continuously updated with the arrival of each news item. As a result of the technological developments at all levels of the trading process, high-frequency trading (HFT) systems can capture and integrate news into their strategies within milliseconds. Investors rebalance their portfolios and consequently make a profit (or loss) depending on their assessment of the market's reaction to certain news. Hence, the increasing speed of news dissemination forces high-frequency traders to have a priori knowledge about the effects of arriving news on market dynamics.

There is a vast literature investigating the relationship between news as a tool of information transmission and the functioning of financial markets. Berry and Howe (1994) provide one of the earliest chapters that analyzes the intraday impact of public information measured by the number of news releases by Reuters' news service per unit of time. By using S&P 500 index returns and the number of shares traded on New York Stock Exchange, they observe a positive relationship between public information and trading volume but an insignificant relationship to price volatility. In a similar

The Handbook of High Frequency Trading
ISBN 978-0-12-802205-4

attempt, Kalev et al. (2004) present a positive and significant relationship between the arrival rate of news and the conditional variance of stock returns by using high-frequency data from the Australian Stock Exchange. Ranaldo (2008) provides a detailed analysis of the market behavior around the time firm-specific news is released. He studies price discovery, liquidity provision, and transaction-cost components by using six months of firm-specific news for 30 highly liquid stocks traded on the Paris Bourse. He finds that although market liquidity decreases with the disclosure of public information, which causes severe price adjustments (e.g., in earnings announcements), most firm-specific news increases liquidity. His results also show slightly lower adverse selection costs around news releases.

Groß-Klußmann and Hautsch (2011) are among the first to investigate the relationship between firm-specific news and high-frequency market dynamics (e.g., returns, volatility, trading intensity, trade sizes, trade imbalances, spreads, and market depth) by analyzing data from an automated news engine. Working with the transaction data of 39 liquid stocks traded on the London Stock Exchange, they show that relevant company-specific news items (excluding earnings announcements) have a significant effect on HFT. By using a similar news dataset, Riordan et al. (2013) analyze the impact of newswire messages on intraday price discovery, trading intensity, and liquidity of stocks traded on the Toronto Stock Exchange. They find that traders show asymmetric reactions to positive, negative, and neutral intraday news arrivals. In particular, negative messages have a more significant impact on high-frequency asset price discovery and liquidity, which is proxied by spread measures. Ho et al. (2013) extend the work of Riordan et al. (2013) by providing a detailed analysis of how and when news sentiment influences high-frequency asset volatility. By using >1200 types of firm-specific and macroeconomic news messages and their sentiment scores at high frequencies for the constituent stocks of Dow Jones Composite Average, they find negative news to have a greater impact on volatility than positive news. They also show that firm-specific news has a greater overall impact than macroeconomic news.

Another study that contributes to the literature by exploring the impact of macroeconomic news on quote adjustments, noise, and informational volatility is provided by Hautsch et al. (2011). Their analysis on intraday data of German Bund futures traded on Eurex reveals that immediately after an announcement, volatility exhibits significant jumps followed by a gradual decline. Erenburg and Lasser (2009) study the dynamics of the Island Electronic Communication Network electronic limit order book (LOB) around the arrival of macroeconomic news for the Nasdaq-100 equity-index tracking stock. They show that traders tend to submit more aggressive orders as early as 3 min before an announcement and the most aggressive orders within the first minute after the announcement.

There are also a number of studies (e.g., Odabasi (1998), Kutan and Aksoy (2003, 2004), Altiok-Yilmaz and Selcuk (2010), Özbebek et al. (2011)), which analyze the relationship between Turkish stock market dynamics and firm-specific or macroeconomics news. However, only a few of these studies investigate the relationship at the intraday level. Among them, Baklaci et al. (2011) examine the impact of firm-specific news on return volatility and trade volume by using stock prices in 15-min intervals for a selection of 20 stocks traded on the Istanbul Stock Exchange. They observe a significant reduction in volatility persistence for a majority of the stocks, which implies stability of prices following a news arrival.

In this chapter, we investigate the effects of firm-specific announcements on the market dynamics for a selection of 42 stocks listed on Borsa Istanbul. These announcements were obtained from the Public Disclosure Platform (Kamuyu Aydinlatma Platformu (KAP)), which is the first official channel for accessing company-related news. Our study contributes to the previous literature by providing a detailed analysis of market quality around the news arrival time. In contrast to the previous studies that only look at a few measures (e.g., trading volume, price volatility, return, and bid–ask spread), we employ many other interesting analytics to better understand and explore market dynamics, and consequently, we try to find profitable strategies that can be used by HFT systems. More specifically, we use 51 different liquidity or trade variables that are based on price, quantity, and time, including weighted bid, ask and midquote prices, spreads obtained from these weighted prices, total quantities available at different price levels in the order book, volume-weighted average price (VWAP), trading volume, number of buyer- and seller-initiated trades, as well as waiting time between orders and transactions. We then compare the results for 5-min intervals before and after the news release time and detect significant changes. To the best of our knowledge, this is the first study to investigate the market behavior of the Turkish stock exchange before and after the release of firm-specific news at high frequency. Based upon our findings, we also discuss the implications to HFT.

The remainder of the chapter proceeds as follows: Section 18.2 describes the data and the methodology, Section 18.3 explores empirical results, Section 18.4 documents the results of certain trading strategies, and Section 18.5 concludes.

18.2 DATA AND METHODOLOGY

Our dataset consists of tick-by-tick transaction prices and LOB aggregates (prices and quantities at the five best levels) as well as Public Disclosure Platform (KAP) announcements with their time stamp to the second.

We cover all the stocks included in the Borsa Istanbul (BIST) 50 index from January 1, 2010, to December 31, 2010. We then prepare two subsets, one for the largest companies (blue chips) and another for large yet relatively smaller companies. More specifically, we select 23 stocks that took part in the BIST 30 index during the entire year 2010 (Group 1 Stocks) and the other 19 stocks that were in the BIST 50 index during all of 2010, but never in the BIST 30 index (Group 2 Stocks).

The stock market of Borsa Istanbul is electronic and order driven (traditionally without market makers), so most of the liquidity is provided through limit orders. Hence, LOB dynamics carry crucial information for traders, especially during periods of high uncertainty caused by the arrival of new public information. The exchange disseminates LOB up to five best prices on both bid and ask sides in real time for each stock. Our analysis depends on the displayed portion of the LOB. This restricts one from investigating the market dynamics in complete depth, yet we believe that the visible portion of the book already contains crucial information to draw important inferences about the market dynamics.

The market is characterized by high percentage tick sizes. This issue is particularly important since high ticks limit any analysis made directly with transaction prices or quoted bid–ask spread. Hence, we mostly work with volume-weighted aggregates (see in variable definitions below).

For most stocks, a continuous trading session exists from 9.35 to 12:30 and 14:15 to 17:30 with a lunch break in the middle. (These hours were from 9:50 to 12:30 and 14:20 to 17:30 in our data period.) The usual price and time priority applies for transactions. There are three call auctions a day, one at the opening of the morning session and the others at the opening and closing of the afternoon session. (However, only the morning call auction existed in our study period.) In order to see the immediate effect of news, we only consider the announcements made during continuous trading.

During 2010, 1839 (1244) announcements were made in the KAP during continuous trading for the 23 (19) Group 1 (Group 2) stocks included in our dataset. However, we select only particular announcements, that is, those that might be more influential on the fundamental value of the firm (see the list of selected announcement types in Table 18.1). We remove all the announcements made during the first and last 5 min of each trading

Table 18.1 Selected announcement types

Group no	Nature
1	Issue or board resolution about the issue of debt securities
2	Merger and acquisition
3	Release of financial reports or annual report
4	Purchase/sale of financial or intangible assets
5	Contract award
6	Board resolution about dividend payment
7	Special announcement (update or repeat)
8	Special announcement

session (i.e., in both the morning and afternoon), since no comparison is possible if data are missing before or after the arrival of the news. We also skip simultaneous or overlapping announcements (i.e., among all the announcements made within a certain time period—actually 5 min—we only consider the first one). Although these steps greatly reduce our dataset, we end up with 325 (188) announcements for 23 (19) stocks that can still be viewed as a considerable number of observations.

We define various price-, quantity-, and time-based variables derived from the LOB and trade data, showing liquidity, price, and volatility dynamics (Table 18.2(A) and (B)). We then compute them for a certain time period (actually 5 min) before and after the arrival of the news and compare these two sets to see if the news has impacted the market dynamics. In order to filter for intraday effects, we first compute from period t to t+1

Table 18.2-A Liquidity variables used in the analysis

Type	Abbreviation	Liquidity variable
Price based	WBP2	Weighted bid price at two best price levels*
	WAP2	Weighted ask price at two best price levels*
	WMP2	Weighted midprice at two best price levels*
	WBP5	Weighted bid price at five best price levels*
	WAP5	Weighted ask price at five best price levels*
	WMP5	Weighted midprice at five best price levels*
	WS2	Weighted spread at the two best price levels (WAP2-WBP2)*
	WS5	Weighted spread at the five best price levels (WAP5-WBP5)*
Quantity based	TBQ2	Total bid quantity at two best price levels*
	TAQ2	Total ask quantity at two best price levels*
	TBQ5	Total bid quantity at five best price levels*
	TAQ5	Total ask quantity at five best price levels*
Time based	MWTO	Mean waiting time between orders
	MedWTO	Median waiting time between orders
	MinWTO	Min waiting time between orders
	MaxWTO	Max waiting time between orders
	MWTBO2	Mean waiting time for a buy order at two best price levels
	MedWTBO2	Median waiting time for a buy order at two best price levels
	MinWTBO2	Min waiting time for a buy order at two best price levels
	MaxWTBO2	Max waiting time for a buy order at five best price levels
	MWTSO2	Mean waiting time for a sell order at two best price levels
	MedWTSO2	Median waiting time for a sell order at two best price levels
	MinWTSO2	Min waiting time for a sell order at two best price levels
	MaxWTSO2	Max waiting time for a sell order at two best price levels

Notes: the asterisk (*) indicates that the variable is calculated by weighting with time. Weighted bid, ask, or midprices are obtained by weighting the prices with the quantities available in LOB.

Table 18.2-B Trade variables used in the analysis

Type	Abbreviation	Trade variable
Price based	VWAP	Volume-weighted average price
	PV	Price variance
	PF	Price fluctuation $((p_{max}-p_{min})/(p_{max} + p_{min})/2)$
	SAR	Sum of absolute returns
	AART	Average absolute returns per trade
Quantity based	NT	Number of trades
	V	Trading volume
	NBIT	Number of buyer-initiated trades
	NSIT	Number of seller-initiated trades
	VBIT	Volume of buyer-initiated trades
	VSIT	Volume of seller-initiated trades
	NCBS	Number of change from buy to sell
	NCSB	Number of change from sell to buy
	MaxNSBIT	Max number of successive buyer-initiated trades
	MaxNSSIT	Max number of successive seller-initiated trades
Time based	MWTT	Mean waiting time between trades
	MedWTT	Median waiting time between trades
	MinWTT	Min waiting time between trades
	MaxWTT	Max waiting time between trades
	MWTBIT	Mean waiting time for a buyer-initiated trade
	MedWTBIT	Median waiting time for a buyer-initiated trade
	MinWTBIT	Min waiting time for a buyer-initiated trade
	MaxWTBIT	Max waiting time for a buyer-initiated trade
	MWTSIT	Mean waiting time for a seller-initiated trade
	MedWTSIT	Median waiting time for a seller-initiated trade
	MinWTSIT	Min waiting time for a seller-initiated trade
	MaxWTSIT	Max waiting time for a seller-initiated trade

(period t (t+1) showing the interval before (after) the arrival of the news) the percentage change in each variable and compare this to the average percentage change of 23 (19) stocks. This step is particularly important and allows us to isolate the effect of the announcement from intraday seasonality or any other effect at the aggregate market level.

Price- and quantity-based liquidity variables are time weighted since they are stock variables. Others (time-based liquidity variables and all the trade variables) are not time weighted since they are flow variables.

We test several hypotheses regarding liquidity, price, and volatility dynamics as listed in Table 18.3(A) and (B). For instance, upon the arrival of the news, we expect to see a significant change (either positive or negative) in the value of the stock relative to other stocks in the market. Hence, we would observe changes in such variables as VWAP as well as weighted bid, ask, or midprices at two or five best price levels (WBP2, WAP2, WMP2, WBP5, WAP5, and WMP5) in the order book. However, we do not make

Table 18.3-A Hypotheses about liquidity variables

Variables	Abbreviation	Null hypothesis (H_0)	Alternative hypothesis (H_1)	Test type
Price based	WBP2	$WBP2_t = WBP2_{t+1}$	$WBP2_t \neq WBP2_{t+1}$	2-tailed
	WAP2	$WAP2_t = WAP2_{t+1}$	$WAP2_t \neq WAP2_{t+1}$	2-tailed
	WMP2	$WMP2_t = WMP2_{t+1}$	$WMP2_t \neq WMP2_{t+1}$	2-tailed
	WBP5	$WBP5_t = WBP5_{t+1}$	$WBP5_t \neq WBP2_{t+1}$	2-tailed
	WAP5	$WAP5_t = WAP5_{t+1}$	$WAP5_t \neq WAP5_{t+1}$	2-tailed
	WMP5	$WMP5_t = WMP5_{t+1}$	$WMP5_t \neq WMP5_{t+1}$	2-tailed
	WS2	$WS2_t = WS2_{t+1}$	$WS2_t < WS2_{t+1}$	1-tailed
	WS5	$WS5_t = WS5_{t+1}$	$WS5_t < WS5_{t+1}$	1-tailed
Quantity based	TBQ2	$TBQ2_t = TBQ2_{t+1}$	$TBQ2_t > TBQ2_{t+1}$	1-tailed
	TAQ2	$TAQ2_t = TQA2_{t+1}$	$TAQ2_t > TAQ2_{t+1}$	1-tailed
	TBQ5	$TBQ5_t = TBQ5_{t+1}$	$TBQ5_t > TBQ5_{t+1}$	1-tailed
	TAQ5	$TAQ5_t = TAQ5_{t+1}$	$TAQ5_t > TAQ5_{t+1}$	1-tailed
Time based	MWTO	$MWTO_t = MWTO_{t+1}$	$MWTO_t > MWTO_{t+1}$	1-tailed
	MedWTO	$MedWTO_t = MedWTO_{t+1}$	$MedWTO_t > MedWTO_{t+1}$	1-tailed
	MinWTO	$MinWTO_t = MinWTO_{t+1}$	$MinWTO_t > MinWTO_{t+1}$	1-tailed
	MaxWTO	$MaxWTO_t = MaxWTO_{t+1}$	$MaxWTO_t > MaxWTO_{t+1}$	1-tailed
	MWTBO2	$MWTBO2_t = MWTBO2_{t+1}$	$MWTBO2_t > MWTBO2_{t+1}$	1-tailed
	MedWTBO2	$MedWTBO2_t = MedWTBO2_{t+1}$	$MedWTBO2_t > MedWTBO2_{t+1}$	1-tailed
	MinWTBO2	$MinWTBO2_t = MinWTBO2_{t+1}$	$MinWTBO2_t > MinWTBO2_{t+1}$	1-tailed
	MaxWTBO2	$MaxWTBO2_t = MaxWTBO2_{t+1}$	$MaxWTBO2_t > MaxWTBO2_{t+1}$	1-tailed
	MWTSO2	$MWTSO2_t = MWTSO2_{t+1}$	$MWTSO2_t > MWTSO2_{t+1}$	1-tailed
	MedWTSO2	$MedWTSO2_t = MedWTSO2_{t+1}$	$MedWTSO2_t > MedWTSO2_{t+1}$	1-tailed
	MinWTSO2	$MinWTSO2_t = MinWTSO2_{t+1}$	$MinWTSO2_t > MinWTSO2_{t+1}$	1-tailed
	MaxWTSO2	$MaxWTSO2_t = MaxWTSO2_{t+1}$	$MaxWTSO2_t > MaxWTSO2_{t+1}$	1-tailed

Table 18.3-B Hypotheses about trade variables

Variables	Abbreviation	H_0	H_1	Test type
Price based	VWAP	$VWAP_t = VWAP_{t+1}$	$VWAP_t \neq VWAP_{t+1}$	2-tailed
	PV	$PV_t = PV_{t+1}$	$PV_t < PV_{t+1}$	1-tailed
	PF	$PF_t = PF_{t+1}$	$PF_t < PF_{t+1}$	1-tailed
	SAR	$SAR_t = SAR_{t+1}$	$SAR_t < SAR_{t+1}$	1-tailed
	AART	$AART_t = AART_{t+1}$	$AART_t < AART_{t+1}$	1-tailed
Quantity based	NT	$NT_t = NT_{t+1}$	$NT_t < NT_{t+1}$	1-tailed
	V	$V_t = V_{t+1}$	$V_t < V_{t+1}$	1-tailed
	NBIT	$NBIT_t = NBIT_{t+1}$	$NBIT_t < NBIT_{t+1}$	1-tailed
	NSIT	$NSIT_t = NSIT_{t+1}$	$NSIT_t < NSIT_{t+1}$	1-tailed
	VBIT	$VBIT_t = VBIT_{t+1}$	$VBIT_t < VBIT_{t+1}$	1-tailed
	VSIT	$VSIT_t = VSIT_{t+1}$	$VSIT_t < VSIT_{t+1}$	1-tailed
	NCBS	$NCBS_t = NCBS_{t+1}$	$NCBS_t < NCBS_{t+1}$	1-tailed
	NCSB	$NCSB_t = NCSB_{t+1}$	$NCSB_t < NCSB_{t+1}$	1-tailed
	MaxNSBIT	$MaxNSBIT_t = MaxNSBIT_{t+1}$	$MaxNSBIT_t < MaxNSBIT_{t+1}$	1-tailed
	MaxNSSIT	$MaxNSSIT_t = MaxNSSIT_{t+1}$	$MaxNSSIT_t < MaxNSSIT_{t+1}$	1-tailed
Time based	MWTT	$MWTT_t = MWTT_{t+1}$	$MWTT_t > MWTT_{t+1}$	1-tailed
	MedWTT	$MedWTT_t = MedWTT_{t+1}$	$MedWTT_t > MedWTT_{t+1}$	1-tailed
	MinWTT	$MinWTT_t = MinWTT_{t+1}$	$MinWTT_t > MinWTT_{t+1}$	1-tailed
	MaxWTT	$MaxWTT_t = MaxWTT_{t+1}$	$MaxWTT_t > MaxWTT_{t+1}$	1-tailed
	MWTBIT	$MWTBIT_t = MWTBIT_{t+1}$	$MWTBIT_t > MWTBIT_{t+1}$	1-tailed
	MedWTBIT	$MedWTBIT_t = MedWTBIT_{t+1}$	$MedWTBIT_t > MedWTBIT_{t+1}$	1-tailed
	MinWTBIT	$MinWTBIT_t = MinWTBIT_{t+1}$	$MinWTBIT_t > MinWTBIT_{t+1}$	1-tailed
	MaxWTBIT	$MaxWTBIT_t = MaxWTBIT_{t+1}$	$MaxWTBIT_t > MaxWTBIT_{t+1}$	1-tailed
	MWTSIT	$MWTSIT_t = MWTSIT_{t+1}$	$MWTSIT_t > MWTSIT_{t+1}$	1-tailed
	MedWTSIT	$MedWTSIT_t = MedWTSIT_{t+1}$	$MedWTSIT_t > MedWTSIT_{t+1}$	1-tailed
	MinWTSIT	$MinWTSIT_t = MinWTSIT_{t+1}$	$MinWTSIT_t > MinWTSIT_{t+1}$	1-tailed
	MaxWTSIT	$MaxWTSIT_t = MaxWTSIT_{t+1}$	$MaxWTSIT_t > MaxWTSIT_{t+1}$	1-tailed

an inference about the direction of change since we do not know the content of each news item. Therefore, we run two-tailed t tests on these variables. By contrast, we suspect that news can cause price volatility, which usually means larger bid—ask spreads. Therefore, we run one-tailed t tests on price-based variables such as PV, PF, SAR, and AART, and also quantity-based variables such as numbers of change from buy to sell and from sell to buy (NCBS and NCSB) as well as liquidity-based variables such as weighted spread measures (WS2 and WS5) derived from order book. This hypothesis is in line with the expectation of a higher proportion of active trading (i.e., more market orders would be submitted than limit orders) with the arrival of news. In fact, we would see higher levels of quantity-based variables such as volumes and number of trades (we also distinguish between buyer- and seller-initiated trades), that is, V, NT, VBIT, VSIT, NBIT, and NSIT, after the news arrive. Similarly, we expect to see higher maximum numbers of successive buyer- and seller-initiated trades (MaxNSBIT and MaxNSSIT). With the last two variables, we argue that successive trades on one side of the trade (i.e., buyer-initiated trades following buyer-initiated trades and seller-initiated trades following seller-initiated trades) are important in detecting if the news is important and well understood by market participants. The fact that with the arrival of the news, more trades (triggered by market orders) would occur than passive (limit) orders implies that pending quantities at LOB would decline. This is why we expect a decrease in TBQ2, TAQ2, TBQ5, and TAQ5 upon the arrival of news.

If the news is material, we would see increased activity in both transactions and order submission. This implies that the duration between trades and orders would decline. Hence, we hypothesize that mean, median, minimum, and maximum waiting times in trades (both buyer and seller initiated) and orders should be lower in the period after the news and we run one-tailed t tests.

Some variables were omitted during the calculation stage. For example, time-based variables as well as some volatility measures could not be calculated if there are less than two trades or two orders in any 5-min interval (assuming the market remains open).

18.3 EMPIRICAL RESULTS

Table 18.4(A) and (B) give the list of Group 1 and Group 2 stocks with their descriptive statistics about market capitalization (average of monthly values >2010), daily turnover (average of 2010) and relevant number of announcements in each type of news. There are 325 (188) selected news in 23 Group 1 (19 Group 2) stocks during 2010. Two hundred forty-eight news items out of 325 in Group 1 stocks (104 news out of 188 in Group 2 stocks) are special announcements. Besides, most announcements (189 out of 325) came for banking corporations that constitute a large portion of Group 1 stocks (9 out of 23) and have a considerable weight in the BIST 30 index. The second most common

Table 18.4-A Descriptive statistics about group 1 stocks and number of related announcements

Stock	Market cap (bn TL)	Daily turnover (mn TL)	News group								Total news
			1	2	3	4	5	6	7	8	
AKBNK	31.36	54	3	0	1	0	0	0	0	45	49
ASYAB	3.22	30	0	0	1	0	0	0	0	2	3
DOHOL	2.64	42	0	0	0	2	0	0	1	1	4
ENKAI	12.50	16	0	0	1	0	0	0	0	6	7
EREGL	7.43	31	0	0	0	1	0	0	1	0	2
GARAN	30.93	234	0	0	5	0	0	0	2	6	13
HALKB	15.07	47	0	0	1	0	0	0	4	20	25
ISCTR	22.97	129	0	0	1	0	0	1	0	1	3
KCHOL	14.44	26	0	0	0	0	0	0	0	5	5
KRDMD	0.67	23	0	0	0	0	0	0	0	1	1
PETKM	2.17	46	0	0	1	0	0	0	0	8	9
SAHOL	13.71	29	0	0	4	0	0	1	0	6	11
SISE	2.43	18	0	0	1	0	0	2	1	16	20
SKBNK	1.23	9	2	0	6	0	0	1	0	8	17
TAVHL	2.40	17	0	0	1	0	0	0	0	4	5
TCELL	21.10	37	0	0	0	0	0	0	0	6	6
TEBNK	2.54	17	0	1	1	0	0	0	0	8	10
THYAO	4.80	51	0	0	3	0	0	0	0	31	34
TKFEN	2.05	15	0	0	2	1	0	0	1	5	9
TTKOM	20.02	12	0	0	2	0	1	0	2	11	16
TUPRS	8.47	20	0	0	5	0	0	0	0	2	7
VAKBN	9.96	81	0	0	8	0	0	0	0	51	59
YKBNK	19.27	70	0	0	2	0	0	1	2	5	10
Total	251.37	1055	5	1	46	4	1	6	14	248	325

Notes: news types (from 1 to 8) are explained in Table 18.1.

Table 18.4-B Descriptive statistics about group 2 stocks and number of related announcements

Stock	Market cap (bn TL)	Daily turnover (mn TL)	News group								Total news
			1	2	3	4	5	6	7	8	
AEFES	8.68	6	0	0	0	2	0	0	0	3	5
AKENR	1.19	10	0	0	4	0	0	1	0	13	18
AKGRT	0.61	21	0	0	2	0	0	0	1	8	11
ANSGR	0.59	7	0	0	4	1	0	0	0	12	17
ARCLK	4.70	12	0	0	6	0	0	0	0	6	12
AYGAZ	2.04	5	0	0	4	0	0	0	0	0	4
BAGFS	0.37	16	0	0	3	0	0	0	1	10	14
BIMAS	6.55	10	0	0	0	0	0	0	0	0	0
DYHOL	1.42	44	0	0	1	0	0	2	12	2	17
ECILC	1.39	13	0	0	5	0	0	0	4	2	11
GSDHO	0.26	9	0	0	6	0	0	0	0	3	9
HURGZ	0.88	12	0	0	1	0	0	0	0	4	5
NTHOL	0.29	6	0	0	0	0	0	0	0	10	10
PTOFS	3.79	5	0	0	1	0	0	0	1	4	6
SELEC	1.50	2	0	0	0	0	0	1	0	0	1
TOASO	3.20	6	0	0	3	0	0	0	0	3	6
TSKB	1.47	7	0	0	4	0	0	2	3	14	23
ULKER	1.12	9	0	0	1	2	0	1	1	4	9
VESTL	0.80	9	0	0	3	1	0	0	0	6	10
Total	40.83	211	0	0	48	6	0	7	23	104	188

news type is the release of financial and annual reports (46 (48) news out of 325 (188) in Group 1 (Group 2) stocks).

Market capitalization and turnover statistics reveal that Group 1 (Group 2) stocks total market value is TRY 251 bn (41 bn) and that the total daily turnover is TRY 1.05 bn (0.21 bn). Again, market cap and turnover are concentrated in banks.

Table 18.5(A) (Table 18.5(B)) gives the statistics about the difference between the percentage change in the liquidity (trade) variables of the stock that is the subject of the announcement and the average percentage change in the liquidity (trade) variables of Group 1 stocks as well as the associated t-test results testing the significance. For example, within the 5-min period after the arrival of the news, WBP2 increased on average 0.02% more than the market average (i.e., the average of the 23 stocks combined) with a maximum differential of 1.62% and minimum differential of -2.05%. The two-tailed t-test score indicates that this positive difference is significant at a 0.11 confidence interval (t-stat is 1.60). Similar results apply for other weighted prices (WAP2, WMP2, WBP5, WAP5, and WMP5). The WS5 measure significantly increases upon news (p-value is 0.019), but the increase in WS2 is not significant since the null hypothesis cannot be rejected (p-value of 0.425).

Any change in total quantities of orders pending on both bid and ask sides at two or five best price levels (TBQ2, TAQ2, TBQ5, and TAQ5) cannot be confirmed since t statistics are very low (p-values vary between 0.277 and 0.896).

As expected, most time-based liquidity variables significantly decrease relative to the market upon the arrival of the news (see the p values in the lower part of Table 18.5(A)). The two exceptions are MedWTO and MinWTBO2[1].

Surprisingly, in Table 18.5(B), VWAP is significantly positive (a p-value of 0.006), signaling that prices tend to rise upon the arrival of news. Among the price-based trade variables designating volatility such as PV, PF, SAR, and AART, increases in PF, and SAR are significant. On the other hand, quantity-based trade variables designating volatility such as NCBS and NCSB significantly increase (p-values are 0.004 and 0.002, respectively) indicating that trade signs change much more frequently upon the arrival of news. However, this finding is in contrast with significant increases in the maximum numbers of successive buyer-initiated and seller-initiated trades (MaxNSBIT and MaxNSSIT) that are significantly higher (p-values of 0.003 and 0.065, respectively) in the period after the news[2].

---

[1] Note that all the median values of time-based liquidity (trade) variables are negative in Table 18.5(A) and (B) although significance is not always attained.

[2] The finding that the percentage change differentials are significant in both NCBS/NCSB couple and MaxNSBIT/MaxNSSIT couple is contradictory since the former define sign changes between trades from buy to sell or from sell to buy while the latter define successive trades (buys following buys and sells following sells). Nevertheless, this can be explained by the increase in overall numbers of transactions upon the arrival of news.

Table 18.5-A Percentage change differential in liquidity variables measured before and after the arrival of news and significance tests results—group 1 stocks

	Variable	Mean	Med	Max	Min	Standard deviation	N	T-stat	p-value (2−t)	p-value (1−t)
Price based	WBP2	0.0002	0.0000	0.0162	−0.0205	0.0027	325	1.60	0.110	0.425
	WAP2	0.0002	0.0000	0.0148	−0.0201	0.0027	325	1.52	0.130	0.019
	WMP2	0.0002	0.0000	0.0155	−0.0203	0.0027	325	1.58	0.115	0.277
	WBP5	0.0001	0.0000	0.0124	−0.0198	0.0024	325	0.89	0.373	0.779
	WAP5	0.0002	0.0000	0.0128	−0.0193	0.0025	325	1.59	0.112	0.518
	WMP5	0.0002	0.0000	0.0125	−0.0196	0.0024	325	1.29	0.198	0.896
	WS2	0.0006	−0.0043	0.2331	−0.2311	0.0574	325	0.19		0.000
	WS5	0.0048	−0.0014	0.2729	−0.1176	0.0416	325	2.08		0.019
Quantity based	TBQ2	−0.0071	−0.0148	1.3807	−0.6478	0.2158	325	−0.59		0.277
	TAQ2	0.0079	−0.0043	1.0180	−0.5416	0.1849	325	0.77		0.779
	TBQ5	0.0003	−0.0060	0.6943	−0.6535	0.1241	325	0.04		0.518
	TAQ5	0.0081	−0.0006	0.9743	−0.3042	0.1157	325	1.26		0.896
Time based	MWTO	−0.18	−0.34	7.51	−2.21	0.92	323	−3.44		0.000
	MedWTO	−0.06	−0.51	34.85	−12.96	2.98	317	−0.38		0.354
	MinWTO	−0.11	−0.23	3.06	−2.03	0.62	323	−3.27		0.001
	MaxWTO	−1.21	−0.87	16.30	−17.89	4.64	94	−2.53		0.007
	MWTBO2	−0.32	−0.57	11.69	−7.54	2.00	234	−2.46		0.007
	MedWTBO2	−0.73	−1.19	18.61	−11.98	3.55	233	−3.14		0.001
	MaxWTBO2	−0.43	−0.37	16.48	−9.75	2.04	234	−3.22		0.001
	MinWTBO2	2.79	−1.38	142.02	−23.93	21.35	151	1.61		0.945
	MWTSO2	−0.47	−0.62	13.59	−13.86	2.09	239	−3.46		0.000
	MedWTSO2	−0.67	−0.96	58.88	−17.06	5.49	239	−1.89		0.030
	MaxWTSO2	−0.29	−0.30	35.28	−13.29	2.89	239	−1.56		0.061
	MinxWTSO2	−2.58	−1.84	82.28	−38.94	11.05	151	−2.86		0.002

Notes: Definitions of the liquidity variables are given in Table 18.2(A). 2−t (1−t) means the test is held two tailed (one tailed).

Table 18.5-B Percentage change differential in trade variables measured before and after the arrival of news and significance tests results—group 1 stocks

	Variable	Mean	Med	Max	Min	Standard deviation	N	T-stat	p-value (2–t)	p-value (1–t)
Price based	VWAP	0.0005	0.0004	0.0119	−0.0153	0.0033	316	2.77	0.006	
	PV	0.18	−0.21	31.26	−6.42	2.50	222	1.09		0.137
	PF	0.19	0.09	6.83	−1.08	0.75	245	3.93		0.000
	SAR	0.42	−0.10	12.53	−3.58	2.07	245	3.22		0.001
	AART	−0.01	−0.21	22.35	−4.45	1.73	245	−0.09		0.537
Quantity based	NT	1.83	−0.13	104.31	−4.09	9.20	320	3.56		0.000
	V	245	−12.69	97,290	−20,046	6765	316	0.64		0.260
	NBIT	2.33	−0.20	144.90	−3.28	13.24	287	2.98		0.002
	NSIT	0.62	−0.28	42.73	−3.68	4.13	283	2.53		0.006
	VBIT	749	−27.01	233,055	−64,952	16,056	287	0.79		0.215
	VSIT	171	−28.74	178,294	−33,562	13,123	283	0.22		0.413
	NCBS	0.34	−0.11	17.84	−1.91	1.91	225	2.67		0.004
	NCSB	0.37	−0.09	17.20	−1.96	1.92	236	2.96		0.002
	MaxNSBIT	1.55	−0.13	91.94	−5.00	9.63	287	2.73		0.003
	MaxNSSIT	0.19	−0.25	22.12	−3.72	2.14	283	1.52		0.065
Time based	MWTT	0.04	−0.42	88.40	−5.13	5.35	293	0.11		0.545
	MedWTT	−0.17	−0.84	87.75	−12.31	6.16	293	−0.47		0.319
	MaxWTT	0.18	−0.29	88.27	−7.14	5.35	293	0.57		0.716
	MinWTT	0.34	−1.45	155.21	−17.88	18.68	154	0.23		0.590
	MWTBIT	−0.20	−0.54	24.97	−5.27	2.40	228	−1.28		0.101
	MedWTBIT	−0.49	−1.04	39.99	−19.43	5.13	228	−1.44		0.076
	MaxWTBIT	−0.22	−0.45	18.27	−9.19	2.29	228	−1.47		0.072
	MinWTBIT	−2.26	−1.92	52.46	−29.12	9.93	139	−2.69		0.004
	MWTSIT	−0.24	−0.62	85.17	−24.29	6.69	212	−0.53		0.300
	MedWTSIT	−0.03	−0.89	84.30	−24.06	7.54	211	−0.06		0.477
	MaxWTSIT	−0.31	−0.43	85.16	−18.10	7.09	212	−0.64		0.263
	MinWTSIT	−1.75	−1.25	81.02	−37.54	11.44	141	−1.82		0.035

Notes: definitions of the trade variables are given in Table 18.2(B). 2–t (1–t) means the test is held two tailed (one tailed).

Interestingly, by contrast to the significant relative increase in trading activity variables defined in terms of numbers, the increases in quantity-based trade variables related to volume, such as V, VBIT, and VSIT, are not statistically significant (p-values are 0.260, 0.215, and 0.413, respectively). Moreover, all the means are positive, whereas all the medians are negative in V, VBIT, and VSIT.

The lower part of Table 18.5(B) shows the results about time-based trade variables. Accordingly, it is not easy to draw inference about relative percentage changes in waiting times between trades. Generally, the hypothesis that waiting time between trades and waiting time between seller-initiated trades stay stable cannot be rejected since p-values are high. However, mean, median, maximum, and minimum waiting times between buyer-initiated trades are all negative and statistically significant to a large extent (p-values are 0.101, 0.076, 0.072, and 0.004, respectively). One can note that all the median values of time-based trade variables are negative in this table.

The corresponding statistics and test results for Group 2 stocks are given in Table 18.6(A) and (B). The tables show that most results are markedly different than those of the Group 1 stocks. For example, the insignificance of relative percentage changes in price-based liquidity variables such as weighted bid, ask, and midprices are confirmed, but with lower t statistics (higher p-values). As opposed to Group 1 stocks, the relative increase in WS2 is statistically significant (p-value of 0.078) while the increase cannot be confirmed for WS5 (p-value of 0.408).

Generally speaking, the relative decrease in time-based liquidity variables cannot be verified. The mean values of MWTO and MedWTO are negative, and p-values are 0.070 and 0.077, respectively, meaning that mean and median waiting times between orders significantly decrease upon the arrival of news, but in all other time-based liquidity variables, the null hypothesis cannot be rejected.

Given in Table 18.6(B), trade variables for Group 2 stocks also have different patterns than those for Group 1 stocks. For instance, VWAP is negative though not significant (p-value is 0.353). Interestingly, neither the changes in price-based variables designating volatility (PV, PF, SAR, and AART) nor the changes in quantity-based variables designating volatility (NCBS, NCSB, MaxNSBIT, and MaxNSSIT) are significant (all the p-values are >0.10). Hence, we fail to reject the null hypothesis of stable volatility upon the arrival of news for Group 2 stocks.

We also fail to reject the null hypothesis of increase in trading volumes (V, VBIT, and VSIT) upon the arrival of news. Conversely, t statistics for VBIT and VSIT are negative and low (-1.90 and -2.92, respectively). This implies that trading volumes tend to relatively decrease upon the arrival of news. The slight increases in NT, NBIT, and NSIT are not confirmed statistically (p-values are 0.137, 0.236, and 0.306, respectively).

Finally, when time-based trade variables are analyzed, one sees that the values about waiting time between trades and waiting time between buyer-initiated trades are mostly negative, whereas the values about waiting time between seller-initiated trades are

Table 18.6-A Percentage change differential in liquidity variables measured before and after the arrival of news and significance tests results—group 2 stocks

	Variable	Mean	Med	Max	Min	Standard deviation	N	T-stat	p-value (2-t)	p-value (1-t)
Price based	WBP2	0.0000	−0.0001	0.0066	−0.0056	0.0017	188	−0.15	0.879	
	WAP2	0.0000	0.0000	0.0076	−0.0065	0.0016	188	0.16	0.871	
	WMP2	0.0000	−0.0001	0.0071	−0.0058	0.0017	188	0.00	0.998	
	WBP5	0.0000	0.0000	0.0060	−0.0057	0.0016	188	0.09	0.925	
	WAP5	0.0000	0.0000	0.0065	−0.0048	0.0014	188	−0.21	0.835	
	WMP5	0.0000	−0.0001	0.0061	−0.0051	0.0014	188	−0.06	0.955	
	WS2	0.0057	0.0015	0.3515	−0.1194	0.0550	188	1.43		0.078
	WS5	0.0008	−0.0014	0.3108	−0.2078	0.0448	188	0.23		0.408
Quantity based	TBQ2	−0.0212	−0.0074	0.3721	−0.7139	0.1247	188	−2.33		0.010
	TAQ2	−0.0013	−0.0089	0.8022	−0.4675	0.1504	188	−0.12		0.453
	TBQ5	−0.0114	−0.0066	0.3854	−0.4314	0.0875	188	−1.79		0.037
	TAQ5	0.0003	−0.0016	0.2719	−0.2280	0.0540	188	0.08		0.533
Time based	MWTO	−0.08	−0.18	2.69	−1.77	0.77	185	−1.48		0.070
	MedWTO	−0.18	−0.43	12.98	−4.89	1.66	182	−1.43		0.077
	MinWTO	−0.03	−0.17	3.62	−2.72	0.73	185	−0.54		0.295
	MaxWTO	0.57	−0.31	56.40	−12.80	7.96	63	0.57		0.714
	MWTBO2	−0.09	−0.30	11.48	−12.88	2.46	129	−0.41		0.340
	MedWTBO2	−0.21	−0.62	16.22	−20.02	4.02	126	−0.58		0.281
	MaxWTBO2	−0.15	−0.26	10.35	−9.63	1.85	129	−0.91		0.183
	MinWTBO2	2.62	−0.64	57.92	−13.19	13.03	93	1.94		0.972
	MWTSO2	0.08	−0.32	20.42	−8.61	2.58	122	0.33		0.630
	MedWTSO2	−0.28	−0.64	24.14	−15.69	4.19	122	−0.74		0.229
	MaxWTSO2	0.50	−0.22	67.03	−6.33	6.33	122	0.88		0.809
	MinxWTSO2	−0.05	−0.69	56.59	−32.28	10.61	83	−0.04		0.484

Notes: definitions of the liquidity variables are given in Table 18.2(A). 2−t (1−t) means the test is held two tailed (one tailed).

Table 18.6-B Percentage change differential in trade variables measured before and after the arrival of news and significance tests results—group 2 stocks

	Variable	Mean	Med	Max	Min	Standard deviation	N	T-stat	p-value (2–t)	p-value (1–t)
Price based	VWAP	-0.0002	-0.0001	0.0113	-0.0093	0.0032	177	-0.93	0.353	0.864
	PV	-0.09	-0.20	3.12	-2.40	0.85	113	-1.10		0.492
	PF	0.00	0.04	1.84	-1.14	0.44	128	0.02		0.475
	SAR	0.01	-0.32	9.41	-2.47	1.46	128	0.06		0.918
	AART	-0.14	-0.28	5.83	-4.84	1.11	128	-1.40		0.137
Quantity based	NT	0.20	-0.29	21.52	-2.30	2.44	182	1.10		0.578
	V	-28.97	-9.74	16,162	-9808	1960	177	-0.20		0.236
	NBIT	0.30	-0.31	62.84	-3.30	5.21	158	0.72		0.306
	NSIT	0.07	-0.20	10.63	-3.39	1.66	156	0.51		0.970
	VBIT	-428	-17.63	11,022	-27,450	2827	158	-1.90		0.998
	VSIT	-1009	-25.76	6475	-41,109	4318	156	-2.92		0.623
	NCBS	-0.03	-0.22	3.22	-1.61	0.95	120	-0.31		0.462
	NCSB	0.01	-0.28	4.85	-1.99	1.12	124	0.10		0.418
	MaxNSBIT	0.04	-0.37	28.85	-4.14	2.66	158	0.21		0.572
	MaxNSSIT	-0.02	-0.18	8.95	-3.45	1.47	156	-0.18		0.248
Time based	MWTT	-0.07	-0.25	7.57	-2.84	1.39	164	-0.68		0.027
	MedWTT	-0.44	-0.66	16.03	-12.40	2.88	161	-1.93		0.419
	MaxWTT	-0.02	-0.24	12.11	-4.04	1.47	164	-0.21		0.427
	MinWTT	-0.17	-0.73	88.67	-23.66	9.78	107	-0.18		0.139
	MWTBIT	-0.25	-0.41	10.03	-9.99	2.34	105	-1.09		0.270
	MedWTBIT	-0.41	-0.90	40.08	-18.47	6.86	104	-0.61		0.023
	MaxWTBIT	-0.55	-0.38	10.28	-14.60	2.77	105	-2.02		0.917
	MinWTBIT	3.24	-0.69	104.16	-31.60	20.45	78	1.40		0.779
	MWTSIT	0.64	-0.53	60.27	-10.25	8.44	105	0.77		0.634
	MedWTSIT	0.34	-0.84	64.68	-10.70	10.04	105	0.34		0.823
	MaxWTSIT	1.50	-0.39	150.24	-10.55	16.51	105	0.93		0.798
	MinWTSIT	2.01	-0.85	177.42	-26.57	21.61	81	0.84		

Notes: definitions of the liquidity variables are given in Table 18.2(A). 2–t (1–t) means the test is held two tailed (one tailed).

positive. However, the only statistically significant changes occur in MedWTT and MaxWTBIT (*p*-values are 0.027 and 0.023, respectively) and both are negative, showing a relative decrease in these waiting times upon the arrival of news.

18.4 IMPLICATIONS FOR HFT

Given all the results in the previous section, one can wonder if it is possible to use them for building HFT strategies. This section tries to briefly answer this question.

We check the profitability of simple momentum or contrarian trading strategies that foresee to purchase or sell a certain amount of Group 1 stocks (1000, 10,000, and 100,000 stocks, respectively) just after the news announcement. We simultaneously assign a take-profit order that is one tick (alternatively two ticks) above (below) the purchase (sales) price. Assuming that transaction costs are negligible and our order does not affect the market prices, if both the initial order and the take-profit order is fulfilled, then the strategy becomes profitable. Marketable limit orders are "all-or-none" type, that is, they are either fully executed soon or canceled, and all the (initial and take-profit) limit orders are valid for the day. In order to keep the strategy simple, we assume that we cancel the initial limit orders if the market moves one tick away from our specified price.

Table 18.7 presents the execution probabilities of initial orders. Accordingly, it is almost always possible to buy or sell up to 10,000 shares at the prevailing quotes, but for larger sizes, this probability is smaller (0.41 for purchases and 0.50 for sales).

Table 18.8 gives the execution probabilities of take-profit orders. It follows that the probabilities of a one-tick gain from a marketable limit order to buy are 0.15, 0.14, and 0.09 for 1000, 10,000, and 100,000 shares, respectively. If the expected gain is two ticks, then these probabilities fall to 0.09, 0.09, and 0.05, respectively. If the gains that cannot be confirmed with the current data are added, the probabilities almost double (e.g., 0.31 for one-tick gain in a small trade).

Obviously, the probabilities are lower for limit orders than marketable limit orders and for two-tick gains than one-tick gains. What is more surprising is that probabilities are higher on the sell side (see the lower part of the table).

Table 18.7 Probability of execution of initial orders

Order Type	Buy			Sell		
	1K	10K	100K	1K	10K	100K
Marketable limit order	1.00	0.99	0.80	1.00	0.98	0.77
Limit order at best price	0.41	0.41	0.41	0.50	0.50	0.50

Notes: 1K, 10K, and 100K show the order sizes (number of shares to be purchased or sold—1000, 10,000, and 100,000, respectively). As we could not check the execution of limit orders at best price with exactitude, orders with different sizes are considered to have the same probability of execution.

Table 18.8 Probability of execution of take-profit orders

Buy

Order type	Execution certainty	Take-profit (1 tick)			Take-profit (2 ticks)		
		1K	10K	100K	1K	10K	100K
Marketable limit order	Certain execution	0.15	0.14	0.09	0.09	0.09	0.05
	Probable execution	0.16	0.16	0.13	0.06	0.05	0.04
	Total	0.31	0.30	0.22	0.15	0.14	0.09
Limit order at best price	Certain execution	0.07	0.07	0.07	0.03	0.03	0.03
	Probable execution	0.06	0.06	0.06	0.04	0.04	0.04
	Total	0.13	0.13	0.13	0.07	0.07	0.07

Sell

Order type	Execution certainty	Take-profit (1 tick)			Take-profit (2 ticks)		
		1K	10K	100K	1K	10K	100K
Marketable limit order	Certain execution	0.20	0.19	0.13	0.14	0.14	0.09
	Probable execution	0.13	0.13	0.09	0.06	0.06	0.04
	Total	0.33	0.32	0.22	0.20	0.19	0.13
Limit order at best price	Certain execution	0.10	0.10	0.10	0.06	0.06	0.06
	Probable execution	0.08	0.08	0.08	0.04	0.04	0.04
	Total	0.18	0.18	0.18	0.10	0.10	0.10

Table 18.9 Conditional probability of execution of take-profit orders

Buy

Order type	Execution certainty	Take-profit (1 tick)			Take-profit (2 ticks)		
		1K	10K	100K	1K	10K	100K
Marketable limit order	Certain execution	0.15	0.15	0.12	0.09	0.09	0.07
	Probable execution	0.16	0.16	0.16	0.06	0.05	0.05
	Total	0.31	0.30	0.28	0.15	0.15	0.12
Limit order at best price	Certain execution	0.18	0.18	0.18	0.07	0.07	0.07
	Probable execution	0.14	0.14	0.14	0.10	0.10	0.10
	Total	0.32	0.32	0.32	0.18	0.18	0.18

Sell

Order type	Execution certainty	Take-profit (1 tick)			Take-profit (2 ticks)		
		1K	10K	100K	1K	10K	100K
Marketable limit order	Certain execution	0.20	0.19	0.17	0.14	0.14	0.12
	Probable execution	0.13	0.13	0.12	0.06	0.06	0.05
	Total	0.33	0.33	0.29	0.20	0.19	0.17
Limit order at best price	Certain execution	0.20	0.20	0.20	0.12	0.12	0.12
	Probable execution	0.15	0.15	0.15	0.08	0.08	0.08
	Total	0.35	0.35	0.35	0.20	0.20	0.20

Table 18.9 shows the execution probability of a take-profit order given the initial order is executed. Interestingly, in this table, the probabilities associated with limit orders are much higher compared to Table 18.8.

18.5 CONCLUSION

This chapter was about the role of firm-specific public announcements on liquidity, price, and volatility dynamics on Borsa Istanbul. It is one of the first studies for discovering market dynamics of Borsa Istanbul at high frequency and at the stock level. Besides, it aims at contributing to the literature about market dynamics during firm-specific public announcements.

We analyzed the effects of 325 (188) selected announcements in eight categories on the dynamics of 23 (19) stocks included in BIST 30 (in BIST 50 but not in BIST 30) stocks called Group 1 (Group 2) stocks. We defined 24 liquidity variables and 27 trade variables that are based on price, quantity, or time. We calculated all these variables for the periods of 5 min just before (t) and after (t+1) the time of the news and compare the two periods. In order to filter out intraday effects and marketwide movements, for each stock for which there is an announcement, we computed excess percentage change (percentage change in the stock minus the average percentage change of 23 (19) stocks) from period t to period t+1.

The results indicate that the percentage change differential is significant in some variables such as VWAP, price variation, PF, numbers of change from buy to sell and from sell to buy, and maximum number of successive buyer-initiated and seller-initiated trades for Group 1 stocks. In general, evidence in Group 2 stocks is weaker. For instance, significance in higher volatility or lower interorder and intertrade durations diminishes or disappears.

Motivated by the significantly higher volume-weighted average prices after the arrival of the news, we subsequently analyzed the profitability of certain order submission strategies. More specifically, we calculated the execution probabilities of marketable limit orders and limit orders at best price on both buy and sell sides as well as their take-profit orders that are one tick or two ticks away. Execution probabilities of take-profit orders seemed to be low, which means that strategies may not be very profitable. However, if the assumptions are relaxed (e.g., allowing the validity to be more than one day for take-profit orders) or the strategies are elaborated, more profitable cases may be obtained.

ACKNOWLEDGMENTS

We thank Borsa Istanbul for providing data.

REFERENCES

Altiok-Yilmaz, A., Selcuk, E.A., 2010. Information content of dividends: evidence from Istanbul. Int. Bus. Res. 3 (3), 126.

Baklaci, H.F., Tunc, G., Aydogan, B., Vardar, G., 2011. The impact of firm-specific public news on intraday market dynamics: evidence from the Turkish stock market. Emerg. Mark. Finance Trade 47 (6), 99–119.

Berry, T.D., Howe, K.M., 1994. Public information arrival. J. Finance 49 (4), 1331–1346.

Erenburg, G., Lasser, D., 2009. Electronic limit order book and order submission choice around macroeconomic news. Rev. Financial Econ. 18 (4), 172–182.

Groß-Klußmann, A., Hautsch, N., 2011. When machines read the news: using automated text analytics to quantify high frequency news-implied market reactions. J. Empir. Finance 18 (2), 321–340.

Hautsch, N., Hess, D., Veredas, D., 2011. The impact of macroeconomic news on quote adjustments, noise, and informational volatility. J. Bank. Finance 35 (10), 2733–2746.

Ho, K.Y., Shi, Y., Zhang, Z., 2013. How does news sentiment impact asset volatility? Evidence from long memory and regime-switching approaches. North Am. J. Econ. Finance 26 (2), 436–456.

Kalev, P.S., Liu, W.M., Pham, P.K., Jarnecic, E., 2004. Public information arrival and volatility of intraday stock returns. J. Bank. Finance 28 (6), 1441–1467.

Kutan, A.M., Aksoy, T., 2004. Public information arrival and emerging markets returns and volatility. Multinatl. Finance J. 8 (3–4), 227–245.

Kutan, A.M., Aksoy, T., 2003. Public information arrival and the Fisher effect in emerging markets: evidence from stock and bond markets in Turkey. J. Financial Serv. Res. 23 (3), 225–239.

Odabasi, A., 1998. Security returns' reactions to earnings announcements: a case study on the Istanbul stock exchange. Rev. Soc. Econ. Adm. Stud. 12 (2), 3–19.

Özbebek, A., Canikli, S., Aytürk, Y., 2011. Does the Turkish stock market react to public announcements of major capital expenditures? Procedia-Social Behav. Sci. 24 (1), 928–934.

Ranaldo, A., 2008. Intraday market dynamics around public information disclosures. In: Lhabitant, F.-S., Gregoriou, G. (Eds.), Stock Market Liquidity. John Wiley and Sons, New Jersey, pp. 199–226 (Chapter 11).

Riordan, R., Storkenmaier, A., Wagener, M., Sarah Zhang, S., 2013. Public information arrival: Price discovery and liquidity in electronic limit order markets. J. Bank. Finance 37 (4), 1148–1159.

CHAPTER 19

Machine News and Volatility: The Dow Jones Industrial Average and the TRNA Real-Time High-Frequency Sentiment Series

David E. Allen[1], Michael J. McAleer[2], Abhay K. Singh[3]

[1]School of Mathematics and Statistics, University of Sydney, and School of Business, University of South Australia, Australia;
[2]Department of Quantitative Finance, College of Technology Management, National Tsing Hua University, Hsinchu, Taiwan, and Econometric Institute, Erasmus School of Economics, Erasmus University, Rotterdam, The Netherlands;
[3]School of Business, Edith Cowan University, Joondalup, WA, Australia

Contents

19.1 INTRODUCTION

There has been a revolution in the speed of news transmission during the twentieth century that began with wire services, whose use spans a period from around World War 1 to the 1940s, during which time the news agencies in the United States transmitted copy over telephone wires to teletypewriters in newspaper offices. In the late 1940s, things changed again with the introduction of Teletypesetter machines. These permitted the use of perforated paper tape, which was fed into typesetting, or linotype, machines, without human intervention, further reducing processing times. Newspapers subsequently switched from linotype to photocomposition in the late 1960s—1970s.

A more recent innovation has been the use of the Internet. Information is now transmitted by satellite service or the Internet, and newspapers reconstruct the information in their own format. News has always been the lifeblood of financial markets, and being the first to know provides a first mover advantage. However, some parties, such as corporate officers, are likely to be the "first in the know," and this has attracted the attention of

The Handbook of High Frequency Trading
ISBN 978-0-12-802205-4

market regulators over the years, who have attempted to ensure that investors face a "level playing field." For example, in the United States, sections 16(b) and 10(b) of the Securities Exchange Act of 1934 address insider trading.

There is also the issue that the information has to be pertinent and value relevant, and other investors also need to be convinced of its value. This brings us to consider Keyne's (1936) famous analogy between choosing investment stocks and a fictional newspaper beauty competition in which entrants are asked to choose from a set of six photographs of women that are the most beautiful. Those who picked the most popular face would then be eligible for a prize. "It is not a case of choosing those [faces] that, to the best of one's judgment, are really the prettiest, nor even those that average opinion genuinely thinks the prettiest. We have reached the third degree where we devote our intelligences to anticipating what average opinion expects the average opinion to be. And there are some, I believe, who practice the fourth, fifth and higher degrees." (Keynes (1936), Chapter 12, p. 100). It follows that, at any given moment in time, a security's price must be a weighted average of investor trading strategies.

Clearly, the information embodied in news items is one information source that has the potential to influence investor opinions. This chapter features an exploration of the impact of a machine-created news series drawn from Thomson Reuters News Analytics (TRNA) that could be termed news sentiment, and which is produced by the application of machine learning techniques to news items. The TRNA system can scan and analyze stories on thousands of companies in real time and translate the results into a series that can be used to help model and inform quantitative trading strategies. The system produces scores for news items on >25,000 equities and nearly 40 commodities and energy topics. We take this real-time high-frequency scoring system and transform it into a daily score for Dow Jones Industrial Average (DJIA) constituent company stocks and then use this series in our analyses.

The work is a companion piece to two other studies by Allen et al. (2013a,b). The first of these papers examines the influence of the Sentiment measure as a factor in pricing DJIA constituent company stocks in a Capital Asset Pricing Model (CAPM) context. The second paper uses these real-time scores aggregated into a DJIA market sentiment score to study the relationship between financial news sentiment scores and the DJIA return series using entropy-based measures. Both studies find that the sentiment scores have a significant information component, which in the former study is priced as a factor in an asset-pricing context. The current work further explores the influence of sentiment scores in the context of their impact on the Dow Jones 30 index's volatility.

The series we use are based on TRNA, which takes news items calibrated into positive, negative, or neutral values per news item, and are used to construct its Sentiment series. The key issue is the extent to which the series influences investors' investment strategies, which, in turn, influence the market and the evolution of stock prices. They are also used as an input to algorithmic trading techniques.

There has been attention recently on the role of market news sentiment, in particular, machine-driven sentiment signals, and their implications for financial market processes. The research on this topic argues that news items from different sources influence investor sentiment, which feeds into asset prices, asset price volatility, and risk (Tetlock, 2007; Tetlock et al., 2008; Da et al., 2011; Barber and Odean, 2008; diBartolomeo and Warrick, 2005; Mitra, Mitra and diBartolomeo, 2009; Dzielinski et al., 2011). The diversification benefits of the information impounded in news sentiment scores provided by RavenPack have been demonstrated by Cahan et al. (2009) and Hafez and Xie (2012), who examined its benefits in the context of popular asset pricing models.

Another important research question is the extent to which the availability of these machine-driven series contributes to market information and the evolution of security prices. Baker and Wurgler (2006) demonstrated a link between investor sentiment and stock returns. Recent work by Hafez and Xie (2012) examines the effect of investor's sentiment using news-based sentiment, generated from the RavenPack Sentiment Index as a proxy for market sentiment in a multifactor model. They report a strong impact of market sentiment on stock price predictability over six- and 12-month time horizons. Allen, McAleer and Singh (2013a) demonstrate, in an analysis of Dow Jones Index constituent companies, that a Sentiment series can make up a distinct factor that is priced in a CAPM framework.

The issue of the news content of sentiment scores for volatility behavior is the central focus of this study. We address it by analyzing the relationship between a commercially available real-time high-frequency company series, the TRNA series, aggregate it to a daily level across the DJIA company stocks, and assess its impact on the volatility behavior of a major index, the DJIA. These large US stocks are likely to be among the most heavily traded and analyzed securities in the world. Therefore, the issue of the relevance of these individual company news feeds to the volatility behavior of this major index is an important one.

We take the real-time high-frequency TRNA news series for the DJIA constituent stocks and aggregate them into a daily time series. This facilitates an analysis of the relationship between the two daily sets of series, TRNA news sentiment on the one hand and the DJIA volatility behavior on the other. We analyze the relationship between the two series using three standard univariate volatility models, namely, GARCH (Generalized Autoregressive Conditional Heteroscedastic)(1,1), GJR (Glosten, Jagganathan and Rundle (1993))(1,1), and EGARCH (Exponential Generalized Autoregressive Conditional Heteroscedasctic)(1,1).

The extent to which these news series have relevant information for volatility behavior is germane for both investors and market regulators. If access to these particular information feeds provides a trading advantage, then the market is no longer a level playing field for all investors. Institutions and algorithmic traders with access to these analytics will have an advantage. However, this chapter does not address the issue of the timing of access to news items, but the more general question of the degree to which these sentiment-based series contain "relevant information," as revealed by an analysis of the volatility of the DJIA and its links to a daily average of the TRNA series. The chapter is a component of three separate analyses of this relationship. Allen, McAleer and Singh (2013a) explore the links between the series in an asset-pricing framework, while Allen, McAleer and Singh (2013b) explore the informational relationship between the two series using entropy-based measures.

This chapter is organized as follows: Section 19.1 provides an introduction. Section 19.2 features an introduction to sentiment analysis and an overview of the TRNA data set, and introduces the research methods adopted. Section 19.3 discusses the major results, and Section 19.4 draws some conclusions.

19.2 RESEARCH METHODS AND DATA

19.2.1 News Sentiment

In this chapter, we examine the sentiment scores provided by TRNA as a single information vector that is added to the mean and variance equations for three commonly used volatility models, GARCH(1,1), GJR(1,1), and EGARCH(1,1), as applied to the volatility behavior of the DJIA. We use daily DJIA market sentiment scores constructed from high-frequency sentiment scores for the various stocks in DJIA. The empirical analysis includes data from the Global Financial Crisis and other periods of market turbulence to assess the effect of financial news sentiment on stock prices in both normal and extreme market conditions. The relationship between stock price movements and news sentiment has recently been examined by Tetlock (2007), Barber and Odean (2008), Mitra, Mitra and diBartolomeo (2009), Leinweber and Sisk (2012), Sinha (2011), and Huynh and Smith (2013).

The scale of competing news sources in the electronic media means that there is scope for the commercial use of sources of preprocessed news. Vendors such as TRNA and RavenPack produce sentiment scores to provide direct indicators to traders and other financial practitioners of changes in news sentiment. They use text-mining tools to electronically analyze available textual news items. The analytics engines of these sources apply pattern recognition and identification methods to analyze words and their patterns, and the novelty and relevance of the news items for a particular industry or sector. These news items are converted into quantifiable sentiment scores.

We use sentiment indicators provided by TRNA in our empirical analysis. Thomson Reuters was a pioneer in the implementation of a sophisticated text-mining algorithm as an addition to its company and industry-specific news database, starting from January 2003, which resulted in the present TRNA data set. The TRNA data guide states that: "Powered by a unique processing system the Thomson Reuters News Analytics system provides real-time numerical insight into the events in the news, in a format that can be directly consumed by algorithmic trading systems."

The data set was available for various stocks and commodities until October 2012. The TRNA sentiment scores are produced from text-mining news items at a sentence level, which takes into account the context of a particular news item. This kind of news analytics makes the resulting scores more usable as they are mostly relevant to the particular company or sector. Every news item in the TRNA engine is assigned an exact time stamp, and a list of companies and topics it mentions. A total of 89 broad fields are reported in the TRNA data set, which are broadly divided into the following five main categories:

1. Relevance: A numerical measure of how relevant the news item is to the asset.
2. Sentiment: A measure of the inherent sentiment of the news item, quantifying it as either negative (-1), positive (1), or neutral (0).
3. Novelty: A measure defining how new the news item is; in other words, whether it reports a news item that is related to some previous news stories.
4. Volume: Counts of news items related to the particular asset.
5. Headline Classification: Specific analysis of the headline.

Figure 19.1 shows a snapshot of the headline text as reported in BCAST_REF field of the TRNA database for General Motors during the year 2007. These are not the sentences that are analyzed by TRNA to produce sentiment scores, but are the headlines for the news item used to generate the TRNA sentiment and other relevant scores.

Figure 19.2 provides another example featuring the Australian company BHP Billiton, which is reported in TRNA as having generated more than 3000 news items in the year 2011. Figure 19.2 shows the sentiment scores $(-1$ to $+1)$ for BHP Billiton during the month of January 2011, where the red line is the moving average of the scores.

Similar to BHP, there are various news stories reported per day for the various DJIA traded stocks. These news stories result in sentiment scores that are positive, negative, or neutral for that particular stock. Figure 19.3 gives a snapshot of the sentiment scores for the DJIA traded stocks during the year 2007. The bar chart of Figure 19.3 shows that the most sentiment scores generated during the year 2007, which marked the beginning of the period of Global Financial Crisis (GFC), were for the Citibank group (C.N), General Motors (GM.N), General Electric (GE.N), and J. P Morgan (JPM.N). This is a reflection of the market sentiment during the GFC period, as these financial institutions were among the most affected during the GFC.

Figure 19.4 shows the number of positive, negative, or neutral sentiment scores stacked against each other in 2007. It is evident that the number of negative and neutral sentiment news was exceeded by the number of positive sentiments for the majority of stocks, as it was only later in the year that the GFC really began to impact. However, Bank of America (BA.N), Citibank (C.N), General Motors (GM.N), Walmart (WMT.N), and Exxon (XOM.N) have a preponderance of negative sentiment during the year.

Applications of TRNA news data sets in financial research have grown recently. Dzielinski (2012), Groß-Kulßman and Hautsch (2011), Smales (2013), Huynh and Smith

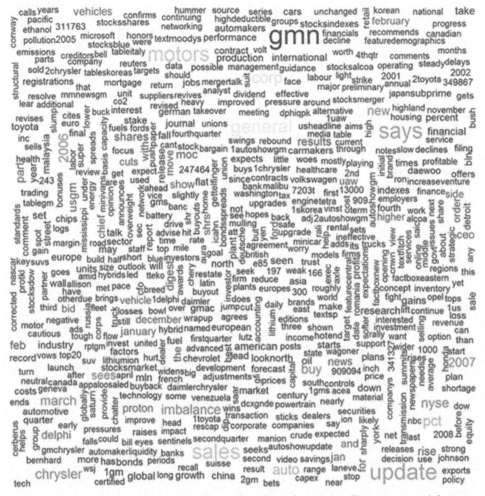

Figure 19.1 Thomson Reuters News Analytics snapshot of news headlines generated for general motors in the year 2007.

(2013), Borovkova and Mahakena (2013). Storkenmaier et al. (2012), and Sinha (2011) have explored the usefulness of the TRNA data set in stock markets and in commodity markets. In this chapter, we use the TRNA data set to analyze the effect of news sentiment on the DJIA daily volatility behavior. We construct daily sentiment index score time series for the empirical exercise based on the high-frequency scores reported by TRNA.

The empirical analysis in this chapter analyzes the effect of news sentiment on stock prices of the DJIA by considering the daily DJIA market sentiment as an additional exogenous factor in volatility models of the DJIA. We construct daily sentiment scores for the DJIA market by accumulating high-frequency sentiment scores of the DJIA

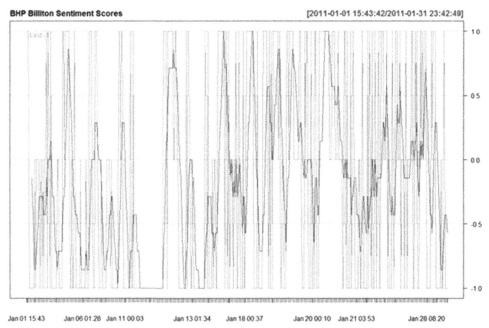

Figure 19.2 Thomson Reuters News Analytics sentiment scores generated for BHP Billiton in January 2011.

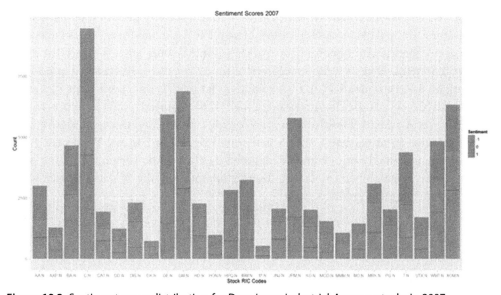

Figure 19.3 Sentiment score distribution for Dow Jones Industrial Average stocks in 2007.

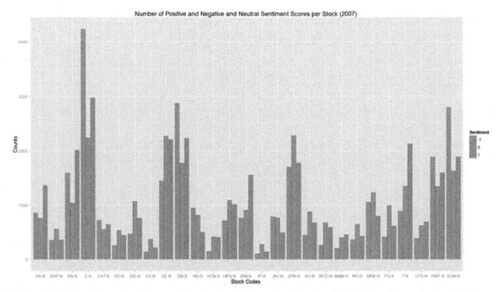

Figure 19.4 Positive, negative, and neutral sentiment score distribution for Dow Jones Industrial Average stocks in 2007.

constituents obtained from the TRNA data set. We use data from January 2007 to October 2012 to analyze the sensitivity of the DJIA daily volatility to the daily market sentiment scores. The daily stock prices for all the DJIA traded stocks are obtained from the Thomson Tick History database for the same time period.

The TRNA provides high-frequency sentiment scores calculated for each news item reported for various stocks and commodities. These TRNA scores for the stocks traded in DJIA can be aggregated to obtain a daily market sentiment score series for the DJIA stock index components. A news item, s_t, received at time t for a stock is classified as positive $(+1)$, negative (-1), or neutral (0). $I_{s_t}^+$ is a positive classifier (1) for a news item, s_t, and $I_{s_t}^-$ is the negative (-1) classifier for a news item, s_t. TRNA reported sentiment scores have a probability level associated with them, $prob_{s_t}^+$, $prob_{s_t}^-$, $prob_{s_t}^0$ for positive, negative, and neutral sentiments, respectively, which is reported by TRNA in the Sentiment field. Based on the probability of occurrence, denoted by P_{s_t} for a news item, s_t, all the daily sentiments can be combined to obtain a daily sentiment indicator. We use the following formula to obtain the combined score:

$$S = \frac{\sum_{q=t-1}^{t-Q} I_{s_q}^+ P_{s_q} - \sum_{q=t-1}^{t-Q} I_{s_q}^- P_{s_q}}{n_{prob_{s_q}^+} + n_{prob_{s_q}^-} + n_{prob_{s_q}^0}} \tag{19.1}$$

The time periods considered are $t - Q,\ldots,t - 1$, which covers all the news stories (and respective scores) for a 24-h period.

19.2.2 Our Sample Characteristics and Preliminary Analysis

Table 19.1 lists the various stocks traded in DJIA, along with their Reuters Instrument Code (RIC) and time periods. We use the TRNA sentiment scores related to these stocks to obtain the aggregate daily sentiment for the market. The aggregated daily sentiment score, S, represents the combined score of the sentiment scores reported for the stocks on a particular date. We construct daily sentiment scores for the DJIA market by accumulating high-frequency sentiment scores of the DJIA constituents obtained from the TRNA data set. We use data from January 2006 to October 2012 to examine the sensitivity of the daily DJIA volatility to the daily market sentiment scores. The daily stock prices for all the DJIA traded stocks are obtained from the Thomson Tick History database for the same time period, and are provided by the Securities Industry Research Center of the Asia Pacific.

Table 19.1 Dow Jones Industrial Average stocks with Thomson Tick History Reuters Instrument Codes (RICs)

RIC Code	Stocks	First Date	Last Date
.DJI	Dow Jones INDU AVERAGE	1-Jan-96	17-Mar-13
AA.N	ALCOA INC	2-Jan-96	18-Mar-13
GE.N	GENERAL ELEC CO	2-Jan-96	18-Mar-13
JNJ.N	JOHNSON&JOHNSON	2-Jan-96	18-Mar-13
MSFT.OQ	MICROSOFT CP	20-Jul-02	18-Mar-13
AXP.N	AMER EXPRESS CO	2-Jan-96	18-Mar-13
GM.N	GENERAL MOTORS	3-Jan-96	18-Mar-13
GMGMQ.PK	GENERAL MOTORS	2-Jun-09	15-Aug-09
JPM.N	JPMORGAN CHASE	1-Jan-96	18-Mar-13
PG.N	PROCTER & GAMBLE	2-Jan-96	18-Mar-13
BA.N	BOEING CO	2-Jan-96	18-Mar-13
HD.N	HOME DEPOT INC	2-Jan-96	18-Mar-13
KO.N	COCA-COLA CO	2-Jan-96	18-Mar-13
SBC.N	SBC COMMS	2-Jan-96	31-Dec-05
T.N	AT&T	3-Jan-96	18-Mar-13
C.N	CITIGROUP	2-Jan-96	18-Mar-13
HON.N	HONEYWELL INTL	2-Jan-96	18-Mar-13
XOM.N	EXXON MOBIL	1-Dec-99	18-Mar-13
MCDw.N	MCDONLDS CORP	6-Oct-06	4-Nov-06
MCD.N	MCDONALD'S CORP	1-Jan-96	18-Mar-13
EK.N	EASTMAN KODAK	1-Jan-96	18-Feb-12
EKDKQ.PK	EASTMAN KODAK	19-Jan-12	18-Mar-13
IP.N	INTNL PAPER CO	2-Jan-96	18-Mar-13
CAT.N	CATERPILLAR INC	2-Jan-96	18-Mar-13
HPQ.N	HEWLETT-PACKARD	4-May-02	18-Mar-13
MMM_w.N	3M COMPANY WI	18-Sep-03	27-Oct-03

Continued

Table 19.1 Dow Jones Industrial Average stocks with Thomson Tick History Reuters Instrument Codes (RICs)—cont'd

RIC Code	Stocks	First Date	Last Date
MMM.N	MINNESOTA MINIhNG	1-Jan-96	18-Mar-13
UTX.N	UNITED TECH CP	2-Jan-96	18-Mar-13
DD.N	DU PONT CO	2-Jan-96	18-Mar-13
IBM.N	INTL BUS MACHINE	2-Jan-96	18-Mar-13
MO.N	ALTRIA GROUP	2-Jan-96	18-Mar-13
WMT.N	WAL-MART STORES	2-Jan-96	18-Mar-13
DIS.N	WALT DISNEY CO	2-Jan-96	18-Mar-13
INTC.OQ	INTEL CORP	20-Jul-02	18-Mar-13
MRK.N	MERCK & CO	2-Jan-96	18-Mar-13

The stocks with insufficient data are removed from the analysis, and the stock prices for EK.N and EKDKQ.PK are combined to obtain a uniform time series.

The summary statistics in Table 19.2 show that the sample of Sentiment scores for the full sample is predominantly negative, with a mean of −0.034532. The minimum score is −0.52787, and the maximum score is 0.28564. It appears that negative news has greater prominence than positive news on the scale running from +1 to −1. The Hurst exponent for the Sentiment score, with a value of 0.925828, suggests that there is a long memory or persistence in the scores, which makes intuitive sense, given that items of news may take several days to unfold, as greater scrutiny of a story leads to greater disclosure of information. When an event is classified as positive or negative, this will tend to occupy the media for several days, and is consistent with trending behavior. The Hurst exponent for DJIA is 0.557638, which suggests that the DJIA shows much less tendency to display memory and, as might be expected, behaves more like a random walk. The significant Jarque-Bera Lagrange multiplier test statistics for both series suggest that both are non-Gaussian.

Table 19.2 Summary statistics, Dow Jones Industrial Average (DJIA) returns, and sentiment scores January 4, 2006, to October 31, 2012

	DJIA return (%)	Sentiment score	Sentiment squared	Sentiment absolute	Sentiment difference
Min	−8.2005	−0.52787	5.38240e-010	2.32000e-005	−0.452678
Median	0.053410	−0.031140	0.00623149	0.0789397	−0.00349615
Mean	0.013971	−0.034532	0.0148177	0.0960405	3.70853e-005
Max	10.5083	0.28564	5.38240e-010	0.527867	0.534308
Standard Deviation	1.3640	0.116762	0.0222546	0.0748150	0.125985
Hurst Exponent	0.557638	0.925828	0.861467	0.853927	0.178098
J-B test	5320.84 (0.00)	18.2197 (0.00)	27737.1(0.00)	489.515(0.00)	14.8959(0.00)

NB: Probabilities in parentheses.

We also used a number of variants of the sentiment score, squared score, absolute value of the score, and the first difference to explore which might better capture the influence of market sentiment scores. The plots of the various series are shown in Figures 19.5 and 19.6. Summary statistics for these series are presented in Table 19.2. The variants of the sentiment score have quite similar values for their Hurst exponent. All suggest trending behavior, apart from the first differences of sentiment scores, which have a low Hurst exponent of 0.178, suggesting a tendency to display reversals. The Jarque-Bera Lagrange multiplier tests strongly reject the null hypothesis of a normal distribution for all series.

19.2.2.1 Volatility Models Utilized

Engle (1982) developed the Autoregressive Conditional Heteroskedasticity (ARCH) model that incorporates all past error terms. It was generalized to GARCH by Bollerslev (1986) to include lagged conditional volatility. In other words, GARCH predicts that the best indicator of future variance is the weighted average of long-run variance, the pre-dicted variance for the current period, and any new information in this period, as captured by the squared return shocks (Engle, 2001).

The framework is developed as follows: consider a time series $y_t = E_{t-1}(y_t) + \varepsilon_t$, where $E_{t-1}(y_t)$ is the conditional expectation of y_t at time $t-1$ and ε_t is the error term. The GARCH model has the following specification:

$$\varepsilon_t = \sqrt{h_t}\eta_t, \quad \eta_t \sim N(0,1) \tag{19.2}$$

$$h_t = \omega + \sum_{j=1}^{p} \alpha_j \varepsilon_{t-j}^2 + \sum_{j=1}^{q} \beta_j h_{t-j} \tag{19.3}$$

in which $\omega > 0$, $\alpha_j \geq 0$ and $\beta_j \geq 0$ are sufficient conditions to ensure a positive conditional variance, $h_t \geq 0$. The ARCH effect is captured by the parameter α_j, which represents the short-run persistence of shocks to returns. β_j captures the GARCH effect, and $\alpha_j + \beta_j$ measures the persistence of the impact of shocks to returns to long-run persistence. A GARCH(1,1) process is weakly stationary if $\alpha_1 + \beta_1 \leq 1$. We explore the impact of the various sentiment series on both the conditional mean and conditional variance equations.

Engle (2001), Nelson (1991), McAleer (2005), and Harris et al. (2007) outline some of the disadvantages of the GARCH model as follows: GARCH can be computationally burdensome and can involve simultaneous estimation of a large number of parameters. The standard GARCH model tends to underestimate risk (when applied to Value at Risk, VaR), as the normality assumption of the standardized residual does not always hold with the behavior of financial returns. The specification of the conditional variance equation and the distribution used to construct the log likelihood may also be incorrect.

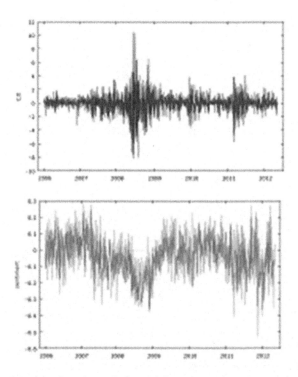

Figure 19.5 Basic series plots: Dow Jones Industrial Average and sentiment scores.

The basic symmetric model rules out, by assumption, the negative leverage relationship between current returns and future volatilities, despite empirical evidence to the contrary. GARCH assumes that the magnitude of excess returns determines future volatility, but not the sign (positive or negative returns), as it is a symmetric model. This is a significant problem as research by Nelson (1991) and Glosten et al. (1993) shows that asset returns and volatility do not react in the same way for negative information, or "bad news," as they do for positive information, or "good news," of equal magnitude.

An alternative asymmetric model is the Glosten, Jagannathan, and Runkle (GJR model, 1993), which is specified as

$$h_t = \omega + \sum_{j=1}^{r} \left(\alpha_j + \gamma_j I\left(\varepsilon_{t-j}^2\right) \right) \varepsilon_{t-j}^2 + \sum_{j=1}^{s} \beta_j h_{t-j} \tag{19.4}$$

where

$$I_{it} = \left\{ \begin{array}{ll} 0, & \varepsilon_{it} \geq 0 \\ 1, & \varepsilon_{it} < 0 \end{array} \right\}$$

and i_{it} is an indicator function that distinguishes between positive and negative shocks of equal magnitude. In this model, when there is only one lag, that is, when $r = s = 1$, the

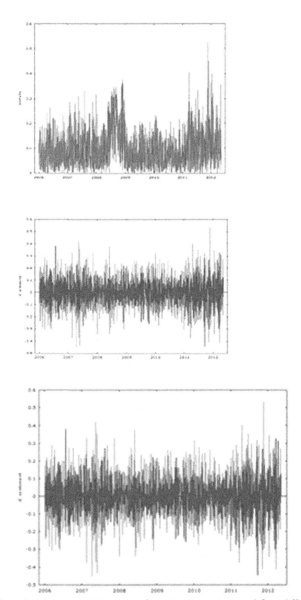

Figure 19.6 Absolute Sentiment series, squared sentiment series, and first differences of sentiment series.

sufficient conditions to ensure that the conditional variance is positive $(h_t > 0)$ are that $\omega > 0$, $\alpha_1 \geq 0$, $\alpha_1 + \gamma_1 \geq 0$, and $\beta_1 \geq 0$ where α_1 and $(\alpha_1 + \gamma_1)$ measure the short-run persistence of positive and negative shocks, respectively, and the given conditions apply for a GJR(1,1) model.

In the EGARCH model, the conditional variance h_t is an asymmetric standardized function of the lagged disturbances, ϵ_{t-1}:

$$ln(h_t) = \omega + \sum_{j=1}^{p} \beta_j ln\left(h_{t-j}\right) + \sum_{i=1}^{g} \alpha_i \left| \frac{\epsilon_{t-1}}{\sqrt{h_{t-i}}} \right| + \sum_{k=1}^{r} \gamma_k \frac{\epsilon_{t-k}}{\sqrt{h_{t-k}}} \qquad (19.5)$$

The fact that the log of the conditional variance is used in Eqn (19.5) implies that the leverage effect may be exponential and guarantees that forecasts of the conditional variance will be nonnegative. The presence of asymmetric effects can be tested by the hypothesis that $\gamma_i = 0$, and the impact is asymmetric if $\gamma_i \neq 0$. A sufficient condition for the stationarity of the EGARCH(1,1) model is that $|\beta| < 1$.

In this chapter, we analyze the impact of the news series on volatility using these three standard variants of the GARCH model and four different measures of the sentiment index, namely, weighted sentiment scores, squared values of the sentiment score, absolute values of the sentiment score, and its first difference. The results of our analysis are shown in the next section. We explore the influence of the sentiment scores on both the conditional mean and conditional variance equations using the methods introduced in Eqns (19.2)−(19.5).

19.3 THE SIGNIFICANCE OF THE SENTIMENT SCORES IN THE GARCH ANALYSIS OF DJIA RETURN SERIES

We commence by estimating a standard GARCH(1,1) model, and augment both the conditional mean and conditional variance equations by adding a vector of the variants of the sentiment scores to assess whether they add information to the basic model. The results are shown in Table 19.3.

In Table 19.3, which represents a standard GARCH(1,1) model under normality, the sentiment series raw scores appear to work the best in that they have the smallest log likelihood value of the four sentiment measures, and the coefficient is highly significant in both the conditional mean and conditional variance equations. Sentiment squared performs the next best, but it is not significant in the conditional variance equation, though it is highly significant in the conditional mean equation. The least effective sentiment metric is the difference of the sentiment scores, which is insignificant in both the conditional mean and conditional variance equations for the GARCH(1,1) model.

We also estimated the GJR model with the student t distribution and report estimates with robust standard errors. The results are shown in Table 19.4.

The variants of the Sentiment series score are significant in all four equations in the conditional mean return specification. They are less influential in the conditional variance equation, but the Sentiment score and the Sentiment in differences are significant in their respective conditional variance equations. The log likelihood statistic again suggests that the most useful form of the Sentiment score is the weighted average.

The final set of GARCH models feature Nelson's (1991) EGARCH model. The results are shown in Table 19.5, and feature a skewed t distribution and robust standard

Table 19.3 GARCH(1,1) model of Dow Jones Industrial Average, with mean and variance equations augmented by sentiment scores

Variable	Sentiment	Sentiment squared	Sentiment absolute value	Sentiment difference
Constant ω	6.9508598	12.0447668	14.3688799	6.9319048
	(0.00)	(0.00)	(0.00)	(0.00)
Sentiment Φ_1	1.7808631	−4.4281874	−0.8853287	−0.0007089
	(0.00)	(0.00)	(0.01)	(0.23)
Constant	268.0133312	156.7162601	101.0827012	192.2448593
	(0.0))	(0.00)	(0.29)	(0.00)
α	0.1088096	0.1041336	0.1033907	0.1043631
	(0.00)	(0.00)	(0.00)	(0.00)
β_1	0.8678536	0.8833507	0.8837965	0.8825165
	(0.00)	(0.00)	(0.00)	(0.00)
Sentiment β_2	−17.4582744	27.9358986	10.5553179	0.0435489
	(0.03)	(0.51)	(0.35)	(0.37)
Log likelihood	−9965.6178	−10,004.9911	−10,008.2604	−10,011.2447

Note: probabilities in parentheses.

errors. The various Sentiment score measures are always highly significant in the conditional mean equation and the first two Sentiment measures, the weighted average score and the square of the score, are highly significant in the conditional variance equation, while the other two Sentiment metrics are significant at the 10% level. The log likelihood statistic suggests that the weighted average Sentiment score is the most informative for the EGARCH specification.

Table 19.4 Glosten, Jagannathan, and Runkle(1,1) model of Dow Jones Industrial Average, with mean and variance equations augmented by sentiment scores

Variable	Sentiment	Sentiment squared	Sentiment absolute	Sentiment difference
Conditional mean equation				
Constant ω	0.0448461 (0.01)	0.0701814 (0.00)	0.0871242 (0.00)	0.0349153 (0.06)
Sentiment	1.57960 (0.00)	3.96032 (0.00)	0.728568 (0.02)	1.16198 (0.00)
Conditional variance equation				
Constant	0.0141329 (0.01)	0.00786521 (0.15)	0.00393231 (0.67)	0.0125011 (0.00)
Sentiment	0.171409 (0.00)	0.700363 (0.13)	0.134351 (0.24)	0.354530 (0.05)
Alpha α	0.0468063 (0.00)	0.0500625 (0.00)	0.0493889 (0.00)	0.0471467 (0.00)
Gamma γ	1.01626 (0.00)	1.00935 (0.00)	1.00936 (0.00)	1.00957 (0.00)
Beta β	0.898544 (0.00)	0.892031 (0.00)	0.893386 (0.00)	0.897946 (0.00)
Likelihood	−2264.05965	−2296.52548	−2300.39130	−2269.12295

Note: probabilities in parentheses.

Table 19.5 EGARCH model of Dow Jones Industrial Average, with mean and variance equations augmented by sentiment scores

Variable	Sentiment	Sentiment squared	Sentiment absolute	Sentiment difference
Conditional mean equation				
Constant ω	0.0128581 (0.46)	0.0676681 (0.00)	0.0902486 (0.00)	0.0298678 (0.00)
Sentiment	1.65606 (0.00)	4.41787 (0.00)	0.838581 (0.00)	1.14923 (0.00)
Conditional variance equation				
Constant	0.107452 (0.00)	0.110305 (0.00)	0.129897 (0.00)	0.0978228 (0.00)
Sentiment	0.433137 (0.00)	0.936212 (0.02)	0.238725 (0.09)	0.742513 (0.07)
Alpha α	0.128429 (0.00)	0.129616 (0.00)	0.129897 (0.00)	0.126812 (0.00)
Gamma γ	0.191717 (0.00)	0.195877 (0.00)	0.194817 (0.00)	0.179412 (0.00)
Beta β	0.966777 (0.00)	0.973785 (0.00)	0.974168 (0.00)	0.981003 (0.00)
Likelihood	−2245.48488	−2290.97489	−2295.05655	−2263.91824

Note: probabilities in parentheses.

19.4 CONCLUSION

In this chapter, we have analyzed the relationship between the TRNA news series for the DJIA constituent stocks after having aggregated them into a daily average Sentiment score time series using all the constituent companies in the DJIA. This was then used in an analysis of the relationship between the two daily sets of series, TRNA news sentiment on the one hand, and DJIA returns on the other. We analyzed the relationship between the two series using the basic GARCH, GJR, and EGARCH models. The conditional mean and conditional variance equations are augmented for each model by including one of the four variants of the sentiment score.

The results for all three models suggested that the weighted average Sentiment score was the most informative in all cases, with the lowest log likelihood score. Nevertheless, all variants of the score contained useful information about factors impacting on the volatility of the DJIA. These findings support our previous work on the topic (Allen et al., 2013a,b), which suggested the usefulness of the sentiment series in an asset-pricing context and the informativeness of the series, as revealed by entropy-based metrics.

ACKNOWLEDGMENTS

The authors gratefully acknowledge the support of the QUANTVALLEY/FdR: "Quantitative Management Initiative," and SIRCA for providing the TRNA data sets. The authors acknowledge the financial support of the Australian Research Council. The second author is also grateful for the financial support of the National Science Council, Taiwan.

REFERENCES

Allen, D.E., McAleer, M.J., Singh, A.K., 2013a. Daily Market News Sentiment and Stock Prices. Working Paper Commissioned by QUANTVALLEY/FdR: "Quantitative Management Initiative". Available at. http://www.qminitiative.org/quantitative-management-initiative.html.

Allen, D.E., McAleer, M.J., Singh, A.K., 2013b. An Entropy Based Analysis of the Relationship between the DOW JONES Index and the TRNA Sentiment Series. Working Paper Commissioned by QUANT-VALLEY/FdR: "Quantitative Management Initiative". Available at. http://www.qminitiative.org/quantitative-management-initiative.html.

Baker, M., Wurgler, J., 2006. Investor sentiment and the cross-section of stock returns. J. Finance 61 (4), 1645—1680.

Barber, B.M., Odean, T., 2008. All that glitters: the effect of attention and news on the buying behavior of individual and institutional investors. Rev. Financial Stud. 21 (2), 785—818.

Bollerslev, T., 1986. Generalized autoregressive conditional heteroscedasticity. J. Econ. 31 (3), 307—327.

Borovkova, S., Mahakena, D., 2013. News, Volatility and Jumps: The Case of Natural Gas Futures. Working Paper. Retrieved From: http://ssrncom/abstract=2334226.

Cahan, R., Jussa, J., Luo, Y., 2009. Breaking News: How to Use News Sentiment to Pick Stocks (MacQuarie Research Report, Sydney, Australia).

Da, Z.H.I., Engelberg, J., Gao, P., 2011. In search of attention. J. Finance 66 (5), 1461—1499.

diBartolomeo, D., Warrick, S., 2005. Making covariance based portfolio risk models sensitive to the rate at which markets react to new information. In: Knight, J., Satchell, S. (Eds.), Linear Factor Models. Elsevier, Burlington, MA.

Dzielinski, M., 2012. Which News Resolves Asymmetric Information? Working Paper NCCR, University of Zurich.

Dzielinski, M., Rieger, M.O., Talpsepp, T., 2011. Volatility Asymmetry, News, and Private Investors. The Handbook of News Analytics in Finance (pp. 255—270). John Wiley and Sons, Hoboken, NJ.

Engle, R.F., 1982. Autoregressive conditional heteroskedasticity with estimates of the variance of United Kingdom inflation. Econometrica 50 (4), 987—1007.

Engle, R.F., 2001. GARCH 101: an introduction to the use of Arch/Garch models in applied econometrics. J. Econ. Perspect. 15 (4), 157—168.

Glosten, L.R., Jagannathan, R., Runkle, D., 1993. On the relation between the expected value and the volatility of the nominal excess return on stocks. J. Finance 48 (5), 1779—1801.

Groß-Klußmann, A., Hautsch, N., 2011. When machines read the news: using automated text analytics to quantify high frequency news-implied market reactions. J. Empir. Finance 18 (2), 321—340.

Hafez, P., Xie, J., 2012. Factoring Sentiment Risk into Quant Models. RavenPack International S.L.

Harris, R.D.F., Stoja, E., Tucker, J., 2007. A simplified approach to modelling the co-movement of asset returns. J. Futur. Mark. 27 (6), 575—598.

Huynh, T.D., Smith, D.R., 2013. News Sentiment and Momentum (FIRN Research Paper).

Keynes, J.M., 1936. The General Theory of Employment, Interest and Money. Palgrave Macmillan, Basingstoke, UK.

Leinweber, D., Sisk, J., 2012. Relating News Analytics to Stock Returns. The Handbook of News Analytics in Finance (pp. 147—172). John Wiley and Sons, Hoboken, NJ.

McAleer, M.J., 2005. Automated inference and learning in modelling financial volatility. Econ. Theory 21 (1), 232—261.

Mitra, L., Mitra, G., diBartolomeo, D., 2009. Equity portfolio risk (Volatility) estimation using market information and sentiment. Quant. Finance 9 (8), 887—895.

Nelson, D.B., 1991. Conditional heteroskedasticity in asset returns: a new approach. Econometrica 59 (2), 347—370.

Sinha, N., 2011. Underreaction to News in the US Stock Market. Working Paper. Retrieved From: http://ssrncom/abstract=1572614.

Smales, L.A., 2013. News Sentiment in the Gold Futures Market. Working Paper. Curtin University of Technology.

Storkenmaier, A., Wagener, M., Weinhardt, C., 2012. Public information in fragmented markets. Financial Mark. Portfolio Manag. 26 (2), 179–215.

Tetlock, P.C., 2007. Giving content to investor sentiment: the role of media in the stock market. J. Finance 62 (3), 1139–1167.

Tetlock, P.C., Macskassy, S.A., Saar-Tsechansky, M., 2008. More than words: quantifying language to measure firms' fundamentals. J. Finance 63 (3), 1427–1467.

PART 5

Impact of Volatility

CHAPTER 20

High-Frequency Technical Trading: Insights for Practitioners

Camillo Lento[1], Nikola Gradojevic[2]
[1]Faculty of Business Administration, Lakehead University, Thunder Bay, ON, Canada; [2]Lille Catholic University, IÉSEG School of Management, Lille, France

Contents

20.1 INTRODUCTION

Technical analysis has a rich and long history. Since its beginnings in the 1700s, many different trading rules have emerged. Moving-average crossover (MACO) rules, filter rules (FRs), trading range breakout rules (TRBO), and Bollinger Bands (BBs) are all examples of the many different types of trading rules (Murphy, 2000). Nowadays, technical analysis is widely used in practice by foreign exchange traders (Menkhoff and Taylor, 2007) and equity fund managers (Menkhoff, 2010).

One of the most important considerations for the technical analyst is in regard to the frequency of the data used to calculate trading rules. Historically, daily data have been the most popular frequency. This is likely due to data availability and the fact that daily data can lead to trading rules being generated with closing prices and executed the following day. Investors now have more and more access to real-time data. These high-frequency data provide more options for the calculation of technical trading rules. Technical trading rules can be calculated with hourly, minute-by-minute, or even millisecond sampled data. The increased use of high-frequency trading has been said to have many negative results, such as the "flash crash" that occurred on May 6, 2010.

The literature on technical trading rules calculated with high-frequency data (or, high-frequency technical trading, "HFTT") is still emerging. Recent research suggests that high-frequency trading can have a positive impact on technical analysis (Manahov et al., 2014). The performance of trading rules at high frequencies has also been shown

The Handbook of High Frequency Trading
ISBN 978-0-12-802205-4

to be related to the speed at which trade is triggered. A delay of as little as 200 ms can negatively impact performance (Scholtus and van Dijk, 2012). For instance, Chaboud et al. (2014) show that computers have an executional advantage over humans in reacting to arbitrage opportunities.

This study has two purposes. The first is to investigate the profitability of HFTT across different market regimes. Specifically, we investigate the profitability of HFTT during a market that is trending upward with lower volatility (2013) and a market that is trending sideways with higher volatility (2011). The second purpose is to test whether VIX (Chicago Board Options Exchange Market Volatility Index) data are related to additional profits from technical trading rules calculated at high frequencies. Kozyra and Lento (2011) calculated technical trading rules with the VIX and buy-and-sold the S&P 500 Index with daily data, and revealed that excess profits could be earned. That is, calculating the buy-and-sell technical trading signals for the S&P 500 Index with VIX data results in improved profitability over calculating the buy-and-sell signals with the S&P 500 Index data. In the same vein, Kho (1996) finds that periods of higher (lower) technical trading returns correspond to high (low) risk premia and volatility. However, Reitz (2006) argues that the information content of a technical trading signal is low when high exchange rate volatility disturbs inference. Gradojevic and Gençay (2013) document that higher volatility is associated with lower profits from pure technical trading strategies in the foreign exchange market, but greater profits from fuzzy technical trading strategies. The current study will investigate the relationship between volatility and HFTT profitability at the 5-min frequency.

The results reveal that technical trading rules are more profitable during periods of high volatility with no definitive upward trend (i.e., in 2011) where nine of the 12 HFTT variants generated profits (before transaction costs). Technical trading rules were not able to generate any returns in excess of the buy-and-hold strategy during the steady upward, lower volatility market of 2013. Unlike with data at the daily frequency (Kozyra and Lento, 2011), technical trading rules calculated with VIX data at high frequencies did not result in any excess profits. Technical trading rules are shown to be more profitable at high frequencies when calculated with the S&P 500 Index data.

There are some other interesting observations that emerge from the results. First, the FR generated very few trading signals with the 1%, 2%, and 5% parameters. Future researchers are encouraged to investigate smaller parameter values that would be more ideal for high-frequency trading rules. Second is that aside from the FRs, the remaining technical trading rules generated a significantly large number of trading signals during a calendar year. Accordingly, transaction costs become of utmost importance. Our results did not include transaction costs due to the highly diverse and unknown nature of the true transaction cost of high-frequency trading; however, the sheer number of trades generated in a single year reveal that transaction costs can have a significant impact on the profitability of high-frequency trading rules.

The remainder of this chapter is organized as follows: Section 20.2 presents the trading rule methodology, Section 20.3 discusses data sets, Section 20.4 analyzes the results, and Section 20.5 provides a summary and the conclusion.

20.2 THE TRADING RULE METHODOLOGY

This section discusses the trading rule methodology as follows: (1) the first subsection presents a discussion of the trading rules tested in this study, along with a detailed discussion of their computations; and (2) the second subsection discusses the methodology used to calculate the profits from the trading rules.

20.2.1 Trading Rule Definitions

This study tests three variants of four technical trading rules. The four rules tested are the MACO, FR, TRBO, and BB. The MACO, BB, and TRBO were selected in order to mitigate the potential biases that can arise from identifying and testing patterns in security returns in the same data set. These are the same common trading rules tested in the seminal work of Brock et al. (1992). Selecting the same trading rules as a seminal, past study reduces the possibility of data snooping as the data sets are not searched for successful trading rules ex post.

The BB strategy has been selected because even though it is a very popular trading model, it has not been tested significantly in the literature, especially in the high-frequency context. Therefore, the BB strategy provides additional insights into the profitability of technical trading strategies at high frequencies. The remainder of this section defines the four trading rules utilized in this study. A more detailed definition of each of these trading rules can be found in Lento (2007) and Lento et al. (2007).

The MACO rule compares a short moving average to a long moving average. The buy-and-sell trading signals generated by the MACO can be models as follows:

Equation 1—MACO Buy Signal

$$\frac{\sum_{s=1}^{S} R_{s,t}}{S} > \frac{\sum_{l=1}^{L} R_{l,t-1}}{L}$$

Equation 2—MACO Sell Signal

$$\frac{\sum_{s=1}^{S} R_{s,t}}{S} < \frac{\sum_{l=1}^{L} R_{l,t-1}}{L}$$

where $R_{s,t}$ is the log return for any given short period of S periods (1 or 5 periods), and $R_{l,t-1}$ is the log return over any given long period of L periods (50, 150, or 200 periods). Note that the previous period's position is carried forward if the short and long moving average equal. The three MACO variants will be defined with the following short, long combinations: (1, 50), (1, 200), and (5, 150). These are the same combinations used in previous studies (e.g., Ratner and Leal, 1999; Lento, 2007), which reduce potential bias and increase comparability with past studies.

FR generates buy-and-sell signals as follows: (1) Buy when the price rises by f percent above the most recent trough; and (2) sell when the price falls f percent below its most recent peak. The filter size (f) is the parameter that defines an FR. This study tests the FR based on three parameters: 1 percent, 2 percent, and 5 percent. Again, these are the same combinations used in previous studies (e.g., Fama and Bloom, 1966; Lento, 2007).

TRBO generates a buy signal when the price breaks out above the resistance level (local maximum) and a sell signal when the price breaks below the support level (local minimum). The buy-and-sell signals from the TRBO are defined as follows:

Equation 3—TRBO Positions

$$Pos_{t+1} = Buy, \quad \text{if} \quad P_t > Max\ \{P_{t-1}, P_{t-2}, ..., P_{t-n}\},$$
$$Pos_{t+1} = Pos_t, \quad \text{if} \quad P_t > Min\ \{P_{t-1}, P_{t-2}, ..., P_{t-n}\}$$
$$\leq P_t \leq Max\ \{P_{t-1}, P_{t-2}, ..., P_{t-n}\},$$
$$Pos_{t+1} = Sell, \quad \text{if} \quad P_t < Min\ \{P_{t-1}, P_{t-2}, ..., P_{t-n}\},$$

where P_t is the stock price at time t.

The local maximum and minimum are measured based on 50, 150, and 200 periods. These are the same periods used in previous studies (e.g., Brock et al., 1992; Lento, 2007).

BBs are trading bands that are plotted two standard deviations above and below a 20-period moving average. When the market touches (or exceeds) one of the trading bands, the market is considered to be overextended (Murphy, 2000).

Modeling the BB trading rule requires two parameters: the 20-period moving average (MA20) and the standard deviation (σ) of the 20-period moving-average line (σ MA20). Buy-and-sell signals are calculated as follows:

Equation 4—BB Trading Rule Strategies

$$\text{Sell: Security Price} > MA_{20} + 2\sigma_{MA20}$$
$$\text{Buy: Security Price} < MA_{20} - 2\sigma_{MA20}$$

The traditional BB definition is tested along with two variants: 30-period moving average, $\pm 2\sigma$ and 20-period moving average, $\pm 1\sigma$. These variants are consistent with those in prior studies (see Lento et al., 2007 for a further discussion on these variants).

20.2.2 Trading Rule Profitability

The profitability of the trading rules is defined as the excess return from the trading signals over a naive buy-and-hold trading strategy. This relatively simple technique is used over a more complicated, nonlinear model in order to mitigate issues such as computational expensiveness, overfitting, data snooping, and difficulties interpreting the results

(White, 2006). The statistical significance of the result is tested by using the bootstrap approach developed by Levich and Thomas (1993).

In regard to the MACO, FR, TRBO, and BB calculations, an investor is assumed to be out of the market at the beginning of the time series. While out of the market, the investor is assumed to earn a notional interest rate (as the data set is not inflation adjusted).

An investor is assumed to be long in the market during the period following the generation of a buy signal. This same period time lag is used when a sell signal is generated. This is consistent with the literature and minimizes the measurement error due to nonsynchronous trading (Scholes and Williams, 1977). If an investor is long (out) of the market, and a buy (sell) signal is generated, the position is carried forward.

The returns generated from the trading rules are not adjusted for transaction costs due to the opaque and unknown nature of transaction costs for high-frequency traders.

20.3 DATA

This study utilizes high-frequency data for the S&P 500 Index and the VIX for 2013 and 2011. The data were obtained from Tick Data, and are at the 5-min frequency and results in 19,548 observations over the year of 2013, and 19,618 observations over the year of 2011. There are approximately 78 observations per trading day.

The years 2013 and 2011 were selected because they provide two macrolevel trends. The 2013 data present a steadily increasing upward trend with declining volatility. For example, the S&P 500 Index began the year at 1453 and ended the year at 1847 for a total increase of 27.1%, while the VIX declined to 14.03 from 15.3 for a total decline of 8.3%. Figure 20.1 presents a visual summary of the 2013 data in the form of a line graph.

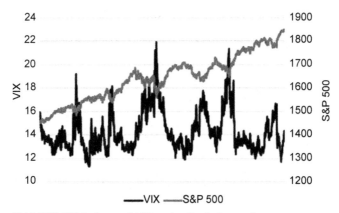

Figure 20.1 The 2013 S&P 500 Index and VIX at the 5-min interval.

Figure 20.2 The 2011 S&P 500 Index and VIX at the 5-min interval.

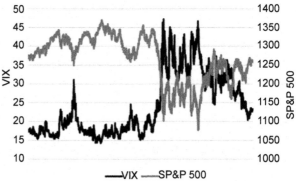

—VIX —SP&P 500

Table 20.1 Data set descriptions

Data set	n	Annual change	Average period change	Standard deviation	Skewness	Kurtosis
VIX, 2011	19,548	27.6%	0.0014%	0.8519%	0.75	−0.73
S&P 500, 2011	19,548	−0.4%	0.0000%	0.1515%	−0.65	−0.56
VIX, 2013	19,618	−8.3%	−0.0004%	0.6252%	1.23	1.45
S&P 500, 2013	19,618	27.1%	0.0012%	0.0736%	0.03	−0.85

The 2011 data present a sideways trend with increasing volatility. The S&P 500 Index began the year at 1268 and ended the year at 1257 for a total decline of 0.4%, while the VIX increased to 17.87 from 23.31 for a total decline of 27.6%. Figure 20.2 presents a visual summary of the 2011 data in the form of a line graph.

Summary descriptive statistics are provided in Table 20.1. Note that the average period change is the average holding period change across the all the 5-min frequencies.

Table 20.1 corroborates the line graphs above in that the VIX measure increased significantly in 2011, while it decreased in 2013. The standard deviation of the VIX average period change is also greater in 2011 than in 2013. In regard to the S&P 500 Index time series, the standard deviation of the average period change is also greater in 2011 than in 2013. Overall, Table 20.1 corroborates the conclusion that 2011 was a more volatile year than was 2013.

20.4 RESULTS

Table 20.2 presents the profits from the four technical trading rule variants before adjusting for transaction costs. Panel A presents the results from the 2011 data set, while Panel B presents the results from the 2013 data set. The results from the 2011 data set reveals that

Table 20.2 Profitability of high-frequency technical trading rules before transaction costs

Market index	MA crossover rule short (periods)/long (periods)			Filter rule (in %)			Trading range breakout (periods of local max/min)			Bollinger bands (MA and σ)		
	1/50	1/200	5/150	1%	2%	5%	50	150	200	20/2	30/2	20/1
Panel A—2011 data set												
S&P 500												
Annual return	7.1%	24.2%	25.2%	17.6%	8.0%	2.0%	10.6%	5.0%	2.3%	-8.0%	-1.3%	-4.1%
Buy-and-hold return	-1.3%	-1.3%	-0.8%	-1.0%	-1.0%	-1.0%	-1.3%	-0.8%	-1.4%	-1.6%	-1.3%	-1.2%
Profits	**8.4%**	**25.5%**	**26.0%**	**18.6%**	**9.0%**	**3.0%**	**11.9%**	**5.8%**	**3.7%**	-6.6%	0%	-3.0%
No. of trades	1308	429	304	128	25	0	1528	923	796	1638	2050	1349
p-Value	0.01[a]	0.01[a]	0.00[a]	0.02[a]	0.05[a]	0.06	0.03[a]	0.05[a]	0.07	0.38	0.23	0.17
VIX												
Annual return	-9.3%	-1.3%	-7.0%	3.7%	-5.0%	-12.3%	-11.2%	-5.8%	4.3%	5.4%	-2.4%	12.8%
Buy-and-hold return	-1.3%	-1.3%	-0.8%	-1.0%	-1.0%	-1.0%	-1.3%	-0.8%	-1.4%	-1.3%	-1.3%	-1.2%
Profits	-8.0%	0%	-6.2%	**4.6%**	-4.0%	-11.3%	-9.9%	-5.0%	**5.7%**	**6.8%**	-1.0%	**14.0%**
No. of trades	908	413	309	2145	765	154	1331	702	588	1237	1506	965
p-Value	0.19	0.34	0.27	0.07	0.25	0.36	0.29	0.65	0.04[a]	0.05[a]	0.73	0.01[a]
Panel B—2013 data set												
S&P 500												
Annual return	12.0%	14.2%	15.0%	9.6%	2.0%	2.0%	16.3%	14.4%	19.6%	17.1%	18.6%	14.3%
Buy-and-hold return	27.4%	26.5%	27.1%	27.2%	27.2%	27.2%	27.4%	27.1%	26.5%	27.4%	27.4%	27.3%
Profits	-15.3%	-12.3%	-12.1%	-17.6%	-25.1%	-25.1%	-11.0%	-12.7%	-6.9%	-10.3%	-8.8%	-12.9%
No. of trades	1288	496	318	15	0	0	1488	890	802	1584	2019	1305
p-Value	0.22	0.34[a]	0.48	0.35	0.57	0.92	0.77	0.25	0.75	0.65	0.52	0.34
VIX												
Annual return	8.9%	6.6%	9.9%	16.1%	14.6%	10.6%	2.3%	3.4%	3.4%	9.9%	10.6%	8.8%
Buy-and-hold return	27.4%	26.5%	27.1%	27.2%	27.2%	27.2%	0.6%	3.7%	2.6%	27.4%	27.1%	26.5%
Profits	-18.4%	-19.9%	-17.1%	-11.0%	-12.6%	-16.6%	**1.7%**	-0.3%	**0.8%**	-17.5%	-16.4%	-17.7%
No. of trades	894	437	365	1377	492	78	202	105	90	1377	718	613
p-Value	0.64	0.37	0.75	0.62	0.35	0.45	0.09	0.55	0.12	0.42	0.45	0.24

[a]Significant at the 5 percent level.

the moving averages, FRs, and trading range breakout rules result in profits (before transaction costs) when calculated with the S&P 500 Index data. The BBs did not result in any profits.

In regard to the technical trading rules calculated with the VIX data[1], the technical trading rules did not generate any consistent profits. Only four of the 12 variants result in profits (before transaction costs).

The results from the 2013 data set reveal that none of the moving averages, FRs, BBs, or trading range breakout rules generated profits when calculated with the S&P 500 Index data. The technical trading rules did not do any better when calculated with the VIX data only two of the 12 variants result in profits (before transaction costs).

Recall the two purposes of this chapter. The first purpose is to investigate the profitability of HFTT rules under different market regimes. The results reveal that technical trading rules are more profitable during periods of high volatility with no definitive upward trend (i.e., in 2011). The technical trading rules were not able to generate any returns in excess of the buy-and-hold strategy during the steady upward, lower volatility market of 2013. Specifically, the buy-and-hold strategy generated returns of approximately 27% in 2013. This significant market upward movement makes it difficult to earn any excess returns.

Figure 20.3 presents a line chart of the MACO (1, 50) versus the buy-and-hold trading rule for 2013, while Figure 20.4 presents the same line graph for 2011. The purpose of the line graphs is to provide a visual description of the technical trading rule profitability at a high frequency.

Figures 20.3 and 20.4 corroborate the conclusion that the trading rules calculated at high frequencies are more profitable during periods of high volatility and sideways

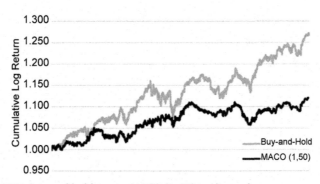

Figure 20.3 The 2013 Buy-and-hold versus MACO (1, 50) trading rule.

---

[1] The VIX Index cannot be traded directly, but several VIX derivatives allow traders to take positions on the VIX without owning the underlying: VIX options, VIX futures, and VIX exchange traded notes.

Figure 20.4 The 2011 Buy-and-hold versus MACO (1, 50) trading rule.

market trends. Figure 20.3 reveals that although the trading rule generated positive returns, it is not able to outperform the buy-and-hold due to the market's strong and continued upward trend. Figure 20.4 reveals that the technical trading rules outperform the buy-and-hold in part by avoiding significant market declines.

The second purpose of this chapter is to investigate whether technical trading rules can lead to excess profits when calculated with the VIX data. Unlike with data at the daily frequency (Kozyra and Lento, 2011), technical trading rules calculated with VIX data at high frequencies did not result in any excess profits. Technical trading rules are shown to be more profitable at high frequencies when calculated with the S&P 500 Index data.

Some additional messages arise from the results of our technical trading exercises. First, the FRs trigger a few trading recommendations at the 5-min frequency and when using the most common FR variants (1%, 2%, and 5%). This may suggest that the standard FRs are inappropriate in a high frequency setting and that future research should focus on testing alternative parameter values. This might result in methodological improvements of the FR approach.

Also, except for the FRs, other technical indicators generated a large number of trading signals in each year. For example, the 1, 50 moving-average rule generated approximately 1200 trading rules in 2013. This suggests that transaction costs could substantially impact the profitability of technical trading. Considering this potential problem, it would be important to extend the pure technical trading approach with learning algorithms that enable traders to determine the order size, given a trading signal (Gradojevic and Gençay, 2013).

20.5 CONCLUSION

This chapter investigates the profitability (before transaction costs) of technical trading rules calculated with high-frequency data. Specifically, this chapter investigates whether technical trading rules are more profitable during periods of high volatility (and sideways trending) relative to the periods of low volatility (and upward trending). The results reveal that technical trading rules at high frequencies are more profitable during the periods of high volatility and sideways trending. In addition, this chapter tests whether the technical trading rules are more profitable when calculated with the S&P 500 Index data as opposed to the VIX data. The results also reveal that the FRs with common daily level parameters do not generate many trades when used at high frequencies, while the moving average, TRBO, and BBs all generate a very large number of signals during a calendar year.

These results are novel in that they apply technical trading rules that are shown to be profitable with daily data in a high-frequency setting. The results show that traders should consider adjustments to the nature of the traditional trading rules used at daily frequencies in order to apply them at high frequencies. Researchers are encouraged to investigate the ideal parameters and metrics from each trading rule at each high-frequency level. In addition, researchers are encouraged to investigate the impact of trading costs on the overall profitability of high-frequency trading rules. Considering the emerging, yet controversial nature of high-frequency finance, more scholarly effort should be concentrated on investigating the overall efficacy of HFTT.

REFERENCES

Brock, W., Lakonishok, J., LeBaron, B., 1992. Simple technical trading rules and the stochastic properties of stock returns. J. Finance 47 (5), 1731−1764. http://www.technicalanalysis.org.uk/moving-averages/BrLL92.pdf.

Chaboud, A., Chiquoine, B., Hjalmarsson, E., Vega, C., 2014. Rise of the machines: algorithmic trading in the foreign exchange market. J. Finance 69 (5), 2045−2084.

Fama, E., Blume, M., 1966. Filter tests and stock market trading. J. Bus. 39 (1), 226−241.

Gradojevic, N., Gençay, R., 2013. Fuzzy logic, trading uncertainty and technical trading. J. Bank. Financ. 37 (2), 578−586.

Kho, B.C., 1996. Time-varying risk premia, volatility, and technical trading rule profits: evidence from foreign currency futures markets. J. Financ. Econ. 41 (2), 249−290.

Kozyra, J., Lento, C., 2011. Using VIX data to enhance technical trading rules. Appl. Econ. Lett. 18 (14), 1367−1370.

Lento, C., 2007. Test of technical analysis in the Asian-Pacific equity markets: a bootstrap approach. Acad. Account. Financ. Stud. J. 11 (2), 51−74.

Lento, C., Gradojevic, N., Wright, C.S., 2007. Investment information content in Bollinger bands? Appl. Financ. Econ. Lett. 3 (4), 263−267.

Levich, R., Thomas, L., 1993. The significance of technical trading rules profits in the foreign exchange market: a bootstrap approach. J. Int. Money Finance 12 (5), 451−474.

Manahov, V., Hudson, R., Gebka, B., 2014. Does high frequency trading affect technical analysis and market efficiency? and if so, how? J. Int. Financ. Mark. Inst. Money 28 (4), 131−157.

Menkhoff, L., 2010. The use of technical analysis by fund managers: international evidence. J. Bank. Financ. 34 (11), 2573−2586.

Menkhoff, L., Taylor, M.P., 2007. The obstinate passion of foreign exchange professionals: technical analysis. J. Econ. Lit. 45 (4), 936−972.

Murphy, J., 2000. Charting Made Easy. John Wiley and Sons Inc., Hoboken, NJ.

Ratner, M., Leal, R.P.C., 1999. Tests of technical trading strategies in the emerging, equity markets of Latin America and Asia. J. Bank. Finance 23 (12), 1887–1905.

Reitz, S., 2006. On the predictive content of technical analysis. N. Am. J. Econ. Finance 17 (2), 121–137.

Scholtus, M.L., van Dijk, D.J.C., February 28, 2012. High-Frequency Technical Trading: The Importance of Speed. Tinbergen Institute. Discussion Paper 12-018/4. Available at SSRN. http://ssrn.com/abstract=2013789.

Scholes, M., Williams, W., 1977. Estimating betas from non-synchronous data. J. Financ. Econ. 5 (3), 309–327.

White, H., 2006. Approximate nonlinear forecasting methods. In: Elliott, G., Granger, C.W.J., Timmerman, A. (Eds.), Handbook of Economics Forecasting, vol. 1 (1), Part II—Chapter 9.

CHAPTER 21

High-Frequency News Flow and States of Asset Volatility

Kin-Yip Ho[1], Yanlin Shi[1], Zhaoyong Zhang[2]

[1]Research School of Finance, Actuarial Studies and Applied Statistics, ANU College of Business and Economics, The Australian National University, Canberra, ACT, Australia; [2]School of Business, Faculty of Business and Law, Edith Cowan University, Joondalup, WA, Australia

Contents

21.1 INTRODUCTION

Clark (1973) proposes the "Mixture of Distributions Hypothesis" (MDH), which suggests that asset volatility is induced by the rate of public information arrival. Based on this theory, many financial studies have been produced to investigate the relationship between news flows and asset volatility. Among them, some focus on the impact of firm-specific news releases (Berry and Howe, 1994; Kalev et al., 2004; Grob-Klubmann and Hautsch, 2011), and others study the impact of macroeconomic news (Andersen et al., 2003; Brenner et al., 2009; Hautsch et al., 2011). Most of these studies limit their discussion to the relatively low-frequency data.

The Handbook of High Frequency Trading
ISBN 978-0-12-802205-4

With increasing data availability, a growing number of recent financial papers have considered the case of high-frequency data. Compared with low-frequency trading, high-frequency trading has the advantages of lowering the cost of trading, increasing the informativeness of quotes, providing liquidity and eliminating arbitrage, and hence reducing asset price volatility (Hendershott et al., 2010). A recent study by Ho et al. (2013) considers both the impacts of firm-specific and macroeconomic news flows and sentiments on asset volatility. Their results suggest that both positive and negative firm-specific and macroeconomic news can significantly and positively affect asset volatility with asymmetrical effects. Further, the effects are different in low-volatility and high-volatility states.

Based on an extension of their study, this chapter aims to address the following set of research questions. How can the flow of high-frequency announcements account for the likelihood of a higher volatility state of intraday asset? Are there any differences between the impact of negative and positive news flows on volatility? Is the impact of firm-specific announcements stronger or weaker than that of macroeconomic news?

Our preliminary analysis apparently suggests that the flows of firm-specific and macroeconomic news could affect states of high-frequency asset volatility. This can be observed from the JPM example in Figure 21.1. The shaded area represents the period of arrival of intraday newswire messages, and macroeconomic (firm-specific) newswire messages are presented on the left (right) side of the plot. As shown in Figure 21.1, after multiple firm-specific and macroeconomic news items are released, asset volatility is subsequently higher and the absolute return is close to 14%.

In this chapter, we study the impact of newswire messages on volatility states of stocks traded on the Dow Jones Composite Average (DJN65). Our sample includes hourly stock returns from the start of 2001 to the end of 2013. Our newswire messages are obtained from the RavenPack News Analytics—Dow Jones Edition, which is a comprehensive database covering >1200 types of firm-specific and macroeconomic news events.[1]

To analyze the relationship between news flow and volatility states of stocks, we need to model how volatility evolves. Over the past few decades, Generalized Autoregressive Conditional Heteroskedasticity (GARCH) family models have become a standard methodology in financial studies to analyze persistence, asymmetric effects, and forecasting of volatility. In order to further extract the latent volatility states, we follow Ho et al. (2013) and employ the Markov Regime-Switching GARCH (MRS-GARCH) model proposed by Haas et al. (2004).

To proxy news flows, we construct two different types of news variables with four specific subcategories for each type. The two types of news variables are the dummy

---

[1] See Ho et al. (2013) for details of RavenPack.

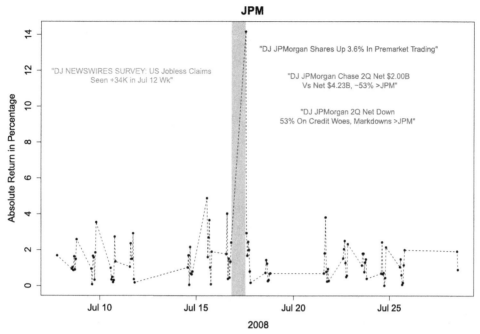

Figure 21.1 *News effects on absolute return.* This figure presents the news effects on the absolute hourly return of the listed company J.P. Morgan (JPM), along with major news headlines of news articles in July 2008. The shaded area represents the period of arrival of intraday newswire messages, and macroeconomic (firm-specific) newswire messages are presented on the left (right) side of the plot.

variable and the number of news stories, and the four subcategories are the negative and positive firm-specific news and negative and positive macroeconomic news. Discrete choice models are then employed to fit stock return volatility and news variables. States of stock return volatility are classified by the smoothing probability extracted from the MRS-GARCH model into calm (low-volatility) and turbulent (high-volatility) states. Our data are first fitted by dummy news variables into binary logit and probit models. The results show that occurrences of news can significantly affect the likelihood of turbulent state. We then constrain our sample to periods during which at least one positive or negative news story is received. In the constrained sample, states are fitted by the number of news variables. We show that the number of news can further significantly affect the likelihood of turbulent state.

Nonparametric tests including the Wilcoxon signed-rank test and Bootstrap percentile confidence interval (BCI) are employed to test the marginal effects of the occurrence of news. In general, macroeconomic news has a greater marginal effect than firm-specific news. More specifically, negative macroeconomic news increases the likelihood of higher level stock return volatility, whereas positive macroeconomic news decreases the chance to a larger degree. Moreover, it is demonstrated that the number of news variables has further significant marginal effects. Overall, the estimated results are consistent with those of occurrences of news. All the above conclusions are roughly robust among classifications based on conditional volatility, fitted via ordered logit and probit models.

Our results suggest that macroeconomic news is more important than firm-specific news on states of stock return volatility. Since macroeconomic news contains information of real-time macroeconomic status, our results also indicate that macroeconomic status is a key factor of the volatility state of individual stock. The results can provide useful information for professional traders who read newswires like Dow Jones. They spend a considerable amount of money on these information sources and emphasize the importance of speed and accuracy of news. Newswire messages represent much of the overall information traders receive on a real-time basis. The intraday impact of these newswire messages will help traders anticipate the potential effects on volatility states of the assets that they are monitoring (Ho et al., 2013).

The rest of the chapter is organized as follows: In Section 21.2, we discuss the RavenPack news database, followed by data description in Section 21.3. Section 21.4 explains the methodology and models used in this chapter. In Section 21.5, we discuss the empirical results from our models. Section 21.6 concludes this chapter.

21.2 DATA AND SAMPLE

21.2.1 Introduction to RavenPack

RavenPack News Analytics—Dow Jones Edition is a comprehensive database covering >1200 types of firm-specific and macroeconomic news events. RavenPack automatically tracks and monitors relevant information on tens of thousands of companies, government organizations, influential people, key geographical locations, and all major currencies and traded commodities. The database includes analytics on >170,000 entities in >100 countries and covers >98% of the investable global market. Among the many benefits, RavenPack delivers sentiment analysis and event data that most likely impact financial markets and trading around the world—all in a matter of milliseconds. It continuously analyzes relevant information from major real-time newswires and trustworthy sources, such as Dow Jones Newswires, regional editions of the *Wall Street Journal* and *Barron's* and internet sources including financial sites, blogs, and local and regional newspapers, to produce real-time news sentiment scores. All relevant news items about entities are classified and quantified according to their sentiment, relevance, topic, novelty, and market impact. In terms of the sentiment, RavenPack uses a proprietary computational linguistic analysis algorithm, which is described in Section 21.2.2, to quantify positive and negative perceptions on facts and opinions reported in the news textual content. The core of the algorithm can be divided into two steps. First, RavenPack builds up a historical database of words, phrases, combinations, and other word-level definitions that have affected the target company, market, or asset class. Then, the text in the specific news story is compared with the historical database, and the sentiment score is generated accordingly.

21.2.2 RavenPack Scores

Among dozens of the analytical outputs in the RavenPack database, we use composite sentiment score (CSS) and event sentiment score (ESS) to construct our news variables.[2] The algorithms to generate those scores are described in Appendix B.

CSS is a sentiment score that ranges from 0 to 100. It represents the news sentiment of a given story by combining various sentiment analysis techniques. The direction of the score is determined by emotionally charged words and phrases embedded in the news story, which is typically rated by experts as having a short-term positive or negative share price impact. A high score (>50) indicates a positive intraday stock price impact, while a low score (<50) indicates a negative impact.

ESS is a granular score that ranges from 0 to 100. It specifies whether the news story conveys positive or negative sentiment about the stock. The score is constructed as follows: First, a set of news (training set) is categorized by a group of financial experts based on the degree to which they have a short-term positive or negative share price impact. Second, their classification is encapsulated in an algorithm that generates a score range from 0 to 100. A high score (>50) indicates positive sentiment, while a low score (<50) indicates negative sentiment.

21.3 DATA AND SAMPLE

21.3.1 Return Series

Our stock price series comprise the hourly data of Dow Jones 65 stocks[3] from January 1, 2001 to December 31, 2013. These series are sourced from the Thomson Reuters Tick History database, which contains high-frequency stock data and is provided by the Securities Industry Research Center of Australasia. Define $\{S_0, S_1,..., S_{T-1}, S_T\}$ as the sequence of hourly closing price for one firm at times $\{0, 1,..., T-1, T\}$. The corresponding hourly return at time t is

$$r_t = 100 \times \log(S_t/S_{t-1}) \tag{21.1}$$

---

[2] For firm-specific news, we use the CSS, and for macroeconomic news, RavenPack only provides the ESS.

[3] To ensure that there are sufficient observations and the datasets are complete over the sample period, 50 out of 65 firms are included in our final sample. Our selection criteria are (1) in each month, there are at least 15 trading days; and (2) there must be no missing month in the whole period. The complete list of the 65 stocks is presented in Appendix A.

21.3.2 News Variables

We use a news database provided by RavenPack News Analytic to proxy for the news flows. Four types of news variables are generated with CSS and ESS. At time t, the number of negative firm-specific and macroeconomic news stories is

$$NN_{f,t} = \sum_{all\ \tau} I\left(CSS_{f,\tau} < 50\right) \tag{21.2}$$

$$NN_{m,t} = \sum_{all\ \tau} I\left(ESS_{m,\tau} < 50\right) \tag{21.3}$$

where subscripts f and m indicate that the corresponding scores (variables) refer to firm-specific and macroeconomic news, respectively, $I(\cdot)$ is the indicator function that gives 1 when the condition inside the brackets is true and gives 0 otherwise, τ is the time at which the news story is received and $\tau \in [t-1,t]$. The numbers of positive firm-specific and macroeconomic news stories at time t are

$$NP_{f,t} = \sum_{all\ \tau} I\left(CSS_{f,\tau} > 50\right) \tag{21.4}$$

$$NN_{m,t} = \sum_{all\ \tau} I\left(ESS_{m,\tau} > 50\right) \tag{21.5}$$

Further, we construct four dummy news variables. Let the dummy variable be 1 when the corresponding number of news variable is not 0, and set it to 0 otherwise. In this way, we use $DN_{f,t}$, $DP_{f,t}$, $DN_{m,t}$, and $DP_{m,t}$ to indicate dummy variables of the negative and positive firm-specific news, and negative and positive macroeconomic news, respectively.

21.4 METHODOLOGY AND MODEL SPECIFICATION

21.4.1 The MRS-GARCH Model

The GARCH family models have enjoyed great popularity because of the ability to model characteristics of financial series such as volatility clustering. However, their main weakness is that they assume that conditional volatility has only one regime over the entire period. Unfortunately, due to reasons like the structural breaks in the real economy and changes in the operators' expectations about the future, financial returns may exhibit sudden jumps and will not stay in the same regime over a long period (Marcucci, 2005).

To retain the advantages of GARCH models and allow structure breaks at the same time, Cai (1994) and Hamilton and Susmel (1994) apply the seminal idea of MRS model into the Autoregressive Conditional Heteroskedasticity (ARCH) specification. Because of the path dependency of the conditional volatility term in the GARCH specifications, many researchers such as Gray (1996) and Klaassen (2002) have generated various algorithms to overcome this issue, and a detailed review can be found in Marcucci (2005).

As to the distribution of innovation, an enormous amount of evidence suggests that financial series is rarely Gaussian but typically leptokurtic and exhibits heavy-tail behavior (Bollerslev, 1987; Susmel and Engle, 1994). In addition, Student-t distribution is a widely used alternative, which can accommodate the excess kurtosis of the innovations (Bollerslev, 1987). On the other hand, as noted by Klaassen (2002), Ardia (2009), and Haas (2009), if regimes of MRS framework are not Gaussian but leptokurtic, the use of within-regime normality can seriously affect the identification of the regime process. The reason can be found in Haas and Paolella (2012), who further argue that quasimaximum likelihood estimation based on Gaussian components does not provide a consistent estimator of models within the MRS framework.

For the above reasons, we employ the two-state MRS-GARCH(1,1) model with Student-t innovations investigated in Haas et al. (2004) as follows:

$$r_t = \mu_{s_t} + \varepsilon_{s_t, t}$$

$$\varepsilon_{s_t, t} = \eta_t \sqrt{h_{s_t, t}} \quad \text{where} \quad \eta_t \stackrel{iid}{\sim} t(0, 1, v)$$

$$h_{s_t, t} = \begin{cases} \omega_{01} + \alpha_1 \varepsilon_{1,t-1}^2 + \beta_1 h_{1,t-1} & \text{when } s_t = 1 \\ \omega_{02} + \alpha_2 \varepsilon_{2,t-1}^2 + \beta_2 h_{2,t-1} & \text{when } s_t = 2 \end{cases} \tag{21.6}$$

where $\varepsilon_{s_t, t}$ is the error at time t in state s_t. η_t is an identical and independent sequence following Student-t distribution, with 0 mean, unit standard deviation, and v degree of freedom. $h_{s_t, t}$ is the conditional volatility in state s_t at time t. Also, the sequence $\{s_t\}$ is assumed to be a stationary, irreducible Markov process with discrete state space $\{1,2\}$ and transition matrix $P = [p_{jk}]$ where $p_{jk} = P(s_{t+1} = k | s_t = j)$ is the transition probability of moving from state j to state k $(j,k \in \{1,2\})$.

As argued by Mullen et al. (2011), Eqn (21.6) can also capture the volatility clustering as in the GARCH model, as well as allow the structure breaks in unconditional variance. In the jth state, the unconditional volatility is

$$\bar{\sigma}_j^2 = \frac{\omega_{0j}}{1 - \alpha_j - \beta_j} \tag{21.7}$$

as long as that $\alpha_j + \beta_j < 1$, that is, the process is covariance stationary (Bollerslev, 1986; Haas et al., 2004). In this chapter, we indicate state 1 as the calm (low-volatility) state and state 2 as the turbulent (high-volatility) state, so that $\bar{\sigma}_1^2 < \bar{\sigma}_2^2$. Also, $\alpha_1 + \beta_1$ and $\alpha_2 + \beta_2$ are the measurements of volatility persistence in calm and turbulent states, respectively.

We estimate parameters of the MRS-GARCH model using maximum likelihood estimation (MLE). The conditional density of $\varepsilon_{s_t, t}$ is given as follows:

$$\Omega_{t-1} = \left\{ \varepsilon_{s_{t-1}, t-1}, \varepsilon_{s_{t-2}, t-2}, \ldots, \varepsilon_{s_1, 1} \right\}$$

$$\theta = (\mu_1, \mu_2, p_{11}, p_{22}, v, \omega_{01}, \omega_{02}, \alpha_1, \alpha_2, \beta_1, \beta_2)'$$

$$f(\varepsilon_{s_t, t} | s_t = j, \theta, \Omega_{t-1}) = \frac{\Gamma[(v+1)/2]}{\Gamma(v/2)\sqrt{\pi(v-2)h_{j,t}}} \left[1 + \frac{\varepsilon_{j,t}^2}{(v-2)h_{j,t}} \right]^{\frac{v+1}{2}} \tag{21.8}$$

where Ω_{t-1} is the information set at time $t-1$. θ is the vector of parameters. $\Gamma(\cdot)$ is the Gamma function and $f(\varepsilon_{s_t,t}|\theta,\Omega_{t-1})$ is the conditional density of $\varepsilon_{s_t,t}$. This stems from the fact that at time t, $\varepsilon_{s_t,t}$ follows a Student-t distribution with mean 0, variance $h_{s_t,t}$, and degrees of freedom ν given time $t-1$.

Plugging the filtered probability in state j at time $t-1$, $\omega_{j,t-1} = P(s_{t-1} = j|\theta,\Omega_{t-1})$, into Eqn (21.8) and integrating out the state variable s_{t-1}, the density function in Eqn (21.8) becomes

$$f(\varepsilon_{s_t,t}|\theta,\Omega_{t-1}) = \sum_{j=1}^{2}\sum_{k=1}^{2} p_{jk}\omega_{j,t-1}f(\varepsilon_{s_t,t}|s_t = j,\theta,\Omega_{t-1}). \tag{21.9}$$

$\omega_{j,t-1}$ can be obtained by an integrative algorithm given in Hamilton (1989). The log-likelihood function corresponds to Eqn (21.9) and is as follows:

$$L(\theta|\varepsilon) = \sum_{t=2}^{T}\ln f(\varepsilon_{s_t,t}|\theta,\Omega_{t-1}) \text{ where } \varepsilon = (\varepsilon_{s_t,1},\varepsilon_{s_t,2},...,\varepsilon_{s_t,T})', \tag{21.10}$$

and the MLE estimator $\widehat{\theta}$ is obtained by maximizing Eqn (21.10).

To identify the volatility states of the return series, we extract the smoothing probability of the calm state as follows (Hamilton, 1988, 1989, 1994):

$$P(s_t = 1|\theta,\Omega_T) = \omega_{1,t}\left[\frac{p_{11}P(s_{t+1} = 1|\theta,\Omega_T)}{P(s_{t+1} = 1|\theta,\Omega_t)} + \frac{p_{12}P(s_{t+1} = 2|\theta,\Omega_T)}{P(s_{t+1} = 2|\theta,\Omega_t)}\right]. \tag{21.11}$$

Using the fact that $P(s_T = 1|\theta,\Omega_T) = \omega_{1,T}$, the smoothing probability series $P(s_t = 1|\theta,\Omega_T)$ can be generated by iterating Eqn (21.11) backward from T to 1.

21.4.2 Discrete Choice Model

The discrete choice model is a branch of Generalized Linear Models and is designed to solve problems that involve choosing between two or more discrete alternatives. In our study, we employ the binary logit and probit models and ordered logit and probit models to investigate how different news affect states of the stock return volatility.

A discrete variable Y_t is defined to indicate different states of the conditional volatility h_t, which is generated from the MRS-GARCH model to proxy the latent stock return volatility. In our study, there are two general types of classifications. First, we broadly divide h_t into just the calm and turbulent states (two-state classification). Then, $Y_t = 1$ indicates that h_t lies in the calm state, while $Y_t = 2$ indicates that h_t lies in the turbulent state. Moreover, to improve the robustness of the results, we create another state intermediate, which lies between calm and turbulent states (three-state classification). In this case, $Y_t = 1,2$, or 3 indicates the calm, intermediate, and turbulent states, respectively. In addition, U_t, the latent utility (continuous and unobservable) at time t, is defined as

$$U_t = \beta_0 + \beta News_t + \varepsilon_t, \tag{21.12}$$

where β_0 is the intercept vector. $\beta = (\beta_1, \beta_2, \beta_3, \beta_4)$ is the coefficient vector of news variables. $News_t$ is the news variable vector at time t, which is composed of a dummy or number of news variables. ε_t is the residual at time t.

For the two-state classification, binary logit and probit models are employed to model Y_t. For the binary logit model, ε_t follows a logistic distribution, with probability density function $\lambda(\varepsilon_t) = \exp(-\varepsilon_t)/[1 + \exp(-\varepsilon_t)]^2$ and cumulative density function $\Lambda(\varepsilon_t) = \exp(\varepsilon_t)/[1 + \exp(\varepsilon_t)]$. Further, we have the following fact:

$$P(Y_t = 1|News_t) = P(U_t > 0|News_t) = \Lambda(-\beta_0 - \beta News_t) \tag{21.13}$$

As a result, the corresponding log-likelihood function is

$$\theta = \{\beta_0, \beta\} \text{ and } \varepsilon = (\varepsilon_1, \varepsilon_2, ..., \varepsilon_T)'$$

$$L(\theta|\varepsilon) = \sum_{t=1}^{T} P(Y_t|News_t) \tag{21.14}$$

$$= \sum_{t=1}^{T} \{Y_t \log[\Lambda(\beta_0 + \beta News_t)] + (1 - Y_t)\log[1 - \Lambda(\beta_0 + \beta News_t)]\}$$

Similarly, for the binary probit model, $\varepsilon_t \sim N(0,1)$ and we have $P(Y_t = 1|News_t) = \Phi(\beta_0 + \beta News_t)$ with the following log-likelihood function:

$$L(\theta|\varepsilon) = \sum_{t=1}^{T} \{Y_t \log[\Phi(\beta_0 + \beta News_t)] + (1 - Y_t)\log[1 - \Phi(\beta_0 + \beta News_t)]\}, \tag{21.15}$$

where $\Phi(\cdot)$ is the cumulative density function of the standard normal distribution.

For the three-state classification, we fit Y_t into ordered logit and probit models. For the ordered logit model, at state m ($m \in \{1,2,3\}$), ε_t follows a logistic distribution and we have

$$P(Y_t = m|News_t) = P(u_{m-1} < U_t < u_m|News_t)$$
$$= \Lambda(u_m - \beta_0 - \beta News_t) - \Lambda(u_{m-1} - \beta_0 - \beta News_t) \tag{21.16}$$

with log-likelihood function:

$$L(\theta|\varepsilon) = \sum_{t=1}^{T} \sum_{m=1}^{3} P(Y_t|News_t)$$

$$= \sum_{t=1}^{T} \sum_{m=1}^{3} \{I(Y_t = m)\{\log[\Lambda(u_m - \beta_0 - \beta News_t) - \Lambda(u_{m-1} - \beta_0 - \beta News_t)]\}\}$$

$$\tag{21.17}$$

Similarly, for the ordered probit model, $\varepsilon_t \sim N(0,1)$, and we have $P(Y_t = m|News_t) = \Phi(u_m - \beta_0 - \beta News_t) - \Phi(u_{m-1} - \beta_0 - \beta News_t)$ with the following log-likelihood function:

$$L(\theta|\varepsilon) = \sum_{t=1}^{T} \sum_{m=1}^{3} \{I(Y_t = m)\{\log[\Phi(u_m - \beta_0 - \beta News_t)$$

$$- \Phi(u_{m-1} - \beta_0 - \beta News_t)]\}\} \tag{21.18}$$

Finally, the coefficient vector θ of binary logit and probit models and ordered logit and probit models can be estimated by maximizing Eqns (21.14), (21.15), (21.17) and (21.18), respectively.

21.5 EMPIRICAL RESULTS AND IMPLICATIONS

21.5.1 Descriptive Statistics of the Dataset

The descriptive statistics of the two sentiment scores $CSS_{f,\tau}$ and $ESS_{m,\tau}$ used to construct our firm-specific and macroeconomic news variables are summarized in Panel A of Table 21.1. The mean $CSS_{f,\tau}$ is very close to 50, indicating that on average, news stories are neutral. The mean $ESS_{m,\tau}$ is 52.90, slightly >50, suggesting from the experts' point of view that overall the news announcements during the entire period are slightly positive.

Table 21.1 Datasets descriptive statistics

	Mean	Standard deviation	Median	Q_1	Q_3	Skew
Panel A: Descriptive statistics of news database						
CSS_τ	49.93	5.04	50	50	52	−1.2187
ESS_τ	52.90	30.16	50	50	89	−0.0937
Panel B: Descriptive statistics of variables						
r_t	0.0016	0.8938	0.0000	−0.3140	0.3200	−4.0284
$|r_t|$	0.5169	0.7291	0.3170	0.1354	0.6473	19.3614
$NN_{f,t}$	0.7900	4.2480	0.0000	0.0000	0.0000	25.2494
$NP_{f,t}$	1.1596	5.5857	0.0000	0.0000	1.0000	15.9065
$NN_{m,t}$	0.1529	0.7607	0.0000	0.0000	0.0000	7.9527
$NP_{m,t}$	0.1865	0.7503	0.0000	0.0000	0.0000	6.2613

Note: This table presents the summary descriptive statistics of all the variables employed in this study. The summary statistics include mean value (*Mean*), median value (*Median*), 25 percentile (Q_1), 75 percentile (Q_3), and Skewness (*Skew*) for each variable. CSS_τ and ESS_τ are the CSS and ESS of each news story, respectively. r_t is the return in percentage at hour t. $|r_t|$ is the absolute percentage return. $NN_{f,t}$ and $NP_{f,t}$ are the number of negative and positive firm-specific news stories, respectively. $NN_{m,t}$ and $NP_{m,t}$ are the number of negative and positive macroeconomic news stories, respectively. The sample period is from January 1, 2001 to December 31, 2013.

The descriptive statistics of our return and news variables are summarized in Panel B of Table 21.1. The mean return (measured in percentage) is around 0, while the mean absolute return is at 0.5169%. In terms of the number of news variables, positive firm-specific news has the greatest mean at 1.1596, much larger than that of negative firm-specific news. The variation of $NP_{f,t}$ is also greater, with the standard deviation 5.5857, compared to 4.2480 for $NN_{f,t}$. The averages of negative and positive macroeconomic news are about the same (<0.2), both are much smaller than the means of firm-specific news though the average of the positive news is slightly larger than that of the negative news. The corresponding variations are also quite close (at around 0.75) and much smaller than that of firm-specific news. Finally, the skewness indicates that the number of firm-specific news variables is generally more right skewed than the number of macroeconomic news variables.

21.5.2 Estimates of the MRS-GARCH Model

As described in Section 21.4.1, we employ the MRS-GARCH model to estimate the stock return volatility and smoothing probability. The results are summarized in Table 21.2. It is observed that $P(s_t = 1|\theta,\Omega_T)$ has a large mean of 0.7650, suggesting that the stock return volatility tends to lie in the calm state most of the time. The large skewness of h_t (with a value of 390.0356) indicates that some extremely large conditional volatility may be present.

The estimated smoothing probability series of the calm state of JPM over the entire period is plotted in Figure 21.2. As suggested by Hamilton (1988, 1989, 1994), if $P(s_t = 1|\theta,\Omega_T) \geq 0.5$, h_t lies in the calm state and otherwise in the turbulent state. Therefore, return volatility of JPM lies in the turbulent state from 2001 to 2003. Then, the volatility switches to the calm state and stays there until 2008, when it switches back to and lies in the turbulent state again. After 2010, the volatility returns to the calm state and stays there. This situation is consistent with the real macroeconomic case: the IT bubble crack event happened at the start of the twenty-first century and lasted for almost 3 years; the Global Financial Crisis took place in 2008, and its impact lasted for around 2 years. Hence, $P(s_t = 1|\theta,\Omega_T)$ can be used to consistently identify the states of the stock return volatility in our study.

Table 21.2 Estimates of the MRS-GARCH model

	Mean	Standard deviation	Median	Q_1	Q_3	Skew
$P(s_t = 1|\theta,\Omega_T)$	0.7650	0.3723	0.9945	0.6060	0.9997	−1.2337
h_t	0.8501	8.6093	0.4259	0.2195	0.8511	390.0356

Note: This table presents the summarized estimates of the MRS-GARCH model. $P(s_t = 1|\theta,\Omega_T)$ is the smoothing probability of the calm state. h_t is the stock return volatility. For the explanation of other variables, see Table 21.1.

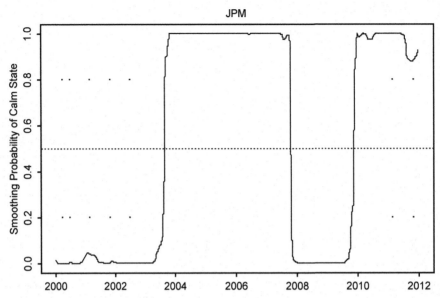

Figure 21.2 *Smoothing Probability of the Calm State.* This figure presents the smoothing probability of the calm state for JPM estimated from the MRS-GARCH model. The sample period is from the beginning of 2001 to the end of 2013.

21.5.3 News Effects on States of Stock Return Volatility

Following the idea of Hamilton (1988, 1989, 1994), we set $Y_t = 1$ when $P(s_t = 1|\theta,\Omega_T) \geq 0.5$ and $Y_t = 2$ otherwise. To confirm the robustness of the classification of states, for each stock, we define the proportion of $P(s_t = 1|\theta,\Omega_T) < 0.5$ as p_0, and then define H_{p0}, to be the p_0th percentile of h_t for each stock. Further, let $Y_t = 1$ when $h_t \geq H_{p_0}$ and $Y_t = 2$ otherwise. In this way, we ensure that the proportion of time for stock return volatility lying in the calm and turbulent states is the same between the two classifications. We use the notations Prob.-2-State and Vol.-2-State to indicate classifications based on $P(s_t = 1|\theta,\Omega_T)$ and h_t, respectively. In this section, the news effects on states of stock return volatility will be studied via discrete choice models.

21.5.3.1 Dummy News Variables on Full Datasets

First, we are interested in whether the occurrence of news can lead to a larger probability of the turbulent state. The following two equations are fitted, respectively, with binary logit and probit models as described in Section 21.4.2:

$$\text{Null model: } U_t = \beta_0 + \varepsilon_t$$
$$\text{Full model: } U_t = \beta_0 + \beta News_t + \varepsilon_t \tag{21.19}$$

Table 21.3 Drop-in-deviance test summary of discrete choice models

	Prob.-2-state		Prob.-3-state		Vol.-2-state		Vol.-3-state	
Variable	Logit	Probit	Logit	Probit	Logit	Probit	Logit	Probit
Panel A: Full datasets								
D.N.	49	49	49	49	50	50	50	50
Panel B: Constrained datasets								
N.N.	49	49	48	49	48	48	49	49

Note: This table presents the number of significant results out of 50 stocks from the drop-in-deviance tests at the 5% significance level with different discrete choice models. The null model is regression without news variables, and the full model is regression with all news variables. Prob.-2-State, Prob.-3-State, Vol.-2-State, and Vol.-3-State indicate states classified by smoothing probability into two states and three states, and states classified by quantiles of volatility into two states and three states, respectively. For two states, data are fitted by binary logit and probit models, while for three states, data are fitted by ordered logit and probit models. D.N. and N.N. stand for the dummy news variable and number of news variables, respectively. Dummy news variables are fitted with full datasets. The number of news variables is fitted with constrained datasets, where at least one positive/negative news of firm-specific or macroeconomic category must be received within the time interval.

where U_t is the latent utility of Y_t, the form of which will be decided by the logit and probit models. $News_t$ is the news variable vector, including $DN_{f,t}$, $DP_{f,t}$, $DN_{m,t}$, and $DP_{m,t}$ in this case. The drop-in-deviance test is then conducted at the 5% significance level. The number of significant results out of 50 stocks of logit and probit models is listed in Panel A of Table 21.3.

Both logit and probit models suggest that in the Prob.-2-State classification, 49 out of 50 models that include the dummy news variables can significantly reduce the deviance. In the Vol.-2-State classification, the number is 50. As a result, we can conclude that dummy news variables have significant overall effects on the states of stock return volatility.

In terms of the estimated β, the results are summarized in Panel A and Panel C of Table 21.4 for Prob.-2-State and Vol.-2-State classifications, respectively. In order to test the statistical significance of the mean estimated β, we employ the Wilcoxon signed-rank test and 95% BCI.[4] From Panel A of Table 21.4, it is observed that most of the mean values β are significantly different from 0 at the 5% level (except for $DP_{f,t}$), as confirmed by both the Wilcoxon test and the BCI. Moreover, the occurrences of negative firm-specific and positive macroeconomic news have negative effects, whereas estimates of $DN_{m,t}$ are positive on average. Further, the marginal effects[5] of

---

[4] The reason why the significance of the estimates in each stock is not reported is that, based on $P(s_t = 1|\theta,\Omega_T)$ and h_t, both states are stationary but have a considerably large autocorrelation (not reported in the chapter and is available upon request). So Y_t is the binary time series with autocorrelation. Therefore, the estimated standard deviation of β is problematic and cannot be used for inference. However, the estimated β itself is still unbiased, so that results of nonparametric tests are valid.

[5] The marginal effect is defined as the effect of one unit increase of the individual news variable on the logarithm of odds of $P(Y_t = 2|News_t)$, given all the other news variables are already included in the model.

Table 21.4 Summary output and nonparametric tests results of dummy news variables

Variable	Logit					Probit				
	Mean	Standard deviation	Median	Skew	Boot-CI	Mean	Standard deviation	Median	Skew	Boot-CI
Panel A: Prob.-2-state models										
$DN_{f,t}$	−0.1696[a]	0.3219	−0.1667	1.7369	[−0.2000, −0.0754][b]	−0.0933[a]	0.1830	−0.0939	1.8895	[−0.1118, −0.0393][b]
$DP_{f,t}$	−0.0475	0.2876	−0.0371	−2.0572	[−0.0734, 0.0239]	−0.0275	0.1711	−0.0163	−2.3130	[−0.0430, 0.0151]
$DN_{m,t}$	0.2300[a]	0.1376	0.2111	1.1062	[0.2165, 0.2712][b]	0.1247[a]	0.0619	0.1247	0.1636	[0.1188, 0.1423][b]
$DP_{m,t}$	−0.2392[a]	0.1259	−0.2334	−0.5216	[−0.2524, −0.2081][b]	−0.1308[a]	0.0609	−0.1335	−0.0646	[−0.1365, −0.1140][b]
Panel B: Prob.-3-state models										
$DN_{f,t}$	−0.1867[a]	0.3028	−0.2249	1.9934	[−0.2208, −0.1001][b]	−0.1061[a]	0.1718	−0.1270	1.9989	[−0.1212, −0.0556][b]
$DP_{f,t}$	−0.0370	0.2892	−0.0332	−2.0696	[−0.0615, 0.0336]	−0.0220	0.1718	−0.0146	−2.3436	[−0.0375, 0.0232]
$DN_{m,t}$	0.2119[a]	0.1046	0.2079	1.0050	[0.2019, 0.2415][b]	0.1188[a]	0.0510	0.1218	0.1337	[0.1147, 0.1332][b]
$DP_{m,t}$	−0.2181[a]	0.1097	−0.2115	0.0497	[−0.2277, −0.1890][b]	−0.1245[a]	0.0566	−0.1281	0.1579	[−0.1302, −0.1093][b]
Panel C: Vol.-2-state models										
$DN_{f,t}$	−0.1302[a]	0.3729	−0.1889	1.3605	[−0.1633, −0.0342][b]	−0.0730[a]	0.2040	−0.1056	1.3086	[−0.0925, −0.0136][b]
$DP_{f,t}$	0.0473[a]	0.2784	0.0985	−2.3891	[0.0243, 0.1142][b]	0.0263[a]	0.1614	0.0581	−2.7581	[0.0127, 0.0642][b]
$DN_{m,t}$	0.2230[a]	0.1881	0.2087	0.6798	[0.2048, 0.2783][b]	0.1181[a]	0.0841	0.1239	0.0338	[0.1109, 0.1423][b]
$DP_{m,t}$	−0.2678[a]	0.1217	−0.2463	−1.0001	[−0.2783, −0.2359][b]	−0.1431[a]	0.0512	−0.1417	−0.5036	[−0.1475, −0.1293][b]

Panel D: Vol.-3-state models

$DN_{f,t}$	-0.1444^a	0.3571	-0.1824	1.3118	$[-0.1796, -0.0389]^b$	-0.0784^a	0.2016	-0.1140	1.2959	$[-0.0974, -0.0224]^b$
$DP_{f,t}$	0.0436^a	0.2766	0.0838	-2.3128	$[0.0213, 0.1116]^b$	0.0254^a	0.1605	0.0504	-2.7026	$[0.0108, 0.0655]^b$
$DN_{m,t}$	0.1995^a	0.1447	0.1966	1.0761	$[0.1859, 0.2436]^b$	0.1126^a	0.0706	0.1231	0.3636	$[0.1058, 0.1337]^b$
$DP_{m,t}$	-0.2341^a	0.1007	-0.2116	-1.2639	$[-0.2441, -0.2078]^b$	-0.1336^a	0.0451	-0.1252	-0.7593	$[-0.1377, -0.1214]^b$

Note: This table presents the summary output along with the results of Wilcoxon signed-rank tests and the BCI of estimates of the dummy news variables in different models. $DN_{f,t}$, $DP_{f,t}$, $DN_{m,t}$, and $DP_{m,t}$ are dummy variables of negative and positive firm-specific and negative and positive macroeconomic news stories, respectively. The fitted models include binary and ordered logit and probit models. *Boot-CI* stands for the 95% BCI.

[a] Indicates that the estimates are significantly different from 0 at the 5% level for Wilcoxon signed-rank test.
[b] Suggests that the estimates lie out of the 95% BCI.
For an explanation of other variables, see Table 21.1.

two macroeconomic news variables are roughly the same and greater than that of $DN_{f,t}$. Similar results can be found in the Vol.-2-State case, though $DP_{f,t}$ has a positively significant marginal effect with a much smaller magnitude. Thus, both negative firm-specific and macroeconomic news can significantly affect the likelihood of the turbulent state of stock return volatility, with negative firm-specific news and positive macroeconomic news decreasing the chance and negative macroeconomic news increasing it. In addition, the occurrences of macroeconomic news have greater marginal effects than that of firm-specific news.

Wilfling (2009) suggests an alternative classification based on the smoothing probability: assuming that stock return volatility lies in extremely low-volatility state when $P(s_t = 1|\theta,\Omega_T)$ is close to 1, lies in an extremely high-volatility state when $P(s_t = 1|\theta,\Omega_T)$ is close to 0, and lies in an intermediate state otherwise. Accordingly, we let $Y_t = 1$ indicate the calm state when $P(s_t = 1|\theta,\Omega_T) \geq 0.8$, $Y_t = 3$ indicate the turbulent state when $P(s_t = 1|\theta,\Omega_T) \leq 0.2$, and $Y_t = 2$ indicate the intermediate state otherwise (the Prob.-3-State classification). To confirm the robustness of the results, for each stock, we define the proportions of $P(s_t = 1|\theta,\Omega_T) \geq 0.8$ and $P(s_t = 1|\theta,\Omega_T) \leq 0.2$ as p_1 and p_2, respectively, then, define H_{p_1} and H_{p_2} to be the p_1th and p_2th percentile of h_t for each stock, and finally, define $Y_t = 1$ when $h_t \leq H_{p_1}$, $Y_t = 3$ when $h_t \geq H_{p_2}$ and $Y_t = 2$ otherwise (Vol.-3-State classification). The two three-state classifications are hence summarized as follows:

$$
Y_t = \begin{cases} 1 & P(s_t = 1|\theta,\Omega_T) \geq 0.8 \\ 2 & 0.2 < P(s_t = 1|\theta,\Omega_T) < 0.8, \\ 3 & P(s_t = 1|\theta,\Omega_T) \leq 0.2 \end{cases} \quad Y_t = \begin{cases} 1 & h_t \leq H_{p_1} \\ 2 & H_{p_1} < h_t < H_{p_2} \quad (21.20) \\ 3 & h_t \geq H_{p_2} \end{cases}
$$

The data are then fitted into Eqn (21.19) with both ordered logit and ordered probit specifications as described in Section 21.4.2. The number of significant results with ordered logit and probit models is as given in Panel A of Table 21.3. Both logit and probit models suggest that in 49 out of 50 models, by including dummy news, variables can significantly reduce the deviance in Prob.-3-State classification. For both the logit and probit models, the number is 50 in the Vol.-3-State case. As a result, we can conclude that dummy news variables have significant overall effects on stock return volatility in the three-state classification. The summary outputs of estimated β are listed in Panels B and D of Table 21.4 for the Prob.-3-State and Vol.-3-State classifications, respectively. The results are found to be highly consistent with those of the two-state case.

In conclusion, for both Prob.-2-State and Prob.-3-State classifications, the results further confirm that the occurrences of negative firm-specific news and both negative and positive macroeconomic news can significantly affect the likelihood of a higher volatility state, with negative firm-specific news and positive macroeconomic news decreasing the chance and negative macroeconomic news increasing it. In addition, occurrences of macroeconomic news have greater marginal effects than that of firm-specific news. The results are found to be generally robust in the Vol.-2-State and Vol.-3-State classifications.

21.5.3.2 Number of News Variables on Constrained Dataset

In Section 21.5.3.1, we have demonstrated that occurrences of different news have various significant effects on the states of stock return volatility. As discussed earlier, the theory of MDH also suggests that news flows can affect asset volatility. Thus, it is expected that news flows should have additional effects on asset volatility as compared with news occurrences.

To test such an argument, we first constrain our dataset from the entire period to the period containing at least one news story. In other words, we construct our sample to time i, where $i \in \{1, 2, \ldots, T\}$ and $I(DN_{f,i} + DP_{f,i} + DN_{m,i} + DP_{m,i} > 0) = 1, \forall i$.

We repeat the procedure in Section 21.5.3.1 for the number of news variables with the above-constrained sample. That is, we first apply all the four different classifications of states to the constrained sample, and then, fit $NN_{f,t}$, $NP_{f,t}$, $NN_{m,t}$, and $NP_{m,t}$ into Eqn (21.19) with binary logit and probit models for two-state classifications and with ordered logit and probit models for three-state classifications. The drop-in-deviance results are summarized in Panel B of Table 21.3. The estimation results of both the logit and probit models show that the number of significant deviance reduction by including the number of news variables is ≥ 48 for all classifications, which confirms that, apart from occurrences of news, number of news can significantly further affect states of stock return volatility.

In terms of the estimated β, the results of Prob.-2-State and Prob.-3-State classifications are summarized in Panels A and B of Table 21.5, respectively. Since the Wilcoxon test and BCI yield slightly different results, we focus on significant estimates confirmed by both methods. Therefore, only the number of negative and positive macroeconomic news has significant estimates, with the former being positive and the latter negative. In addition, $NP_{m,t}$ has a much larger marginal effect than $NN_{m,t}$ (>0.12 vs <0.05). All the results are robust in Vol.-2-State and Vol.-3-State classifications. In conclusion, apart from occurrences of news, the number of both negative and positive macroeconomic news has further significant marginal effects on the likelihood of a higher volatility state, with the former increasing the chance and the latter substantially decreasing it.

Table 21.5 Summary output and nonparametric tests results of the number of news variables

Variable	Logit					Probit				
	Mean	Standard Deviation	Median	Skew	Boot-CI	Mean	Standard Deviation	Median	Skew	Boot-CI
Panel A: Prob.-2-state models										
$NN_{f,t}$	−0.0109	0.1091	0.0123	−1.2964	[−0.0216, 0.0182]	−0.0053	0.0586	0.0073	−1.4869	[−0.0104, 0.0098]
$NP_{f,t}$	−0.0079	0.0598	−0.0085	1.3778	[−0.0136, 0.0090]	−0.0024	0.0332	−0.0048	1.8081	[−0.0060, 0.0073]
$NN_{m,t}$	0.0414[a]	0.0464	0.0449	−0.4745	[0.0371, 0.0536][b]	0.0228[a]	0.0248	0.0271	−0.6362	[0.0207, 0.0298][b]
$NP_{m,t}$	−0.1407[a]	0.0640	−0.1380	−0.8019	[−0.1471, −0.1232][b]	−0.0748[a]	0.0299	−0.0718	−0.3237	[−0.0776, −0.0663][b]
Panel B: Prob.-3-state models										
$NN_{f,t}$	−0.0170	0.1010	0.0033	−0.8063	[−0.0269, 0.0106]	−0.0090	0.0547	0.0029	−1.1170	[−0.0145, 0.0056]
$NP_{f,t}$	−0.0019	0.0584	−0.0067	1.3824	[−0.0081, 0.0138]	0.0000	0.0334	−0.0035	1.6217	[−0.0032, 0.0095]
$NN_{m,t}$	0.0390[a]	0.0367	0.0443	−0.4780	[0.0352, 0.0488][b]	0.0225[a]	0.0211	0.0260	−0.4762	[0.0206, 0.0281][b]
$NP_{m,t}$	−0.1273[a]	0.0572	−0.1165	−0.4702	[−0.1324, −0.1124][b]	−0.0711[a]	0.0287	−0.0697	−0.2471	[−0.0736, −0.0631][b]

Panel C: Vol.-2-state models

$NN_{f,t}$	0.0003	0.1213	0.0165	−0.8106	[−0.0116, 0.0329]	0.0012	0.0638	0.0085	−1.0000	[−0.0049, 0.0183]
$NP_{f,t}$	0.0083	0.0572	0.0055	0.5726	[0.0033, 0.0249][b]	0.0059	0.0317	0.0032	0.7346	[0.0028, 0.0150][b]
$NN_{m,t}$	0.0205[a]	0.0570	0.0319	−1.2987	[0.0151, 0.0355][b]	0.0114[a]	0.0300	0.0163	−1.2156	[0.0084, 0.0196][b]
$NP_{m,t}$	−0.1558[a]	0.0607	−0.1571	−0.2351	[−0.1616, −0.1392][b]	−0.0814[a]	0.0272	−0.0804	0.1381	[−0.0838, −0.0739][b]

Panel D: Vol.-3-state models

$NN_{f,t}$	−0.0050	0.1190	0.0117	−0.5066	[−0.0156, 0.0266]	−0.0007	0.0644	0.0067	−0.8309	[−0.0066, 0.0161]
$NP_{f,t}$	0.0090	0.0572	0.0051	0.6396	[0.0037, 0.0247][b]	0.0061	0.0317	0.0037	0.8852	[0.0030, 0.0143][b]
$NN_{m,t}$	0.0173[a]	0.0449	0.0260	−0.6543	[0.0133, 0.0294][b]	0.0103[a]	0.0259	0.0155	−0.8625	[0.0078, 0.0170][b]
$NP_{m,t}$	−0.1378[a]	0.0541	−0.1378	−0.4955	[−0.1428, −0.1229][b]	−0.0765[a]	0.0256	−0.0769	−0.1362	[−0.0790, −0.0695][b]

Note: This table presents the summary output along with the results of Wilcoxon signed-rank tests and Bootstrap percentile confidence interval of estimates of the number of news variables in different models. $NN_{f,t}$, $NP_{f,t}$, $NN_{m,t}$ and $NP_{m,t}$ are the number of news variables of negative and positive firm-specific and negative and positive macroeconomic news stories.
[a]Indicates that the estimates are significantly different from 0 at the 5% level for Wilcoxon signed-rank test.
[b]Suggests that the estimates lie out of the 95% BCI.
For an explanation of other variables, see Tables 21.1 and 21.5.

21.6 CONCLUSION AND IMPLICATIONS

This chapter investigates the impact of intraday firm-specific and macroeconomic news flow on states of stock return volatility for the constituent stocks of Dow Jones Composite Average. By using the MRS-GARCH model to generate smoothing probability and proxy stock return volatility and employing discrete choice models to study the impacts of news, we estimate and demonstrate how public news flow can influence states of asset volatility using data spanning from January 1, 2001 to December 31, 2013. The results show that occurrences of different types of news have various significant effects on the likelihood of a higher volatility state. Further, flows of macroeconomic news have additional impacts. These findings are robust across different models and classifications of volatility states.

Moreover, nonparametric tests including the Wilcoxon signed-rank test and Bootstrap percentile confidence interval are used to test the marginal effect of news variables. Overall, the occurrence of macroeconomic news has a greater marginal effect than that of firm-specific news. More specifically, the occurrence of negative macroeconomic news increases the likelihood of higher-level stock return volatility, whereas that of positive macroeconomic news decreases the chance to a larger degree. Besides, it is demonstrated that the number of news occurrences have further significant marginal effects. Overall, the estimated results are consistent with those of news occurrences and robust across different classifications of volatility states.

Our results also suggest that compared with firm-specific news, macroeconomic news contributes more to volatility state. Since macroeconomic news contains information of the real-time macroeconomic state, our results also indicate that the macroeconomic state is a key factor for the volatility state of individual stock. This empirical result can provide useful information for professional traders who read newswire messages. The intraday impact of these newswire messages will help traders anticipate the potential effects on the state of macroeconomy, which can further affect the volatility of the assets that they are monitoring. Since both the occurrence and number of news have significant marginal effects, traders can adjust their strategies proactively in response to the changes in news flows. In today's electronic trading environment, passive algorithmic trading strategies primarily based on automating the trading process may require a closer monitoring of news flows to manage unexpected market risk (Ho et al., 2013).

APPENDIX A: DOW JONES COMPOSITE AVERAGE 65 STOCKS

Name	Ticker
American Electric Power Co., Inc.	AEP
The AES Corporation	AES
Alaska Air Group, Inc.	ALK
American Express Company	AXP

Name	Ticker
The Boeing Company	BA
Caterpillar Inc.	CAT
CH Robinson Worldwide Inc.	CHRW
CenterPoint Energy, Inc.	CNP
Con-way Inc.	CNW
Cisco Systems, Inc.	CSCO
CSX Corp.	CSX
Chevron Corporation	CVX
Dominion Resources, Inc.	D
Delta Air Lines Inc.	DAL
E. I. du Pont de Nemours and Company	DD
The Walt Disney Company	DIS
Duke Energy Corporation	DUK
Consolidated Edison, Inc.	ED
Edison International	EIX
Exelon Corporation	EXC
Expeditors International of Washington Inc.	EXPD
FedEx Corporation	FDX
FirstEnergy Corp.	FE
General Electric Company	GE
GATX Corp.	GMT
The Goldman Sachs Group, Inc.	GS
The Home Depot, Inc.	HD
International Business Machines Corporation	IBM
Intel Corporation	INTC
JB Hunt Transport Services Inc.	JBHT
JetBlue Airways Corporation	JBLU
Johnson & Johnson	JNJ
JPMorgan Chase & Co.	JPM
Kirby Corporation	KEX
The Coca-Cola Company	KO
Kansas City Southern	KSU
Landstar System Inc.	LSTR
Southwest Airlines Co.	LUV
Matson, Inc.	MATX
McDonald's Corp.	MCD
3M Company	MMM
Merck & Co. Inc.	MRK
Microsoft Corporation	MSFT
NextEra Energy, Inc.	NEE
NiSource Inc.	NI
Nike, Inc.	NKE

Continued

Name	Ticker
Norfolk Southern Corporation	NSC
PG&E Corporation	PCG
Public Service Enterprise Group Inc.	PEG
Pfizer Inc.	PFE
The Procter & Gamble Company	PG
Ryder System, Inc.	R
Southern Company	SO
AT&T, Inc.	T
The Travelers Companies, Inc.	TRV
United Continental Holdings, Inc.	UAL
UnitedHealth Group Incorporated	UNH
Union Pacific Corporation	UNP
United Parcel Service, Inc.	UPS
United Technologies Corp.	UTX
Visa Inc.	V
Verizon Communications Inc.	VZ
Williams Companies, Inc.	WMB
Wal-Mart Stores Inc.	WMT
Exxon Mobil Corporation	XOM

APPENDIX B: RAVENPACK ALGORITHMS

1. Market response methodology

   RavenPack's Market Response methodology underpins the CSS and is based on a Rule Base that identifies and maps individual words or word combinations in the story headline to the price impact on stocks of companies mentioned in the headline. The price impact is measured in the hours ahead of the arrival of the news item and is transformed into an impact score using advanced machine learning techniques.

   Step One: A Classification Base is defined: Develop a Classification Base, or define the types of stories that contain the content relevant for tagging.

   Step Two: A large sample is analyzed to create a Rule Base: A sample set of stories in the Classification Base developed in step one is drawn from RavenPack's news database for a fixed date range. The headlines of these stories are extracted and parsed into words to form a list of candidates of individual words and word combinations that are typical for such headline stories.

   Step Three: Create an Impact Score using the Rule Base: Different advanced machine learning techniques are applied with the objective of creating an Impact Score that identifies the probability of the volatility of a particular stock to be either higher or lower than the volatility of the market.

Step Four: Generate historical analysis and enable real-time tagging: This process involves several consistency checks of historical data and generation of volume statistics. When this process is complete, the series is published.

Step Five: Quarterly reevaluation: Classifiers are reevaluated on a quarterly basis. This process involves completing step two for stories sampled outside of the date range of the original sample or most recent quarterly reevaluation. If the accuracy level is 10% lower than the level when the series was originally released, a new series is developed.

2. Expert consensus tagging methodology

RavenPack's Expert Consensus Methodology underpins the ESS and entails a group of financial experts manually tagging a set of stories that is later used as a basis for automated computer classification using a Bayes Classifier.

Step One: A Classification Base is defined: Develop a Classification Base, or define the types of stories that contain the content relevant for tagging.

Step Two: Experts build an internal Tagging Guide: A team of in-house experts with extensive backgrounds in linguistics, finance, and economics first develop and agree upon a set of parameters and basic assumptions that will guide sentiment tagging.

Step Three: A large sample is tagged: A sample set of stories in the Classification Base developed in step one is drawn from RavenPack's news database for a fixed date range. Stories are randomly selected for tagging. A group of experts read and classify the sample using the Tagging Guide developed in step two.

Step Four: Software is trained from sample to automate tagging: A Bayes Classifier uses supervised learning to discern patterns in expert tagging and establish rules for future automation. This automated tagging process must meet exceptional levels of accuracy in order to be made available to clients. In cases when accuracy is not sufficiently high, step three is repeated with a larger sample set.

Step Five: Generate historical analysis and enable real-time tagging: Historical analysis is generated and real-time tagging is enabled. This process involves several consistency checks of historical data and generation of volume statistics. When this process is complete, the series is published.

Step Six: Quarterly reevaluation: Classifiers are reevaluated on a quarterly basis. This process involves completing step three for stories sampled outside of the date range of the original sample or most recent quarterly reevaluation. The results of this expert classification are compared to the results of automated classification. If the accuracy level is 10% lower than the level when the series was originally released, a new series is developed.

3. Factors in the ESS

In addition to the expert consensus survey data, the ESS has a strength component that is influenced by a variety of factors, depending on the type of event. RavenPack systematically extracts information from every news story to model these factors and determine how positive or negative each event should be. Here is a list of some of these factors:

Emotional Factor. There are five scales containing groups of words and phrases in the RavenPack emotional magnitude component of ESS: Low, Moderate, Substantial, Severe, and Critical Magnitude. Each component contains words that signify the magnitude of an event as described by the author of the story.

Weather and Climate Factor. Tracks official scales to measure extreme weather such as the Richter scale or the Volcanic Eruption Index.

Analyst Rating Factor. Covers >150 different broker and analyst rating scales for stocks (e.g., strong buy, buy, hold, sell, and strong sell).

Credit Rating Factor. Consolidates the three main credit ratings scales by Moody's, Fitch, and S&P (e.g., AAA, AA, BB, and C) into one normalized scale.

Fundamental Comparison Factor. Extracts and calculates numerical differences between actual or estimated values in earnings, revenues, dividends, macroeconomic indicators, and any other financial or economic announcement. Performs arithmetic and translates fundamental percentage changes into a normalized score within the ESS ranges.

Casualties Factor. Identifies how many people are dead or injured as a result of an event and uses this as sentiment strength factor, particularly for natural disasters and industrial accidents.

REFERENCES

Andersen, T.G., Bollerslev, T., Diebold, F., Vega, C., 2003. Micro effects of macro announcements: real-time price discovery in foreign exchange. Am. Econ. Rev. 93 (1), 38–62.

Ardia, D., 2009. Bayesian estimation of a Markov-switching threshold asymmetric GARCH model with Student-t innovations. Econom. J. 12 (1), 105–126.

Berry, T., Howe, K., 1994. Public information arrival. J. Finance 49 (4), 1331–1346.

Bollerslev, T., 1986. Generalized autoregressive conditional heteroskedasticity. J. Econom. 31 (3), 307–327.

Bollerslev, T., 1987. A conditional heteroskedastic time series model for speculative prices and rates of return. Rev. Econ. Stat. 69 (3), 542–547.

Brenner, M., Pasquariello, P., Subrahmanyam, M., 2009. On the volatility and comovement of U.S. financial markets around macroeconomic news announcements. J. Financ. Quant. Anal. 44 (6), 1265–1289.

Cai, J., 1994. A Markov model of unconditional variance in ARCH. J. Bus. Econ. Stat. 12 (3), 309–316.

Clark, P., 1973. A subordinated stochastic process model with finite variance for speculative prices. Econometrica 41 (1), 135–155.

Gray, S., 1996. Modelling the conditional distribution of interest rates as a regime-switching process. J. Financ. Econ. 42 (1), 27–62.

Grob-Klubmann, A., Hautsch, N., 2011. When machines read the news: using automated text analytics to quantify high-frequency news-implied market reactions. J. Empir. Financ. 18 (2), 321–340.

Haas, M., 2009. Value-at-risk via mixture distributions reconsidered. Appl. Math. Comput. 215 (6), 2103–2119.

Haas, M., Paolella, M.S., 2012. Mixture and regime-switching GARCH models. In: Bauwens, L., Hafner, C., Laurent, S. (Eds.), Handbook of Volatility Models and Their Applications. Willey, United Kingdom.

Haas, M., Mittnik, S., Paolella, M.S., 2004. A new approach to Markov-switching GARCH models. J. Financ. Econom. 2 (4), 493–530.

Hamilton, J.D., 1988. Rational-expectations econometric analysis of changes in regime: an investigation of the term structure of interest rates. J. Econ. Dyn. Control 12 (2–3), 385–423.

Hamilton, J.D., 1989. A new approach to the economic analysis of nonstationary time series and the business cycle. Econometrica 57 (2), 357—384.

Hamilton, J.D., 1994. Time Series Analysis. Princeton University Press, Princeton.

Hamilton, J.D., Susmel, R., 1994. Autoregressive conditional heteroskedasticity and changes in regime. J. Econom. 64 (1), 307—333.

Hautsch, N., Hess, D., Veredas, D., 2011. The impact of macroeconomic news on quote adjustments, noise, and informational volatility. J. Bank. Financ. 35 (10), 2733—2746.

Hendershott, T., Jones, C.M., Menkveld, A.J., 2010. Does algorithmic trading improve liquidity? J. Finance 66 (1), 1—33.

Ho, K.Y., Shi, Y., Zhang, Z., 2013. How does news sentiment impact asset volatility? Evidence from long memory and regime-switching approaches. N. Am. J. Econ. Financ. 26, 436—456.

Kalev, P.S., Liu, W.M., Pham, P.K., Jarnecic, E., 2004. Public information arrival and volatility of intraday stock returns. J. Bank. Financ. 28 (6), 1441—1467.

Klaassen, F., 2002. Improving GARCH volatility forecasts with regime-switching GARCH. Empir. Econ. 27 (2), 363—394.

Marcucci, J., 2005. Forecasting stock market volatility with regime-switching GARCH models. Stud. Nonlinear Dyn. Econom. 9 (4), 1—53.

Mullen, K.M., Ardia, D., Gil, D.L., Windover, D., Cline, J., 2011. DEoptim: an R package for global optimization by differential evolution. J. Stat. Softw. 40 (6), 1—26.

Susmel, R., Engel, R., 1994. Hourly volatility spillovers between international equity markets. J. Int. Money Financ. 13 (1), 3—25.

Wilfling, B., 2009. Volatility regime-switching in European exchange rates prior to monetary unification. J. Int. Money Financ. 28 (2), 240—270.

CHAPTER 22

News Releases and Stock Market Volatility: Intraday Evidence from Borsa Istanbul

M. Nihat Solakoglu, Nazmi Demir
Department of Banking & Finance, Bilkent University, Bilkent, Ankara, Turkey

Contents

22.1 INTRODUCTION

The effect of public information arrival on asset prices and volatility has been investigated extensively in the past using different markets, asset prices, and most importantly different proxies for information arrival. One line of research utilized macroeconomic announcements to investigate the effect of information arrival on asset returns and return volatility (e.g., Ederington and Lee, 1993; Andersen and Bollerslev, 1998; Almeida et al., 1998; Pearce and Roley, 1985; Pearce and Solakoglu, 2007; Kutan and Aksoy, 2004). Another line of research focused on market information as a measure of news arrivals, such as trading volume, floor transactions, the number of price changes, and executed order imbalances, to investigate the same hypothesis (Lamoureux and Lastrapes, 1990; Andersen, 1996; Bollerslev and Domowitz, 1993; Locke and Sayers, 1993). In the last line of research, new information arrival is measured by the frequency of public news that arrives to the market. These studies use either the number of news headlines obtained from newspapers (Berry and Howe, 1994) or those released by companies that provide data services, such as Dow Jones and Company or Reuters, to count the number of news items (Kalev et al., 2004; Mitchell and Mulherin, 1994; Janssen, 2004; Chang and Taylor, 2003; Baklacı et al., 2011).

This study follows the last line of research and utilizes the number of economic news headlines that arrives to the market to investigate the effect of news arrival on market return and return volatility. This study differs from earlier studies in three ways. First, we use intraday data, specifically 60-min returns, and focus on economic news only. Moreover, we separate news originating from the United States, Turkey, and a subsegment of

Europe that consists of the United Kingdom, France, Spain, Germany, and Italy (which we call Europe in this study)[1] and try to identify whether the source of the news is important for investors. Second, we analyze the effect of real economy news and inflation news on return and return volatility separately. In addition, since expected news should not have an impact on asset prices under the efficient market hypothesis, we count the number of unexpected surprises in the GDP and CPI news headlines and evaluate the effect of surprises on return and return volatility. Finally, we focus our analysis on the return and return volatility of two different stock market indices: BIST100 and Second National Market (SNM). In BIST100, there is a widespread existence of institutional investors, and hence we assume that these investors are more informed and have better access to both market- and firm-level information than those of the SNM. We also expect them to have better resources relative to the SNM investors to analyze information content. In the SNM index, the presence of institutional investors is much smaller relative to BIST100, and hence we assume investors are less informed. As a result, we aim to investigate whether this difference influences our results significantly.

Our findings show that the arrival of economic news causes return volatility to decline. However, there is no significant effect on index returns. We also find that return volatility reacts mostly to negative GDP and inflation surprises. Moreover, our results indicate that investors, whether well-informed or not, respond similarly to news arrival as documented by same-sign coefficients and by a comparable decline in volatility persistence.

The remainder of this study is organized as follows. In Section II, we discuss data sources and present descriptive statistics. The model specification is also discussed in this section. Our findings and discussion are left for Section III. The last section presents our main conclusions and suggestions for further research.

22.2 MODEL SPECIFICATION AND DATA

This study uses the hourly number of economic news headlines provided by *Foreks Data Terminal* to proxy the arrival of new information for the period between October 3, 2013 and March 31, 2014. News coverage is only included during weekdays and hence there is no data available for weekends.[2] To measure return volatility, we utilize two indexes—BIST100 and SNM index—of Borsa Istanbul (BIST). Hourly index data are obtained from *Matriks Data Terminal*. The BIST100 covers the largest 100 firms in Turkey, mostly with foreign portfolio investments that account for about 60% of traded shares, while the SNM covers small-to-medium-sized firms as well as those

---

[1] The share of Turkish exports to these countries within the 28 European Union countries is around 77% for 2013.
 Source: Turkish Government Ministry of Economy Web page (http://www.economy.gov.tr).
[2] The analysis uses 961 observations.

Table 22.1 Descriptive statistics

	Mean	Standard deviation	Minimum	Maximum	Skewness	Kurtosis
Total economic news	10.08	9.31	0.00	52.00	1.29	4.56
US economic news	1.90	4.94	0.00	36.00	3.49	16.73
US news on real economy	0.55	1.70	0.00	15.00	4.13	23.25
US news on inflation	0.10	0.70	0.00	12.00	9.18	112.82
Europe economic news	1.63	3.34	0.00	25.00	2.75	11.96
Europe news on real economy	0.63	1.60	0.00	10.00	3.02	12.41
Europe news on inflation	0.41	1.68	0.00	16.00	6.16	49.27
Turkish economic news	1.99	4.81	0.00	33.00	2.88	11.71
Turkish news on real economy	0.23	1.09	0.00	14.00	6.68	58.20
Turkish news on inflation	0.21	1.06	0.00	10.00	6.17	46.48

In the table, the number of economic news headlines is provided. Europe news includes news on a sample of European countries. These countries are: UK, France, Germany, Spain, and Italy.

delisted from the National Index.[3] Hence, while BIST100 includes large institutional holdings of securities, the SNM index is mostly for local investors, and by including these two indexes we want to identify differences in how the news arrival are evaluated by these two distinct investor groups.[4] A recent study by Solakoglu and Demir (2014) provides sample evidence that shows the existence of sentimental herding for SNM investors and not for better-informed investors of BIST100.

Table 22.1 reports descriptive statistics on news arrivals. On average, 10 news headlines arrive to the market per hour, with a maximum of 52 news headlines per hour. The average number of daily news arrivals, not reported, is 80 during our sample, with a minimum of 29 and a maximum of 157. For both Europe and the USA, more news on output arrives to the market than inflation. For Turkish news, there does not seem to be a significant difference between news on inflation and news on output. In addition,

---

[3] For details on these two indexes, see http://www.borsaistanbul.com.

[4] For example, in 2012, the average holding period was 316 days for foreign investors and only 37 days for local investors, showing the differences in investment strategies (Bourse Trend Report, January 2013, http://www.tuyid.org/tr/).

the highest number of hourly news arrivals seems to be on Thursdays, with an average of 13.3 news headlines per hour for our sample period. The least number of news arrives on Tuesdays, with an average of 7.7 news items per hour. Although not presented in the table, the average daily return for SNM appears to be higher than for BIST100. However, the range is also much larger for SNM. In addition, the SNM index returns are more leptokurtic than for BIST100 index returns, indicating that it is more likely to observe extreme ups and downs in the market, thus pointing out that the SNM is riskier with higher return on the average than is the BIST100.

Following earlier studies, we utilize the Generalized Autoregressive Conditional Heteroscedasticity (GARCH) models introduced by Engle (1982) and Bollerslev (1986) to test the effect of new information arrival on return and return volatility. Through the use of the GARCH model, we also expect volatility persistence to decline. That is, we will be able to observe whether some of the volatility clustering observed in the conditional volatility is due to new information. The model we estimate is provided below.

$$R_{i,t} = \mu + \phi_1 D_1 + \phi_2 D_2 + \phi_3 D_3 + \phi_4 D_4 + \phi_5 Open + \sum \lambda_j N_{jt}$$

$$+ \varepsilon_t, \text{ where } \varepsilon_t \sim N(0, \sigma_t^2)$$

$$\sigma_t^2 = \alpha_0 + \alpha_1 \varepsilon_{t-1}^2 + \beta \sigma_{t-1}^2 + \sum \lambda_j N_{jt} \qquad [22.1]$$

In this equation, $R_{i,t}$ is the hourly index return, calculated as the log difference. The mean equation includes day-of-the-week effect as represented by day dummies D_1 to D_4, with Friday being the base, as well as a dummy, *Open*, that represents the opening hour for BIST. In both the mean and the conditional variance equation, N_{jt} denotes measures of new information arrivals at time t for measure j, and λ_j denotes the associated coefficients. If the new information arrival is important, we expect λ_j to be statistically significant for the jth news measure. Moreover, with the new information arrival, we expect a decline in volatility persistence, as defined by the sum of coefficient estimates, α_1 and β.

22.3 RESULTS AND DISCUSSION

We reported the estimation results for Eqn (22.1) in Table 22.2 for both BIST100 and SNM returns. Base model reports the estimation results when no news arrival measure is used. When the news arrival is measured by the total number of economic news, our findings indicate that return volatility declines for BIST100 and not for SNM index. In addition, there seems to be no impact on returns itself. The last columns present results when the news is segmented based on country of origin. For both index returns, the number of economic news arriving from the US, Europe, and Turkey causes return volatility to decline. Although this result seems puzzling as one expects return volatility to increase due to news arrival, it is not unique to our study. For example, Kutan and Aksoy

Table 22.2 New information arrival and return volatility

	BIST100			SNM		
	Base model	Model 1	Model 2	Base model	Model 1	Model 2
Return equation						
Total economic news	—	0.000004	—	—	−0.000009	—
		(0.000015)			(0.000013)	
US economic news	—	—	0.000031	—	—	0.000064**
			(0.000042)			(2.008843)
Europe economic news	—	—	0.000102	—	—	0.000127
			(0.000092)			(1.655401)
Turkey economic news	—	—	0.000003	—	—	0.000005
			(0.000059)			(0.112800)
Conditional Variance equation						
g	0.000002***	0.000011***	0.000026***	0.000001***	0.000003***	0.000023***
	(0.000000)	(0.000001)	(0.000004)	(0.000000)	(0.000000)	(0.000003)
d_1	0.026173***	0.059396***	0.149867***	0.090068***	0.112992	0.149952***
	(0.004823)	(0.012601)	(0.049291)	(0.007881)	(0.011541)	(0.030456)
d_2	0.954729***	0.753705***	0.599660***	0.897270***	0.843588	0.599626***
	(0.007605)	(0.024490)	(0.081638)	(0.008125)	(0.015449)	(0.066174)
Opening hour	−0.000013***	0.000000	−0.000017***	−0.000002	−0.000002	−0.000013***
	(0.000003)	(0.000000)	(0.000006)	(0.000002)	(0.000002)	(0.000005)
Total economic news	—	−0.000004***	—	—	0.000000	—
		(0.000003)			(0.000000)	
US economic news	—	—	−0.000001***	—	—	−0.000001***
			(0.000000)			(0.000000)
Europe economic news	—	—	−0.000002***	—	—	−0.000002***
			(0.000000)			(0.000000)
Turkey economic news	—	—	−0.000001***	—	—	−0.000001***
			(0.000000)			(0.000000)
Function value	3666.58	3678.44	3612.35	3868.56	3875.84	3725.24
AIC	−7.59	−7.61	−7.47	−8.01	−8.02	−7.70

***, **, * denotes statistical significance at 1%, 5%, and 10%, respectively. Standard errors are provided in parentheses. For brevity, we did not provide coefficient of the constant and day-of-the-week dummies in the return equation. Opening hour corresponds to first hour where the trading starts to represent the effect of accumulated news on return and return volatility. Function value is the log likelihood value, and AIC denotes Akaike Information Criteria. BIST, Borsa Istanbul; SNM, Second National Maret.

(2004a, b) also find a decline in return volatility using data from BIST. Moreover, for both bearish and bullish periods, Baklaci et al. (2011) show that news arrival causes return volatility to decline for several firms. If the arrival of news causes information asymmetry to decline, then it is plausible also to observe return volatility to decline (Diamond and Verrechia, 1991). In other words, investors/traders are clearer about the market, and hence their confusions or questions are removed as the news (positive or negative) arrives. As a result, return volatility declines as they are in line with one another following market fundamentals.

The information content of news that arrives to the market will be different if the news is on output or on inflation. Therefore, in Table 22.3, we provide estimation results when the news headlines are separated by whether the news is on the real economy or on inflation. As before, we do not find any significant relationship between return and news arrival. However, for the BIST100 index, regardless of the type of news, return volatility and news arrival are negatively related. For the SNM index, our results indicate that US and Europe news on output causes a decline in return volatility. However, neither inflation news nor news on the Turkish economy with respect to output or inflation has a significant influence on return volatility. Given that investors in the firms listed under the SNM index are mostly local investors with much lower average holding periods, this finding does not seem to be a surprise. Perhaps the SNM investors, being frequent sellers and buyers, are buying the past winners and selling the past losers with no particular attention to news arrivals.

If the markets are efficient, anticipated news should provide no new information to investors/traders, while unanticipated news contains new information that changes investment/trading behavior. In other words, news headlines that indicate an expected output growth can have a different interpretation than a headline announcing a surprise output growth. Moreover, news arrival that indicates a surprise output growth or a surprise rise in price levels can have a different impact on return volatility than a surprise decline in output growth or a surprise decline in price level.

Therefore, for CPI and GDP news, we identify surprises by comparing actual and expected announcements provided by *Foreks Data Terminal*. We also distinguish surprise news as either a positive surprise or a negative surprise. Although we define positive surprises when the actual value is greater than the expected value, we do not intend to associate positive surprises with good news or bad news all the time. As discussed in Pearce and Solakoglu (2007) and Birz and Lott (2011), the same news headlines can send different signals when the economy is in a recession as opposed to overheating. For instance, news on surprise output growth can be interpreted as bad news in an overheating economy, while the same news can be interpreted as good news when the economy is in recession. Given that our sample period does not correspond to a crisis period, we believe that both surprise growth in output and surprise decline in inflation represent signals of good news for the Turkish economy.

Table 22.3 Type of information and return volatility

	BIST100		SNM	
	X = Real	X = Inflation	X = Real	X = Inflation
Return equation				
US news on X economy	0.000062	−0.000119	0.000209★★	−0.000037
	(0.606543)	(0.000439)	(0.000086)	(0.000350)
Europe news on X economy	0.000060	0.000073	−0.000077	0.000015
	(0.193720)	(0.000057)	(0.000111)	(0.000178)
Turkey news on X economy	−0.000073	−0.000139	0.000098	0.000002
	−(0.212380)	(0.000146)	(0.000184)	(0.000227)
Conditional variance equation				
g	0.000028★★★	0.000026★★★	0.000011★★★	0.000025
	(0.000008)	(0.000005)	(0.000001)	(0.000006)
d_1	0.149605★★	0.149162★★	0.150534★★★	0.149760
	(0.066503)	(0.058623)	(0.023091)	(0.042670)
d_2	0.598895★★★	0.597579★★★	0.595804★★★	0.597969
	(0.126722)	(0.094998)	(0.048324)	(0.099808)
Opening hour	−0.000016	−0.000024★★★	−0.000005	−0.000021
	(0.000009)	(0.000009)	(0.000004)	(0.000009)
US news on X economy	−0.000003★★★	−0.000002★★	−0.000001★★★	−0.000002
	(0.000001)	(0.000001)	(0.000000)	(0.000001)
Europe news on X economy	−0.000003★	−0.000003★★★	−0.000002★★★	−0.000003
	(0.000002)	(0.000001)	(0.000000)	(0.000000)
Turkey news on X economy	−0.000003★★★	−0.000004★★★	−0.000001	−0.000003
	(0.000001)	(0.000001)	(0.000001)	(0.000001)
Function value	3549.81	3560.89	3795.16	3638.39
AIC	−7.34	−7.36	−7.85	−7.52

★★★, ★★, ★ denotes statistical significance at 1%, 5%, and 10%, respectively. Standard errors are provided in parentheses. For brevity, we did not provide coefficient of the constant and day-of-the-week dummies in the return equation. Opening hour corresponds to first hour where the trading starts to represent the effect of accumulated news on return and return volatility. Function value is the log likelihood value, and AIC denotes Akaike Information Criteria. BIST, Borsa Istanbul; SNM, Second National Maret.

Table 22.4 provides estimation results for GDP and CPI surprises. Consistent with our earlier results, we do not observe a significant association between surprise news and returns in general. However, we provide some evidence that negative surprises, whether it is related to output or inflation, lead to a decline in return volatility. On

Table 22.4 PI and GDP surprises and return volatility

	BIST100				SNM			
A: Return equation	Model 1	Model 2	Model 3	Model 4	Model 1	Model 2	Model 3	Model 4
Surprise CPI announcements	−0.000649 (0.001146)	—	—	—	0.000069 (0.000810)	—	—	—
Positive CPI surprises	—	−0.001530 (0.002898)	—	—	—	0.000223 (0.001378)	—	—
Negative CPI surprises	—	−0.000406 (0.002516)	—	—	—	0.000874** (0.000387)	—	—
Surprise GDP announcements	—	—	0.002180* (0.001273)	—	—	—	0.002551 (0.001626)	—
Positive GDP surprises	—	—	—	−0.000266 (0.002174)	—	—	—	0.001521 (0.002175)
Negative GDP surprises	—	—	—	0.000399 (0.007507)	—	—	—	0.001745 (0.002408)
B: Conditional variance equation								
g	0.000002*** (0.000000)	0.000024*** (0.000001)	0.000023*** (0.000002)	0.000026*** (0.000009)	0.000001*** (0.000000)	0.000001*** (0.000000)	0.000014*** (0.000002)	0.000023*** (0.000005)
d_1	0.026269*** (0.005211)	0.143223*** (0.045575)	0.140714*** (0.042958)	0.145278** (0.068690)	0.093729*** (0.008774)	0.085933*** (0.009644)	0.159740*** (0.026459)	0.148508*** (0.037781)
d_2	0.955229*** (0.008373)	0.583938*** (0.023855)	0.584064*** (0.008469)	0.588012*** (0.156037)	0.893191*** (0.009175)	0.891845*** (0.010133)	0.563065*** (0.055657)	0.587324*** (0.087025)

Opening hour	−0.000012***	−0.000032***	−0.000028***	−0.000028***	−0.000001	−0.000001	−0.000019***	−0.000026***
	(0.000003)	(0.000006)	(0.000007)	(0.000009)	(0.000002)	(0.000002)	(0.000002)	(0.000005)
Surprise CPI announcements	0.000003**	—	—	—	−0.000001	−0.000001	—	—
	(0.000002)	—	—	—	(0.000001)	(0.000002)	—	—
Positive CPI surprises	—	−0.000013	—	—	−0.000001	0.000004	—	—
	—	(0.000016)	—	—	(0.000001)	(0.000002)	—	—
Negative CPI surprises	—	−0.000035***	—	—	—	−0.000004***	—	—
	—	(0.000003)	—	—	—	(0.000001)	—	—
Surprise GDP announcements	—	—	−0.000027***	—	—	—	0.000000	—
	—	—	(0.000010)	—	—	—	(0.000009)	—
Positive GDP surprises	—	—	—	−0.000036	—	—	—	−0.000014
	—	—	—	(0.000025)	—	—	—	(0.000014)
Negative GDP surprises	—	—	—	−0.000034***	—	—	—	−0.000031***
	—	—	—	(0.000008)	—	—	—	(0.000005)
Function value	3667.84	3579.13	3573.78	3552.64	3868.79	3871.65	3735.26	3648.28
AIC	−7.59	−7.40	−7.40	−7.35	−8.01	−8.01	−7.73	−7.55

***, **, * denotes statistical significance at 1%, 5% and 10%, respectively. Standard errors are provided in parentheses. For brevity, we did not provide coefficient of the constant and day-of-the-week dummies in the return equation. Opening hour corresponds to first hour where the trading starts to represent the effect of accumulated news on return and return volatility. Function value is the log likelihood value, and AIC denotes Akaike Information Criteria. BIST, Borsa Istanbul; SNM, Second National Maret.

the other hand, positive surprises have no significant effect on return volatility. We can link this interesting finding with the herding intentions of investors/traders. It is possible that investors/traders observe lower than expected output growth as a signal for market stress (bad news) and hence decide to act together, which leads to a decline in return volatility (see, for example, Hwang and Salmon, 2004; Christie and Huang, 1995; Chang et al., 2000).

The mixture of distribution hypothesis states that if news arrival is important for return volatility, the inclusion of news arrival into the conditional volatility equation should cause a decline in volatility persistence. With the inclusion of economic news headline counts, volatility persistence drops about 17% for the BIST100 index and only about 3% for the SNM index. However, when news is separated by country of origin, for both indices, we observe a decline of about 24% in volatility persistence. In addition, the decline in persistence is over 30% when the news arrival is measured by the news on output or inflation separately, or by the positive and negative surprises. As a result, even though investor characteristics are different for both indices, the reaction of investors/traders to news arrival appears to be similar.

22.3 CONCLUSION

In this study, we try to understand the role of news arrival on return and return volatility for two types of investors, informed versus not-informed, using hourly data for the Turkish stock market. News arrival is measured by the number of economic headlines received from the US, a sample of European countries and Turkey. News is classified based on the country of origin and type of news headlines. Moreover, for GDP and inflation news, we identify positive and negative surprises for the countries we considered during our sample period.

Our results are surprising in two fronts. One is the lack of significant response of returns to news arrival. The second one is the significant decline in return volatility due to news arrival. We believe that news arrival leads information asymmetry to decline among investors which, in turn leads to a decline in return volatility (Diamond and Verrechia, 1991). Given that return volatility declines significantly only under negative GDP and inflation surprises, we can also reference herding behavior as a possible explanation for the decreased return volatility. In addition, our findings imply that the information asymmetry is lower and hence investors/traders are clearer about the market when news arrival is about negative surprises on GDP and inflation. Although we consider two types of investors, our results do not provide strong evidence that indicate the differences in the usage of information arrivals between the two groups. Overall, both groups seem to be affected similarly, both for the effect of news arrival on return and return volatility and decline in volatility persistence.

REFERENCES

Almeida, A., Goodhart, C., Payne, R., 1998. The effects of macroeconomic news on high frequency exchange rate behavior. J. Financial Quantitative Analysis 33 (3), 383—408.

Anderson, T.G., Bollerslev, T., 1998. Deutsche Mark—dollar Volatility: Intraday activity patterns, macro-economic announcements, and longer run dependencies. J. Finance 53 (1), 219—265.

Anderson, T.G., 1996. Return volatility and trading volume: an information flow interpretation of stochastic volatility. J. Finance 51 (1), 169—204.

Baklacı, H.F., Gokce Tunc, G., Aydogan, B., Vardar, G., 2011. The impact of firm-specific public news on intraday market dynamics: evidence from the turkish stock market. Emerg. Mark. Finance Trade 47 (6), 99—119.

Berry, T.D., Howe, K.M., 1994. Public information arrival. J. Finance 49 (4), 1331—1346.

Birz, G., Lott Jr, J.R., 2011. The effect of macroeconomic news on stock returns: new evidence from news-paper coverage. J. Bank. Finance 35 (11), 2791—2800.

Bollerslev, T., 1986. Generalized autoregressive conditional heteroscedasticity. J. Econ. 31 (3), 307—326.

Bollerslev, T., Domowitz, I., 1993. Trading patterns and prices in the interbank foreign exchange market. J. Finance 48 (4), 1421—1444.

Chang, Y., Taylor, S.J., 2003. Information arrivals and intraday exchange rate volatility. J. Int. Financial Mark. Institutions Money 13 (2), 85—112.

Chang, E.C., Cheng, J.W., Khorana, A., 2000. An examination of herd behavior in equity markets: an international perspective. J. Bank. Finance 24 (10), 1651—1679.

Christie, W.G., Huang, R.D., 1995. Following the pied piper: do individual returns herd around the market. Financial Analysts J. 51 (4), 31—37.

Diamond, D.W., Verrechia, R.E., 1991. Disclosure, liquidity, and cost of capital. J. Finance 46 (40), 1325—1359.

Ederington, L.H., Lee, J.H., 1993. How markets process information: news releases and volatility. J. Finance 48 (4), 1161—1191.

Engle, R.F., 1982. Autoregressive conditional Heteroskedasticity with estimates of the variances of UK inflation. Econometrica 50 (4), 987—1008.

Hwang, S., Salmon, M, 2004. Market stress and herding. J. Empir. Finance 11 (4), 585—616.

Janssen, G., 2004. Public information arrival and volatility persistence in Financial markets. Eur. J. Finance 10 (3), 177—197.

Kalev, P.S., Liu, W.M., Pham, P.K., Jarnecic, E., 2004. Public information arrival and volatility of intraday stock returns. J. Bank. Finance 28 (6), 1441—1467.

Kutan, A.M., Aksoy, T., 2004a. Public information arrival and emerging, markets returns and volatility. Multinatl. Finance J. 8 (3—4), 227—245.

Kutan, A.M., Aksoy, T., 2004b. Public information arrival and gold market, returns in emerging markets: evidence from the istanbul gold exchange. Sci. J. Adm. Dev. 2 (2), 13—26.

Lamoureux, C.G., Lastrapes, W.D., 1990. Heteroscedasticity in stock return Data: Volume versus GARCH effects. J. Finance 45 (1), 221—229.

Locke, P.R., Sayers, C.L., 1993. Intraday futures Price Volatility: Information effects and variance persistence. J. Appl. Econ. 8 (1), 15—30.

Mitchell, M.L., Mulherin, J.H., 1994. The impact of public information on stock market. J. Finance 49 (3), 923—950.

Pearce, D.K., Solakoglu, M.N., 2007. Macroeconomic news and exchange rates. J. Int. Financ. Mark. Institutions Money 17 (4), 307—325.

Pearce, D.K., Roley, V.V., 1985. Stock prices and economic news. J. Bus. 58 (1), 49—67.

Solakoglu, M.N., Demir, N., 2014. Sentimental herding in borsa Istanbul: Informed versus uninformed. Appl. Econ. Lett. 21 (14), 965—968.

CHAPTER 23

The Low-Risk Anomaly Revisited on High-Frequency Data

Kris Boudt[1], Giang Nguyen[1], Benedict Peeters[2]
[1]Solvay Business School, Vrije Universiteit Brussel, Brussels, Belgium; [2]Finvex Group, Brussels, Belgium

Contents

23.1 INTRODUCTION

A growing number of investment practitioners and academics have stepped away from stock portfolio construction based on joint forecasts of expected returns and risk to equity risk-based strategies that rely only on risk views to manage risk and increase diversification. An interesting empirical finding is that, over longer investment horizons, investing in portfolios that dynamically invest in low-risk stocks tends to outperform the market capitalization-weighted portfolio (e.g., Leote de Carvalho et al. (2012), Baker and Haugen (2012), Frazzini and Pedersen (2014)).

These low-risk equity portfolios that, through stock selection and weighting, aim at reducing the portfolio risk have become increasingly popular since the 2008 financial crisis and mostly use daily, weekly, or monthly return data to estimate the portfolio risk.

At the same time, the financial econometrics literature has recommended the use of high-frequency (also called intraday) data for the estimation of financial risk (e.g., Engle (2000), Ghysels et al. (2006)). Because of recent advances in information

The Handbook of High Frequency Trading
ISBN 978-0-12-802205-4

technology, these data are more easily available and pose less computational challenges. Since they offer access to more observations, they offer the opportunity to estimate in a more accurate and timely way the risk of equity investments.

The literature seems to suggest that there is an economic value for the investor to use intraday data in daily portfolio allocation. Most of the research has followed the volatility timing approach in Fleming et al. (2001) in which portfolio weights are determined to minimize the portfolio variance. De Pooter et al. (2008) and Hautsch et al. (2013) document that for investors in large capitalization US stocks, the use of high-frequency data reduces the out-of-sample volatility.

It is unfortunately, for several reasons, unclear whether this result extends to realistic portfolio allocations. The first reason is that the daily rebalancing frequency analyzed in previous research is a mismatch with the usual monthly or quarterly frequency at which low-risk portfolios are rebalanced. The second reason is that these studies have a substantial survivorship bias as they do not take the dynamic evolution of the investment universe into account, but restrict it to those stocks that never drop out of the universe (the S&P 100 for de Pooter et al. (2008)) or have the longest continuous trading history (of the S&P 500 stocks in Hautsch et al. (2013)). The third explanation is that they focus on the estimation of the covariance matrix, but most real low-risk portfolios use simple univariate and bivariate risk measures to select low-risk stocks and weight them (Amenc et al., 2013). Finally, most authors present the differences in performance without any formal test of the statistical significance of the observed difference in performance, making it difficult to conclude whether the observed differences are large enough to distinguish them from (good or bad) luck.

This chapter is the first to study the economic value of high-frequency data for low-risk portfolio allocation in a realistic framework. We mimic the MSCI low-volatility index by a two-step investment process. On the last trading day of every month, the 100 lowest risk stocks are selected from the S&P 500 universe at that moment, and the selected stocks are then market capitalization weighted, equal weighted, or inverse risk weighted. For all five risk measures considered, we find no statistically significant difference in average return, standard deviation, or Sharpe ratio between portfolios using daily data and high-frequency data. We do find a confirmation of the low-risk anomaly that the low-risk portfolio out of sample outperforms the market capitalization-weighted portfolio over the period 2007−2012, mostly because of a statistically significant lower volatility and because of its superior relative performance during the financial crisis.

The remainder of this chapter is organized as follows: Section 23.2 summarizes the literature about the low-risk anomaly, and the utilization of high-frequency data in risk-return analysis and portfolio optimization. Then, Section 23.3 introduces our methodology to construct low-risk portfolios and estimate the different risk measures using daily data and high-frequency data. The data collection process is described in Section 23.4. Our findings are presented in Section 23.5. Finally, Section 23.6 concludes and sketches directions for further research. Appendices contain technical details on the implementation of the high-frequency data–based risk estimates and additional output from the out-of-sample performance evaluation.

23.2 LITERATURE REVIEW

Our research question is at the intersection of two strands of the literature: the literature on the low-risk anomaly and the literature on the utilization of high-frequency data to study the risk-return relationship, to optimize the portfolio allocation.

23.2.1 The Low-Risk Anomaly

The fundamental principle in finance is that a high-risk exposure should be compensated with a higher (expected) return. This prediction is both intuitive and backed by several financial theories such as the Capital Asset Pricing Model (CAPM) developed by Sharpe (1964) and Lintner (1965), and the Intertemporal Capital Asset Pricing Model (ICAPM) of Merton (1980). At the same time, it has been contested by several empirical studies that find that the risk-return relationship is flat or even negative and that portfolios of low-risk stock outperform on the long run portfolios with high-risk stocks (see e.g., Baker et al. (2011) and the references therein).

Under the CAPM model, conditional on the return of the market portfolio, the required (expected) rate of return on a risky asset (in excess of the risk free rate) is proportional to the excess market return with the proportionality factor equal to the asset's beta. In CAPM theory, only the systematic risk (i.e., the asset's beta defined as the covariance between the asset and the market return divided by variance of the market return) is rewarded. A positive beta implies a positive relation between risk and return.

The ICAPM model studies the risk-return relation for the aggregate market portfolio. In the ICAPM model, Merton (1980) shows that the equilibrium conditional excess return on the market can be approximated by a linear function of its conditional variance. This establishes the dynamic relation that investors require a larger risk premium at times when the stock market is riskier (Bali and Peng, 2006). This mechanism is also called the volatility feedback effect since it predicts that, if volatility is priced, an anticipated increase in volatility raises the required rate of return, and therefore implies an almost immediate stock price decline in order to allow for higher future returns (Bollerslev et al., 2006).

Several empirical studies have questioned the principle of a risk-return trade-off. Haugen and Heins (1975) show that US stocks with smaller volatility exhibit larger returns over a period ranging from 1926 to 1971. Clarke, de Silva and Thorley (2006) find that minimum variance portfolios based on the 1000 largest US stocks during 1968–2005 achieve a volatility reduction of about 25%, while delivering comparable or even higher average returns than the market portfolio. Blitz and Van Vliet (2007) report that when global stocks are ranked by historical volatility into deciles, the average returns in 1986–1995 of each decile portfolio is comparable, but the volatility of the highest volatility decile portfolio is twice the volatility of the lowest decile portfolio. Similarly, Baker et al. (2011) show that in 1968–2008 the lowest decile volatility and beta US stocks both possess higher returns than their top decile counterparts. As noted already by Haugen and Heins (1975), the long evaluation periods are needed to balance the bearish and bullish periods. As a result of its less-than unity market beta, the low-risk investment style is expected to underperform the market in market rallies. However, low-volatility strategies tend to outperform market cap-weighted benchmarks during downmarkets. Pettengill et al. (1995) illustrate that the outperformance in bear markets is more consistent and larger in magnitude and find that, as a result, low-volatility strategies outperform in the long run.

The empirical evidence against the presence of a substantial risk premium in equities is now supported by several financial theories especially in the field of behavioral finance. Investors tend to accept a too low return for risky stocks because they are subject to the lottery-effect (attracted to high-risk stocks seeking for high returns). Also, institutional investors' performance is likely to be benchmarked with the tracking error of market cap-weighted indices. Baker et al. (2011) argue that, as low-risk investing increases the tracking error, these securities are anticipated as unattractive. Institutional investors are often constrained with respect to leveraged investments. Frazzini and Pedersen (2014) attribute the existence of the anomaly to the fact that many investors are constrained in the leverage they can take and therefore overweight risky securities instead of using leverage, leading to lower risk-adjusted returns for risky high-beta assets.

23.2.2 The Use of High-Frequency Data in Risk-Return Analysis and Portfolio Allocation

Several papers have recently investigated the risk-return trade-off by using high-frequency data for the estimation of risk measure. The rationale for this is that the use of high-frequency data leads to more accurate volatility estimation and therefore more precision in the analysis of the risk-return relationship than when using daily data.

The study of Bali and Peng (2006) on the Center for Research in Security Prices value-weighted index, S&P 500 cash index, S&P 500 index futures, seems to indicate a significantly positive relation between the conditional volatility and conditional mean of market returns at the daily level, and this both for the cases where volatility is estimated using daily and intraday data.

Dufour et al. (2012) combine high-frequency data with option price data and propose to use the difference between the implied and realized volatility (called the variance risk premium) to predict future returns. They also state that the use of implied volatilities rather than realized volatilities is essential to assess the volatility feedback effect.

Neri and Notini (2006) study the Sao Paulo stock exchange index (IBOVESPA), during the period 01/02/1998 to 07/09/2001 (covering the Russian crisis in 1998) and also find a positive relationship between daily risk (estimated on 15-min return data) and return. Finally, Lee et al. (2011) use a wavelet analysis to study the return—volatility relationship in high-frequency price data for the S&P 500 index from January 1997 to March 2005 but find mixed results on the presence of a risk-return relationship. Overall, we can conclude that the majority of the studies currently available on applying high-frequency data into measuring volatilities, seem to confirm the presence of a positive intertemporal relation between conditional mean and variance of return series, supporting the ICAPM of Merton (1980).

The previously mentioned results are for the market capitalization-weighted index. Another strand of research has investigated the use of high-frequency data for portfolio allocation. As mentioned in the Introduction, most of the research on the use of high-frequency data in portfolio allocation has focused on the prediction of the daily covariance matrix and its use in the minimum variance portfolio allocation. Unfortunately, those studies do not reflect actual investment practice as they do not consider weight constraints and/or are subject to a serious survivorship bias. De Pooter et al. (2008), for example, tested their strategies on the sample of 78 surviving S&P 100 constituents over the period 1997—2004.

Liu (2009) uses the high frequency-based covariance forecast methodology to create minimum tracking error portfolios for the 30 DJIA stocks between 1993 and 2000. She finds that there is an economic benefit of using high-frequency data when the estimation horizon is <6 months or the portfolio manager rebalances his portfolio at a daily frequency. The portfolios that we will consider are long-only portfolios. Similarly, as in Amaya et al. (2011), the portfolios are based on ranking stocks according to a univariate proxy for risk. For the stocks listed on NASDAQ, New York Stock Exchange (NYSE), and AMEX (subject to a liquidity filer of at least 80 transactions per day and a minimum price requirement of 5 USD), Amaya et al. (2011) find that, between 1993 and 2008, there is no relation between the realized volatility and future stock returns, while there is a negative relation between realized skewness and return and a positive relation between realized kurtosis and return.

23.3 METHODOLOGY

This section aims at describing the portfolio construction methodology, the risk measures used, and the performance evaluation framework applied to assess the economic value of high-frequency data for low-risk portfolio allocation. Within the family of low-risk equity portfolios, we focus on those that follow the two-step design of the MSCI low-volatility index, in which first the universe of the S&P 500 constituents is reduced to the 100 most interesting stocks in terms of low risk. Next, the stocks are weighted. In Section 23.3.1, this allocation scheme is described in more detail. More information on the five risk measures used (standard deviation, beta, semivariance, and first- and second-order Cornish–Fisher value at risk) is given in Section 23.3.2. Finally, Section 23.3.3 describes the procedure used for the out-of-sample performance evaluation of the low-risk portfolios.

23.3.1 Portfolio Construction

The portfolio allocation proceeds in two steps: First, the stocks are selected that will be included in the portfolio; second, the weights of those selected stocks are determined. The selection and weighting steps need to be analyzed separately, as emphasized, for example, by Amenc et al. (2013).

In the selection step, we apply the following dummy variables:

- I_Universe$_{it}$: 1 if stock i belongs to the investment universe on rebalancing date t, and 0 otherwise;
- I_LowRisk$_{it}$: 1 if stock i belongs to the 100 stocks with the lowest risk and for which I_Universe$_{it}$ is 1, and 0 otherwise.

Next, we consider three weighting schemes, namely, the widespread market capitalization-weighting methods and the alternative equal-weighted and inverse risk weighting approaches.

Weighting stocks by market capitalization is the most popular weighting scheme in portfolio management. It is used by many well-known indices such as the S&P 500 index and the NASDAQ composite index. It is popular because this approach offers broad diversification, high liquidity, a low transaction cost, and is mean-variance efficient under the CAPM assumptions. Yet its disadvantages are a lack of diversification, an overconcentration on overpriced stocks (Perold, 2007), and that the efficiency property of the portfolio is based on unrealistic assumptions (e.g., unlimited borrowing, same investment preference among investors; see, e.g., Goltz and Le Sourd (2011)). The market capitalization weight for the low-risk portfolios on a rebalancing date t is given by

$$ w_{it} = \frac{mc_{it} * I\_LowRisk_{it}}{\sum_{i=1}^{n_t} mc_{it} * I\_LowRisk_{it}}, \qquad [23.1] $$

where mc_{it}: market capitalization of stock i on date t from COMPUSTAT, and n_t is the number of stocks on date t in the universe.

Second, we will consider the equal-weight approach (often also called 1/N allocation). This methodology assigns an equal weight to each selected stock. It has no estimation risk and, compared to the market capitalization weighting method, will overweight small stocks compared to large stocks. Because it does not exploit any model structure, there is a so-called optimality risk of being far off from the theoretically optimal portfolio (Amenc et al., 2013). The actual relative performance of the equal-weighting method compared to optimized portfolio weights is in principle case dependent, but DeMiguel et al. (2009) provide several empirically relevant applications in which the equal-weighted portfolio outperforms all other portfolios using estimations or portfolio constraints. Nowadays, the equal-weight allocation is used in the S&P 500 equal weight index.[1] Under the equal-weight approach, stock weights in the low-risk portfolio are defined as

$$w_{it} = \frac{I\_LowRisk_{it}}{100}.$$ [23.2]

A third and final method of equity weighting that we consider in the portfolio allocation is inverse risk weighting. This method is applied in the S&P Low-volatility index (S&P Dow Jones index, 2014) and the MSCI risk-weighted index.[2] Under this approach and for a risk measure z_{it} for stock i at time t, the weight is given by

$$w_{it} = \frac{max\left(0, \frac{1}{z_{it}}\right) * I\_LowRisk_{it}}{\sum_{i=1}^{n} max\left(0, \frac{1}{z_{it}}\right) * I\_LowRisk_{it}}.$$ [23.3]

The normalization ensures that the portfolio will be fully invested. To avoid overconcentration on a few low-risk stocks, we cap the weight at the 5% level, as in Leote de Carvalho et al. (2012).

Note that there exist course alternative weighting methods that use accounting data such as the fundamental weighting method in Arnott, Hsu and Moore (2005) or methods that take the dependence between the stocks directly into account. Examples are the mean-variance portfolio allocation in Markowitz (1952), the equal-risk-contribution allocation in Maillard et al. (2010), the maximum diversification approach of Choueifaty and Coignard (2008), and the risk-efficient portfolio in Amenc et al. (2011).

23.3.2 Risk Measures Used for Portfolio Allocation

For stock selection and inverse risk weighting, we will use the usual volatility and beta risk measures as "normal" risk measures and semivariance, first- and second-order Cornish–Fisher value at risk as downside risk measures. We thus consider for each stock five risk measures that are estimated on the stock's daily or intraday 5-min return data. The stock's beta is computed with respect to the S&P 500 index when using daily data, while in the application with high-frequency data, the price data of the SPY index (an extremely liquid exchange traded fund that tracks the S&P 500) are used.

All returns are simple returns, except for the construction of high frequency-based risk measure where the input values are 5-min logarithm returns. The 5-min frequency is also

---

[1] A more complete description of the S&P 500 equal weight index can be found at http://us.spindices.com/indices/equity/sp-500-equal-weighted.

[2] The product sheet of the MSCI risk-weighted index is available at http://www.msci.com/products/indexes/strategy/factor/risk_weighted/.

used by Amaya et al. (2001), Fleming et al. (2001), and Liu (2009). This frequency strikes a balance between a fine-grained sampling and robustness to the contamination by market microstructure frictions such as price discreteness, infrequent trading, and bid—ask bounce.

As measures accounting for the nonnormality in the return series, we consider the stock returns' semivariance and their value at risk computed under the first- and second-order Cornish—Fisher expansion. These are downside risk measures since they measure the risk of extreme negative returns. On daily data, the calculation of these measures is standard (Boudt et al., 2007). Detailed formulas of these indicators computed on intraday data are presented in Appendix 1.

Under the high frequency-based approach, the ex post risk measure for day t is based on the intraday data only, while for the daily data, the ex post risk measure is obtained from the returns in the 250 days trailing window. In the base case, the portfolio is rebalanced at the end of the month. To reduce the sensitivity to events on that particular day, we average the ex post risk estimates over the last 5 days. The disadvantage of the equal-weighting approach is that it is backward looking.

Alternatively, we will use the predicted risk measure obtained using the exponential weighted moving average (EMA) approach as a robustness check of our findings obtained with the simple averaging. Under the EMA formula, the predicted risk follows an autoregressive equation with updates given by the realized risk measure and decaying weights:

$$Risk_{t+1|t} = K^* Risk_t + (1 - K)^* Risk_{t|t-1}; \qquad [23.4]$$

with $Risk_t$ being the value of the risk measure on day t, the weight $K = 2/(p + 1)$, and $p = 20$ since we average over a month of 20 trading days. The process is initialized at the simple moving average value of the past period.

23.3.3 Out-of-Sample Performance Evaluation

We evaluate the return performance on seven dimensions: i) annualized average return; ii) annualized volatility; iii) Sharpe ratio; iv) skewness; v) historical value at risk; vi) maximum drawdown; and vii) the Alpha of the factor model, all computed on the time series of out-of-sample monthly returns. Besides the evaluation for the complete period (2007–2012), we also perform the analysis on subperiods corresponding to a bullish market regime (January to September 2007, March 2009 to December 2012) and the bearish regime of the great financial crisis (October 2007 to February 2009).

To test whether differences in returns and volatilities are due to luck or significantly different from zero, we follow Engle and Colacito (2005) by testing significant differences between the monthly portfolio returns and squared returns using a Diebold and Mariano (1995) type test. It regresses the monthly differences between the performance measures of two portfolio methods on a constant, and tests whether the estimated constant is significantly different from zero using a Newey—West standard error. The significance of the difference in Sharpe ratios is evaluated using the test of Jobson and Korkie (1981), Memmel (2003) and Ledoit and Wolf (2008) in which Newey–West standard errors are used to account for the serial correlation and heteroskedasticity in the return series.

We use the Carhart four-factor model to decompose excess returns of low-risk portfolios into its abnormal return component and the return explained by the exposure to the market, size, value, and momentum factors. The estimated abnormal return α (alpha) is the least squares estimation of the regression of the excess portfolio return (ER_t) on the four factors in Fama and French (1992) and Carhart (1997):

$$ER_t = \alpha + \beta_1 MKT_t + \beta_2 SMB_t + \beta_3 HML_t + \beta_4 MOM_t + \varepsilon_t, \qquad [23.5]$$

where MKT_t is the market excess return on date t; SMB_t is the size factor on date t (i.e., is the average return on the three small portfolios minus the average return on the three big portfolios); HML_t is the book-to-market factor on date t (is the average return on the two value portfolios minus the average return on the two growth portfolios), and MOM_t is the momentum factor on date t (is the average return on the two high prior return portfolios minus the average return on the two low prior return portfolios) (Bauer et al., 2005; Barber and Lyon, 1997). Data of the four factors are retrieved from the K. French data library. Note that in [23.5] alpha can typically be interpreted as a measure of outperformance or underperformance relative to market proxy and the size, value, and momentum risk factors. Of course, the higher alpha is, the better the performance is. Its statistical significance will be tested using the t-test.

23.4 INVESTMENT UNIVERSE AND DATA COLLECTION

We will track the S&P 500 composition as closely as possible for the period 2007–2012. As mentioned in the Introduction, this is important since investment universes of most current research on high-frequency data-based portfolio allocation do not correspond to the actual investment universe used by professionals, because they impose special ex post liquidity and survival conditions, which an investor would not have done in real time. This will lead to survivorship bias in the sense of overestimating average return and underestimating the actual risk (Brown et al., 1992). Indeed, only the relatively well-performing fund will survive in market capitalization-based universes. According to the research of Carpenter and Lynch (1999), survivorship bias has an impact not only on performance but also on persistence. For a realistic evaluation of the portfolio performance, it is important that the analysis is free of survivorship bias.

We thus aim at considering the investment universe composed of S&P 500 constituents over the period 2007–2012 and collect data for this universe from two sources. End of day-adjusted stock prices are obtained from COMPUSTAT and corrected for dividend payouts and stock splits (Fama et al., 1969), while high-frequency stock prices

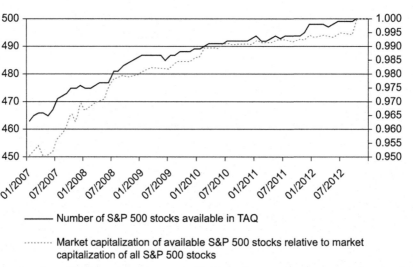

Number of S&P 500 stocks available in TAQ

········· Market capitalization of available S&P 500 stocks relative to market capitalization of all S&P 500 stocks

Figure 23.1 Number of S&P 500 Constituents Available in the TAQ Database and Their Market Capitalization Relative to all S&P 500 Stocks. Note: This figure presents, for each end of the month selection date in 2007–2012, the total number of stocks belonging to the S&P 500 for which data are available in the TAQ database (full line) and the corresponding percentage of market capitalization of all S&P 500 stocks (dashed line). Data were downloaded in January 2014 through the WRDS portal.

are retrieved from the Trades and Quotes (TAQ) database accessed through the Wharton Research Data Service (WRDS). Unfortunately, for the TAQ data, some of the price data are missing. The total data availability and total market capitalization weights of the S&P 500 stocks available in the TAQ database are shown in Figure 23.1. The full line and dashed line show the number of available stocks and their market capitalization in percent of the market capitalization of all S&P 500 stocks. We see that availability on TAQ is especially an issue at the beginning, where in January 2007 the price data for only 463 stocks are available, corresponding to 95% of the total market capitalization. This availability then gradually improves as the selection dates are more recent.

23.5 FINDINGS

In this section, we summarize the results of the out-of-sample analysis of the performance of the various portfolios considered. We hereby distinguish between the effect of stock selection and the weight allocation in the reported output tables, and a bearish vs bullish market regime.

To start off, we present in Panel A of Table 23.1 the summary performance statistics of the benchmark portfolios that do not select but are invested in all S&P 500 stocks with either market capitalization weights or equal weights. Regarding those selection-free

Table 23.1 Summary performance statistics of the monthly rebalance benchmark and low-risk portfolios implemented with volatility and beta as risk measure

Weights	Market cap				Equal weight				Inverse risk			
Criteria	All	Period 1	Period 2	Period 3	All	Period 1	Period 2	Period 3	All	Period 1	Period 2	Period 3
Panel A: Benchmark (S&P 500)												
Return	2.90%	11.98%	−37.32%	20.95%		7.18%	−40.48%	28.42%				
Std	17.92%	9.86%	19.39%	15.97%		9.74%	24.27%	19.51%				
Sharpe	0.16	1.21	−1.92	1.31		0.74	−1.67	1.46				
Skewness	−0.57	−0.26	−0.71	−0.18		−0.41	−0.82	0.37				
His.VaR	−8.19%	−2.59%	−11.54%	−6.33%		−3.29%	−13.74%	−6.92%				
Max.DD	−49.28%	−4.41%	−49.28%	−17.71%		−5.86%	−52.65%	−19.84%				
Panel B: Daily volatility												
Return	4.46%	6.03%	−25.55%	16.86%	6.39%	2.21%	−26.85%	21.23%	8.68%	1.00%	−30.54%	27.32%
Std	***12.14%	9.80%	14.48%	9.74%	***12.93%	9.09%	17.05%	9.37%	16.73%	8.67%	20.39%	13.95%
Sharpe	0.37	0.62	−1.76	1.73	0.49	0.24	−1.57	2.27	0.52	0.12	−1.5	1.96
Skewness	−0.89	−0.51	−0.8	−0.27	−1.29	−1.42	−1	−0.11	0.23	−1.25	−0.66	2.58
His.VaR	−6.35%	−3.16%	−9.36%	−2.21%	−5.79%	−4.01%	−11.86%	−2.22%	−6.14%	−3.85%	−13.93%	−1.61%
Max.DD	−35.15%	−6.01%	−35.15%	−9.16%	−38.12%	−7.32%	−36.27%	−6.78%	−42.77%	−7.13%	−40.85%	−6.98%
Panel C: Daily beta												
Return	7.27%	8.47%	−23.65%	19.37%	5.68%	6.33%	−28.97%	20.66%	5.11%	6.96%	−34.72%	23.47%
Std	***11.73%***	9.34%	14.63%	8.94%	***13.33%***	9.86%	18.27%	9.05%	16.34%	9.30%	21.18%	12.45%
Sharpe	0.62	0.91	−1.62	2.17	0.43	0.64	−1.59	2.28	0.31	0.75	−1.64	1.89
Skewness	−1.01	−0.33	−0.85	−0.08	−1.41	−1.19	−0.89	0.03	−0.6	−1.1	−0.71	1.62
His.VaR	−5.41%	−2.88%	−9.31%	−1.64%	−6.12%	−3.90%	−11.62%	−1.69%	−6.90%	−3.54%	−12.98%	−1.85%
Max.DD	−32.35%	−5.47%	−32.35%	−7.73%	−40.47%	−6.98%	−38.88%	−6.41%	−46.66%	−6.35%	−45.75%	−8.22%
Panel D: Realized volatility												
Return	4.83%	8.38%	−25.94%	17.18%	5.74%	6.25%	−27.65%	19.95%	5.62%	6.35%	−27.34%	19.57%
Std	***12.05%	9.10%	14.52%	9.56%	***12.73%	8.34%	16.73%	9.27%	***12.44%	8.08%	16.12%	9.17%
Sharpe	0.4	0.92	−1.79	1.8	0.45	0.75	−1.65	2.15	0.45	0.79	−1.7	2.13
Skewness	−1.04	−0.17	−1.09	−0.27	−1.51	−0.93	−1.31	−0.42	−1.31	−0.97	−1.13	−0.1
His.VaR	−5.74%	−2.52%	−9.60%	−2.57%	−5.77%	−3.11%	−10.56%	−2.44%	−5.90%	−3.00%	−10.48%	−1.66%
Max.DD	−34.85%	−4.77%	−34.85%	−7.25%	−38.24%	−5.49%	−37.71%	−7.29%	−37.67%	−5.28%	−37.39%	−8.11%
Panel E: Realized beta												
Return	6.89%	9.60%	−28.75%	21.61%	7.77%	8.95%	−31.70%	25.05%	5.71%	3.35%	−38.06%	27.60%
Std	***13.08%***	10.15%	14.75%	10.46%	***14.72%***	9.64%	18.10%	11.21%	19.49%	8.46%	19.57%	18.09%
Sharpe	0.53	0.95	−1.94	2.07	*0.53	0.93	−1.75	2.23	0.29	0.4	−1.95	1.53
Skewness	−0.84	−0.3	−0.89	−0.22	−1.04	−0.64	−0.95	0.03	1.14	−0.53	−0.63	2.84
His.VaR	−6.49%	−3.20%	−9.23%	−2.25%	−6.52%	−3.32%	−11.44%	−3.57%	−8.79%	−3.22%	−12.88%	−3.89%
Max.DD	−39.25%	−6.12%	−38.59%	−9.86%	−43.79%	−5.95%	−42.69%	−8.22%	−51.71%	−6.42%	−50.33%	−10.32%

Note: Std: Standard deviation; His. VaR: Historical VaR; Max. DD: Maximum drawdown; Both return, standard deviation and Sharpe ratio are annualized; historical VaR is calculated at confidence level of 95%; equality tests are done for return, standard deviation, and Sharpe ratio; ***, **, * on the left-hand side: comparison between low-risk portfolios and the benchmark (using market capitalization-weighted scheme) with 1%, 5%, and 10%, significance level, respectively; ***, **, * on the right-hand side: comparison between low-risk portfolios using daily data and high-frequency data with 1%, 5%, and 10% significance level, respectively.

portfolios, we see in Panel A of Table 23.1 that over the whole 2007–2012 period, the equal-weighted portfolio outperforms the market capitalization-weighted benchmark in terms of a higher return (5.55% vs 2.90%) and Sharpe ratio (0.26 vs 0.16), but offers at the same time a higher volatility (21.72% vs 17.92%) and downside risk (as shown by a higher absolute value of the portfolio's historical VaR and maximum drawdown). The choice between equal weighting and market cap weighting in the case of no selection thus seems to be consistent with the standard result in financial theory that a higher return comes at the price of a higher risk.

We next compare these performance results with the low-risk portfolios invested in the 100 least risky stocks. In panels B and C of Table 23.1, we consider first the low-risk portfolio based on the traditional standard deviation and beta as risk measure, computed using daily data. The main result is that low-risk portfolios, using market cap weights or equal weights (Panels B and C of Table 23.1), have a higher (but not statistically significant) average return and Sharpe ratio, and significantly reduce the portfolio volatility in comparison with the market capitalization-weighted benchmark (hereafter called the benchmark).

Table 23.2 shows in above-diagonal elements the percentage number of stocks that are selected simultaneously by two risk measures. For daily beta and volatility, the overlap is on average around 70%. There is no clear dominance between using beta or volatility for stock selection. In terms of weighting, the market capitalization approach leads to a slightly lower volatility than does the equal weighting. The inverse risk weighting is clearly not recommended in this setting, since it substantially increases the volatility profile of the portfolio.

Turning to the subperiod analysis, we further see that the outperformance over the 2007–2012 period of low-risk portfolios in terms of a higher return is because the low-risk portfolios suffered a lower loss during the bearish market (period 2), which compensates the lower return during the bullish market (period 3). These results are consistent with the findings of Pettengill et al. (1995) and Baker et al. (2011) about the performance of low-risk portfolios during upmarket/downmarket and the importance of a long-term investment horizon for low-risk investors (offering diversification across the different market regimes).

We thus find a confirmation of the low-risk anomaly using daily data. The next question that we address in panels D and E of Table 23.1 is the impact of using high-frequency data. First of all, we can confirm that the low-risk anomaly is robust to the evaluation with high-frequency data. In fact, as for the low-risk portfolios using daily return data, we find that low-risk portfolios using high-frequency data have higher (but not statistically significant different) returns and Sharpe ratios than the benchmark and a significantly lower volatility (at the 1% significance level). There does not seem any gain in performance that compensates the operational costs of using high frequency. On the contrary, we see that the use of high-frequency data instead of daily data does not improve

Table 23.2 Overlap in selected stocks across daily and realized volatility, beta, semivariance, first- and second-order Cornish–Fisher values at risk (upper diagonal elements), and the correlation between the inverse risk weights (below the diagonal)

Overlap weight cor.	D.vol	D.beta	R.vol	R.beta	D.SV	D.1stVaR	D.2ndVaR	R.SV	R.1stVaR	R.2ndVaR
D.vol	–	72.2%	67.9%	52.4%	88.3%	80.2%	76.7%	67.1%	65.3%	62.3%
D.beta	0.55	–	60.7%	56.8%	70.0%	67.1%	66.4%	59.6%	59.7%	59.2%
R.vol	0.52	0.44	–	56.0%	65.8%	63.0%	61.8%	86.3%	86.4%	81.3%
R.beta	0.33	0.38	0.37	–	50.9%	50.5%	50.2%	53.7%	55.7%	55.7%
D.SV	0.54	0.52	0.37	0.31	–	86.1%	80.7%	64.5%	63.6%	61.1%
D.1stVaR	0.45	0.42	0.34	0.30	0.60	–	89.4%	62.1%	60.8%	58.9%
D.2ndVaR	0.37	0.39	0.32	0.32	0.54	0.57	–	60.5%	59.6%	57.8%
R.SV	0.46	0.43	0.75	0.32	0.31	0.36	0.32	–	76.4%	71.1%
R.1stVaR	0.45	0.49	0.62	0.35	0.39	0.33	0.29	0.64	–	87.9%
R.2ndVaR	0.38	0.54	0.69	0.40	0.38	0.35	0.33	0.62	0.69	–

Note: This table presents for each pair of risk estimates the average percentage number of stocks that are selected jointly by both risk estimates (above the diagonal) and the average correlation in weights between the inverse risk-weighted low-risk portfolios (below the diagonal). The risk estimates considered are daily volatility, daily beta, realized volatility, realized beta, daily semivariance, daily first-order VaR, daily second-order VaR, realized semivariance, realized first-order VaR, and realized second-order VaR, respectively.

the performance of low-risk portfolios and sometimes even increases the level of risk of the low-risk portfolios. Up to now, we have focused on low-risk portfolios using "normal" risk measures (standard deviation and beta). As shown by, for example, Officer (1972) and Ane and Geman (2000), stock returns are usually nonnormally distributed. In Table 23.3, we consider the performance of downside risk-based low-risk portfolios.

In Table 23.2, we see that the overlap between the volatility and semivariance is extremely high (88%) and also the overlap with the Cornish—Fisher Value at Risk-based selections is high (around 80%). The correlation between the inverse risk weights is around ≤50%. The change from using a normal to downside risk measure will thus mostly affect the inverse risk weighted portfolios. This is confirmed in Table 23.3 where the equal-weight and market cap-weighted downside risk portfolios have a similar performance, and where the inverse risk-weighted downside risk portfolio has a lower out-of-sample risk (volatility of 14% vs 16%, drawdown of 38% vs 42%).

As for beta and volatility, we do not find a relevant gain in performance of using high-frequency data to estimate the risk of the individual stocks. Market cap weighting seems to outperform equal weighting and inverse risk weighting. The low-risk anomaly is also present for the downside risk estimates used. Except for the low-risk portfolio using the second-order Cornish—Fisher VaR as risk measure and inverse risk weighting scheme, all other low-risk portfolios report a significant lower volatility than the benchmark (at the 5% significance level) and offer a similar out-of-sample return.

In Appendix 2, we report the results of a sensitivity analysis to the choice of risk prediction method used (averaging over the last five days vs EMA over the past 20 days) and the rebalancing frequency applied (monthly vs daily frequency). The details on the out-of-sample performance for these variations are presented in Tables A1—A4 in Appendix 2. We find that the switch to the exponentially weighted moving average has hardly any effects on the out-of-sample performance and that switching from a monthly to daily rebalancing frequency especially improves the performance of the inverse risk-weighted portfolios.

These additional results confirm the main findings of a superior risk-adjusted performance of low-risk portfolios and that there is no economic gain in using high-frequency data for the construction of the low-risk portfolios considered. One caveat is that the superior performance in terms of returns and risk of the low-risk portfolios is not robust to controlling for exposure to the Carhart four risk factors, as we show in Table 23.4. We find indeed that for all low-risk portfolios the intercept is not significantly different from zero.

The exposure to the market return and the size factor dominate. The low-risk portfolios have, by design, a lower than unity exposure to the market return. In the case of market capitalization weighting, the exposure to the size factor is negative. It is less negative or positive for the equal-weighting and inverse risk weighting. For market cap-weighted stocks, the exposure to momentum is positive, while for the

Table 23.3 Out-of-sample performance of monthly rebalanced low-risk portfolios implemented with a downside risk measure

Criteria	Market cap				Equal weight				Inverse risk			
	All	Period 1	Period 2	Period 3	All	Period 1	Period 2	Period 3	All	Period 1	Period 2	Period 3
Panel A: Daily semivariance												
Return	4.47%	4.99%	−25.04%	16.77%	6.00%	3.60%	−25.57%	19.60%	6.48%	4.38%	−26.64%	20.79%
Std	★★★12.23%	9.69%	15.03%	9.71%	★★★12.19%★	8.99%	16.57%	8.48%	★★13.78%	7.56%	17.84%	10.91%
Sharpe	0.37	0.52	−1.67	1.73	0.49	0.4	−1.54	2.31	0.47	0.58	−1.49	1.91
Skewness	−0.94	−0.47	−0.84	−0.21	−1.48	−1.28	−1.11	−0.16	−0.25	−1.01	−0.77	2.29
His.VaR	−6.05%	−3.27%	−9.62%	−2.15%	−5.74%	−3.79%	−11.04%	−2.09%	−5.36%	−2.96%	−11.21%	−1.36%
Max.DD	−34.11%	−6.11%	−34.11%	−8.57%	−36.05%	−6.97%	−34.76%	−6.23%	−36.49%	−5.58%	−36.01%	−5.30%
Panel B: Daily first-order VaR												
Return	5.06%	3.96%	−24.64%	17.60%	5.71%	2.57%	−27.01%	20.24%	6.92%	3.42%	−27.96%	22.46%
Std	★★★12.37%	10.07%	14.97%	9.94%	★★★12.48%	8.80%	16.48%	8.90%	★★14.28%	5.87%	17.63%	11.80%
Sharpe	0.41	0.39	−1.65	1.77	0.46	0.29	−1.64	2.28	0.48	0.58	−1.59	1.9
Skewness	−0.84	−0.38	−0.75	−0.19	−1.4	−1.32	−1.1	−0.22	−0.1	−0.92	−0.8	2.05
His.VaR	−6.38%	−3.43%	−9.37%	−2.58%	−5.49%	−3.78%	−10.99%	−2.08%	−5.95%	−2.26%	−11.31%	−1.75%
Max.DD	−34.01%	−6.37%	−34.01%	−8.66%	−37.97%	−6.76%	−36.35%	−6.55%	−38.36%	−3.95%	−37.45%	−5.41%
Panel C: Daily second-order VaR												
Return	5.15%	4.85%	−25.90%	18.30%	5.66%	0.79%	−26.76%	20.39%	6.04%	−3.35%	−26.13%	21.45%
Std	★★★12.36%	10.29%	15.00%	9.63%	★★★12.75%	9.32%	16.98%	9.08%	14.64%	8.55%	16.82%	12.86%
Sharpe	0.42	0.47	−1.73	1.9	0.44	0.08	−1.58	2.25	0.41	−0.39	−1.55	1.67
Skewness	−0.96	−0.36	−0.86	−0.24	−1.37	−1.51	−1.05	−0.18	0.74	−0.32	−0.65	2.9
His.VaR	−6.06%	−3.33%	−9.59%	−2.21%	−5.62%	−4.21%	−11.13%	−2.22%	−6.00%	−3.61%	−11.15%	−1.63%
Max.DD	−35.48%	−6.20%	−35.48%	−7.83%	−38.39%	−7.48%	−35.86%	−6.67%	−39.18%	−7.63%	−35.19%	−8.31%
Panel D: Realized semivariance												
Return	4.31%	6.97%	−26.46%	16.99%	6.65%	6.23%	−26.86%	20.81%	9.19%	5.66%	−25.34%	23.75%
Std	★★★12.16%	9.14%	14.90%	9.51%	★★★12.97%★	8.49%	17.32%	9.44%	★14.35%	7.59%	16.90%	12.36%
Sharpe	0.35	0.76	−1.78	1.79	★0.51	0.73	−1.55	2.2	★0.64	0.75	−1.5	1.92
Skewness	−1.06	−0.15	−1.04	−0.25	−1.48	−0.72	−1.31	−0.21	−0.12	−0.94	−1.22	1.66
His.VaR	−5.79%	−2.74%	−10.01%	−2.74%	−5.54%	−3.10%	−10.97%	−2.44%	−5.98%	−2.82%	−10.41%	−1.92%
Max.DD	−35.43%	−5.30%	−35.30%	−8.30%	−37.30%	−5.58%	−36.59%	−7.48%	−35.18%	−4.96%	−34.48%	−7.73%

Continued

Table 23.3 Out-of-sample performance of monthly rebalanced low-risk portfolios implemented with a downside risk measure—cont'd

Weights	Market cap				Equal weight				Inverse risk			
Criteria	All	Period 1	Period 2	Period 3	All	Period 1	Period 2	Period 3	All	Period 1	Period 2	Period 3
Panel E: Realized VaR first-order												
Return	5.97%	9.40%	−24.18%	17.61%	6.55%	7.58%	−27.34%	20.69%	7.25%	7.43%	−29.11%	22.87%
Std	★★★11.90%	9.55%	14.14%	9.59%	★★★13.12%	8.45%	17.35%	9.66%	★★★14.43%	7.93%	18.87%	11.03%
Sharpe	0.5	0.98	−1.71	1.84	0.5	0.9	−1.58	2.14	0.5	0.94	−1.54	2.07
Skewness	−0.88	−0.05	−0.82	−0.29	−1.37	−0.77	−1.06	−0.34	−1.01	−1.01	−1.04	0.63
His.VaR	−5.82%	−2.51%	−9.09%	−2.58%	−6.04%	−3.00%	−10.38%	−2.70%	−6.44%	−2.87%	−11.25%	−2.20%
Max.DD	−33.58%	−4.80%	−33.58%	−7.04%	−37.61%	−5.35%	−37.37%	−7.54%	−39.56%	−5.03%	−39.45%	−8.20%
Panel F: Realized VaR second-order												
Return	3.90%	10.40%	−26.75%	15.92%	5.45%	6.87%	−28.00%	19.62%	4.27%	5.42%	−28.11%	18.21%
Std	★★★12.52%	9.29%	15.55%	9.86%	★★★12.94%	8.35%	17.11%	9.44%	★★★13.30%	7.90%	16.44%	10.72%
Sharpe	0.31	1.12	−1.72	1.61	0.42	0.82	−1.64	2.08	0.32	0.69	−1.71	1.7
Skewness	−1.04	−0.14	−0.98	−0.18	−1.29	−1.02	−0.86	−0.29	−0.37	−0.96	−0.35	1.08
His.VaR	−6.06%	−2.49%	−10.29%	−2.83%	−6.00%	−3.12%	−10.94%	−2.74%	−6.07%	−2.99%	−10.26%	−2.59%
Max.DD	−37.01%	−4.78%	−37.01%	−8.24%	−38.66%	−5.52%	−38.06%	−7.81%	−39.20%	−5.26%	−38.35%	−7.14%

Note: See note in Table 23.1 for more information.

Table 23.4 Multifactor analysis of the 2007–2012 out-of-sample returns of low-risk portfolios

Weighting scheme	Data	Risk measure	Alpha	Market	SMB	HML	MOM	R²
Market cap weighted	Daily	Std	0.002 [0.002]	0.667*** [0.042]	−0.297*** [0.09]	0.076 [0.076]	0.074** [0.034]	0.827
		Second-order VaR	0.002 [0.002]	0.673** [0.042]	−0.268* [0.092]	0.078* [0.078]	0.072** [0.035]	0.827
	High-frequency	Std	0.002 [0.002]	0.668 [0.041]	−0.295*** [0.089]	0.074* [0.076]	0.093* [0.035]	0.828
		Second-order VaR	0.002 [0.002]	0.689*** [0.04]	−0.238*** [0.089]	0.106 [0.076]	0.104* [0.034]	0.853
Equal weighted	Daily	Std	0.003 [0.002]	0.637*** [0.044]	−0.079*** [0.096]	0.079 [0.081]	−0.013** [0.036]	0.828
		Second-order VaR	0.002 [0.002]	0.623** [0.043]	−0.007* [0.093]	0.055* [0.079]	−0.012** [0.035]	0.835
	High-frequency	Std	0.002 [0.002]	0.666*** [0.04]	−0.076*** [0.093]	0.053* [0.079]	0.042* [0.035]	0.855
		Second-order VaR	0.002 [0.002]	0.668*** [0.038]	−0.032*** [0.087]	0.078 [0.074]	0.037* [0.033]	0.874
Inverse risk weighted	Daily	Std	0.005 [0.003]	0.612*** [0.06]	0.009*** [0.129]	0.206 [0.11]	−0.245** [0.049]	0.813
		Second-order VaR	0.002 [0.002]	0.493** [0.056]	0.167* [0.129]	0.13* [0.11]	−0.227** [0.046]	0.788
	High-frequency	Std	0.003 [0.002]	0.585 [0.044]	−0.071*** [0.12]	0.157* [0.102]	−0.015* [0.046]	0.817
		Second-order VaR	0.001 [0.002]	0.552*** [0.048]	0.181*** [0.104]	0.098 [0.089]	−0.074* [0.039]	0.807

Note: The table presents the results from estimating the Carhart four-factor model. The data are taken on a monthly basis. The time period ranges from 2007 to 2012. SMB, HML, and MOM represent, respectively, the size, value, and momentum premium. The estimated coefficients are presented together with the corresponding standard errors between square brackets. ***, **, and * indicate a significance level of 1%, 5%, and 10%, respectively.

inverse risk-weighted portfolio, it is negative. This opposite exposure is as expected since a relatively high-risk value can often be associated with a stock that has lost value, while the market cap will increase for a winning stock. All low-risk portfolios tend to also have a positive exposure on the value risk factor, which is as expected and in line with the results of Leo De et al. (2012), but the exposure is often not significant.

23.6 CONCLUSION

An increasing number of ETFs track low-risk indices such as the MSCI low-volatility index, in which first the universe of the S&P 500 constituents is reduced to the 100 least risky stocks, and then the selected stocks are either market capitalization, equally or inverse risk weighted. The popularity of low-risk portfolios stems from their superior risk-adjusted return over long investment horizon compared to the traditional market capitalization-weighted portfolio. This is the so-called low-risk anomaly. In this chapter, we revisit the low-risk anomaly and contribute to the literature by considering the use of high-frequency data for the estimation of equity risk.

Applying the traditional two-step investment procedure of selection and weighting on low-risk portfolios invested in the S&P 500 universe over the period 2007–2012, we confirm that low-risk portfolios outperform market capitalization-weighted portfolios in the sense of offering a similar return at a significantly lower volatility. This result holds irrespective of using daily or high-frequency data and for both daily and monthly rebalancing and for both the traditional normal risk measures (volatility, beta) as for the downside risk measures (semivariance, Cornish–Fisher value at risk).

In our setting, there does not seem to be a gain of using high-frequency data compared to using daily data. For the portfolio design that we consider, we therefore do not recommend to use one of the examined methods using high-frequency data, but to construct the monthly rebalanced low-risk portfolios based on screening the universe using the different risk measures on daily data and then weight each stock using either market capitalization weighting or equal weighting.

Several aspects can be considered for future research. Regarding the methodology, it would be interesting to consider multivariate risk measures and a combination of daily and high-frequency data. On the empirical side, it would be useful to consider a longer time span and a different universe than the S&P 500. A particular interesting direction is to consider the interaction between sustainability and low risk, as commercially available in ETFs and structured products linked to the Finvex Sustainable Efficient and for which Bertrand and Lapointe (2014) show that the use of a socially responsible investment universe seems to improve the performance of risk-based allocations.

APPENDIX 1

In this appendix, we present the formulas used to calculate the risk measures using high-frequency data. Prior to the analysis, the price data obtained from the TAQ database are first cleaned and only prices during the regular trading time of NYSE and NASDAQ stock exchanges (i.e., 9.30 ET to 16.00 ET, i.e., 6.5 h) are retained. Cleaning is needed, since as shown, for example, by Brownlees and Gallo (2006), the raw high-frequency data contain many errors. Therefore, we cleaned these data following the procedure described by Barndorff-Nielsen et al. (2009) before using it for the estimation of the risk of the stocks. Because some high-frequency indicators require at least three observations per day, we ignored stocks having less than five observations per day to ensure that indicators are calculable.

We used the five-min frequency to compute the equispaced returns that enter into the high-frequency risk measures. As such, there is a maximum of $N = 78$ equispaced returns on trading day t. Let $r_{t,i}$ be the ith 5-min log return (with $i = 1,\ldots,N$) in trading day t.

For the realized volatility, we use medRV in this chapter. The medRV of day t is defined by Andersen et al. (2012) as

$$medRV_t = \frac{\pi}{6 - 4\sqrt{3} + \pi}\left(\frac{N}{N-2}\right)\sum_{i=2}^{N-1} median\left(\left|r_{t,i-1}\right|, \left|r_{t,i}\right|, \left|r_{t,i+1}\right|\right)^2. \qquad [23.6]$$

The realized beta of a stock on trading day t is calculated as the ratio between the realized covariance with the SPY (ETF) and the realized variance of the SPY (ETF):

$$\beta_t = \frac{RCOV_t}{RV_t^{SPY}} = \frac{\sum_{i=1}^{N}\left(r_{t,i} \times r_{t,i}^{SPY}\right)}{\sum_{i=1}^{N}\left(r_{t,i}^{SPY}\right)^2}, \qquad [23.7]$$

where $r_{t,i}^{SPY}$ is the ith return series of SPY (ETF) on trading day t; $RCOV_t$ the realized covariance of stock and SPY in trading day t, and RV_t^{SPY} the realized variance of the SPY on trading day t (Barndorff-Nielsen and Shephard, 2004).

For the realized skewness and realized kurtosis, we follow Amaya et al. (2011) and compute those as

$$rSkew_t = \frac{\sqrt{N}\sum_{i=1}^{N}(r_{t,i})^3}{RV_t^{3/2}} = \frac{\sqrt{N}\sum_{i=1}^{N}(r_{t,i})^3}{\left\{\sum_{i=1}^{N}(r_{t,i})^2\right\}^{3/2}},$$ [23.8]

$$rKurt_t = \frac{\sqrt{N}\sum_{i=1}^{N}(r_{t,i})^4}{RV_t^{2}} = \frac{\sqrt{N}\sum_{i=1}^{N}(r_{t,i})^4}{\left\{\sum_{i=1}^{N}(r_{t,i})^2\right\}^{2}}.$$ [23.9]

For the realized semivariance, we follow Barndorff-Nielsen et al. (2010) and compute it as

$$rSV_t = \sum_{i=1}^{N}(r_{t,i})^2 \times I\left[r_{t,i} < 0\right].$$ [23.10]

For realized Cornish–Fisher value at risk, we use the Cornish–Fisher estimation method in which the value at risk is a function of the realized volatility, skewness, and kurtosis with coefficients that depend on the standard normal quantiles (Boudt et al., 2007). We use both first and second Cornish–Fisher VaR in this chapter. Under the first-order Cornish Fisher expansion, the realized Cornish Fisher VaR is given by

$$VaR^{1st\ order}(\alpha) = -\sqrt{medRV_t}\left[z_\alpha + \frac{1}{6}(z_\alpha^2 - 1)rSkew_t\right].$$ [23.11]

Under the second-order Cornish Fisher VaR expansion,

$$VaR^{2nd\ order}(\alpha) =$$

$$-\sqrt{medRV_t}\left[z_\alpha + \frac{1}{6}(z_\alpha^2 - 1)rSkew_t + \frac{1}{24}(z_\alpha^3 - 3z_\alpha)rKurt_t - \frac{1}{36}(2z_\alpha^3 - 5z_\alpha)rSkew_t^2\right],$$ [23.12]

where z_α is the value of the α-quantile under the standard normal distribution. We use $\alpha = 5\%$ in this chapter, for which $z_\alpha = -1.645$. Compared to the first-order Cornish Fisher VaR, the second-order Cornish–Fisher VaR takes into account excess kurtosis. In case the excess kurtosis is different from zero and accurately estimated, the second-order Cornish Fisher VaR is usually a better estimation of the VaR.

APPENDIX 2

Table A1 Out-of-sample performance of monthly rebalanced low-risk portfolios implemented with an exponentially moving average-based estimate of volatility and beta

Weights	Market cap				Equal weight				Inverse risk			
Criteria	All	Period 1	Period 2	Period 3	All	Period 1	Period 2	Period 3	All	Period 1	Period 2	Period 3
Panel A: Daily volatility												
Return	5.32%	6.02%	−24.77%	17.66%	5.96%	2.12%	−27.14%	20.79%	2.64%	1.92%	−36.52%	21.97%
Std	★★★12.19%	9.87%	14.93%	9.62%	★★★13.14%	9.05%	17.40%	9.61%	17.51%★★	8.79%	22.02%	14.17%
Sharpe	0.44	0.61	−1.66	1.84	0.45	0.23	−1.56	2.16	0.15	0.22	−1.66	1.55
Skewness	−0.87	−0.52	−0.71	−0.12	−1.22	−1.36	−0.92	−0.03	−0.22	−1.25	−0.58	1.79
His.VaR	−5.94%	−3.20%	−9.36%	−2.17%	−6.17%	−3.97%	−11.58%	−2.37%	−7.71%	−3.83%	−14.14%	−2.47%
Max.DD	−34.00%	−6.07%	−34.00%	−8.39%	−38.48%	−7.27%	−36.53%	−6.82%	−49.37%	−7.09%	−47.88%	−9.01%
Panel B: Daily beta												
Return	7.11%	9.55%	−23.94%	19.11%	5.63%	5.98%	−29.13%	20.76%	2.27%	4.92%	−37.63%	21.58%
Std	★★★11.75%	9.37%	14.79%	8.88%	★★★13.75%	9.88%	18.94%	9.49%	17.94%	9.36%	23.21%	14.16%
Sharpe	0.61	1.02	−1.62	2.15	0.41	0.61	−1.54	2.19	0.13	0.53	−1.62	1.52
Skewness	−1.05	−0.46	−0.87	−0.05	−1.31	−1.16	−0.86	0.32	−0.27	−0.97	−0.5	1.98
His.VaR	−5.36%	−2.88%	−9.51%	−1.67%	−5.96%	−3.93%	−12.32%	−1.69%	−7.79%	−3.70%	−14.61%	−2.38%
Max.DD	−32.77%	−5.47%	−32.77%	−7.50%	−41.05%	−7.07%	−39.16%	−6.38%	−50.81%	−6.78%	−49.29%	−9.02%
Panel C: Realized volatility												
Return	4.61%	9.90%	−25.41%	16.27%	5.15%	6.11%	−28.97%	19.91%	1.98%	5.23%	−34.37%	18.81%
Std	★★★11.88%	8.82%	14.76%	9.28%	★★★13.32%	8.13%	18.02%	9.54%	15.84%★★	7.45%	19.89%	12.85%
Sharpe	0.39	1.12	−1.72	1.75	0.39	0.75	−1.61	2.09	0.12	0.7	−1.73	1.46
Skewness	−1.07	−0.21	−0.93	−0.28	−1.44	−0.97	−1.12	−0.09	−0.37	−0.92	−0.82	1.66
His.VaR	−5.71%	−2.43%	−9.86%	−2.31%	−5.67%	−3.05%	−11.56%	−2.47%	−6.80%	−2.78%	−13.09%	−2.11%
Max.DD	−34.71%	−4.62%	−34.71%	−7.28%	−39.70%	−5.39%	−39.10%	−7.26%	−46.17%	−4.88%	−45.59%	−8.69%
Panel D: Realized beta												
Return	5.80%	6.76%	−26.76%	19.39%	5.87%	6.08%	−30.50%	21.96%	0.32%	3.80%	−40.60%	20.94%
Std	★★★12.45%	10.73%	14.50%	9.77%	★★★14.11%	9.14%	19.29%	9.80%	18.11%	7.88%	23.31%	14.14%
Sharpe	0.47	0.63	−1.85	1.99	0.42	0.67	−1.58	2.24	0.02	0.48	−1.74	1.48
Skewness	−0.89	−0.69	−1.06	0.02	−1.34	−1.08	−0.73	−0.17	−0.77	−1.13	−0.97	1.16
His.VaR	−6.07%	−3.95%	−8.87%	−2.15%	−7.42%	−3.53%	−11.09%	−2.81%	−7.71%	−3.18%	−14.52%	−3.58%
Max.DD	−37.68%	−7.36%	−37.56%	−8.02%	−42.38%	−6.30%	−41.52%	−7.93%	−53.70%	−5.88%	−53.30%	−9.15%

Note: See note in Table 23.1 for more information.

Table A2 Out-of-sample performance of monthly rebalanced low-risk portfolios implemented with an exponentially moving average-based estimate of downside risk

Weights	Market cap				Equal weight				Inverse risk			
Criteria	All	Period 1	Period 2	Period 3	All	Period 1	Period 2	Period 3	All	Period 1	Period 2	Period 3
Panel A: Daily semivariance												
Return	4.69%	4.28%	−24.76%	17.07%	5.78%	2.99%	−25.48%	19.80%	2.93%	4.40%	−29.68%	17.39%
Std	★★★12.21%★	9.88%	14.96%	9.70%	★★★12.45%	8.66%	16.37%	8.87%	★★14.36%	6.27%	18.25%	11.80%
Sharpe	0.38	0.43	−1.65	1.76	0.46	0.35	−1.56	2.23	0.2	0.7	−1.63	1.47
Skewness	−0.93	−0.46	−0.85	−0.18	−1.56	−1.32	−1	−0.05	−0.35	−1	−0.67	1.43
His.VaR	−5.73%	−3.36%	−9.43%	−2.25%	−5.42%	−3.71%	−10.75%	−2.03%	−6.33%	−2.41%	−11.17%	−1.61%
Max.DD	−33.86%	−6.29%	−33.86%	−8.30%	−37.03%	−6.82%	−34.82%	−6.41%	−40.13%	−4.49%	−39.92%	−7.92%
Panel B: Daily first-order VaR												
Return	5.13%	4.50%	−25.01%	17.81%	5.96%	1.93%	−26.13%	20.21%	2.77%	2.64%	−29.38%	17.31%
Std	★★★12.32%★	9.76%	14.85%	9.88%	★★★12.34%	8.45%	15.94%	9.12%	★★14.20%★★	5.23%	16.90%	12.30%
Sharpe	0.42	0.46	−1.68	1.8	0.48	0.23	−1.64	2.22	0.2	0.51	−1.74	1.41
Skewness	−0.84	−0.36	−0.75	−0.15	−1.2	−1.27	−0.95	−0.11	0.02	−0.39	−0.64	1.62
His.VaR	−6.14%	−3.22%	−9.07%	−2.25%	−5.70%	−3.68%	−10.14%	−2.17%	−6.41%	−1.97%	−10.62%	−2.27%
Max.DD	−34.58%	−6.02%	−34.58%	−8.31%	−37.14%	−6.65%	−35.39%	−6.64%	−40.30%	−3.61%	−39.46%	−7.73%
Panel C: Daily second-order VaR												
Return	5.34%	6.75%	−25.80%	18.14%	5.98%	0.05%	−26.50%	20.86%	2.07%	−2.24%	−29.31%	17.22%
Std	★★★12.24%	10.28%	14.59%	9.65%	★★★12.84%	8.81%	16.99%	9.33%	★14.76%★	6.95%	17.86%	12.72%
Sharpe	0.44	0.66	−1.77	1.88	0.47	0.01	−1.56	2.24	0.14	−0.32	−1.64	1.35
Skewness	−0.83	−0.32	−0.72	−0.11	−1.19	−1.35	−0.85	−0.04	−0.05	0.35	−0.83	1.58
His.VaR	−5.69%	−3.22%	−9.41%	−2.31%	−6.00%	−3.99%	−10.82%	−2.21%	−6.50%	−2.64%	−12.26%	−2.72%
Max.DD	−35.45%	−5.61%	−35.45%	−7.50%	−38.17%	−7.10%	−35.61%	−6.30%	−41.79%	−5.97%	−38.88%	−8.58%

Panel D: Realized semivariance

Return	5.20%	9.39%	−25.00%	16.97%	5.16%	−28.04%	19.49%	1.91%	4.87%	−32.26%	17.39%
Std	★★★12.08%	9.00%	14.92%	9.56%	★★★13.14%	17.96%	9.32%	★14.95%	7.57%	19.16%	11.95%
Sharpe	0.43	1.04	−1.68	1.78	0.39	−1.56	2.09	0.13	0.64	−1.68	1.46
Skewness	−1.1	−0.3	−1.03	−0.38	−1.54	−1.15	−0.33	−0.65	−1.06	−0.99	1.24
His.VaR	−5.81%	−2.55%	−10.14%	−2.52%	−6.05%	−11.67%	−2.39%	−6.49%	−2.96%	−13.37%	−1.97%
Max.DD	−33.81%	−4.97%	−33.81%	−8.12%	−39.15%	−38.25%	−7.87%	−43.90%	−5.31%	−43.21%	−8.88%

Panel E: Realized first-order VaR

Return	4.81%	9.45%	−24.98%	16.39%	5.62%	−28.47%	20.05%	2.28%	6.36%	−33.99%	18.78%
Std	★★★11.90%★	9.12%	14.84%	9.28%	★★★13.29%	17.89%	9.60%	15.80%★★	7.55%	19.77%	12.86%
Sharpe	0.4	1.04	−1.68	1.77	0.42	−1.59	2.09	0.14	0.84	−1.72	1.46
Skewness	−1	−0.13	−0.78	−0.26	−1.39	−1.03	−0.14	−0.36	−0.91	−0.8	1.61
His.VaR	−5.72%	−2.47%	−9.88%	−2.45%	−5.70%	−11.55%	−2.71%	−6.67%	−2.75%	−13.05%	−2.26%
Max.DD	−35.28%	−4.72%	−35.28%	−6.80%	−38.91%	−38.72%	−7.68%	−45.57%	−4.83%	−45.28%	−8.56%

Panel F: Realized second-order VaR

Return	5.75%	10.70%	−24.94%	17.50%	6.03%	−28.76%	20.84%	2.29%	6.43%	−34.22%	18.95%
Std	★★★12.26%	8.77%	15.53%	9.57%	★★★13.37%	17.48%	9.87%	15.94%★	7.74%	19.60%	13.17%
Sharpe	0.47	1.22	−1.61	1.83	0.45	−1.65	2.11	0.14	0.83	−1.75	1.44
Skewness	−1.07	−0.15	−0.88	−0.23	−1.22	−0.93	−0.06	−0.25	−0.95	−0.76	1.65
His.VaR	−5.31%	−2.44%	−10.42%	−2.47%	−5.71%	−11.77%	−2.71%	−6.63%	−2.85%	−13.15%	−2.64%
Max.DD	−35.34%	−4.62%	−35.34%	−7.50%	−39.56%	−38.91%	−7.84%	−46.04%	−5.01%	−45.46%	−8.56%

Note: See note in Table 23.1 for more information.

Table A3 Summary performance statistics of daily rebalanced low-risk portfolios using volatility and beta as risk measure

Weights	Market cap				Equal weight				Inverse risk			
Criteria	All	Period 1	Period 2	Period 3	All	Period 1	Period 2	Period 3	All	Period 1	Period 2	Period 3
Panel A: Benchmark (S&P 500)												
Return	3.08%	13.08%	-37.30%	20.68%	7.42%	10.20%	-38.54%	28.96%				
Std	17.80%	9.30%	19.40%	15.97%	21.43%	9.46%	23.74%	19.68%				
Sharpe	0.17	1.41	-1.92	1.29	0.35	1.08	-1.62	1.47				
Skewness	-0.58	-0.41	-0.71	-0.17	-0.28	-0.75	-0.73	0.38				
His.VaR	-8.19%	-2.58%	-11.53%	-6.33%	-9.46%	-3.24%	-13.31%	-6.92%				
Max.DD	-49.28%	-4.45%	-49.28%	-18.20%	-51.52%	-5.90%	-50.48%	-19.93%				
Panel B: Daily volatility												
Return	4.55%	4.37%	-24.93%	16.84%	6.16%	4.45%	-25.12%	19.28%	6.24%	4.31%	-24.61%	19.14%
Std	12.30%***	9.50%	14.93%	10.00%	12.37%***	8.86%	16.53%	9.11%	12.09%***	8.70%	16.18%	8.84%
Sharpe	0.37	0.46	-1.67	1.68	0.5	0.5	-1.52	2.12	0.52	0.5	-1.52	2.17
Skewness	-0.92	-0.4	-0.87	-0.32	-1.4	-1.38	-1.11	-0.34	-1.41	-1.29	-1.11	-0.36
His.VaR	-6.03%	-3.33%	-9.63%	-2.71%	-5.67%	-3.90%	-11.19%	-2.75%	-5.60%	-3.80%	-11.01%	-2.56%
Max.DD	-34.38%	-6.41%	-34.38%	-9.56%	-35.65%	-7.33%	-34.15%	-7.12%	-34.85%	-7.16%	-33.49%	-6.67%
Panel C: Daily beta												
Return	6.87%	8.53%	-24.70%	19.19%	5.80%	6.51%	-27.25%	19.57%	5.69%	6.39%	-26.89%	19.22%
Std	11.81%***	8.56%	14.23%	9.38%	12.68%***	9.06%	17.11%	9.00%	12.45%***	8.64%	17.12%	8.67%
Sharpe	0.58	1	-1.74	2.05	0.46	0.72	-1.59	2.17	0.46	0.74	-1.57	2.22
Skewness	-0.88	-0.5	-0.78	-0.06	-1.35	-1.16	-0.91	-0.15	-1.36	-1.08	-0.79	-0.15
His.VaR	-5.40%	-2.82%	-9.37%	-1.68%	-5.49%	-3.71%	-11.14%	-1.88%	-5.75%	-3.49%	-11.03%	-1.78%
Max.DD	-33.86%	-5.49%	-33.86%	-8.34%	-39.02%	-6.96%	-37.09%	-6.63%	-38.27%	-6.60%	-36.55%	-6.49%
Panel D: Realized volatility												
Return	6.36%	8.49%	-27.11%	19.89%	6.56%	8.22%	-29.30%	21.59%	6.88%	7.40%	-27.20%	20.94%
Std	12.52%***	8.91%	15.76%	9.51%	13.71%***	8.26%	18.91%	9.70%	12.94%***	8.19%	17.89%	9.08%
Sharpe	0.51	0.95	-1.72	2.09	0.48	1	-1.55	2.23	0.53*	0.9	-1.52	2.31
Skewness	-1.18	-0.13	-0.95	-0.41	-1.84	-1.03	-1.57	-0.54	-1.84	-1.22	-1.55	-0.53
His.VaR	-6.05%	-2.76%	-10.26%	-2.22%	-6.23%	-2.88%	-11.41%	-2.63%	-5.70%	-3.04%	-11.11%	-2.40%
Max.DD	-36.64%	-4.25%	-36.64%	-8.77%	-40.08%	-5.08%	-39.72%	-8.88%	-37.86%	-5.39%	-37.20%	-8.17%
Panel E: Realized beta												
Return	4.62%	10.04%	-33.75%	21.21%	5.61%	12.66%	-36.01%	23.72%	6.03%	9.99%	-33.87%	23.44%
Std	13.46%***	10.69%	14.37%	10.52%	15.86%***	9.21%	20.80%	11.58%	16.71%***	9.87%	22.34%	12.75%
Sharpe	0.34	0.94	-2.35	2.02	0.35	1.37	-1.73	2.05	0.36	1.01	-1.52	1.84
Skewness	-0.77	0.62	-0.7	-0.36	-1.4	0.09	-1.11	-0.22	-1.41	0.94	-1.4	-0.13
His.VaR	-6.24%	-2.52%	-10.64%	-2.85%	-7.65%	-2.28%	-12.65%	-3.46%	-5.56%	-2.29%	-14.08%	-4.64%
Max.DD	-45.17%	-3.84%	-45.17%	-10.02%	-47.52%	-4.11%	-47.52%	-10.80%	-45.38%	-4.71%	-45.35%	-12.75%

Note: See note in Table 23.1 for more information.

Table A4 Summary performance statistics of daily rebalanced low-risk portfolios using a downside risk measure

Weights	Market cap				Equal weight				Inverse risk			
Criteria	All	Period 1	Period 2	Period 3	All	Period 1	Period 2	Period 3	All	Period 1	Period 2	Period 3
Panel A: Daily semivariance												
Return	4.49%	4.20%	−25.83%	17.31%	5.77%	4.11%	−26.50%	19.60%	5.91%	4.10%	−25.81%	19.41%
Std	***12.40%	8.99%	15.51%	9.81%	***12.53%	8.64%	16.99%	8.95%	***12.22%	8.46%	16.59%	8.69%
Sharpe	0.36	0.47	−1.67	1.76	0.46	0.48	−1.56	2.19	0.48	0.48	−1.56	2.23
Skewness	−1.03	−0.25	−0.93	−0.28	−1.52	−1.25	−1.2	−0.31	−1.53	−1.17	−1.2	−0.34
His.VaR	−6.28%	−3.11%	−9.81%	−2.34%	−5.73%	−3.77%	−11.42%	−2.24%	−5.64%	−3.65%	−11.22%	−2.16%
Max.DD	−35.39%	−5.93%	−35.39%	−8.56%	−37.29%	−7.10%	−36.09%	−6.82%	−36.27%	−6.90%	−35.19%	−6.52%
Panel B: Daily first-order VaR												
Return	4.38%	1.81%	−25.93%	17.75%	4.97%*	1.58%	−28.02%	19.92%	4.64%***	2.36%	−28.36%	19.46%
Std	***12.89%	9.30%	16.43%	10.17%	***13.01%*	9.01%	18.01%	8.98%	***12.84%***	8.55%	17.82%	8.80%
Sharpe	0.34	0.2	−1.58	1.75	0.38*	0.18	−1.56	2.22	0.36***	0.28	−1.59	2.21
Skewness	−1	−0.31	−0.8	−0.26	−1.63	−1.23	−1.25	−0.32	−1.63	−0.88	−1.18	−0.36
His.VaR	−6.48%	−3.51%	−9.97%	−2.59%	−85.92%	−4.13%	−11.57%	−2.48%	−5.97%	−3.70%	−11.42%	−2.43%
Max.DD	−35.95%	−6.75%	−35.64%	−8.94%	−40.22%	−7.70%	−37.77%	−7.01%	−40.20%	−6.96%	−38.18%	−6.83%
Panel C: Daily second-order VaR												
Return	4.41%	3.78%	−26.25%	17.54%	4.90%	2.71%	−28.58%	19.90%	5.11%*	5.14%	−29.64%	20.34%
Std	***12.90%	9.26%	17.20%	9.73%	***13.17%*	8.99%	18.28%	9.07%	***13.33%*	9.75%	18.51%	8.93%
Sharpe	0.34	0.41	−1.53	1.8	0.37	0.3	−1.56	2.19	0.38*	0.53	−1.6	2.28
Skewness	−1.22	−0.22	−0.95	−0.28	−1.63	−1.4	−1.18	−0.37	−1.63	−0.75	−1.08	−0.43
His.VaR	−6.47%	−3.11%	−10.51%	−2.54%	−5.96%	−4.05%	−12.14%	−2.43%	−6.00%	−3.85%	−12.04%	−2.37%
Max.DD	−36.06%	−5.95%	−36.06%	−8.75%	−40.57%	−7.50%	−38.31%	−7.22%	−41.52%	−7.08%	−39.69%	−7.16%
Panel D: Realized semivariance												
Return	6.25%	6.98%	−25.20%	18.90%	6.80%	6.64%	−28.29%	21.67%	7.44%	5.32%	−24.27%	20.46%
Std	***11.71%	8.66%	13.52%	9.49%	***13.59%	8.59%	18.51%	9.78%	***12.33%	8.44%	17.06%	8.77%
Sharpe	0.53	0.81	−1.86	1.99	*0.50	0.77	−1.53	2.22	*0.60*	0.63	−1.42	2.33
Skewness	−0.72	−0.23	−0.51	−0.16	−1.6	−0.8	−1.26	−0.51	−1.64	−1.22	−1.29	−0.47
His.VaR	−5.28%	−2.67%	−9.36%	−2.58%	−6.40%	−3.12%	−11.50%	−2.71%	−5.28%	−3.37%	−11.00%	−2.38%
Max.DD	−34.76%	−4.41%	−34.76%	−8.35%	−39.76%	−5.61%	−38.88%	−8.67%	−35.36%	−6.06%	−33.86%	−7.52%

Continued

Table A4 Summary performance statistics of daily rebalanced low-risk portfolios using a downside risk measure—cont'd

Weights	Market cap				Equal weight				Inverse risk			
Criteria	All	Period 1	Period 2	Period 3	All	Period 1	Period 2	Period 3	All	Period 1	Period 2	Period 3
Panel E: Realized first-order VaR												
Return	7.49%	10.51%	−28.20%	21.79%	★★★9.31%★	12.63%	−28.94%	24.50%	★★★11.60%★★★	12.80%	−26.72%	26.43%
Std	★★★12.94%	8.54%	15.92%	9.96%	★★★14.35%★	7.96%	19.24%	10.66%	★★★13.79%★★★	8.14%	18.06%	10.34%
Sharpe	★★0.58	1.23	−1.77	2.19	★★★0.65★	1.59	−1.5	2.3	★★★0.84★★★	1.57	−1.48	2.56
Skewness	−1.28	0.15	−1.23	−0.55	−1.82	−0.79	−1.87	−0.49	−1.68	−0.92	−1.71	−0.54
His.VaR	−5.78%	−2.32%	−9.98%	−2.28%	−6.28%	−2.42%	−10.66%	−2.60%	−5.94%	−2.49%	−10.08%	−2.35%
Max.DD	−37.86%	−3.37%	−37.86%	−9.18%	−39.41%	−4.30%	−39.41%	−9.25%	−36.95%	−4.35%	−36.95%	−9.15%
Panel F: Realized second-order VaR												
Return	7.18%	10.88%	−27.49%	20.80%	★7.68%	12.18%	−31.47%	23.83%	★9.17%★	12.45%	−27.90%	23.67%
Std	★★★12.73%	8.69%	15.38%	10.01%	★★15.00%★	8.16%	20.28%	11.01%	★★★14.61%★★	9.05%	19.82%	10.94%
Sharpe	★★0.56	1.25	−1.79	2.08	★0.51	1.49	−1.55	2.16	★★0.63★	1.38	−1.41	2.16
Skewness	−1.12	0.06	−1.05	−0.48	−1.78	−0.78	−1.77	−0.28	−1.64	−0.82	−1.69	−0.14
His.VaR	−6.80%	−2.35%	−9.49%	−2.61%	−6.64%	−2.57%	−11.43%	−3.01%	−6.01%	−2.83%	−11.36%	−2.86%
Max.DD	−37.24%	−3.99%	−37.24%	−8.97%	−42.35%	−4.63%	−42.35%	−9.83%	−38.81%	−5.36%	−38.81%	−9.01%

Note: See note in Table 23.1 for more information.

ACKNOWLEDGMENTS

Financial support from Vrije Universiteit Brussel (VUB) and the Doctiris program of the Brussels Institute for Research and Innovation (Innoviris) is gratefully acknowledged.

REFERENCES

Ane, T., Geman, H., 2000. Order flow, transaction clock, and normality of asset returns. J. Finance 55 (5), 2259—2284.

Amaya, D., Christoffersen, P., Jacobs, K., Vasquez, A., 2011. Do realized skewness and kurtosis predict the cross-section of equity returns. SSRN Electron. J.

Amenc, N., Goltz, F., Martellini, L., Ketkowsky, P., 2011. Efficient indexation: an alternative to cap-weighted indices. J. Invest. Manag. 9 (4), 1—23.

Amenc, N., Goltz, F., Martellini, L., 2013. Smart Beta 2.0. EDHEC (Risk Position Paper).

Andersen, T.G., Dobrev, D., Schaumburg, E., 2012. Jump-robust volatility estimation using nearest neighbor truncation. J. Econometrics 169 (1), 75—93.

Arnott, R.D., Hsu, J., Moore, P., 2005. Fundamental indexation. Financial Analysts Journal 61 (2), 83—99.

Baker, M., Bradley, B., Wurgler, J., 2011. Benchmarks as limits to arbitrage: understanding the low volatility anomaly. Financ. Anal. J. 67 (1), 40—54.

Baker, N.L., Haugen, R.A., 2012. Low Risk Stocks Outperform within All Observable Markets of the World. Available at SSRN 2055431.

Bali, T.G., Peng, L., 2006. Is there a risk—return trade-off? evidence from high-frequency data. J. Appl. Econ. 21 (8), 1169—1198.

Barber, B.M., Lyon, J.D., 1997. Firm size, book-to-market ratio, and security returns: a holdout sample of financial firms. J. Finance 52 (2), 875—883.

Barndorff-Nielsen, O.E., Hansen, P.R., Lunde, A., Shephard, N., 2009. Realized kernels in practice: trades and quotes. Econ. J. 12 (3), C1—C32.

Barndorff-Nielsen, O.E., Kinnebrock, S., Shephard, N., 2010. Measuring downside risk: realized semivariance. In: Volatility and Time Series Econometrics. Oxford University Press, Oxford, UK.

Barndorff-Nielsen, O.E., Shephard, N., 2004. Econometric analysis of realized covariation: high-frequency based covariance, regression, and correlation in financial economics. Econometrica 72 (3), 885—925.

Bauer, R., Koedijk, K., Otten, R., 2005. International evidence on ethical mutual fund performance and investment style. J. Bank. Financ. 29 (7), 1751—1767.

Bertrand, P., Lapointe, V., 2014. How Performance of Risk-based Strategies Is Modified by Socially Responsible Investment Universe? Available at: http://papers.ssrn.com/sol3/papers.cfm?abstract_id=2282372.

Blitz, D., Van Vliet, P., 2007. The volatility effect. J. Portfol. Manage. 34 (1), 102—113.

Bollerslev, T., Litvinova, J., Tauchen, G., 2006. Leverage and volatility feedback effects in high-frequency data. J. Financ. Econ. 4 (3), 353—384.

Boudt, K., Peterson, B., Croux, C., 2007. Estimation and decomposition of downside risk for portfolios with non-normal returns. J. Risk 11 (2), 79—103.

Brown, S.J., Goetzmann, W., Ibbotson, R.G., Ross, S.A., 1992. Survivorship bias in performance studies. Rev. Financ. Stud. 5 (4), 553—580.

Brownlees, C.T., Gallo, G.M., 2006. Financial econometric analysis at ultra-high- frequency: data handling concerns. Comput. Stat. Data Anal. 51 (4), 2232—2245.

Carhart, M.M., 1997. On persistence in mutual fund performance. J. Finance 52 (1), 57—82.

Carpenter, J.N., Lynch, A.W., 1999. Survivorship bias and attrition effects in measures of performance persistence. J. Financ. Econ. 54 (3), 337—374.

Choueifaty, Y., Coignard, Y., 2008. Toward maximum diversification. J. Portfol. Manage. 35 (1), 40—51.

Clarke, R.G., De Silva, H., Thorley, S., 2006. Minimum-variance portfolios in the US equity market. J. Portfol. Manage. 33 (1), 10—24.

DeMiguel, V., Garlappi, L., Uppal, R., 2009. Optimal versus naive diversification: how inefficient is the 1/N portfolio strategy? Rev. Financ. Stud. 22 (5), 1915—1953.

De Pooter, M.D., Martens, M., Dijk, D.V., 2008. Predicting the daily covariance matrix for S&P 100 stocks using intraday data- but which frequency to use? Econ. Rev. 27 (1–3), 199–229.

Diebold, F., Mariano, R., 1995. Comparing predictive accuracy. J. Bus. Econ. Stat. 13 (3), 253–263.

Dufour, J.M., Garcia, R., Taamouti, A., 2012. Measuring high-frequency causality between returns, realized volatility, and implied volatility. J. Financ. Econ. 10 (1), 124–163.

Engle, R.F., 2000. The econometrics of Ultra-high-frequency data. Econometrica 68 (1), 1–22.

Engle, R.F., Colacito, R., 2005. Testing and valuing dynamic correlations for asset allocation. J. Bus. Econ. Stat. 24 (2), 238–253.

Fama, E.F., Fisher, L., Jensen, M., Roll, R., 1969. The adjustment of stock prices to new information. Int. Econ. Rev. 10 (1), 1–21.

Fama, E.F., French, K.R., 1992. The cross- section of expected stock returns. J. Finance 47 (2), 427–465.

Fleming, J., Kirby, C., Ostdiek, B., 2001. The economic value of volatility timing. J. Finance 56 (1), 329–352.

Frazzini, A., Pedersen, L.H., 2014. Betting against beta. J. Financ. Econ. 111 (1), 1–25.

Ghysels, E., Santa-Clara, P., Valkanov, R., 2006. Predicting volatility: getting the most out of return data sampled at different frequencies. J. Econ. 131 (1), 59–95.

Goltz, F., Le Sourd, V., 2011. Does finance theory make the case for capitalisation-weighted indexing? J. Index Invest. 2 (2), 59–75.

Haugen, R., Heins, A.J., 1975. Risk and the rate of return on financial assets: some old wine in new bottles. J. Financ. Quant. Anal. 10 (05), 775–784.

Hautsch, N., Kyj, L.M., and Malec, P. (2013). Do high-frequency data improve high- dimensional portfolio allocations? J. Appl. Econ. forthcoming.

Jobson, J., Korkie, B., 1981. Performance hypothesis testing with the Sharpe and Treynor measures. J. Finance 36 (4), 889–908.

Ledoit, O., Wolf, M., 2008. Robust performance hypothesis testing with the Sharpe ratio. J. Empir. Financ. 15 (5), 850–859.

Lee, J., Kim, T.S., Lee, H.K., 2011. Return-volatility relationship in high-frequency data: multi-scale horizon dependency. Stud. Nonlinear Dyn. Econ. 15 (1), 60–101.

Leote de Carvalho, R., Lu, X., Moulin, P., 2012. Demystifying equity risk–based strategies: a simple alpha plus beta description. J. Portfol. Manage. 38 (3), 56–70.

Lintner, J., 1965. The valuation of risk assets and the selection of risky investments in stock portfolios and capital budgets. Rev. Econ. Stat. 47 (1), 13–37.

Liu, Q., 2009. On portfolio optimization: how and when do we benefit from high-frequency data? J. Appl. Econ. 24 (4), 560–582.

Maillard, S., Roncalli, T., Teiletche, J., 2010. The properties of equally weighted risk contribution portfolios. J. Portfol. Manage. 36 (4), 60–70.

Markowitz, H., 1952. Portfolio selection. J. Finance 7 (1), 77–91.

Memmel, C., 2003. Performance hypothesis testing with the Sharpe ratio. Financ. Lett. 1 (1), 21–23.

Merton, R.C., 1980. On estimating the expected return on the market: an exploratory investigation. J. Financ. Econ. 8 (4), 323–361.

Néri, B.D.A.P., Notini, H.H., 2006. Evidences of Risk-return Trade-off in IBOVESPA Using High-frequency Data. Available at: https://files.nyu.edu/bpn207/public/Research/High_Frequency/Risk-Return_Trade-Off.pdf.

Officer, R.R., 1972. The distribution of stock returns. J. Am. Stat. Assoc. 67 (340), 807–812.

Perold, A.F., 2007. Fundamentally flawed indexing. Financ. Anal. J. 63 (6), 31–37.

Pettengill, G.N., Sundaram, S., Mathur, I., 1995. The conditional relation between beta and returns. J. Financ. Quant. Anal. 30 (01), 101–116.

Sharpe, W.F., 1964. Capital asset prices: a theory of market equilibrium under conditions of risk. J. Finance 19 (3), 425–442.

S&P Dow Jones index. S&P Low Volatility Index Methodology, 2014. Retrieved from http://us.spindices.com/indices/strategy/sp-500-low-volatility-index.

CHAPTER 24

Measuring the Leverage Effect in a High-Frequency Trading Framework

Imma Valentina Curato[1], Simona Sanfelici[2]
[1]Ulm University, Ulm, Germany; [2]Department of Economics, University of Parma, Parma, Italy

Contents

24.1 INTRODUCTION

The models used to describe the dynamics of the financial time series have to incorporate the speed and complexity of the modern financial markets. Since 1999 after the US Securities and Exchange Commission (SEC) authorized electronic exchanges, high-frequency trading accounts approximatively for 50% of all trading volume just taking into account the US equity market.[1] Nowadays, technological progress, along with the growing dominance of electronic trading, allows one to record market activity with high precision leading to advanced and comprehensive data sets. The historical data analysis of the financial time series, therefore, cannot avoid the use of the aforementioned data as long as their underlying models have to show a richer structure in the price/volatility dynamics in order to fit the features of data with time aggregation of minutes and seconds. In this direction, a first fundamental step is reinterpreting the classical stylized facts of the financial time series in order to improve our understanding of the matters concerned.

The *leverage effect* is one of the classical stylized facts observed in the security return distributions, along with the well-known fat tails, skewness, and heteroscedasticity, and it is closely related to the stochastic nature of the volatility dynamics. It refers to

---

[1] *Equity Market Structure Literature Review, Part II: High Frequency Trading*, Staff of the Division of Trading and Markets (US SEC), March 18, 2014. *Market microstructure confronting many view points*, F. Abergel, J.P. Bouchaud, T. Foucault, C.A. Lehalle, M. Rosenbaum, 2012.

The Handbook of High Frequency Trading
ISBN 978-0-12-802205-4

the relationship between returns and their corresponding volatilities, which tends to be negatively correlated. One possible economic interpretation of this phenomenon was developed in Black (1976) and Christie (1982), and it is connected with the concept of *financial leverage* (debt-to-equity ratio). As asset prices decline, companies become automatically more leveraged since the relative value of their debts rises relative to that of their equities. The probability of default rises, and then, their stocks become riskier, and hence more volatile. As discussed in Ait-Sahalia et al. (2013), being the most prevalent economic interpretation in the literature, the name *leverage* is also used to describe the statistical correlation between the prices and their corresponding volatilities.

In order to capture the leverage effect in modeling terms, a classical approach consists of using a constant correlation structure between the price and its corresponding volatility, for example, Heston (1993) and Barndorff-Nielsen and Shepard (2002). Recent empirical works, however, emphasized that this effect is not constant, but itself evolves in time, see Yu (2005) and Bollerslev et al. (2006) among others. Moreover there may be important asymmetries in the way in which the volatility responds to price changes. For instance, Carr and Wu (2007), Bandi and Renò (2012) show how in the presence of positive shocks (positive returns) the volatility may not change or even change positively. These findings motivate the growth of sophisticated models like the class of the multi-factor stochastic volatility models. The correlation structure between price and volatility can be modeled as a state space-dependent variable or as in Veraart and Veraart (2012) as a stochastic process itself.

Generally, calibrating these models to market information is rather complicated because estimation procedures of the leverage and of the variance of the volatility processes have not been extensively studied under general hypotheses and an inference on these models cannot avoid estimations of these quantities. We will introduce a nonparametric procedure for the leverage estimation based on the Fourier analysis developed in Malliavin and Mancino (2002, 2009), showing the versatility of this estimation procedure and its effectiveness when dealing with high-frequency data. The Fourier methodology has already been applied in estimating second-order latent quantities like the variance of the volatility in Curato et al. (2014).

We assume that the underlying dynamics of the price and volatility processes are governed by two continuous semi-Martingales, correlated by means of a stochastic process $\rho(t)$. We do not assume any specific functional form for the volatility, for the variance of the volatility and for the correlation processes between the Brownian motions driving the price and volatility. In particular, the Heston (H) model and the Generalized Heston (GH) model proposed in Veraart and Veraart (2012) are included in our framework. With respect to the other nonparametric estimators present in the literature that involved the use of high-frequency data (Barucci and Mancino (2010), Cuchiero and Teichmann (2015), Bandi and Renò (2012), Mykland and Wang (2014)), we define integrated and spot estimations of the leverage in a novel way, that is, by using only a preestimation of the Fourier coefficients of the *latent* volatility process. In Barucci and Mancino (2010) and Cuchiero and Teichmann (2013), two different nonparametric procedures with several features in common are presented. First, the authors estimate the spot volatility process using, respectively, the Fourier estimator developed in Malliavin and Mancino (2009) and a Fourier estimator constructed starting by a jump-robust estimation of the covariance process. Second, they estimate the leverage function using the estimated spot volatility instead of its unknown paths. Bandi and Renò (2012) and Mykland and Wang (2014) develop nonparametric procedures suitable for *local* stochastic leverage models. Also, these methods are based on the preestimation of the spot volatility function since the leverage is defined as a state space-dependent function of the volatility process. These estimators, however, do not take into account the microstructure contamination effects that might appear when dealing with data having time aggregation <5-min (Hautsch, 2012). These effects might spoil the estimation process, as the spot volatility estimators are quite sensitive to noise. Avoiding the estimation of the spot volatility allows us to define consistent estimators that, without any manipulation of the data, are robust under microstructure noise and irregular trading (uneven observations of the price path).

We investigate the robustness to microstructure effects of the integrated estimator via numerical simulations. We generate two data sets by means of an Euler discretization of the H model and the GH model, and we study the performances of the leverage estimator in different scenarios. The simulation results corroborate the theoretical results and also show the features of the Fourier methodology in realistic frameworks. We are able to construct efficient estimations of the integrated leverage and to conduct an analysis on the sensitivity to the choice of the cutting parameters. An empirical application to S&P 500 index futures is also presented.

The chapter is organized as follows: The model setting is carefully described in Section 24.2. In Section 24.3, we define the Fourier estimators of the spot and integrated leverage and prove their consistency. Finally, in Section 24.4, the Monte-Carlo and empirical results are shown. Section 24.5 concludes.

24.2 MODEL SETTING

We consider the log price and the volatility processes defined on a probability space $(\Omega, (\mathcal{F}_t)_{t \in [0,T]}, \mathbb{P})$ satisfying the usual conditions and following the Itô stochastic differential equations:

$$\begin{cases} dp(t) = \sigma(t)dW(t) + a(t)dt \\ dv(t) = \gamma(t)dZ(t) + b(t)dt, \end{cases} \qquad [24.1]$$

where $v(t) = \sigma^2(t)$ and $W(t)$ and $Z(t)$ are correlated Brownian motions. The correlation process between the Brownian motions is defined as

$$< dW(t), dZ(t) > = \rho(t)dt,$$

where the brackets stand for the Itô contraction and $\rho(t)$ is a process with value in $[-1,1]$.

A standard no-arbitrage condition suggests that the security price must be a semimartingale as prescribed by Back (1991) and Delbaen and Schachermayer (1994). These types of processes obey the fundamental theorem of asset pricing and, as a result, are used extensively in financial econometrics, (see Ghysels et al. (1996) for a review). We think of this model as the model governing an underlying efficient price process, that is, the price that would be observed in the absence of market frictions. We do not assume any specific functional form of the volatility, of the variance of the volatility, and of the correlation processes; thus, we are working in a model-free setting. In particular, parametric models such as H, CEV, and the GH Models defined in Veraart and Veraart (2012) fit our assumptions.

Scaling the unit of time, we can always reduce ourselves to the case in which the time window $[0,T]$ becomes $[0,2\pi]$. For this reason, in what follows, we will consider the time window to be $[0,2\pi]$, which is the most suitable choice if we want to apply Fourier analysis. We make the following hypotheses on the processes that appear in Eqn (24.1):

- **H.1** $a(t)$, $b(t)$, $\sigma(t)$, $\gamma(t)$, $\rho(t)$ are continuous in $[0,2\pi]$ and adapted to the filtration $\mathcal{F}_t$ with values in $\mathbb{R}$.

- **H.2** $\forall \, p \geq 1$

$$E\left[\sup_{t \in [0,2\pi]} |a(t)|^p\right] < \infty, \quad E\left[\sup_{t \in [0,2\pi]} |b(t)|^p\right] < \infty,$$

$$E\left[\sup_{t \in [0,2\pi]} |\sigma(t)|^p\right] < \infty, \quad E\left[\sup_{t \in [0,2\pi]} |\gamma(t)|^p\right] < \infty,$$

$$E\left[\sup_{t \in [0,2\pi]} |\rho(t)|^p\right] < \infty.$$

- **H.3** $\forall p \geq 1$, the processes $a(t), b(t), \sigma(t), \gamma(t) \in \mathbb{D}^{1,p}$, and

$$E\left[\sup_{s,t \in [0,2\pi]} |\mathscr{D}_s a(t)|^p\right] < \infty, \quad E\left[\sup_{s,t \in [0,2\pi]} |\mathscr{D}_s b(t)|^p\right] < \infty,$$

$$E\left[\sup_{s,t \in [0,2\pi]} |\mathscr{D}_s \sigma(t)|^p\right] < \infty, \quad E\left[\sup_{s,t \in [0,2\pi]} |\mathscr{D}_s \gamma(t)|^p\right] < \infty,$$

where $\mathbb{D}^{1,p}$ is the Sobolev space of the generalized derivative in the sense of Malliavin and $\mathscr{D}$ stands for the Malliavin derivative (Nualart, 2006).

We are interested in estimating the *spot leverage process* $\eta(t)$, which is defined by means of the Itô contraction between the price and volatility as

$$< dp(t), dv(t) > = \eta(t)dt, \qquad [24.2]$$

and the *integrated* quantity

$$\eta^{[1]} = \int_0^{2\pi} \eta(t)dt. \qquad [24.3]$$

24.3 COMPUTATION OF LEVERAGE USING FOURIER METHODOLOGY

The leverage process represents the covariance between the price and the volatility process as stated in Eqn (24.2). The Fourier methodology developed by Malliavin and Mancino (2002, 2009) for the estimation of the covariance between asset returns can be adapted to get estimations also in this context. Before proceeding, we recall some definitions from harmonic analysis theory, see e.g. Malliavin (1995).

Given ϕ defined on the Hilbert space $L_2([0,2\pi])$ of the complex valued functions, we consider its *Fourier coefficients*, defined on the group of the integers $\mathbb{Z}$ by the formula

$$c_h(\phi): = \frac{1}{2\pi} \int_0^{2\pi} e^{-iht}\phi(t)dt \quad \text{for all } h \in \mathbb{Z}. \qquad [24.4]$$

The set of Fourier coefficients represents the *coordinates* of ϕ with respect to the orthonormal basis $\{e_h(t) = e^{iht} s.t. h \in \mathbb{Z}\}$ of the Hilbert space $L_2([0,2\pi])$. Thus, starting with an arbitrary number of Fourier coefficients as $(c_1,...,c_N)$, we can reconstruct a trigonometric approximation of ϕ by means of the orthogonal projection of the function onto the space $< e_1,...,e_N>$

$$\pi_N(\phi) = \sum_{i=1}^N e_i c_i(\phi)$$

that can be interpreted as an *estimation* of the function ϕ with arbitrary precision; see the works of De La Vallée Poussin (1919), Favard (1937), and Zamansky (1949) for further details. Therefore, *an arbitrary sequence of Fourier coefficients includes the necessary information to get an estimation of ϕ*. Given two functions Φ and Ψ on the integers $\mathbb{Z}$, we say that the *Bohr convolution product* exists if the following limit exists for all integers h:

$$(\Phi * \Psi)(h): = \lim_{N \to \infty} \frac{1}{2N+1} \sum_{|l| \leq N} \Phi(l)\Psi(h-l).$$

Then, the following identity relating the Fourier coefficients of dp and dv to the Fourier coefficients of the process $\eta(t)$ holds:

$$c_h(\eta) := \lim_{N \to \infty} \frac{2\pi}{2N+1} \sum_{|l| \leq N} c_l(dv) c_{h-l}(dp), \qquad [24.5]$$

where the convergence is attained in probability, see Theorem 2.1 in Malliavin and Mancino (2009). The above identity is feasible only when continuous observations of the price and volatility process are available. Before turning to a more realistic framework, we need the following considerations.

We start from the definition of the approximate Fourier coefficients, obtained in Eqn (24.5) by dropping the limit operator:

$$c_h(\eta_N) := \frac{2\pi}{2N+1} \sum_{|l| \leq N} c_l(dv) c_{h-l}(dp), \qquad [24.6]$$

where the Fourier coefficients

$$c_l(dp) = \frac{1}{2\pi} \int_0^{2\pi} e^{-ilt} dp(t), \qquad [24.7]$$

for all $|l| \leq 2N$ and $c_l(dv)$ can be defined by means of the integration by part formula for all $|l| \neq 0$ as

$$c_l(dv) = il c_l(v) + \frac{1}{2\pi} (v(2\pi) - v(0)). \qquad [24.8]$$

It is evident from Eqn (24.8) that preestimating the volatility path is a necessary step in order to define coefficients (24.6). This is the methodology followed in Barucci and Mancino (2010).

In the present work, we modify the Bohr convolution product leading to definition (24.6) by replacing the coefficients $c_l(dv)$ with $il c_l(v)$ for all $l \neq 0$. Therefore, we propose the following:

$$\widehat{c}_h(\eta_N) := \frac{2\pi}{2N+1} \sum_{|l| \leq N} il\, c_l(v) c_{h-l}(dp), \qquad [24.9]$$

in which only a preestimation of the Fourier coefficients of the volatility is required.

We note that spot volatility enters implicitly in definition (24.9) because its Fourier coefficients define a trigonometric approximation of $v(t)$. The effectiveness of definition (24.9) shows when we observe the log-price process at discrete unevenly spaced times. In fact, the instability of the spot volatility estimations at the boundary of a finite sample is a well-known result (end effects). Even the Fourier spot volatility estimators used in Barucci and Mancino (2010) and Cuchiero and Teichmann (2013), that are more suitable to deal with unevenly spaced data, introduce a bias term if evaluated at the boundary of the time window $[0,2\pi]$. Definition (24.9) overcomes the above problems allowing one to define a consistent estimator. We now define the procedure that allows one to define the Fourier coefficients of the leverage starting by *discrete observations* of the price process.

- **Step 1:** we start by preestimating the Fourier coefficients of the volatility. We assume that $p(t)$ is observed at a discrete unevenly spaced grid

$$S_n := \left\{ 0 = t_{0,n} \leq t_{1,n} \leq .. \leq t_{i,n} \leq .. \leq t_{k_n,n} = 2\pi \right\}, \quad \text{for all}$$
$$i = 0, \ldots k_n \text{ and } k_n \leq n,$$

and we define $\rho(n) := \max_{i=0,\ldots,k_n-1} |t_{i+1,n} - t_{i,n}|$ and the discrete observed return as $\delta_{i,n}(p) = p(t_{i+1,n}) - p(t_{i,n})$ for all $i = 0, \ldots, k_n - 1$.

Therefore, by means of the classical definition of the discrete Fourier transform, we estimate $c_s(dp)$ as

$$c_s(dp_n) = \frac{1}{2\pi} \sum_{i=0}^{k_n-1} e^{-ist_{i,n}} \delta_{i,n}(p), \qquad [24.10]$$

for any integer s such that $|s| \leq 2M + N$.

We define the Fourier coefficient estimators of the volatility process as in Malliavin and Mancino (2002):

$$c_l(v_{n,M}): \frac{2\pi}{2M + 1} \sum_{|s| \leq M} c_s(dp_n) c_{l-s}(dp_n) \qquad [24.11]$$

for any integer l such that $|l| \leq 2N$.

- **Step 2:** by means of definition (24.9) and estimations (24.10) and (24.11), we get the estimators of the Fourier coefficients of the leverage processes for any integer h such that $|h| \leq N$:

$$\widehat{c}_h(\eta_{n,M,N}) := \frac{2\pi}{2N + 1} \sum_{|l| \leq N} il \ c_l(v_{n,M}) c_{h-l}(dp_n). \qquad [24.12]$$

The consistency of estimator (24.12) is proved in the following Theorem:

Theorem 3.1. For all $|h| \leq N$, let $\widehat{c}_h(\eta_{n,M,N})$ be the hth Fourier coefficient estimator of the leverage process defined in Eqn (24.12). We assume that hypotheses (**H**) and

$$\frac{N^2}{M} \to 0 \text{ and } M\rho(n) \to a \qquad [24.13]$$

with $a \in \left(0, \frac{1}{2}\right)$ hold true as $n, N, M \to \infty$ and $\rho(n) \to 0$. Then,

$$\widehat{c}_h(\eta_{n,M,N}) \xrightarrow{\text{P}} \frac{1}{2\pi} \int_0^{2\pi} e^{-iht} \eta(t) dt. \qquad [24.14]$$

Remark 3.2. The range prescribed for the parameter a is connected with the Nyquist frequency. In this context, the cutting frequencies M and N that denote, respectively, the number of the Fourier coefficients of the return and of the volatility process to use in definition (24.12) has an order of magnitude less than $n/2$—the so-called Nyquist frequency—in order to avoid aliasing effects.

Proof (Theorem 3.1.):

Hereafter, let $\phi_n(t) := \sup_{i=0,\dots,k_n} \{t_{i,n}: t_{i,n} \leq t\}$. We will then refer to the discrete Fourier coefficients of the return process by using the following equivalent integral definition:

$$c_s(dp_n) = \frac{1}{2\pi} \int_0^{2\pi} e^{-is\phi_n(t)} dp(t) \qquad [24.15]$$

for all $|s| \leq 2M + N$.

The notation D_M stands for the normalized Dirichlet kernel. In its continuous definition, it is defined as

$$D_M(s) = \frac{1}{2M+1} \sum_{|k| \leq M} e^{-iks}, \quad \text{for all } M \in \mathbb{N},$$

and by substituting $\phi_n(s)$ instead of s, we will refer to its discrete version.

We can decompose

$$\widehat{c}_h(\eta_{n,M,N}) - \frac{1}{2\pi} \int_0^{2\pi} e^{-iht} \eta(t) dt$$

$$= \frac{2\pi}{2N+1} \sum_{|l| \leq N} il c_l(v_{n,M}) c_{h-1}(dp_n) - \frac{2\pi}{2N+1} \sum_{|l| \leq N} il c_l(v) c_{h-1}(dp) \qquad [24.16]$$

$$+ \frac{2\pi}{2N+1} \sum_{|l| \leq N} il c_l(v) c_{h-1}(dp) - \frac{1}{2\pi} \int_0^{2\pi} e^{-iht} \eta(t) dt. \qquad [24.17]$$

In what follows, the constant C will denote a suitable constant that may not necessarily be the same.

Applying the Cauchy–Schwartz inequality to Eqn (24.16), we have that in L_1-norm

$$
E\left[\left|\frac{2\pi}{2N+1}\sum_{|l|\leq N} il\, c_l(v_{n,M})c_{h-l}(dp_n) - \frac{2\pi}{2N+1}\sum_{|l|\leq N} il\, c_l(v)c_{h-l}(dp)\right|\right]
$$

$$
= E\left[\left|\frac{2\pi}{2N+1}\sum_{|l|\leq N} il\, c_l(v_{n,M})\left(c_{h-l}(dp_n) - c_{h-l}(dp)\right) + il\, c_{h-l}(dp)\left(c_l(v_{n,M}) - c_l(v)\right)\right|\right]
$$

$$
\leq \frac{2\pi}{2N+1}\sum_{|l|\leq N}|l|\left(E\left[c_l(v_{n,M})^2\right]^{\frac{1}{2}}E\left[\left(c_{h-l}(dp_n) - c_{h-l}(dp)\right)^2\right]^{\frac{1}{2}}\right.
$$

$$
\left. + E\left[c_{h-l}(dp)^2\right]^{\frac{1}{2}}E\left[\left(c_l(v_{n,M}) - c_l(v)\right)^2\right]^{\frac{1}{2}}\right)
$$

$$
(24.18)
$$

The Fourier coefficients of the return process are bounded under the hypotheses (**H**) and

$$
E\left[\left(c_l(dp_n) - c_l(dp)\right)^2\right] \leq E\left[\left(\frac{1}{2\pi}\int_0^{2\pi}\left(e^{-il\phi_n(t)} - e^{-ilt}\right)\sigma(t)dW(t)\right.\right.
$$

$$
[24.19]
$$

$$
\left.\left. + \frac{1}{2\pi}\int_0^{2\pi}\left(e^{-il\phi_n(t)} - e^{-ilt}\right)a(t)dt\right)^2\right] \leq CN^2\rho^2(n)
$$

for each $|l| \leq 2N$ after using the Itô identity and Taylor's formula.

From definition (24.11) and by applying the Itô formula to the product $c_s(dp_n)$ $c_{l-s}(dp_n)$, we obtain the following decomposition regarding the discrete Fourier coefficients of the volatility process:

$$
c_l(v_{n,M}) = \frac{1}{2\pi}\int_0^{2\pi}e^{-il\phi_n(t)}v(t)dt + I_{M,n} + \tilde{I}_{M,n} + H^1_{M,n} + H^2_{M,n} + H^3_{M,n} + \tilde{H}^1_{M,n}
$$

$$
+ \tilde{H}^2_{M,n} + \tilde{H}^3_{M,n}
$$

where $I_{M,n}$ and $\tilde{I}_{M,n}$ are the contributions due to the diffusion part of dp in Eqn (24.1):

$$I_{M,n} = \frac{1}{2\pi} \int_0^{2\pi} \int_0^t e^{-il\phi_n(u)} D_M(\phi_n(t) - \phi_n(u))\sigma(u)dW(u)\sigma(t)dW(t) \qquad [24.20]$$

$$\tilde{I}_{M,n} = \frac{1}{2\pi} \int_0^{2\pi} e^{-il\phi_n(t)} \int_0^t D_M(\phi_n(t) - \phi_n(u))\sigma(u)dW(u)\sigma(t)dW(t).$$

and the other terms are the contributions of the drift part

$$H_{M,n}^1 = \frac{1}{2\pi} \int_0^{2\pi} \int_0^t e^{-il\phi_n(u)} D_M(\phi_n(t) - \phi_n(u))a(u)du\, \sigma(t)dW(t) \qquad [24.21]$$

$$H_{M,n}^2 = \frac{1}{2\pi} \int_0^{2\pi} \int_0^t e^{-il\phi_n(u)} D_M(\phi_n(t) - \phi_n(u))\sigma(u)dW(u)a(t)dt \qquad [24.22]$$

$$H_{M,n}^3 = \frac{1}{2\pi} \int_0^{2\pi} \int_0^t e^{-il\phi_n(u)} D_M(\phi_n(t) - \phi_n(u))a(u)du\, a(t)dt \qquad [24.23]$$

and $\tilde{H}_{M,n}^1$, $\tilde{H}_{M,n}^2$, and $\tilde{H}_{M,n}^3$ are defined in a symmetric way.

Using the Itô identity subsequently, the Cauchy–Schwartz and the Burkholder–Gundy inequalities, term (24.20) becomes in L_2-norm

$$E\left[(I_{M,n})^2\right] = E\left[\frac{1}{4\pi^2}\int_0^{2\pi} \left(\int_0^t e^{-il\phi_n(u)} D_M(\phi_n(t) - \phi_n(u))\sigma(u)dW(u)\right)^2 v(t)dt\right]$$

$$\leq C E\left[\sup_{t \in [0,2\pi]} v^2(t)\right] \int_0^{2\pi} \int_0^t D_M^2(\phi_n(t) - \phi_n(u))du\, dt \leq \frac{C}{M}$$

because of hypotheses (**H.2**) and the properties of the discretized Dirichlet kernel proved in Clément and Gloter (2011). By using the same tools, it is possible to prove that the L_2-norm of Eqns (24.21) and (24.23) is

$$E\left[\left(H_{M,n}^1\right)^2\right] \leq \frac{C}{M^{\frac{2}{p}}} \text{ and } E\left[\left(H_{M,n}^3\right)^2\right] \leq \frac{C}{M^{\frac{2}{p}}}$$

for a $p \in (1,2)$.

By defining

$$\Gamma(t) = \int_0^t e^{-il\phi_n(u)} D_M(\phi_n(t) - \phi_n(u)) \sigma(u) dW(u),$$

we can rewrite term (24.22) in L_2-norm as

$$E\left[\left(H_{M,n}^2\right)^2\right] = \iint_0^{2\pi} E\left[\Gamma(t)\overline{\Gamma(t')}a(t)a(t')\right] dt\, dt'.$$

Using the duality for the stochastic integrals and formula (1.65) in Nualart (2006), we get that

$$E\left[\Gamma(t)\overline{\Gamma(t')}a(t)a(t')\right]$$

$$= E\left[\int_0^t e^{-il\phi_n(u)} D_M(\phi_n(t) - \phi_n(u)) \sigma(u) \mathscr{D}_u\left(\overline{\Gamma(t')}a(t)a(t')\right) du\right]$$

$$= E\left[a(t)a(t') \int_0^t D_M(\phi_n(t) - \phi_n(u)) D_M(\phi_n(t') - \phi_n(u)) 1_{\{u \le t'\}} v(u) du\right]$$

$$+ E\left[a(t)a(t') \int_0^t e^{-il\phi_n(u)} D_M(\phi_n(t)\right.$$

$$\left. - \phi_n(u)) \left(\int_u^{t'} e^{il\phi_n(v)} D_M(\phi_n(t') - \phi_n(v)) \mathscr{D}_u(\sigma(v))\right) dW(v)\right) du\right]$$

$$+ E\left[\overline{\Gamma(t')} \int_0^t e^{-il\phi_n(u)} D_M(\phi_n(t) - \phi_n(u)) \sigma(u) \mathscr{D}_u(a(t)a(t')) du\right].$$

Then, we can consider

$$E\left[\left(H_{M,n}^2\right)^2\right] = E_{M,n}^1 + E_{M,n}^2 + E_{M,n}^3$$

Let us consider $p \in (1,2)$ in what follows. Using Fubini's theorem,

$$E_{M,n}^1 \leq C \iint_0^{2\pi} \int_0^t |D_M(\phi_n(t) - \phi_n(u))D_M(\phi_n(t') - \phi_n(u))|1_{\{u \leq t'\}} du \, dt \, dt'$$

$$= C \int_0^{2\pi} \left(\int_u^{2\pi} |D_M(\phi_n(t) - \phi_n(u))| dt \int_u^{2\pi} |D_M(\phi_n(t') - \phi_n(u))| dt' \right) du$$

$$\leq C \sup_{u \in [0,2\pi]} \left(\int_0^{2\pi} |D_M(\phi_n(t) - \phi_n(u))|^p dt \right)^{\frac{2}{p}} \leq \frac{C}{M^{\frac{2}{p}}}$$

where the properties of the Dirichlet kernel and hypothesis (**H.2**) allow one to get the estimation.

We need hypotheses (**H.2**) and (**H.3**) and the Cauchy–Schwartz inequality to estimate the addend $E_{M,n}^2$:

$$E_{M,n}^2 \leq C \iint_0^{2\pi} \left| \int_0^t e^{-il\phi_n(u)} D_M(\phi_n(t) \right.$$

$$\left. - \phi_n(u)) E\left[\int_u^{t'} D_M^2(\phi_n(t') - \phi_n(v)) \mathscr{D}_u(\sigma(v))^2 dv \right]^{\frac{1}{2}} du \right| dt \, dt'$$

$$\leq CE\left[\sup_{u,v \in [0,2\pi]} \mathscr{D}_u(\sigma(v))^2 \right]^{\frac{1}{2}} \iint_0^{2\pi} \int_0^t |D_M(\phi_n(t) - \phi_n(u))| du$$

$$\times \left[\int_0^{t'} D_M^2(\phi_n(t') - \phi_n(v)) dv \right]^{\frac{1}{2}} dt \, dt' \leq \frac{C}{M^{\frac{2+p}{2p}}}.$$

As above, the same estimation can be obtained for the addend $E_{M,n}^3$:

$$E_{M,n}^3 \leq C \iint_0^{2\pi} E\left[\int_0^{t'} D_M^2(\phi_n(t') - \phi_n(u))v(u) du \right]^{\frac{1}{2}} \int_0^t |D_M(\phi_n(t) - \phi_n(u))| du \, dt \, dt'$$

$$\leq C \iint_0^{2\pi} \left(\int_0^{t'} D_M^2(\phi_n(t') - \phi_n(u)) du \right)^{\frac{1}{2}} \left(\int_0^t |D_M(\phi_n(t) - \phi_n(u))|^p du \right)^{\frac{1}{p}} dt \, dt' \leq \frac{C}{M^{\frac{2+p}{2p}}}$$

by means of the Cauchy–Schwartz inequality and the properties of the discretized Dirichlet kernel.

Concerning the symmetric terms $\tilde{I}_{M,n}$, $\tilde{H}^1_{M,n}$, $\tilde{H}^2_{M,n}$, and $\tilde{H}^3_{M,n}$, respectively, the same estimations can be carried out.

Therefore, the Fourier coefficients $c_l(\nu_{n,M})$ are bounded in L_2-norm, the difference

$$E\left[\left(c_l(\nu_{n,M}) - c_l(\nu)\right)^2\right] \leq CE\left[\left(\int_0^{2\pi}\left(e^{-il\phi_n(u)} - e^{-ilu}\right)\nu(t)dt\right)^2\right] + \frac{C}{M}$$

$$\leq CN^2\rho^2(n) + \frac{C}{M}$$

and the L_1-norm of Eqn (24.16) is an $O\left(N^2\rho(n) + C\dfrac{N}{\sqrt{M}}\right)$ that tends to zero as N, M, $n \to \infty$ and $\rho(n) \to 0$ under hypotheses (24.13).

It remains to study the convergence in the probability of addend (24.17).

For any integer $|h| \leq N$,

$$\frac{2\pi}{2N+1}\sum_{|l|\leq N} il c_l(\nu)c_{h-l}(dp) - \frac{1}{2\pi}\int_0^{2\pi}e^{-iht}\eta(t)dt$$

[24.24]

$$= \frac{2\pi}{2N+1}\sum_{|l|\leq N}\left(c_l(d\nu) - c_0(d\nu)\right)c_{h-l}(dp) - \frac{1}{2\pi}\int_0^{2\pi}e^{-iht}\eta(t)dt$$

because of relation (24.8). Applying the Itô formula to the products $c_l(d\nu)c_{h-l}(dp)$ and $c_0(d\nu)c_{h-l}(dp)$, Eqn (24.24) becomes in L_1-norm

$$E\left[\left|\frac{1}{2\pi}\int_0^{2\pi}\int_0^{s}e^{-ihu}D_N(s-u)dp(u)d\nu(s)\right.\right.$$

$$+ \frac{1}{2\pi}\int_0^{2\pi}e^{-ihs}\int_0^{s}D_N(s-u)d\nu(u)dp(s)$$

$$- \frac{1}{2\pi}\int_0^{2\pi}\int_0^{s}e^{-ihu}D_N(u)dp(u)d\nu(s)$$

$$\left.\left.- \frac{1}{2\pi}\int_0^{2\pi}e^{-ihs}\int_0^{s}D_N(s)d\nu(u)dp(s) - \frac{1}{2\pi}\int_0^{2\pi}e^{-ihu}D_N(u)\eta(u)du\right|\right]$$

$$\leq \frac{C}{\sqrt{N}} + \frac{C}{N^{\frac{1}{p}}}$$

where p is an integer >1. The above estimation is obtained under hypotheses (**H**) and using the classical properties of the continuous Dirichlet kernel. Therefore, we can conclude that also addend (24.17) converges to zero in L_1-norm as $N \to \infty$, which concludes the proof.

QED

We conclude the section by studying the consistency of *spot* and *integrated leverage* estimators.

For all $t \in (0, 2\pi)$,

$$\eta_{n,M,N}(t) = \sum_{|h| \leq N} \left(1 - \frac{|h|}{N}\right) e^{iht} \widehat{c}_h(\eta_{n,M,N}) \qquad [24.25]$$

The random function $\eta_{n,M,N}(t)$ will be called the *Fourier spot estimator* of the leverage function $\eta(t)$. The defined spot estimator uses all the information along the observed path to infer the value of $\eta_{n,M,N}(t)$, and by means of the Cesaro summation, it allows one to preserve the sign of the estimated function (see Remark 2.3 in Malliavin and Mancino (2009)).

An estimation of the integrated quantity (24.3) can be simply obtained by means of definition (24.12) for $h = 0$.

$$\eta^{[1]}_{n,M,N}(t) = 2\pi \widehat{c}_0(\eta_{n,M,N}). \qquad [24.26]$$

Theorem 3.3. We assume that hypotheses (**H**) and

$$\frac{N^2}{M} \to 0 \text{ and } M\rho(n) \to a$$

with $a \in \left(0, \frac{1}{2}\right)$ hold true as $n, N, M \to \infty$ and $\rho(n) \to 0$. We then have the following convergence in probability:

$$\eta^{[1]}_{n,M,N} \to \eta^1, \qquad [24.27]$$

$$\lim_{n,N,M \to \infty} \sup_{t \in (0,2\pi)} \left|\eta_{n,M,N}(t) - \eta(t)\right| = 0. \qquad [24.28]$$

Proof (Theorem 3.3):

In Theorem 3.1, we have proved that for any fixed h, the convergence in probability of $\widehat{c}_h(\eta_{n,M,N})$ to the Fourier coefficient $c_h(\eta)$ as $n, N, M \to \infty$. Then, proving the convergence in Eqn (24.27) is straightforward and the uniform convergence in Eqn (24.28) follows by the Féjer Theorem for the continuous function.

QED

Remark 3.4. The extension of the estimation of the leverage in a multiasset scenario is essentially contained in the proposed theory. Following the procedure described in

Malliavin and Mancino (2002) for the estimation of multivariate integrated and spot volatility, it is possible to generalize this issue to the leverage estimation. We do not develop this theory in the present work. Nevertheless, the availability of a multivariate extension is an important feature of estimators (24.25) and (24.26).

24.4 NUMERICAL RESULTS

In this section, we simulate discrete data from a continuous time stochastic volatility model with and without microstructure contaminations. From the simulated data, Fourier estimates of the integrated leverage can be compared to the value of the true quantity and to estimates obtained with other methods proposed in the literature.

As a benchmark for our estimator, we use the preestimated spot variance-based realized leverage, which we call *Realized Leverage* in the following, which is based on a suitably normalized sum of the products of the high frequency-estimated spot variance increments and the log returns (Mykland and Zhang, 2009). The spot volatility is estimated on a finer time scale than the one used for computing the realized covariance between volatility and returns. This estimator relies on a preliminary estimation of the spot volatility path. It is well known that spot volatility estimation is particularly difficult and quite unstable, especially in the presence of microstructure effects. To obtain roughly unbiased and valid estimates of the integrated leverage when microstructure effects play a role, we can resort to low-frequency sampling. However, the well-known bias-variance trade-off comes up as sparse sampling eliminates information contained in the available data.

On the contrary, the Fourier estimator can reconstruct the Fourier coefficients of the leverage process starting from the observable log prices. Therefore, our estimate is obtained by iterated convolutions of the Fourier coefficients of the log returns, without resorting explicitly to any proxy of the latent spot variance of returns. We think that this can represent the strength of our approach, as will be highlighted by the following numerical simulations.

Our analysis is threefold:. First, we analyze the sensitivity of the Fourier estimator to the choice of the parameters M and N, to which the consistency of the estimator is related. Second, we test the robustness of the estimator with respect to several noise settings and for two different data-generating processes. Finally, we consider an empirical application to S&P 500 index futures.

In order to account for the leverage effect in the data, most of the well-known stochastic volatility models allow for correlation between the Brownian motions driving the logarithmic asset price and the volatility processes. In particular, these correlations are usually assumed to be constant and not time varying. A recent model proposed in Veraart and Veraart (2012) introduces stochastic correlation by adding a further source of randomness in the H model. We will prove the efficiency of our estimator assuming that the underlying dynamics of the price process is described by two different models: the classical *H model* presented in Heston (1993) and the *GH model* proposed in Veraart and Veraart (2012).

We simulate second-by-second return and variance paths over a daily trading period of $T = 6$ h, for a total of 100 trading days and $n = 21,600$ observations per day.

The first data set is simulated by the model,

$$(\text{H}): \begin{cases} dp(t) = \sigma(t)dW_1(t) \\ d\sigma^2(t) = \alpha(\beta - \sigma^2(t))dt + v\sigma(t)dW_2(t), \end{cases}$$

where W_1 and W_2 are correlated Brownian motions. The parameter values used in the simulations are $\alpha = 0.01$, $\beta = 1.0$, $v = 0.05$ and the correlation parameter is chosen as $\rho = -0.2$.

The second data set is simulated by the model,

$$(\text{GH}): \begin{cases} dp(t) = \sigma(t)dX(t) \\ dX(t) = \rho(t)dW_1(t) + \sqrt{1 - \rho^2(t)}dW_2(t) \\ d\sigma^2(t) = \alpha(\beta - \sigma^2(t))dt + v\sigma(t)dW_1(t), \end{cases}$$

where the infinitesimal variation of $\rho(t)$ is given by

$$d\rho(t) = \left((2\xi - \eta) - \eta\rho(t)\right)dt + \vartheta\sqrt{(1 + \rho(t))(1 - \rho(t))}dW_0(t)$$

and η, ξ, and ϑ are positive constants and W_0 is a Brownian motion. The processes W_0, W_1, and W_2 are assumed to be independent. The parameter values used in the simulation are $\alpha = 0.01$, $\beta = 1.0$, $v = 0.05$, and $\xi = 0.2$, $\eta = 0.5$, $\vartheta = 0.5$, where the last three parameters are chosen in the range prescribed in Veraart and Veraart (2012) such that $\rho \in [-1,1]$. We set the initial values as $\sigma^2(0) = 1$, $p(0) = log100$, and $\rho(0) = 0.04$. Moreover, when microstructure effects are considered, we consider the logarithm of the observed price given by

$$\tilde{p}(t) = p(t) + \zeta(t),$$

where $p(t)$ is the efficient log price in the equilibrium defined in (H model/GH model) and $\zeta(t)$ is the microstructure noise. The random shock ζ is Gaussian i.i.d. and independent from p.

To perform an estimation of $\eta^{[1]}$, we have to choose the highest frequency of the coefficients that have to be included in formula (24.12). Parameters M and N, respectively, identify the numbers of the Fourier coefficients of the return process $c_s(dp_n)$ and of the volatility process $c_l(v_{n,M})$ appearing in $\eta^{[1]}_{n,M,N}$ and will be called *cutting frequencies*. Therefore, it is important to analyze the sensitivity of the estimator to the choice of parameters M and N in both the absence and the presence of microstructure noise.

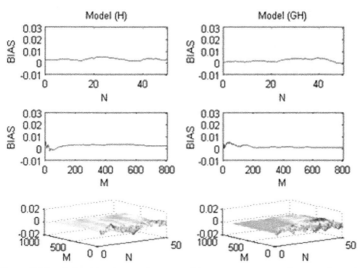

Figure 24.1 True BIAS of the Fourier estimator of leverage, averaged over the whole data sets (100 days) as a function of M and N, in the absence of microstructure effects.

In Figure 24.1, we plot the true BIAS of the Fourier estimator averaged over 100 days as a function of M and N, respectively, and of any combination (M,N) in the absence of microstructure effect, for the H model (left panel) and the GH model (right panel). We notice that the Fourier estimator turns out to be quite robust to the choice of N and for $M > 200$ for both models.

Figure 24.2 shows the true BIAS in the presence of microstructure effects with noise-to-signal ratio $\lambda = \frac{std(\zeta)}{std(r)} = 3$, where r is the $1 - s$ returns, for the H-model (left panel) and the GH model (right panel). The plots are qualitatively the same as in Figure 24.1. On the whole, we can conclude that the Fourier estimator is quite stable with respect to the choice of the parameters M and N, although some instability can be observed for very small values of M.

We study the performances of the Fourier estimator $\eta_{n,M,N}^{[1]}$ in comparison to the Realized Leverage focusing our attention on 12 different scenarios that also include noise and irregular trading times of observations. The results obtained are listed in Tables 24.1 and 24.2. In Mancino and Sanfelici (2008, 2012), an optimal Mean Squared Error (MSE) based approach is designed in order to determine the optimal cutting frequencies.

When estimating the leverage effect, a larger variability in the estimates can be observed if compared to other quantities such as volatility or quarticity. This may penalize the MSE computation, so that the MSE minimization criterion may not be useful to determine the optimal values of M and N. For this reason, in our simulations, the optimal parameters that the Fourier and Realized Leverage estimators depend on are chosen by minimization of the true BIAS. The optimal M values turn out to be much smaller than

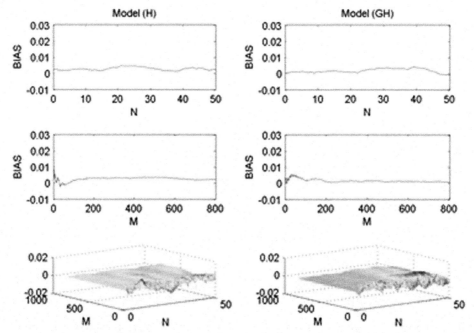

Figure 24.2 True BIAS of the Fourier estimator of leverage, averaged over the whole data sets (100 days) as a function of M and N, in the presence of microstructure effects, with $\lambda = 3$.

Table 24.1 H model

Noise-to-signal ratio	Fourier estimator		Realized leverage	
	BIAS	MSE	BIAS	MSE
0.0	−3.05e−007	4.80e−004	−1.07e−005	1.66e−002
1.0	3.52e−007	6.52e−004	−1.48e−006	1.72e−004
1.5	3.42e−007	5.98e−004	1.72e−006	8.02e−004
2.0	−8.65e−008	8.75e−004	−6.43e−007	2.07e−004
2.5	−1.80e−007	4.31e−004	−1.03e−007	1.73e−004
3.0	8.48e−008	3.92e−004	9.72e−007	6.98e−004

the Nyquist frequency (i.e., $M \ll n/2$), whereas N is very small in complete agreement with Theorem 3.3.

We consider six different levels of the noise-to-signal ratio λ ranging from 0 (no-noise case) to 3. Table 24.1 shows the results obtained for the H model, while Table 24.2 gives the results for the GH model. The tables highlight that, in all the scenarios under consideration, the Fourier estimator allows one to achieve smaller level of BIAS with respect to the Realized Leverage. The corresponding MSE levels are comparable. The only

Table 24.2 GH model

Noise-to-signal ratio	Fourier estimator		Realized leverage	
	BIAS	MSE	BIAS	MSE
0.0	−3.64e−008	5.25e−005	3.36e−006	4.79e−003
1.0	5.62e−008	2.67e−004	−9.28e−007	5.38e−004
1.5	−2.83e−007	2.07e−004	−2.00e−007	1.00e−004
2.0	−1.52e−007	1.14e−003	1.29e−006	1.67e−004
2.5	−8.31e−008	2.51e−004	1.84e−007	2.54e−004
3.0	−1.12e−007	2.76e−004	−5.65e−007	4.40e−004

exception is the pure diffusive case ($\lambda = 0$), where the Realized Leverage estimate is obtained using tick-by-tick prices at the first level (spot volatility estimation) and by using 2- and 7-min returns at the second level (covariance estimation) for the H and GH models, respectively. This sparse sampling induces a much larger MSE for the Realized Leverage estimation. Moreover, the estimates obtained by the Realized Leverage are quite sensitive to the choice of the sampling frequency.

We now consider a case study based on tick-by-tick data of the S&P 500 index futures recorded at the Chicago Mercantile Exchange (CME). The sample covers the period from January 3, 2006 to December 31, 2007, a period of 500 trading days, having 1,074,825 tick-by-tick observations. The price ranges in the interval [1229.70, 1586.5], with an average value of 1401.8 and standard deviation 99.28. Table 24.3 describes the main features of our data set.

Days with a trading period <5 h have been removed. Jumps have been identified and measured using the Threshold Bipower Variation method of Corsi et al. (2010), which is based on the joint use of bipower variation and threshold estimation (Mancini, 2009). This method provides a powerful test for jump detection, which is employed at the significance level of 99.9%. We refer the reader to Mancino and Sanfelici (2012) for further details on the jump removal procedure. The number of days remaining after jump removal and filtering is 333, for a total of 727,137 tick-by-tick data. The contribution coming from overnight returns is neglected.

Table 24.3 Summary Statistics for the sample of the traded CME S&P 500 index futures in the period January 3, 2006 to December 31, 2007 (1,074,825 trades)

Statistics	Mean	Standard deviation	Min	Max
S&P 500 index futures	1401.80	99.28	1229.70	1586.50
No. of ticks per minute	5.62291	3.60078	1.00000	36.0000

Sparse sampling needed for the Realized variance estimator can be performed either in calendar time, for instance, with prices sampled every 5 or 15 min, or in transaction time, where prices are recorded for every *m*th transaction. When we sample in calendar time, the x-minute returns are constructed using the nearest neighbor to the x-minute tag.

Figure 24.3 shows the average integrated leverage estimated over the full sample period obtained by the Fourier estimator as a function of the cutting frequency M (Panel A) and by the realized Leverage estimator for different sampling frequencies in calendar (Panel B) and transaction time (Panel C).

The leverage signature plots clearly indicate that the bias induced by market micro-structure effects is relatively small for the highly liquid S&P 500 index futures, and dies out very quickly. Note that with a transaction taking place on average about every 17.93 s, the 1-min sampling interval corresponds to around the third tick presented in the figure, with a large variability across the whole data set. The market microstructure effects on the 5-min realized leverage measure for the S&P 500 index futures over the period 2006–2007 can therefore be regarded as negligible. However, the estimates obtained by transaction time sampling (Panel C) are quite unstable and irregular as the sampling frequency decreases. When sampling in calendar time (Panel B), we observe a bias toward zero as the sampling frequency decreases. For low frequencies, the Realized

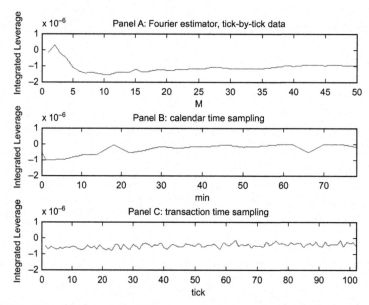

Figure 24.3 S&P 500 index futures. Panel A shows the average integrated leverage computed by means of the Fourier estimator, using tick-by-tick data, as a function of the parameter *M*. *N* is set equal to 5. Panels B and C show the average integrated leverage obtained by the realized leverage estimator for different frequencies measured in minutes and in the number of ticks, respectively.

Leverage estimator becomes downward biased because sparse sampling has a severe impact on the cardinality of the database. On the contrary, the Fourier estimator (Panel A) uses tick-by-tick data. The value of the parameter N is set to 5, and we show the leverage signature plot as a function on the parameter M. We can see that for $M > 40$, the estimates become very stable.

24.5 CONCLUSION

We have proposed new estimators of the stochastic leverage function based on the use of the Fourier transform. The methodology used is nonparametric and model-free and relies only on the preestimation of the Fourier coefficients of the volatility function.

By means of the choice of an appropriate number of Fourier coefficients of the return and of the volatility process to be included in the estimation, we prove in our numerical simulations the efficiency of the integrated estimator of the leverage in finite samples.

In conclusion, we define consistent estimators—*integrated and spot*—that show robustness in the presence of microstructure noise and irregular trading without any manipulation of the data.

ACKNOWLEDGMENTS

We would like to thank Maria Elvira Mancino and Arnaud Gloter for the helpful discussions and their comments.

REFERENCES

Ait-Sahalia, Y., Fan, J., Li, Y., 2013. The leverage effect puzzle: disentangling sources of bias at high frequency. J. Financ. Econ. 109 (1), 224–249.

Back, K., 1991. Asset prices for general processes. J. Math. Econ. 20 (4), 371–395.

Bandi, F., Renò, R., 2012. Time-varying leverage effects. J. Econ. 169 (1), 94–113.

Barndorff-Nielsen, O.E., Shepard, N., 2002. Econometric analysis of realized volatility and its use in estimating stochastic volatility models. J. R. Stat. Soc. Ser. B 64, 253–280.

Barucci, E., Mancino, M.E., 2010. Computation of volatility in stochastic volatility models with high frequency data. Int. J. Theor. Appl. Finance 15 (5), 767–787.

Black, F., 1976. Studies of stock market volatility changes. In: Proceedings of the Business and Economic Statistic Section. American Statistical Association, pp. 177–181.

Bollerslev, T., Litvinova, J., Tauchen, G., 2006. Leverage and volatility feedback effects in high frequency data. J. Financ. Econ. 4 (3), 353–384.

Carr, P., Wu, L., 2007. Stochastic skew in currency options. J. Financ. Econ. 86 (1), 213–247.

Christie, A.A., 1982. The stochastic behavior of common stock variances. J. Financ. Econ. 10 (2), 407–432.

Clément, E., Gloter, A., 2011. Limit theorems in the Fourier transform method for the estimation of multivariate volatility. Stoch. Process. Appl. 121 (5), 1097–1124.

Corsi, F., Pirino, D., Renò, R., 2010. Threshold bipower variation and the impact of jumps on volatility forecasting. J. Econ. 159 (2), 276–288.

Cuchiero, C., Teichmann, J., 2015. Fourier Transform Methods for Pathwise Covariance Estimation in the Presence of Jumps. Stochastic Processes and their Applications 125 (1), 116–160.

Curato, I.V., Mancino, M.E., Sanfelici, S., 2014. High frequency volatility of volatility free from spot volatility estimates. Forthcom. Quant. Finance.

De La Vallèe Poussin, C., 1919. Lecons Sur L'Approximation D'Une Variable Rèelle. Gauthier-Villars Paris.

Delbaen, F., Schachermayer, W., 1994. A general version of the fundamental theorem of asset pricing. Math. Ann. 300 (1), 463–520.

Favard, J., 1937. Sur les Meilleurs Proceeds D'approximation de Certaines Classes de Fonctions par de Polynomes Trigonométriques. Bull. Sci. Math. LXI, 2nd series.

Ghysels, E., Harvey, A.C., Renault, E., 1996. Stochastic volatility. Handb. Statistics 14 (2), 119–191.

Hautsch, N., 2012. Econometrics of Financial High-frequency Data. Springer, New York, NY.

Heston, S.L., 1993. A closed-form solution for options with stochastic volatility with applications to bond and currency options. Rev. Financ. Stud. 6 (2), 327–343.

Malliavin, P., 1995. Integration and Probability. Springer-Verlag, New York, NY.

Malliavin, P., Mancino, M.E., 2002. Fourier series method for measurement of multivariate volatility. Finance Stochastics 6 (9), 49–61.

Malliavin, P., Mancino, M.E., 2009. A Fourier transform method for nonparametric estimation of volatility. Ann. Statistics 37 (4), 1983–2010.

Mancini, C., 2009. Non-parametric threshold estimation for models with stochastic diffusion coefficient and jumps. Scand. J. Statistics 36 (2), 270–296.

Mancino, M.E., Sanfelici, S., 2008. Robustness of Fourier estimator of integrated volatility in the presence of microstructure noise. Comput. Statistics Data Anal. 52 (6), 2966–2989.

Mancino, M.E., Sanfelici, S., 2012. Estimation of quarticity with high frequency data. Quant. Finance 12 (4), 607–622.

Mykland, C.D., Wang, P.A., 2014. The estimation of leverage effect with high frequency data. J. Am. Stat. Assoc. 109 (505), 197–215.

Mykland, P.A., Zhang, L., 2009. Inference for continuous semimartingales observed at high frequency. Econometrica 77 (5), 1403–1445.

Nualart, D., 2006. The Malliavin Calculus and Related Topics. Springer-Verlag, New York, NY.

Veraart, A.E.D., Veraart, L.A.M., 2012. Stochastic volatility and stochastic leverage. Ann. Finance 8 (2–3), 205–233.

Yu, J., 2005. On leverage in stochastic volatility model. J. Econ. 127 (2), 165–178.

Zamansky, m, 1949. Classes de saturation de certains proceeds d'approximation des séries de Fourier des fonctions continues et applications à quelques problems d'approximation. Ann. Sci. 66 (2), 19–23 l'E.N.S. 3-Séries.

INDEX

Note: Page numbers followed by "f" and "t" indicate figures and tables respectively.

Printed in the United States
By Bookmasters